Drafting Contracts

Aspen Coursebook Series

DRAFTING CONTRACTS
How and Why Lawyers Do What They Do

Second Edition

Tina L. Stark

Visiting Professor
Fordham University School of Law

Wolters Kluwer
Law & Business

Wolters Kluwer Law & Business serves customers worldwide with CCH, Aspen Publishers, and Kluwer Law International products. (www.wolterskluwerlb.com)

To contact Customer Service, e-mail customer.service@wolterskluwer.com, call 1-800-234-1660, fax 1-800-901-9075, or mail correspondence to:

Wolters Kluwer Law & Business
Attn: Order Department
PO Box 990
Frederick, MD 21705

Printed in the United States of America.

5 6 7 8 9 0

ISBN 978-0-7355-9477-7

Library of Congress Cataloging-in-Publication Data

Stark, Tina L., 1953- author.
  Drafting contracts : how and why lawyers do what they do / Tina L. Stark, Visiting Professor, Fordham University School of Law.
      p. cm.
  Includes bibliographical references and index.
  ISBN 978-0-7355-9477-7 (alk. paper)
  1. Contracts--United States. 2. Contracts--United States--Language. 3. Legal composition. I. Title.
KF807.S73 2013
346.7302'2--dc23

2013039766

ABOUT WOLTERS KLUWER LAW & BUSINESS

Wolters Kluwer Law & Business is a leading global provider of intelligent information and digital solutions for legal and business professionals in key specialty areas, and respected educational resources for professors and law students. Wolters Kluwer Law & Business connects legal and business professionals as well as those in the education market with timely, specialized authoritative content and information-enabled solutions to support success through productivity, accuracy and mobility.

Serving customers worldwide, Wolters Kluwer Law & Business products include those under the Aspen Publishers, CCH, Kluwer Law International, Loislaw, ftwilliam.com and MediRegs family of products.

CCH products have been a trusted resource since 1913, and are highly regarded resources for legal, securities, antitrust and trade regulation, government contracting, banking, pension, payroll, employment and labor, and healthcare reimbursement and compliance professionals.

Aspen Publishers products provide essential information to attorneys, business professionals and law students. Written by preeminent authorities, the product line offers analytical and practical information in a range of specialty practice areas from securities law and intellectual property to mergers and acquisitions and pension/benefits. Aspen's trusted legal education resources provide professors and students with high-quality, up-to-date and effective resources for successful instruction and study in all areas of the law.

Kluwer Law International products provide the global business community with reliable international legal information in English. Legal practitioners, corporate counsel and business executives around the world rely on Kluwer Law journals, looseleafs, books, and electronic products for comprehensive information in many areas of international legal practice.

Loislaw is a comprehensive online legal research product providing legal content to law firm practitioners of various specializations. Loislaw provides attorneys with the ability to quickly and efficiently find the necessary legal information they need, when and where they need it, by facilitating access to primary law as well as state-specific law, records, forms and treatises.

ftwilliam.com offers employee benefits professionals the highest quality plan documents (retirement, welfare and non-qualified) and government forms (5500/PBGC, 1099 and IRS) software at highly competitive prices.

MediRegs products provide integrated health care compliance content and software solutions for professionals in healthcare, higher education and life sciences, including professionals in accounting, law and consulting.

Wolters Kluwer Law & Business, a division of Wolters Kluwer, is headquartered in New York. Wolters Kluwer is a market-leading global information services company focused on professionals.

For Bobby and Mort Weisenfeld, my mother- and father-in-law, who have always treated me as if I were their daughter

For their son Dave, my best friend and beloved husband

and

For their grandson Andy, my wondrous treasure

About the Author

Tina L. Stark is a Visiting Professor at Fordham University School of Law, where she was an adjunct from 1993-2007. In 2012, the Burton Foundation honored her with its Award for Outstanding Contributions to Legal Writing Education for her work on contract drafting. In 2011, she was one of 26 professors chosen from a nationwide search to be included in the study *What the Best Law Teachers Do.*[1]

From 2007-2011, Professor Stark taught at Emory University School of Law, where she was a Professor in the Practice of Law and the first Executive Director of that school's Center for Transactional Law and Practice. While there, she created a multi-year, integrated transactional skills curriculum designed to graduate students with both a doctrinal foundation and the skills to provide an employer value beginning on Day 1. During the 2011-2012 academic year, Professor Stark was a Professor of the Practice of Law at Boston University School of Law and the Founding Director of that school's Transactional Program.

Professor Stark is a former corporate partner at Chadbourne & Parke LLP. While there, she had a broad-based transactional practice that included acquisitions, dispositions, recapitalizations, and financings. In addition, she developed and implemented the firm's corporate training program. Before entering law school, Professor Stark was a commercial banker at Irving Trust Company.

When teaching, Professor Stark emphasizes the relationship between law and business, drawing on her experience as a corporate partner at Chadbourne and as a commercial banker at Irving Trust Company. In addition to teaching at law schools, Professor Stark has lectured on law and business issues for CLE organizations and at firms, corporations, and government agencies in the United States, Canada, England, Italy, China, and Poland. As a consultant, she assisted a London law school in creating and implementing its transactional skills curriculum.

After receiving her A.B., with honors, from Brown University, Professor Stark earned her J.D. from New York University School of Law, where she was a contributing editor to the *Journal of International Law & Politics.* Following law school, she clerked for Judge Jacob D. Fuchsberg of the New York State Court of Appeals and was an associate with Barrett Smith Schapiro Simon & Armstrong.

Professor Stark is the editor-in-chief and co-author of *Negotiating and Drafting Contract Boilerplate,* publisher, American Lawyer Media (2003).

---

1. Michael Hunter Schwartz, Gerald F. Hess, & Sophie M. Sparrow, *What the Best Law Teachers Do* (Harv. U. Press 2013).

Summary of Contents

Contents

Preface to the Second Edition

The following discussion occurred in 2005 between the publisher's editors and me—before I signed the contract for the First Edition:

Person 1: It's a great idea.
Person 2: But there's no market.
Persons 1 and 2 and me: If we build it, they will come.

And you came—in numbers I never thought possible. Enough of you came, you could *almost* say that Contract Drafting has become a mainstream course. Indeed, enough of you came, that the publisher said, "Write a second edition." So, here it is.

Highlights of the Second Edition

1. The Second Edition retains the same organizational structure and pedagogy as the First Edition, but with two additions. First, students will spend more time learning how to work with precedents. For example, the textbook includes a well-drafted House Purchase Agreement that students can use as a precedent for the Car Purchase Agreement. Second, students will learn contract analysis—how to read a contract. The Teachers' Manual includes the pedagogy and many of the textbook's exercises do double-duty, so teaching this new skill will fit easily into most syllabi.

2. Most chapters have expanded discussions of their respective content, along with new exercises.

3. The Second Edition virtually completely overhauls Chapter 15—Endgame. It now discusses in detail common contractual remedies and provides a multitude of exemplars. The exemplars come from a host of contracts, so students can see the provisions at work. Among the contracts from which the provisions have been taken are a grocery supply agreement, a construction agreement, a theater lease, and a movie distribution agreement.

4. Chapter 16—General Provisions now includes examples of well-drafted provisions, so that students have basic precedents going forward.

5. Scattered throughout the book and in Chapter 32 are multiple well-drafted exemplars for students. These exemplars are more than bare bones contracts. The Chapter 32 exemplars are populated with annotations that explain associated business and legal issues and ask questions designed to help students problem solve the agreement's drafting. These annotations give students context for what they are reading and help avert a *mindless markup*. I call the pedagogy for using the annotations *guided reading*.

6. The textbook has revised the *Aircraft Purchase Agreement* exercise. By omitting some provisions and redrafting others, the APA more directly addresses the significant issues. The memos giving instructions are also more targeted. In addition, Chapter 32 includes exemplars of action sections and endgame sections in acquisition agreements so that students gain practice working with precedents. This move reduces the textbook's narrative discussions on acquisitions—a topic not all professor want to teach.

7. The poorly drafted, much-maligned *Asset Purchase Agreement* appears no longer in the textbook's appendices. But it's on the website for anyone who grew attached to it.

8. The website will include significant new material:

   (a) Multiple exercises not included in the textbook

   (b) Standard comments that you can use when grading some of the more significant exercises. They are in a Word document, listed in order by section number. All you need to do is copy and paste the comment into a Word Comment bubble — and then tailor as necessary. These standard comments work because students regularly make the same mistakes because provisions target a specific pedagogic issues. So, when a student errs in her drafting, the error probably resembles the same error of previous students. I update these comments regularly, so please check the website right before you use the comments.

   (c) Proposed grading suggestions. The grading document allocates to each drafting, business or legal issue a number of points reflective of the issue's difficulty; for example, fewer points for the preamble and more points for the action sections. The website provides detailed information on how to use the grading documents.

Tina L. Stark
November 2013

Preface to the First Edition

Drafting Contracts brings a new approach to the teaching of contract drafting. It emphasizes the nexus between the business deal and the contract, both in the material taught and in the exercises students work on. In addition, it teaches students to think critically about the law and the transaction they are memorializing.

To draft a contract well, a drafter must know the rules of good writing—and more. Among other things, a drafter must

- understand the business deal;
- know how to use the contract concepts to reflect the parties' deal accurately; and
- be able to draft and recognize nuances in language that change the deal.

In addition, a good drafter knows how to add value to a deal by discerning and resolving business issues.

Drafting Contracts reflects a real world approach to contract drafting, bringing together years of real world contract drafting experience and law school teaching. Although new to the market, the materials in *Drafting Contracts* have been used in law school classrooms for more than 13 years, including use of the manuscript at more than ten schools.

Drafting Contracts teaches students through narration and drafting exercises. The exercises are numerous, permitting a professor to choose the ones most appropriate for his or her class. As designed, the exercises in later chapters incorporate material from earlier chapters, so that students practice what they have already learned while integrating new skills. Professors need not, however, teach the materials in *Drafting Contracts* in the order set out. The book is sufficiently flexible that professors can reorder the chapters to suit any curriculum.

This book's organization reflects its pedagogy. Part 1 teaches the material that is the course's foundation. Its chapters introduce students to the building blocks of contracts: representations and warranties, covenants, rights, conditions, discretionary authority, and declarations. These chapters do more, however, than define the terms. They show how and why a drafter chooses a specific contract concept by teaching the analytic skill of *translating the business deal into contract concepts*.

In Part 2, *Drafting Contracts* sets out the framework of an agreement and works through it from the preamble to the signature lines, in each instance discussing the business, legal, and drafting issues that occur in each part of a contract. After these chapters, in Part 3, *Drafting Contracts* turns to the rules for good drafting and to techniques to enhance clarity and to avoid ambiguity. Although the chapters in this Part concentrate on more traditional drafting issues, they nonetheless remain sensitive to how the business deal affects drafting in subtle ways.

In Part 4, students learn how to look at a deal from the client's business perspective and how to add value to a transaction by identifying business issues using the five-prong framework of money, risk, control, standards, and endgame.

In Part 5, students learn the drafting process, from organizing the initial contract to amending the signed agreement. Students also learn how to analyze and comment on a contract that another lawyer has drafted.

Drafting Contracts directly addresses ethical issues unique to contract drafting, both through textual material and exercises in Part 6. The book's final part, Part 7, provides supplementary exercises.

Drafting Contracts is designed for use in an upper-level drafting course but can be integrated into a variety of other courses, including a first-year writing or contracts course, a mergers and acquisitions course, a transactional simulation course, a transactional clinic, and an upper-level writing survey course. The Teachers Manual suggests appropriate chapters and exercises for each of these uses.

The Teachers Manual is detailed. For exercises that require the redrafting of a provision, the TM includes the original provision, a mark-up showing the changes, the final version, and Notes explaining the answer. For exercises that require free drafting, the TM includes an example of a good answer along with Notes explaining the answer. In addition, the TM provides answers to commonly asked questions and tips on how to present material.

The *Drafting Contracts* website will also be a resource available to professors and students. First, professors will have access to an electronic version of the TM, so anything in it can be copied and incorporated into class notes. Second, professors will be able to download PowerPoint slides and additional exercises. Third, the website will include Word and WordPerfect versions of each provision in a large, readable font. These provisions can be projected on a screen in the same way that a PowerPoint slide can be projected. Once projected, the professor and students can work through the revision together. The website will also have additional exercises to give professors even more choices for assignments. Finally, to minimize the word processing that students do, the website will include electronic versions of the longer exercises.

Drafting Contracts teaches contract drafting in a new way. It teaches students how to think like deal lawyers and how to reflect that thinking in the contracts they draft.

Tina L. Stark
May 2007

Acknowledgments to the Second Edition

I first thank my adopters and would-be adopters. You waited patiently for this second edition. Unfortunately, life intervened, and earlier publication was not a realistic possibility. During this time, my publisher graciously delayed publication and supported me through a difficult time. The mantra was, "We will publish when you are ready." I will always be most grateful to Carol McGeehan (Publisher, Aspen Publishers) and Dana Wilson (my editor) for the many kindnesses they showed during my extended illness.

I also thank my adopters for taking the time to send me suggestions. As for my students, it was a joy to teach them, and the book is better because of their uncensored critiques—which were always given with a smile.

During the writing of this edition, I had superb help from my research assistants, both those from Emory and BU: Connor Alexander, Kasey Chow, Trey Flaherty, Roy Hakimian, Blake Kamaroff, Lisa Prestamo, Melissa Softness, and Sam Taylor. I particularly thank Anna Katz who worked with me at the pressured end of the writing process, juggling multiple projects with panache and good humor.

I give most special thanks to Nancy Stein who read every word, commented on substance and style, and worked tirelessly to make the book right. She also provided solace and dear friendship during difficult times. I am delighted to call her my friend.

I also thank Terry Lloyd, my longtime friend and colleague. His financial acumen added depth and accuracy to Chapter 22—Numbers and Financials Provisions. Any errors are mine.

Only a publisher who values and pursues excellence can publish a quality textbook. For me, Aspen is that publisher. Dana Wilson skillfully guided me throughout the writing process, providing wise counsel, good humor, and compassion. I look forward to working with her on the third edition. Julie Nahil copy edited the book, paying extraordinary attention to substance, style, and formatting. Her questions were perceptive and her proposed changes often added elegance to the text. Sharon Ray, the compositor, did a wonderful job designing and formatting the book. The exemplars in Chapter 32 required formatting work rarely seen in textbooks. Sharon inserted, by hand, each annotation, revising repeatedly until each page was correct. No computer program could accomplish what I envisaged. Sharon did.

Finally, I have three family members to thank.

First, to my mother, Cookie Stark. In 2007, she told me that I had to take the Emory job because it was what I always wanted. That permission was a gift. She was 75 years old, when daughters are supposed to be hanging around. But she gave me her blessing to leave. It was a gift that only a special mother could give.

Second, to my husband, Dave. Your love embraces me and makes possible everything I do. My words are inadequate.

Finally, to my son, Andy. Your pursuit of life inspires me and brings me a mother's joy. You are happy, and I could want nothing more. Besides, you're a stitch.

The author gratefully acknowledges permission from the following sources to use excerpts from their works:

ABA Model Rules of Professional Conduct, 2013 Edition. Copyright © 2013 by the American Bar Association. Reprinted with permission. Copies of ABA Model Rules of

Shaw, Alan, excerpts from Fordham Law School course materials. Reprinted by permission.

Stark, Tina L., *Thinking Like a Deal Lawyer,* 54 J. Leg. Educ. 223, 223-224 (June 2004). Excerpts appear in *Drafting Contracts* Sections 2.3 and 3.1. Reprinted by permission.

Stark, Tina L. et al. eds, *Negotiating and Drafting Contract Boilerplate,* ALM Properties, Inc. 2003. All material from *Negotiating and Drafting Contract Boilerplate* is used with permission of the publisher—ALM Publishing (www.lawcatalog.com); copyright ALM Properties, Inc. 2003. All Rights Reserved.

Acknowledgments to the First Edition

I began this book in 1993 when I first began teaching at Fordham Law School. Unfortunately, the text was only in my head. It took another ten years before I began to put the words on a page. This lengthy gestation has led to a long list of people to thank.

I begin by thanking my students. They were the first to encourage me to write this book. Through the years, their comments and insights challenged me to rethink and clarify my ideas.

While writing this book, I had the help of the following practitioners and professors: Helen Bender, Robin Boyle, Ruthie Buck, Sandra Cohen, Carl Felsenfeld, John Forry, Eric Goldman, Morton Grosz, Carol Hansell, Charles Hoppin, Vickie Kobak, Terry Lloyd, Lisa Penland, Nancy Persechino, and Sally Weaver. Their input and that of Aspen Publishers's anonymous reviewers greatly improved this book's quality.

I thank my colleague Alan Shaw for his intellectual generosity and careful review of the manuscript. In addition, I am grateful to Peter Clapp, someone whom I have never met, but who gave me line-by-line comments on almost every chapter.

Richard Green at Thelen Reid Brown Raysman & Steiner LLP was most helpful. He not only reviewed chapters, but also graciously arranged for his firm's word processing wonders to turn my typed pages into a manuscript.

While working on this book, I had the enthusiastic and dedicated support of my student research assistants: Hannah Amoah, Stephen Costa, Sarah Elkaim, and Noel Paladin-Tripp. I thank Fordham Law School for its generous support of this book.

I also thank Rick Garbarini for his good work and friendship.

Richard Neumann of Hofstra Law School played a pivotal role in this book's publication by introducing me to Richard Mixter at Aspen Publishers. I thank them and Carol McGeehan at Aspen for having had the imagination to envisage a contract drafting textbook market, even when one barely existed.

Others at Aspen also played important roles. Barbara Roth expertly shepherded me through the writing and design process, and Sarah Hains and Meri Keithley artfully designed the book's pages to showcase the contract provision examples. In addition, Kaesmene Harrison Banks skillfully guided the book through production on a tight timeframe, and Lauren Arnest meticulously copy-edited the manuscript.

Finally, I thank my husband Dave and son Andy. Their unwavering love, support, and encouragement make everything I do possible. They also make me laugh—at myself.

The author gratefully acknowledges permission from the following sources to use excerpts from their works:

American Bar Association, ABA Informal Opinion 86-1518. © 1986 by the American Bar Association. Reprinted with permission. Copies of ABA Ethics Opinions are available from Service Center, American Bar Association, 321 North Clark Street, Chicago, IL 60610, 1-800-285-2221.

American Bar Association, ABA *Model Rules of Professional Conduct,* 2006 Edition. © 2006 by the American Bar Association. Reprinted with permission. Copies of ABA *Model*

Rules of Professional Conduct, 2006 Edition are available from Service Center, American Bar Association, 321 North Clark Street, Chicago, IL 60610, 1-800-285-2221.

Gulfstream Aerospace Corporation, Gulfstream G550 photo and technical data. © Gulfstream Aerospace Corporation. Reprinted by permission.

Shaw, Alan, excerpts from Fordham Law School course materials. Reprinted by permission.

Stark, Tina L., *Thinking Like a Deal Lawyer,* 54 J. Leg. Educ. 223, 223-224 (June 2004). Excerpts appear in *Drafting Contracts* Sections 2.3 and 3.1. Reprinted by permission.

Stark, Tina L. et al. eds, *Negotiating and Drafting Contract Boilerplate,* ALM Properties, Inc. 2003. All material from *Negotiating and Drafting Contract Boilerplate* is used with permission of the publisher — ALM Publishing (www.lawcatalog.com); copyright ALM Properties, Inc. 2003. All Rights Reserved.

PART ONE

Translating the Business Deal into Contract Concepts

A Few Words About Contract Drafting and This Book

1.1 INTRODUCTION

A well-drafted contract is elegant. Its language is clear and unambiguous, and its organization cohesive and thoughtful. But drafting a contract requires more than good writing and organizational skills. A drafter should have keen analytical skills; a superior ability to negotiate; a sophisticated understanding of business, the business deal, and the client's business; a comprehensive knowledge of the law; and a discerning eye for details. It also helps to have formidable powers of concentration, physical stamina, mental acuity, tenacity, the ability to multitask, and a sense of humor. Finally, a drafter must enjoy working with colleagues to create a product—the contract.

1.2 WHAT DOES A CONTRACT DO?

A contract establishes the terms of the parties' relationship. It reflects their agreement as to the rules that will govern their transaction. The rules generally include

- the statements of facts that each party made that induced the other to enter the transaction;
- each party's promises as to its future performance;
- each party's rights;
- the events that must occur before each party is obligated to perform;
- each party's discretionary authority;
- how the contract will end, including the events that constitute breach and the remedies for breach; and
- the general policies that govern the parties' relationship.

These rules are the parties' private laws, which the courts will enforce, subject to public policy exceptions found in statutes and common law. Indeed, commentators speak of contracts as **private law**. They also refer to them as **planning documents**. Unlike litigation, which looks back in time, contracts look forward to the parties' future relationship and reflect their joint plans.

A contract also helps the parties to problem solve. Often parties will have the same goal but differ as to how to resolve a specific business issue. A well-written contract can bridge this difference, giving each party enough of what it needs to agree to the contract.

1.3   WHAT ARE A CONTRACT'S GOALS?

When drafting, you are trying to create a document that serves multiple purposes. Sometimes, you may not be able to accomplish all of them, but you should try. A well-written contract should do the following:

- Accurately memorialize the business deal.
- Be clear and unambiguous.
- Resolve problems pragmatically.
- Be sufficiently specific that the parties know their rights and obligations, but be flexible enough to cope with changed circumstances.
- Advance the client's goals and reduce its risks.
- Give each side enough of what it needs so that each leaves the table feeling that it negotiated a good deal.
- Be drafted well enough that it never leaves the file drawer.
- Prevent litigation.

1.4   WHAT IS THE CONTEXT WITHIN WHICH CONTRACTS ARE DRAFTED?

Most contracts are drafted in a different atmosphere from that in which litigators draft memoranda and briefs. Litigators are out to win. They want to defeat their adversaries in court; cooperation is not generally a big part of their playbook. But doing deals and drafting contracts differ from litigation. Neither party wants to give away the candy store, but each looks for a way to get the deal done.

The argot of deal lawyers also differs from that of litigators. While litigators talk about their **adversaries**—those with whom they will battle through a war of words—deal lawyers and their clients talk about **the other side** or **the principals**. These phrases acknowledge that the parties are not aligned, but they are softer than *adversaries* and reflect a different relationship. The parties are competitive, but in the context of a cooperative venture.[1] Each may be willing to walk away from the deal, but each has incentive to find a way to get the deal done.

1.5   DOES THIS BOOK COVER ALL KINDS OF CONTRACTS?

This book focuses on the drafting of **business contracts**, not standard form consumer contracts. The scope of the phrase *business contracts* is intended to be broad and encompassing. It is intended to cover all negotiated contracts, whatever the topic or dollar amount. Within its reach are contracts for the sale of a used car, the construction of an office tower, and a settlement agreement between litigating adversaries. It does not cover a standard form contract that a corporation puts to a consumer. The distinction matters because it affects a drafter's contract drafting style and a contract's substance.

Today, most consumer contracts are drafted in plain English, a style of drafting in which simplicity and clarity prevail. This book will not teach you to draft in plain English. Instead, for business contracts, this book espouses a style of drafting that

---

1. Settlement and divorce negotiations are two notorious exceptions.

this author calls **contemporary commercial drafting**. It resembles plain English, but it is not the same. It draws on the principles of plain English and promotes clarity through, among other things, simpler language, shorter sentences, and formatting. It differs from plain English, however, in important ways.

First, plain English drafters make their contracts more reader friendly by, for example, adopting an informal tone. Although the business world is more informal than it used to be (think business casual dress), it is hard to imagine a multimillion dollar contract between Apple and Intel in which Apple is referred to as *we* and Intel as *you*. But more important than tone is the approach to the contract's substance. A plain English contract's provisions are pared down to their bare essentials, while a business contract's are hefty, retaining all provisions that might add value or protect against risk. Carl Felsenfeld, one of the first proponents of plain English, explained the difference between the two kinds of contracts as follows:

> The plain English movement requires a new drafting approach. Each provision [of a consumer contract] must be analyzed one at a time against the specific transaction and the type of protection required. Many of the traditional legal provisions may well be found essentially unnecessary.
>
> It is basic to this approach that one must regard drafting for a consumer transaction as quite different from drafting for a business transaction. . . . One does not yet, for example, see it taken seriously, in the teaching of contract law. Traditionally, [promissory] notes were not divided in this way and many of the carefully drafted provisions that cluttered up consumer documents, while important, perhaps even essential, to a business transaction really added very little to the typical consumer loan. . . . The point is that consumer drafting must be regarded as a separate process from business drafting. A legal principle derived from this, while perhaps extreme, does lead the way: "In a business transaction, if a risk can be perceived draft for it. In a consumer transaction, unless a risk seems likely, forget it."[2]

1.6 WHY SHOULD YOU LEARN TO DRAFT IF YOU PLAN TO LITIGATE?

If you plan to litigate, you should learn to draft for two reasons. First, you will regularly draft contracts as a litigator. Litigating parties settle more often than they go to trial. The settlement they reach is a business deal, just like any other, and it must be memorialized clearly and accurately. Failure to do so can lead to another dispute and further litigation. Second, knowing how to draft will make you a better litigator. Many of the cases that you litigate will grow out of contract disputes. To represent your client properly, you must be able to analyze a contract and its provisions. If you understand how and why a drafter wrote a provision in a specific way, you will be able to craft more persuasive legal arguments.

1.7 WHAT WILL THIS BOOK TEACH YOU?

This book will teach you how to write a contract and how to think about writing a contract. The first requires that you learn basic principles of contract drafting: For example, use recitals sparingly; limit the number of definitions; avoid ambiguity; do not use the false imperative; tabulate to promote clarity; and say the same thing the

---

2. Carl Felsenfeld, *Language Simplification and Consumer Legal Forms,* remarks made at program on simplified legal drafting, American Bar Association, New York City, Aug. 7, 1978, in F. Reed Dickerson, *Materials on Legal Drafting* 267 (2d ed., Little, Brown & Co. 1986). *See also* Carl Felsenfeld & Alan Siegel, *Writing Contracts in Plain English* 28-29 (West 1981).

same way. Learning how to *think* about writing a contract will require you to learn how business people and their lawyers think about a transaction and the contract that memorializes it. Some of the questions that lawyers and their clients think about include the following:

- What are the client's business goals?
- How can the contract frustrate or further those goals?
- What risks inhere in the transaction?
- What business issues does a provision raise and how can the drafting resolve them?
- Does a provision give the other side too much control?
- Do the representations and warranties allocate too much risk to the client?
- How can the drafter change a covenant's standard of liability to reduce the client's risk?
- Should a particular event result in a breach?
- What remedies are appropriate if a party breaches the contract?

Asking and answering these and other questions are the fun part of contract drafting. They are what make you more than "a mere scrivener"—the ultimate insult to a contract drafter.

1.8   HOW IS THIS BOOK ORGANIZED?

Part 1, composed of Chapters 1 through 4, provides the framework for the course. It introduces you to the building blocks of contracts: representations and warranties, covenants, rights, conditions, discretionary authority, and declarations. Part 1, however, does more than define these terms. It shows how and why a drafter chooses a specific contract concept. It does this by teaching you the analytic skill of **translating the business deal into contract concepts**.

The translation skill is the analytic skill that deal lawyers use when drafting. It differs from that used in writing a persuasive document—whether a memorandum or a brief. Rather than applying the law to the facts, a deal lawyer translates the client's business concerns (a deal lawyer's facts) into contract concepts and then into contract provisions. By learning this skill in the beginning of the course, you will later be able to layer knowledge of *how* to draft on top of a framework that has taught you *what* you are drafting.

Part 2 begins with Chapter 5. That chapter provides an overview of Part 2 by introducing you to a contract's parts.

- **Preamble**—name of agreement, date, and the parties.
- **Recitals**—why the parties are entering the contract.
- **Words of agreement**—statement that the parties agree to the provisions that follow.
- **Definitions**.
- **Action sections**—promise to perform the subject matter of the contract and monetary provisions.
- **Other substantive business provisions**.
- **Endgame provisions**—specific business provisions dealing with the contract's end.

- **General provisions**—the "boilerplate" provisions.
- **Signature lines**.
- **Schedules**.
- **Exhibits**.

This chapter also shows you how the contract concepts you learned in Chapters 3 and 4 are integrated into a contract's parts.

In the remainder of Part 2, Chapters 6 through 17, you will learn how to draft each of the listed parts. Some of this will entail learning detailed drafting rules, but much of it will require you to learn to think like a deal lawyer.

Chapters 18 through 24, which compose Part 3, will teach you rules and techniques to enhance clarity and to avoid ambiguity. You will learn, among other things, about formatting, clarity through sentence structure, tabulation, and common causes of and cures for ambiguity. You will also learn how to draft formulas and provisions that use accounting concepts.

Chapter 25, the only chapter in Part 4, will teach you how to look at a deal from the client's business perspective and how to add value to a transaction by identifying business issues.

In Part 5, Chapters 26 through 29, you will learn the drafting process, from organizing the initial contract to amending the signed agreement. You will also learn how to analyze and comment on a contract that another lawyer has drafted. Part 6, which consists of Chapter 30, addresses ethical issues unique to contract drafting. Part 7, which consists of Chapter 31, contains additional exercises for you to work on. Part 8 contains the final chapter, Chapter 32. That chapter provides exemplars of well-drafted contracts and guided reading exercises. In addition, the exemplars will serve as precedents for some of the exercises you do for class.

This book concludes with several exhibits. Each exhibit provides background on specific issues not appropriate for the body of the textbook.

1.9 STYLISTIC MATTERS

As you read this book, you will see that some words and phrases are in bold and others in italics. Words or phrases in a **bold** font signal important terms, many of which are defined. *Italics* are used for three purposes: to signal contract language, to provide supplementary information, and to emphasize a word or phrase.

You will also notice that the book uses two kinds of boxes to highlight contract language. Short provisions are inside shaded boxes.

> **Successors and Assigns**. This Agreement binds and benefits the parties and their respective permitted successors and assigns.

When two or more provisions are within a shaded box, each is numbered to distinguish where one ends and the other begins.

Longer provisions are inside an unshaded box—to show you how the provision would look on a contract page.

This Noncompetition Agreement, dated March 16, 20XX, is between Attorney Staffing Acquisition Co., a Delaware corporation (the "**Company**"), and Maria Rodriguez (the "**Executive**").

Background

1. Attorney Staffing Inc., a Delaware corporation (the "**Seller**"), provides temporary lawyers to law firms in the greater Chicago area.
2. The Seller is selling substantially all of its assets to the Company in accordance with the Asset Acquisition Agreement, dated February 1, 20XX (the "**Acquisition Agreement**").
3. The Executive is the sole stockholder of the Seller and its President.
4. The Executive has extensive knowledge of the Seller's business, including its client base and pool of temporary lawyers.
5. It is a condition to the consummation of the Acquisition Agreement that the Executive enter into this Noncompetition Agreement.

Accordingly, the parties agree as follows:

1.10 SOME FINAL WORDS

This course is a lot of work. But it is a great deal of fun (or so my students have told me). You will be learning the quintessential deal-lawyering skills: You will be learning to think and draft like a lawyer. Have fun.

The Building Blocks of Contracts: The Seven Contract Concepts

2.1 INTRODUCTION

To draft a contract, you must use contract concepts. These concepts are the foundation of every contract, the building blocks that, when properly assembled, express the parties' business deal. In this chapter, you will be introduced to those concepts. Once you understand why contract concepts are used in a specific way, you can learn how to assemble them to create a contract and how to express a contract provision clearly and unambiguously.

Here are the seven contract concepts, which when integrated into a contract's parts, result in a contract:

- Representations.
- Warranties.
- Covenants.
- Rights.
- Conditions.
- Discretionary authority.
- Declarations.

You already know something about these concepts from your first-year contracts course. Now you will learn in more depth how deal lawyers use them.

2.2 CAPSULE DEFINITIONS

These are quick definitions of the seven contract concepts. You will learn more about each of them in Chapters 3 and 4.

- A **representation** is a statement of a past or present fact, made as of a moment in time to induce a party to act.
- A **warranty** is a promise that if the statement in the representation is false, the maker of the statement will indemnify the other party for any damages suffered because of the false statement.
- A **covenant** is a promise to do or not to do something. It creates a duty to perform.

- A **right** is the flipside of a covenant. A right entitles a party to the other party's performance.
- A **condition to an obligation** is a state of facts that must exist before a party is obligated to perform.
- **Discretionary authority** gives a party a choice or permission to act. Sometimes the exercise of discretionary authority is subject to the satisfaction of a condition.
- A **declaration** is a fact as to which both parties agree, generally a definition or a policy for the management of the contract. Sometimes a declaration is subject to the satisfaction of a condition.

2.3 TRANSLATING THE BUSINESS DEAL INTO CONTRACT CONCEPTS

Each contract concept serves a different business purpose and has different legal consequences. Accordingly, drafters choose from among these concepts when memorializing the business deal. The analytical skill of determining which contract concept best reflects the business deal is the **translation skill**; it requires the drafter to look at each specific agreement of the business deal and to translate it into contract concepts. Only then can a drafter memorialize the business deal in a contract provision.

The analytical skill of translating the business deal into contract concepts fundamentally differs from the analytical skill that litigators use. Litigators take the law and apply it to the facts to create a persuasive argument. They then memorialize that argument in a brief or a memo or otherwise use it to sway another, be it the other party or the court. In this paradigm, litigators seek a certain legal result by working backward from the law to a static set of facts.

For example, imagine that a driver is going 80 miles an hour and hits a pedestrian; the pedestrian dies, and his heirs bring a lawsuit against the driver. The legal issue is whether the driver was negligent. To determine this, a litigator looks at the components of the cause of action for negligence and then to see whether each of the components can be matched up with the facts. The law is applied to the facts. Depending on whom the litigator represents, the conclusion may vary.

The analytical skill of deal lawyers stands this paradigm on its head. Deal lawyers start from the business deal. The terms of the business deal are the deal lawyer's facts. The deal lawyer must then find the contract concepts that best reflect the business deal and use those concepts as the basis for drafting the contract provisions.

Chapters 3 and 4 teach the translation skill by looking at each of the contract concepts and examining its role in an agreement. Although we will be using the purchase of a house as the factual basis of much of our discussion of contract concepts, these same concepts are the building blocks of all contracts.

Translating the Business Deal into Contract Concepts: Part 1 (Representations and Warranties & Covenants and Rights)

3.1 INTRODUCTION

Before deal lawyers begin to draft, they learn the terms of the business deal. Those terms are the deal lawyer's facts. The lawyer must then find the contract concepts that best reflect the business deal and use those concepts as the basis of drafting the contract provisions. This skill is known as **translating the business deal into contract concepts**, often referred to in its truncated form as the **translation skill**. It is the foundation of a deal lawyer's professional expertise and ability to problem solve. Without it, negotiating and drafting are abstractions. By learning this skill first, you will be able to layer knowledge of how to draft on top of a framework that has taught you what you are drafting.

This chapter and the next discuss the seven contract concepts in depth and demonstrate how to use them in a contract. This chapter deals with representations and warranties, then covenants and rights. Chapter 4 deals with conditions, discretionary authority, and declarations. As part of this discussion, you will learn not only the legal aspects of each contract concept, but also its business purpose. Chapter 4 ends with two appendices that summarize the material in Chapters 3 and 4. You can use them as a quick reference.

3.2 REPRESENTATIONS AND WARRANTIES

3.2.1 DEFINITIONS

Imagine that Sally Seller has listed her house for sale and that Bob Buyer is interested in purchasing it. But before Bob agrees to buy the house, he wants to learn more about it. All that he knows now is that the house is a two-story Cape Cod painted brown. He asks Sally the following questions during a telephone call:

- When was the house built?
- How old is the roof?
- Do all the appliances work?
- Is the house wired for Internet and cable television and is the wiring functioning properly?
- Is there a swimming pool?

- Is there a swimming pool water heater? Does it use propane gas for fuel?
- How much propane gas is in the tank?
- What color are the living room walls, and when were they last painted?
- How much property comes with the house?

Sally responds to Bob by telling him the following:

- The house was built in 1953 along with other houses in the neighborhood.
- The roof is four years old.
- All the appliances are in excellent condition.
- The house is wired for Internet and cable television, and the wiring is functioning properly.
- Yes. A swimming pool is on the property.
- Yes. A swimming pool water heater is on the property, and it uses propane gas for fuel.
- The tank is exactly one-half full with propane gas.
- The living room's walls are painted eggshell white and were painted one year ago. Sally mentions that she has been thinking of painting them a pale blue to coordinate with her furniture.
- The house is on a one-acre lot.

After hearing Sally's answers, Bob visits the house and immediately decides that it is perfect for him. He and Sally agree on a $200,000 purchase price. Bob then calls his lawyer and asks her to draw up the contract and to include within it the information that Sally has told him. He tells his lawyer that he relied on Sally's answers when deciding to buy the house.

How does the lawyer include the information in the contract? The answer is that she will use **representations and warranties**.

A representation

- is a statement[1] of a past or present fact[2]
- as of a moment in time[3]
- intended to induce reliance.[4]

Assume that Sally and Bob sign a contract today for the sale of the house and that in the contract Sally tells Bob the following:

- The roof is four years old.

Sally's statement is a representation. She made that statement (*a statement*) today (*a moment in time*). (Had she made the statement a year ago, the roof would have been three years old, and if she were to make the statement in a year, it would

---

1. *See Restatement (Second) of Contracts* § 159 (1981) (Section 159 states that "[a] misrepresentation is an assertion that is not in accord with the facts."). Turning the definition from a negative statement to a positive one, we obtain a definition of representation: a true assertion of fact. The *Restatement* uses *assertion* and *statement* synonymously. This textbook will use *statement*.

2. *Id.* at cmt. c ("[F]acts include past events as well as present circumstances but do not include future events."); *see Misrepresentation by Promisor of Real Intention as Misstatement of Existing Fact*, 4 U. N.Y.U. L. Rev. 5, 5 (1926) (author not listed). ("Misrepresentations, in order to support an action in fraud, must, among other things, relate *to a fact existing or past.* Statements as to future events, merely promissory in character, are not actionable.") (citations omitted; emphasis added).

3. *Id.* at cmt. c ("An assertion must relate to something that is a fact at the time the assertion is made in order to be a misrepresentation."); *see Spreitzer v. Hawkeye State Bank*, 779 N.W.2d 726, 735 (Iowa 2009) ("[A] representation must be false at the time it was made to support a claim of fraud, and a representation that twas true cannot serve as the basis for a claim of fraud. . . . (citation omitted)").

4. *See Harold Cohn & Co., Inc. v. Harco Int'l, LLC*, 804 A.2d 218, 223-224 (Conn. App. 2002).

be five years old.) In addition, she made the statement to convince Bob to purchase the house (*to induce reliance*).

The representation that the roof is four years old is a statement about a present fact. Sally also made representations with respect to facts concerning the past: *The house was built in 1953 along with other houses in the neighborhood.* Although a party can make representations with respect to present and past facts, it generally cannot do so with respect to future facts.[5] Those are mere statements of opinion. Chapter 9 discusses this issue in more depth.

For Bob to have a cause of action for fraudulent misrepresentation, also known as *the tort of deceit,* Sally must have known that her statement was false when she made it; Bob must have relied on Sally's statement; and that reliance must have been justifiable.[6] That is, Bob must not have known that Sally's statement was false. So, for example, if Bob purchases the house after his contractor inspects the roof and tells Bob that the roof is much older than four years, Bob cannot justifiably rely on Sally's representation that the roof is four years old. Accordingly, Bob would not have a cause of action in tort for fraudulent misrepresentation as to the roof's age. He might, however, have a separate cause of action for breach of **warranty** based on Sally's statement in the representation about the roof's age.[7]

Do not equate a statement in a representation with a representation. A representation is more than a bald statement of fact. It must be a past or present fact intended to induce the reliance of the person receiving the statement.

As you proceed through this chapter, focus on the salient role of reliance in establishing the tort cause of action for breach of warranty.

A warranty differs from a representation.

> A **warranty** is a promise by the maker of a statement that the statement is true.[8]

In the context of a contract with both representations and warranties, the *statements* referenced in the definition of warranty are those the maker made *in* the representation. Thus a warranty requires the statement's maker to pay damages to the statement's recipient if the statement was false and the recipient damaged. The warranty acts as an indemnity.[9] Generally, it does not matter whether the recipient knew the statement was false and did not rely on it.

> The critical question is not whether the buyer believed in the truth of the warranted information, as [the seller] would have it, but "whether [the buyer] believed [it] was purchasing the [seller's] promise [as to its truth]."[10]

The dispute as to reliance's role in a cause of action for breach of warranty stems from the oddity of its birth as a creature of tort law. English lawyers created war-

---

5. *See supra* n. 2 and accompanying text.

6. *See Restatement (Second) of Torts* § 537 (1977) ("The recipient of a fraudulent misrepresentation can recover against its maker for pecuniary loss resulting from it if, but only if . . . (a) he relies on the misrepresentation in acting or refraining from action, and (b) his reliance is justifiable.").
See generally 37 Am. Jur. 2d *Fraud and Deceit* § 239 (2001) for a list of cases from multiple jurisdictions addressing the issue of justifiable reliance.

7. *See S. Broad. Group, LLC v. Harco Int'l, LLC*, 145 F. Supp. 2d 1316, 1321-1324 (M.D. Fla. 2001), *aff'd*, 49 Fed. Appx. 288 (11th Cir. 2002) (table); *see also Shambaugh v. Lindsay*, 445 N.E.2d 124, 125-127 (Ind. App. 1983).

8. *See CBS Inc. v. Ziff-Davis Publg. Co.*, 554 N.Y.S.2d 449, 452-453 (1990). This is not the Uniform Commercial Code definition of a warranty, but the common law one on which this book will focus.

9. *Metro. Coal Co. v. Howard*, 155 F.2d 780, 784 (2d Cir. 1946) (Judge Learned Hand).

10. *CBS Inc. v. Ziff-Davis Publg. Co.*, *supra* n. 8, at 453 (*quoting Ainger v. Mich. Gen. Corp.*, 476 F. Supp. 1209, 1225 (S.D.N.Y. 1979), *aff'd*, 632 F.2d 1025 (2d Cir. 1980)).

ranties centuries ago to tackle the common law's inflexibility. At the time, no contract-related writ permitted a plaintiff to sue the other side if it had not performed its obligations under the contract. The ever-inventive common law lawyers solved the problem by transforming nonperformance of a contract into a tort—an action of deceit that required reliance. Over time, a suit for breach of warranty became an action of *assumpsit,* a contract action.[11] Nonetheless, through the centuries the contours of the cause of action remained uncertain and controversial. Warranty's birth as a tort haunted it.

American scholars extensively debated and analyzed warranties concerning the sale of goods during much of the twentieth century.[12] Codification of the law of warranty concerning the sale of goods in the Uniform Sales Act, and subsequently in the Uniform Commercial Code, did little to quell the debate about whether reliance was a required element of a cause of action for breach of warranty.[13] Outside the context of the sale of goods, academic writing about warranties appears nonexistent, despite the use of warranties in all kinds of commercial agreements (e.g., leases, licenses, and acquisition, credit, settlement, and entertainment agreements).[14]

The evolution of warranties outside the U.C.C. context pivots on the 1990 case of *CBS Inc. v. Ziff-Davis Publishing Company.* In that case, New York's highest court held unequivocally that a warranty was contractual, and that reliance was not an element in a cause of action for its breach.[15] (The Second Circuit has qualified the *CBS* decision by holding that a party waives its cause of action for breach of warranty if the party knows of a warranty's falsity and does not explicitly preserve its rights.[16] Nonetheless, the breadth of the *CBS* decision leaves open whether New York's Court of Appeals would concur with the Second Circuit.[17])

---

11. *See generally* James B. Ames, *History of Assumpsit,* 2 Harv. L. Rev. 1 (1888).

12. *See e.g.* James J. White, *Freeing the Tortious Soul of Express Warranty Law,* 72 Tul. L. Rev. 2089 (June 1998); George Gleason Bogert, *Express Warranties in Sale of Goods,* 33 Yale L. J. 14 (1923); Samuel Williston, *What Constitutes an Express Warranty in the Law of Sales?,* 21 Harv. L. Rev. 555 (1908); *see also* Thomas Williams Saunders, *Warranties and Representations: Fraudulent Representations on the Sale of Personal Chattels,* 10 W. Jurist 586 (1876) (discussing then contemporary English cases).

13. *See generally* White, *supra* n. 12, at 2094-2098; Sidney Kwestel, *Freedom from Reliance: A Contract Approach to Express Warranty,* 20 Suffolk U. L. Rev. 959 (Winter 1992).

14. The author found no mid- to late-20th century scholarly writing on warranties outside the U.C.C. context before the *CBS* decision. But proving the negative is, of course, problematic. After *CBS,* scholarly and practitioner writing on reliance's role as an element in a cause of action for breach of warranty outside the U.C.C. context blossomed. *See e.g.* Bill Payne, *Representations, Reliance & Remedies: The Legacy of Hendricks v. Callahan,* 62 Bench & Bar Minn. 30 (Sept. 2005); Robert J. Johannes & Thomas A. Simonis, *Buyer's Pre-Closing Knowledge of Seller's Breach of Warranty,* 75 Wis. Law. 18 (July 2002); Sidney Kwestel, *Express Warranty as Contractual—The Need for a Clear Approach,* 53 Mercer L. Rev. 557 (Winter 2002); Matthew J. Duchemin, *Whether Reliance on the Warranty is Required in a Common Law Action for Breach of an Express Warranty?,* 82 Marq. L. Rev. 689 (Spring 1999); Frank J. Wozniak, *Purchaser's Disbelief in, or Nonreliance upon, Express Warranties Made by Seller in Contract for Sale of Business as Precluding Action for Breach of Express Warranties,* 7 A.L.R.5th 841 (1992).

15. *CBS Inc. v. Ziff-Davis Publg. Co., supra* n. 8.

16. *See Galli v. Metz,* 973 F.2d 145, 151 (2d Cir. 1992) (holding that where a buyer closes with full knowledge that the facts disclosed by the seller are not as warranted, the buyer may not sue on the breach of warranty, unless it expressly preserves the right to do so); *Rogath v. Siebenmann,* 129 F.3d 261, 264-265 (2d Cir. 1997) (requiring the express preservation of rights when the seller is the source of knowledge of the warranties' falsity).

17. *CBS Inc. v. Ziff-Davis Publg. Co., supra* n. 8, at 454, *505-506, **1002 ("We see no reason why Ziff-Davis should be absolved from its warranty obligations under these circumstances. A holding that it should be because CBS questioned the truth of the facts warranted would have the effect of depriving the express warranties of their only value to CBS—i.e., as continuing promises by Ziff-Davis to indemnify CBS if the facts warranted proved to be untrue (*see Metropolitan Coal Co. v. Howard, supra,* at 784). . . . Ironically, if Ziff-Davis's position were adopted, it would have succeeded in pressing CBS to close despite CBS's misgivings and, at the same time, would have succeeded in *defeating* CBS's breach of warranties action because CBS harbored these *identical misgivings.*") (emphasis in the original).

Since the seminal *CBS* decision, the majority of courts addressing the issue of reliance have agreed with the *CBS* court and held that reliance is not an element of a cause of action for breach of warranty.[18] In addition, courts have roundly criticized the small number of decisions holding to the contrary.[19] Thus the modern view is that warranty has shed its tort origins[20] and is a promise like any other in a contract.[21] This book goes forth on that basis. (Because state Law governs this issue, be sure you know the law in the state whose law governs the transaction.) Chapter 9 discusses the consequences of this now bright-line distinction between representations and warranties.

With this context, let's return to our house purchase hypothetical. As stated previously, Bob would not have a cause of action for misrepresentation with respect to the roof's age because his contractor had told him that it was older than Sally represented. Nonetheless, because Sally also warranted the roof's age, Bob would be able to sue for a breach of warranty post-closing—so long as he told Sally when they were closing that he was reserving his right to make a claim.[22]

Deal lawyers almost always negotiate for both representations and warranties.[23] For example, in the house purchase agreement between Sally and Bob, the representations and warranties article would be introduced with the following language:

> The Seller *represents and warrants* to the Buyer as follows:

By virtue of this one line, every statement in the sections that followed would be both a representation and a warranty.

In the purchase agreement between Sally and Bob, Sally's representations and warranties would resemble the following:

---

18. *See Grupo Condumex, S.A. v. SPX Corp.*, 2008 WL 4372678 at *4 (No. 3:99CV7316, N.D. Ohio, Sept. 19, 2008) ("Declining to impose an obligation on a party claiming damages for breach of warranty to prove reliance on the warranty conforms to the current views of a majority of other jurisdictions. *Mowbray v. Waste Mgmt. Holdings, Inc.*, 189 F.R.D. 194, 200 (D. Mass.); *see Power Soak Sys. v. EMCO Holdings, Inc.*, 482 F. Supp. 2d 1125, 1134 (W.D. Mo. 2007) ('The modern trend is that a buyer need not rely on a seller's express warranty in order to recover for the seller's subsequent breach of the express warranty.'); *Southern Broadcast Group, LLC v. GEM Broadcasting, Inc.*, 145 F. Supp. 2d 1316, 1321-1324 (M.D. Fla. 2001) (citing cases applying Illinois, Pennsylvania, Connecticut, Montana, New York, New Mexico, Indiana, and Massachusetts law); *Norcold Inc. v. Gateway Supply Co.*, 154 Ohio App. 3d 594, 601, 798 N.E.2d 618 (2003) (also recognizing that a 'decisive majority of courts' have held that reliance is not an element for claim of breach of warranty).")

19. Cases holding to the contrary: *Hendricks v. Callahan*, 972 F.2d 190 (8th Cir. 1992) (applying Minnesota law); *Land v. Roper Corp.*, 531 F.2d 445 (10th Cir. 1976) (applying Kansas law); *Middleby Corp. v. Hussman*, 1992 WL 220922 (N.D. Ill. 1992) (applying Delaware law); *Kazerouni v. De Satnick*, 228 Cal. App. 3d 871 (2d Dist. 1991).

Cases criticizing *Hendricks* and *Land*: *Giuffrida v. Am. Family Brands, Inc.*, 1998 WL 196402 at *4 (E.D. Pa. Apr. 23, 1998); *S. Broad. Group, LLC v. GEM Broad., Inc.*, 145 F. Supp. 2d 1316, 1321 (M.D. Fla. 2001); *Mowbray v. Waste Mgt. Holdings, Inc.*, 189 F.R.D. 194, 200 (D. Mass. 1999).

Case criticizing *Middleby*: *Vigertone AG Prods., Inc. v. AG Prods. Inc.*, 316 F.3d 641, 649 (7th Cir. 2002) (Judge Posner).

Case distinguishing *Kazerouni*: *Telephia v. Cuppy*, 411 F. Supp. 2d 1178 (N.D. Cal. 2006).

20. *CBS Inc. v. Ziff-Davis Publg. Co.*, *supra* n. 8, at 453, 503, 1001 ("This view of 'reliance'—i.e., as requiring no more than reliance on the express warranty as being a part of the bargain between the parties—reflects the prevailing perception of an action for breach of express warranty as one that is no longer grounded in tort, but essentially in contract."); *see also Ainger v. Mich. Gen. Corp.*, 476 F. Supp. 1209, 1224-1225 (S.D.N.Y. 1979), *aff'd*, 632 F.2d 1025 (2d Cir. 1980) ("Transporting tort principles into contract law seems analytically unsound.").

21. *Glacier Gen. Assur. Co. v. Cas. Indem. Exch.*, 435 F. Supp. 855, 860 (D. Mont. 1977) ("The warranty is as much a part of the contract as any other part, and the right to damages on the breach depends on nothing more than the breach of warranty.").

22. *See supra* nn. 16 and 17 and accompanying text.

23. Chapter 9 discusses situations when it might be appropriate to ask for just warranties.

> **Seller's Representations and Warranties**. The Seller represents and warrants to the Buyer as follows:
>
> (a) The house was built in 1953, along with the other houses in the neighborhood.
> (b) The roof is four years old.
> (c) All the appliances are in excellent condition.
> (d) The house is wired for Internet and cable television, and the wiring is functioning properly.
> (e) A swimming pool is on the property.
> (f) A swimming pool water heater is on the property, and it uses propane gas for fuel. The propane gas tank is on the property.
> (g) The tank is exactly one-half full with propane gas.
> (h) The living room's walls are painted eggshell white and were painted one year ago.
> (i) The house is on a one-acre lot.

Finally, when determining whether a party made a misrepresentation and breached a warranty, a statement's truthfulness is always determined by comparing the statement to reality as of the moment in time when the statement was made, not when the determination of truthfulness is made.[24] Therefore, Sally's representation and warranty are truthful so long as the living room walls were painted eggshell white when she stated that they were that color. It would be irrelevant with respect to claims for misrepresentation and breach of warranty that she painted the walls pale blue after she made the representation in the contract for sale but before she sold the house to Bob. Of course, the painting of the walls would not be irrelevant to Bob. But to obtain a remedy, he would need to rely on a cause of action other than misrepresentation and breach of warranty. He would need a covenant and perhaps a condition.[25]

3.2.2   REMEDIES

Representations and warranties are common law concepts. As such, they carry with them common law remedies. The differences in these remedies can directly affect which cause of action is the most favorable for a plaintiff to plead.

A party can make three types of misrepresentations: innocent,[26] negligent,[27] and fraudulent.[28] A litigation alleging any of these misrepresentations is a suit in tort.

Typically, innocent and negligent misrepresentations must be material to support a remedy.[29] The law with respect to fraudulent misrepresentations depends on the jurisdiction. In some jurisdictions, a misrepresentation need not be material for it to constitute a fraudulent misrepresentation,[30] while in others it must.[31]

---

24. *See Union Bank v. Jones*, 411 A.2d 1338, 1342 (Vt. 1980) and footnote 3 in this chapter.

25. See §§ 3.3 and 4.2.

26. *See Bortz v. Noon*, 729 A.2d 555, 563-564 (Pa. 1999); *Restatement (Second) of Torts* § 552C (1977) (misrepresentations in sales, rental, or exchange transactions).

27. *See Liberty Mut. Ins. Co. v. Decking & Steel, Inc.*, 301 F. Supp. 2d 830, 834 (N.D. Ill. 2004); *Restatement (Second) of Torts* § 552 (1977) (information negligently supplied for the guidance of others).

28. *See Skurnowicz v. Lucci*, 798 A.2d 788, 793 (Pa. Super. 2002).

29. *See Restatement (Second) of Contracts* § 164 (1981).

30. *See Sarvis v. Vt. State Colleges*, 772 A.2d 494, 498 (Vt. 2001). *Compare Restatement (Second) of Contracts* § 164 (1981) (providing that a fraudulent misrepresentation need not be material to make it voidable) *with Restatement (Second) of Torts* § 538 (1977) (providing that reliance on a fraudulent representation is not justifiable unless the matter misrepresented is material).

31. *See Skurnowicz v. Lucci, supra* n. 28.

If a misrepresentation is innocent or negligent, the usual remedies are **avoidance** and **restitutionary recovery**.[32] Avoidance permits the injured party to unwind the contract.[33] Both lawyers and courts often refer to it as *rescission*. Restitutionary recovery requires each party to return to the other what it received, either in kind or, if necessary, in money.[34]

A misrepresentation may also be fraudulent—a misstatement made with knowledge of its falsity (**scienter**).[35] In this case, an injured party has a choice of remedies. First, it may void the contract and seek restitution,[36] just as with innocent and negligent misrepresentations. Alternatively, it may affirm the contract, retain its benefits, and sue for damages based on a claim of fraudulent misrepresentation,[37] sometimes referred to as the tort of deceit. The injured party's damages claim could also include punitive damages,[38] which, of course, can be significantly larger than general damages. (Lawyers sometimes refer to affirming the contract as **standing on the contract**.)

If an injured party decides to affirm the contract by suing for fraudulent misrepresentation, the measure of damages depends on which state's law governs the contract. Most states use the **benefit of the bargain** measure of damages,[39] with the minority using the **out-of-pocket** measure of damages.[40]

The benefit of the bargain measure of damages results in a higher damages award and is the measure of damages that a party generally receives on a contract breach. It is equal to the value that the property was represented to be minus the actual value. So, if the property was represented to be worth $10,000 but was actually only worth $3,000, the damages would be $7,000.

Value if as represented	$10,000
Actual value	-3,000
Damages	$7,000

Out-of-pocket damages are equal to the amount the plaintiff paid for the property minus the actual value. Thus, if the plaintiff paid $5,000 for property that was only worth $3,000, it could recover only $2,000 in damages.

Amount paid	$5,000
Actual value	-3,000
Damages	$2,000

---

32. *See Norton v. Poplos*, 443 A.2d 1, 4-5 (Del. 1981) (innocent misrepresentation); *Patch v. Arsenault*, 653 A.2d 1079, 1081-1083 (N.H. 1995) (negligent misrepresentation). Damages have been awarded in cases of innocent and negligent misrepresentation. *See Restatement (Second) of Torts* §§552B and 552C (1977); *see generally* Dan B. Dobbs, *Dobbs' Law of Remedies* vol. 2, §9.2(2), 554-556 (2d ed., West 1993) [*Dobbs' Law of Remedies*].

33. *See Kavarco v. T.J.E., Inc.*, 478 A.2d 257, 261 (Conn. App. 1984); *see generally* E. Allan Farnsworth, *Farnsworth on Contracts* vol. 1, 495-496 (3d ed., Aspen Publishers 2004).

34. *Farnsworth on Contracts, supra* n. 33, at 499. Some cases hold that the injured party is also entitled to reliance damages. *See In re Letterman*, 799 F.2d 967, 974 (5th Cir. 1986).

35. *See Bortz v. Noon*, 729 A.2d 555, 560 (Pa. 1999).

36. *See Smith v. Brown*, 778 N.E.2d 490, 497 (Ind. App. 2002).

37. *See Stebins v. Wells*, 766 A.2d 369, 372 (R.I. 2001); *A. Sangivanni & Sons v. F. M. Floryan & Co.*, 262 A.2d 159, 163 (Conn. 1969) ("Fraud in the inducement of a contract ordinarily renders the contract merely voidable at the option of the defrauded party, who also has the choice of affirming the contract and suing for damages. . . . [in which event] the contract remains in force. . .").

38. *See generally Dobbs' Law of Remedies* vol. 2, § 9.2(5), 565-568.

39. *See e.g. Lightning Litho, Inc. v. Danka Indus., Inc.*, 776 N.E.2d 1238, 1241-1242 (Ind. App. 2002).

40. *See Reno v. Bull*, 124 N.E. 144, 146 (N.Y. 1919). Some states follow neither rule exclusively, but instead have a more flexible approach that varies the damage award based on specific factors. *See e.g. Selman v. Shirley*, 85 P.2d 384, 393-394 (Or. 1938).

The difference in recovery between the benefit of the bargain damages and out-of-pocket damages can be an important factor when a plaintiff decides whether to sue for fraudulent misrepresentation or breach of warranty. Specifically, if an injured party asserts a claim for breach of warranty, a contract claim, the remedy for that breach is full benefit of the bargain damages.[41] Therefore, in a state that follows the out-of-pocket rule of damages for fraudulent misrepresentations, a plaintiff would probably be better off pursuing a breach of warranty claim, as its benefit of the bargain damages would be greater.[42] A claim for fraud might become the preferable claim, however, if a plaintiff could successfully argue for punitive damages.

The following chart summarizes the remedies associated with representations and warranties.

INNOCENT AND NEGLIGENT MISREPRESENTATIONS	FRAUDULENT MISREPRESENTATIONS	WARRANTIES
Avoidance and restitutionary recovery	Avoidance and restitutionary recovery *or* Damages: • Out-of-pocket damages *or* • Benefit of the bargain damages • Punitive damages (possibly)	Benefit of the bargain damages

In this discussion, false representations have been referred to as *misrepresentations.* Although some lawyers colloquially speak of *breaches of representations,* that terminology is incorrect. A breach is a violation of a promise. Because representations are not promises, they cannot be breached. Instead, a party makes *misrepresentations.* It is correct, however, to speak of *breaches of warranties,* as warranties are promises.

3.2.3 WHY A PARTY SHOULD RECEIVE BOTH REPRESENTATIONS AND WARRANTIES

As the preceding sections have made clear, multiple benefits accrue to a party who receives both representations and warranties. To summarize, these benefits are the following:

■ **First**, a party may void the contract and receive restitution only if that party receives representations.

■ **Second**, a party may sue for punitive damages only by claiming a fraudulent misrepresentation.

■ **Third**, if a party cannot prove justifiable reliance on a representation, that party can still sue for breach of warranty.

■ **Fourth**, if a state follows the out-of-pocket rule for damages for fraudulent misrepresentations, a party can still recover the greater benefit of the bargain damages by suing for breach of warranty.

---

41. *See Nunn v. Chem. Waste Mgt., Inc.*, 856 F.2d 1464, 1470 (10th Cir. 1988).
42. *See Ainger v. Mich. Gen. Corp., supra* n. 20, at 1233-1234.

■ **Fifth**, a breach of warranty claim may be easier to prove than a fraudulent misrepresentation claim. As noted earlier, to prove fraudulent misrepresentation, a plaintiff must demonstrate *scienter,* that the defendant knowingly made a false representation.[43] As proving a party's state of mind can be difficult, a breach of warranty claim, which has no such requirement, may be the easier claim to win.[44]

3.2.4 RISK ALLOCATION

Each representation and warranty establishes a standard of liability. If a statement is false — if the statement does not reflect reality — then the standard has not been met and the party making the statement is subject to liability.

By establishing standards of liability, representations and warranties serve an important business purpose. They are a **risk allocation** mechanism. This means that the degree of risk that each party assumes with respect to a statement varies depending on how broadly or narrowly the statement is drafted.

Recall that Sally told Bob that the propane gas tank was exactly one-half full. That is a precise statement. It is posited as an absolute, without any kind of wiggle room. It is a **flat representation**. It is a high-risk statement for Sally because if she is even a little wrong, Bob has a cause of action for misrepresentation and breach of warranty. He might not have a claim for a great deal of money, but he could certainly bring a nuisance suit and hope for a quick settlement/price reduction.

Sally could have reduced her risk by making a less precise statement. She could have made a **qualified representation**. For example, she could have said, "[T]he tank is *approximately* half-filled." Then if the propane gas tank had been less than one-half its capacity, Sally might still have been able to contend that her statement was true. Her risk of having made a false statement would have been reduced. Bob, however, would have assumed a greater risk with respect to Sally's statement about the amount of fuel in the tank. Originally, Bob would have had a cause of action if the tank was even a little less than half full. Now, in order to prove a misrepresentation and breach of warranty, Bob must argue what *approximately* means. The risk allocation has shifted more of the risk to Bob.[45]

To see how risk allocation works in a more sophisticated context, imagine that you are general counsel of a $100 million company that is selling all of its shares in a wholly owned subsidiary (the Target). Your current task is to negotiate the *no litigation* representation and warranty that appears in the stock purchase agreement.[46] You know the statement needs to be qualified. But how?

Immediately following this paragraph are five versions of a *no litigation* representation and warranty. The first version is the language in the agreement. The subsequent versions represent the evolution of your thinking with respect to what kind of qualifications would be appropriate. Read all of the versions and see if you can explain how each version changes the risk allocation.

---

43. See §3.2.2 n. 35.

44. *See* W. Page Keeton, Dan B. Dobbs, Robert E. Keeton & David G. Owen, *Prosser and Keeton on Torts* §107, 741 (5th ed. West 1984).

45. If this issue arose in the real world, the parties would most likely deal with it by a purchase price adjustment. It is used here to demonstrate risk allocation.

46. In an acquisition agreement, a *no litigation* representation and warranty details what litigation exists so that a buyer can determine if that litigation presents a significant risk to the business it is buying. Similar representations and warranties exist in other agreements. For example, in a license agreement, the licensor generally represents and warrants that there are no litigations challenging the licensor's ownership of the trademark.

Version 1

No Litigation. No litigation is pending or threatened against the Target.

Version 2

No Litigation. Except as stated in **Schedule 3.14**, no litigation is pending or threatened against the Target.

Version 3

No Litigation. Except as stated in **Schedule 3.14**, no litigation is pending or, to the Seller's knowledge, threatened against the Target.

Version 4

No Litigation. Except as stated in **Schedule 3.14**, no litigation is pending or, to the knowledge of any of the Seller's officers, threatened against the Target.

Version 5

No Litigation. Except as stated in **Schedule 3.14**, no litigation is pending or, to the knowledge of any of the Seller's three executive officers, threatened against the Target. For the purpose of this representation and warranty, "knowledge" means, cumulatively,

(a) each executive officer's actual knowledge; and

(b) the knowledge that each executive officer would have had after a diligent investigation.

Again, Version 1 is how the representation and warranty appears in the stock purchase agreement. It is a flat representation and warranty. You immediately recognize its most obvious flaw: It is false. Virtually every company has some litigation, and the Target is no exception. If the representation and warranty is not changed, the Seller is at great risk because it knows that the statement is false. A cause of action for misrepresentation could allege fraud. Therefore, the first qualification is that the representation and warranty must indicate pending litigations. The typical way to do this is to list them on a **disclosure schedule** and then to refer to the schedule in the representation and warranty. Version 2 does this. For a more detailed discussion of schedules, see § 5.10.

The easy part is now over. On further review, you see that the representation and warranty actually makes two statements: one about pending litigation and the other about threatened litigation. At first, you do not see this as a concern as the disclosure schedule can qualify the representation and warranty not only with respect to pending litigation, but also with respect to known, threatened litigation. But what if the Seller does not know of an existing, threatened litigation against the Target? Perhaps someone is claiming that a product malfunctioned and intends to sue. It is an unknown, threatened litigation. After concluding that this is an unfair risk for the Seller to assume, you ask the Buyer's counsel for a knowledge qualification with respect to unknown, threatened litigation.[47] He acquiesces, and the representation and warranty is redrafted as set forth in Version 3.[48]

While the form of the Version 3 representation and warranty decreases the Seller's risk of liability, it increases the Buyer's risk. Because the Seller is no longer making a representation and warranty about unknown, threatened litigation, the Buyer will have no cause of action if unknown, threatened litigation against the Target actually exists.

Version 4 addresses the problem of what constitutes the Seller's knowledge. In the hypothetical, the Seller is a corporation, a juridical entity formed when its certificate of incorporation was filed with the appropriate governmental authority. As it is not a living, breathing human being, what constitutes its knowledge is not immediately apparent. Is it the knowledge of the company's managers, or the knowledge of everyone from the president to the employees on the shop floor?

From your perspective as general counsel (to put words in your mouth), it undoubtedly is an unfair risk for the Seller to be liable for the knowledge of every company employee. Accordingly, you request that the representation and warranty be further qualified so that the Seller is responsible only for its officers' knowledge.[49] With this change, the Seller no longer takes a risk as to the knowledge of an employee on the shop floor. However, the Seller's decrease in risk means that the Buyer's risk has commensurately increased. If an employee on the shop floor, in fact, knows of a threatened litigation, the Buyer will have no cause of action against the Seller because its representation and warranty is true: No officer knew. Thus, should the threatened litigation turn into an actual litigation and result in an award of damages, the Buyer would be obligated to pay it.

At this point, you are on a roll. You decide that even *knowledge of any of the Seller's officers* is too great a risk. Therefore, you go to the well again and ask the Buyer's counsel to change the qualification so that it reads *knowledge of any of the Seller's three executive officers*. This is the language in the first sentence of Version 5.

At this point, however, the Buyer's counsel says: "Enough. If knowledge is limited to three executive officers, they could walk around with blinders on doing their best to acquire no knowledge of threatened litigation. This is too much risk for the Buyer to assume." The Buyer's counsel instead proposes to define *knowledge* as the aggregate actual knowledge of each of the executive officers and their **imputed knowledge**; that is, the knowledge each executive would have had if the executive had performed a diligent inquiry. This is the compromise language in the remainder of Version 5. The Seller has limited its risk to the knowledge of the three executive officers, while, concurrently, the Buyer has eliminated its risk of the executive officers' intentional oblivion.

Understanding the impact of risk allocation is essential to fulfilling your role as a counselor. Clients too often misunderstand the purpose of representations and

---

47. Another common qualification of representations and warranties is **materiality**. That qualifier is discussed in §9.3 and is the subject of Exercise 9-1.

48. Agreeing to this qualification is so common that a buyer's first draft often includes it. The parties do, however, often negotiate the definition of *knowledge*.

49. The qualification in Version 4 uses the phrase "to the knowledge of *any* of the Seller's officers." Thus, if any one or more of the Seller's officers knows of any threatened litigation, that alone creates a misrepresentation and breach of warranty. If *any* were replaced with *each*, however, then all three of the Seller's officers would have to know of the threatened litigation to cause a misrepresentation and breach of warranty.

warranties and think that the time spent negotiating them is mere **wordsmithing**.[50] By explaining to a client that the wording of the representations and warranties can affect potential liability, you have explained that money is on the table, something that clients readily understand.

3.3 COVENANTS

3.3.1 DEFINITIONS AND USES OF COVENANTS

We will first look at covenants in the context of the sale of Sally's house to Bob and then in other contexts.

Imagine that after Sally and Bob have agreed to a price, Bob tells Sally that he cannot immediately purchase the house as he first needs to obtain a mortgage. A delayed closing is acceptable to Sally, and they agree to close the sale on the last day of the next month. This delay creates a gap period between the signing of the purchase contract and the closing.[51] (A **closing** is when parties exchange the agreed performances. Typically, closings occur only in acquisitions and financings. In an acquisition, it would be the day the seller transfers its property to the buyer, and the buyer pays the seller; in a financing, it would be the day the bank makes the loan to the borrower, and the borrower agrees to repay it.)

As Bob and Sally finalize their agreement, Bob tells Sally that he is concerned about what will happen to the house during the gap period. Specifically, he does not want the living room walls painted, and he wants to make sure that the propane gas tank is at least one-third full with propane gas when he moves in on the closing date. Sally agrees. To incorporate Sally's agreement into the purchase contract, the lawyers use **covenants**, called **promises** in the argot of *Restatement (Second) of Contracts*.[52]

> A **covenant** is a promise to do or not to do something.[53] It creates a duty to perform if a contract has been formed.[54] The duty to perform is sometimes called an **obligation**.[55]

In the purchase agreement between Sally and Bob, the covenants will resemble the following:

> **Seller's Covenants.** The Seller
>
> (a) shall not paint the walls between the signing and the Closing; and
>
> (b) shall cause the propane gas tank to be at least one-third full with propane gas on the Closing Date.

---

50. **Wordsmithing** has a pejorative connotation. It suggests that a lawyer redrafts language for no substantive reason, wasting time and money.

51. A gap period between signing and closing is routine in acquisition transactions. It arises for multiple reasons. First, the buyer may need to obtain financing. Second, the parties may need to obtain consents to the transaction or to the transfer of particular assets. Finally, the buyer may want to perform **due diligence** if it did not previously do so. Due diligence is the corporate equivalent of test-driving a car before purchasing it. (To be sure that a target company is worth purchasing, the buyer-to-be examines, among other things, the seller's contracts, equipment, and financial statements.)

52. *Restatement (Second) of Contracts* § 2(1).

53. *Id.*

54. *Restatement (Second) of Contracts* §§ 1 and 2 cmt. a.

55. *Id.* at § 1 cmt. b.

Although the need for these covenants in the purchase agreement arose because of the gap period between signing and closing, covenants are used in multiple other contexts. One of the most important is in the subject matter performance provision. In this provision, each side covenants to the other that it will perform the main subject matter of the contract. So, in our house contract hypothetical, the main subject matter of the contract is the purpose and sale of the house. The subject matter performance provision would be stated as follows:

> At the Closing, the Seller shall sell the house to the Buyer, and the Buyer shall buy the house from the Seller.

The following timelines of an acquisition agreement and a license agreement show how covenants can be used at difficult stages in a transaction.

Example 1. Acquisition Agreement

Gap period:
1. Covenants relating to the gap period
2. Other covenants

Post-closing period
Post-closing covenants

Signing date:
Representations and warranties

Closing date:
1. Conditions
2. Covenants to be performed at closing

Example 2. License Agreement

Contract term:
Covenants

Covenants after the end of the contract term

Signing date:
1. Representations and warranties
2. Conditions (if any)

End of the contract term

Example 1 is the timeline of an acquisition agreement. As we have seen, in this type of transaction, the parties use covenants during the gap period to control the seller's actions with respect to the subject matter of the contract (e.g., the house).[56] However, an acquisition agreement also has covenants that are unrelated to the gap period. Some covenants, such as confidentiality provisions, apply both before and after closing. Other covenants apply only at closing; for example, the promise to pay the purchase price and the promise to transfer the assets (the subject matter performance covenants). And finally, some covenants apply only to the post-closing period. Indemnities and noncompetition provisions are classic examples.

The timeline of a license agreement, Example 2, differs from the timeline of an acquisition agreement. The license agreement has no gap period. Its term begins and ends on agreed-on dates.[57] Each party covenants to the other as to its behavior during the term. The licensee promises to use its commercially reasonable efforts to manu-

---

56. Buyers also give covenants, such as promising to obtain any necessary consents.

57. Sometimes the parties sign on a date before the term begins. The period between the signing and the beginning of the term differs from the gap periods in acquisition agreements. During the license agreement's "gap period," generally, no covenants must be performed or conditions satisfied. Instead, the delayed beginning of the term is for administrative ease, so that the term begins either on the first day of a month or immediately after one party's relationship with a third party concludes. For example, a licensor and a licensee may negotiate and sign a license agreement in October, but the license term will not begin until January 1, the day after the licensor's current arrangement with another licensee terminates.

facture and market products using the trademark, to pay license fees, and to submit for approval a prototype of each product. In turn, the licensor promises not to license the trademark to anyone else, to defend the trademark, and to promptly approve or disapprove each prototype submitted for approval. Occasionally, covenants relate to the period after the term. For example, the contract will typically set out the parties' obligations post-term with respect to any unsold inventory that the licensee owns at the end of the term.

3.3.2 DEGREES OF OBLIGATION

In the same way that representations and warranties are a risk allocation mechanism, so too are covenants. The allocation manifests itself in terms of how absolute a party's promises are. The business differences between the different ways of expressing a party's obligations are **degrees of obligation**.[58]

Consider a transaction in which the buyer hopes to acquire a lease for property that the seller uses in its business operations. To effect this acquisition, the seller must assign its rights under the lease to the buyer, but the seller's lease prohibits it from doing so. Therefore, the buyer insists that the seller must promise to obtain the landlord's consent to the assignment. Review the following covenants and see if you can determine how the risk allocation shifts depending on the degree of the seller's obligation.[59]

Version 1

Consents. The Seller shall obtain the consent of Landlord Corp. to the Seller's assignment of the Lease to the Buyer.

Version 2

Consents. The Seller shall use commercially reasonable efforts to obtain the consent of Landlord Corp. to the Seller's assignment of the Lease to the Buyer.

Version 3

Consents. The Seller shall use commercially reasonable efforts to obtain the consent of Landlord Corp. to the Seller's assignment of the Lease to the Buyer. For purposes of this provision, the Seller is deemed to have used its commercially reasonable efforts if it offers Landlord Corp. at least $10,000 as an inducement to consent to the assignment.

Version 4

Consents. The Seller shall request that Landlord Corp. consent to the Seller's assignment of the Lease to the Buyer.

Version 1 is the equivalent of a flat representation. It is the Seller's absolute promise to obtain consent. The promise is dangerous for the Seller to make as it has no

---

58. I thank my former Fordham Law School colleague, Alan Shaw, for coining this most useful phrase, *degrees of obligation.*

59. These covenants are based on covenants that Alan Shaw drafted.

control over the outcome: Landlord Corp. has no obligation to consent, and it could just as easily refuse consent as grant it. Because the Seller has no control, it risks breaching the covenant. The Seller, therefore, wants to reduce its risk by reducing its degree of obligation.

From the Buyer's perspective, Version 1 is a terrific covenant. If the Seller obtains Landlord Corp.'s consent, the Buyer is in position immediately to continue the Seller's business on the same premises. If the Buyer does not obtain consent, however, the Buyer should still come out whole as it has the right to sue for damages. If the current lease's rent is under market value, the Buyer's damages might be equal to the rent the Buyer would have to pay for comparable leased property minus the rent the Seller is paying under its lease.

Versions 2 through 4 each change the Seller's risk but in a different way. Version 2 does not require the Seller to obtain consent. Instead, the standard is that the Seller must have tried to obtain consent and must have used commercially reasonable efforts in that endeavor. That is, the Seller must do what the reasonable business-person would do. This change substantially reduces the degree of the Seller's obligation and, therefore, its risk. Now, the focus is on the degree of effort, rather than the result. So long as the Seller uses commercially reasonable efforts to obtain consent, the Buyer has no cause of action for breach if the consent is not obtained. Any difference between the cost of the existing lease and a new lease is for the Buyer's account. The decrease in the Seller's risk has shifted risk to the Buyer.

From the Seller's perspective, Version 2 is definitely better than Version 1. Nonetheless, the precise degree of effort is vague. What does *commercially reasonable efforts* mean? How much money must the Seller spend to induce Landlord Corp. to grant consent?[60] Version 3 directly addresses this issue by capping, at $10,000, the amount that the Seller needs to spend to comply with the covenant.

The cap shifts risk to the Buyer. To see this more vividly, assume the Seller offers Landlord Corp. $10,000 to consent, but Landlord Corp. refuses to consent and demands $10,500. In this event, the Seller has performed its covenant and, therefore, is not in breach, even though it did not obtain consent. Accordingly, the Buyer is on the hook for any increased lease expense—even though a slightly increased payment to Landlord Corp. would have resulted in a consent.

Finally, Version 4 eliminates the Seller's obligation to obtain consent. Instead, the Seller must merely request that consent. Its degree of obligation is minimal, and the Buyer assumes almost all the risk with respect to the Seller's failure to obtain consent.

3.3.3 REMEDIES

In the same way that representations and warranties carry with them their own common law remedies, so too do covenants. In general, breach of a covenant entitles the injured party to sue for damages[61] and, if the facts are appropriate, specific performance.[62] The measure of damages is full benefit of the bargain damages. (If the breach is so material that it is a breach of the whole contract that cannot be cured, then a party may have a right to cancel as well as other remedies.[63])

---

60. *See e.g. Bloor v. Falstaff Brewing Corp.*, 601 F.2d 609 (2d Cir. 1979).
61. *See generally Dobbs' Law of Remedies* vol. 3, § 12.2, 21-50.
62. *See generally id.* at § 12.8, 189-245.
63. *See* U.C.C. §§ 2-106(4), 2-612, 2-703 (2004).

If a party breaches a covenant, that party need not also have made a misrepresentation and breached a warranty. First, as is often the case, the party may not have made a representation and warranty on the same topic. Second, even if it has, the truthfulness of a representation and warranty is determined as of the time it was made. So, if a representation and warranty was true at the time that it was made, no misrepresentation or breach of warranty would occur just because the related covenant was breached.

To put this in context, assume that, at the signing of the contract, Sally represents and warrants that the walls of the living room are eggshell white and covenants to maintain their color. Then, during the gap period, Sally decides that she wants blue walls for her last few weeks in the house, and she paints them. By doing so, Sally breaches her covenant not to paint the walls, giving Bob a cause of action for breach of the covenant. Bob will not, however, have a cause of action for misrepresentation or breach of warranty because the walls were eggshell white when Sally represented and warranted their color.[64]

3.4 RIGHTS

A contract **right** flows from another party's duty to perform; that is, it flows from a covenant. The person to whom the performance is owed has a right to that performance. Therefore, if there is a duty, there is a correlative right. More colloquially, the flip side of every duty is a right. Because of this relationship, a right's business purpose is the same as a duty's: to allocate risk by establishing standards of liability.

Although a duty is generally expressed as a covenant for business and legal reasons, that duty can alternatively be expressed as a right. For example:

Version 1

Payment of Purchase Price. The Buyer shall pay the Seller $200,000 at Closing. *(Drafted as the Buyer's duty.)*

Version 2

Entitlement to Purchase Price. The Seller is entitled to be paid $200,000 at Closing. *(Drafted as the Seller's right.)*

In both examples, the Buyer must pay $200,000. The difference is the focus: the Buyer's duty to pay versus the Seller's right to payment.

When determining whether a particular business point is a right, the correlative duty is not always immediately apparent. For example:

Entitlement to Deposit. If the Buyer fails to close because it did not obtain financing, the Seller is entitled to keep the deposit.

---

64. See §3.2.1.

In this instance, the correlative duty would be the Buyer's obligation not to seek return of the deposit.[65] (The use of *may* here to indicate discretionary authority would be wrong. *May* indicates a choice between alternatives, but it's hard to imagine a seller choosing to give the deposit back to a buyer.) A seller might be quite nonplussed to find it has discretionary authority as opposed to the absolute right. This is another example of *is entitled* being used to express a remedy. Some commentators might opt for *may* in these situations, but *may* insufficiently expresses the business deal. If clients are wronged, discretion doesn't cut it. They want a right.

---

65. See Chapter 10, Guideline 3 and § 12.1.2, pp. 176-178 for a further discussion of the drafting of rights in the context of endgame provisions.

Translating the Business Deal into Contract Concepts: Part 2 (Conditions, Discretionary Authority, and Declarations)

4.1 INTRODUCTION

This chapter continues teaching you how to translate the business deal into contract concepts. It discusses conditions, discretionary authority, and declarations.

4.2 CONDITIONS TO OBLIGATIONS

4.2.1 THE BASICS

Let's continue with the Sally Seller/Bob Buyer house purchase hypothetical that we discussed in Chapter 3.

After negotiating the purchase price, Bob tells Sally that he needs to obtain a mortgage and that the application process will take about six weeks. He also tells her that while he is quite confident that he will obtain the mortgage, he does not want to be obligated to buy the house if he cannot obtain it. Sally agrees.

To establish the mortgage as a contractual prerequisite to Bob's obligation to buy the house, the purchase contract will use a **condition.**

> A **condition** is a state of facts that must exist before a party is obligated to perform.[1]

If that state of facts does not exist, the obligation to perform is not triggered. Uncertainty is a hallmark of a condition. For a state of facts to be a condition, those facts cannot be certain to occur. Thus, the passage of time cannot be a condition because it will occur.[2] Conditions may appear in any type of agreement. They are not limited to acquisition agreements.

---

1. The *Restatement (Second) of Contracts* §224 (1981) defines a condition as "an event, not certain to occur, which must occur, unless its nonoccurrence is excused, before performance under a contract becomes due." However, this book uses the shorthand definition in the text. In addition, this chapter discusses two other types of conditions: conditions to discretionary authority and conditions to declarations. See §4.3 (conditions to discretionary authority) and §4.4 (conditions to declarations).

2. *Restatement (Second) of Contracts* §224 cmt. b.

A condition is not a condition to the making of a covenant. Instead, a condition is a state of facts that must exist before a party must perform the obligation that flows from a covenant.

Although many lawyers refer to a condition as a condition precedent, the *Restatement (Second) of Contracts* has eliminated the use of that term.[3] Previously, a condition was labeled either a **condition precedent** or a **condition subsequent**. While a **condition precedent** was defined as a state of facts that had to exist before there was an obligation to perform, a **condition subsequent** was a state of facts that took away a preexisting obligation.[4] As a lawyer could draft most provisions as either a condition precedent or a condition subsequent, distinguishing between the conditions was problematic. The difference, however, remained important because the type of condition determined which party had the evidentiary burden of proving the condition. The *Restatement* has recharacterized the condition subsequent as the discharge of an obligation.[5] So now, conditions precedent are referred to simply as conditions.[6]

In the contract between Bob and Sally, the condition to the obligation and the obligation to perform might look something like the following:

> **If the Buyer obtains a mortgage, then the Buyer shall buy [is obligated to buy] the House.**

Obtaining the mortgage triggers Bob's obligation to purchase.

The condition to an obligation and the obligation need not be in the same sentence. They can be in different sections of the contract. But for every condition to an obligation, the contract must include an obligation. They are a matched pair.

To decide whether a condition is the appropriate contract concept, determine if a relationship exists between two events and whether one must precede the other temporally. Try to fit the fact pattern into an *if/then* formulation. *If* this happens, *then* and only then is a party obligated to perform. If you can do that, draft a condition.

When creating an if/then statement, the *then* clause should state who has the obligation to perform.

> **Correct**
>
> **Mortgage.** If the Buyer obtains a mortgage, the Buyer shall [is obligated to] purchase the House on the Closing Date.

Do not craft the sentence so that it states what happens if the condition is not satisfied.

> **Wrong**
>
> **Mortgage.** If the Buyer does not obtain a mortgage, the Buyer is not obligated to purchase the House on the Closing Date.

---

3. *Restatement (Second) of Contracts* § 224, Reporter's Note.

4. *Restatement of Contracts* § 250 (1932).

5. *Restatement (Second) of Contracts* § 224, Reporter's Note.

6. That said, many practitioners continue to use the argot they have always used: *condition precedent*.

This formulation states the common law consequences of the failure to satisfy a condition, not the condition to an obligation and the obligation to be performed if the condition is satisfied. When you find a condition drafted in the negative, restructure it so that the *then* clause states that a party has an obligation to perform. The revised formulation clarifies who has an obligation and under what circumstances it is triggered. It will also facilitate the proper drafting of the contract provision.

Because a right is the flip side of a covenant,[7] parties can provide for a condition to the exercise of a right. Here is the same business term drafted first as a condition to an obligation, along with the obligation, and then as a condition to a right, along with the right.

Version 1

Painting of Bedroom. If the Seller paints the bedroom, the Buyer shall pay an additional $1,000 in purchase price.

Version 2

Painting of Bedroom. If the Seller paints the bedroom, the Seller is entitled to an increase in purchase price of $1,000.

Whether the language in the first version or the second is used, the result remains the same: no additional payment unless the bedroom is painted. Better drafting is to state the condition to the obligation. If the provision containing the right were challenged, a brief would need an extra section to clarify the relationship between covenants and rights. (First, how an entitlement (a right) is the flip side of a covenant and, second, why the contract provision does not even mention the party who has the obligation to perform.)

4.2.2 ONGOING CONDITIONS AND WALK-AWAY CONDITIONS

Conditions can be divided into two subcategories, **walk-away conditions** and **ongoing conditions.** A condition's category depends on the type of obligation that must be performed if the condition is satisfied. This book uses the terms **ongoing conditions** and **walk-away conditions** as a pedagogical aid; they are not technical contract law terms.

- A **walk-away condition** is a condition that must be satisfied before a party is obligated to perform its subject matter performance obligation.
- An **ongoing condition** is a condition that must be satisfied before a party is obligated to perform an obligation that *is not* a subject matter performance obligation.

As Sections 5.4 and 8.2 explain in more depth, the subject matter performance provisions, generally speaking, are the covenants in which the parties promise to perform the main subject matter of the contract. Therefore, for example, in an acquisition agreement, where the main subject matter of the contract is the purchase and sale of the business, the subject matter performance provisions are the parties' reciprocal promises to buy and sell that business. Similarly, in a lease where the main subject matter of the contract is the rental of specific premises, the subject matter perfor-

---

7. See § 3.4.

mance provisions are the landlord's promise to lease the premises to the tenant and the tenant's reciprocal promise to rent the premises from the landlord.

Walk-away conditions benefit a party who wants them satisfied before that party is obligated to perform its subject matter performance obligation. They are most frequently seen in acquisition and financing agreements.

In contrast, ongoing conditions can appear in any kind of contract. We will return once again to our house purchase hypothetical for an example.

Let's assume that the $200,000 purchase price for the house takes into account water damage to the living room ceiling resulting from a leaky roof. Not unreasonably, Bob worries that the leaks could cause extensive damage during the period between the signing and the closing. Therefore, he offers Sally the following deal: He will pay 110 percent of the cost of repairs if Sally has the roof repaired no later than ten business days after the contract's signing. Sally agrees. Here's the condition and the obligation.

Roof Repair. If the Seller repairs the roof to the Buyer's reasonable satisfaction no later than ten business days after the date of this Agreement's signing, the Buyer shall pay the Seller at Closing

(a) the Purchase Price *plus*
(b) an amount equal to 110% of the cost of the repairs, as evidenced by receipts.

In contract terms, Sally's timely repair of the roof is a condition to Bob's obligation to pay 110% of the cost of repairs as additional purchase price. Bob's obligation to pay this additional purchase price is separate from his obligation to buy the house—his subject matter performance obligation. Therefore, the failure to satisfy the condition as to roof repairs affects only Bob's obligation to pay the additional purchase price, not any other provision, including Bob's subject matter performance promise to buy the house. Because the remainder of the contract provisions continue and have ongoing relevance, this condition is dubbed an **ongoing condition**.

In contrast, Bob's securing a mortgage is a walk-away condition. If he does not secure it, the condition is not satisfied, and Bob is not obligated to perform his subject matter performance obligation—the purchase of the house.

Now, here is the tricky part: At this juncture, although not obligated to perform, Bob may choose whether to perform. Deal lawyers call this choice a **walk-away right**. Here are Bob's options:

1. Bob may choose not to perform, that is, choose not to buy the house. That nonperformance would not be a breach because Bob had no obligation to purchase the house. The obligation to perform was never triggered by the satisfaction of the condition.
2. Bob may choose to perform by buying the house despite the absence of an obligation to purchase it. Why would he do so? The purchase of the house may ultimately be more important to him than the satisfaction of the condition. If Bob does buy the house,[8] as a technical legal matter, he waives the failure to satisfy the condition.

---

8. Bob's circumstances may have changed. He may have inherited money or decided to sell some stock to raise cash.

The choice is not contractual.[9] It is the *common law consequence* of a failed walk-away condition. Accordingly, many agreements do not explicitly state that a party may choose whether to perform in these circumstances. Nonetheless, the agreement may explicitly provide additional consequences that flow from the existence of the choice not to perform.[10] For example, the agreement could automatically terminate. Alternatively, the agreement could give one or both parties the discretionary authority to terminate immediately, thereby permitting immediate termination, but not requiring it. By not requiring termination, the agreement extends the deadline by which the walk-away condition may be satisfied.[11] Often, the agreement terminates automatically if the condition is not satisfied by the new deadline.

The following diagram depicts the relationship between

- the satisfaction of a walk-away condition and the obligation to perform, on the one hand, and
- the failure to satisfy the walk-away condition and the choice whether to walk or perform, on the other hand.

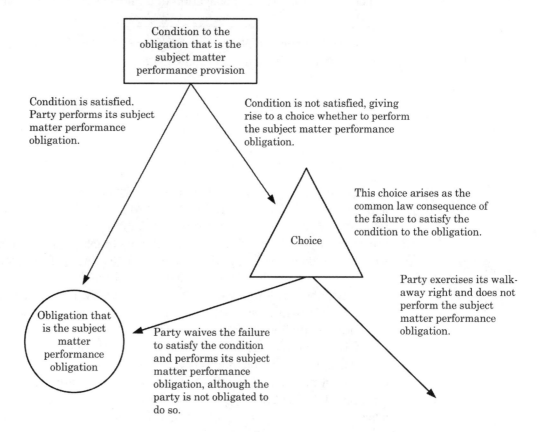

The rectangle represents the condition to the obligation to perform the subject matter performance provision. If the condition is satisfied (the left side of the diagram), the party must perform the subject matter performance obligation (the circle). If the condition is not satisfied (the right side of the diagram), the party has a choice (the triangle) that is the common law consequence of the failure to satisfy the con-

---

9. This choice—although a form of discretionary authority—differs from the discretionary authority to be discussed in §4.3. That is *contractual* discretionary authority. Contractual discretionary authority exists because the parties agreed to it as a business term. It is not the common law consequence of the failure to satisfy a walk-away condition.

10. See Document 1 in Chapter 32.

11. See §8.5 for a discussion of rolling closing dates.

dition. In this event, the party may choose to perform (ending up at the circle), or it may walk away, not perform, and not be in breach—despite its nonperformance. Again, the nonperformance is not a breach because the obligation to perform was never triggered.

4.2.3 RELATIONSHIP BETWEEN CONDITIONS AND COVENANTS IN ACQUISITION AGREEMENTS AND FINANCINGS

Walk-away conditions and walk-away rights are *sometimes* related to a party's performance of a covenant. This is particularly true in acquisitions and financings. We will use the house purchase as an example.

Suppose the kitchen is a wreck, and Bob wants Sally to renovate it before the closing date. If Sally agrees to do the work, the parties can use both covenants and conditions to implement and memorialize their business deal. First, Sally can promise to renovate the kitchen before the closing date. Second, performance of that covenant can be a condition to Bob's obligation to perform; that is, to buy the house.

> **Obligation to Renovate the Kitchen**. The Seller shall renovate the kitchen no later than the Closing Date.
>
> *and*
>
> **Condition to Closing**. It is a condition to the Buyer's obligation to buy the House that the Seller must have performed her covenant to renovate the kitchen, as stated in Section X.[12]

Because the parties have used two provisions to implement their business deal, both provisions must be consulted to determine the consequences if Sally does not renovate the kitchen. Let's assume that Sally never renovates the kitchen, thereby breaching her covenant. In that event, Bob has a cause of action for breach and may sue Sally for damages. But Bob has an additional remedy. The covenant breach means that the related condition was not satisfied. Therefore, on the closing date, Bob may choose whether to perform or walk away. No matter which of these actions he chooses, he retains his right to sue Sally for damages because she breached her covenant to renovate the kitchen. Two contract concepts were involved, so Bob has two sets of rights. Each contract concept exists independently of the other.[13]

Although satisfaction of a walk-away condition may rest on the performance of a covenant, it need not. A condition can be completely unrelated to any covenant. For example, Bob might quite reasonably insist that before closing he must have received a licensed engineer's report stating that the house has no structural problems.

> It is a condition to the Buyer's obligation to buy the House that the Buyer must have received a licensed engineer's report stating the House has no structural damage.

---

12. Bob would probably be quite unhappy with this vague standard. In a real world situation, the parties would negotiate alternative language, providing more detailed standards.

13. In either scenario, as a matter of good practice, the buyer should formally notify the seller that it is reserving its right to sue for breach.

The role of misrepresentations would also be considered independently, assuming the contract included misrepresentations.

Securing the clean report would then be a walk-away condition, giving Bob a walk-away right if not satisfied. It would not, however, be based on Sally's performance of a covenant.

4.2.4 RISK ALLOCATION

Parties use conditions in several ways to allocate risk. First, the agreement to include a condition is itself a risk allocation. By agreeing to a condition, the parties have agreed that the *performing party* has no duty to perform if the condition is not satisfied. Thus, the contract allocates the risk of the failure to satisfy the condition to the party who would have been entitled to performance. For example, if the parties have agreed that Bob is not obligated to purchase the house if he does not obtain a mortgage, Sally bears the risk that the condition might not be satisfied.

Second, parties allocate risk by choosing to frame a business issue as a condition rather than as a covenant. A classic example occurs in the insurance context where an insured must notify its insurer of a loss.

Let's assume that Bob purchases the house and that shortly afterward someone breaks in and steals his large-screen television. Bob reviews his homeowner's insurance policy and discovers that the insurance company must receive notice of the loss no later than ten days after it occurs. Unfortunately, the notice Bob sends is received 12 days late. If the notice provision is a covenant, then Bob has breached the contract. In that event, the insurance company remains obligated to pay Bob for his loss, but it is entitled to damages, if any. For example, its damages might be the additional expense it incurs when it purchases the replacement television at full price, rather than at a sale that took place during the initial ten-day period.

The result differs dramatically, however, if the provision is a condition. Then, if the notice is late, Bob fails to satisfy the condition to the insurance company's obligation to perform. This failure means that the insurance company's obligation to pay Bob is never triggered, and Bob forfeits his right to receive the insurance proceeds. Thus, the use of a condition places the risk of a late notice squarely on Bob, the homeowner. (Courts dislike forfeitures and regularly construe them as covenant provisions even though the language suggests that the provisions are conditions.[14])

Third, parties allocate risk by choosing the standard that establishes the state of facts that must exist before the obligation to perform arises. For example, assume that as a condition to Bob's obligation to close, Sally's lawyer must deliver an opinion addressing, among other things, environmental matters. That condition could be formulated in several ways. Here are three. (Note how even minor "drafting" revisions change the standard and shift risk.)

> **Version 1**
>
> **Opinion of Seller's Counsel**. The Seller's lawyers must have delivered to the Buyer an opinion of counsel *satisfactory* to the Buyer.
>
> **Version 2**
>
> **Opinion of Seller's Counsel**. The Seller's lawyers must have delivered to the Buyer an opinion of counsel *reasonably satisfactory* to the Buyer.

---

14. Samuel Williston, *Williston on Contracts* vol. 13, § 38.13 (Richard A. Lord ed., 4th ed., West 2000), and the cases cited therein.

> **Version 3**
>
> **Opinion of Seller's Counsel.** The Seller's lawyers must have delivered to the Buyer an opinion of counsel *substantially in the form of Exhibit B.*

Version 1 is high risk for Sally as the standard of *satisfactory to the Buyer* seems to give Bob unfettered discretion in deciding whether the opinion is acceptable. Version 2 is somewhat less risky to Sally as it constrains Bob's determination. Here, the reasonable person standard of torts has been imported into the contract. The opinion must be *reasonably satisfactory.* Version 3 substantially reduces Sally's risk as she and her lawyer will know what is required because they will have negotiated and agreed on the opinion that the lawyer must give.

Fourth, parties allocate risk by deciding whose obligations are subject to the satisfaction of which conditions. For example, Bob may insist that before he is obligated to buy the house, he wants an appropriate test to conclude that the house's water meets certain safety standards. To incorporate that requirement into the contract, the parties might use the following condition:

> **Water Safety.** It is a condition to the Buyer's obligation to buy the House that the Buyer must have received test results that conclude that the House's water is safe to use for all residential purposes.

This condition would be a condition only to Bob's obligation to close, not to Sally's. The rationale is that the test is for Bob's benefit only. It is part of his due diligence, part of his risk assessment. If the water is not satisfactory and he is willing to waive the failure of the condition, Sally should not be able to scuttle the deal by having a walk-away right.

Although some conditions may be conditions for only one party, other conditions are conditions to both parties' performance. A classic example in an acquisition agreement is receipt of specific governmental approvals.

4.3   DISCRETIONARY AUTHORITY

Discretionary authority gives its holder a choice or permission to act.[15] The holder may exercise that authority but is not required to do so. Once it does, the other party is bound by the holder's decision. A person who has discretionary authority is sometimes said to have a **privilege**.[16]

The discretionary authority being discussed in this section is *contractual* discretionary authority. The parties have negotiated and agreed that one or both of them should have a choice under specific facts. It is not the same as the choice that a party has when there has been a failure to satisfy a condition to a subject matter performance obligation. That choice arises as *a common law consequence* of the unsatisfied condition, not through *contractual agreement.*

As with the other contract concepts, a grant of discretionary authority allocates risk. It subjects the party without the discretion to the consequences of the actions of the party with the discretionary authority.

---

15. *See Aroostook Valley R.R. Co. v. Bangor & Aroostook R.R. Co.*, 455 A.2d 431, 433 (Me. 1983).

16. *See e.g. Armstrong Paint & Varnish Works v. Contl. Can Co.*, 301 Ill. 102, 107-108 (1921); *Smith v. St. Paul & D. R. Co.*, 60 Minn. 330, 332 (1895).

The following provisions from Bob and Sally's contract demonstrate how discretionary authority can be used:

> ### Example 1
>
> **Use of House**. During the period between this Agreement's signing and the Closing, the Seller may rent the House to one or more third parties.
>
> ### Example 2
>
> **Notice**. A party sending notice shall use one of the following methods of delivery, but may choose which method: registered mail, personal delivery, or overnight courier.

In Example 1, Sally Seller has the absolute discretion to rent her house to anyone she chooses. In contrast, in Example 2, the parties have curtailed the exercise of discretion. There, the party giving notice may choose how to notify the other party, but it must be one of the previously agreed-on methods. The notifying party has discretion, but within limited parameters.

A grant of discretionary authority often appears as an exception to a prohibition. The party exercising the discretion can be either the party prohibited from acting or the other party. Thus, the risk of how the discretionary authority is exercised depends on how a provision is drafted.

In Versions 1 and 2 that follow, the house purchase agreement prohibits Bob from assigning his rights under the agreement but grants Sally the discretionary authority to consent to an assignment. Thus, these versions allocate to Bob the risk of how Sally will exercise her discretionary authority. In Version 1, Bob has the greater risk because the agreement imposes no constraints on how Sally may exercise her discretion. In contrast, in Version 2, the agreement limits Bob's risk because it requires Sally to act reasonably.[17]

Version 3 differs from the other versions because now Bob has the discretionary authority. That authority is permission to assign, which Bob may exercise without constraint. It is an exception to the prohibition against assignment, and it allocates to Sally the risk of whether Bob will exercise his discretionary authority.

> ### Version 1
>
> The Buyer shall not assign any of his rights under this Agreement without the Seller's prior written consent.
>
> ### Version 2
>
> The Buyer shall not assign any of his rights under this Agreement without the Seller's prior written consent, which consent the Seller shall not unreasonably withhold.
>
> ### Version 3
>
> The Buyer shall not assign any of his rights under this Agreement, except that he may assign his rights to his wife, Lara Raskin.

---

17. In some states, a party's right to exercise its discretion in these circumstances is curbed by the implied obligations of good faith and fair dealing, even if the provision does not explicitly do so. *See* E. Allan Farnsworth, *Farnsworth on Contracts* vol. 3, § 11.4, 88, n. 35 (3d ed., Aspen 2004).

The exercise of discretionary authority is often subject to a state of facts having first occurred. Here, the "condition" is a **condition to discretionary authority**.

> A **condition to discretionary authority** is a state of facts that must exist before a party may exercise its discretionary authority.

As with conditions to obligations, an *if/then* temporal sequence is a hallmark of conditions to discretionary authority. A classic example of the interplay between a condition and discretionary authority occurs in a loan agreement. Assume that to finance his purchase of the house, Bob takes out a loan and mortgages the house. In one of the later sections of the bank's loan agreement, that agreement lists the events that constitute an Event of Default. It then provides what happens if one of those events occurs.

> **Remedies.** If an Event of Default occurs and is continuing, then the Bank may accelerate the Loan, foreclose on its security [Bob's house]. . . .

Here, the Bank has no authority to accelerate the Loan and to foreclose unless an Event of Default has occurred and is continuing.[18] Once this state of facts exists, the Bank must decide whether it wishes to exercise its remedies. It need not; it has discretion. Alternatively, it could sue on the note, waive the default, or grant Bob extra time to comply with the loan covenant.

A condition to discretionary authority allocates risk. Without the condition, the Bank could exercise its remedies at any time. Bob, of course, would find this unacceptable. By subjecting the exercise of remedies to the occurrence of a condition, Bob eliminates the risk of the Bank unjustifiably exercising its remedies.

In analyzing whether a party has discretionary authority, do not be lured into characterizing discretionary authority as a *right* or an *entitlement*. Drafters often colloquially refer to discretionary authority as *having a right or being entitled to do something*. For instance, in the preceding example, some practitioners might characterize the Bank's choice whether to exercise its remedies as a right. But, if it were a right, the borrower would have a correlative duty, but none exists.

4.4 DECLARATIONS

A declaration is a statement of fact or policy that the parties agree will govern their actions during the agreement. But neither party has stated the fact to induce the other party to act. A party cannot sue on a declaration to obtain damages. No rights or remedies are associated with it.[19]

Some declarations have **legal** effect on their own, but no **substantive** contractual effect, except when inserted into another provision; other declarations have a substantive effect on their own.

All definitions are declarations. These declarations have no substantive contractual effect on their own. For instance, the following definition of purchase price might appear in Sally and Bob's purchase agreement:

---

18. The agreement's requirement that the Event of Default be continuing favors the borrower. It precludes the bank from exercising its remedies if the borrower cures the default. See §6.2.1.

19. *See Third-Party "Closing" Opinions: A Report of the TriBar Opinion Committee*, 53 Bus. Law. 592, 605-606, 620 (1998).

> **"Purchase Price"** means $200,000.

Although the parties have declared a legal result by including the definition in the contract, standing alone, the definition of Purchase Price has no substantive consequences within the contract.[20] It cannot be breached because, in the definition, neither party has made a representation and warranty or promised to do anything. Instead, the definition must be "kicked into action" by its inclusion in another provision—for example, Bob's covenant to pay the Purchase Price at the closing.

> **Payment of Purchase Price**. The Buyer shall pay the Seller the Purchase Price at the Closing.

Only by including this second provision does Bob have a duty to pay the Purchase Price and Sally a remedy on Bob's failure to pay.

Declarations that have substantive effect on their own establish policies to which the parties must adhere during their contractual relationship. A classic example is the governing law provision.

> **Governing Law**. The laws of Michigan govern all matters arising under or relating to this Agreement, including torts.

This provision establishes the policy that the courts are to use Michigan law to interpret the contract when a dispute arises.

As with a definition standing on its own, the governing law provision has no rights or remedies associated with it; it cannot be breached. But, unlike definitions that must be kicked into action to have a substantive effect, the governing law provision is a contract policy and has a substantive effect by its mere inclusion in the contract.

Declarations are not immune to litigation. Here is a common provision from a website agreement.

> **Rights to Programming**. The Website is a work made for hire and all rights in it vest in the Client. Despite the preceding sentence, the Developer retains all rights to all Developer Programming.

Both sentences are declarations. Were the parties to dispute who owned a piece of code, they would litigate whether that code was part of the "work made for hire" or Developer Programming. The determination could have substantial financial consequences, but the damages award would not be because of a statement a party made to induce the contract or because of a breach of a party's obligation to perform.[21]

---

20. It is akin to a stipulated fact in a negligence case. Both parties agree that Patty fell down the stairs on June 3, 20X5, but how that fact is woven into the litigation is open.

21. Similarly, although neither party could sue the other for damages based on a governing law provision, a party could sue, claiming that the governing law should be that of another state, say Wisconsin. The determination of that claim alone would not subject a party to liability. Liability might result, however, when a court adjudicated the substantive claim (e.g., negligence) according to Wisconsin law, rather than Michigan law.

In the same way that obligations and discretionary authority can be subject to conditions, so too can a declaration that is a policy.

> A **condition to a declaration** is a state of facts that must exist before a policy has substantive consequences.

For example:

> **Consequences of Assignment**. If any party assigns its rights under this Agreement in violation of this Section, that assignment is void.

Here, the entire provision establishes a policy, but the policy consists of a condition and the declaration, together. That policy does not have substantive contractual consequences for the parties until the condition is satisfied.

To test whether a provision is a declaration, ask yourself whether a party would want monetary damages if the legal consequences were not as stated. If the answer is *yes*, then the provision must be either a representation and warranty or a covenant because only these contract concepts have monetary remedies if there is a breach. If the answer is *no*, then the provision is a declaration.

4.5 A CONTRACT'S BUILDING BLOCKS

Representations, warranties, covenants, rights, conditions, discretionary authority, and declarations are a contract's building blocks. Once a drafter knows which contract concept best expresses the business deal, the drafter can begin drafting and memorializing the contract provision.

In the next chapter, we will see how drafters integrate the building blocks into a contract's parts and assemble them to create a contract.[22]

---

22. See Chapter 5.

APPENDICES

Appendix 1: Contract Concepts

Use the following questions as a quick reference to help guide your decision as to which contract concept will memorialize a specific business term properly.

1. **Representation and warranty**: Has a party said something on which the other party is relying?

2. **Covenant**: Has a party promised to do something in the future? A covenant creates a *duty to perform,* also known as an *obligation.*

3. **Discretionary authority**: Does a party have a choice or has it been given permission (a kind of choice) to do something?

4. **Declaration**: Is the business term a definition? Does it establish a policy?

   (a) To test whether a business term is a declaration, ask whether a party would want a monetary remedy if it were not true.

   (b) If a party would want a monetary remedy, the business term is not a declaration. It must be either a representation and warranty or a covenant.

5. **Conditions**: Does the business term require that one thing must happen before another thing happens? Stated differently, must events occur in a chronological sequence?

   (a) **Condition to an obligation (and the obligation)**. If an event occurs, X has an obligation.

      (i) *Ongoing condition*: The condition is not a condition to the performance of a subject matter performance obligation.

      (ii) *Walk-away condition*: The condition is a condition to the performance of a subject matter performance obligation. If a walk-away condition is not satisfied, the party for whose benefit the condition exists may

         (A) choose to waive the failure of the condition and perform the subject matter performance obligation;

            or

         (B) choose not to perform the subject matter performance obligation without being in breach and walk away from the contractual relationship.

      Although the failure of the condition creates a choice for the party that would have had the obligation, the contract provision to be identified is not discretionary authority. It is the condition to an obligation and the obligation. The choice arises as the *common law consequence of the failure to satisfy the condition to the subject matter performance obligation*, not because of contractual agreement.

   (b) **Condition to discretionary authority (and the discretionary authority)**: Must an event occur before a party may exercise discretionary authority?

(c) **Condition to a declaration (and the declaration)**: Must an event occur before the policy has substantive consequences?

(d) ***If/then* test**: When creating an *if/then* statement, the *then* clause should state who has the obligation to perform or who has the discretionary authority.

> **Correct**
>
> If X happens, Y is obligated to perform

Do not use the following formulation:

> **Wrong**
>
> If X does not happen, then Y is not obligated to . . .

This formulation states the common law consequences of the failure to satisfy a condition, not the condition to an obligation and its obligation.

Appendix 2: Summary Chart

	DEFINITION	BUSINESS PURPOSE	REMEDY
Representation	Statement of fact as of a moment in time intended to induce reliance.	To induce reliance; to establish standards of liability; to allocate risk.	Only available if the recipient justifiably relies on the fact. For a material, innocent or negligent misrepresentation, avoidance and restitutionary recovery. For a fraudulent misrepresentation, either • avoidance and restitutionary recovery or • damages (either out-of-pocket or benefit of the bargain) and possibly punitive damages.
Warranty	A promise that a statement is true (generally the statement in the misrepresentation).	To provide an indemnity if a statement is not true, regardless of the recipient's knowledge of the statement's falsity; to allocate risk.	Damages.
Covenant	A promise to do or not to do something. A covenant establishes a duty, also called an obligation to perform.	To require or prohibit action; to establish standards of liability; to allocate risk.	Damages and, if appropriate, specific performance. If the breach is so material that it is a breach of the whole contract that cannot be cured, then a party may have a right to cancel as well as other remedies.
Right	A party's entitlement to the other party's performance of a covenant. A right is the flip side of a covenant.	To require or prohibit action; to establish standards of liability; to allocate risk.	The same as for a covenant.
Condition to an Obligation	A state of facts that must exist before a party is obligated to perform. The occurrence of the condition must be uncertain.	To establish when a party is obligated to perform a covenant; to allocate risk.	A condition to an obligation cannot be breached. Its failure to occur means that the obligation to perform is not triggered. If the condition is a condition to an obligation that is not the subject matter performance obligation, then the condition is an on-going condition. If the condition is a condition to a subject matter performance obligation then the condition is a walk-away condition.

	DEFINITION	BUSINESS PURPOSE	REMEDY
Discretionary Authority	The right to choose what action to take; permission to act.	To provide choice or permission; to allocate risk.	Not applicable.
Condition to Discretionary Authority	A state of facts that must exist before a party may exercise discretionary authority.	To establish when discretionary authority may be exercised; to allocate risk.	Not applicable.
Declaration	A definition or a policy.	To create definitions and establish policies.	Not applicable.
Condition to a Declaration	A state of facts that must exist before a policy has substantive consequences.	To establish when a policy is applicable.	Not applicable.

Drafting a Contract's Parts

A Contract's Parts

5.1 INTRODUCTION

In Chapters 3 and 4, you learned how to translate the business deal into contract concepts. This chapter introduces you to the contract parts into which the contract concepts and business deal are integrated. While subsequent chapters detail how to draft each of these contract parts, having an overview will give you a perspective about how the parts work together.

Look at the list of contract parts that follows. They are organized in the order in which they typically appear in an agreement. Although contracts can be on radically different topics, their organization is remarkably similar.

Parts of an Agreement

1. Preamble.
2. Recitals.
3. Words of agreement.
4. Definitions.
5. Action sections.
6. Other substantive business provisions (representations and warranties, covenants, rights, conditions, discretionary authority, and declarations).
7. Endgame provisions (a kind of substantive provision).
8. General provisions.
9. Signature lines.
10. Schedules.
11. Exhibits.

The remaining sections in this chapter introduce you to each of these contract parts.

5.2 INTRODUCTORY PROVISIONS

The **introductory provisions** are composed of the preamble, the recitals, and the words of agreement. They precede the agreement of the parties and provide the contract's reader with important information, such as who the parties are and why they are entering into the agreement.

5.2.1 PREAMBLE

The **preamble** is the first paragraph of the contract. Its purpose is to identify the contract. The preamble sets forth the name of the agreement, the parties, and the date the parties signed the contract. For example:

> **This License Agreement**, dated April 17, 20XX, is between Hong Licensing Corp., a California corporation ("**Hong**"), and Browne Manufacturing, Inc., an Alabama corporation ("**Browne**").

5.2.2 RECITALS

The **recitals** explain the background of the contract and why the parties are entering into it. They are not enforceable provisions, so they do not provide rights or remedies. The following recitals are from a guaranty.

> **Background**
>
> 1. The Bank has agreed to lend funds to the Borrower in accordance with the Credit Agreement that they are signing today.
> 2. The Borrower is a wholly owned subsidiary of the Parent.
> 3. The Bank will lend to the Borrower only if the Parent guarantees the Borrower's debt.
> 4. The Parent and the Borrower are engaged in related businesses, and the Parent will derive substantial direct and indirect benefit from the Bank's loans to the Borrower.
> 5. The Parent is willing to guarantee the Borrower's debt.

5.2.3 WORDS OF AGREEMENT

The **words of agreement** do what they say: They state, for the record, that the parties have agreed to the terms of the contract. Historically, these words had a secondary function, to recite the contract's consideration. But today, that recitation is archaic and superfluous in many instances. Lawyers who continue to use the more traditional language often refer to the words of agreement as the **statement of consideration**. Here are three examples:

> **Example 1 — Contemporary**
>
> Accordingly, the parties agree:
>
> **Example 2 — Contemporary/Traditional**
>
> Accordingly in consideration of the mutual promises stated in this Agreement, the parties agree as follows:
>
> **Example 3 — Traditional**
>
> NOW, THEREFORE, in consideration of $10 paid in hand and other good and valuable consideration, the receipt of which is hereby acknowledged, the parties hereto hereby agree as follows:

5.3 DEFINED TERMS AND DEFINITIONS

Although it is not always the case (and some contend it should never be the case), **defined terms** and their **definitions** often follow the words of agreement. Defined terms are a shorthand way of referring to complex concepts and ensure that the same concept is referred to the same way throughout an agreement. Definitions are used for multiple purposes, including expanding or narrowing the ordinary meaning of a word or phrase. As noted in Chapter 4, definitions are drafted as declarations. An example of a defined term and its definition follows:

> **"Litigation Expense"** means any expense incurred in connection with asserting, investigating, or defending any claim arising out of or relating to this Agreement, including without limitation, the fees, disbursements, and expenses of attorneys and other professionals.

5.4 ACTION SECTIONS

This textbook refers to the next part of an agreement as the **action sections**.[1] The action sections earn their name because they are *where the action is* from the client's perspective. In the action sections, the parties

- agree to perform the main subject matter of the contract;
- agree to pay the financial consideration, if any (be it purchase price, rent, or royalties);
- state the term of the contract (if any);
- state the closing date (if any); and
- list the closing deliveries (if any).

Paragraphs 2 through 4 of the Website Development Agreement (Version 1) (see Chapter 32, Document 2) contain that agreement's action sections.

5.4.1 SUBJECT MATTER PERFORMANCE PROVISIONS

The first section of the action sections is the **subject matter performance provision**. In this provision, each side covenants to the other that it will perform the main subject matter of the contract.

> **Example 1**
>
> **Purchase and Sale**. At the Closing, Sally Seller *shall sell* the house to Bob Buyer, and Bob Buyer *shall buy* the house from Sally Seller.
>
> **Example 2**
>
> **License**. During the Term, the Licensor *shall license* the Trademark to the Manufacturer, and the Manufacturer *shall manufacture and market products* with the Trademark.

---

1. The author coined the phrase *action sections* because no name existed that one could use to refer to these sections collectively.

These reciprocal, executory covenants, each given in exchange for the other's covenant, establish the agreement's primary consideration.[2]

A subject matter performance provision does not always consist of **reciprocal covenants** of future performance. Sometimes, it is a **self-executing provision**.

Contract promises that are to be performed in the future are often called *executory promises*.[3] With a self-executing provision, a party does not promise performance. Instead, that performance is achieved through the signing of the contract.

> **Grant of Security Interest**. By signing this Security Agreement, the Borrower grants a security interest in its assets to the Bank.

Here, the main subject matter of the contract is the creation of the security interest. The Borrower does not promise to grant a security interest. The parties do not intend for performance to be in the future. Instead, the signing of the agreement causes the grant of the security interest, which is the Borrower's performance of the agreement.

5.4.2 PAYMENT PROVISIONS

The next provision of the action sections usually sets out the **financial consideration**, be it the purchase price, salary, or royalties. Financial consideration is generally drafted in one of two ways. The first way states what the financial consideration is and then, in a separate section or sentence, a party covenants to pay the financial consideration. The second way combines the statement of what the financial consideration is with the covenant to pay it.

> **Version 1**
>
> **Rent**. The rent for each calendar month of the Term is $700. The Tenant shall pay the Landlord the rent for each calendar month no later than the first day of that calendar month. *(Drafted as a declaration and a covenant.)*
>
> **Version 2**
>
> **Royalties**. With respect to each calendar month of the Term, the Tenant shall pay the Landlord rent of $700 no later than the first day of that calendar month. *(Drafted as a covenant.)*

5.4.3 TERM

Another common provision of the action sections states **the term of the contract**—the period of time that the contract will govern the parties' relationship. Not all contracts have terms. Some contracts contemplate a one-time transaction, such as an acquisition, and terminate on the consummation of that transaction. Colloquially, lawyers refer to these transactions as **one-off** transactions. Other contracts, however, are intended to govern the parties' relationship for multiple years. Supply agreements, software licensing agreements, and leases are all agreements that commonly

---

2. Jeff Ferriell, *Understanding Contracts*, 72-73 (2d ed. LexisNexis 2009).

3. Joseph M. Perillo, *Calamari and Perillo on Contracts* § 1.2 (6th ed., Thomson Reuters 2009).

have terms. The following examples illustrate two of the possible ways to incorporate a term into the action sections.

Version 1

Term. The term of this Lease is three years. It begins on the date that the parties sign and deliver this Agreement and ends at 5:00 p.m. on the day immediately preceding the third anniversary of the date that the parties sign and deliver this Agreement. *(The term is stated as a declaration in a stand-alone provision.)*

Version 2

Term. The Landlord shall lease the Premises to the Tenant, and the Tenant shall rent the Premises, for a term of three years. The term begins on the date that the parties sign and deliver this Agreement and ends at 5:00 p.m. on the day immediately preceding the third anniversary of the date that the parties sign and deliver this Agreement. *(This provision integrates the contract's term into the reciprocal covenants that compose the subject matter performance provision. The next sentence, a declaration, states the term's beginning and ending dates.)*

5.5 CLOSING-RELATED PROVISIONS

Some transactions, not all, have a closing. Generally, they are necessary only in acquisitions and financings, where there is a moment when the transaction is consummated (that is, the moment when the asset is sold or the loan is extended). When a transaction has a closing, the agreement will include a **closing date** provision and **closing deliveries** provisions. In the closing date provision, the parties state when and where the closing is to take place. In the closing deliveries provisions, each party covenants to the other how it will deliver its performance at closing. For example, in an acquisition agreement, the seller promises to execute and deliver conveyancing documents, and the buyer promises to deliver the purchase price. Similarly, in a financing agreement, the bank promises to deliver the loan amount, and the borrower promises to execute and deliver a note.

5.6 OTHER SUBSTANTIVE BUSINESS PROVISIONS

The **other substantive business provisions** follow the action sections. In the House Purchase Agreement (Document 1, Chapter 32), the provisions are organized by contract concept and appear in order of their chronology on the transaction's timeline: first are the representations and warranties (made at the time of the signing of the agreement), then covenants (to govern during the gap period between signing and closing), and finally conditions (to provide walk-away rights at closing). Other agreements use different organizational schemes, such as subject matter in decreasing order of importance.[4] For example, take a look at the Website Development Agree-

---

4. For a detailed discussion of how to organize a contract, see Chapter 26.

ment in Document 2, Chapter 32. It is organized almost wholly by subject matter. Only the parties' representations and warranties are set out by contract concept and they are towards the end of that agreement, reflecting their relative lack of importance.

5.7 ENDGAME PROVISIONS

The **endgame provisions** are additional substantive business provisions, but are sufficiently important to warrant a brief discussion devoted just to them. These provisions generally are the next-to-last provisions of a contract. They state the business terms that govern the end of the parties' contractual relationship. They require a drafter to determine the different ways that a contract can end and how the contract will deal with each of the scenarios.

Contracts can end either happily or unhappily. The joint venture can be successfully concluded, or the borrower can fail to pay principal when due. In either event, the contract must deal with the consequences of the end of the contract. If a contract ends happily, the endgame provisions will set out any final payments that need to be made or state any covenants that survive the termination of the relationship. For example, an employment agreement might include a confidentiality covenant that continues past the end of the term of the contract. If a contract ends unhappily, the endgame provisions will state what constitutes a default and the agreed-on remedies. As these provisions invariably involve money, they are often hotly negotiated.

Endgame provisions are often drafted as conditions to an obligation to perform and the statement of the obligation, or conditions to discretionary authority and the statement of the discretionary authority. Occasionally, they are drafted as conditions to a right and a statement of the right.

Example 1

Release of Collateral. After the Borrower has paid all of the outstanding principal and accrued interest, the Bank shall sign any documents necessary to release the Collateral. *(Condition to an obligation and the obligation.)*

Example 2

Late Submission of Manuscript. If the Author does not submit his manuscript before November 1, 20XX, the publisher may refuse to publish the Book. *(Condition to discretionary authority and the discretionary authority.)*

Example 3

Return of Deposit. If the Tenant does not return the Premises in broom-clean condition, the Landlord is entitled to retain the amount of the Deposit equal to the cost of appropriately cleaning the Premises.[5] *(Condition to a right and the right.)*

---

5. See Chapter 10, Guideline 3 and §12.1.2, pp. 176-178, for explanations of why a *right* is appropriate here rather than *discretionary authority.*

5.8 GENERAL PROVISIONS

The final provisions of an agreement are the **general provisions**, often referred to as the **boilerplate provisions**. These provisions tell the parties how to govern their relationship and administer the contract. Classic general provisions include notice, governing law, forum selection, anti-assignment, merger, waiver of the right to a jury trial, and severability provisions.

The phrase *boilerplate provisions* sometimes misleads drafters because the phrase suggests that the provisions are standardized and in no need of tailoring. Treating these provisions this way courts disaster. Each of these provisions raises important business and legal issues that you must address.

Some general provisions are covenants, while others are declarations.

Example 1

> **Assignment and Delegation**. The Tenant shall not assign its rights or delegate its performance under this Lease to any person. *(A covenant.)*

Example 2

> **Successors and Assigns**. This Agreement binds and benefits the parties and their respective permitted successors and assigns. *(A declaration.)*

5.9 SIGNATURE LINES

A contract concludes, of course, with the parties' **signatures**. (Although signatures are not required to create a contract, they are good to have.) While generally both parties sign a contract because both make promises, in some contracts, such as a guaranty, only one party makes promises. In that case, only that party signs.

5.10 SCHEDULES AND EXHIBITS

5.10.1 INTRODUCTION

Schedules and exhibits are additional materials not within the body of a contract but are nonetheless part of a contract. Although some drafters use the terms *schedules* and *exhibits* interchangeably, they have different purposes.

Schedules and exhibits generally gain their status as part of an agreement by being referred to in the agreement or in the interpretive section of the definition article. Under the common law, if the reference is specific enough, then an explicit incorporation by reference is unnecessary.[6] That said, including them within the defi-

---

6. *See United Cal. Bank v. Prudential Ins. Co. of Am.*, 681 P.2d 390, 420 (Ariz. App.1983) ("While it is not necessary that a contract state specifically that another writing is 'incorporated by this reference herein,' the context in which the reference is made must make clear that the writing is part of the contract."); *see also New Park Assoc., LLC v. Blardo*, 906 A.2d 720, 725 (Conn. App. 2006) (stating that "the language of the contract clearly and unambiguously refers to A205 as part of the contract."); *see CJS Contracts* § 402, Separate writings—Incorporation by reference (Westlaw, database updated June 2013) ("A reference to another document must be clear and unequivocal, and the terms of the incorporated document must be known or easily available to the parties. . . . [A] mere reference to another document is not sufficient to incorporate that other document into a contract; the writing to which reference is made must be described

nition of *Agreement* or interpretive section precludes any technical argument that they are not part of the agreement. Drafters generally do not separately define these terms, although they often appear with their first letters capitalized.

Example 1

"**Agreement**" means this Power Purchase Agreement and the Schedules and Exhibits to it, each as amended from time to time.

This definition intentionally does not state that the schedules and exhibits are "attached." Sometimes these documents are so large that attaching them becomes unwieldy. As drafted, this definition prevents any technical interpretive problems that might arise because the documents are not physically attached to the agreement.[7]

5.10.2 SCHEDULES

Parties typically use **schedules** (also known as **disclosure schedules**) to disclose information that would otherwise be in representations and warranties. Sometimes the schedules contain additional information that supplements a party's representations and warranties; other times schedules list exceptions.[8]

Example 1

Material Contracts. Schedule 3.10 lists all the material contracts to which the Borrower is a party.

Example 2

Defaults. Except as stated in **Schedule 3.18**, the Borrower is not in default under any agreement.[9]

Properly or improperly scheduling information directly affects liability under an agreement. If a borrower fails to schedule a material contract to which it is a party, it will have misrepresented the facts, subjecting it to liability.[10] Therefore, you must meticulously prepare schedules and vet them with the client.

Parties put information into schedules for several reasons.

---

in such terms that its identity may be ascertained beyond reasonable doubt."); *but see Rosenblum v. Travelbyus.com Ltd.*, 299 F.3d 657, 664-665 (7th Cir. 2002) ("There is no doubt that the Acquisition Agreement refers to the Employment Agreement, but there is no 'intention to incorporate the document and make it a part of the contract' on the face of the Acquisition Agreement itself. (citations omitted). Indeed, Article 1.4 is not an incorporation clause at all; rather, it is a merger clause.").

7. *See United Cal. Bank v. Prudential Ins. Co. of Am.*, *supra* n. 5, at 420 ("While the parties recognize that physical attachment is not necessary *if* the document to be incorporated is *clearly and unambiguously* incorporated by reference, there was no such clear and unambiguous incorporation by reference in this case.") (emphasis in original).

8. Lou R. Kling & Eileen T. Nugent, *Negotiated Acquisitions of Companies, Subsidiaries and Divisions* vol. 2, § 10.01 (Law Journal Press 1992, 2012).

9. See § 23.3.2. It is common practice to begin representations and warranties with the exception stated first: "Except as specified in Schedule 3.18, ..."

10. *See Gildor v. Optical Solutions, Inc.*, 2006 WL 4782348 (Del. Ch. June 5, 2006) (drafter's failure to prepare and annex schedule with stockholders' addresses resulted in defendant sending insufficient notice under the stockholders' agreement).

- First, it unclutters the agreement and makes it easier to read.
- Second, it simplifies the logistics of preparing the agreement. The lawyers responsible for drafting the schedules are not necessarily the lawyers drafting the agreement. For example, a bank's lawyers invariably draft the loan agreement, but the borrower and its counsel compile and draft the schedules used to expand or qualify the borrower's representations and warranties. Having the schedules in a separate word-processing document simplifies the drafting process.

When drafting an agreement, do not provide for a schedule if it will not list any information. Similarly, if only one or two short items are to be listed, include them in the representation and warranty. Readers quickly become frustrated if they turn to a schedule that provides little or no information.

Each schedule in a contract is identified by a number. The number is usually the same as the section number of the provision that requires the schedule. So, if Section 4.12 requires the seller to disclose all litigations, the list of litigations will appear in Schedule 4.12. Drafters often bold schedule references the first time they are used to visually alert the reader to a schedule: **Schedule 4.12**. It also acts as a reminder to the drafter to prepare the schedule.

Putting together a disclosure schedule can be a sophisticated task. Before finalizing any schedules, make sure that you assess the business and legal issues and deal with them appropriately.[11]

5.10.3 EXHIBITS

Exhibits are agreements or other documents relating to the contract that the parties want treated as part of the contract. They may or may not have already been signed when the parties sign the contract. For example, when a loan agreement is signed, it will include as exhibits a form for each of the following: the promissory note, the security agreement, the pledge agreement, and the opinion that borrower's counsel must deliver. By "attaching" the forms as exhibits at the contract's signing, the parties establish an objective standard as to the agreements' and the documents' content. They are exactly what the parties will sign at closing. All that needs to be done at closing to turn them into agreements is to delete the title *Exhibit,* date the document, and have the parties sign it. With luck, these exhibits will preclude any negotiation or dispute at closing as to their substance.

Exhibits of unsigned documents and agreements are often first referenced in the definitions article.

> **"Pledge Agreement"** means the Pledge Agreement by the Borrower in favor of the Bank, *substantially in the form of **Exhibit F**.*

Drafters include the italicized language above (but not in italics) to handle the possibility that the Pledge Agreement might differ slightly from the exhibit. This could occur either because the parties must complete blanks in the form, such as the date, or because the parties agree to a minor change.

As indicated, parties may also include as an exhibit an agreement that has been previously signed. Parties often do this if the agreement directly relates to the agreement's purpose. For example, the parties might attach to an assignment and assump-

---

11. *See generally* Kling & Nugent, *supra* n. 7, Ch. 10.

tion agreement a copy of the contract being assigned. Again, the rationale is to prevent a dispute, in this instance, as to which contract is being assigned. In the United States, parties would not generally attach as an exhibit a letter of intent or a confidentiality agreement signed before the signing of the main agreement. Outside the United States, customs differ, so be sensitive to local practice.

Occasionally, parties also use exhibits to display technical information or to demonstrate how a mathematical formula works.[12] The sample computations act as a form of legislative history that the parties or a court can use to resolve disputes.

Exhibits are generally given sequential numbers or letters based on the order in which they appear in an agreement. Exhibit A, Exhibit B, and Exhibit C, or Exhibit 1, Exhibit 2, and Exhibit 3. To facilitate keeping track of the exhibits, some drafters bold the references to them the first time they are used: **Exhibit A**.

12. See Chapter 22.

EXERCISES

Exercise 5-1

Draft a car purchase agreement using the following facts. Do not include any other provisions. Assume that no statutes apply to the transaction.

Use the House Purchase Agreement (Chapter 32, Document 1) as a precedent. It is available in Microsoft Word on the book's website.

Facts

1. The parties are Barbara Balram, the seller, and Tom Rogers, the buyer.
2. The car is a red, 20XX Acura.
3. It has been driven 26,000 miles.
4. The purchase price is $11,000. The buyer will pay the seller with a certified check.
5. The seller owns the car, and it is not subject to any liens.
6. The car has been maintained in accordance with the owner's manual and is in good operating condition, normal wear and tear excepted.
7. The closing will take place on the last day of the month that follows the month in which the car purchase agreement is signed.
8. With respect to the period beginning on the day the agreement is signed and ending on the closing date, the seller promises not to paint the car and not to drive it more than 500 miles. The seller also promises to garage the car and to continue to maintain it.
9. The buyer only has to close if the seller has performed its covenants and if the seller's representations and warranties are true on the date that they were made and on the closing date as if they were made on that date, except to the extent the agreement contemplates that specific facts might change.
10. The date of the agreement is the date that this assignment is due.

Exercise 5-2

Follow the instructions supplied in the following memorandum from Senior Associate to Overworked Junior Associate. For the purposes of this exercise, assume that it is March 1, 20X8.

From: Senior Associate

To: Overworked Junior Associate

Date: March 1, 20X8

    As you know, Corporate Partner went on vacation last week and left me in charge of one of her matters. As I will be conducting the negotiations, I need your assistance in churning out the docu-

---

ments. Please review the deal terms and determine how you would translate each of them into contract concepts. Specifically, determine which of the following contract concepts best expresses each business term. Several of the business terms require more than one contract concept. It will not help me to tell me that a business term belongs in the action sections or the endgame provisions. What I really need to know is which contract concept to use.

Put your answer on the line that follows each numbered paragraph. Don't worry about Paragraph 12. We will deal with that information later on in the transaction.

- Representation and warranty
- Covenant
- Right
- Condition
  - ➤ Condition to an obligation and the related obligation (on-going or walk-away?)
  - ➤ Condition to discretionary authority and the related discretionary authority
  - ➤ Condition to a declaration and the related declaration
- Discretionary authority
- Declaration

We will review your work as soon as you finish. (It is fine with me, in fact I prefer, if you consult with other associates in the firm.)

Our client, Healthy Hearts Inc., an immediate care medical facility, has been conducting an extensive search for a new chief executive officer. Last week, it reached a handshake deal with Adele Administrator. The salient provisions of the contract follow.

1. Healthy Hearts agrees to hire Administrator, and Administrator agrees to work for Healthy Hearts.

_____

2. Administrator will be engaged as Chief Executive Officer of Healthy Hearts.

_____

3. Administrator is currently executive vice president at Holistic Hospitals Corp. and is party to an Employment Agreement with Holistic that is dated April 1, 20X6, and purportedly ends March 31, 20X8. Healthy Hearts is very concerned about that agreement. According to Administrator, its terms do not permit her to show it to anyone other than her advisors. Healthy Hearts does not want to tortiously interfere with that agreement. Administrator insists that she is free to enter into the employment agreement with Healthy Hearts and that doing so will not breach her employment agreement with Holistic. Please see if you can put in one provision that will give Healthy Hearts comfort on this point. Specifically:

(a) Healthy Hearts wants to show that it entered into its employment agreement with Administrator in the good faith belief that it was not causing her to breach her agreement with Holistic Hospitals. (As you may recall from law school, a party can defend against a claim of tortious interference by demonstrating that it had no intent to interfere with the other contract. Other than Healthy Hearts self-servingly stating it entered into the contract with Administrator in the good faith belief that it was not causing her to breach her contract, what could demonstrate our client's good faith?)

(b) Healthy Hearts wants to be able to sue Administrator if the employment agreement with Healthy Hearts in fact causes a breach under her employment agreement with Holistic.

4. The term of employment will be for three years, beginning on April 1, 20X8.

5. Healthy Hearts negotiated for the right to terminate Administrator's employment for "cause," in which event Healthy Hearts would pay Administrator her salary through the date of termination, plus reimbursement of any expenses incurred through the date of termination. Healthy Hearts must make such payment on the date of the termination.

6. Administrator will be paid $25,000 per month, payable on the first business day of each month.

7. During her negotiations with Healthy Hearts, Administrator stated that she received her A.B. from Brown University in 20X1 and her M.D. from Harvard University in 20X5. She also advised Healthy Hearts that she is enrolled in the MBA program at Fordham University and is specializing in Hospital Administration. Healthy Hearts is very "hung up" on credentials and is also concerned about what it calls "résumé fraud." It therefore wants to be able to sue Administrator if she in fact does not have the credentials she claims. In addition, Healthy Hearts does not want to be obligated under the Employment Agreement if Administrator has not been awarded her MBA by the time her employment under the Employment Agreement is to begin.

8. Administrator shall perform all duties that are customary for an officer of a corporation holding the office of Chief Executive Officer.

9. During her negotiations with Healthy Hearts, Administrator insisted on two things to which Healthy Hearts agreed:

(a) She wants Healthy Hearts to employ Samuel Samaritan as her Administrative Assistant no later than March 31, 20X8. (Healthy Hearts agreed that Administrator would not only have the right to sue if Healthy Hearts failed to employ Samaritan by March 31, 20X8, but also the right not to go forward with Healthy Hearts.)

(b) Administrator can back out of the deal if Phil Philanthropic has not contributed $5 million to the Healthy Hearts capital fund-raising program by March 31, 20X8.

10. Administrator agreed that she would devote her attention and energies on a full-time basis to the business of Healthy Hearts, except for her work at the animal shelter.

11. If Healthy Hearts terminates Administrator's employment "without cause," it must pay Administrator any salary currently payable, plus $100,000, plus reimbursement of any expenses incurred through the date of termination. Healthy Hearts must make such payment on the date of termination.

---

12. In case you need to know for any reason, Healthy Hearts is incorporated in Michigan, and Adele Administrator lives in Detroit, Michigan.

Exercise 5-3

This exercise once again asks you to translate the business deal into contract concepts. Please follow the instructions in the memorandum.

From: Senior Associate

To: Overworked Junior Associate

Date: April 20, 20X8

I really appreciated your help on that last project. As you know by now, the reward for excellent work is more work. . . .

Our client is Ralph Products LP. Ralph LP owns all rights in the cartoon character Ralph — a short, frumpy, bespectacled, eight-year-old for whom life never goes quite right. For reasons that no one can fathom, anything with a likeness of Ralph on it sells like hotcakes. Ralph LP has been making millions by licensing the trademark rights to use this character to different companies who manufacture and then market products bearing Ralph's likeness.

Our client and Merchandisers Extraordinaire, Inc., have agreed to enter into a license agreement with the terms stated in this memorandum. Please tell me how you would translate these business terms into contract concepts. For each numbered paragraph, choose the correct contract concept or concepts from the list that you used in the last assignment. Then, write your answer on the lines following the paragraph. Don't worry about Paragraph 11. We will deal with that information later.

1. Ralph LP will grant Merchandisers a license for caps and t-shirts bearing the Ralph likeness, and Merchandisers will be obligated to market and merchandise them in Maine, New Hampshire, and Vermont. ✓

---

2. As you might well understand, Ralph LP has an ongoing concern about the financial condition of its licensees. It is willing to enter into this agreement only because Merchandisers's most recent financial statements showed substantial financial strength. Ralph LP wants the contract to reflect its reliance on those financial statements. In addition, Ralph LP wants the right to terminate this agreement if Merchandisers' net worth—as at the end of any fiscal year during the term of the contract—drops below $15 million. ✓ ⊘

3. The agreement will have a three-year licensing term, to begin on the first day of the month after the end of this month. Please assume that we'll be able to execute this agreement tomorrow. ✓ ⊘

4. Merchandisers is to have an obligation to use commercially reasonable efforts to market the Ralph merchandise. If Merchandisers has any unsold merchandise on hand at the time the term ends, Ralph LP will buy that merchandise at its cost. ✓

5. Merchandisers wants some kind of assurance in the contract

   (a) that Ralph LP actually owns what it is licensing; and ✓
   (b) that during the term of the license, Ralph LP will
       (i) enforce its intellectual property rights against all third parties; and ✓
       (ii) defend its licensees against all intellectual property claims of third parties. ✓

6. The parties have agreed that with respect to each year of the term of the contract, Merchandisers must pay royalties equal to 15% of all net sales. ✓

7. Ralph LP has a reputation for being quality crazy and always requires its licensees to submit samples of any item it intends to manufacture at least 30 days before the item is to go into production. Ralph LP then must either accept or reject the item. If Ralph LP approves the item, then Merchandisers must manufacture it. If Ralph LP rejects the sample, it must explain in detail why it did so. After the receipt of the rejection notice, Merchandisers may revise the sample and resubmit it for approval. If Ralph LP approves the revised sample, then Merchandisers must manufacture it. ✓

8. Merchandisers wants Ralph LP to give assurances that Merchandisers is the only one now with the right to sell trademarked caps and t-shirts in its territory and that during the term of the contract Ralph LP will not grant anyone else a competing right. ✓

9. Merchandisers was concerned that its territory was relatively small. Our client agreed to extend the territory to include Delaware and Rhode Island if Merchandisers's sales for the first year of the term exceeded $7 million. ✓

10. Please provide that Virginia law will govern. ✓

11. In case you need to know for any reason, Ralph Products LP is a Virginia limited partnership, and Merchandisers Extraordinaire, Inc., is an Oregon corporation. ✓

Exercise 5-4

Through this exercise, you will begin to learn how to read a contract. To do so, you will need to read the Website Development Agreement (Version 1), which is Document 2, Chapter 32.

In the previous two exercises you translated the business deal into contract concepts. In this exercise, you must determine from the contract language what contract part it is or which contract concepts were used to memorialize the business deal.

Here's how the exercise works: The first column has a series of boxes that asks you to identify a contract part or the language used to express the contract concept that formed the basis of a provision. Review the Website Development Agreement (Chapter 32, Document 2) to find the answer and then write your answer in the box immediately adjacent to the box that tells you what to find.

Contract Part or Concept	Reference
Preamble	
Recitals	
Words of agreement	
Subject matter performance provision. Covenant or self-executing?	
In the financial provisions, a declaration, a covenant, and discretionary authority.	S. 4.2.1 Declarat S.4.3.1 discretionary authority (2nd Sentence) S. 4.3.1 Declaration S. 4.3.2 J S.4.3.2 Covenant

In Paragraph 5 (other than Paragraph 5.6) three covenants, a condition to discretionary authority and the related discretionary authority. In Paragraph 5.6, a condition to a declaration and a declaration. (It's tricky.)	5.3 - discretionary authority (2nd Sentence)
In Paragraph 8, a self-executing provision.	8.2.2.
Representations and warranties. (This one is SO easy.)	Paragraph 10
In the endgame provisions, a condition to discretionary authority and discretionary authority.	

Introductory Provisions: Preamble, Recitals, and Words of Agreement

6.1 INTRODUCTION

The first three provisions of a contract are introductory and set the stage for the remainder of the contract. They identify the agreement, explain its purpose, and state that the parties agree to the provisions that follow. Although seemingly basic, they can bind the wrong party and affect a contract's meaning.

Unfortunately, many drafters continue to draft these introductory provisions in a traditional style, one that is verbose, replete with legalese, and evocative of eighteenth-century England. What follows is typical:

Version 1

THIS NONCOMPETITION AGREEMENT, made the 16th day of March, 20XX, by and between ATTORNEY STAFFING ACQUISITION CO., a corporation organized under the laws of Delaware (hereinafter, the "Company"), and MARIA RODRIGUEZ, residing at 21 Melmartin Road, Chicago, Illinois 60606 (hereinafter, the "Executive"),

WITNESSETH:

WHEREAS, Attorney Staffing Inc., a Delaware corporation (hereinafter, the "Seller"), provides temporary lawyers to law firms in the greater Chicago area;

WHEREAS, the Seller is selling substantially all of its assets to the Company in accordance with the Asset Acquisition Agreement, dated the first day of February 20XX (hereinafter, the "Acquisition Agreement");

WHEREAS, the Executive is the sole stockholder of the Seller and its President;

WHEREAS, the Executive has extensive knowledge of the Seller's business, including its client base and pool of temporary lawyers; and

continued on next page >

WHEREAS, it is a condition to the consummation of the Acquisition Agreement that the Executive enter into this Noncompetition Agreement;

NOW, THEREFORE, in consideration of the mutual promises herein contained and other good and valuable consideration, the receipt of which is hereby acknowledged, the parties hereto hereby agree:

Note that the provisions are actually part of one long sentence.

> **This Agreement . . . witnesseth [the following things] and therefore, the parties agree to what follows:**

This format is archaic and can be revised without any change in substance or effect. For example:

Version 2

This Noncompetition Agreement, dated March 16, 20XX, is between Attorney Staffing Acquisition Co., a Delaware corporation (the "**Company**"), and Maria Rodriguez (the "**Executive**").

Background

1. Attorney Staffing Inc., a Delaware corporation (the "**Seller**"), provides temporary lawyers to law firms in the greater Chicago area.
2. The Seller is selling substantially all of its assets to the Company in accordance with the Asset Acquisition Agreement, dated February 1, 20XX (the "**Acquisition Agreement**").
3. The Executive is the Seller's sole stockholder and its President.
4. The Executive has extensive knowledge of the Seller's business, including its client base and pool of temporary lawyers.
5. It is a condition to the consummation of the Acquisition Agreement that the Executive enter into this Noncompetition Agreement.

Accordingly, in consideration of the mutual promises stated in this Agreement, the parties agree as follows:

In the remainder of this chapter, we will look at how to draft each of these introductory provisions.

6.2 PREAMBLE

The **preamble** is the first paragraph of an agreement. Some drafters refer to it as the **introductory paragraph**. It identifies the agreement by stating its name, its date, and the parties. The following is a well-drafted, contemporary preamble. Commentators usually recommend this format.

Version 1

This Supply Agreement, dated March 3, 20XX, is between Carpetmakers, Inc., an Indiana corporation (the "**Manufacturer**"), and Big Retail Corp., a Florida corporation (the "**Retailer**"). (*Using a bold font for the name of the agreement and the parties' defined terms quickly alerts the reader to the preamble's salient information. Ordinarily, typographers suggest that bold and regular font not be used together because the combination is jarring to the eye. From a contract drafting perspective, bold in the preamble is a good exception to the general rule.*)

Version 2 is another contemporary way of drafting the preamble. It has the same information as in Version 1, but it is no longer a sentence. More traditional, yet somewhat contemporary, many drafters still use this version. This book uses both, so that you can be familiar with what you'll see in practice.

Version 2

Supply Agreement, dated March 3, 20XX, between Carpetmakers, Inc., an Indiana corporation (the "**Manufacturer**"), and Big Retail Corp., a Florida corporation (the "**Retailer**").

The remainder of this section details the rules for drafting the preamble.

6.2.1 NAME OF THE AGREEMENT

Typically, the preamble begins with the name of the agreement indented five spaces and typed in all capital letters to make the title conspicuous and the contract easy to identify. Although multiple lines of capital letters impede a document's readability, sparing use of capital letters brings attention to the capitalized words.[1] Some drafters also put the title in a bold font. That said, this author prefers the alternative, more contemporary style in which the agreement's name is in upper and lowercase letters and a bold font. Bold is sufficient to make the title conspicuous.

Lease, dated November 14, 20XX, between Real Estate, Inc., a Florida corporation (the "**Landlord**"), and Red Shoes LLC, a Texas limited liability company (the "**Tenant**").

Most drafters precede the preamble with the name of the agreement on a separate line. This additional title further helps the reader to identify the agreement quickly.

---

1. Carl Felsenfeld & Alan Siegel, *Writing Contracts in Plain English* 194-195 (West 1981).

If you include the name of the agreement as a title, it should be precisely the same as that which appears in the preamble. The title should be centered and the letters in bold and a larger font than the letters in the body of the agreement. The combination of the two will make the title conspicuous. Consistent with the preamble, only the first letter of each word should be capitalized. (If the style being used is to draft the title in the preamble in all capital letters, then the centered title should be done the same way.)

A separate title is particularly useful in a transaction where the parties sign multiple agreements of the same type, but where one party differs in each agreement. This might occur, for example, in a financing transaction where multiple subsidiaries guarantee the parent corporation's debt. To expedite the agreements' identification, drafters title the agreement as described and then put below the agreement's name, in brackets, the name of the subsidiary that is a party.

Guaranty
[Subsidiary A]

Guaranty, dated October 15, 20XX, by Subsidiary A, an Arkansas corporation (the "**Guarantor**"), in favor of Big Bank, N.A., a national banking corporation (the "**Bank**").

An agreement's name should describe its subject matter—for example, **Supply Agreement**. Some drafters simply use *Agreement*, but that defeats the purpose of the preamble, which is to identify the agreement. A truncated agreement name becomes especially problematic if multiple agreements in a transaction are named *Agreement*. In that case, a reader may have to wade through the agreement to learn its subject matter. A truncated name can further frustrate a reader if one agreement refers to another. A cross-reference to the *Agreement* conveys no meaningful information.

6.2.2   DATE

Drafters can date an agreement in one of two ways:

Version 1

, dated January 6, 20XX,

Version 2

, dated *as of* January 1, 20XX,

Drafters use the Version 1 format when the parties reach agreement on the same day that they sign the agreement. In contrast, drafters use the Version 2 format when parties reach an agreement on the *as of* date, but do not sign their agreement until a later date.

For example, if a senior executive begins work on May 23, 20XX, without a written contract, the parties will want the agreed-on business terms to be effective as of that date. Accordingly, the employment agreement will be dated *as of May 23, 20XX*, even if it is not signed until July 1, 20XX. That the effective date and the signing date differ causes no legal problem.[2] Nonetheless, to state what should be self-evident, an

---

2. *See Brewer v. Nat'l Sur. Corp.*, 169 F.2d 926, 928 (10th Cir. 1948).

as of date should never be used to deceive a third party such as the government. That would be fraud.[3]

Using an *as of* date can affect the accuracy of representations and warranties and the effective date of covenants. Recall that representations and warranties speak as of the moment in time when they are given.[4] If a contract has an *as of* date, then the representations and warranties speak as of that date, not the date the contract is signed.

Suppose, for example, that on October 15, 20XX, Bob Buyer agreed to buy Sally Seller's car and on that day Sally represented and warranted that the fuel tank was one-half full. If the contract is signed on October 20, 20XX, without being effective as of October 15, 20XX, then the representations and warranties speak as of October 20, 20XX. In that case, the representation and warranty with respect to the fuel tank is probably wrong. Fuel may have been used or the tank refilled. Therefore, to keep the representation and warranty accurate, the parties should date the contract *as of* the date of their agreement, October 15, 20XX. Alternatively, the parties could date the contract October 20, 20XX, and update the representations and warranties.

An *as of* date can raise a similar issue with respect to covenants. Specifically, when an *as of* date is used, covenants must be effective as of that date rather than on the signing date. If they are not, a party could do as it pleased from the agreement date (the *as of* date) until the signing date. So, for example, if Bob and Sally agree on October 15, 20XX, that Sally may drive the car no more than 100 miles before the closing, that covenant must limit Sally's driving beginning on that date. If instead the covenant begins on October 20, 20XX, the signing date, Sally can drive as much as she wants from October 15 to October 20 without breaching her covenant.

When drafting a contract with an *as of* date in the preamble, you should also indicate its actual signing date somewhere in the contract. This might be important for tax or other reasons. Although some drafters put a date line under each signature, this approach is not recommended unless the effective date of the contract is tied to the date that the last party signs the contract.[5] Courts have concluded that dated signatures can create an ambiguity as to the contract's effective date.[6] A better alternative is to put the *as of* date in the preamble and in the concluding language, and to include an effective date provision in the action sections that distinguishes the signing date from the effective date.

Version 1

Step 1—as of *date in the preamble*

Settlement Agreement, dated as of January 5, 20XX, between Cartoon Characters LLC, a Pennsylvania limited liability company ("**Cartoon**"), and Specialty Manufacturing, Inc., a Texas corporation ("**Specialty**").

and

---

3. *See U.S. v. Bourgeois*, 950 F.2d 980, 982-983 (5th Cir. 1992).

4. See § 3.2.1.

5. See § 17.3.

6. *Am. Cyanamid Co. v. Ring*, 286 S.E.2d 1, 2-3 (Ga. 1982); *Sweetman v. Strescon Indus., Inc.*, 389 A.2d 1319, 1322 (Del. Super. 1978).

Step 2—*effective date provision in the action sections*

Effective Date. The parties executed and delivered this Agreement on February 27, 20XX, but it is effective as of January 5, 20XX.

and

Step 3—*effective date stated in the concluding paragraph*

To evidence the parties' agreement to this Agreement, the parties have executed and delivered this Agreement *as of the date stated in the preamble.*

An alternative is to put the *as of* date in the preamble *and* the *as of* date *and* the signing date in the concluding paragraph.

Version 2

Settlement Agreement, dated as of January 5, 20XX, between Cartoon Characters LLC, a Pennsylvania limited liability company ("**Cartoon**"), and Specialty Manufacturing, Inc., a Texas corporation ("**Specialty**").

and

To evidence the parties' agreement to this Agreement, the parties have executed and delivered this Agreement *on February 27, 20XX, but it is effective as of the date stated in the preamble.*

This author prefers Version 1 because of the explicit action section provision—a provision within the body of the contract—as opposed to the concluding paragraph.

If the parties decide that they want the agreement to be effective on the date that the last party signs, omit the date from the preamble and include an effective date provision in the action sections that states what determines the effective date. In addition, conform the concluding language. Including a date in the preamble, but leaving it blank until the date is known and can be inserted invites trouble. What happens if the date is never inserted or the wrong date is inserted? Just don't go there.

Some drafters put the effective date provision in the counterparts provision in the General Provisions article but that is insufficiently conspicuous. It works, but the action sections are a better option.

Here is an example of the suggested provisions and suggested signature line to be used if the agreement's date is the date that the last party signs the agreement.

Settlement Agreement between Cartoon Characters LLC, a Pennsylvania limited liability company ("**Cartoon**"), and Specialty Manufacturing, Inc., a Texas corporation ("**Specialty**").

and

Effective Date. This Agreement is effective on the date that the last party executes and delivers this Agreement as indicated by the date stated under that party's signature line. *(This is Section X.)*

and

> To evidence the parties' agreement to this Agreement, each party has executed and delivered it on the date stated under that party's name, with this Agreement being effective on the date stated in Section X [*the Effective Date section*].
>
> *and*
>
> Cartoon Characters LLC
>
> By: _____
>
> Ann Chin, Manager
>
> Dated: [*date to be inserted*]

Do not put a future date in the preamble. If parties want provisions to be effective on a future date, use the signing date in the preamble and include an effective date provision in the action sections. This results in the contract being in force on the signing date stated in the preamble but the effectiveness of provisions being postponed until the effective date.

> **Effective Date**. The provisions of this Agreement (other than this Section [list any provisions that should be enforceable immediately; e.g., dispute resolution provisions]) are effective on the third day after the Contractor receives all municipal approvals. This Section [and the previously listed provisions] are effective on the date stated in the preamble.

Whether an agreement is dated based on the agreement date or the signing date, drafting the date is straightforward. Either offset the date with two commas, or use no commas. Either style is acceptable.

> **Version 1 — two commas**
>
> . . . , dated January 6, 20XX, . . .
>
> *or*
>
> . . . , dated as of January 1, 20XX, . . .
>
> **Version 2 — no commas**
>
> . . . dated January 6, 20XX . . .
>
> *or*
>
> . . . dated as of January 1, 20XX . . .

6.2.3 PARTIES

After the date, the preamble states who the parties are.

> **This Settlement Agreement**, dated as of January 10, 20XX, is *between Cartoon Characters LLC, a Pennsylvania limited liability company* ("**Cartoon**"), and *Specialty Manufacturing, Inc., a Texas corporation* ("**Specialty**").

Although some drafters precede the first party's name with *by and between*, the words *by and* are superfluous, and you should omit them.

Some lawyers use *between* if a contract has two parties and *among* if it has three or more. This is wrong. *Between* is correct whenever two or more parties are in a direct, reciprocal relationship with each other. In contrast, *among* should be used to express a less direct relationship with a group.[7]

Consider the example of a stockholders' agreement whose parties are the seven stockholders and the corporation. In this instance, an agreement exists between each stockholder and each of the other stockholders and between each stockholder and the corporation. Accordingly, *between* is the correct preposition to use in the preamble. Distinguish this example from the following: *The Clean Air Act is among the environmental laws that have been enacted.* Here, the laws do not have a direct, reciprocal relationship with each other. Instead, they are members of a group. Thus, *among* is correct.

If you intend to use *between* in all instances in a preamble, beware. You may have an uphill battle convincing your colleagues that you are right. The improper use of *among* in this context is deeply ingrained. But, keep in mind that using *between* or *among* in the preamble does not affect a contract's substance.[8] Therefore, do not waste negotiating capital on this point.

6.2.3.1 Identifying the Parties

When drafting the preamble, take the time to be sure that you properly identify the parties. Using the wrong name may, at a minimum, start a litigation to determine who the correct party to the contract is. To ascertain an entity's name, check its organizational document—for example, its certificate of incorporation. That will give you the entity's legal name, including such details as whether a comma precedes *Inc.* If the party is an individual, confirm that you have that person's full legal name, rather than a nickname or professional name.[9] Some drafters put the parties' names in all capital letters, but this is unnecessary; it is stylistic.

> *Drafting tip:* Draft the preamble and signature lines at the same time, so you focus in both these critical places on the parties' names.

After an entity's name, state what type of entity it is, along with its jurisdiction of organization (together, its **organizational identity**). Some drafters omit this information, believing it to be inappropriate in a preamble. That may be correct in the

---

7. *The Oxford English Dictionary* 154-155 (2d ed., Clarendon Press Oxford 1989); *see also* H. W. Fowler, *A Dictionary of Modern English Usage* 57 (Sir Ernest Gowers ed., 2d ed., Oxford U. Press 1965).

In New York City, lawyers used to circulate a Cleary Gottlieb newsletter from 1981. (The author is voluntarily dating herself and expects readers to be kind.) In it, one of the firm's lawyers argues fervently in favor of the use of *between* in all instances in a preamble, regardless of the number of parties. *See* Andrew Kull, *Between You, Me and the Gatepost* in *Cleargolaw News* vol. XXIII, No. 4 (Mar. 19, 1981) (copy on file with the author). Serendipitously, 30 years later, Andrew Kull was Professor Kull, my colleague at Boston University School of Law.

8. The choice between these terms can matter in a contract's substantive provisions, so make sure you understand when each should be used.

9. Some women use their given surname for professional purposes, but their married name for legal purposes, such as passports and drivers' licenses.

context of consumer agreements being drafted in plain English. However, in the context of sophisticated parties entering into a complex commercial agreement, other concerns take priority.

Specifically, the jurisdiction of organization may be necessary to identify an entity and to prevent confusion as to which entity is a party to the contract. Although no two entities organized in the same state may have the same name, entities organized in different states may have the same name. Indeed, some holding companies intentionally give their subsidiaries the same name so that they have the same public persona.

For example, ABC Inc., a holding company incorporated in Delaware, may have 49 subsidiaries, each of which is named ABC Inc., and each of which is incorporated in a different state. If the preamble lists ABC Inc. as a party, but omits its state of incorporation, a nonparty might not know which ABC Inc. is the party to the agreement. Including an entity's organizational identity clarifies any ambiguity. Here are two examples of an entity's name followed by its organizational identity.

Example 1

Internet Inc., a Delaware corporation,

Example 2

Colossal Construction LP, a New York limited partnership,

Note that a comma precedes and follows the organizational identity. Grammar dictates this punctuation because the organizational identity is an **appositive**: a word or phrase following a noun that further describes the noun. Note also that neither *corporation* nor *limited partnership* is capitalized. Capitalize these terms only if they are part of an entity's name.

Wrong

Hong Corporation, a California Corporation,

Correct

Hong Corporation, a California corporation,

In addition, avoid the old-fashioned, elongated version of an entity's organizational identity.

Wrong

Internet Inc., a corporation organized under the laws of the State of Delaware,

Instead, truncate the appositive as in the previous examples.

Correct

Internet Inc., a Delaware corporation,

Including an entity's organizational identity in the preamble does not substitute for including that information in the agreement's representations and warranties. There, the information becomes part of a substantive provision, giving a party a remedy if the information is incorrect. Banks, for example, often want this information so that they know where to file to perfect their security interests in a borrower's assets.

Entities sometimes operate through divisions with names that differ from the entity's legal name. A division differs from a subsidiary. A subsidiary is a separate legal entity. A division is not. It is merely an organizational tool designed to refer to a group dedicated to a specific purpose. For example, Bushwick Electric Co. might have two divisions: the first, Bushwick Appliances, dedicated to the manufacturing of kitchen appliances and the second, Bushwick Engines, dedicated to the manufacturing of aircraft engines. As neither Bushwick Appliances nor Bushwick Engines is a legal entity, neither can bind Bushwick Electric Co. Therefore, the divisions should not be listed as parties to the agreement. Instead, the preamble must name Bushwick Electric Co., as should the signature block. If the parties want to refer to the division, the drafter can include the information in the recitals and even give each division a defined term.[10]

When one of the parties is an individual, some drafters state that the party is an individual and give the state where the individual lives.

> **Maria Rodriguez, an individual residing in Oregon,**

This drafting is technically correct because it makes the identifying information parallel to the information about the other party. That said, for pragmatic reasons, the information can be omitted.[11] First, stating that a person is an individual is superfluous. It provides no identifying information. (Cyborgs are not yet sufficiently prevalent.) Although distinguishing an entity by its state of organization and its form identifies the entity, stating that a person is an individual does not. Second, the state of residence may not help in a person's identification because more than one person with a given name may reside in the same state. In addition, stating a person's state of residence may have unwanted tax or other substantive implications. If a person's name does not narrow the universe of people to one person, the person's address will.

Drafters differ on the wisdom of including the parties' addresses in the preamble — even when a party is an individual. The better practice is to put that information in the notice section or at the end of the contract either under a party's signature line or in a schedule. It keeps the preamble short and easy to read. It also reduces the likelihood of inadvertently including inconsistent addresses.[12]

6.2.3.2 Defining the Parties

To define the parties in the preamble (which is the usual practice), first, insert parentheses after the organizational identity. By inserting the parentheses, the second comma of the appositive precedes the open parenthesis (Version 1). But this placement violates the stylistic rule that a comma never precedes an open parenthesis. Therefore, move that comma so that it immediately follows the close parenthesis (Version 2).

---

10. See §6.3, Guideline 11, for information about how to create a defined term in recitals.

11. If you are a junior lawyer, following the precedent is the better alternative.

12. *See Gildor v. Optical Solutions, Inc.*, 2006 WL 4782348 at *1-2 (Del. Ch.).

Version 1 — Wrong

Colossal Construction LP, a New York limited partnership, ([defined term to be inserted])

Version 2 — Correct

Colossal Construction LP, a New York limited partnership ([defined term to be inserted]),

Next, with respect to the first party, choose a defined term that either relates to the party's role in the transaction or is a shorthand name for the individual or entity. Good shorthand names include an individual's last name and a significant word from an entity's name. Be careful when choosing a defined term that is role-related as the term may affect the agreement's interpretation.[13] Capitalize the defined term, bold it, insert quotation marks around it, and then use it capitalized (but in regular font) throughout the agreement to signal that it is a defined term.

Example 1

   (**"Contractor"**)

Example 2

   (**"Dell"**)

Example 3

   (**"Josephson"**)

Avoid acronyms — words formed from initials. Readers generally find it difficult to remember what the letters stand for. However, if an entity is commonly referred to by an acronym (e.g., IBM), then you may use it.

As a guiding principle in choosing defined terms, choose a term that makes it easy for the reader to follow who is doing what to whom. First, consider who the audience is. Ask yourself, "Which will be easier for the audience — names or role-related terms?" Whatever the answer is, you can easily change an agreement's existing defined terms by using a word-processing program's "Find and Replace" function.

Next, consider whether the terms relating to the parties' roles are confusing. Classic baffling terms are *mortgagor* and *mortgagee, lessor* and *lessee,* and *licensor* and *licensee.* Instead of these terms, use the parties' names or other terms that indicate a party's role, such as *bank* and *borrower* or *landlord* and *tenant.* Using these alternative terms can also reduce typographical errors.

Also take into account the number of parties. If more than two, using role-related defined terms is often the better choice. For example, in a credit agreement, the parties often include the borrower, multiple lending banks, and an agent bank (a bank that acts on behalf of the other banks). In this instance, a reader will probably find it easier to keep track of the parties if the contract uses role-related defined terms.

---

13. *See In re Taxes, Aiea Dairy, Ltd.*, 380 P.2d 156, 160-161 (Haw. 1963) (finding that the parties' choice of role-related defined terms (*producer* and *distributor*) was evidence that the parties had an agency relationship, rather than that of buyer and seller).

Finally, consider whether others will use this agreement as a precedent. If so, role-related terms are preferable, as they will facilitate the drafting of future agreements.

Once you choose the first party's defined term, choosing the other parties' defined terms is easy. Choose a term that parallels the term chosen for the first party.

Example 1

Landlord and Tenant

Example 2

IBM and General Foods

Example 3

Josephson and Martinez

If you choose a role-related defined term, you must decide whether the word *the* will precede each use of it within the agreement.

Version 1

    Rent. *The* Tenant shall pay *the* Landlord the Rent no later than the first business day of each month.

Version 2

    Rent. *Tenant* shall pay *Landlord* the Rent no later than the first business day of each month.

Both formats are acceptable, although drafters disagree over which to use. Some drafters omit *the* on the theory that it shortens the agreement. Other drafters include it, reasoning that the agreement will not be that much longer and that its absence is jarring to lay readers who are accustomed to articles preceding nouns. This author prefers the use of *the* for the reason stated.

If *the* will precede the defined term, insert it inside the parentheses, **but before** the open quotation marks. If *the* will not precede the defined term, only the defined term should be inside the parentheses.

Version 1

    (the "**Executive**")

Version 2

    ("**Executive**")

Do not precede the defined term with *hereinafter referred to as* or some variant.

Wrong

(hereinafter referred to as the "**Executive**")

> **Correct**
>
> (the "**Executive**")

The language is legalese and surplusage. Also, do not create two defined terms for a party, such as *IBM* and the *Company*. That will confuse the reader. Create only one defined term, and then use it capitalized, without quotation marks in the rest of the contract.

> **Wrong**
>
> (hereinafter "**IBM**" or the "**Company**")
>
> **Correct—Version 1**
>
> ("**IBM**")
>
> **Correct—Version 2**
>
> (the "**Company**")

Some drafters do not bold the defined terms in a preamble. That is inconsistent with bolding defined terms in a definitions section[14] and in the body of the agreement. As an alternative, the defined terms are left unbolded or are placed in all capitals. The latter is the less favorable alternative because it creates three font styles in one paragraph.

The punctuation at the end of the preamble is a period, regardless of whether you use the sentence or nonsentence format.

The following are examples of complete preambles, each of which uses a different style for the defined terms.

> **Version 1**
>
> **This Employment Agreement**, dated October 10, 20XX, is between Internet Inc., a Delaware corporation (the "**Company**"), and Joe Hacker (the "**Executive**").
>
> **Version 2**
>
> **This Employment Agreement,** dated October 10, 20XX, is between Internet Inc., a Delaware corporation ("**Company**"), and Joe Hacker ("**Executive**").
>
> **Version 3**
>
> **This Employment Agreement**, dated October 10, 20XX, is between Internet Inc., a Delaware corporation ("**Internet**"), and Joe Hacker ("**Hacker**").

---

14. In this book, the author refers to the definitions section. Whether the definitions are contained in a section or an article of an agreement, the same rules apply.

Occasionally, an agreement will have multiple parties in the same role. In this event, define each party in the role by name and include an inclusive defined term for all the parties in the same role.

Version 1

Shareholders' Agreement, dated July 18, 20XX, between Cuddle Blankets Inc., a Maine corporation (the "**Corporation**"), and Investment Corp., an Ohio corporation ("**Investment**"), Barbara Steckler ("**Steckler**"), Shanice Washington ("**Washington**"), and Andrew Yates ("**Yates**") (Investment, Steckler, Washington, and Yates, individually, a "**Shareholder**" and collectively, the "**Shareholders**").

As an alternative to listing in the preamble all the parties in the same role, put the information concerning those parties in a schedule and refer to the schedule in the preamble. It unclutters the preamble, making it easier to read.

Version 2

Shareholders' Agreement, dated July 18, 20XX, between Cuddle Blankets Inc., a Maine corporation (the "**Corporation**"), and each shareholder listed in **Schedule A**[15] (individually, a "**Shareholder**" and collectively, the "**Shareholders**").

In sophisticated transactions, an entity may play more than one role. For example: A bank may play two roles in a financing transaction—lender to the borrower and agent for the group of banks lending to the borrower.[16] In that event, the preamble must include defined terms that indicate each role the entity plays.

. . . New York Bank, a New York banking corporation, as a lender (in that capacity, a "**Lender**")[17] and as administrative agent (in that capacity, the "**Administrative Agent**") . . .

Some practitioners include in the contract a defined term *Parties*. Better drafting is to leave the term undefined. First, the undefined term suffices if the intent is to clarify that *parties* refers to the parties to the agreement being drafted—as opposed to the parties of some other agreement. Second, *signatories* is the better choice if

---

15. Many drafters bold references to Schedules and Exhibits. This makes it easier for the reader to determine what other documents need to be read and easier for the drafter when collating the full agreement.

16. Multiple banks often act together as lenders to one borrower to spread the credit risk.

17. When a credit agreement has multiple lenders, the preamble may not separately list each lender and define it. Instead, the preamble may use the defined term "Lenders" and include a cross-reference to a schedule or the definitions section. In that event, individual banks will be listed in the preamble to the extent they play a secondary role.

the drafter intends to refer only to those signing the agreement and not to third-party beneficiaries[18] or successors and assigns. It explicitly states what the drafter intends.

6.2.4 DEFINING THE AGREEMENT

You may define the agreement being drafted either in the preamble or in the definitions section.

In the preamble

Version 1

Shareholders' Agreement (this "**Agreement**"), dated as of July 18, 20XX, between Cuddle Blankets Inc., a Maine corporation (the "**Corporation**"), and each shareholder listed in **Schedule A** (individually, a "**Shareholder**" and collectively, the "**Shareholders**").

Version 2

Shareholders' Agreement (including all schedules, exhibits, and amendments, this "**Agreement**"), dated as of July 18, 20XX, between Cuddle Blankets Inc., a Maine corporation (the "**Corporation**"), and each shareholder listed in **Schedule A** (individually, a "**Shareholder**" and collectively, the "**Shareholders**").

Version 3

In the definitions section

"**Agreement**" means this Shareholders' Agreement and all Schedules and Exhibits, as any one or more is amended from time to time.

Some drafters prefer to define the agreement in the definitions section because it shortens the preamble, especially if the definition includes schedules, exhibits, and amendments. They will do this even if they use the defined term Agreement in the recitals or the words of agreement. Although this violates the traditional rules relating to the use of defined terms, it is customary in the legal community. If an agreement does not have a definitions section, define the agreement in the preamble. Including the schedules and exhibits in the defined term precludes any dispute as to whether they are part of the agreement.[19] The reference to amendments eliminates the need to amend the definition of *Agreement* to include amendments, if the Agreement is amended.

---

18. *See Props. Inv. Group v. Applied Commun. Inc.*, 495 N.W.2d 483 (Neb. 1993) (finding that "parties" included third-party beneficiaries); *see also Bush v. Brunswick Corp.*, 783 S.W.2d 724 (Tex. App. 1990) (finding that "person" included shareholders who were not signatory to a merger agreement).

19. See § 5.10.1, nn. 5 and 6.

6.3   RECITALS

Recitals follow the preamble. They describe the background and purpose of a contract. For example:

Escrow Agreement

This Escrow Agreement (this "**Escrow Agreement**"), dated July 1, 20XX, is between Pretty Pearls, Inc., a Delaware corporation ("**Pearls**"), Bijoux Extraordinaires Co., a New York corporation ("**Bijoux**"), and Big Bank Corp., a New York banking corporation, as escrow agent (the "**Escrow Agent**").

Background

1. Each of Bijoux and Pearls is a general partner in Gems & Jewels, a New York general partnership (the "**Partnership**").
2. Bijoux and Pearls have decided to dissolve the Partnership and have memorialized their decision in the Dissolution Agreement, dated the date of this Agreement (the "**Dissolution Agreement**").
3. In accordance with the Dissolution Agreement,

    (a) Bijoux has executed and delivered to Pearls a certificate, dated the date of this Agreement and attached as **Exhibit A** (the "**Warranty Certificate**"), in which Bijoux makes representations and warranties with respect to specific matters; and
    (b) Bijoux and Pearls have agreed that the Partnership will deposit with the Escrow Agent into the Escrow Account (as defined in Section 2(f)) $250,000 that the Partnership would otherwise pay to Bijoux as a distribution in respect of Bijoux's general partnership interest in the Partnership.

Accordingly, the parties agree as follows:

If this escrow agreement had no recitals, its title would give information as to the agreement's general purpose, but not its specific purpose. By using recitals, the drafter explains to the reader the parties' relationship and *why* they have entered into the escrow agreement. Recitals are particularly useful if the parties want to inform interested third parties about an agreement's purpose.[20] Drafters also use recitals to buttress a contract term that might otherwise be unenforceable. Look again at the first example of introductory provisions in this chapter.[21] Here, the recitals tell the reader that the noncompetition agreement is part of a larger transaction, the sale of a business. As courts are more likely to enforce restraints on a person's ability to work if they arise in the context of an acquisition,[22] this information could tip the balance in

---

20. *See Ohio Valley Gas, Inc. v. Blackburn*, 445 N.E.2d 1378, 1383 (Ind. App. 4th Dist. 1983).
21. See §6.1, pp. 65-66.
22. *See Purchasing Assocs., Inc. v. Weitz*, 196 N.E.2d 245, 247 (N.Y. 1963).

favor of enforceability. Therefore, by setting the stage for a provision in the recitals, a drafter can explain its factual predicate, giving the court a basis on which to ground its decision.

Recitals are also used to clarify the parties' intent. This can occur either because the parties explicitly state their intent in the recitals or because the courts use the recitals to interpret ambiguous operative provisions.

A classic example of the use of recitals to interpret a contract's provisions is *Wood v. Lucy, Lady Duff-Gordon*,[23] a case you might recall from your contracts course. In that case, Lady Duff-Gordon granted Wood an exclusive license to market her designs and to place her endorsement on the designs of others. The contract, however, did not include a return promise that Wood would use his best efforts in this endeavor. Nonetheless, the court held that the contract included an implied promise to this effect, and relied, in part, on the contract's recitals to reach its decision.[24]

Drafters may also use recitals to identify a contract's consideration. For example, when a party guarantees another person's debt, the return consideration to the guarantor may not be immediately apparent. In this case, the drafter should specify the consideration in the recitals to dispel any notion that the consideration flows in only one direction.[25] For example:

Guaranty

Guaranty, dated March 18, 20XX, by Handicrafts Corp., a Missouri corporation (the "**Guarantor**"), in favor of Big Bank Corp., a Missouri banking corporation (the "**Lender**").

Background

1. Baskets Inc., a Missouri corporation (the "**Borrower**"), and the Lender have entered into a loan agreement, dated March 18, 20XX (the "**Loan Agreement**"), under which the Lender will make loans to the Borrower.
2. The Guarantor owns all of the issued and outstanding shares of the Borrower.
3. The Guarantor and the Borrower are engaged in related businesses, and the Guarantor will derive substantial direct and indirect benefit from the Lender's loans to the Borrower.
4. The Loan Agreement requires as a condition to the making of any loans by the Lender that the Guarantor guarantee the Borrower's obligations under the Loan Agreement.

In consideration of the Lender making loans to the Borrower, the Guarantor agrees as follows:

---

23. *Wood v. Lucy, Lady Duff-Gordon*, 118 N.E. 214 (N.Y. 1917).
24. *Id.*
25. *See State v. Larsen*, 515 N.W.2d 178, 180-181 (N.D. 1994).

Recitals are part of a contract in that they are included in the document that is the contract. But they are not part of the contract that binds the parties.[26] Therefore, they cannot create enforceable, operative provisions of a contract, unless the parties explicitly incorporate them into the contract and make them so.[27] Therefore, do not put representations and warranties, covenants, or conditions in the recitals because they probably will not be enforceable. For example, return to the recitals in the Escrow Agreement at the beginning of this section. If the following "recital" were added to the recitals already in that agreement, a court would probably not enforce what is actually a condition to an obligation and an obligation.[28]

> 5. The Escrow Agent shall release funds to Bijoux only if
>
> (a) Pearls delivers a certificate to the Escrow Agent stating that the Warranty Certificate has no misrepresentations or breaches of warranties; or
>
> (b) Pearls and Bijoux deliver a certificate to the Escrow Agent stating the amount that the Escrow Agent should release to Bijoux.

As noted, the general rule is that recitals are not part of the contract unless specifically incorporated—which is not generally a good idea to do.[29] That said, some courts have held that a specific recital provides evidence of the material facts stated.[30] In addition, statutes sometimes apply, making the recitals prima facie or conclusive evidence of the facts stated.[31]

Finally, the recitals and the operative provisions of a contract are sometimes inconsistent. In that case, the following rules of interpretation govern:

> If the recitals are clear and the operative part is ambiguous, the recitals govern the construction. If the recitals are ambiguous and the operative part is clear, the operative part must prevail. If both the recitals and the operative part are clear, but they are inconsistent with each other, the operative part is to be preferred.[32]

Use the following guidelines when drafting recitals.

---

26. *See Williams v. Barkley*, 58 N.E. 765, 767 (N.Y. 1900) ("The promise is what the parties agreed to do, and hence is the operative part of the instrument, while the recital states what led up to the promise and gives the inducement for making it"); *see also e.g. Fugate v. Town of Payson*, 791 P.2d 1092, 1094 (Ariz. App. 1990) ("A recital . . . is not strictly part of the contract . . .").

27. *See In re Taxes, Aiea Dairy Ltd.*, 380 P.2d 156, 163 (Haw. 1963).

28. Of course, if the operative provisions of the contract restate or incorporate what is in the recitals, those provisions are enforceable.

29. See § 6.3, Guideline 7.

30. *Det. Grand Park Corp. v. Turner*, 25 N.W.2d 184, 188-189 (Mich. 1946) ("[P]articular recitals in a contract involving a statement of fact are as a rule to be treated as conclusive evidence of the fact stated, while general recitals may not be."); *see Union Pac. Resources Co. v. Texaco, Inc.*, 882 P.2d 212, 222 (Wyo. 1994).

31. *See Rosenberg v. Smidt*, 727 P.2d 778 (Alaska 1986) (finding recital of compliance with notice requirements to be "'conclusive evidence of compliance. . .'") (quoting Alaska Stat. Ann. §34.20.090(c) (1957)).

32. *Jamison v. Franklin Life Ins. Co.*, 136 P.2d 265, 269 (Ariz. 1943), quoting *Williams v. Barkley*, 58 N.E. 765, 767 (N.Y. 1900), quoting English case law (citations omitted).

Guidelines for Recitals

1. *Do not overuse recitals.* Use them only if they add something to the agreement. Lawyers have a long and sordid history of overusing recitals. The practice began in England hundreds of years ago when clients paid their lawyers based on the length of the document.[33]

2. *Determine the content of the recitals by their purpose.* Thus, as with the drafting of anything else, you must determine what you want to accomplish before you write. Consider who the audience is. It may be only the parties and their lawyers. However, it may also include, among others, the parties' shareholders, financial analysts, a judge, and the judge's clerk. If the audience is only the parties and their lawyers, the recitals may be quite short or even omitted. For example, some bank loan agreements no longer include recitals. After reading the agreement's title, no one needs to know much more about the background of the agreement. However, if the anticipated audience is wider, the recitals should be expansive enough to explain the contract's background and the parties' intent.

3. *If the agreement includes expansive recitals, they should tell a story.* They should explain the parties' relationship and the reason for the agreement.

4. *When stating facts in the recitals that relate to the party's past relationship, make sure that they are accurate.* If they are wrong, they might damage your client's case in a litigation. Courts have held recitals to be conclusive evidence of the material facts stated.[34] Specific recitals, rather than general recitals, are more likely to be deemed conclusive evidence of the facts stated.[35]

5. *If the background surrounding the agreement is complicated, consider stating the facts in chronological order.* Chronology can often be a helpful organizing principle.

6. *Do not put operative provisions in the recitals.* Representations and warranties, covenants, and conditions all belong in the body of the agreement—after the words of agreement. A court will not enforce operative provisions that are in recitals.

7. *Do not incorporate the recitals into the body of the agreement.* If you draft the recitals properly and omit all substantive provisions, incorporating the recitals into the agreement by reference serves no purpose. If the recitals are not drafted properly and are incorporated by reference, they become cannon fodder for ambiguity: Who made the representation and warranty? Who made the covenant? Was the incorporated language intended as a covenant or condition? As noted, recitals can be problematic because a court may deem them to be conclusive evidence of the facts stated. Incorporation by reference only exacerbates this problem.

8. *Generally, do not put information concerning the purchase price or consideration in the recitals.* They are not the place to state the purchase price. But if the consideration's adequacy is unclear, then use the recitals to explain what the consideration is and why it is adequate. For example, look at the recitals for the Guaranty set out earlier in this section. In addition, use recitals to buttress a contract term that might otherwise be unenforceable, e.g., a noncompete clause.

9. *Draft recitals in a contemporary format.*
  (a) Do not introduce recitals with the archaic *Witnesseth.* Instead, either proceed directly from the preamble to the recitals or indicate that the recitals follow by using either the word *Recitals* or *Background.*

---

33. David Mellinkoff, *The Language of the Law* 190-191 (Little, Brown & Co. 1963).
34. *See Union Pac. Resources Co. v. Texaco, Inc.*, *supra* n. 30.
35. *See Det. Grand Park Corp. v. Turner*, *supra* n. 30, at 188.

(b) Do not precede each recital with *Whereas*. As with *Witnesseth*, it is archaic. Instead, write one or more well-drafted paragraphs or a series of numbered sentences. Which to use depends on which format will facilitate the reading of the recitals.

10. *Avoid drafting the recitals as reciprocal statements of the parties:*

> **Wrong**
>
> The Company desires to employ the Executive, and the Executive desires to work for the Company.

That is archaic. Try a simpler sentence.

> **Correct**
>
> This Agreement provides for the Company's employment of the Executive.

In either event, if this recital were the only one in the employment agreement, it would be superfluous as the title of the agreement would convey the necessary information.

11. *If you define a term in the recitals, bold the defined term inside quotation marks surrounded by parentheses and precede the defined term with the word* the, *unless the defined term is a person's name.*

> **Example 1**
>
> (the "**Defined Term**")
>
> **Example 2**
>
> ("**Danowski**")

The recitals in the introductory provisions of the Escrow Agreement at the beginning of this section have several examples of how to define terms in recitals.

12. *Avoid using defined terms in the recitals if they are not defined in the preamble or recitals.* Rarely, it is appropriate to use a defined term in the recitals, even though the definition for that term appears in the definitions section. Do this only if the defined term clearly conveys the definition's substance, and if including the definition in the recitals is awkward. Any defined term used without a definition should cross-reference the location of the definition immediately following the defined term's first use. The cross-reference should be inside a set of parentheses.

Look at the recitals in the introductory provisions of the Escrow Agreement at the beginning of this section. There, in subsection 3(b), the defined term *Escrow Account* is used. But the defined term and the cross-reference muddy the recitals. At this stage of contract review, the reader does not need to know the exact meaning of the term. Using *escrow agreement*, uncapitalized, conveys just as much information without interrupting the flow of the recitals.[36]

---

36. The recital in the Website Development Agreement (Chapter 32, Document 2) uses the undefined term "website" as it provides sufficient information to the reader for the purpose of the recital. *Website* is then defined in Section 1 so that its subsequent use in the agreement conveys the information provided in its related definition.

As noted earlier, practitioners commonly violate this rule by using the phrase *this Agreement* in the recitals without a cross-reference to the definitions section.

6.4 WORDS OF AGREEMENT

The **words of agreement** follow the recitals. Some drafters refer to them as the **statement of consideration**, a term that reflects their historical role. These provisions are often verbose and replete with legalese. For example:

Example 1

NOW, THEREFORE, in consideration of the premises[37] and of the mutual agreements and covenants hereinafter set forth, the Owner and the Contractor hereby agree as follows:

Example 2

NOW, THEREFORE, in consideration of $10 paid in hand, and other good and valuable consideration the receipt of which is hereby acknowledged, the parties agree as follows:

Example 3

NOW, THEREFORE, in consideration of the mutual representations, warranties, covenants, and agreements, and on the terms and conditions hereinafter set forth, the parties hereto do hereby agree as follows:

Do not use these provisions—unless you are working for a superior who has one foot rooted in the eighteenth century. Usually, a better choice is one of the following:

Example 4

Accordingly, in consideration of the mutual promises stated in this Agreement, the parties agree as follows:

Example 5

Accordingly, the parties agree as follows: *(For use after recitals.)*

or

The parties agree as follows: *(For use when the agreement has no recitals.)*

Look at Examples 1 through 4. Each provision has two parts.

■ A recitation of the consideration.
■ A statement that the parties agree to the provisions that follow.

The first part is archaic, and in most states it no longer serves a legal purpose. A drafter cannot turn into consideration something that cannot be consideration.

---

37. *Premises* is not a typographical error. It means that which came before—i.e., the information provided in the recitals.

As stated by Professor Farnsworth, "[An] employer cannot transform an unenforceable promise to give an employee a gold watch into an enforceable one simply by reciting, 'In consideration of your past service, I promise. . . .'"[38] Accordingly, in most instances the recitation of consideration can be omitted from the words of agreement. That said, a contract's content and reducing the risk of litigation should be salient. In some states, a recitation of consideration creates a rebuttable presumption of consideration.[39] Although the presumption is rebuttable, litigators tend to appreciate any advantage. In these states, use the language in Example 4. It has the distinct advantage of generally being accurate.

If the consideration's adequacy is in doubt, draft recitals explaining what the consideration is and tailor the words of agreement to reflect the recitals. Drafters do this regularly with guaranties and options where the return consideration for the guaranty and option is unclear.[40] Look, for example, at the recitals of the Guaranty in Section 6.3.[41] In this situation, it is also helpful for the words of agreement to reflect the actual consideration.

The second part of the words of agreement is useful. It evidences the parties' agreement to the contract provisions that follow. This statement can be quite simple as in Example 5.

6.5   COVER PAGE AND TABLE OF CONTENTS

Long contracts often have a **cover page** and a **table of contents** that precede the agreement. The cover page typically states the name of the agreement, the date and the parties, all centered on the page (both horizontally and vertically). The font should be larger than the regular font. If the regular font size is 12 points, 20 points might be appropriate for the cover page.

**Revolving Credit Agreement between
Printing and Graphics Inc.
and
Tribeca Banking N.A.**
April 10, 20X7

The table of contents should immediately follow the cover page and list the agreement's articles, sections, schedules, and exhibits and provide page referents for each. Most word-processing programs can create a table of contents with relative ease.

---

38. E. Allan Farnsworth, *Farnsworth on Contracts* vol. 1, 157 (3d ed., Aspen 2004).

39. *See, e.g. Earl v. St. Louis U.*, 875 S.W.2d 234, 237 (Mo. App. 1994); *Finegan v. Prudential Ins. Co.*, 14 N.E.2d 172, 175-176 (Mass. 1938). In some states, statutes provide that a written instrument is presumptive evidence of consideration. *See* Okla. Stat. tit. 15, § 114 (1996); Idaho Code § 29-104. *See also Farnsworth on Contracts*, *supra* n. 38, vol. 1, 158, and the cases cited therein.

40. *See* Arthur L. Corbin, *Corbin on Contracts* vol. 2, 84-88 (Joseph M. Perillo & Helen Hadjiyannakis Bender eds., rev. ed., West 1995). In some states, it may also be necessary to recite the consideration in land contracts. *See generally* W. W. Allen, *Necessity and Sufficiency of Statement of Consideration in Contract or Memorandum of Sale of Land, Under Statute of Frauds*, 23 A.L.R.2d 164 (1952).

41. See § 6.3.

EXERCISES

Exercise 6-1

Review Chapter 6 and create a top ten list of rules for drafting a contemporary preamble. Each rule should be no more than one sentence. (No run-on sentences or semi-colons.) (Think David Letterman. If David Letterman is too old media, humor your professor and the author and Google *David Letterman top 10 lists*.)

Exercise 6-2

Return to Exercise 5-3, and using the facts in that exercise, draft the preamble to the agreement described in that exercise.

Exercise 6-3

Mark up the following introductory provisions so that they follow the guidelines in Chapter 6.

EXCLUSIVE MANUFACTURING AND SUPPLY AGREEMENT

THIS AGREEMENT made as of April 12, 20X4, by and between THE STEIGER DIVISION OF THE JOHNSON GROUP, INC., a Delaware corporation, ("Steiger") and CREATIVE PARTIES GROUP CORP., a Delaware Corporation, ("CPG").

W I T N E S S E T H :

WHEREAS, CPG designs, promotes, distributes, and sells disposable party goods, including the Products (as hereinafter defined); and

WHEREAS, in accordance with a Sales Agreement between the parties, CPG has concurrently herewith sold to Steiger all of CPG's rights in the machinery and equipment that CPG used to manufacture the Products; and

WHEREAS, Steiger and CPG have determined that they will mutually benefit from an exclusive manufacturing and distribution relationship in accordance with which CPG will use Steiger exclusively to manufacture the Products to CPG's specifications and in accordance with which Steiger will manufacture the Products for sale to CPG.

NOW, THEREFORE, for good and valuable consideration, the receipt and sufficiency of which are hereby acknowledged, Steiger and CPG hereby agree as follows:

Exercise 6-4

Memorandum[42]

To: Leslie Lawyer

From: Brad S. Dennison

Subject: Indemnity Agreement

As you know, I am Vice President in charge of sales for Locomotive Transportation, Inc., a New York corporation (Locomotive). Three months ago, after negotiations with Rapid Trains Corp., a Massachusetts corporation (Rapid), Locomotive sold Rapid 2,100 30-ton coal cars — everything that we had in stock. About a week later, Anne Winsom (a new sales representative) met with Coal Transportation, Inc., a New Jersey corporation (Coal Transportation), and signed a contract with Coal Transportation. That contract committed Locomotive to deliver 300 30-ton coal cars within one week. Obviously, we didn't meet that schedule, as we had no more cars in stock. Coal Transportation sued, alleging breach of contract.

Yesterday, I got a call from Sally Milton, President of Rapid. According to Sally, Rapid would love to purchase an additional 300 cars. As we now have at least that number of cars in stock, I want to do this deal. The proverbial fly in the ointment is that Rapid has heard about Coal Transportation's suit against us and is afraid Coal Transportation will sue Rapid for tortious interference. After I told Rapid that Locomotive would indemnify it, Sally agreed that Rapid would do the deal. (I'm not worried about the lawsuit. According to David Fein in your Litigation Department, the damages we may have to pay are minimal. Our profit on the deal will more than cover anything we have to pay to Coal Transportation. Apparently, it purchased the cars from another manufacturer at approximately the same price as our contract price.)

Please draft the preamble, recitals, and the words of agreement for the indemnity agreement. I would like to review the draft as soon as possible. Please be sure that the agreement is effective as of today, no matter when we sign it.

B.S.D.

---

42. This exercise is based on *Hocking Valley Ry. Co. v. Barbour*, 192 N.Y.S. 163 (App. Div. 3d Dept. 1920), *aff'd without op.*, 130 N.E. 909 (N.Y. 1921).

Exercise 6-5

Memorandum

To: D. Fender
From: H. Flighty
Date: August 31, 20X2
Re: Purchase of Sam Samson's Icarus I-800

Last evening, while sharing a bottle of Chablis with Sam Samson, I finally agreed to buy his jet for $21 million! The Chablis must have been a better vintage than I thought, because I had no intention of agreeing to a price in excess of $15 million. Nonetheless, I signed a Purchase Offer in my capacity as President of Fly-by-Night Aviation, Inc. (Aviation). (A copy of the Purchase Offer is attached.) In my current financial situation, I am simply unable to consummate this transaction. It would, of course, be most embarrassing if I had to admit my current financial straits to Sam.

There is a solution.

I know that Sam's archrival, Rob Robertson, has coveted Sam's Icarus I-800 for years and that Robertson would be willing to purchase the I-800 for a price in excess of $21 million. I'm sure that I can strike a deal with him under which Aviation will

(a)   assign all of its rights in the Purchase Offer to Robertson's holding company, The Robertson Jet Corp., a Delaware corporation (Robertson Jet); and

(b)   delegate its performance to Robertson Jet, which would assume Aviation's performance under the Purchase Offer and contemporaneously pay Aviation $1,000,000.

I plan to speak to Robertson about this transaction in the next week or so. When I meet with him, I would like to show him at least part of the Assignment and Assumption.

Accordingly, please draft the preamble, recitals, and words of agreement for the Assignment and Assumption and have it ready for my review as soon as possible. Also, be sure to check whether my company can delegate its duty to execute the promissory note. If there's an issue, write me a one-paragraph explanation of the law and how we can deal with the problem. In case you don't remember, your drafting textbook from law school had an example of an Assignment and Assumption [Document 3, Chapter 32].

                                                           H.F.

Purchase Offer Attached

Fly-by-Night Aviation, Inc.
987 West 48th Street
New York, New York 10036

Purchase Offer   August 30, 20X2

Fly-by-Night Aviation, Inc. ("**Buyer**") hereby offers to purchase the Icarus Aerospace Corporation I-800 aircraft, bearing United States Registration No. N765BW and Manufacturer's Serial No. 8181, equipped with two Rolls-Royce engines, Model No. BR710, Serial Numbers 72725 and 72726 (the "**Aircraft**"), from Supersonic Wings Corp. ("**Seller**") for $21 million, subject to the following terms and conditions:

1. Negotiation and execution of a definitive Aircraft Purchase Agreement satisfactory to both parties.
2. $5 million of the purchase price shall be paid by delivery of Buyer's promissory note to Seller. The note will bear interest at 9% per annum and will be due in a single bullet payment on December 31, 20X8.
3. Aircraft to be delivered with title free and clear of all liens and encumbrances of any nature whatsoever.
4. At Closing, Aircraft to have no more than 2,500 hours total flying time, exclusive of any flying time necessary to deliver the Aircraft to the location specified in Paragraph 5.
5. On the Closing Date, the Aircraft must be at Reagan National Airport in Washington, D.C., or such other reasonable and mutually convenient location as Buyer shall designate.
6. Seller to execute a bill of sale and any other documents necessary to convey good title to the Buyer.
7. Maintenance Agreement, dated as of April 3, 20X0, with Greasemonkeys, Inc., to be assigned by Seller to Buyer. Buyer is to assume all liabilities arising on or after the date of closing.
8. Pilot Agreement, between Ace Pilots, Inc. and Seller, dated as of May 12, 20X1, to be assigned to Buyer. Buyer is to assume only those liabilities that arise on or after the closing date.
9. Closing to occur on November 25, 20X2, at the offices of Workhard & Playlittle LLP, 1133 Avenue of the Americas, New York, New York, or on another date to which the parties agree. If the Closing does not occur on or before November 25, 20X2, because of Buyer's fault, Buyer shall pay Seller a $3 million termination fee.

On acceptance of this offer, Buyer will cause a deposit of $300,000 to be placed in escrow with Harold C. Astor & Associates, Oklahoma City, Oklahoma (HCA). (The escrow deposit will be governed by the terms of the escrow agreement being entered into by the parties and HCA concurrently with the execution of this Purchase Offer. The Escrow Agreement is attached.) The deposit will be used in partial payment of the purchase price. If the Closing does not occur and Buyer is not at fault, then Buyer is entitled to the return of its deposit, including accrued interest.

Very truly yours,

Fly-by-Night Aviation, Inc.

By: _Horatio Flighty_
Horatio Flighty, President

Accepted by:

Supersonic Wings Corp.

By: _Sam Samson_
Sam Samson, President

Escrow Agreement[43]

Escrow Agreement (this "**Escrow Agreement**"), dated August 30, 20X2, is between Supersonic Wings Corp., a Delaware corporation (the "**Seller**"), Fly-by-Night Aviation, Inc., a New York corporation (the "**Buyer**"), and Harold C. Astor & Associates, an Oklahoma partnership, as escrow agent (in that capacity, the "**Escrow Agent**").

Background

The Seller and the Buyer have executed a Purchase Offer dated August 30, 20X2 (the "**Purchase Offer**"), that provides for the Seller's sale to the Buyer of an Icarus Aerospace Corporation I-800 aircraft. Among other things, the Purchase Offer requires the Buyer to deposit $300,000 in escrow with the Escrow Agent. This Escrow Agreement states the terms relating to the escrow.

The Seller, the Buyer, and the Escrow Agent agree as follows:

1. **Escrow Deposit.** Simultaneously with the execution and delivery of this Escrow Agreement, the Buyer shall deliver $300,000 in immediately available funds to the Escrow Agent. The $300,000 delivered to the Escrow Agent, together with all interest that it earns, is referred to as the "**Escrow Amount.**" Immediately on receipt of the Escrow Amount, the Escrow Agent shall invest it in an interest-bearing money market account at the Bank of Oklahoma City. Afterwards, the Escrow Agent shall hold and dispose of the Escrow Amount as provided in this Escrow Agreement.

2. **Payment of the Escrow Amount.** The Escrow Agent shall dispose of the Escrow Amount in one of the following two ways:

    2.1 **In Accordance with Notice of the Seller and Buyer.** The Escrow Agent shall dispose of the Escrow Amount in the manner instructed in accordance with a notice, substantially in the form of **Exhibit A,** that both the Seller and the Buyer execute and then deliver to the Escrow Agent.

    2.2 **In Accordance with a Court Order.** The Escrow Agent shall dispose of the Escrow Amount when and in the manner that a court of competent jurisdiction instructs in an order that is final and no longer subject to appeal in the opinion of the Escrow Agent's counsel.

3. **Compensation.** The Escrow Agent's fees for its services under this Escrow Agreement are to be determined in accordance with its publicly announced fee schedule as in effect from time to time. The Seller and the Buyer shall each

    3.1 pay 50% of the Escrow Agent's fees for its services under this Escrow Agreement; and

    3.2 reimburse the Escrow Agent for 50% of the Escrow Agent's reasonable out-of-pocket expenses incurred in providing its services under this Escrow Agreement.

4. **Indemnification.**

    4.1 **Indemnity Obligation.** The Seller and the Buyer, jointly and severally, shall indemnify and defend the Escrow Agent against any loss, liability, obligation, claim, damage, or expense (including, without limitation, reasonable attorneys' fees and expenses) arising from or relating to acting under this Escrow Agreement, unless caused by the Escrow Agent's gross negligence or willful misconduct.

    4.2 **Right of Setoff.** Without limiting the Escrow Agent's other rights and remedies against the Seller and the Buyer, the Escrow Agent may satisfy all or part of the Seller and the Buyer's indemnity obligations under subsection 4.1 by setoff against the Escrow Amount. The

---

43. This Escrow Agreement is based, in part, on an escrow agreement that my Fordham colleague Alan Shaw drafted.

Escrow Agent shall promptly notify the Seller and the Buyer of any setoff.

5. **Escrow Agent's Role.** The Seller and the Buyer acknowledge that the Escrow Agent is acting solely as a stakeholder and that, in this capacity, it is not the Seller's or the Buyer's agent. The Escrow Agent has no obligations under this Escrow Agreement, except as expressly stated in this Escrow Agreement.

6. **Escrow Agent's Liability.**

   6.1 **Gross Negligence and Intentional Misconduct.** The Escrow Agent is not liable for any loss arising because it acted or refrained from acting in connection with the transactions this Escrow Agreement contemplates, except for any loss arising because of its gross negligence or intentional misconduct.

   6.2 **Advice of Counsel.** The Escrow Agent is not liable for any loss arising because it acted or refrained from acting in connection with the transactions this Escrow Agreement contemplates if it relied in good faith on its counsel's advice.

7. **Resignation and Discharge of the Escrow Agent.**

   7.1 **Resignation.** The Escrow Agent may resign from its duties under this Escrow Agreement by notifying the Seller and the Buyer in writing that it is resigning and stating in that notice the effective date of the resignation.

   7.2 **Discharge.** The parties may discharge the Escrow Agent from its duties under this Escrow Agreement by a written agreement that
   (a) the Seller and the Buyer execute;
   (b) is delivered to the Escrow Agent; and
   (c) states the effective date of the discharge.

   7.3 **Successor Escrow Agent.** If the Escrow Agent resigns or is discharged, the Seller and the Buyer shall jointly and promptly appoint a successor escrow agent. If they are unable to agree, then a court of competent jurisdiction is to appoint the successor escrow agent.

8. **General Provisions.**

   8.1 **Assignment and Delegation.** The Escrow Agent shall not assign its rights or delegate its performance under this Escrow Agreement without the other parties' written consent. The Seller and the Buyer may each assign its rights and delegate its performance under this Escrow Agreement. Any assignment or delegation in violation of this Section is void.

   8.2 **Amendments.** The parties may not amend this Escrow Agreement, except by an agreement that all the parties execute.

   8.3 **Merger.** This Escrow Agreement is the final and exclusive expression of the parties in connection with the transactions this Escrow Agreement contemplates.

Fly-by-Night Aviation, Inc.

By: _____
    Horatio Flighty, President

Supersonic Wings Corp.

By: _____
    Sam Samson, President

Harold C. Astor & Associates,
a general partnership
(in its capacity as Escrow Agent)

By: _____
    Harold C. Astor, General Partner

Exhibit A to Escrow Agreement

Harold C. Astor & Associates
1911 Main Street
Oklahoma City, Oklahoma 73110

[Insert date]

Ladies and Gentlemen:

We refer to the Escrow Agreement (the "**Escrow Agreement**"), dated August 30, 20X2, between Supersonic Wings Corp., a Delaware corporation (the "**Seller**"), Fly-by-Night Aviation, Inc., a New York corporation (the "**Buyer**"), and Harold C. Astor & Associates, an Oklahoma partnership, as escrow agent (in that capacity, the "**Escrow Agent**").

Each capitalized term used in this letter without definition has the meaning assigned to it in the Escrow Agreement.

By this letter, the Seller and the Buyer instruct the Escrow Agent to wire transfer in immediately available funds to the Seller's bank account or the Buyer's bank account or to both accounts, based on the information in the chart that follows:[44]

	Wire transfer amount	Location at which the funds are to be immediately available	Account information
Payment to Seller			
Payment to Buyer			

Very truly yours,

Supersonic Wings Corp.

By: _____
    Title:

Fly-by-Night Aviation, Inc.

By: _____
    Title:

---

44. Note the use of the chart as a way of organizing information.

Definitions and Defined Terms

7.1 INTRODUCTION

7.1.1 DEFINITIONS

A definition states the meaning of a word or phrase. Drafters use them primarily to create clarity and prevent ambiguity. They do so in the following ways:

First, a definition may expand or limit the dictionary meaning of a word. So, for example, the dictionary meaning of *lake* is "a considerable inland body of standing water."[1] In a contract dealing with the bottling of water from a specific lake, the definition of *lake* might limit its meaning to the specific lake from which water is to be taken for bottling.

Second, a definition may clarify the meaning of a word or phrase, such as *business day.* Although Monday, Tuesday, Wednesday, Thursday, and Friday are typically thought of as business days, the parties might want to clarify that if a holiday falls on any of those days, that day is not a business day.

Third, a definition may resolve the meaning of a word that is ambiguous. The word *dollar* is a classic example. In a contract between two U.S. companies, *dollar* would clearly refer to U.S. money. But in a contract between a Canadian and a U.S. company, *dollar* would be ambiguous. It could refer to either Canadian or U.S. dollars. A definition would eliminate this ambiguity by stipulating the correct meaning.

Fourth, a definition may explain the meaning of a technical word or phrase. For example, *capitalized lease* has a specific meaning under the accounting rules. To avoid any doubt as to the meaning of this phrase, the parties might want to spell out the specifics of those rules or refer to them.[2]

Fifth, a definition can be used to express a concept that is specific to the transaction. For instance, in a loan agreement, the bank might want to limit the borrower's investments to those that are liquid, that is, easily convertible into cash.[3] This is a contract-specific concept. To draft the definition for this concept, the parties might list all of the permitted investments.

---

1. *Merriam-Webster's Collegiate Dictionary* 652 (10th ed., 1999).

2. See § 7.5.2, Guideline 21, for a discussion of the issues relating to referring to materials outside the agreement.

3. A bank would want a borrower's investments to be liquid so that the borrower would always have ready access to cash to pay the bank.

Sixth, as indicated in the immediately preceding paragraph, a definition can list all the things to which a word or phrase refers. This list might specify only one thing, such as the pledge agreement between a bank and its borrower, or it could specify multiple things, such as all of the permitted investments.

Seventh, a definition can explain the meaning of a word or phrase by listing its significant characteristics. For example, the dictionary defines *computer* to be "a programmable electronic device that can store, retrieve, and process data."[4]

7.1.2   DEFINED TERMS

Defined terms are shorthand expressions of definitions. Drafters use them as an easy way of saying the same thing the same way. Failure to say the same thing the same way is an open invitation to the other side and the court to construe two provisions differently. Moreover, without defined terms, drafters would have to repeat the full-blown definition each time a concept was needed in a contract. This would make the agreement onerous to read. For instance, compare the following two versions of the same provision. The first version does not use a definition for *storage space,* while the second does.

Version 1

Condition of Storage Space. When the Tenant takes possession of the 2,500 square feet of storage space shown on the drawing attached to this Lease as Exhibit A, that possession is conclusive evidence that the 2,500 square feet of storage space shown on the drawing attached to this Lease as Exhibit A was in the condition that the Tenant and Landlord agreed on.

Version 2

The definition

"Storage Space" means the 2,500 square feet of storage space shown on the drawing attached to this Lease as Exhibit A.

The provision

Condition of Storage Space. When the Tenant takes possession of the Storage Space, that possession is conclusive evidence that the Storage Space was in the condition that the Tenant and Landlord agreed on.

Now imagine what Version 1 would be like if Tenant and Landlord had not been defined!

7.2   STRATEGIC CONCERNS IN DEFINING TERMS[5]

Strategic concerns affect how a term is defined. For example, consider the strategic concerns that might come into play when parties decide whether to define *force*

---

4. *Merriam-Webster's Collegiate Dictionary, supra* n. 1, at 237.
5. Class materials of Alan Shaw suggested this section.

majeure event by listing the events that constitute a *force majeure* event or by listing the criteria that an event must meet. Look at the following two definitions:[6]

Definition 1

"***Force Majeure* Event**" means war, flood, lightning, drought, earthquake, fire, volcanic eruption, landslide, hurricane, cyclone, typhoon, tornado, explosion, civil disturbance, act of God or the public enemy, terrorism, military action, epidemic, famine or plague, shipwreck, action of a court or public authority, or strike.

Definition 2

"***Force Majeure* Event**" means any act or event, whether foreseen or unforeseen, that meets all three of the following tests:

(a) The act or event prevents a party (the "**Nonperforming Party**"), in whole or in part, from

    (i) performing any obligation under this Agreement; or

    (ii) satisfying any condition to any obligation of the other party (the "**Performing Party**") under this Agreement.

(b) The act or event is beyond the reasonable control of and not the fault of the Nonperforming Party.

(c) The Nonperforming Party has been unable to avoid or overcome the act or event by the exercise of due diligence.

Which of these definitions will better serve your client depends on whether your client is more likely to be the nonperforming party or the performing party. If your client is more likely to be the nonperforming party, Definition 2 may be more appealing. Because it lists criteria, Definition 2 is elastic without clear limits. This might enable your client to argue that a *force majeure* event includes an event not listed in Definition 1. If Definition 1 with its exclusive list of *force majeure* events had instead been included as the definition, your client would have no basis for its argument—which is exactly why the party most likely to be the performing party would prefer it.

7.3 DEFINITIONS AS STANDARD-SETTING TOOLS

Definitions establish standards that affect the parties' rights and obligations. For example, assume that a stockholders' agreement has a defined term *Affiliate* and that a contract provision prohibits assignments *except to Affiliates*. In this context, the defined term *Affiliates* is a standard that is integral to the contract's business purpose. Depending on whether the term is defined broadly or narrowly, the brother of the president of a subsidiary might or might not be included within the scope of the definition. Therefore, you must exercise great care when crafting definitions and think through the consequences of each definition the same way you would if you were crafting a full provision.

---

6. These definitions are from Nancy F. Persechino, *Force Majeure,* in *Negotiating and Drafting Contract Boilerplate* Ch.11, 201-202 (Stark et al. eds., ALM Publg. 2003).

7.4   PLACEMENT OF DEFINITIONS

If an agreement is short or informal, or has only a few definitions, drafters often omit a separate definitions section[7] and define terms in context—that is, where they are used. But, most sophisticated commercial transactions do not fall within this category, thus inexorably leading to the question: Where do the definitions go?

Commentators and drafters disagree as to the answer to this question. Some lawyers champion putting the definitions section immediately after the words of agreement, so that the definitions appear in the beginning pages of an agreement. Others urge that the definitions section appear as the next-to-last section of an agreement, preceding the contract's general provisions. Finally, some lawyers advocate that definitions should appear in context, even if the contract is lengthy and sophisticated. Let's look briefly at the pros and cons of each approach.

The most common approach is to put the defined terms and their definitions in a separate section after the words of agreement. This way, terms used throughout the body of an agreement are easily accessible at the beginning of the contract, facilitating a reader's ability to find them. This placement also reminds a reader who might otherwise ignore the definitions that they often contain deal-critical concepts. A reader cannot help but stumble on them. Finally, having all of the definitions in one place near the front permits the sophisticated practitioner to skim them to see how the contract treats specific issues. For example, loan agreements often include financial covenants, such as requiring the borrower to maintain a certain ratio of cash flow to its debt obligations. As these financial covenants generally are drafted using defined terms, a practitioner can often quickly learn about the covenants by reading the definitions.

Some drafters disagree with this approach. They prefer to define each term in the body of the agreement—generally, the first time it is used but not necessarily. They believe this format yields at least three benefits. First, readers will garner a better understanding of a defined term by seeing its definition in context. Second, readers will no longer need to shuffle through a contract's pages looking for a term's definition in the definitions section. Third, the definitions section will no longer interrupt the flow of the contract. Instead, the business provisions of the action sections would immediately follow the words of agreement.

Although this approach has a superficial appeal, a realistic concern is that defining terms in context can lead to ambiguity. Specifically, the parameters of the definition may be unclear because of the defined term's placement. Typically, the defined term is placed immediately after the language that constitutes the definition, even if it is in the middle of a sentence.[8] This placement can lead to disputes as to how much of the preceding or succeeding[9] language is intended to be included in the definition. Look at the following recital, where an ambiguity concerning two definitions led to litigation:

> WHEREAS, Seller possesses technical information and know-how (the "Technical Information") relating to the production and manufacture of food products which look similar to the thin, crispy crust of 'french bread' from which the dough has been removed (the "Products"). . . .[10]

---

7. In this book, the author generally refers to the provisions containing defined terms and definitions as the *definitions section*. In some agreements, drafters might alternatively use the phrase *definitions article*. Regardless of the provisions' appellation, the same rules apply.

8. *Olympus Ins. Co. v. Aon Benfield, Inc.*, 2012 WL 1072334 at *4, No.11-CV-2607 (D. Minn. Mar. 30, 2012).

9. *Id.* (holding that defined term not limited by language following it).

10. *G. Golden Assocs. of Oceanside, Inc. v. Arnold Foods Co., Inc.*, 870 F. Supp. 472, 474 (E.D.N.Y. 1994).

In the lawsuit over the meaning of *Products,* the plaintiff argued that the definition of *Products* began with the words *food products* and that *Products* was not limited to *Products* produced in accordance with the *Technical Information* being transferred. The defendant, however, asserted that *Products* was limited to those produced in accordance with the *Technical Information.* Realistically, it is likely that neither party noticed this issue when drafting the recital. It was a subtlety that both sides missed. But if the parties had been forced to construct a definition for a definitions section, they would have been much more likely to confront the issue as to how much of the language preceding the word *Products* was included in the definition of that defined term.

If you define terms in context, one possible way to reduce the risk of ambiguity is to put the defined term at the end of the sentence and indicate within the parentheses the noun or phrase to which the defined term refers. Yet even when this approach works, it is not a panacea. Sometimes too much information needs to be included inside the parentheses. For example, assume that the recital from the litigated case *were* rewritten as follows:

> WHEREAS, Seller possesses technical information and know-how relating to the production and manufacture of food products which look similar to the thin, crispy crust of 'french bread' from which the dough has been removed *(the technical information and know-how, the "Technical Information;" the food products manufactured in accordance with the Technical Information, the "Products").* . . .

Here, the parenthetical is almost as long as the recital. It is cumbersome and interrupts the flow of the contract. An alternative would be to write the recital without any definitions, but then to include the definitions in the definitions section. These definitions would trump any ambiguity in the recitals.

Drafters who prefer not to define terms in context also point out that doing so does not end the shuffling of pages to find the appropriate definition. Specifically, a reader who wants to check the meaning of a term that was previously defined must still find the first use of that term in the, say, 100-page document. Those who prefer to define terms in context address this concern by creating an alphabetical index of all the defined terms and listing the page on which each term is defined. Arguably, this index increases a reader's work. Rather than simply turning to the definitions section and then returning to the contract provision, a reader must go to the index, then back to the body of the agreement where the term is defined, and finally back to the provision that includes the defined term. This may even need to be done the first time a reader encounters a defined term because, in some instances, a term is not defined the first time it is used.

Drafters promote two other alternative locations for definitions. Some drafters put them in a separate section at the end of the contract. They agree that it is easier for the reader if all of the definitions are in one place but believe that they should be at the end of the contract. This way, they will not hinder the reader who wishes to read the action sections immediately. These drafters also often believe that placing the definitions at the end of the contract expedites negotiations by making the parties focus first on substantive provisions rather than the definitions.

The second alternative puts the definitions in an appendix or other stand-alone document. Drafters often do this in transactions in which multiple agreements rely on the same definitions. For example, a credit agreement, a security agreement, and a pledge agreement all need terms to refer to the debt outstanding, the agent bank, and the maturity of the loan. If the defined terms are not the same in all three agreements, litigation follows almost inevitably. To ensure that the agreements all use the same defined terms with the same definitions, the parties use an appendix, whose defined terms are incorporated into each agreement.

So, what do you do if you are a junior lawyer and the designated drafter? The real world answer is that you follow the precedent you are given or the style of the person for whom you are working. You should be a chameleon until you are in charge. Then, you can decide.

On balance, this author believes that, in most instances, definitions should be placed in a separate section at the beginning of the contract—where they are easy to find and hard not to trip over (making it ever so much more likely that readers will give them the attention they deserve). Readers who wish to begin with the action sections, or any other section, may easily do so by obtaining the appropriate page number from the contract's table of contents.

There are some exceptions to this general rule. In the appropriate transaction, defining the terms in an appendix or other stand-alone document is a viable option. In addition, it may make sense to define all the terms in context if an agreement is short, informal, or includes only a few definitions.

Even if a contract includes a definitions section, it is appropriate to define a particular term in context in three instances.

- First, when the words of a provision cannot be easily reordered to turn them into an independent definition and defined term.
- Second, when a defined term is used multiple times, but in only one section.[11]
- Third, when you use a defined term in the monetary provisions and the defined term and its definition can be placed in a subsection by themselves.[12] By isolating the definition, the risk of ambiguity is reduced. In addition, it facilitates the reading of some of the agreement's more sophisticated provisions.

7.5 GUIDELINES FOR DRAFTING DEFINITIONS AND DEFINED TERMS

7.5.1 GENERAL GUIDELINES

No hard-and-fast rules govern when definitions should be drafted. If you use a precedent to draft the agreement, you will begin your draft with some definitions that probably work perfectly well—that is one of the benefits of using a precedent. (Of course, you can only be sure that no change is required by reviewing each instance in which the defined term is used.) Other definitions in the precedent will need to be tailored to the specific transaction. For example, in a contract for the sale of real property, the definition of *Premises* will need to be changed (obviously) so that it refers to the property being sold in that transaction. Finally, you will be able to craft some definitions only in the middle of the drafting process when you discover that you have a new concept (the definition) for which you need a new defined term.

Before finalizing a defined term and its definition, check every use of it. Sometimes a definition that works perfectly in three provisions does not work in the fourth. The computer is a terrific tool for this task. Most word-processing applications can search a document for specific words. This automates the task, making it much easier to complete. If you subsequently decide to change a definition, repeat the search to make sure that each provision still makes sense with the new definition.

---

11. See § 7.5.3, Guideline 1.

12. See Chapter 32, Document 4, The Action Sections of an Asset Purchase Agreement, § 2.2(a)(ii).

7.5.2 SPECIFIC GUIDELINES: DEFINING TERMS IN THE DEFINITIONS SECTION OR ARTICLE

Here are guidelines for drafting definitions and defined terms in a definitions section or article.

1. *Introduce the definitions and their defined terms with words to the following effect:*

> **Definitions and Defined Terms.** Each term defined in the preamble and the recitals of this Agreement has its assigned meaning, and each of the following terms has the meaning assigned to it:

If no terms are defined in the recitals, do not refer to the recitals in this introductory language. Many drafters continue to use the term recitals although the information is contained in the *Background or an untitled paragraph.* The better practice is to use the term/title that preceded the recitals, if any. If there was no title, you can refer to the *preceding introductory paragraph.*

2. *Do not create a defined term unless you will use it more than once, and once you create it, use it each time the definition is appropriate.* Despite the preceding sentence, you may use a defined term only once if its use will enhance a provision's readability. Specifically, sometimes a concept is so complicated that putting it in the middle of a provision makes the provision difficult to understand. If the defined term sufficiently encapsulates the concept, using it in the provision may permit a reader to understand better an otherwise thorny provision. If you do this, break the provision down into two subsections. Put the defined term and its definition in the first subsection and the substantive provision in the second.[13] Drafters sometimes take this approach in credit agreements when stating complex accounting concepts.[14]

3. *Create only one defined term for each definition, and use it exclusively.*

4. *List the defined terms alphabetically.* Including subsection referents, such as (a), (b), or (c), is unnecessary but not wrong. Getting your word-processing program to stop its automatic lettering is not worth the trouble.

5. *Include all terms defined in the agreement in the list of defined terms, other than terms defined in the preamble or the recitals.* These latter terms are already incorporated by reference in the language Guideline 1 suggests. If you define a term in context,[15] the alphabetical listing should cross-reference the definition's location.

> **"Rent"** has the meaning assigned to it in Section 2.2.
>
> *or*
>
> **"Rent"** is defined in Section 2.2.

6. *When defining a term, capitalize the first letter of each word. Put the entire defined term in bold and surround it with quotation marks:*

> **"Mechanical Failure"**

---

13. See § 7.5.3, Guideline 1, for an example.

14. For an example, see § 22.3.3, text accompanying n. 10.

15. See § 7.5.3.

If you are working for someone who drafts in a plain English style, that style might include omitting the quotation marks. Other drafters underline defined terms rather than use boldface. But boldface is the preferred way to make words prominent. Underlining is a holdover from the days when contracts were typed on typewriters and boldface was not an option.[16]

7. *When in the body of a contract, signal that a term is defined by capitalizing the first letter of each word* — just as was done when the term was defined in the definitions section.

Be careful. Occasionally, a defined term should not be capitalized because it is not intended to signal a definition. For example, *Agreement* is generally the word chosen as the defined term that refers to the parties' contract. Capitalizing *agreement* would be incorrect, however, in the following representation and warranty:

> **Agreements. Schedule 4.12** lists each agreement to which the Borrower is a party.

In this instance, *agreement* refers to contracts other than the parties' contract.

8. *Follow the defined term with the verb* means. *Shall mean* is incorrect. *Shall* is the language of obligation, and only parties can be obligated to do something.[17] As the defined term is not promising to do anything, *shall* is wrong. If it is used in this way, it is known as the *false imperative.*

> **Wrong**
>
> > **"Mechanical Failure"** shall mean
>
> **Correct**
>
> > **"Mechanical Failure"** means

9. *If a definition is not intended as an exclusive listing or description, follow the defined term with the verb* includes.

> **"Breach"** includes a cross-default.[18]

Take care when using *includes* to think through whether any exclusions are appropriate.[19]

10. *Never use* means *and* includes *together.* If *means* is the verb, it signals that the defined term and the definition are equivalents. Logically, no additional matters can be part of the definition. *Includes* indicates that the defined term refers not only to matters stated in the definition, but also to matters outside the definition. Therefore, *means* and *includes* are inconsistent and cannot be used together.

11. *To exclude something that would ordinarily be within the contemplation of a defined term, follow the defined term with* excludes.

---

16. Bryan A. Garner, *Legal Writing in Plain English: A Text with Exercises* § 44, 126-127 (U. Chi. Press 2001).

17. See § 10.2, Guideline 1.

18. A **cross-default** is a default that occurs in the subject agreement because of a default in another agreement. For example, a credit agreement may specify that a default under that agreement occurs if a borrower fails to pay when due any material liability under any other agreement.

19. See § 23.5 for a discussion of *including* and *including without limitation.*

> **Version 1**
>
> **"Telephone"** excludes a cellular telephone that does not take photographs.

Note that this definition does not state what a *telephone* is. It relies on the parties' understanding of this everyday term. An alternative is to state what a telephone is and to follow it with the exclusion.

> **Version 2**
>
> **"Telephone"** means an instrument for reproducing sound at a distance,[20] but excludes cellular telephones that do not take photographs.

12. *Choose as the defined term words that convey information to the reader about the substance of the definition.* Thus, *Residence* would be a good defined term if the definition were *house, townhouse, apartment, cooperative, houseboat,* and *condominium.*

Similarly, the substance of a definition should not include concepts unrelated to the other concepts in a definition. Thus, the definition of *Residence* should not include *office towers.*

13. *If a definition varies the usual meaning of a word or phrase, choose a defined term that signals the variation.* For example, a good defined term for an electronic book would be *E-book,* not *Book.*

14. *Include a defined term in the definition of another defined term if one definition builds on another definition.* For example, the following definition is from a website-linking agreement under which one company agrees to include in its website a hyperlink to another company's website.[21]

> **"Company A Users"** means users accessing Company B's Website through the Link.

If the definition of *Company A Users* could not include the defined terms *Company B's Website* and *Link,* then, on eliminating the defined term *Company A Users,* the replacement language would be as follows:

> . . . users accessing [definition of *Company B's Website*] through [definition of the *Link*]

Great care would be required to ensure that the definitions were completely and accurately transferred each time the concept of *Company A Users* was needed. Any deviation would open the door to a claim that the parties intended the deviation to be a substantive change. In addition, integrating the definitions would make the provision lengthier and more difficult to understand. As drafted, the defined terms nicely signal their meaning, permitting a short definition.

---

20. "[A]n instrument for reproducing sound at a distance" is a quotation from *Merriam-Webster's Collegiate Dictionary, supra* n. 1, at 1211.

21. This definition is based on a definition in Gregory J. Battersby & Charles W. Grimes eds., *License Agreements: Forms and Checklist* 4-27 (Aspen Publishers 2003).

Although including a defined term in another defined term's definition is a useful drafting technique, it can be overdone, forcing a reader to go on a scavenger hunt to understand a defined term's definition. If the defined term in the definition is used only in that definition, follow the exception to Guideline 15.

Do not cross-reference a defined term in a definition even if it is defined later in the definitions section. Cross-references are unnecessary because the language introducing the definitions tells a reader that this is where the agreement's definitions are. (This practice differs from what you should do if you use a defined term without definition in the recitals.[22] Then, you must tell the reader where to find the definition of any undefined terms, as the recitals precede the language introducing the definitions.)

Wrong

"**Consent**" means any consent of, approval by, authorization of, notice to, designation of, or filing with any Person (as subsequently defined in this Article 1).

Correct

"**Consent**" means any consent of, approval by, authorization of, notice to, designation of, or filing with any Person.

---

15. *Do not define a defined term in another term's definition.* If you do, you will frustrate the poor reader who searches for the definition after reading its defined term later in the contract. The reader will look for the defined term and its definition in the alphabetical list of defined terms, but they will not appear in the expected location—they will be hidden in another definition.

Wrong

"**Royalty Period**" means each calendar quarter in the three-year term that begins on January 1, 20X3 and ends on December 31, 20X5 (the "**Term**").

Correct

"**Royalty Period**" means each calendar quarter in the Term.

and

"**Term**" means the three-year term that begins on January 1, 20X3 and ends on December 31, 20X5.

Despite the general rule, you may define a defined term within a definition if that term is used only in that definition. Alternatively, put the definition in a paragraph immediately following the definition.

For the purposes of the preceding definition of [insert the defined term], "**X**" means . . .

If you take advantage of the exception, do not include the defined term in the alphabetical list of defined terms as the reader will have no reason to look for it there.

---

22. See § 6.3, Guideline 11.

16. *Avoid definitions that apply to more than one person at one time.* For example, the definition of *Contract* in a share purchase agreement is often intended to apply to the Seller, the Buyer, and the Target. This definition can be cumbersome.

Version 1

   "**Contract**" means any contract, lease, arrangement, commitment, or understanding to which the Seller, the Buyer, or the Target is a party or by which the Seller, the Buyer, or the Target or any of their respective properties may be bound or affected.

A simpler version applies the definition to *a Person*, thereby applying it to only one person at a time, but making the definition generally applicable.

Version 2

   "**Contract**" means, with respect to a Person, any contract, lease, agreement, license, arrangement, commitment, or understanding to which that Person is a party or by which that Person or any of its properties is bound or affected.

---

17. *Do not define a term when the ordinary meaning of the word or phrase expresses the concept.* For example, the following definition of *Resume Performance* is superfluous.

   "**Resume Performance**" means to restart performance after it was suspended because of a *Force Majeure* Event.

Similarly, a definition of Parties is generally unnecessary.[23]

18. *Write a definition as narrowly as possible so that additional information may be included as part of a substantive provision, such as a representation and warranty or a covenant.* A party may sue on a representation and warranty or a covenant, but not on a definition.

Wrong

Definition

   "**Shares**" means the 1,000 issued and outstanding common shares of the Company, par value $1 per share.

and

Representation and warranty

   Shares Outstanding. The Company has 1,000 issued and outstanding Shares [1,000 issued and outstanding common shares of the Company, par value $1 per share], each of which has a par value of $1 per share.

---

   23. One instance when it might be useful to define *parties* is if Nebraska law governs the contract and the contract includes a third-party beneficiary provision. *See Props. Inv. Group v. Applied Commun. Inc.*, 495 N.W.2d 483, 489-490 (Neb. 1993) (holding that *party* refers to nonsignatories).

Because the information as to the number of shares and their par value is included in the definition of *Shares,* a representation and warranty as to the number and par value of the *Shares* presents the same information twice, explicitly and through the use of the definition of *Shares.* If the number of issued and outstanding shares and the par value are omitted from the definition of Shares, then the representation and warranty works as it should.

Correct

Revised definition

"**Shares**" means the Company's common shares.

and

Representation and warranty

Shares Outstanding. The Company has issued and outstanding 1,000 Shares [the Company's common shares], each of which has a par value of $1 per share.

Although the author believes that this guideline states the correct way to draft these definitions, she recognizes that some drafters respectfully disagree and are not bothered by the circularity created.

19. *Do not create a circular definition; that is, do not define a term by using the same term.* For example, do not do the following:

Wrong

"**Subsidiary**" means a subsidiary.

A better definition is as follows:

Correct

"**Subsidiary**" means any corporation with respect to which the Borrower owns more than 50% of the issued and outstanding shares.

Despite the general rule, you may include the defined term in the definition *if* the definition is intended to narrow the general meaning of the term so that it applies to a specific instance. For example:

"**Song**" means any song that the Beatles recorded and included on any of their albums.

---

20. *Do not include substantive provisions, such as representations and warranties, covenants, and conditions, in a definition.* Their inclusion may create an ambiguity as to the substantive provision's purpose. For example, consider the following definition of *Intellectual Property* from an agreement of sale:

> **"Intellectual Property"** means patents, copyrights, trade secrets, registered trademarks and service marks, trade names, and Internet domain names, *all of which are to be unencumbered as of the Closing Date.*

Are the italicized words a condition to closing, a preclosing covenant, or both? The proper way to draft the definition would be to omit the italicized words. Then, insert them into the appropriate article or articles of the agreement.

Including substantive provisions in a definition increases the likelihood that a reader will miss the provision when reviewing the contract. For example, a reader trying to find all of the conditions to closing in an acquisition agreement will look at the conditions article, not the definitions article.[24] If the reader has a wonderful memory, she may remember that a definition had a substantive provision, but that's only if she remembers. It's far better to put the substantive provision where it belongs.

21. *Be leery of defining a legal term by referring to a source outside the contract if the information in that source can be easily restated in the contract.* A reference to an outside source means that the contract does not stand on its own, making it more difficult for a reader to understand the contract's full implications.

Sometimes, however, it is appropriate to define a term by referring to an outside source. For example, a real estate lease may need to refer to various environmental laws. As restating those laws in the contract would be unwieldy, a cross-reference is appropriate. If the outside legal source changes over time, the definition must indicate whether it is referring to the source as it exists on the day of the agreement's signing or as it exists from time to time (that is, including past and future amendments). This detail is indispensible, because unless otherwise stated, a contract incorporates the law as it exists at the time the contract is signed.[25]

> **"CERCLA"** means the federal Comprehensive Environmental Response, Compensation, and Liability Act of 1980, as amended [as of the date of this Agreement] [from time to time].

Drafters regularly use the phrases *as in effect from time to time* and *as amended from time to time* synonymously. Neither phrase is controversial nor a regular source of litigation. A Westlaw® "ALLCASES" *words and phrases* field search for each of the two phrases yielded no cases.[26] A search for the abbreviated phrase *from time to time* yielded fewer than a dozen cases, all of which interpreted the phrase in its most common usage.[27]

---

24. Definitions typically appear in an article in an acquisitions agreement.

25. *See generally* Samuel Williston, *Williston on Contracts* vol. 11, § 30:19 (Richard A. Lord ed., 4th ed., West 2000).

26. Westlaw, ALLCASES database, wp ("as amended from time to time") and wp ("as in effect from time to time") (May 27, 2013).

27. Westlaw, ALLCASES database, wp ("from time to time") (May 27, 2013). Selected representative cases are the following: *Union Constr. Co., Inc. v. Beneficial Stand. Mortg. Investors*, 610 P.2d 67 (Ariz. Div. 1 1980) (holding that a consent-to-extension provision authorizing extensions "from time to time" permitted multiple extensions of time); *Rogers v. W. Riverside 350-Inch Water Co.*, 124 P. 447, 450 (Cal. App. 1912) (holding that "The words 'from time to time,' as used in the contract, were intended by the parties to apply to and mean the successive irrigation seasons, which may or may not be coextensive with the year."); *Bay Nat'l Bank & Trust Co. v. Mason*, 349 So. 2d 810 (Fla. App. 1st Dist. 1977) (holding that language permitting two notes to be extended "from time to time without notice . . ." must be held to mean the parties consented in advance to additional extensions of the notes without further notice); *TMG Life Ins. Co. v. Ashner*, 898 P.2d 1145, 1155-1156 (Kan. App. 1995) (holding that the phrase "from time to time" means

22. *Define an agreement, other than the agreement being drafted, by using the information in the preamble of the agreement being defined: the name of that agreement, its date, and the parties.* Some drafters precede the name of the agreement in the definition with the words *that certain.* Those are **pointing words**, and they make the definition no more specific. Omit them.

Wrong

"**Credit Agreement**" means *that certain* Credit Agreement, dated April 11, 20XX, between the Borrower and the Lender, as amended from time to time.

Correct

"**Credit Agreement**" means the Credit Agreement, dated April 11, 20XX, between the Borrower and the Lender, as amended from time to time.

The definition should indicate whether references to the agreement are to the agreement's provisions as they exist on the day of that agreement's signing (Version 1) or as they may exist from time to time (Version 2).

Version 1

"**Credit Agreement**" means the Credit Agreement, dated April 11, 20XX, between the Borrower and the Lender as of the date of its signing.

Version 2

"**Credit Agreement**" means the Credit Agreement, dated April 11, 20XX, between the Borrower and the Lender, as amended from time to time.

Which of these versions is used has substantive consequences. For example, pledge agreements and other security agreements often incorporate by reference the credit agreement's definitions. This saves time and paper and ensures that the definitions in the two agreements are exactly the same.

Definitions. Capitalized terms used in this Pledge Agreement without definition have the meanings assigned to them in the Credit Agreement.

The definitions of the two agreements will fall out of sync if the pledge agreement includes a definition of *Credit Agreement* that freezes it as of the date of signing (Version 1) and if the parties subsequently amend the credit agreement's definitions. This disconnect could cause conflicting obligations. To ensure that the two agreements always work in tandem, the pledge agreement's definition of the *Credit Agreement* must refer to that agreement *as it exists from time to time* (Version 2).

"as occasion may arise," "at intervals," "now and then occasionally," and that use of the phrase "from time to time" in a guaranty did not give the lender the "right to enforce the guaranty at one time to the exclusion of another").

A different approach may be appropriate, however, when drafting an acquisition agreement. Then, the buyer may want to freeze the provisions of the seller's contracts so that it knows what is being assigned to it. Accomplishing this business goal requires a two-step process. First, the parties must narrowly define the contracts, so that their definitions exclude future amendments. Second, the seller must promise that it will not amend the contracts.

> **Wrong**
>
> **"Maintenance Agreement"** means the Maintenance Agreement, dated March 13, 20XX, between the Seller and ABC Inc., as amended from time to time.
>
> **Correct**
>
> **"Maintenance Agreement"** means the Maintenance Agreement, dated March 13, 20XX, between the Seller and ABC Inc., as amended to the date of this Agreement.
>
> *and*
>
> **Amendments to Contracts**. The Seller shall not amend the Maintenance Agreement.

23. *Once a term is defined, do not repeat any part of the definition when using the defined term.* For example, assume that a contract includes the following definition of *Shares:*

> **"Shares"** means the issued and outstanding common shares of the Company.

In the substantive provisions that follow, the phrase *of the Company* should not be included when the defined term *Shares* is used.

> **Wrong**
>
> *A* shall deliver 500 Shares *of the Company* to *B.*
>
> **Correct**
>
> *A* shall deliver 500 Shares to *B.*

7.5.3 SPECIFIC GUIDELINES: DEFINING TERMS IN CONTEXT

1. *To define a term in context, define it, and then put the defined term immediately after the language that constitutes the definition.* The format is fairly straightforward. Follow the rules for defining parties in the preamble. Capitalize the defined term, surround it with quotation marks, put it in bold, and precede it with *the* if it is a noun other than a person's name.

> **Version 1**
>
> **Post-decree Sale of the House.** Lisa and Edward Boswick shall put their house and property at 496 Maple Avenue, Glen Street, Maryland (the "**House**") on the market no later than 30 days after their divorce decree is final.

As discussed earlier in this chapter, the key to defining terms in context is their proper placement. Be sure to look carefully at any sentence that includes a defined term for any possible ambiguities in its definition. For example, in the previous definition, does the defined term include both the house and the property? If the definition could be ambiguous, consider indicating within the parentheses the noun or phrase to which the defined term refers. Also consider putting the defined term with an explanatory noun or phrase at the end of the sentence.[28]

> **Version 2**
>
> **Post-decree Sale of the House.** Lisa and Edward Boswick shall put their house and property at 496 Maple Avenue, Glen Street, Maryland (the house and the property, the "**House**") on the market no later than 30 days after their divorce decree is final.

Alternatively, carve the section into subsections and put the definition in the first subsection and the substantive provision in the second subsection. Also, use this format if a defined term is used multiple times but only used in one section.

> **Version 3**
>
> **Sale of the House.**
>
> (a) **Definition.** "**House**" means the house and property at 496 Maple Avenue, Glen Street, Maryland.
>
> (b) **Post-decree Sale of the House.** Lisa and Edward Boswick shall put the House on the market no later than 30 days after their divorce decree is final.

2. *List alphabetically in the definitions section any term defined in context and cross-reference the section in which the term is defined.*

> "**Competition**" has the meaning assigned to it in Section 5.3.
>
> *or*
>
> "**Competition**" is defined in Section 5.3.

By including the cross-reference, the reader will be able to find the defined term's definition easily.

---

28. See § 7.4, p. 99.

7.6 OTHER PROVISIONS IN THE DEFINITIONS SECTION

In many sophisticated commercial agreements, the definitions section sometimes has a second part. Often entitled *Interpretive Provisions* or *Other Definitional Provisions,* these provisions are of general applicability. The following is typical:

1.2 Interpretive Provisions.

(a) Each term defined in this Agreement has its defined meaning when used in any other Deal Document, unless the term is otherwise defined in that Deal Document. In that event, the term has the meaning that the Deal Document assigns it. *(Prevents ambiguity.)*

(b) References to "Sections," "Exhibits," and "Schedules" are to Sections of, and Exhibits and Schedules to, this Agreement, unless otherwise specifically stated. *(Eliminates references to this Agreement after each reference to a Section, Exhibit, or Schedule; and expressly acknowledges that the Schedules and Exhibits are part of the Agreement, regardless of whether they are attached.[29])*

(c) The words "including," "includes," and "include" are deemed to be followed by the words "without limitation." *(Prevents ambiguity by deeming all variations of includes to be nonrestrictive.)*

(d) References to a "Person" include that Person's permitted successors and assigns and, in the case of any governmental Person, the Person succeeding to the relevant functions of that governmental Person. *(Prevents ambiguity in changed circumstances.)*

(e) All references to statutes and related regulations include

    (i) any past and future amendments of those statutes and related regulations; and

    (ii) any successor statutes and related regulations.[30]

(f) All references in this Agreement to "Dollars" or "$" refer to lawful currency of the United States of America. *(This subsection is generally needed only in agreements with non-U.S. parties.)*

(g) When "must" is used in this Agreement, it signals a condition. *(Clarifies drafting and prevents ambiguity.)*

---

29. See generally § 5.10.1.
30. See Guideline 21.

EXERCISES

Exercise 7-1

Return to Exercise 5-3. Define the territory that Merchandisers will have under the license agreement. To properly do so, review the provisions that follow. They are the provisions that would use the defined term *Territory*. To test whether your definition works, try replacing the defined term with the definition in each of the provisions. Consider whether more than one defined term is necessary.

Definitions

"**Licensed Products**" means caps and t-shirts bearing the Trademark.
"**Term**" has the meaning assigned to it in Section 2.1.
"**Trademark**" means a pictorial representation of the cartoon character Ralph.

Subject matter performance provisions

2.1 Grant of License. By signing this Agreement, Ralph LP grants Merchandisers an exclusive license to manufacture and sell Licensed Products during the period beginning January 1, 20X3 and ending on December 31, 20X5 (the "Term") in [insert defined term]. [*This is only one side of the subject matter performance provision.*]

Representation and warranty

3.1 Other Licenses. Ralph LP has not granted any other license with respect to the [insert defined term] for the manufacture and sale of Licensed Products.

Covenants

4.3 No Other Grants. Ralph LP shall not grant any license to any other Person for the manufacture and sale of Licensed Products with respect to the [insert defined term].

4.4 Licenses in Delaware and Rhode Island. Ralph LP shall terminate or cause to terminate any license that it has granted with respect to Delaware and Rhode Island no later than the last day of the Term's first year, but only if Merchandisers may manufacture and sell Licensed Products in the

[insert the defined term] during the Term's second and third years.

Exercise 7-2

Draft a defined term and definition for a definitions section for the financial statements described in the following representation and warranty. In addition, mark up the provision so that the financial statements are defined in context.

> **Financial Statements.** The balance sheet of the Company as of December 31, 20X4 and
>
> December 31, 20X3 and the related statements of income, cash flows, and shareholders' equity for
>
> each of the two years in the period ended December 31, 20X4, reported on by Debit & Credit LLP,
>
> independent accountants, present fairly, in all material respects, the financial position of the Company
>
> as of December 31, 20X4 and December 31, 20X3, and the results of its operations and its cash
>
> flows for each of the two years in the period ended December 31, 20X4, in conformity with account-
>
> ing principles generally accepted in the United States of America.

Exercise 7-3

Create a defined term for *Purchase Price* based on the sentence that follows. Does it work when included in the contract provision? In addition, state where you would place the defined term if you were to define it in context.

The purchase price for the House is $250,000.

Exercise 7-4

Assume that your client wants to exclude industry-wide strikes from the definition of *Force Majeure* Event. How would you redraft this provision?

> "***Force Majeure* Event**" means any act or event that
>
> (a) prevents the affected party, in whole or in part, from
>
> > (i) performing its obligations under this Agreement or
> >
> > (ii) satisfying any conditions required by the other party under this Agreement;
>
> (b) is beyond the reasonable control of and not the fault of the affected party; and
>
> (c) the affected party has been unable to avoid or overcome by the exercise of due diligence,

including, without limitation: war, flood, lightning, drought, earthquake, fire, volcanic eruption, land-

slide, cyclone, typhoon, tornado, explosion, civil disturbance, act of God or the public enemy,

epidemic, famine or plague, shipwreck, action of a court or public authority, or strike, work-to-rule

action, go-slow or similar labor difficulty, each on an industry-wide, region-wide or nationwide basis.[31]

Exercise 7-5

The following is a monetary provision from a license agreement. How much of what precedes the defined term is part of the definition?

> **Royalties**. The royalties for each calendar month are the amount equal to 2% times Net Sales for that calendar month (the "**Monthly Royalties**").

Exercise 7-6

In choosing between the following definitions, what would you consider?

Version 1

"Breach" means a misrepresentation, breach of warranty, and breach of covenant.

Version 2

"Breach" includes any breach of warranty or covenant.

---

31. This definition is from Nancy F. Persechino, *Force Majeure,* in *Negotiating and Drafting Contract Boilerplate* 201-202 (Tina L. Stark et al. eds., ALM Publg. 2003).

Exercise 7-7

Memorandum

To: D. Fender

From: H. Flighty

Date: September 14, 20X2

Re: Purchase of Aircraft

As it is our responsibility to draft the purchase agreement, we need to get moving on it. To save some money and give you a head start, I wrote some of the contract last night. Please take a look at it. I think I did a pretty good job, but if you find any errors, correct them.

Remember that you have the Purchase Offer if you need it (Exercise 6-3). One other thing: I used an October 30 date in the preamble because that's the date Samson and I want to sign the agreement.

AIRCRAFT PURCHASE AGREEMENT

between

AGREEMENT, dated October 30, 20XX, by and ~~among~~ Supersonic Wings Corp., a Delaware corporation, (the "Seller") and Fly-by-Night Aviation, Inc., a New York corporation having its principal place of business at 987 East 48th Street, New York, New York 10036 (~~the~~ "Buyer"). *(where shaw the addss be)*

Recital:

~~WHEREAS~~, the Seller desires to sell to Buyer, and Buyer desires to purchase from the Seller, the Aircraft; and

~~WHEREAS~~, the Buyer hereby agrees to pay the Seller $23,000,000 in immediately available funds. *— (amount doesnt belong in recitals.*

Accordingly the parties agree as follow

~~NOW, THEREFORE, in consideration of the mutual promises herein set forth and~~ subject to the terms and conditions hereof, the parties agree as follows:

Article 1 — Definitions

1.1 Defined Terms. As used in this Agreement, terms defined in the preamble and recitals of this Agreement have the meanings set forth therein, and the following terms have the meanings set forth below:

Air Graft Purchase Agreement:

"**Agreement**" means this Agreement of Sale and all Schedules and Exhibits ~~hereto~~, as ~~the~~ *each are* ~~same may~~ be amended from time to time.

"**Aircraft**" means the Airframe, equipped with ~~two Rolls-Royce~~ engines Model No. MK611-8 bearing Serial Nos. 72725 and 72726, together with all appliances, avionics, furnishings, and other components, equipment, and property incorporated in or otherwise related to the Airframe or engines. *Bolden terms thatll be defined later*

"**Airframe**" means the Icarus Aerospace Corporation I-800 aircraft, bearing United States Registration No. N765BW and Manufacturer's Serial No. 8181.

"**Assigned Contracts**" means the Maintenance Agreement (~~as hereafter defined~~) and the Pilot Agreement (~~as hereafter defined~~).

"**Assumed Liabilities**" means, collectively, all liabilities and obligations of the Seller that arise under either (a) the Maintenance Agreement on or after the Closing Date or (b) the Pilot Agreement on or after the date of the Closing. *(Closing date or date of closing, be consistent)*

"**Aviation Fuel**" means the gas or liquid that is used to create power to propel the Aircraft. At the time of the Seller's delivery of the Aircraft to Buyer, the fuel gauge of the Aircraft shall register as full. *– Covenant not definition.*

"**Closing**" means the closing of the sale of the Aircraft contemplated by this Agreement in New York, New York on the Closing Date.

"**Closing Date**" has the meaning specified in Section 2.04(a).

"**Consent**" ~~shall~~ mean*s* any consent of, approval of, authorization of, notice to, or designation, registration, declaration or filing with, any Person.

"**Contract**" ~~shall~~ mean*s* any contract, lease, agreement, license, arrangement, commitment or understanding to which the Buyer or ~~any~~ *the* Seller is a party or by which it or any of its properties or assets may be bound or affected.

"**Engines**" means the two Rolls-Royce engines, Model No. BR710, bearing Serial Nos. 72725 and 72726.

"**Laws**" means all federal, state, local or foreign laws, rules and regulations.

"**Lien**" means any lien, charge, encumbrance, security interest, mortgage, or pledge.

"**Maintenance Agreement**" means that ~~certain~~ *the* Maintenance Agreement, dated as of April 3, 20X0, between Greasemonkeys, Inc., and Seller, as ~~the same~~ *each* may be amended from time to time.

"**Order**" *means* any judgment, award, order, writ, injunction or decree issued by any federal, state, local or foreign authority, court, tribunal, agency, or other governmental authority, or by any arbitrator, to which ~~any~~ *the* Seller or its assets are subject, or to which the Buyer or its assets are subject, as the case may be.

"**Person**" ~~shall~~ mean*s* any individual, partnership, joint venture, corporation, trust, unincorporated organization, government ~~(and any department or agency thereof)~~ *and any of its departments or agencies* or other entity.

"**Pilot Agreement**" means ~~that certain~~ *the* Pilot Agreement between *the* Seller and Ace Pilots, Inc., dated as of May 12, 20X1, as of the date of this Agreement.

Action Sections

8.1 INTRODUCTION

The **action sections** tell the parties how to perform the principal objective of the contract. The two primary components are

- the provisions in which the parties agree to perform the main subject matter of the contract; and
- the financial provisions, generally the payment of money.

If appropriate, the action sections also include the closing date, the closing deliveries, and a contract's term.

Reminder: *Action sections* is not a technical contract term. This book uses that phrase to refer to the provisions that this chapter discusses.

8.2 SUBJECT MATTER PERFORMANCE PROVISION

The first section of the action sections is always the **subject matter performance provision**. In this provision, the parties promise to accomplish a contract's primary objective.

Imagine that a client receives her dream job offer and that her prospective employer asks her to sign an employment agreement. The primary subject matter of that agreement is her employment. The contract will deal with other significant topics, such as salary, duties, and benefits, but the agreement's primary purpose is to obligate the employer to hire your client and to obligate her to work for the employer. These obligations are the promises that comprise the subject matter performance provision. Similarly, if a client decides to write a book, the primary subject matter of the agreement with the client's publisher is the book's publication. So, in this instance, the subject matter performance provision contains the client's agreement to write the book and the publisher's agreement to publish it. In both instances these provisions are classic consideration: bargained for, reciprocal, executory promises. The following examples show how these provisions might appear in a contract.

Example 1

Employment. Subject to the provisions of this Agreement, the Company shall hire the Executive, and the Executive shall work for the Company for the Term.

Example 2

Agreement to Write and Publish. Subject to the provisions of this Agreement, the Author shall write a book on seals in the Galapagos Islands, and the Publisher shall publish that book.

Note that both provisions include **reciprocal promises** and are introduced with qualifying language, *Subject to the provisions of this Agreement*. The reciprocal promises reflect the mutuality of the transaction. The qualifying language makes explicit that the reciprocal promises must be read in conjunction with the contract's other provisions. Thus, the publisher's promise to publish the book may be subject to a condition—for example, the author must have written a summary and detailed outline that the publisher finds acceptable.

Although the subject matter performance provision often takes the form of mirror image reciprocal promises that reflect the flip sides of a transaction—*hire* and *work for, write* and *publish*—this is not always the case. In some agreements, a party's principal promise cannot be reduced to a few words that can easily be juxtaposed with the other party's promise. The return promise may be much more elaborate and require multiple provisions. In addition, the structure of the transaction may not allow for the mirror image promises. Thus, in a loan agreement, while the bank promises to lend money, the borrower does not promise to borrow it. Instead, it generally has the discretion to borrow on an as-needed basis. The borrower's reciprocal promise would be its promise to repay the principal with interest. Moreover, other provisions may provide consideration. The entire contract is a bargained for exchange. But the subject matter performance promises play a unique role.

Although the subject matter performance provisions in many contracts are promises, that is not the case for all contracts. In these contracts, rather than a party promising to perform in the future, the party performs when it signs the contract because of the nature of the words in the contract. The words in the subject matter performance provision constitute the performance. These provisions are **self-executing**. As noted earlier, contract promises that are to be performed in the future are often called *executory promises*.[1] With a self-executing provision, a party does not promise performance. Instead, that performance is achieved through the signing of the contract and the words of the provision. Classic examples are guaranties, waivers, releases, options, and grants of security interests.

Example 1

Guaranty. By signing this Guaranty,[2] Conglomerate Corp. guarantees to Big Bank the debt of its subsidiary, Oliveira Manufacturing Inc.

---

1. See § 5.4.1.

2. Historically, the words *By signing this Agreement* were encapsulated in *X hereby. Hereby* is legalese, and therefore, is not usually a drafter's first choice. It does have the merit of being succinct.

Example 2

Grant of Security Interest. By signing this Security Agreement, the Borrower grants the Lender a security interest in the Borrower's assets.

Example 3

Appointment of Escrow Agent. By signing this Agreement, the parties appoint Vivienne Kim as Escrow Agent.

Finally, the subject matter performance provision of a contract need not contain reciprocal promises or be self-executing. Instead, one party might promise to perform, while the other might perform by signing. This is the case with the Website Development Agreement (Version 1) (Chapter 32, Document 2).

8.3   PAYMENT PROVISIONS

The payment provision of a contract sets forth its financial terms, which practitioners often refer to as *the consideration*. In this section, one party promises to pay the other in exchange for whatever that party has promised to do. In a publishing agreement, the publisher promises to pay the author royalties for the book the author will write; while in a lease, the tenant promises to pay the landlord rent in exchange for the use of the leased premises.

Money is not the only form of payment that parties use. They can also pay with monetary equivalents such as shares, a promissory note, an assignment of rights, an assumption of liabilities, or any other agreed-on medium of exchange. For example, parties could agree to a barter exchange in which one party promises to deliver ten bushels of apples in exchange for five bushels of corn. Similarly, Henry can promise to paint Moesha's living room in return for Moesha's promise to tutor Henry's son. This section will refer to the different forms of payment, when referred to together, as *payment*.

Every payment provision must state the amount of the payment and include a promise to pay it. You can draft the provision as two sentences or sections, one a declaration stating the amount of the payment, and the other a promise to pay it. Alternatively, you can combine the statement of the amount and the promise to pay into a single sentence.

Example 1

Rent. The rent is $2,500 per month (the "**Rent**"). With respect to each month of the Lease, the Tenant shall pay the Landlord the Rent no later than the first day of that month. *(Two sentences: the first is a declaration and the second is a covenant.)*

Example 2

Fee. The Owner shall pay the Contractor a $35,000 fee for renovating the House, $10,000 contemporaneously with the signing of this Agreement and $25,000 no later than three days after the Contractor completes the renovation. *(A single sentence, including the amounts to be paid and the obligation to pay them.)*

When drafting payment provisions, keep the following guidelines in mind.

Guidelines for Payment Provisions

1. *Follow the cash.*[3] Make certain that you keep track of all the money in the transaction: Make a flowchart so that you can visualize the flow of money. Who has it? Why? What triggers its payment? Is there a deposit? Who is entitled to it when the contract ends? Are multiple payments being made to one or more parties?

2. *The payment provision should answer the questions of* ***who*** *is paying* ***what*** *to* ***whom, when, why,*** *and* ***how***. Create a chart that lists each payment and how it is to be made. If money is to be deposited to a bank account, include the name of the bank and the account number.

3. *State the* ***amount*** *of the payment payable.* (This answers the ***what*** question.)

Example 1

Purchase Price. The purchase price is $40 million.

Example 2

Rent. The monthly rent is $2,500.

Example 3

Purchase Price. The purchase price is 20,000 shares of the Company's Class A Common Stock.

Some drafters put defined terms relating to the payment of consideration in the payment provision, as this is often the only place they are used. To prevent ambiguity, define any needed terms in a separate section or in a subsection devoted exclusively to the term being defined.

Purchase Price. The Buyer shall pay the Seller $100,000 for the House by

   (a) paying the Seller $50,000 at Closing by wire transfer of immediately available funds; and

   (b) executing and delivering at Closing the Buyer's promissory note in the principal amount of $50,000, substantially in the form of **Exhibit B** (the "**Note**").

If the transaction involves international parties, state the currency in which payment is to be made.

As noted earlier, payment is typically money, shares, or promissory notes, but it can also be an assignment of rights or an assumption of liabilities. If a party assigns its rights, it transfers to a third person its right to the other party's performance. Imagine that Colossal Construction Corp. owes Tong's Machinery LLC $100,000, but the payment is not due until year-end. If Tong's Machinery needs cash immediately, it can assign to its bank its right to payment from Colossal Construction. In exchange, the bank will pay Tong's Machinery a discounted amount, say, $90,000. The consideration

---

3. The phrase, *follow the cash,* is the mantra of my former partner, Donald Schapiro.

is the assignment of the right to payment and the return payment of $90,000. Big Bank earns a $10,000 profit when Colossal Construction pays it the $100,000 originally owed to Tong's Machinery LLC.

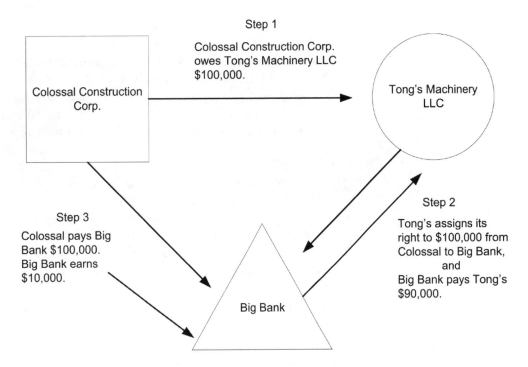

Step 1

Colossal Construction Corp.

Colossal Construction Corp. owes Tong's Machinery LLC $100,000.

Tong's Machinery LLC

Step 3

Colossal pays Big Bank $100,000. Big Bank earns $10,000.

Step 2

Tong's assigns its right to $100,000 from Colossal to Big Bank, and Big Bank pays Tong's $90,000.

Big Bank

An assumption of liabilities is the converse of an assignment of rights. In this situation, a third party takes on a party's duty to perform. To see how this works, we will first look at a transaction without an assumption, and then, we will compare it to the same transaction but with an assumption.

Imagine that Darnell Winston purchased Blackacre last year for $80,000 and paid $50,000 with his own money and the remaining $30,000 with money that he borrowed from a bank. After completing the purchase, Darnell has a $30,000 liability, the amount he owes to the bank. Because the real estate market is hot, Darnell decides a year later to sell Blackacre for $100,000 to Phyllis Wright. If Phyllis pays Darnell $100,000, Darnell must use $30,000 of that amount to repay the bank. After that payment, he has $70,000 in cash. But to determine his profit, his cash out-of-pocket investment of $50,000 must be subtracted from the $70,000, giving him a profit of $20,000.

Darnell's cash from Phyllis	$100,000
Darnell's cash repayment to the bank	(30,000)
Darnell's cash after repayment to the bank	$ 70,000
Darnell's cash out-of-pocket cost for the initial investment	(50,000)
Darnell's cash profit	$ 20,000

Alternatively, if the bank agrees, Phyllis could assume (become legally obligated to pay) Darnell's $30,000 liability to the bank. (Stated differently, Phyllis could take over Darnell's obligation to pay the $30,000 loan.) If she does so, her total out-of-pocket cost does not change; the recipients change. Phyllis will still pay $100,000, but she will pay $30,000 to the bank as a loan repayment, either immediately or on a future date. In addition, Phyllis must pay Darnell $70,000. That amount is, of course, what he would have netted if Phyllis had paid him $100,000 and he then paid the bank $30,000. But does Darnell end up in the same position as before with a $20,000 cash profit? Yes. To determine his cash profit, his cash out-of-pocket cost for the initial investment is subtracted from the cash he received.

Darnell's cash from Phyllis	$ 70,000
Darnell's cash out-of-pocket cost for the initial investment	(50,000)
Darnell's cash profit	$ 20,000

So, whether the payment is $100,000 in cash, or $70,000 in cash, plus the assumption of $30,000 in debt, both parties end up in essentially the same financial position.[4]

When stating what the payment is, think through the consequences of a term starting on a date other than January 1. The contract might require a specially calculated payment to deal with the stub period. A **stub period** is a period less than a calendar year that occurs when a contract term either begins after January 1 or ends before December 31 of a calendar year. For example, if an executive begins work on September 15, the midyear start date creates two stub periods. The first occurs in the first year of the contract term. It begins on September 15 and ends on December 31. The second stub period occurs in the contract's final year. It begins on January 1 and ends on September 14, the last day of the contract term. In both instances, if the executive is entitled to a bonus based on the company's performance for each calendar year, the parties might need to provide special rules to calculate the bonus for the stub periods.[5]

4. *State **who** is paying **what** to **whom***. Draft a party's obligation to pay in the active voice.

> **Payment of Rent**. With respect to each month of the Term, the Tenant shall pay the Rent to the Landlord.

Some drafters violate this rule by providing that a payee has a right to payment. Although this is technically correct as every obligation to perform includes a right to that performance, better drafting is to state who has the obligation to perform; that is, what would need to be proven in a litigation that alleged breach of performance.

Do not use euphemisms for an obligation to pay. State explicitly that *X shall pay Y.*

> **Wrong**
>
> **Fee**. The Producer is responsible for paying the Screenwriter $6,000 for the script.
>
> **Correct**
>
> **Fee**. The Producer shall pay the Screenwriter $6,000 for the script.

---

4. In the real world, a buyer is in a slightly different financial position if it assumes a seller's liabilities to third parties. First, a buyer may not have to pay the seller's liabilities immediately. Instead, the buyer may be able to pay them over time, either in accordance with the seller's agreements with the third parties or in accordance with an arrangement it can negotiate. This delayed payment could be a substantial advantage to a buyer. Second, a buyer could also negotiate with the third parties to reduce the amount to be paid, thus obtaining a discount. Third, a buyer may have to pay interest that it would not have had to pay if it had paid the full amount owed.

5. See Guideline 7 for more about *stub periods.*

5. *Calculate any amounts that can be calculated before signing, rather than including a mathematical formula.* For example, if possible, state the amount each party is to be paid, rather than stating that each party is to be paid its allocable share. This explicit statement of amount should reduce the likelihood of a dispute because the parties will check the calculations before signing the agreement. Do not state the formula and the results of the formula; it will create an ambiguity if the calculation does not comport with the formula.

If a party will be using more than one form of payment to more than one party, create a chart that specifies the type and amount of payment payable to each party. For example:

Wrong

> **Consideration.** The Purchase Price is $100 million in immediately available funds,[6] $25 million in subordinated debt, and 5 million Class A Shares, each Shareholder to be paid that Shareholder's allocable share.

Correct

> **Consideration.** The Purchase Price is $100 million in immediately available funds, $25 million in subordinated debt, and 5 million Class A Shares, payable to each Shareholder as follows:

	Immediately Available Funds	Subordinated Debt	Equity
Shareholder A	$20 million	$5 million	1 million Class A Shares
Shareholder B	$70 million	$17.5 million	3.5 million Class A Shares
Shareholder C	$10 million	$2.5 Million	.5 million Class A Shares

6. *State **when** the consideration is payable.*

> **Rent.** With respect to each month of the Term, the Tenant shall pay the Rent to the Landlord *no later than the fifth day of that month.*

7. *If a contract term creates any stub periods, provide for appropriate payments.* Also, consider what timing issues are created if the contract term does not coincide with the fiscal year.[7] For example, if a license agreement term begins on March 15, are payments to be made

- at the end of every three months based on a term beginning on March 15 (i.e., June 14, September 14, December 14, and March 14) or
- at the end of each calendar quarter (i.e., March 31, June 30, September 30, and December 31)?

---

6. See Guideline 8 for a discussion of *immediately available funds.*

7. A company's fiscal year is the one-year period that the company uses to determine its annual revenues, etc. Generally, the fiscal year is a calendar year, but that does not hold true in all industries.

Consider also whether any payment should be accelerated or delayed. Loan agreements often require mandatory prepayments of principal if the borrower sells equity securities, borrows more money, or sells substantially all of its assets.

8. *State **how** a party is to pay money: personal check, company check, cashier's check, certified check, or immediately available funds.*

> **Rent.** With respect to each month of the Term, the Tenant shall pay the Rent to the Landlord *by certified check* no later than the fifth day of that month.

The form of payment determines when a recipient has access to the money and reflects an allocation of risk between the parties. Some forms of payment are more risky for a recipient than others. The most risky are personal checks and company checks. When a party pays by check, the recipient does not have immediate access to the funds. It must first deposit the check at its bank, and that bank must (technically) receive payment from the paying party's bank. The delay that this process entails creates a credit risk: The paying party might not have money in its account at the time payment is required. Thus, even if the recipient has performed, it might not get paid. Despite this risk, many recipients are willing to accept a personal or company check. For example, Internet service providers, telephone companies, and electric utilities all accept their customer's personal checks—although most would prefer an online payment.

Less risky for a payee are cashier's checks (also known as bank checks) and certified checks. A **cashier's check** is a check that a bank issues from its own account. It is the bank's promise to pay the recipient.[8] (The paying party applies to its bank for a cashier's check, at which time the bank takes the money from that party's account and issues its own check payable to the order of the recipient.) Therefore, when a recipient accepts a cashier's check as payment, it no longer takes a risk as to the paying party's creditworthiness. Instead, its credit risk is the bank's creditworthiness. Although the recipient's credit risk is significantly reduced, it still does not have access to the funds until the business day after the banking day on which the cashier's check was deposited.[9] In addition, the check is subject to final clearing and reversal if it is dishonored because of fraud or some other issue.

A **certified check** is a check as to which a bank has set aside sufficient funds from the paying party's account to ensure full payment of the check. The bank *certifies* the check by having an authorized employee sign the check.[10] Again, while the recipient has reduced its credit risk, the funds are not available until the business day after the banking day on which the certified check was deposited.[11] In addition, the bank can take back its payment if it discovers that the check was fraudulently issued.

Parties often use cashier's checks or certified checks when the parties know the payment amount several days before the transaction, the amount is relatively large, and the recipient wants to reduce its credit risk. Car dealers often insist on one of these forms of payment.

In complex, sophisticated transactions with significant sums at risk, many recipients refuse to take any risk of nonpayment and, in addition, want immediate access

8. 12 C.F.R. § 229.2(i) (2006).

9. 12 C.F.R. § 229.10(c)(v) (2003).

10. 12 C.F.R. § 229.2(j) (2006).

11. 12 C.F.R. § 229.10(c)(v) (2003).

to the money for investment or other purposes. In these transactions, the paying party can **wire transfer** immediately available funds from its bank account to the recipient's.[12] The recipient need not make a deposit because the wire transfer accomplishes that, and the funds do not need to clear because the funds transferred were immediately available funds. Although wire transfers can be made through different systems,[13] generally the parties use a system that the Federal Reserve System maintains.[14] Parties speak colloquially of a **Fed funds** transfer.

If a wire transfer involves multinational parties or parties located in different cities, determine where the funds are to be sent and the currency for payment. Are funds being transferred to an account in New York City, Detroit, or Tokyo? Funds immediately available in New York City are not immediately available in Tokyo because of the difference in time zones. An obligation to pay by a Fed funds wire transfer is generally along the following lines:

> **Payment of Purchase Price.** The Buyer shall pay the Seller the Purchase Price by wire transfer of [immediately available funds] [funds immediately available in Chicago] [immediately available funds in pound sterling]. The Seller shall notify the Buyer of the bank account into which the funds are to be transferred no later than two business days before the Closing Date.

Some drafters provide that a paying party must pay the consideration in *cash*. Do not do this. **Cash** is currency (bills and coins), and it is most unlikely that the parties intend the paying party to arrive with bushels of dollar bills. Although some courts have interpreted *cash* to mean immediately available funds,[15] other courts have held that *cash* means currency.[16] While using the word *cash* is unlikely to cause a problem, when drafting, say what you mean.

9. *If money is payable for more than one reason, the terms for each payment should conform to this section's guidelines.* For example, if a company is obligated to pay an executive both a salary and a bonus, create separate payment sections for each payment, and then in each section, state the appropriate amount, when the payment is due, etc. Treating the two types of payments separately will help you analyze the possibly different business issues associated with each of the payments (e.g.: Under what circumstances is the bonus paid? Is it paid if the company terminates the executive for cause?).

10. *If payment is based on a formula, state the formula accurately.* While a formula may appear simple at first, it often requires sophisticated drafting, especially if tax or accounting issues are implicated.[17]

---

12. 12 C.F.R. § 229.2(ll) (WL current through June 7, 2012) ("Wire transfer means an unconditional order to a bank to pay a fixed or determinable amount of money to a beneficiary on receipt or on a day stated in the order, that is transmitted by electronic or other means through Fedwire, the Clearing House Interbank Payments System, other similar network, between banks, or on the books of a bank.").

13. *Id.*

14. *See generally Fedwire Funds Servs.*, http://www.federalreserve.gov/paymentsystems/fedfunds_about.htm (accessed June 16, 2013).

15. *Upchurch v. Chaney*, 635 S.E.2d 124, 125 (Ga. 2006) (holding that in context of a judicial sale cash meant immediately available funds).

16. *Nance v. Schoonover*, 521 P.2d 896, 897 (Utah 1974) (holding that parties intended cash to mean currency).

17. See Chapters 22 and 25, specifically § 25.2.6.

8.4 TERM

Some contracts relate to a specific transaction, for example, the sale of Blackacre. Although it may take time for the parties to consummate this transaction, their contract has a limited time horizon. Colloquially, some lawyers refer to these transactions as **one-off deals**. In other contracts, however, the parties anticipate a relationship that will span an extended time period. Their contract will govern their relationship for an agreed-on number of years—that is, a specific **term**. Leases and license agreements are examples of contracts that have terms.

When drafting a contract for a term of years, the beginning and ending dates of the term must be unambiguous. The easiest way to accomplish this is to state the term's beginning and ending dates.[18] You may do this either by drafting a stand-alone section or by incorporating the dates into the subject matter performance provision. In either case, drafters often define *Term* in the action sections.[19]

Example 1

Term. This Agreement's term begins on January 1, 20X5 and ends on December 31, 20X7 (the "**Term**"). *(Stand-alone section.)*

Example 2

Term. Subject to the provisions of this Agreement, the Supplier shall supply the Manufacturer with the Materials listed in **Exhibit A**, and the Purchaser shall purchase those Materials, during a three-year term beginning on January 1, 20X5 and ending on December 31, 20X7 (the "**Term**"). *(Incorporated into the subject matter performance provision.)*

If you are drafting a precedent for use in multiple transactions, you may want a contract that requires minimal changes each time it is used. In this case, key the beginning of the term to the date the parties sign the contract. The ending date then keys off the anniversary date[20] of the contract's signing.

Term. This Agreement's term begins on the date that the parties execute and deliver this Agreement and ends at 5:00 p.m. [on the day preceding the third anniversary] [on the third anniversary] of the date the parties execute and deliver this Agreement (the "**Term**").

A contract need not state the specific date on which a term begins. Instead, the contract can provide that the first day of the term coincides with a future event. Here, the parties distinguish the creation of a binding contract from the first day of the term. That is, although a binding contract comes into existence on the date the parties sign the contract, the term does not begin until a later date when a specified event occurs.

---

18. Provisions dealing with dates are, unfortunately, often rife with ambiguity. See Chapter 21, which discusses how to avoid ambiguity when drafting contract provisions that include time periods.

19. If you define *Term* in the action sections, remember to include it in the contract's alphabetical listing of defined terms, along with a cross-reference to the section where you define it.

20. *Anniversary date* is preferable because of its precision. References to years can be ambiguous. See §21.5.2.

For example, a lease term may begin on the first day of the month after the month during which a tenant pays its deposit.

When drafting the ending date of the contract, some drafters provide for the contract's early termination in the action sections.

> **Term**. The Agreement's term begins on the date that the parties execute and deliver this Agreement and ends at 5:00 p.m. on the day preceding the third anniversary of the day the parties execute and deliver this Agreement (the "**Term**"), *unless sooner terminated in accordance with the provisions of this Agreement.*

Other drafters believe the additional language is superfluous. The advantage of the language is that it signals the parties' intent by explicitly recognizing that the term could prematurely end. To complete the circle, the termination provisions should include language such as the following:

> **Termination for Cause**. The Company may terminate the Executive's employment for Cause before the end of the Term.

When drafting contracts with a term, discuss with the client whether the contract should include an **evergreen provision**. These provisions automatically renew a contract's term. When drafting an evergreen provision, consider the following issues:

- Does the term automatically renew, unless one party notifies the other that it is terminating the contract?
- Does the term automatically end, unless a party exercises its option to renew?
- Does each party have the authority to renew?
- How long should the renewal period be: the same length of time as the original period or shorter?

The following is an example of an evergreen provision:[21]

> **Term**. This Agreement's term begins on January 1, 20X5 and ends on December 31, 20X7. It automatically renews for successive one-year terms, unless either party exercises its option to terminate this Agreement. (The initial three-year period and each successive one-year renewal, a "**Term**.") To exercise its option to terminate the Agreement at the end of the then-existing Term, a party must deliver a written notice of termination to the other party that is received no later than 30 days before the last day of the then-existing Term.

When drafting an evergreen provision, do not provide that the parties will agree on a price increase at the time of a renewal. Agreements to agree are unenforceable.[22] Instead, provide a contractual mechanism for determining the amount of the increase (e.g., a stated percentage increase or a percentage increase tied into cost-of-living

---

21. For an excellent discussion of the term provisions, *see* David C. Burgess, *Duration of the Agreement*, in *Drafting Business Contracts: Principles, Techniques, and Forms* ch. 6 (Cal. CEB 1994).

22. *Joseph Martin, Jr., Delicatessen, Inc. v. Schumacher*, 417 N.E.2d 541, 543-544 (N.Y. 1981).

increases). If the parties want to be able to negotiate the increase at the end of a term, the contract can require the parties to negotiate in good faith. Counsel should advise the parties, however, that if they do not reach an agreement, the renewal right may be unenforceable.[23]

Careless drafting of evergreen provisions is a prescription for litigation. Consider the following provision, which engendered a lawsuit:

> **Term**. This Agreement continues in force for a period of five years from the date it is made, and thereafter for successive five-year terms, unless and until terminated by one-year prior notice in writing by either party.

The *unless* clause at the end of the sentence was the culprit. Did the discretionary authority apply only to its immediate antecedent (the successive five-year terms) or also to the initial term? Two sentences rather than a comma would have made all the difference.

> **Term**. This Agreement continues in force for a period of five years from the date it is made. After the initial term, the Agreement continues in force for successive five-year terms, unless and until terminated by one-year prior notice in writing by either party.[24]

8.5   SPECIAL PROVISIONS IN ACQUISITIONS AND FINANCINGS

8.5.1   ACTION SECTIONS IN ACQUISITIONS

The action sections of an acquisition agreement can be quite complex because of the payments and the conveyancing deliveries. Document 4 in Chapter 32 is an exemplar of the action sections of an asset purchase agreement. It includes notes and comments, and you may use it as a precedent.

8.5.2   CLOSINGS AND THE CLOSING DATE IN ACQUISITIONS AND FINANCINGS

Recall from Chapter 3 that a closing is the consummation of a transaction at which time the parties exchange financial consideration.[25] It is the final step in actuating certain transactions. Usually, closings are necessary only in acquisitions[26] and financings—both are one-off transactions where the parties sign multiple documents, exchange significant sums, and the relationship terminates at closing. In the context of the Sally and Bob house sale described in Chapters 3 and 4, the closing will occur when Sally delivers the deed (which conveys the property) and Bob pays the purchase price. In a financing, the closing occurs when the bank funds the loan and the borrower signs the note.[27]

---

23. *Id.* at 544.

24. See §21.4.1. This provision could also use a substantial rewrite to clean up the language.

25. See Chapter 3.

26. *Acquisitions* has a broad meaning in this context. It refers to any purchase transaction, including the sales of assets or shares, underwritings, and the purchase of asset-backed securities.

27. In a financing, the loan is the consummation of the lending part of the transaction. The parties continue to have a relationship because the borrower has the use of the loan for a specified time period and covenants to do certain things so long as the loan is outstanding.

Most transactions do not require a closing. For example, the Website Development Agreement (Version 1) (Chapter 32, Document 2) does not require a closing; neither does a trademark licensing agreement. Similarly, no closing is necessary in most leasing transactions. Generally, the parties must just sign the lease and the tenant pay the deposit. The parties need not even get together to sign the lease; they can exchange signature pages by PDFs attached to e-mails. Hard copies of the signatures can be exchanged by snail mail, and the parties may not insist on that.

If the transaction will have a closing, the contract should state its place, date, and time. The statement of the time should take into account where the parties are located because they might be in different time zones. If they are in the same time zone, a reference to *local time* is sufficient. If they are in different time zones, refer to the time at the location where the closing is to be held. In addition, when drafting that provision, consider whether the closing date should be fixed or whether it should be determined by the happening of an event. For example, the closing date in the following Example 2 ties into the date that the parties receive all the consents to their transaction. The closing date provision should be drafted in the present tense as a declaration. It reflects the parties' policy decision as to the closing's date, time, and location. The parties are not obligated to close because this provision is in the agreement. Rather, the provision memorializes when and where the parties have agreed that they will appear—if they hold a closing.

Example 1

From the definitions article

"**Closing**" means the consummation of the transactions that this Agreement contemplates.

"**Closing Date**" means the date stated as such in Section X.

From the action sections

Closing. The Closing is to occur on December 22, 20X2, beginning at 9:00 a.m. local time (the date and time, the "**Closing Date**"). It is to take place at the offices of Workhard & Playlittle LLP, 1180 Avenue of the Americas, New York, New York.

Example 2

From the definitions article

"**Closing**" means the consummation of the transactions that this Agreement contemplates.

"**Closing Date**" means the date and time determined in accordance with Section X.

From the action sections (Section X)

Closing. The Closing is to occur on the third business day after the parties receive the last of the consents listed in **Schedule 3.7**. It is to take place at the offices of Workhard & Playlittle LLP, 8000 Sears Tower, Chicago, Illinois, at 10:00 a.m. Chicago time (the date and time of the Closing, the "**Closing Date**").[28]

---

28. The location of the defined term in this paragraph is tricky. It includes not only the time in the immediately preceding sentence, but also the date in the first sentence. To avoid ambiguity, the paren-

If the contract provides for a specific closing date, determine with your client whether the parties must close on that date. If so, consider a time-of-the-essence clause, but be sure that you and your client understand the consequences of that provision in your jurisdiction. If time is not of the essence, provide that the parties may jointly postpone the closing date. It is awkward to need an amendment or a waiver if documenting the transaction takes longer than expected. Many deals have what are colloquially referred to as **rolling closing dates**. For example, the parties agree to close, say, on March 15, but the documentation is not ready then, so the parties postpone day by day until they are ready to close.

If the agreement permits postponements, consider whether the contract should include a **drop-dead date**—a date after which the parties may no longer postpone the closing. A drop-dead date might be appropriate, for instance, in an acquisition that needs to close before year-end so that the seller can include the income in its year-end financial statements. A drop-dead date might also be appropriate in the purchase and sale of a house if a seller has another buyer waiting in the wings. The following provision provides for a rolling closing date with a drop-dead date:

> **Closing.** The Closing is to take place on June 15, 20XX at 10:00 a.m. local time or on another date and time as to which the parties agree, but in no event later than June 30, 20XX (the date and time of the Closing, the "**Closing Date**"). It is to be held at the offices of Workhard & Playlittle LLP, 200 Peachtree Street, Atlanta, Georgia.

If a contract includes a drop-dead date, include endgame provisions that provide for the contract's termination and that spell out the consequences of a failure to close. Do not put this information in the action sections.

8.5.3 CLOSING DELIVERIES IN ACQUISITIONS AND FINANCINGS

The phrase **closing deliveries** has both a narrow and a broad meaning. Its narrow meaning arises in the context of an acquisition or a financing agreement and refers to the exchange of documents and consideration necessary to consummate the transaction. Thus, in a sale of assets, the seller's closing deliveries are the documents that convey the assets being sold. Each type of asset needs its own conveyancing document. A bill of sale conveys most assets.[29] An assignment is used to convey rights under a contract, while a deed conveys Blackacre. The buyer's closing deliveries are the delivery of the purchase price (whether immediately available funds, a promissory note, or shares of the buyer) and, if appropriate, an assumption of liabilities.

Deal lawyers also use *closing deliveries* in a broader sense in acquisitions and financings to refer to all of the documents that a party delivers at closing. These documents include bring-down certificates,[30] incumbency certificates, certified resolutions, and opinion letters.

Where the closing deliveries are listed depends on what is being delivered. In an acquisition agreement, the action sections will include a closing delivery section in

---

thetical creating the defined term expressly indicates that both the date and time are components of the definition.

29. See Chapter 32, Documents 3 and 5, which are exemplars of conveying documents. Document 3 is an assignment and assumption and Document 5 is a bill of sale.

30. Lou R. Kling & Eileen T. Nugent, *Negotiated Acquisitions of Companies, Subsidiaries, and Divisions* vol. 2, § 14.02 [5].

which the buyer and seller obligate themselves to exchange the documents and consideration necessary to consummate the transaction. These are the *closing deliveries* as that term is used in its narrow sense—the documents and payments necessary to consummate the transaction. The following closing delivery section excerpt comes from an acquisition agreement. As you read the provision, note the italicized language that establishes the standard as to the form of the conveyancing document. The more specific the standard is, the more favorable it is to the Buyer because it reduces the risk that the conveyancing document will fail or otherwise not be satisfactory to the Buyer.

Closing Deliveries.

(a) **Seller's Deliveries.** At the Closing, the Seller shall execute and deliver to the Buyer the following:

   (i)   *A bill of sale* for the Purchased Assets.

   (ii) An assignment of each real property lease under which the Seller is lessee, *each assignment to be satisfactory to the Buyer*.

   (iii) Assignments for all funds on deposit with banks or other Persons that are Purchased Assets, *each assignment to be reasonably satisfactory to the Buyer*.

   (iv) A general warranty deed for each real property interest owned by the Seller, *drafted in the manner customarily used in commercial transactions in the place where the real property is located*.

   (v)   Assignments for each Assigned Contract, each to be *substantially in the form of Exhibit C*.

As to the other closing deliveries (*closing deliveries* as used in its broader sense), some are included in the action sections and others in the conditions article. Where a closing delivery is listed has contractual consequences. If the delivery is listed in the action sections, a party covenants to deliver the document. Any failure to deliver it breaches the agreement, entitling the other party to damages. In addition, the other party would have a walk-away right because, in an acquisition agreement, a condition to closing is the performance of every covenant to be performed *on or before the Closing Date*—and that would include the delivery obligations in the action sections. The contractual consequences differ, however, if the closing delivery is listed only in the conditions article. Then, the buyer's sole remedy is a walk-away right.

In deciding where to list a closing delivery, determine whether the party responsible for the delivery has control over its delivery. If the party can control its delivery, list the closing delivery in the action sections. In this event, the delivering party accepts the risk of breaching its covenant to deliver the document. If the party cannot control the delivery, list it as a condition to closing, so that a walk-away right is the other party's only remedy.

For example, drafters always carefully provide that the delivery of a legal opinion is a condition to closing, not an action section covenant. This protects the parties because they cannot control whether their lawyers will deliver the opinion. A peculiarity in the transaction's structure or a new court opinion can make a specific opinion difficult, if not impossible, to give. By listing the delivery of the opinion in the conditions article, an opinion's nondelivery creates only a walk-away right—not a right to damages.

In contrast, deliveries that properly appear in the action sections include certified resolutions of a party and agreements that the delivering party must sign—for example, a noncompetition agreement. Parties can control whether they sign and deliver these types of documents.

CHAPTER EIGHT

EXERCISES

Exercise 8-1

Which are the action sections in the Escrow Agreement in Exercise 6-5?

Exercise 8-2

Memorandum

To: Portia Porter

From: Sam Samson

Date: September 22, 20X2

Re: Sale of Aircraft

While we can't take over the drafting of the whole agreement, I convinced Flighty to let us draft the action sections. I told him that it would save him money. That guy is so cheap, he said yes immediately. Of course, the real reason I want you to do the drafting is that I don't trust Flighty. He is just a little too "sharp."

You may recall that several years ago his company bought a helicopter from Rich Lefkowitz's company. The purchase price was to be paid partially in cash and the rest in notes. In addition, as part of the business deal, Flighty was supposed to personally guarantee his company's notes. As I heard the story, he signed the guaranty and then took it off the table while the money was being wired. It wasn't until Lefkowitz threatened to sue for fraud that Flighty delivered the guaranty. What a bum.

I would appreciate your getting me the draft of the action sections as soon as possible. You probably know this, but to draft those provisions, you will need information from the Purchase Offer and the Escrow Agreement [Exercise 6-5] and a few defined terms from the first draft of the Aircraft Purchase Agreement [Exercise 7-7]. You may want to take a look at Document 4 in Chapter 32 from your law school drafting textbook. It is an example of the action sections in an acquisition agreement. It also includes comments to explain various terms. Thanks.

Document 4 is also available on the textbook's website.

Exercise 8-3

Below are two versions of the same provision based on the facts that follow. Read the facts and the first version. Find the substantive and nonsubstantive drafting errors. How would you correct them? Hold off on the second version for now, but when you do review it, determine the drafting problem with Section 3.1(a)(ii)(B).

Facts

1. Assume that it is October 18, 20X6. Your client, the employer, is entering into an agreement on this day for the employment of an executive.
2. The executive is to begin work on January 1, 20X7. The last day of the employment term is December 31, 20X9.
3. The salary is at a rate of $85,000 per year for the first year. The company will pay the employee every two weeks. The salary will increase each year over the previous year's salary by at least 7½%. The increase takes effect on January 1 of each year.
4. The executive is entitled to a bonus of $15,000 each year. The bonus will be paid on December 31, 20X7, December 31, 20X8, and December 31, 20X9.
5. The company will pay the executive with its company check.

Version 1

From the definitions section

"Employment Term" means the three-year period beginning on January 1, 20X7 and ending on December 31, 20X9.

The contract provision

3.1 Salary. For the first year of the Employment Term, the Company shall pay the Executive a salary of $85,000 (the "**Base Salary**") in biweekly installments of $3,269.23. Beginning on the first anniversary of this Agreement and on each subsequent anniversary during the Employment Term, the Base Salary of the Executive increases by an amount not less than 7½% of the preceding year's Base Salary.

3.2 Bonus. In addition to the Base Salary, with respect to each year that the Executive is employed under this Agreement, the Company shall pay the Executive a $15,000 bonus (the "**Bonus**") on the last day of that year.

Version 2

From the definitions section

"Employment Term" means the three-year period beginning on January 1, 20X7 and ending on December 31, 20X9.

The contract provision

3.1 Compensation.

(a)   **Salary**. During the Employment Term, the Company shall pay the Executive a salary (the

"**Salary**") in an amount computed as follows:

(i) With respect to the first year of the Employment Term, the Salary is $85,000.

(ii) With respect to each year of the Employment Term, other than the first year of the Employment Term, the Salary is the amount equal to the *sum* of

(A) the Salary for the immediately preceding year *plus*

(B) an amount equal to 7½% of the Salary for the immediately preceding year or such greater amount as the Company determines in its sole discretion. [The Company shall pay the Executive the Salary for each year in the Employment Term in equal, biweekly installments.]

(b) **Bonus.** During the Employment Term, the Company shall pay the Executive a $15,000 bonus (the "**Bonus**") no later than the last day of each year of the Employment Term.

Exercise 8-4

Redraft the compensation provisions in Exercise 8-3 to correct the errors.

Exercise 8-5

Draft the action sections of the trademark licensing agreement in Exercise 5-3. Remember that the territory may change, so the action sections will need to provide the appropriate provisions.

Exercise 8-6

Arthur Wright, a quarterback for the San Jose Dragons, has hired Davis Reynolds to represent him in contract negotiations with the Dragons. The parties have agreed that the representation will begin on the day that their contract is signed and is to continue during the term of any contract that Reynolds negotiates with the Dragons and thereafter until either party gives notice of termination. Termination of the representation is effective on the 20th day after a party receives notice of termination. It may help if you define Wright's contract with the Dragons.

Draft the term provision, including the definition of the term in the provision you draft.

Representations and Warranties

9.1 INTRODUCTION TO CHAPTERS 9 THROUGH 14

As you learned in Chapters 3 and 4, the building blocks of contracts are the following contract concepts: representations and warranties, covenants, rights, conditions, discretionary authority, and declarations. By using these building blocks as the starting point for the drafting of contract provisions, a drafter can accurately memorialize the parties' business deal.

Chapters 9 through 12 discuss the drafting of the building blocks from two perspectives. First, when appropriate, a chapter explains the considerations to take into account from a business perspective. Second, it details the rules relating to the drafting of each building block—for example, what tense and voice are appropriate. Chapter 13 explains when you can use *will* and provides a nongrammatical framework for determining whether the use of *shall* is correct. Chapter 14 provides a chart that summarizes the key information in Chapters 9 through 13.

Each chapter, other than Chapter 13, has exercises that apply to the material in that chapter. Chapter 14's exercises require you to draft and mark up provisions using all the contract concepts.

9.2 GENERAL COMMENTS ON DRAFTING REPRESENTATIONS AND WARRANTIES

The language introducing representations and warranties is simple and results in each statement of fact being both a representation and a warranty.

> Party A represents and warrants to Party B as follows:

Nothing else is needed, and individual statements of fact do not need to reiterate that a party is making both representations and warranties.

Using *represents and warrants* together, rather than either term alone, precludes any ambiguity as to the contract's meaning. It plainly states the parties' intent: that a party both represents and warrants the statements that follow.

The phrase represents and warrants differs from other couplets and triplets where the words are synonymous.[1] With respect to those phrases, a drafter can safely omit all but one of the words without changing the phrase's meaning. But using just *represents* or just *warrants* could create different legal consequences because those terms have different substantive meanings. Using only one of them raises the possibility that the parties intended the consequences of only that term. It invites litigation. However, preventing litigation is one of a drafter's crucial jobs.[2] A careful drafter anticipates the business and legal problems that a provision might pose and then drafts to foreclose the possibility of that problem occurring. By using both *represents* and *warrants,* a drafter reduces a client's litigation risk by explicitly saying what the parties mean—a cardinal principle of good drafting.

The standard language introducing the representations and warranties makes them speak as of the date in the preamble. The parties, however, might want a different or additional date. For example, if a bank and its borrower are restating their credit agreement,[3] absent any change in the introductory language, the representations and warranties would speak as of the date in the restated agreement's preamble. The bank, however, might insist that the borrower's representations and warranties be true as of two dates: the date of the restated agreement and the date of the original credit agreement. This way the restated agreement does not eliminate any of the bank's rights or remedies arising from any misrepresentation or breach of warranty in the original credit agreement. Revised introductory language might look like the following:

> **The parties represent and warrant the following as of the date of this Restated Agreement and as of the date of the Original Agreement:**

The following sections discuss considerations specific to representations and warranties.

9.3   DRAFTING THE SUBSTANCE OF REPRESENTATIONS

This section discusses what you should consider when drafting the statements of fact that constitute representations. By virtue of the introductory language referred to earlier, these statements do double duty and will also serve as warranties. This section focuses, however, on how to craft the representations, the statements of fact, from a client's business perspective.

When drafting a representation, remember that it allocates risk by establishing a standard of liability. That standard is the statement of fact. If it is false, the maker of the representation is liable. Recall from Chapter 3 how the standard of liability—and, therefore, the risk—shifted each time the knowledge qualifier in the no litigation representation changed. The same process of risk allocation occurs each time a drafter changes a representation. If the statement changes, the standard changes, and the risk shifts. Therefore, when drafting the substance of representations, look closely at each word and ask whether it establishes the appropriate standard.

---

1. See § 18.3.

2. *See* Louis M. Brown, *The Law Office—A Preventive Law Laboratory,* 104 U. Pa. L. Rev. 940, 945-946 (May 1956).

3. For a discussion of restated agreements, see § 29.4.

When drafting representations, your strategic approach will differ, depending on whether you represent the party making the representations or the party receiving them. If you represent the party making the representations, minimize the number of representations and qualify them as much as possible. This reduces your client's potential liability. But, if you represent the party receiving the representations, your client's business interests are best served by receiving representations that are as broad and as unqualified as possible. These representations increase the risk that the maker will misstate a fact, thereby making it easier for the recipient to claim a misrepresentation.

As noted, drafters often use *knowledge* qualifiers to reduce a maker's risks. They also frequently use **materiality qualifiers**. A materiality qualifier reduces a maker's risks by limiting a representation's focus to the most important facts. Something is material if it would affect a person's decision.[4] Compare the following:

Version 1

Defaults. The Borrower is not in default under any agreement.

Version 2

Defaults. The Borrower is not in default under any *material* agreement.

Under Version 1, a borrower with $200 million in sales misrepresents the facts if it has failed to pay the rent for even one month on one of its 450 photocopiers. But it will not have misrepresented the facts if the representation is that in Version 2. Exercise 9-1 looks at the various ways in which materiality qualifiers can be drafted.

9.3.1 REPRESENTATIONS WITH RESPECT TO THE PAST, PRESENT, AND FUTURE

Generally, the facts in a representation must relate to a state of affairs that exists in the present or existed in the past.[5] With respect to those facts that presently exist, draft the representation and warranty in the present tense.

Organization; Good Standing. The Seller *is* a corporation duly organized, validly existing, and in good standing under the laws of the state of its incorporation as stated in **Schedule 4.1**, with all requisite corporate power and authority to own, operate, and lease its properties, and to carry on its business as now being conducted.

Be careful not to use *currently* or *presently* in a representation. Their use affects the meaning of a condition that provides that representations must also be true on the closing date. If a representation includes one of these words, the maker probably intends that the representation speak only as of the date of signing. But a condition that requires a repetition of the representation as of the date of the closing would frustrate the maker's intent because the condition would require the representation to be true currently — that is, as of the date of the closing. With respect to those facts

---

4. *See Barrington Press, Inc. v. Morey*, 752 F.2d 307, 310 (7th Cir. 1985).

5. *Restatement (Second) of Contracts* § 159 cmt. c (1981).

that relate to the past, draft the representation in a tense that expresses that time horizon.[6]

> **Tax Returns and Payments.** The Parent and each Subsidiary *have duly filed* all federal, state, and local tax returns and reports required to be filed and each of them *has duly paid or established* adequate reserves for the proper payment of all taxes and other governmental charges on it or its properties, assets, income, franchises, licenses, or sales.

The question arises: Can representations be drafted with respect to the future? Typically, the cases say *no*, holding that statements about future events are opinions or speculation.[7] Thus, a recipient of a representation with respect to the future usually cannot justifiably rely on it.[8]

There are, of course, exceptions. A recipient of a representation may rely on a future "fact"—an opinion—if the speaker purports to have special knowledge of the "fact," stands in a fiduciary relationship to the recipient, and has secured the recipient's confidence.[9] In addition, a statement has been held to be one of existing fact if

> a quality is asserted which inheres in the article so that, at the time the representation is made, the quality may be said to exist independently of future acts or performance of the one making the representation, independently of other particular occurrences in the future, and independently of particular future uses or requirements of the buyer.[10]

Moreover, a party has a cause of action when another party promises to perform, but knows it will not.[11] This is known as **promissory fraud**. In this context, the promise as to the future fraudulently misrepresents a present fact—the misrepresenting party's state of mind.[12] While this cause of action exists, courts disfavor it because it risks converting ordinary breach of contract claims into tort actions, which bring with them the potential award of punitive damages.[13]

The following representation from an acquisition agreement shows an error with respect to "future facts" that drafters commonly make.

> **Wrong**
>
> **3.8 Consents.** The Seller has obtained all consents required in connection with the execution and delivery of this Agreement. The Seller *will have obtained* before Closing all consents required in connection with the consummation of the transactions that this Agreement contemplates.

---

6. Representations with respect to the past are generally drafted in the past tense (e.g., "The Borrower's board of directors *authorized* the Borrowings on September 26, 20XX.") or the present perfect tense (e.g., "The Executive *has completed* her doctoral dissertation in biochemical engineering."). It is not necessary to remember the names of the tenses. Instead, remember that a party may make a representation with respect to the past.

7. *See e.g. Next Cent. Commun. Corp. v. Ellis*, 171 F. Supp. 2d 1374, 1379-1380 (N.D. Ga. 2001).

8. *Glen Holly Ent., Inc. v. Tektronix, Inc.*, 100 F. Supp. 2d 1086, 1093 (C.D. Cal. 1999).

9. *Outlook Windows Partn. v. York Int'l Corp.*, 112 F. Supp. 2d 877, 894 (D. Neb. 2000) (citing *Burke v. Harman*, 574 N.W.2d 156, 179 (Neb. App. 1998)).

10. *Nyquist v. Foster*, 268 P.2d 442, 445 (Wash. 1954).

11. *Levin v. Singer*, 175 A.2d 423, 432 (Md. 1961); *but see Bower v. Jones*, 978 F.2d 1004, 1011-1012 (7th Cir. 1992) (stating that Illinois does not recognize promissory fraud as a cause of action, except if the promise is part of a scheme to accomplish fraud; but noting, however, that the exception has been viewed as swallowing the rule); *see generally* Ian Ayres & Gregory Klass, *Insincere Promises: The Law of Misrepresented Intent* (Yale U. Press 2005).

12. *Palmacci v. Umpierrez*, 121 F.3d 781 786-787 (1st Cir. 1997).

13. *See Rosenblum v. Travelbyus.com, Ltd.*, 2002 WL 31487823 at *3 (N.D. Ill.).

As the second sentence is with respect to the future, a recipient cannot justifiably rely on it. That sentence was included, however, with the best of intentions. The seller intended to comfort the buyer by stating that it would obtain all the consents before closing, even though it had not yet done so. In essence, the seller was *promising* the buyer that it would obtain them. Indeed, representations with respect to the future are generally disguised covenants. Therefore, to carry out the seller's intent, the provision should be redrafted as two provisions: one a representation and the other a covenant.

Correct

3.8 Consents. The Seller has obtained all consents required in connection with the execution and delivery of this Agreement. Except as listed in **Schedule 3.8**, the Seller has obtained all consents required in connection with the consummation of the transactions that this Agreement contemplates. *(The representation.)*

4.6 Consents. The Seller shall obtain all the consents listed in **Schedule 3.8** before the Closing. *(The covenant.)*

By breaking out the covenant from the representation, a risk hidden in the representation becomes evident. The seller courts danger with the covenant as drafted in Section 4.6 in the example because it cannot control whether it will receive all the consents. To protect itself, the seller must change the covenant's degree of obligation so that it promises to exert a stated degree of effort to obtain the consents.[14]

9.3.2 ACTIVE VS. PASSIVE VOICE

Treatises and commentators usually advise drafters to prefer the active voice over the passive. When using the active voice, the subject of the sentence acts on an object. When the passive voice is used, the subject of the sentence is acted on by an actor. Sometimes the actor is even dropped from the sentence, creating the possibility of an ambiguity. Sentences in the active voice tend to be shorter, easier to read, and have a stronger impact.

Active

Taxes. The Seller paid its taxes when due.

Passive

Version 1

Taxes. The taxes were paid when due by the Seller.

Version 2

Taxes. The taxes were paid when due.

---

14. With the change in the covenant, a buyer would probably insist on a condition that all consents be obtained by closing. This would be its ultimate protection with respect to the consents.

While you should generally draft representations in the active voice, that is not always the case. Sometimes the voice used makes a substantive difference: A change in the subject of the sentence can change its meaning. For example, when purchasing a used parachute, a buyer wants to know the total number of times the parachute has been used, not how many times the seller has used it.

> **Active**
>
>   **Prior Use**. The Seller has used the parachute three times.
>
> **Passive**
>
>   **Prior Use**. The parachute has been used five times.

When the issue is the action rather than the actor, the passive voice is appropriate. You can use settings in a word-processing application to help you spot the use of the passive voice.

9.4 WARRANTIES

9.4.1 WARRANTIES WITH RESPECT TO THE FUTURE

When a warranty is coupled with a representation, one party promises to indemnify the other with respect to a state of facts currently existing or that existed in the past. A party may also warrant that a state of facts will exist in the future.[15] It may do so because the issue of the recipient's justifiable reliance disappears with respect to a warranty.

For example:

> **Warranty**. The Manufacturer warrants to the Retailer [and the eventual consumer] that the Product as packaged and shipped from the Manufacturer's plant *will be free* from defects in material and workmanship and *will function and perform* in accordance with Manufacturer's specifications for a period of one year from the date of retail purchase.[16]

Here, the Retailer is not relying on the truthfulness of the underlying statements (the future facts) but instead is relying on the Manufacturer's promise that it will pay damages if the state of facts does not exist in the future.[17] Thus, a statement that cannot be a representation because it deals with the future can be a warranty.

9.4.2 RISK ALLOCATION

Occasionally, but not often, as a matter of risk allocation, a party might make only a warranty. Typically, this occurs when a party refuses to represent a "fact" because it

---

15. *See S. Cal. Enters., Inc. v. D.N. & E. Walter & Co.*, 178 P.2d 785, 757-758 (Cal. App. 2d Dist. 1947).

16. *See* James J. White, Robert S. Summers & Robert A. Hillman, *Uniform Commercial Code* vol. 1, §12:18 (6th ed., West 2012) (discussing what constitutes warranty of future performance under U.C.C. §2-725(2)).

17. *See Wright v. Couch*, 54 S.W.2d 207, 209-210 (Tex. App.—Eastland 1932).

is false, but the parties agree that the would-be maker should be liable if the fact is not as stated. Colloquially, deal lawyers refer to this practice as *representing over the fact*.

For example, suppose the buyer of a manufacturing business asks the seller to represent and warrant that existing claims under the seller's warranties for its products do not exceed $1.5 million. If the seller does not know, it might quite reasonably refuse to make the representation. Nonetheless, the parties might agree that, as a matter of risk allocation, the seller should be financially responsible for any claims on the product warranties that exceed $1.5 million. In this circumstance, some lawyers would permit their clients to make the requested representation and warranty without qualification. As an alternative, the seller could warrant, but not represent, the dollar amount of the claims. This would accomplish the risk allocation, without the seller making a misrepresentation.

This author believes that the better practice is not to make the representation, but to accomplish the desired risk allocation through alternative means.[18] First, as a matter of policy, parties should understand that truthfulness in a contract matters. Second, a seller could be blindsided if its buyer "forgets" that the representation was merely risk allocation and sues for fraudulent misrepresentation, including punitive damages. Third, a buyer might not even have a cause of action for misrepresentation if its seller successfully argues that the buyer could not justifiably rely on the representation. Ironically, in that event, the buyer ends up where it could have started—with a cause of action for breach of warranty.

The use of a warranty on a stand-alone basis has increased since the *CBS, Inc. v. Ziff-Davis Publishing Co.*[19] decision. It made clear that a warranty was a separate contract concept with a separate cause of action. For example, lawyers drafting software contracts are advised to draft only warranties.[20]

---

18. The parties could address this matter in two additional ways. First, the seller could make the representation and warranty to its knowledge—assuming it had the knowledge. Then, it could indemnify the buyer with respect to the representation and warranty, but without regard to the knowledge qualifier. That is, for the purposes of the indemnity, the representation and warranty would be flat. Second, the parties could address this issue only in the indemnity, where the seller would agree to indemnify the buyer for claims in excess of $1.5 million. Both these methods accomplish the parties' business goals without the seller misrepresenting the facts.

19. *See generally CBS, Inc. v. Ziff-Davis Publg. Co.*, 553 N.E.2d 997 (N.Y. 1990).

20. H. Ward Classen, *A Practical Guide to Software Licensing for Licensees and Licensors* at 48-50 (4th ed., ABA 2011) (generally with respect to the differences between representations and warranties) and at 49 (while noting the differences between representations and warranties, the author states that "given that most licensees are willing to accept only a warranty and not require the licensor to provide a representation in the belief one is as good as the other, the licensor should refrain from including any representations in its agreement.").

EXERCISES

Exercise 9-1

In the same way that parties use a knowledge qualification as a risk allocation mechanism, they also use a **materiality** qualification. Materiality is a vague term, requiring a facts and circumstances test. There is no easy or pat definition. What may be material in one context may not be material in another. Generally, something is material if it would affect a person's decision. In essence, a materiality qualification means that the parties will not nitpick. The focus is on the important issues.[21]

In the examples that follow, the provisions are representations and warranties and a definition from a loan agreement. In a loan agreement, a bank requires representations and warranties from a borrower in the same way that a buyer requires representations and warranties from a seller. Both the buyer and the bank are making investments. The buyer is investing in the seller by buying it, and the bank is investing in the borrower by making a loan to it. Both the buyer and the bank need as much information as possible before they make their respective decisions to invest. In addition, the bank will use the representations and warranties as a risk allocation mechanism, to establish standards of liability, which, if breached, will provide the bank with remedies.

Each of the examples has a materiality qualification, but each differs from the others. This exercise is intended to familiarize you with these differences and how they affect the business deal. Although most of the examples are of different representations and warranties, several examples are different versions of the same representation and warranty. In reality, of course, only one version would actually appear in an agreement.

Part 1

Review Examples 1 through 3. Is Example 1 a flat or qualified representation and warranty? Would the bank or the borrower have asked for the change in language from Example 1 to Example 2? What would have been its argument to support its request for the change? If the first draft of the contract used the representation and warranty in Example 2, which party would have asked to change it to the language in Example 3? If the bank were to agree to the language in Example 3, what risk would it be taking?

Example 1

> **Purchase and Sale Orders**. Listed in **Schedule 3.10** is each purchase and sale order to which the Borrower is a party.

Example 2

> **Purchase and Sale Orders**. Listed in **Schedule 3.10** is each material purchase and sale order to which the Borrower is a party.

---

21. *See Barrington Press, Inc. v. Morey*, 752 F.2d 307, 310 (7th Cir. 1985).

Example 3

> **Purchase and Sale Orders**. Listed in **Schedule 3.10** is each purchase and sale order to which the Borrower is a party and that involves future payments in excess of $100,000.

Part 2

The representations and warranties in Examples 4 and 5 both deal with the possibility of defaults. Example 4 answers the question of whether entering into the agreement creates a conflict or a default under any other agreement to which the Borrower is a party. Example 5 answers the question of whether the Borrower is currently in default under any other agreement to which it is a party. Both examples include materiality qualifications. Which qualifications are more favorable to the borrower and why?

Example 4

> **Noncontravention**. The Borrower's execution and delivery of this Agreement do not conflict with or create a default under any agreement to which the Borrower is a party, except for any conflict or default that would not materially adversely affect the business or financial condition of the Borrower.

Example 5

From the definitions

> "**Material Agreement**" means any agreement that involves future payments in excess of $50,000.

The provision

> **Other Material Agreements**. The Borrower is not in default under any Material Agreement, except for any default that does not materially adversely affect the Borrower.

Part 3

Would the borrower prefer the language in Example 6 or Example 7? Why?

Example 6

> **Regulatory Compliance**. The Borrower is in compliance in all material respects with all federal, state, local, and foreign laws and regulations applicable to it.

Example 7

> **Regulatory Compliance**. The Borrower is in compliance with all federal, state, local, and foreign laws and regulations applicable to it, except for those instances of noncompliance that would not materially adversely affect the Borrower's financial condition, business, or results of operations.

Part 4

In Example 8, would the borrower prefer the *material adverse change* qualification in subsection (a) or subsection (b)? Why? What is the effect of the words *severally or in the aggregate* in Example 9?

Example 8

> **No Material Adverse Change**. Since the date of the Financial Statements,
> (a) no material adverse change has occurred in the financial condition, opera-
>   tions, or business of the Borrower and the Subsidiaries taken as a whole; and
> (b) no property or asset of the Borrower or any Subsidiary has suffered material
>   damage, destruction, or loss.

Example 9

> **Leases**. With respect to each lease listed in **Schedule 3.11**,
> (a) no default has occurred and is continuing; and
> (b) no event has occurred and is continuing which, with notice or lapse of time
>   or both, would constitute a default on the Borrower's part, except for those
>   defaults, if any, that
>   (i) are not material in character, amount, or extent; and
>   (ii) do not, severally or in the aggregate, materially detract from the value,
>   or interfere with the present use, of the property subject to the lease.

Part 5

List all of the qualifications in Example 10. What are the most important words or
phrases in the definition of "Material" in Example 11?

Example 10

> **Litigation**. Except as set forth in **Schedule 3.14**, no litigation is pending
> or, to the knowledge of any of the Borrower's officers, threatened that might,
> severally or in the aggregate, materially adversely affect the financial condition
> of the business, assets, or prospects of the Borrower and the Subsidiaries taken
> as a whole.

Example 11

> **"Material"** means an event, condition, matter, change, or effect (either
> alone or in combination with any one or more other events, conditions, matters,
> changes, or effects) that impacts or that is reasonably likely to impact the Bor-
> rower's condition (financial or otherwise), in an amount in excess of $10,000.

Exercise 9-2

Determine the drafting errors and mark up the provisions to correct the errors.

> **Compliance with Applicable Law**. The Seller has complied with, is cur-
> rently in compliance with, and will be in compliance with on the Closing Date, all
> laws, rules, and regulations, except for any noncompliance that would not have a
> material adverse effect on the Seller.

_____

_____

_____

_____

Unacceptable Content. The Book will contain no matter that invades any person's privacy or that is scandalous, libelous, obscene, or otherwise unlawful.

_____

_____

_____

_____

Exercise 9-3

If you were selling the Horse, which of the following two representations and warranties would you prefer and why?

Version 1

Additional Races. Sam Jockey has not raced the Horse since the Kentucky Derby.

Version 2

Additional Races. The Horse has not raced since the Kentucky Derby.

Covenants and Rights

10.1 DRAFTING THE SUBSTANCE OF COVENANTS

As with representations and warranties, covenants allocate risk and establish standards of liability. Recall from Chapter 3 how a drafter can change a covenant's import by using different degrees of obligation.[1] Should the equipment be maintained *in good condition, ordinary wear and tear excepted*, or should it be maintained *in accordance with industry standards*? As the obligation changes, so too does the standard of liability. The covenant becomes harder or easier for the promisor to perform, and therefore it becomes more or less likely that the promisor might be found in breach of the standard. Good drafting requires that you carefully examine each covenant in the context of the client's business deal to determine the appropriate standard of liability. As a general rule, if your client is making the covenant, the degree of obligation should be as weak as possible, while the reverse would be true if your client has the right to receive the performance.

To help you determine the substance of a covenant, use the *who, what, when, where, why, how,* and *how much* tests. Each time you answer one of the questions, ask yourself whether a variation might be more helpful to your client.

- **Who** is obligated to whom?
- **What** is the obligation?
- By **when** must the obligation be performed?
- **Where** will the performance take place?
- **Why** must a party perform?
- **How** is the obligation performed?
- If performance involves money, **how much**?

Example 1

Samples. No later than 60 days before an Item is to be shipped to the Retail Stores [*when—Should it be shorter or longer?*], the Manufacturer [*who*] shall submit a sample of that Item [*what*] to the Licensor [*to whom*] for its approval. The Licensor [*who*] shall approve or reject the sample and

---

1. See §3.3.2.

notify [*what*] the Manufacturer [*who*] of its decision by telephone [*how*] no later than three business days after the date of its receipt of the Item [*when*] for approval.

Example 2

Delivery of Disputed Amount. No later than five days after its receipt of the Release Notice [*when—Should it be later or sooner?*], the Escrow Agent [*who*] shall deliver [*to whom?*] a certified check [*how—Would a wire transfer be better?*] in an amount equal to the Disputed Amount [*how much?*], payable to the order of the party set forth in the Release Notice.

Example 3

Condition of Premises at End of Term. The Tenant [*who*] shall leave the Premises broom clean [*what—Is this the proper standard if representing the Landlord?*] when it vacates the Premises at the end of the Term [*when and why—What if the Tenant leaves earlier?*].

When analyzing the substance of a covenant, be wary if it asks your client to promise something that your client cannot control. This is a high-risk covenant because an outside event or third party controls whether your client breaches it. For example, imagine that Herald Stadium Productions asks your client, Preston Presentations Inc., to sign a contract that includes the following provision:

McCrary Concert. Preston Presentations Inc. shall present a concert on July 4, 20XX at Herald Stadium at which Sir Paul McCrary is the lead act.

This covenant presents no problem if your client has already arranged that Sir Paul will perform. If it has not, your client is in serious risk of breaching this covenant. Sir Paul could just say "No."

As noted in Chapter 3, covenants include promises both to do and not to do something. Some drafters refer to these promises as affirmative and negative covenants. This nomenclature is generally not useful, except in the context of a loan agreement where covenants are classified for convenient reference.[2] There, affirmative covenants generally require a borrower "to maintain prudent business practices,"[3] including payment of taxes, maintenance of equipment, maintenance of existence, compliance with laws, and the keeping of proper business and financial records. Other affirmative covenants require the borrower to provide the bank with current financial information. In contrast, negative covenants typically prohibit actions that the borrower might take if the loan agreement were not in effect and that would significantly change the borrower's structure or business operations.[4] For example, negative covenants prohibit

---

2. *See* Richard Wight, Warren Cooke & Richard Gray, *The LSTA's Complete Credit Agreement Guide* § 7.1 (1st ed., McGraw-Hill 2009) ("Covenants can be divided into three categories: financial covenants, affirmative covenants, and negative covenants. . . . There is no substantive effect to these classifications; they are purely a matter of convenience of reference.").

3. Michael A. Leichtling, Barry A. Dubin & Jeffrey J. Wong (1943-2001), *Commercial Loan Documentation Guide* vol. 1, § 11.01 (Matthew Bender 2012).

4. Sandra Schnitzer Stern, *Structuring and Drafting Commercial Loan Agreements* vol. 1, ¶¶ 5.01[1], 6.01[1] (A.S. Pratt & Sons 2012).

mergers, debt, and the granting of security interests. Breaches of these covenants generally require that the borrower intended to perform the act that violated the covenant. Banks generally grant a borrower a grace period to cure a breach of an affirmative covenant as it may be inadvertent.[5] Breaches of negative covenants generally result in an immediate event of default.[6] Once a company has merged, for instance, the merger can rarely be undone.

10.2 DRAFTING GUIDELINES

Adhere to the following guidelines when drafting covenants:
   1. *To obligate a party to perform, use **shall**.*

> **Regular Exercise**. The Athlete *shall* exercise regularly in order to maintain himself in top physical condition.

Most commentators agree that sophisticated commercial contracts should use *shall* to signal a covenant.[7] Nonetheless, some commentators ardently advocate banning *shall* from the legal lexicon.[8] They believe that lawyers have used it improperly so many times and in so many ways, it can no longer do its job. For example, courts have interpreted *shall* to mean *will*,[9] *may*, and a *condition*. The proposed alternatives are *will* and *must*. However, neither of those alternatives is a panacea. The suggested solutions replace one set of problems with another.

Assume that drafters banish *shall* from their contracts. In that event, a drafter would need to use either *will* or *must* to signal a covenant. But as *will* is already reserved for the future,[10] it would then need to do double duty, creating again the possibility of ambiguity. The use of *must* creates the same problem because drafters use it to signal a condition. The issue of whether *shall* signals the future or discretionary authority will not go away if *will* is used instead of *shall*. It will merely be transformed. Instead, courts will need to construe *will*.[11] Imagine the irony of a court using as precedent the cases analyzing whether *shall* was intended to signal a covenant, the future, or discretionary authority. Analogous issues would arise if *must* were to replace *shall*. To cure the problematic use of *shall*, drafters must reform and reserve the use of *shall* for duties.

The following example demonstrates a proper use of *will*. It appears in a covenant, but does not signal the obligation. Instead, it describes what the nonparty limited

---

5. Stern, *supra* n. 4, at ¶ 8.01[2]; Leichtling et al., *supra* n. 3, at § 11.01.

6. Stern, *supra* n. 4, at ¶ 8.05[2].

7. *See* Kenneth A. Adams, *A Manual of Style for Contract Drafting* 43-44 (3d ed., ABA 2013); Scott J. Burnham, *Drafting and Analyzing Contracts* §§ 16.2 and 17.6.1 (3d ed., Matthew Bender 2003); Robert C. Dick, *Legal Drafting in Plain Language* 93 (3d ed., Carswell 1995) (Canada); F. Reed Dickerson, *The Fundamentals of Legal Drafting* 214 (2d ed., Little, Brown & Co. 1986); Lenné Espenschied, *Contract Drafting, Powerful Prose in Transactional Practice* 139 (ABA 2010).

8. *See* Bryan A. Garner, *A Dictionary of Modern Legal Usage* 940 (2d ed., Oxford U. Press 1995); Joseph Kimble, *The Many Misuses of "Shall,"* 3 Scribes J. Leg. Writing 61, 69-71 (1992).

9. *E.g. Cunningham v. Long*, 135 A. 198, 201 (Me. 1926) (stating that when looked at in the context of the other contract provisions, "shall" plainly had an element of futurity).

10. See Chapter 13, which discusses in detail when to use *will*. It also provides a set of nongrammatical rules to ensure the proper use of *shall*.

11. *See Doe v. Wal-Mart Stores, Inc.*, 572 F.3d 677, 681-682 (9th Cir. 2009) (issue whether the phrase "will undertake" created a covenant or discretionary authority).

partners will do in the future. The future tense is correct here because the nonparties are not making promises in this sentence. Those promises will be somewhere else in the agreement or in some other agreement.

> **Obligation to Find Investors**. The General Partner *shall* use commercially reasonable efforts to find at least ten limited partners, each of whom *will* invest $1 million in the Partnership.

Although lawyers should not use *will* to signal an obligation in commercial contracts, it has its place in consumer contracts where different drafting rules prevail. Commercial lawyers also use *will* in letter agreements. For example, employment agreements are sometimes drafted as letters to make the tone more friendly and less intimidating. As part of this process, drafters often use *will* instead of *shall*.

2. *As a general rule, do not state what a party has a right to; state what the other party's obligation is.* Recall from Chapter 3 that a right is the flip side of a covenant.[12] Therefore, you could draft these provisions as either a covenant or a right. You should, however, draft them as covenants for two reasons.

- **First**, a covenant is easier to litigate because it explicitly states that a party has an obligation to perform. The statement of a right does not always do so. When a provision is cast as a right, a litigator must first establish who has the obligation to perform. While hardly an insurmountable task, it adds an unnecessary issue to the litigation.
- **Second**, a covenant facilitates the drafting of the full contours of a party's obligations.

> **Acceptable**
>
> **Air-conditioning**. The Tenant *has the right* to air-conditioning for the Premises during the summer.
>
> **Much better**
>
> **Air-conditioning**. The Landlord *shall air-condition* the Premises until 5:00 p.m. each weekday during the summer, unless the Tenant requests that the air-conditioning remain on longer on a weekday or turned on for one or both weekend days. The Landlord shall comply with the Tenant's request and shall bill the Tenant at the regular rate plus 15%. The Tenant may make one or more requests, all of which this Section governs.

If a party insists on a statement of its rights, state the right but pair it with a covenant—except as discussed next. But be careful, if the covenant and the right are inconsistent, the contract will be unambiguous.

> **Author's Right to Book Copies**. The Author has the right to receive 20 free copies of the Book, and the Publisher *shall provide* the Author with those copies no later than ten days before the Publication Date.

---

12. See Chapter 3.

Generally, state just a party's rights if you are stating that it has an entitlement as a remedy.

Example 1

Equitable Relief. If the Executive breaches her duty of confidentiality, the Company *has the right* to equitable relief.

Example 2

Return of Deposit. If the Tenant does not return the Premises in broom clean condition, the Landlord *has the right* to retain the amount of the Deposit equal to the cost of the appropriate cleaning.

In Example 1, the flip side of the Company's right is the Executive's implied promise not to contest that equitable relief is appropriate.[13] Similarly, in Example 2, the flip side of the Landlord's right to the Deposit is the Tenant's implied promise not to seek the Deposit's return.

As *has the right to* and *is entitled to* are often misused to signal discretionary authority, check your drafting to confirm that the party indeed has a right and not a choice between remedies.

Wrong

If the Borrower makes a material misrepresentation, the Bank [has the right] [is entitled] to accelerate the Loan or to take any other action that law or this Agreement permits. *(This sentence should be drafted using language of discretionary authority. The bank has a choice of remedies.)*

Correct

If the Borrower makes a material misrepresentation, the Bank *may* accelerate the Loan or take any other action that law or this Agreement permits. *(May is the correct term to signal discretionary authority in a remedy when the remedies include a choice.)*

---

3. *Do not use any form of **agree***. It is superfluous because the words of agreement state that *the parties agree*.

Wrong

Capital Contribution. Each Limited Partner *agrees* to contribute $100,000 to the limited partnership before January 1, 20XX.

Correct

Capital Contribution. Each Limited Partner *shall* contribute $100,000 to the limited partnership before January 1, 20XX.

---

13. *See* Thomas R. Haggard, *Legal Drafting: Process, Technique, and Exercises* 409 (West 2003).

4. *Do not say that a party* **is responsible** *for doing something.*

Wrong

 Costumes. The Performer *is responsible* for designing and making her own costume.

Correct

 Costumes. The Performer *shall* design and make her own costume.

5. *To obligate a party not to do something, use* **shall not**, *except as stated in Guideline 6.*

 Participation in Other Sports. The Athlete *shall not* participate in any sport other than baseball.

6. *If the sentence uses a negative subject, use* **may** *instead of* **shall not**. Negative subjects include *neither party* and *no party*.

 Anti-assignment. Neither party may assign any of its rights under this Agreement.

If *shall* were used instead of *may*, the substantive meaning of the sentence would change: *Neither party shall assign any of its rights under this Agreement* means that *neither party is obligated to assign its rights*. It does not prohibit assignments.

7. *To negate a duty to perform, use* **is not obligated to**. The duty negated is a subset of the duties that a party is obligated to perform. A duty negated is in essence an exception. In Example 1, the monetary limit is an exception to the general duty to *use commercially reasonable efforts*. In Example 2, another provision obligates the Company to provide an indemnity. Example 2 states the circumstances of the exception.

Example 1

 Landlord's Consent. The Seller shall use commercially reasonable efforts to obtain the Landlord's consent, but in using those efforts, the Seller *is not obligated to* spend more than $10,000.

Example 2

 No Obligation to Indemnify. The Company *is not obligated to* indemnify the Executive for her actions if they were outside the scope of her duties as stated in Section 3.

8. *Draft covenants using the active voice.*

> **Wrong**
>
> **End of Term Repairs**. The premises *shall be painted* by the Tenant in the last month of the lease term.

> **Correct**
>
> **End of Term Repairs**. The Tenant *shall paint* the premises in the last month of the lease term.

9. *Beware of covenants posing as declarations.* Sometimes drafters write a provision so that it appears to be a declaration. Test whether a declaration is appropriate by asking whether remedies should flow from the provision. If the answer is *yes*, then recast the provision as a covenant. (It might also be a representation and warranty, depending on the context.)

> **Version 1 — Wrong**
>
> **Security Deposit**. The security deposit will be $3,000, due concurrently with the parties' execution and delivery of this Agreement.

A quick read of Version 1 gives the impression that the provision is a declaration, that it defines the amount of the security deposit. However, a closer read reveals that the provision should be drafted to include both a declaration and a covenant, as in Version 2, or as a covenant that includes the information in the declaration, as in Version 3.

> **Version 2 — Correct**
>
> **Security Deposit**. The security deposit is $3,000, and the Tenant shall pay the security deposit to the Landlord by certified check concurrently with the parties' execution and delivery of this Agreement.

> **Version 3 — Correct**
>
> **Security Deposit**. The Tenant shall pay the Landlord a $3,000 security deposit by certified check concurrently with the parties' execution and delivery of this Agreement.

10. *Do not draft a provision so that it appears to bind a nonparty, whether it be human or otherwise.* For example, contracts often include arbitration provisions in which the parties state the arbitrators' obligations. A typical provision might be as follows:

> **Version 1 — Wrong**
>
> **Choice of Law**. The arbitrators shall interpret all controversies arising under or relating to this Agreement, including torts, in accordance with the laws of Missouri.

The use of *shall* is inappropriate because the arbitrators are not parties to the agreement and cannot be obligated to do anything. Here is an appropriate redraft:

Version 2 — Correct

Choice of Law. The arbitrators are to interpret all controversies arising under or relating to this Agreement, including torts, in accordance with the laws of Missouri.

This wording creates a declaration, a policy statement. As an alternative, the agreement can obligate the parties to instruct the arbitrators how to act.

Version 3 — Correct

Choice of Law. The parties shall instruct the arbitrators to interpret all controversies arising under or relating to this Agreement, including torts, in accordance with the laws of Missouri.

Some drafters prefer this version because it reflects the reality of what will happen if the parties arbitrate their controversies.

Another common error is to follow a party's covenant to give notice with language that obligates the notice to give specific information.

Wrong

Purchase of Shares. If a Stockholder wants to purchase any of the Shares referred to in the Offer, it shall give notice no later than three days after it receives the Offer, and *the notice shall state* . . . .

Because *the notice* is not a party, it cannot obligate itself or anyone else to take or refrain from an action. Instead, the obligation must be the promisor's.

Correct

Purchase of Shares. If a Stockholder wants to purchase any of the Shares referred to in the Offer, the Stockholder shall deliver a notice no later than three days after receiving the Offer. The Stockholder shall include the following information in the notice:

---

11. *Use* **shall cause** *or* **shall not permit** *when a party is responsible for a result*. This guideline is a variation on the preceding one. Occasionally, a party wants a contract to state explicitly that, while it is responsible for achieving a specific result, it will not perform the act that brings about the result. Instead, a generally unidentified third party will do it.[14] For example, suppose that a contractor is obligated to construct a building on land that has an underground gas tank. Part of the deal might

---

14. If you drafted the action sections of the Aircraft Purchase Agreement, you may recall that the Buyer promised to *deliver, or cause to be delivered*, the full consideration. The *cause to be delivered* language was included to take into account the escrow agent's obligation under the escrow agreement to deliver part of the consideration.

be that the gas tank is to be removed before construction begins. In the negotiations, the owner might object to a covenant that *it* is obligated to remove the tank. From its perspective, the issue is the removal of the tank, not who removes it. A provision like this is often drafted—incorrectly—in the passive voice without stating who is to perform. But covenants *should* establish who has the obligation to perform.

Wrong

> **Removal of Gas Tank**. The underground gas tank shall be removed from the Land no later than five Business Days before the Start Date. *(Passive voice with unstated actor.)*

Correct

> **Removal of Gas Tank**. The Owner shall cause the underground gas tank to be removed from the Land no later than five Business Days before the Start Date. *(Active voice with Owner responsible for result.)*

A similar problem occurs when a parent corporation sells the shares of a subsidiary. A buyer often wants the subsidiary to take various actions during the gap period, but the parent, not the subsidiary, is party to the agreement. To achieve the desired result, have the parent *cause* the subsidiary to perform in a certain way.[15]

> **Equipment**. The Seller shall cause the Target to maintain its equipment in accordance with industry standards.

The covenant is the Seller's. Its obligation is to cause a certain result: the Target's maintenance of the equipment in accordance with industry standards.

10.3 COVENANT ARTICLES IN ACQUISITION AGREEMENTS

The modern acquisition agreement often combines pre- and post-closing covenants into one article. Because each covenant may relate to a different time period, each covenant must state the time period to which it applies. The following excerpt from a purchase and sale agreement is typical. The italicized language has been added to emphasize the time-period-related language.

---

15. As an alternative, some buyers require the target to become a party to the stock purchase agreement and to agree to perform certain obligations during the gap period.

ARTICLE VIII[16]
COVENANTS

8.1 **Access to Information.** *Prior to Closing*, Sellers shall permit Purchaser . . . to have reasonable access, during normal business hours and on reasonable advance notice, to the Books and Records and senior management personnel of Sellers pertaining to the Purchased Assets . . .

8.2 **Conduct of the Business Pending the Closing.** Except as otherwise expressly contemplated by this Agreement . . . , *during the period from and after the date hereof until the Closing Date*, Sellers:

(a) shall use commercially reasonable efforts to conduct the Business in the Ordinary Course of Business . . .

(c) will maintain in full force and effect policies of insurance that provide casualty, property damage and general liability coverage for the Purchased Assets comparable in all material respects in amount and scope of coverage to that now maintained by or on behalf of Sellers . . . .

8.3 **Cooperation; Consents and Filings.**

(a) *From and after the date hereof until the Closing Date*, Sellers, Purchaser and Guarantor will each cooperate with each other and use (and will cause their respective representatives to use) commercially reasonable efforts . . . (i) to take, or to cause to be taken, all actions, and to do, or to cause to be done, all things reasonably necessary, proper or advisable on its part under this Agreement . . . to consummate and make effective the transactions contemplated by this Agreement as promptly as practicable . . . .

8.4 **Preservation of Records.** Subject to the other provisions of this Agreement, Purchaser and Guarantor shall . . . preserve and keep in their possession all records held by them on and after the date hereof relating to the Purchased Assets, *for a period of seven years or such longer period as may be required by Applicable Law* . . . .

The alternative drafting style for covenant articles in acquisition agreements begins the article with an unnumbered introductory paragraph. It states that a party promises to perform the following obligations from signing to closing. Numbered sections follow the introductory paragraph, each section addressing a different subject. Post-closing covenants generally appear in separate articles.

---

16. Excerpt from Article VIII of the Settlement and Purchase and Sale Agreement among ASARCO LLC, AR Silver Bell, Inc., Copper Basin Railway, Inc., ASARCO Santa Cruz, Inc., Sterlite (USA), Inc. and Sterlite Industries (Inia) LTD, dated as of March 6, 2009, http://www.bloomberglaw.com/s/dealmaker _document/10c942bccf8d339dfdbca569eab522dc/document/XLFP3JG5GVG0?search32=C9P6UQR5E9FN 6PB1E9HMGNRKCLP6QFB3DTR6ARJ1DPQ3MER2DTNMOPB1DPFN6PB1E9HMGNRKCLP6QF9SCHM LUP3FCDFN0OBIEHSLUR31ETFMCQBIDKUIGSR8CLGN4RB1DOG76T35E9M6IRJ754V209H07HI6QP 3FCDQ7IS357KH36C1H60O328HU7CTMSRQVD5MN0NRGD1P62SR5ECUJ2EPREDSMSRREF5MN6F9H (accessed Aug. 17, 2013).

Article 4 — Seller's Covenants

The Seller shall do the following beginning on the date of this Agreement and ending on the Closing Date:

4.1 **Consents.** The Seller shall use commercially reasonable efforts to obtain all consents.

4.2 **Maintenance of Machinery.** The Seller shall maintain the Machinery in its current condition.

EXERCISES

Exercise 10-1

Which of the following covenants would a seller prefer and why? Which would a buyer prefer and why?

Version 1

> **Maintenance.** Seller shall maintain its plants, structures, and equipment in good operating condition and repair.

Version 2

> **Maintenance.** Seller shall maintain its plants, structures, and equipment in good operating condition and repair, subject only to ordinary wear and tear.

Version 3

> **Maintenance.** Seller shall maintain its plants, structures, and equipment in customary operating condition and repair.

Version 4

> **Maintenance.** Seller shall maintain its plants, structures, and equipment in accordance with industry standards.

Version 5

> **Maintenance.** Seller shall steam clean, oil, and otherwise maintain each piece of equipment as prescribed in Exhibit B.

Version 6

> **Maintenance.** Seller shall not permit its plants, structures, and equipment to be in a state of operating condition and repair that would materially and adversely affect the operations of Seller.

Exercise 10-2

Mark up the following provision to correct the drafting errors:

> **Use of Proceeds.** The Borrower shall not use, and hereby specifically agrees not to use,
>
> directly or indirectly, the Borrowing's proceeds for any purpose, except that stated in this Section 3.4.

Fees and Expenses. The fees of the Escrow Agent and all expenses reasonably incurred by the Escrow Agent in performing its obligations hereunder shall be borne one-half by Rapid Transportation and one-half by Eagle.

Discharge. No employee may be discharged without two weeks' notice.

Exercise 10-3

Draft the following provisions. You may need more than one sentence. Do not draft any definitions; just use a defined term that you think works in context.

1. Sam Student wants to rent an apartment. The landlord was leery of renting it to a student, but he agreed to do so because Sam said that he would return the apartment in good condition and broom clean.

   Tenant Shall _____

   _____

   _____

   _____

2. Same facts as in Paragraph 1 plus the following: Sam wanted it made clear that he had not agreed to repair any damage that existed when he moved in. Draft this provision as a nonobligation. It should be a follow-on sentence to the provision you wrote for the previous exercise.

   The tenant is not obligated _____

   _____

3. Private Equity LLP is borrowing money from Big Bank N.A. The bank doesn't want the borrower to merge or sell substantially all of its assets without the bank's consent. The bank agreed it would not unreasonably withhold its consent.

   _____

   _____

   _____

Exercise 10-4

Mark up the following provision to correct the drafting errors:

Disputes. The parties have decided to submit all disputes arising under or relating to this Agreement to binding arbitration before the American Arbitration Association and under the rules of that Association. The lawyers' expenses related to the arbitration shall be paid as the arbitrators may

direct.

Exercise 10-5

A seller and buyer have entered into a Confidentiality Agreement in accordance with which each party has agreed "to hold in strict confidence and not disclose to any nonsignatory information acquired in connection with the transaction." The seller is concerned that the buyer has three subsidiaries and that word will leak. How can you protect the seller with a buyer's covenant?

_____

_____

_____

Conditions to an Obligation

11.1 INTRODUCTION

For this chapter's purposes, a condition is a state of facts that must exist before a party is obligated to perform. Chapter 12 discusses discretionary authority and conditions to discretionary authority, and declarations and conditions to declarations.[1]

11.2 DRAFTING THE SUBSTANCE OF A CONDITION TO AN OBLIGATION

Once the parties have decided that a condition is appropriate, they must decide on the state of facts—the standard—that must exist before a party is obligated to perform. Each party's risk then depends on how difficult or easy it is to meet the standard.

For example, assume that a landlord and a tenant (a store owner) have agreed that the landlord will maintain the premises in the ordinary course of business, but that the landlord will make immediate repairs under certain circumstances. The parties and the drafter must then determine those circumstances—the standard. Here is the provision before the parties have negotiated the standard.

> **Maintenance of the Premises**. The Landlord shall maintain the Premises in the ordinary course of business. Despite the preceding sentence, if [state of facts to be inserted], the Landlord shall make immediate repairs.

The tenant, wary of liability, might propose that the landlord's obligation be activated whenever an *unsafe condition* exists. The landlord might object to this standard, noting its vagueness and the failure to consider a danger's extent or immediacy. Consistent with these concerns, the landlord might propose instead that its obligation be activated only when a *significant, imminent danger* exists. This alternative standard would reduce the landlord's risk that it would be obligated to perform. Here are the two versions of the provision:

---

1. See Chapter 12.

> **Version 1**
>
> **Maintenance of the Premises.** The Landlord shall maintain the Premises in the ordinary course of business. Despite the preceding sentence, if an unsafe condition exists, the Landlord shall make immediate repairs.
>
> **Version 2**
>
> **Maintenance of the Premises.** The Landlord shall maintain the Premises in the ordinary course of business. Despite the preceding sentence, if a significant, imminent danger exists, the Landlord shall make immediate repairs.

Although many conditions depend on facts occurring, a condition can also be based on the failure of facts to occur.[2] For example, a condition to a bank's obligation to lend could be the absence of product liability litigation against the borrower.

When deciding the substance of a condition, keep in mind the following:

- A party's own actions cannot be a condition to its obligations. If they could, the party would be in control of whether the condition could be satisfied. Stated differently, a party cannot fail to perform, claiming that a condition was not satisfied if the failure to satisfy the condition resulted from the party's own action or inaction.[3]
- The passage of time cannot be a condition because it is certain to occur.[4]

11.3 SIGNALING A CONDITION OUTSIDE OF A CONDITIONS ARTICLE IN AN ACQUISITION OR FINANCING AGREEMENT

When a drafter wants to craft a condition outside a conditions article, she usually uses one of the following words or phrases: *if/then, must, when, subject to, provided that,*[5] *if, conditioned on,* and *on.*[6] Unfortunately, using these words does not guarantee that a court will construe the provision as a condition.[7] Courts dislike conditions because they often result in a party forfeiting a right.[8] So, when given a choice between construing a provision as a condition or a covenant, courts regularly inter-

---

2. *Restatement (Second) of Contracts* § 224 cmt. b (1981).

3. *Rogier v. Am. Testing & Engr. Corp.*, 734 N.E.2d 606, 621 (Ind. App. 2000) ("[A] party may not rely on the failure of a condition precedent to excuse performance where that party's own action or inaction caused the failure. When a party retains control over when the condition will be fulfilled, it has an implied obligation to make a reasonable and good faith effort to satisfy the condition. [Citation omitted.] 'The *Hamlin* doctrine prevents a party from acts of contractual sabotage or other acts in bad faith by a party that cause the failure of a condition.' [Citation omitted.]").

4. *Restatement (Second) of Contracts* § 224 cmt. b.

5. Despite *provided that*'s regular use to signal a condition, drafters should avoid it because of its potential to create an ambiguity. See § 21.7.

6. *Ross v. Harding*, 391 P.2d 526, 531 (Wash. 1964); *see Restatement (Second) of Contracts* § 226 cmt. a.

7. *Cedar Point Apts., Ltd. v. Cedar Point Inv. Corp.*, 693 F.2d 748 n. 9 (8th Cir. 1982), *cert. denied*, 461 U.S. 914 (1983).

8. See § 4.2.4 for an example of how a condition can result in a forfeiture. *See Restatement (Second) of Contracts* § 227(2) and cmt. d.

pret the provision to be a covenant.[9] Then, the nonbreaching party must still perform, but the breaching party must pay it damages.

To ensure — as much as possible — that a court will construe a provision as a condition, do one or more of the following:

- State that a provision is a condition.
- Use *must*[10] and insert an interpretive provision that *must* signals a condition.
- Construct the sentence using an *if/then* formulation, drafting the *if* clause in the present tense.
- State the consequences of the failure to satisfy a condition. (For example, *if* the condition is not satisfied, Y is not obligated to perform.)

Example 1

Conversion of Preferred Stock. To convert its preferred stock to common stock, a preferred stockholder must submit the Required Documents to the Corporation no later than May 15, 20XX.

and

Add the following as part of the general provisions or the interpretive section of a definitions article:

The use of *must* in this Agreement signals a condition.

Example 2

Excerpt from an insurance agreement

Claims. If the Owner suffers a loss because of theft or unintentional damage, then the Owner must give the Insurer written notice of the claim no later than ten days after the loss. The Owner's failure to deliver a timely notice relieves the Insurer of its obligation to pay the Owner for any loss. *(Provision explicitly states the consequences of the failure to satisfy the condition.)*

Example 3

Excerpt from an insurance agreement

Claims. It is a condition to the Insurer's obligations under this Agreement that the Owner must give the Insurer written notice of any Loss no later than ten days after the Loss. *(Explicit statement of condition, plus use of must.)*

Example 4

Termination. If the Contractor completes construction before the Deadline, then the Owner shall pay the Contractor a $5,000 bonus no later than

---

9. *See* Samuel Williston, *Williston on Contracts* vol. 13, § 38.13 (Richard A. Lord ed., 4th ed., 2000), and the cases cited therein.

10. *See In re Kirkbride*, 409 B.R. 354, 357-358 (E.D.N.C. 2009); *Stewart-Smith Haidinger, Inc. v. Avi-Truck, Inc.*, 682 P.2d 1108, 1115 (Alaska 1984).

> five Business Days after the construction is complete. *(If/then formulation establishing a temporal sequence.)*

In Example 1, the condition is that the preferred stockholder must submit the required documents. Although most commentators agree that the sentence standing on its own is a condition because of the use of the signal *must*, the better practice is to pair the sentence with an interpretive provision that *must* signals a covenant. Using *must* this way has not yet become commonplace and some courts have previously interpreted *must* as *shall* in contracts.[11] The additional language substantially reduces the likelihood that a court would do so.

Example 2 is a bit tricky. Both the *if* clause and the *then* clause establish conditions to the Insurer's liability. The obligation to which these conditions apply is the Insurer's obligation to pay. That obligation is elsewhere in the contract. (The condition to an obligation and the obligation need not appear in the same provision.) This example also includes an explicit statement of the consequence of the failed condition: that the Insurer is relieved of its obligation to pay.

Example 3 is straightforward and signals that the provision is a condition by saying so explicitly.

Example 4 uses the classic *if/then* formulation, with the *if* clause stating the condition. In this instance, the Owner's obligation to pay appears in the *then* clause. It signals that obligation by using *shall*.

Note that the *if* clauses in Examples 2 and 4 are properly drafted in the present tense. The *shall* in the following provision is wrong because the *if* clause does not state a covenant.

Wrong

> **Notice.** If the Owner *shall have suffered* a loss because of theft or unintentional damage, the Owner must give the Insurer written notice of the claim no later than ten days after the loss.

Correct

> **Notice.** If the Owner *suffers* a loss because of theft or unintentional damage, the Owner must give the Insurer written notice of the claim no later than ten days after the loss.

A provision that uses an *if/then* formulation typically begins with the *if* clause that establishes the condition to reflect the temporal sequence of events.[12] But if the *if* clause contains multiple conditions, the sentence may become difficult to read because too much information precedes the *then* clause. In this instance, the order of the clauses may be reversed.[13]

---

11. *See Jacob & Youngs, Inc. v. Kent*, 129 N.E. 889 (N.Y. 1921). Although courts regularly interpret *must* to be an obligation in statutes, they do so substantially less frequently in cases involving contracts.

12. See § 21.5 for a discussion of how an *if/then* formulation can create an ambiguity.

13. See § 20.3.2 for an example.

11.4 CONDITIONS INSIDE A CONDITIONS ARTICLE IN AN ACQUISITION OR A FINANCING AGREEMENT

11.4.1 SIGNALING A CONDITION INSIDE A CONDITIONS ARTICLE IN AN ACQUISITION OR A FINANCING AGREEMENT

Conditions articles appear almost exclusively in acquisition and financing agreements. Generally, these articles begin with an unnumbered introductory paragraph along the following lines:

> **The Buyer is obligated to consummate the transactions that this Agreement contemplates only if each of the following conditions has been satisfied or waived on or before the Closing Date.**

The introductory paragraph establishes that each section that follows contains a condition to the buyer's obligation to perform the buyer's subject matter performance obligation to purchase the business. The words *satisfied* or *waived* address the possibility that although a condition may not be satisfied, the buyer's obligation can still be triggered if the buyer waives the failed condition. The contractual statement that the buyer may waive is not technically necessary because the buyer may waive as a matter of common law.[14]

The proper way to signal a condition in a conditions article is to join the word *must* with another verb in one of the following three ways:

- *must* + *be*, to indicate a fact that must exist on the closing date.
- *must* + *have* + *the past tense of a verb*, to indicate something that someone must have caused to happen on or after the signing date, but no later than the closing date.
- *must have been* + *the past tense of a verb*, to indicate something that must have occurred on or after the signing date, but no later than the closing date; this is the passive version of the preceding use of *must* and should be used when the focus of the provision is the action, not the actor.

Two versions of the same set of conditions from an acquisition agreement follow. In Version 1, the conditions are properly stated, using *must*. Version 2 replaces *must* with *shall*—typical contract drafting—but analytically, *shall* is incorrect. A condition is not a promise of performance; it is an *if* clause. It is all about possibilities—whether an event not certain to occur will occur. Only if it does occur, does a party have an obligation to perform. To distinguish linguistically between covenants (promises) and conditions (possibilities), drafters should reserve *shall* for covenants and use *must* for conditions.

---

14. *See* Williston, *supra* n. 9, at vol. 13, §39.17; *Restatement (Second) of Contracts* §225(1).

Version 1

Article 8 — Conditions to the Buyer's Obligations

The Buyer is obligated to consummate the transactions that this Agreement contemplates only if each of the following conditions has been satisfied or waived on or before the Closing Date.

8.1 Seller's Representations and Warranties. The representations and warranties of the Seller set forth in this Agreement

(a) *must have been* true on the date this Agreement was executed and delivered; and

(b) *must be* true on and as of the Closing Date with the same force and effect as though made on and as of the Closing Date, except as affected by transactions that this Agreement contemplates.

8.2 Seller's Covenants. The Seller *must have performed* all of its covenants contained in this Agreement to be performed by it on or before the Closing Date.

8.3 Seller's Closing Certificate. The Buyer *must have received* a certificate of the Seller, executed on behalf of the Seller by the President or any Vice President of the Seller, dated the Closing Date, reasonably satisfactory to the Buyer's counsel, certifying the satisfaction of the conditions in Section 8.1 and Section 8.2.

8.4 Seller's Trademark and Patent Counsel's Opinion. The Seller's trademark and patent counsel must have delivered to the Buyer an opinion, dated the Closing Date, reasonably satisfactory to the Buyer's counsel.

8.5 The Manufacturing Facility. The Manufacturing Facility *must have been* demolished and all debris removed.

Version 2

Article 8 — Conditions to the Buyer's Obligations

The Buyer is obligated to consummate the transactions that this Agreement contemplates only if each of the following conditions has been satisfied or waived on or before the Closing Date.

8.1 Seller's Representations and Warranties. The representations and warranties of the Seller set forth in this Agreement

(a) *shall have been* true on the date this Agreement was executed and delivered; and

(b) *shall be* true on and as of the Closing Date with the same force and effect as though made on and as of the Closing Date, except as affected by transactions that this Agreement contemplates.

8.2 Seller's Covenants. The Seller *shall have performed* all of its covenants contained in this Agreement to be performed by it on or before the Closing Date.

8.3 Seller's Closing Certificate. The Buyer *shall have received* a certificate of the Seller, executed on behalf of the Seller by the President or any Vice President of the Seller, dated the Closing Date, reasonably satisfactory to the Buyer's counsel, certifying the satisfaction of the conditions in Section 8.1 and Section 8.2.

8.4 Seller's Trademark and Patent Counsel's Opinion. The Seller's trademark and patent counsel *shall have* delivered to the Buyer an opinion, dated the Closing Date, reasonably satisfactory to the Buyer's counsel.

8.5 The Manufacturing Facility. The Manufacturing Facility *shall have* been demolished and all debris removed.

In the preceding examples, the introductory language specifies the Closing Date as the date by which all of the conditions must have been satisfied. This specificity eliminates the need to include a deadline in each condition, but it presupposes that all of the conditions must be satisfied by the same date. If one or more of the conditions has its own deadline, then the introductory language must be general and the individual conditions specific.

Article 8 — Conditions to the Buyer's Obligations

The Buyer is obligated to consummate the transactions that this Agreement contemplates only if each of the following conditions has been satisfied or waived.

[*Sections 8.1 and 8.2 intentionally omitted*.]

8.3 Seller's Closing Certificate. The Buyer shall have received *on the Closing Date* a certificate of the Seller, executed on behalf of the Seller by the President or any Vice President of the Seller, dated the Closing Date, reasonably satisfactory to the Buyer's counsel, certifying to the satisfaction of the conditions in Section 8.1 and Section 8.2.

[*Section 8.4 intentionally omitted*.]

8.5 The Manufacturing Facility. The Manufacturing Facility must have been demolished and all debris removed *on or before the Closing Date*.

8.6 Shareholder Approval. The Seller's shareholders must have authorized the sale that this Agreement contemplates *no later than December 23, 20XX*.

Note that all three versions of Section 8.5 use the passive voice rather than the active. The passive voice is correct because the focus of the condition is not on who must do the demolishing (the actor), but rather on the fact that the Manufacturing Facility must have been demolished (the action). The promisor is willing to be responsible for a specific result but does not want to be obligated to perform the act causing the result.[15] This use of the passive parallels the use of the passive in representations and warranties.[16]

11.4.2 CONTRACTUAL CONSEQUENCES OF A FAILED CONDITION

When drafting conditions in a conditions article, omit from that article the contractual consequences of failing to satisfy a specific condition. The language introducing the conditions already provides that a party is obligated to perform only if all of the conditions are satisfied or waived. Put all consequences relating to the failure to satisfy a condition in the endgame provisions.[17]

11.4.3 RELATIONSHIP BETWEEN COVENANTS AND CONDITIONS IN AN ACQUISITION AGREEMENT[18]

In acquisition agreements, a common condition to the buyer's obligation to close is that the seller must have performed all of its covenants to be performed on or before the closing.[19] But not every condition in an acquisition agreement is tied into a covenant. Sellers often try to limit their risk by insisting that certain matters be handled with just a condition, not a condition and a covenant. For example, delivery of an opinion letter from the seller's lawyers is generally a condition to a buyer's obligation to close. A seller is generally willing to risk the buyer's refusal to close if the seller's lawyers refuse to deliver their opinion. If that happens, the seller's risk is probably limited to its transaction costs. But if the seller also *promises* that its lawyers will deliver their opinion letter, the seller's risk substantially increases. Then, the lawyers' failure to deliver their opinion puts the seller in breach, making it liable for damages to the buyer.

11.4.4 IN AN ACQUISITION AGREEMENT, WHOSE CONDITION SHOULD IT BE?

Parties also negotiate whether a condition should be a condition to only one party's obligation to close or to both parties' obligations to close. For example, if a private equity firm is buying the assets of the seller, it may well want to have a signed employment contract with the seller's key executive to be a condition to its obligation to close. That condition should, however, be a condition only to the buyer's obligation to close because the executive's signed contract benefits the buyer exclusively. The seller should not be able to walk away and end the deal if the buyer is willing to waive the failure of the condition. In contrast, receipt of a governmental consent may well be a condition to each party's obligation to close as neither party would want to close in violation of law.

---

15. Chapter 10, Guideline 11.

16. See § 9.3.2.

17. See Chapter 15.

18. For a detailed discussion of conditions in an acquisition agreement, *see* Lou Kling & Eileen Nugent, *Negotiated Acquisitions of Companies, Subsidiaries and Divisions* ch. 14 (Law Journal Press 1992).

19. *See id.* at § 4.02[3], which further discusses this relationship. *See generally id.* at § 14.02[7]. Acquisition agreements generally also provide that as a condition to the buyer's obligation to perform, all of the representations and warranties must have been true on the signing date and must be true on the closing date. This condition often provides an exception for any change in facts that the parties anticipate. *See generally id.* at § 14.02.

CHAPTER ELEVEN

EXERCISES

Exercise 11-1

Tom Payne and Georgia Washington are negotiating their prenuptial agreement. Tom has agreed to pay Georgia $100,000 if they divorce before they have been married five years. They have agreed, however, that Tom is not obligated to pay Georgia if the couple divorces because Georgia wants to marry someone else.

Draft the provision.

Exercise 11-2

Ralph LP owns all rights in the cartoon character Ralph—a short, frumpy, bespectacled, eight-year-old for whom life never goes quite right. Ralph LP has agreed to indemnify its licensee, Merchandisers, Inc., if a third party claims that Merchandisers, Inc., is violating that party's trademark in Ralph. Ralph LP insists that it will be liable, however, only if it receives notice from Merchandisers, Inc. no later than ten business days after it receives notice of the claim.

Draft this provision.

Exercise 11-3

Draft the following sentence as a condition, using an *if/then* formulation.

The Law Firm will not allow Alan Associate to work on client matters until he has been sworn in as an attorney before the Ohio bar.

Exercise 11-4

Part 1

Redraft the following sentence to correct the drafting errors:

Expense Reimbursement. The Company is willing to reimburse the Executive's business expenses in accordance with the Company's regular payroll practices in the instances that the Executive shall have submitted appropriate receipts no later than five business days after the last day of the month in which the Executive shall have incurred them.

_____

_____

_____

Part 2

Redraft your redraft using the language that follows as the beginning of the first sentence.

Expense Reimbursement. To be reimbursed for business expenses that the Executive incurs, _____

_____

_____

Exercise 11-5

Mark up the following provision so that it includes a condition.

Notices. All notices to be effective shall be sent by nationally recognized overnight courier and will be effective when they are received.

Exercise 11-6

Barbara Rodriguez has hired Carl Contractor to build the addition to her house. Contractor insists that he won't start work on the house until Rodriguez receives the Housing Department's approval. Draft the provision.

_____

_____

_____

Discretionary Authority and Declarations

12.1 DISCRETIONARY AUTHORITY

12.1.1 DRAFTING THE SUBSTANCE OF A DISCRETIONARY AUTHORITY PROVISION

A provision grants discretionary authority if it gives a party a choice or the permission or authorization to do something. Occasionally, the exercise of discretionary authority is subject to the satisfaction of a condition.

When drafting a provision that grants discretionary authority, consider how broad or narrow the grant should be. It is an allocation of risk. If your client will be exercising the discretionary authority, then draft the grant as broadly as possible; that is, to give the client as much discretionary authority as possible. (Reduces risk because of the expansive latitude the party will have to act.) Also, draft broadly any condition to the exercise of discretionary authority, so that it can be easily satisfied. (Reduces risk by facilitating the exercise of discretionary authority when desired.) If the other party will be exercising the discretionary authority, narrow the grant as much as possible. (Reduces the risk that your client will be subject to the other party's discretionary authority.) In addition, draft any condition to the exercise of the discretionary authority so that it applies only in the most limited circumstances. (Reduces the risk of what may happen when discretionary authority is exercised.)

When drafting a grant of discretionary authority, you must determine whether to provide for

- an unfettered grant of discretionary authority [Version 1], or
- a grant that constrains discretion by requiring that a party be reasonable in the exercise of its discretion [Version 2].

Version 1

Anti-assignment. The Tenant shall not assign its rights under this Lease, without the prior written consent of the Landlord, and the Landlord may give or withhold that consent in its sole discretion. *(Unfettered grant of discretion.)*

> **Version 2**
>
> **Anti-assignment**. The Tenant shall not assign its rights under this Lease, without the prior written consent of the Landlord, and the Landlord shall not unreasonably withhold that consent. *(Exercise of discretion subject to reasonableness standard.)*

In some jurisdictions, courts hold that public policy considerations override an unlimited grant of discretionary authority. These courts have concluded that such grants must be exercised in good faith in order to effect the parties' intent.[1] The courts reach these decisions relying on the implied covenant of good faith and fair dealing.

12.1.2   SIGNALING DISCRETIONARY AUTHORITY

Use *may* to signal a grant of discretionary authority[2] rather than *is entitled to, has the right to,* or *is permitted.* An entitlement and a right technically are the flip side of a covenant, so using language associated with a covenant only muddies the drafting. Moreover, the alternatives are just a long way of saying *may.*[3]

> **Example 1**
>
> **Events of Default**. If an Event of Default occurs and is continuing, the Bank *may* waive the Event of Default or exercise its remedies. *(Choice.)*
>
> **Example 2**
>
> **Capital Expenditures**. The Borrower shall not make any capital expenditures, except that it *may* make capital expenditures in connection with the Bridge Project. *(Permission/authorization.)*

Although most provisions use *may* to signal a grant of discretionary authority, sometimes a provision only implies that grant, as in the following anti-assignment provision:

> **Anti-assignment**. The Tenant shall not assign its rights under this Lease, without the prior written consent of the Landlord.

---

1. *See e.g. White Stone Partners, LP v. Piper Jaffray Cos., Inc.*, 978 F. Supp. 878, 882 (D. Minn. 1997).

2. *See In re Oneida Ltd.*, 400 B.R. 384, 391 (Bankr. S.D.N.Y. 2009); *Burgess Mining & Constr. Corp. v. City of Bessemer*, 312 So. 2d 24, 28 (Ala. 1975); *McMaster v. McIlory Bank*, 654 S.W.2d 591, 594 (Ark. App. 1983). *See also N.W. Traveling Men's Ass'n v. Crawford*, 1906 WL 1865 (Ill. App. 1 Dist.) ("'May' does not mean 'shall,' and is not so construed in private contracts. It is only in the case of statutes by which public rights are involved that this construction is sometimes adopted *ex debito justiticœ*."); *but see Carleno Coal Sales, Inc. v. Ramsay Coal Co.*, 270 P.2d 755, 756 (Colo. 1954) (en banc) (construing the clause "[T]he party not at fault *may* give to the defaulting party 60 days written notice [of termination]." (emphasis in the original)). The drafting error in this clause is that *may* was intended to give the party not at fault discretionary authority to give a notice of termination, but the 60 days was intended to be mandatory. The ambiguity arose because the two matters were merged into one sentence.

3. *See e.g. Kattas v. Sherman*, 32 A.D.2d 496, 498 (N.Y. 2d Dept. 2006) (quoting the following contract language: "[S]hould said Certificate of Occupancy not be able to issue as a matter of right, then and in that event, either party shall be entitled to cancel this Contract . . .") (emphasis in opinion omitted).

Here the Landlord's right to consent implies a grant of discretionary authority to decide whether it will permit the assignment.

Occasionally, using *may* alone does not properly express the parties' intent. Assume that a retailer and a manufacturer agree that the latter will manufacture a product in one of two colors, with the manufacturer to decide which color. Look at the proposed provision.

> **Wrong**
>
> **Color of the Product**. The Manufacturer may manufacture the Product in green or blue.

This provision does not say what it means: that the Manufacturer is obligated to make the Product in one of the two colors, but it may choose between the two. As drafted, the provision does not prohibit the Manufacturer from making the Product in colors other than green or blue. In similar situations, courts have refused to interpret a provision as if the word *only* had been included in the sentence.[4] Inserting *only* does not fix the problem.

> **Wrong**
>
> **Color of the Product**. The Manufacturer may manufacture the Product *only* in green or blue.

Now the provision limits the colors, but it still does not obligate the Manufacturer to make the Product in green or blue. Using *shall* does not work either, as can be seen in the following provision. Now, although the Manufacturer is obligated to manufacture the Product, the provision does not state who has the discretionary authority to determine the Product's color.

> **Wrong**
>
> **Color of the Product**. The Manufacturer shall manufacture the Product in green or blue.

Curing this drafting problem is actually simple. The provision should say what it means.

> **Correct**
>
> **Color of the Product**. The Manufacturer shall manufacture the Product in green or blue and may choose which color.

When drafting a provision of discretionary authority that gives a party permission, consider whether the exercise of that permission acts as a condition to the performance of the other party. If so, the correlative obligation must be drafted. For example, consider the following provision:

---

4. *See Pravin Banker Assocs., Ltd. v. Banco Popular Del Peru*, 109 F.3d 850, 856 (2d Cir. 1997).

> **Nonselling Stockholder Purchases**. On receipt of a Sales Notice, each Nonselling Stockholder may purchase from the Selling Stockholder the number of Shares equal to [insert formula] by delivering a Purchase Notice to the Selling Stockholder.

This provision gives a Nonselling Stockholder permission (discretionary authority) to purchase Shares, which permission it may or may not exercise. If it does exercise its discretionary authority (as to some or all of the Shares), the Selling Stockholder is then obligated to sell the number of Shares that the Nonselling Stockholder wants to purchase. The key here is that one party having discretionary authority is not the same as the other party having an obligation to perform. The contract must include a specific covenant obligating the other party to perform.

Drafters should know that a provision granting discretionary authority to do something does not prohibit a party from doing anything else. For example, here is language that resulted in litigation.

> **Assignment and Delegation**. The Bank may assign all or any part of its rights in the Loan to any Qualified Bank Transferee.[5]

The court interpreted this as explicit permission to assign to Qualified Bank Transferees, but not to the exclusion of other transferees. The grant of permission to assign did not imply a prohibition on other assignments.

This provision could have been fixed in two ways.

> **Version 1**
>
> **Assignment and Delegation**. The Bank may assign all or any part of its rights in the Loan *but only* to a Qualified Bank Transferee.
>
> **Version 2**
>
> **Assignment and Delegation**. The Bank shall not assign all or any part of its rights in the Loan to any Person, except to a Qualified Bank Transferee.

Version 2 is preferable because it creates a duty for the Bank not to assign. Therefore, any assignment in contravention of the provision would be a breach entitling the borrower to damages.

Lawyers sometimes negotiate whether an equitable remedy can or should be drafted as a right rather than discretionary authority.[6]

> **Version 1**
>
> **Equitable Relief**. If the Executive breaches her duty of confidentiality, the Company *may* seek equitable relief.

---

5. Tina L. Stark, *Assignment and Delegation*, in *Negotiating and Drafting Contract Boilerplate* ch.3, 71-72 (Stark et al. eds., ALM Publg. 2003); *see Pravin Banker Assocs., Ltd. v. Banco Popular Del Peru*, 109 F.3d 850, 856 (2d Cir. 1997). The provision is from the case. It could be more concisely drafted.

6. See § 12.1.2.

Here *may* is being used in the sense of permission. Restating the provision: *The Company has the Executive's permission to seek equitable relief.* Many parties in the Company's position would be quite unhappy with this provision in that it states no more than a Truism: the Company can go into court to seek a temporary injunction or it cannot seek one. From a business perspective, the Company wants more from this endgame provision. It wants an acknowledgement that if it goes into court, the Executive agrees that the court should award equitable relief. In essence, the Company wants a liquidated damages provision that's about equitable relief rather than money. To provide the Company with this remedy, the drafter should change the provision from one of discretionary authority/permission to one of right. In that case, the Company would have the right to equitable relief and the Executive the obligation not to interfere with that right.

Version 2

Equitable Relief. If the Executive breaches her duty of confidentiality, the Company *has the right* to equitable relief.

The enforceability of the equitable relief provision is questionable. As a general matter, parties cannot change the standard for equitable relief by an agreement: damages must be inadequate.[7] In accordance with this rule, many courts have held that a contractual provision for equitable relief does not bind a court. Nonetheless, some cases suggest that such a provision may influence a court's decision. If the parties include a right to equitable relief, stating facts in the agreement that justify this relief may be helpful.[8]

This issue also arises in endgame provisions outside the context of equitable relief.

Version 1

Deposit. The Landlord *may* keep the entire Deposit if the Tenant remains in possession after the Term.

Technically, the provision could be read as a condition to discretionary authority and the related discretionary authority. Under the stated circumstances, the Landlord has the Tenant's permission to keep the Deposit, but the discretionary authority to return it. But both parties would probably agree that the previous sentence inaccurately memorializes their intent and agreement. Somewhat reasonably, the Landlord would argue that, in reality, there is no choice involved in this remedy because no reasonable business person would give away money. Therefore, the proper way to describe the Landlord's legal relationship with the Deposit is that the Landlord has a right to the Deposit that cannot be abrogated. That is, the Tenant would have the flip-side obligation not to seek the return of the Deposit. Some lawyers might disagree with this drafting decision. This author's bottom line is that discretionary authority mischaracterizes the intent of this business deal and that we as drafters must respond to our clients' needs. This provision should be drafted as a right.

---

7. *Restatement (Second) of Contracts* § 359 cmt. a (1981).

8. For an excellent discussion of this issue and case citations, *see* Edward Yorio, *Contract Enforcement: Specific Performance and Injunctions* §§ 19.2-19.3 (Aspen Law & Business 1989).

> **Version 2**
>
> **Deposit.** The Landlord *has the right to* keep the entire Deposit if the Tenant remains in possession after the Term.

12.1.3   CONDITIONS TO DISCRETIONARY AUTHORITY

A party's exercise of discretionary authority may be subject to the satisfaction of one or more conditions. Drafters often establish the relationship between a condition and the exercise of discretionary authority by using an *if/then* formulation. Draft the *if* clause in the present tense.

> **Example 1**
>
> **Sales to Other Persons.** If the Manufacturer *builds* more than 500 units of the Product in any month, the Manufacturer may sell the units in excess of 500 to a Person other than the Retailer. *(Permission.)*
>
> **Example 2**
>
> **Publication of Paperback Edition.** If the Book *earns* net sales in excess of $30 million, the Publisher *may* publish the paperback edition of the Book at any time afterwards. *(Permission.)*

12.1.4   DISCRETIONARY AUTHORITY POSING AS A DECLARATION

In the same way that covenants can pose as declarations, a grant of discretionary authority can pose as a declaration.

> **Wrong**
>
> **Counterparts.** Execution of this Agreement in counterparts is permissible. *(Posing as a declaration.)*
>
> **Correct**
>
> **Counterparts.** The parties may execute this Agreement in counterparts. *(Permission to execute in counterparts and the choice whether to execute in counterparts.)*

12.2   DECLARATIONS

Draft declarations in the present tense, as these provisions have continuing effect throughout a contract's life.[9] If drafted this way, a declaration always applies to the

---

9. As stated by Reed Dickerson, "[A provision should speak] as of the time it is being read, not merely as of the time it took effect." F. Reed Dickerson, *The Fundamentals of Legal Drafting* 185 (2d ed., Little, Brown & Co. 1986).

current situation, no matter when it occurs during the life of the contract and the transaction.

Example 1

Governing Law. The laws of Idaho govern all matters, including torts, arising under or relating to this Agreement.

Example 2

Salary. The Executive's salary is at the rate of $3,000 per week.

Example 3

Merger. This Agreement is the parties' complete and exclusive agreement on the matters contained in this Agreement.

Example 4

Termination. This Agreement terminates on the date that is the later of the date that the Lender releases the Collateral and the date the Lender returns to the Borrower its Note marked "Paid."

Some declarations have substantive consequences only if a condition is satisfied. In the following provision, the full second sentence is the policy (even though it begins with a condition), but it applies only if the condition in that sentence is satisfied. Both the condition and the declaration should be drafted in the present tense.

Anti-assignment. Neither party may assign its rights under this Agreement. If either party purports to assign its rights under this Agreement, that purported assignment is void.

CHAPTER TWELVE

EXERCISES

Exercise 12-1

Mark up the following provisions to correct the drafting errors:

Alterations. The Tenant shall be permitted to alter the Premises if the Tenant shall have submitted its architectural plans to the Landlord at least 60 days before it wants to begin construction.

Termination. If the Retailer shall fail to pay the Manufacturer when Payment is due, the Manufacturer shall be entitled to terminate this Agreement.

Withdrawal from LP. No limited partner shall have right to withdraw from the LP without the previous written consent of all the other partners.

Will and Shall

13.1 INTRODUCTION

This chapter discusses when to use *shall* and when to use *will*. It also gives you a nongrammatical framework for testing whether you are using *shall* properly.

The basic rules are simple: Use *shall* to indicate a covenant and *will* to indicate the future. If you do that, you will create a bright-line distinction in meaning between the two words. If you do not follow this rule, you will eventually draft an ambiguous provision. The only exception is a covenant with a negative subject. Then, you should use *may*.

13.2 WHEN TO USE *WILL*

Although you should not use *will* in representations or to signal a covenant, you may use it in limited circumstances.

1. *Use* will *if a provision states a party's opinion, determination, or belief about the future.*

> **Amendments**. As a condition to the effectiveness of each amendment, each party must obtain the authorization of
>
> (a) its Board of Directors and
> (b) its stockholders
>
> if, in the judgment of that party's Board of Directors, the amendment *will* have a material adverse effect on the benefits intended under this Agreement to that party and its stockholders.

This rule makes sense when viewed in the context of the rule that representations cannot be in the future because they would be opinions. Here, in a condition, an opinion about the future is called for and it is appropriately used.

2. *Use* will *when the provision states that a party or a nonparty (Person A) will take action in the future and Person A is not the contract party promising to perform a covenant or to whom discretionary authority has been granted.*

Example 1

Subcontractor for Painting. The Contractor shall use its commercially reasonable efforts to find a subcontractor who *will* paint the House for less than $5,000.

In Example 1, the Contractor, a party, promises to find a subcontractor (Person A) who *will do* something in the future (*paint the house*). *Shall* is an incorrect signal to follow the subcontractor because this is not the provision that obligates the subcontractor to paint the house for less than $5,000.

Example 2

Choice of Color. The Owner may choose the color that the Contractor will paint the House.

Example 2 involves both signatories, but the provision's primary purpose is to describe the Owner's discretionary authority, which is choosing the paint color that the subcontractor (Person A) will use in the future. *Shall* is not the correct signal to follow Contractor. That part of the provision is not a promise by the Contractor to paint the House the chosen color. That requires a separate covenant.[1]

3. *Use* will *if a provision contrasts the present with the future or the past with the future.*

Right to Deposit on Termination. When the Lease terminates, the Landlord has the right to retain the Deposit to pay for expenses that it has incurred or will incur to repair the Tenant's damage to the Premises. The Landlord shall return any retained proceeds that it does not use no later than three days after repairing the damage.

---

4. *Use* will *if a provision warrants future performance of a good or a future state of facts.*

Warranty. The Manufacturer warrants to the Retailer [and the eventual consumer] that the Product as packaged and shipped from the Manufacturer's plant *will be free* from defects in material and workmanship and *will function and perform* in accordance with Manufacturer's specifications for a period of one year from the date of retail purchase.

In this provision, the manufacturer promises that if a state of facts does not exist in the future, then it is responsible as described in the warranty's other provisions.

---

1. See § 12.1.2, which describes how the exercise of discretionary authority can be a condition to an obligation.

Shall would be incorrect in this provision because the Product is not promising anything about its future performance.

13.3 WHEN TO USE *SHALL* AND TESTING WHETHER *SHALL* IS CORRECT

As discussed in Section 10.2, you should use *shall* only to signal an obligation. But drafters incorrectly use *shall* so frequently that they think they are using it correctly, even when they are not. Although you could rely on grammatical tests to confirm whether you are using *shall* correctly, this section provides easy, nongrammatical rules to help you. To ensure that you correctly apply these rules, use your word-processing program to find each instance of *shall*.

Here are the rules:

Rule 1

If a party does not precede the word shall, then shall is wrong. Different corrections are appropriate depending on the parties' intent and the sentence's construction. Specifically, you must determine whether the parties intended the sentence to be

- a covenant (as in Example 1);
- a statement of discretionary authority or permission (as in Example 2);
- a present tense declaration (as in Example 3);
- a provision purporting to bind a nonparty (as in Example 4); or
- a condition (as in Example 5).

Example 1

Wrong

Maintenance of the Premises. The outside of the Premises shall be maintained by the Landlord, and the inside of the Premises shall be maintained by the Tenant.

Correct

Maintenance of the Premises. The Landlord shall maintain the outside of the Premises, and the Tenant shall maintain the inside of the Premises.

With the change, the provision is now in the active voice, rather than the passive voice.

Example 2

Wrong

Forum. An action shall be permitted to be filed to enforce this Agreement in the Supreme Court of the State of New York.

Correct

Forum. A party may file and maintain an action to enforce this Agreement in the Supreme Court of the State of New York.

With the change, the provision is now in the active voice and uses the correct verb (may) to signal permission.

Example 3

Wrong

> **Governing Law**. This Agreement shall be governed by the laws of Nebraska, without regard to its conflict of laws principles.

Correct

> **Governing Law**. Without regard to Nebraska's conflict of laws principles, its laws govern all matters arising under or relating to this Agreement, including torts.

With the change, the provision becomes a declaration stated in the present tense. It also makes substantive changes to broaden the coverage of the provision.[2]

Example 4

Wrong

> **Arbitration**. The arbitrators shall render a decision promptly.

Correct

Version 1

> **Arbitration**. The parties shall instruct the arbitrators to render a decision promptly.

Version 2

> **Arbitration**. The arbitrators are to render a decision promptly.

With the change, the first revision properly requires the parties to perform, rather than the arbitrators, who, as nonparties, cannot be bound. The second revision restates the provision as a declaration.

Example 5

Wrong

> **Notice**. The Event Notice shall be given to the Insurance Company no later than ten days after the Insured Event.

Correct

> **Notice**. The Insured must give the Event Notice to the Insurance Company no later than ten days after the Insured Event.

---

2. See § 16.4.

With the change, the provision unambiguously states that the giving of the Event Notice is a condition to the Insurance Company's performance.

Rule 2

If a party precedes the word shall, shall *is usually correct, but there are at least three exceptions.*

First, the use of *shall* is wrong if a party precedes *shall* and *shall* is coupled with a form of the verb *to have*.[3] Different corrections are appropriate depending on the intent and construction of the sentence. For example, if the parties intended to create a condition, replace *shall* with *must*.

> **Wrong**
>
> **Consent**. The Seller shall have obtained the Landlord's consent.[4]

> **Correct**
>
> **Consent**. The Seller must have obtained the Landlord's consent.

Alternatively, if the parties intended the sentence to be a statement of discretionary authority, replace *shall* with *may*.

> **Wrong**
>
> **Termination**. The Publisher *shall have the right* to terminate this Agreement if the Author does not complete the Work by the Deadline.

> **Correct**
>
> **Termination**. The Publisher *may* terminate this Agreement if the Author does not complete the Work by the Deadline.

Second, the use of *shall* is wrong if a party precedes *shall* and *shall* is coupled with a form of the verb *to be*.[5] Delete *shall* and change the verb *to be* to its present tense form.

> **Wrong**
>
> **Suspension of Performance**. If a *Force Majeure* Event occurs and is continuing, the Affected Party shall be excused from the performance to the extent prevented from performing.

> **Correct**
>
> **Suspension of Performance**. If a *Force Majeure* Event occurs and is continuing, the Affected Party is excused from the performance to the extent prevented from performing.

---

3. Technically, *to have* as used in this way is an **auxiliary verb**, also known as a **helping verb**.

4. This provision's drafting reflects the way drafters typically craft a condition in an acquisition agreement. See §11.3.2.

5. *To be* when used in this way is also an auxiliary verb. See n. 3.

Once redrafted, you can see that the provision is a condition to a declaration and the declaration. (The full sentence is the policy, but that policy applies only if the condition is satisfied.)

Third, the use of *shall* is wrong if a party precedes *shall* in a clause that establishes a condition or other circumstances under which an event may occur. Clue words and phrases that begin these clauses include *when, if, in the event of, provided,* and *that.* These clauses are properly drafted in the present tense so that the clause reads as presently applying whenever the circumstances occur.

Wrong

Late Payment. If the Borrower shall fail to pay interest when due, the Bank may declare the Borrower to be in default.

Correct

Late Payment. If the Borrower fails to pay interest when due, the Bank may declare the Borrower to be in default.

Wrong

Deposit of Funds. The Bank shall deposit the funds to any account that the Borrower shall designate in a written notice.

Correct

Deposit of Funds. The Bank shall deposit the funds to any account that the Borrower designates in a written notice. *(Here, the designation of the account is a condition to the Bank's obligation to deposit the funds.)*

Finally, do not consider these three exceptions the only exceptions. Contracts are nuanced. See Example 2 on page 182 for an exception that does not fall within any of the three stated exceptions. Always test each use of *shall* by asking whether a party is promising to do or not to do something. If no party is making a promise, the use of *shall* is incorrect.

The chart that follows summarizes the tests in this section.

If a Party Does Not Precede **Shall**	*If a Party Precedes* **Shall**
Shall is always wrong.	*Shall* is generally correct, but at least three exceptions exist.
	1. If *shall* is coupled with the verb *to be*, *shall* is wrong.
	2. If *shall* is coupled with the verb *to have*, *shall* is wrong.
	3. If *shall* is in a clause that establishes a condition, *shall* is wrong (clue words: *when, if, as, in the event of, that, and provided*).

Drafting the Contract Concepts — A Summary Chart

The following chart summarizes the material in Chapters 9 through 13. Reading it does not replace reading the chapters. Use it as a handy, quick reference tool.

Contract Concept	Drafting Considerations
Representations and Warranties—Chapter 9	■ If representing the maker, draft the representations and warranties narrowly, and qualify them as much as possible. ■ If representing the recipient, draft the representations and warranties broadly and with as few qualifications as possible. ■ Representations and warranties may deal with past or the present facts, but not with future "facts." ■ Draft in the active voice, unless the focus is on the action rather than the actor. Then, use the passive voice.
Covenants—Chapter 10	■ Determine the appropriate degree of obligation, using qualifiers as appropriate. ■ Use the *who, what, when, where, why, how,* and *how much* tests to help determine a provision's substance. ■ Use *shall* to signal a covenant, except if the sentence has a negative subject. Then use *may.*

Conditions to an Obligation—Chapter 11	■ If your client must satisfy the condition, draft it so that the client can satisfy it easily. If the other party must satisfy the condition, consider how difficult it should be in the context of the transaction.
	■ Outside a conditions article,
	  ➢ use *must* and include an interpretive provision; or
	  ➢ state that a provision is a condition;
	  ➢ state the consequences of the failure to satisfy the condition;
	  ➢ use some combination of these methods.
	■ Inside a conditions article, use *must* with another verb in one of three ways:
	  ➢ *must + be,* to indicate a fact that must exist on the closing date.
	  ➢ *must + have +* the *past tense of a verb,* to indicate something that must have happened after the signing date but no later than the closing date.

continued on next page >

Contract Concept	Drafting Considerations
	➤ *must have been* + the *past tense of a verb*, this is the passive version of the preceding use of *must* and should be used when the issue is the action, not the actor. ■ Real-world note: Most firms continue to use *shall* instead of *must* within conditions articles.
Discretionary Authority — Chapter 12	■ Consider how broad or narrow the grant of discretionary authority should be and to what degree it will be fettered. Will your client have the discretionary authority (a broad grant) or will the other party have the discretionary authority (a narrow grant)? ■ Use *may* to signal discretionary authority. ■ If a party may exercise discretionary authority only on the satisfaction of a condition, consider how difficult it should be to satisfy it. Again, consider whether it is your client or the other party who must satisfy the condition.
Declarations — Chapter 12	■ Draft declarations in the present tense. Any condition to a declaration should also be drafted in the present tense.
Proper Use of *Shall* — Chapter 13	■ If a party does not precede *shall*, *shall* is always wrong. ■ If a party precedes *shall*, *shall* is generally correct with three exceptions: ➤ If *shall* is coupled with the verb *to be*, *shall* is wrong. ➤ If *shall* is coupled with the verb *to have*, *shall* is wrong. ➤ If *shall* is in a clause that establishes a condition or other circumstance, *shall* is wrong (clue words: *when, if, as, in the event of, that, and provided*).
Proper Use of *Will* — Chapter 13	Use *will* in the following circumstances: ■ If a provision states a party's opinion, determination, or belief about the future. ■ When a provision states that a party or a nonparty ("Person A") will take action in the future and Person A is not the contract party promising to perform a covenant or to whom discretionary authority has been granted. ■ If a provision contrasts the present with the future or the past with the future. ■ If a provision warrants future performance of a good or a future state of facts.

CHAPTER FOURTEEN

EXERCISES

Exercise 14-1

Polly Producer is the producer of an off, off, off-Broadway musical, *Passing the Bar*. It will run from August 1 through September 30 and will be presented at the Williston Theater. She would like you to draft the business terms of an agreement with Serious Scenery, Inc., the owner of the scenery she would like to rent. Each numbered paragraph should be a new section. Use the following defined terms, as necessary: Owner, Producer, Scenery, Theater, and Musical. If you need additional defined terms and definitions, you may draft them. The business terms are listed below. Use only the information in this paragraph and provided in the business terms.

1. Serious Scenery is to deliver the scenery on July 1, 20X5.

2. Polly must, of course, return the scenery. She would like not to have to do that until three days after the run concludes.

3. The scenery can be used only in connection with *Passing the Bar* at the specific theater discussed.

4. The scenery is not to be altered or added to, although it is okay to make minor repairs and adjustments.

5. Polly must make sure that the scenery is insured at her expense for all loss or damage.

6. Serious Scenery is willing to give assurances that it owns the scenery and has the right to rent it.

Exercise 14-2

Mark up the following provisions so that they use the proper verb forms. Make any other appropriate changes.

Effects of Termination. If the transactions that this Agreement contemplates shall not have

been consummated on or before July 18, 20XX, this Agreement shall terminate on July 18, 20XX,

and thereafter, neither party shall have any rights or obligations under it, and Buyer will continue to

perform all of its obligations under the Confidentiality Agreement.

Publicity. The parties agree that no publicity release or announcement concerning the transac-

tions contemplated hereby shall be issued by any party without the advance consent of the other, except as such release or announcement may be required by law, in which case the party making the release or announcement shall show the release or announcement in advance to the other party.

Delays. The Contractor agrees that it shall be accountable for promptly notifying the Owner in writing of any event that may delay completion of the Building. The notice shall explain why the delay has occurred and its estimated duration.

Compliance. The Tenant must comply in all material respects with any law the violation of which could have a material adverse effect on the Landlord.

Article and Section Headings. Article and Section headings and the Table of Contents contained in this Agreement shall be for reference purposes only and shall not affect in any way the meaning or interpretation of this Agreement.

Change of Control. A change in control of the Licensee will constitute a default under this License.

Restrictions on Transfer. During the term of this Agreement, none of the Shares now owned or hereafter acquired by any of the Stockholders may be transferred unless such transfer of Shares shall be made in accordance with the provisions of this Agreement. *(This provision is from a Stockholders' Agreement.)*

Endgame Provisions

15.1 INTRODUCTION

A contract may end for a myriad of reasons, some neutral, some friendly, some unfriendly: a decision to change to a less expensive supplier, the successful conclusion of a joint venture, the end of a lease term, the consummation of a transaction, the sale of a partnership interest, the breach of an agreement, or the death of a party.

Deal lawyers find endgame provisions difficult to negotiate and draft. They are not cookie-cutter provisions. They often require significant tailoring to refine them to make them deal-appropriate. While clients may not read an entire contract, they often devote considerable time and effort (transaction costs) to these provisions. They are the go-to provisions when the parties have disputes—frequently involving money, something about which clients are acutely sensitive. Thus, these provisions can typically be sophisticated in both their conceptualization and drafting, and unfortunately, are often a source of litigation.[1]

The author prefers the term **endgame provisions** to **termination provisions**.[2] First, it echoes the argot clients often use. Second, and more importantly, endgame provisions contemplate a broader range of provisions than termination provisions. Endgame provisions include not only default, remedy, and termination provisions, but also exit strategies for the venture capitalist and provisions that tie up loose ends in successful transactions. In this book, the term also includes contractual remedy provisions that directly address a specific problem that the parties anticipated during negotiations. For example, the parties could provide a 5% decrease in purchase price for a delay in delivery. Finding these contractual solutions during the negotiation process requires, first, the imagination to conjure the problem and, second, the ingenuity

---

1. *See generally United Rentals, Inc. v. RAM Holdings, Inc.*, 937 A.2d 810 (Del. Ch. 2007) (dueling endgame provisions resulted in protracted litigation, with court finding that one of the drafters was not a forthright negotiator).

2. Some contracts distinguish between **termination** and **expiration**. Specifically, a contract terminates if it ends prematurely because a specified event occurs. In contrast, a contract expires on the last day of its term. U.C.C. §2-106 U.L.A. §2-106 (2013) distinguishes *termination* from *cancellation*. Here, termination occurs when a party ends a contract other than for breach, while cancellation occurs when a party ends a contract because of a breach. *Termination* is not used in either of its technical senses in this chapter. Instead, it refers to the end of a contract for any reason.

to craft a workable solution. These types of analysis and drafting are two of the most valuable ways that a lawyer can add value to the deal.

In general, a lawyer should consider six points when drafting endgame provisions.

1. The termination events (or the events triggering a contractual remedy).
2. The contractual consequences (both monetary and nonmonetary) of receipt of the termination notice.
3. The date the contract terminates, which may depend on the type of termination event and its contractual consequences.
4. Whether common law rights survive.
5. Whether any specific contract provisions survive.
6. Dispute resolution provisions.

This chapter first discusses the uncertainty created by the terms *notice of termination* and *termination notice.* It then turns to the business and legal issues associated with drafting the first five points in the context of neutral terminations, friendly terminations, and unfriendly terminations, as well as where to locate these provisions and how to organize them. The chapter separately discusses dispute resolution provisions. Document 6 in Chapter 32 discusses the intricacies of endgame provisions in acquisition agreements.

15.2 SOME GENERAL COMMENTS ON THE TERMS *NOTICE OF TERMINATION* AND *TERMINATION NOTICE*

The terms **notice of termination** and **termination notice** are regrettable terms that drafters regularly dragoon other drafters into using—generally because the lawyers know no viable alternatives. The terms mislead the reader and create uncertainty and ambiguity. They suggest that mere receipt of the notice terminates the contract. That is wrong. Mere receipt might terminate an agreement, but it just as easily might not. The notice might instead trigger contractual consequences that the parties must address before the agreement actually terminates. When contracts use these terms, clients and lawyers should interpret them as meaning notices that provide information regarding possible termination or the exercise of remedies, not notices that necessarily terminate an agreement. What should be the exact content and effect of these notices? The answer is not very satisfying. They should be transaction specific.[3] Were the drafting world perfect, some potential, viable alternatives for these terms could be *Termination Event Notice, Notice of Intent to Terminate, or Notice of Intent to Exercise Remedies.*

Many termination notice provisions state that all notices must be in writing. That condition may be superfluous if the agreement's general provision on notices already requires written notices. (As a matter of good drafting, the general provision on notice trumps the other provisions, eliminating the condition in any other provision that notices must be in writing.)

Because termination notices have substantial consequences, drafters should insist that they be effective only on receipt and be sent by national courier or delivered personally, so the date of receipt is undisputed. The receipt date might have contractual consequences in determining other time periods and deadlines, so certainty of receipt

---

3. See § 15.6 for some insight into how to draft unfriendly termination notices.

and knowledge of the notice have their virtues.[4] Some drafters may also be comfortable with e-mail delivery if the drafter or the client has the appropriate software to ensure security and receipt verification.

15.3 GENERAL COMMENTS ON GROUNDS FOR TERMINATION

As noted, a contract may end for multiple reasons: some neutral, some friendly, and some unfriendly. Preliminarily, a drafter must determine the grounds (the categories of events) that will bring the endgame provisions into play. If the parties dispute which category an event belongs in, their different perspectives will affect the negotiation and drafting.

15.4 NEUTRAL TERMINATIONS

15.4.1 WHAT CONSTITUTES NEUTRAL TERMINATION

Neutral terminations arise in contracts that provide the parties the ability to discontinue a relationship, absent fault of either party. For example, a grocery store could decide to end a relationship with a long-term supplier because it wants to purchase only organic vegetables from a new supplier.

> **Example 1—Excerpt from a Supply Agreement**
>
> **Termination.** The Grocer may terminate this Agreement at any time by notifying the Supplier of termination and by payment of all outstanding accounts. Termination occurs on the later to occur of the receipt of the notice of termination and receipt by the Supplier of payments sufficient to satisfy all outstanding accounts.

Alternatively, a neutral termination event would be the failure to satisfy a non-fault condition to closing an acquisition. For example, perhaps a seller cannot obtain a consent. Here the contract ends and the parties walk away without common law rights or remedies continuing—a neutral ending.

Contracts sometimes explicitly provide that the parties may agree to terminate.

> **Example 2—Excerpt from an Acquisition Agreement**
>
> **Termination by Written Agreement.** The parties may terminate this Agreement at any time by written agreement.

Often such a provision appears as part of the section that lists the grounds for termination. Under the common law, the provision is superfluous; parties may agree to terminate without it. Nonetheless, parties include these provisions to memorialize their intent and to notify third parties of that intent. These provisions are typically

---

4. Notice provisions are risk allocation provisions. If a notice were effective when sent, or a stated number of days after deposit with the U.S. Postal Service, the intended recipient could be at risk that the sender has rights against the recipient about which the recipient does not yet know.

bare bones. The future seems the appropriate time to negotiate the consequences of terminating the contract, given that the parties are agreeing that, if they agree, they can terminate the agreement in the future. If they can't agree in the future, then termination by agreement is not happening.

15.4.2 CONTRACTUAL CONSEQUENCES OF RECEIPT OF NOTICE OF TERMINATION; TERMINATION DATE

Receipt of a termination notice of a neutral termination can have contractual consequences. Example 1 in the previous section is paradigmatic. Here's the provision again.

Example 1 — Excerpt from a Supply Agreement

Termination. The Grocer may terminate this Agreement at any time by notifying the Supplier of termination and by payment of all outstanding accounts. Termination occurs on the later to occur of the receipt of the notice of termination and receipt by the Supplier of payments sufficient to satisfy all outstanding accounts. On termination, neither party has any rights or remedies against the other party.

If the Grocer were able to terminate the agreement merely by sending notice, the Supplier might need to argue for the money due it. If the contract has terminated, where is the contractual obligation to pay? The Supplier might well find a way to recover its money, but why make work for the litigators? Therefore, the receipt of the notice of termination triggers not the agreement's termination, but the Grocer's contractual obligation to pay all outstanding accounts. Termination hinges on the Grocer performing this obligation. When it does, the contract terminates.

Neutral termination scenarios may also include contractual provisions that tie up loose ends. For example, in a construction contract, the owner might need to end the project because financing has disappeared. The contractor is not at fault, but the parties must address the monetary consequences of the termination.

Example 2 — Excerpt from a Construction Agreement

Owner's Termination of Contractor Without Cause. If the Owner terminates this Agreement, except for Cause, the Owner shall pay the Contractor for all completed construction work on the Project and for all proven loss or expense in connection with the Project's construction. On the date of the Contractor's receipt of payment in full, this Agreement terminates, and neither party has any other rights or remedies against the other.

15.4.3 SURVIVAL OF COMMON LAW RIGHTS AND OBLIGATIONS AND SPECIFIED CONTRACTUAL PROVISIONS

In the two examples in Section 15.4.2, the provisions stipulated that after the agreement terminated, neither party would have any rights or obligations against the other. That's logical. By definition, the termination is without fault of a party, so neither party has any right or incentive to pursue remedies. As to the survival of specific contractual provisions, that's transaction specific. Confidentiality provisions often present themselves as candidates for survival.

15.5 FRIENDLY TERMINATIONS

15.5.1 WHAT CONSTITUTES A FRIENDLY TERMINATION

The classic, friendly termination results from the successful consummation of a transaction, completion of a project, or the conclusion of a multi-year term relationship: Parties close an acquisition, the developer completes the website, or a lease term ends.

15.5.2 TERMINATION NOTICE, CONTRACTUAL CONSEQUENCES OF RECEIPT OF TERMINATION NOTICE, AND TERMINATION DATE

Friendly terminations sometimes require a notice from one party to the other, but generally not. If a tenant has a three-year lease term, the parties know when the term ends. (No notice generally need be given unless a statute requires one or the contract provides for renewal terms.) Nonetheless, parties still need to articulate the parties' contractual obligations at the end of the term. Here, a termination notice is not the triggering event for the contractual obligations. Instead, the success of the contract triggers these obligations. And as noted before, not until those obligations are performed does the contract terminate. Therefore, although a trademark *license* may terminate at the end of a three-year term, parties may need to perform post-term obligations before the *agreement* terminates.

Once you determine what constitutes a friendly termination, you and your client must decide the contractual consequences. They usually fall into one of three categories:

- Obligations that return the parties to their *status quo* before the contract.
- Contractual performances necessary to tie up loose ends.
- Exit strategies.

Examples of obligations that return the parties to their pre-transaction *status quo* include the following:

- On payment in full of its loan, a bank's obligation to release the collateral it holds and to execute any documents necessary to reflect its release of the collateral.
- A landlord's obligation to return a security deposit (e.g., in connection with the termination of a lease).
- A tenant's obligation to return the premises to the landlord in broom-clean condition.

Contractual performances necessary to tie up loose ends include the following:

- Monetary obligations (e.g., a licensee's final, post-term payment to its licensor; an employer's obligation to reimburse an executive for travel expenses).

Common exit strategies include the following:

- Going public (a favorite of venture capitalists).
- Take-out financing (e.g., long-term lenders take over the debt of a lender that provided construction financing).
- Buyouts (e.g., shareholders purchasing another shareholder's equity interest).

15.5.3 SURVIVAL OF COMMON LAW RIGHTS AND OBLIGATIONS AND SPECIFIED CONTRACTUAL PROVISIONS

In friendly terminations, specific contract provisions often survive.

■ Noncompetition obligations (e.g., in connection with an acquisition).
■ Confidentiality obligations (e.g., in connection with a termination of employment).
■ Further assurances obligations (e.g., in connection with an acquisition).

Common law rights and obligations do not survive. The parties are not quarreling over misrepresentations or breaches of warranties or covenants, so the common law causes of action serve no function.

15.6 UNFRIENDLY TERMINATIONS

Clients do not always want to discuss or negotiate the endgame provisions that address unfriendly terminations. When negotiating the contract, they anticipate a successful working relationship. Either consciously or unconsciously, they prefer to avoid or postpone thinking about what could go wrong. As a counselor, you must ensure that your client understands the consequences of the business transaction succeeding or failing. Some clients contend that these provisions are unnecessary because the principals will work it out based on the strong personal relationship they have forged. That works until the other side's principal changes jobs. (It is, however, a legitimate negotiating perspective, one that the Japanese have long practiced.)

15.6.1 WHAT CONSTITUTES AN UNFRIENDLY TERMINATION AND DETAILS OF A TERMINATION NOTICE

15.6.1.1 What Constitutes an Unfriendly Termination

Contracts approach the listing of unfriendly events in two ways. First, the contract may merely refer to breach of the contract—a down-and-dirty approach for a contract that may not warrant significant transaction costs.

> **Example 1**
>
> **Termination.** Each party may terminate this Agreement by written notice to the other party of that party's misrepresentation, breach of warranty, or breach of covenant.[5] In that event, the parties have the rights and remedies provided at law and at equity.
>
> **Example 2**
>
> **Termination.** This Software License terminates without notice on the first day you breach its terms. The Software License's termination does not preclude the Font Owner from suing you for damages for breach of the Software License.

Alternatively, if the principals want to extend the contract's grounds for termination beyond the common law causes of action, the lawyers have significant work to do.

---

5. This provision is incomplete. It fails to address the contract termination date.

They must think through not only the consequences of a contract breach, but also what else could affect the parties' relationship.

Lawyers use the umbrella-term **breaches** to refer to misrepresentations, breaches of warranties, and breaches of covenants, the grounds for termination that are contract related. But *breaches* is a subset of the more general term **default**. A default need not be contract related. For example, death, bankruptcy, merger, change of control, and **cross-defaults** often give rise to remedies. (A *cross-default* is a default that arises under one agreement because a party is in default under another agreement.) Therefore, when reflecting on what events might entitle your client to remedies, think beyond the four corners of the contract. Consider what non-contract-related events could affect the parties sufficiently to warrant grounds for termination or a remedy. This analysis requires an understanding of business, the client's business, and the business deal.

Again, the question is, *what if*? *What if* the author wants to publish other books under a pseudonym?[6] *What if* the parent company files for bankruptcy? *What if* a natural disaster prevents delivery of time-critical construction material? *What if* a competitor wants to open a store in the same shopping mall? *What if* the play closes and two months later the producer wants to reopen in the same city but at a different theater?

As part of this *what if* exercise, think through what circumstances could frustrate your client's assumptions and expectations.[7] For example, if a pharmaceutical company hires a sales representative, it expects that the person will generate a certain sales volume. If the person does not, the client's expectations are frustrated, and the client will want the right to terminate the contract to cut its losses. This analysis requires more than looking at a specific provision and determining how it works. You must understand the "mechanics" of how the parties will work together, and what could destabilize that relationship.

Lawyers often excel at asking *what if*? Their training instills the need to test assumptions and to discover and expose risk. But the transaction costs of addressing every *what if* question are high. As a counselor you must help your client assess the *what if* questions to determine whether addressing them is worth the time and money. The answer may well depend on the risk analysis discussed in Chapter 25.[8] U.S. lawyers tend to have a penchant for addressing most issues. The proclivity stems partly from our common law system that does not have a set of rules to address common business issues, as in civil law countries.[9]

Finally, when analyzing what events should result in a termination notice, analyze whether those events should be the same for both parties. They need not be. A credit agreement is an extreme example of how termination events differ. Those agreements will have an entire article devoted to the borrower's defaults but will be silent with respect to the lender's defaults.

---

6. I confess that I've always liked the French, *nom de plume*, but it's not even close to plain English.

7. My colleague, Alan Shaw, suggested this analysis.

8. See §25.3.

9. Barbara J. Beveridge, *Legal English—How It Developed And Why It Is Not Appropriate for International Commercial Contracts*, 6 (Sept. 13-15, 2000), included in *The Development of Legal Language: Papers from an International Symposium at the University of Lapland* ("[W]e do not have general code provisions governing the matters between the parties. Because of this everything must be dealt with in the contract itself. One problem that arises from this is that the drafter must include wording which will deal with every situation and cover off every possible contingency that could happen in the future.").

15.6.1.2   Some Details of a Termination Notice

Unlike some other terminations, if a party has grounds for an unfriendly termination or for a remedy, that party must notify the party who allegedly breached the contract. To prevent ambiguity, the drafter's notice should explicitly state

- the grounds for termination and the contract provisions giving the nonbreaching party the right to send the notice of termination;
- the contract provisions triggering monetary or other contractual obligations, if any;
- details with respect to the payment of money (who, what, when, where, how, and how much);
- whether the notice terminates the agreement on receipt;
- the date the agreement terminates if either or both parties must first satisfy specific conditions to the termination;
- whether any common law rights and obligations survive termination; and
- whether specific contractual provisions survive termination.

15.6.2   CONSEQUENCES OF TERMINATION NOTICE OF AN UNFRIENDLY TERMINATION

The consequences of a receipt of a termination notice involving an unfriendly termination depend on multiple factors, including the grounds for termination and whether the contract has provided for contractual consequences—monetary or otherwise—or perhaps specific enforcement. But before addressing consequences and remedies, the parties must decide whether the contract should give the party who allegedly breached the contractual opportunity to fix the problem. In legal terms, "Should the contract include a grace period and the opportunity to cure?"

15.6.2.1   Grace Period and the Opportunity to Cure

A **grace period** is a period of time, past the time of a default's occurrence, during which the allegedly breaching party has the opportunity to **cure** the default—that is, it may do what it should have done before and thereby thwart the nondefaulting party's exercise of remedies. Generally, for the grace period to begin, the nondefaulting party notifies the allegedly defaulting party of the breach, but sometimes the cure period begins without formal notice. Of course, not all defaults can be cured. The death of a chief operating officer is usually final.

Here is a classic termination provision that provides for a cure. It is unedited from the original.[10]

> **Termination**. If either Party believes that the other Party is in material breach of this Agreement . . . , then the non-breaching Party may deliver notice of such breach to the other Party. In such notice, the non-breaching Party will identify the actions or conduct that it wishes such Party to take for an acceptable and prompt cure of such breach (or will otherwise state its good faith belief that such breach is incurable); provided, however, that such identified actions or conduct will not be binding upon the other Party with respect to the actions that it may need to take to cure such breach. If the breach is curable, the allegedly breaching Party will have ninety (90) days to either cure such breach (except to the extent such breach involves the failure to make

---

10. Sec. Exch. Comm'n, *License and Co-Development Agreement by and between Genzyme Corporation and Isis Pharmaceuticals, Inc.*, http://www.sec.gov/Archives/edgar/data/732485/000104746908009073/a2186974zex-10_7.htm (accessed Aug. 8, 2013).

> a payment when due, which breach must be cured within thirty (30) days following such notice) or, if a cure cannot be reasonably effected within such ninety (90) day period, to deliver to the non-breaching Party a plan for curing such breach which is reasonably sufficient to effect a cure within a reasonable period. If the breaching Party fails to (a) cure such breach within the ninety (90) day or thirty (30) day period, as applicable, or (b) use Commercially Reasonable Efforts to carry out the plan and cure the breach, the non-breaching Party may terminate this Agreement by providing written notice to the breaching Party.

Credit agreements often permit a borrower a **grace period** during which the borrower can cure a default. For example, a credit agreement may grant a borrower a five-day grace period to cure a breach arising from a failure to comply with an affirmative covenant (e.g., an obligation to deliver financial statements no later than the third business day of each month). If the borrower provides the financial statements within the grace period, it is as if the default had never occurred. The bank is "gracious" because it recognizes that the borrower may have inadvertently breached the covenant.[11] The length of grace periods varies depending on the type of default.

If a credit agreement provides for notice of a default, a grace period, or both, the agreement may definitionally distinguish between a **Default** and an **Event of Default**. A **Default** is a ground for termination before or after notice to the allegedly defaulting party, but before the grace period ends without a cure. If the grace period ends without a cure, the **Default** ripens into an **Event of Default**, entitling the non-defaulting party to exercise its remedies.

Definition 1

   "**Default**" means any of the events specified in Section . . . , whether or not any requirement for the giving of notice, the lapse of time, or both has [sic] been satisfied.[12]

Definition 2

   "**Event of Default**" means any of the events specified in Section . . . , provided that any requirement for the giving of notice, the lapse of time, or both has [sic] been satisfied.[13]

Contracts regularly require a representation and warranty that no event exists which with notice and a lapse of time will constitute a default. Parties often insist on this representation because it factors heavily into their risk assessment. If notice has been given to a party under one transaction, the counterparty has fair warning that something is not right. It's an early warning system.

The choice of *Default* as a defined term is unfortunate for the new lawyer and uninitiated client. Defined terms should signal the content of their definitions.[14] *Default* suggests something that has gone irretrievably wrong, not something that has gone wrong but with the potential to be fixed. *Prospective, possible,* and *potential* are all adjectives that could precede *Default* as part of the defined term, guiding a

---

11. Sandra Stern, *Structuring and Drafting Commercial Loan Agreements* vol. 1, ¶ 8.01[2], 8-2–8-3 (rev. ed., A.S. Pratt 2012).

12. *Id.* at 8-4.

13. *Id.*

14. See § 7.5.

reader as to a contract's intent. The term *default* is well-ingrained in legal practice, so a change to clearer language unhappily remains for the future.

(Depending on the contract, the events that permit a termination or remedy may not be termed *defaults*. Instead, the contract may instead simply state the events that permit termination or remedy without categorizing them.)

As another way of alchemizing defaults into nondefaults, some credit agreements constrain a bank's exercise of remedies by requiring that a default must have *occurred* and be *continuing* at the time the bank is to exercise its remedies. That is, while a borrower may well have been in breach, a bank loses its discretionary authority to exercise its remedies if a borrower cures the breach, so that it is no longer continuing/ongoing. Banks are not huge fans of this borrower-friendly language.[15] They often want the right to exercise their remedies, worrying that a breach, even if cured, portends bad things to come.

15.6.2.2 Contractual Consequences of Receipt of Termination Notice — Monetary and Nonmonetary

The consequences of a default are as varied as the contracts themselves. This section provides exemplars for some of the most common types of consequences/remedies.

15.6.2.2.1 Price Adjustments

When first analyzing how a contract should treat a specific ground for termination, the parties should address whether a contractual solution short of contract termination will suffice. What remedy will provide both parties with the economics they need, yet leave the contractual relationship intact? For example, in a long-term supply contract, the supplier might give a discount for late delivery.

The following provision is an unedited provision from an international supply agreement:[16]

> **Price Adjustment**. In case of delayed delivery except for force majecure [sic] cases, the Seller shall pay to the Buyer for every week of delay a penalty amounting to 0.5% of the total value of the goods whose delivery has been delayed. Any fractional part of a week is to be considered a full week. The total amount of penalty shall not, however, exceed 5% of the total value of the goods involved in late delivery. The Seller grants a grace period of four weeks from the delivery date before penalties shall be applied.

Here, the parties combined a grace period with an economic remedy. That reflects the reality in which the parties negotiate a package of remedies and obligations appropriate to each situation.

15.6.2.2.2 Self-help

Some parties believe that if something needs doing, they might as well do it themselves. The excerpt that follows is from a construction contract.

---

15. Stern, n. 11, at ¶ 8.02, 8-5.

16. Sec. Exch. Comm'n, *Contract between Shanghai Ja Solar Technology Co., Ltd. and Roth & Rau AG,* http://www.sec.gov/Archives/edgar/data/1385598/000119312507009458/dex1012.htm (accessed Aug. 1, 2013).

> **Owner's Right to Perform Contractor's Obligations**. If the Contractor persistently fails to perform any of its obligations under this Agreement, the Owner may
>
> (a) give the Contractor five days' written notice of its failure to perform and the Owner's intent to perform the Contractor's obligations; and
>
> (b) perform any one or more of the Contractor's obligations if five days after the Contractor's receipt of this notice the Contractor continues to fail to perform any of its obligations under this Agreement.
>
> The Contract Sum is reduced by the Owner's cost of performing the Contractor's obligations.

As with many remedy provisions, this provision is not limited to just one fix. The parties have combined it with an economic remedy to compensate the Owner. The provision could provide for the Contractor to begin work again or for the contract to terminate. It's up to the parties.

Here's another self-help provision, this one adapted from a theater license agreement.[17] It is again paired with economic consequences.

> **Restoration of Theater**.
>
> (a) **Theater Owner's Rights**. If the Production Company does not remove its equipment and property before the end of 24 hours after the last performance,
> (i) the Production Company is deemed to have abandoned its equipment and property (collectively, the "Property");
> (ii) title to the Property passes immediately to the Theater Owner, but regardless of title to the Property, the Theater Owner may dispose of the Property as it sees fit, inclusive of the right (but not the obligation) to remove or store the Property, or to do both.
> (b) **Production Company's Monetary Obligations**. The Production Company shall pay the Theater Owner for
> (i) all damages the Theater Owner sustains because the Production Company failed to timely vacate the Theater; and
> (ii) all expenses incurred in doing any one or more of the following: removing, disposing, and storing the Property.

15.6.2.2.3 Default Interest

Some types of agreements have relatively standard remedies provisions. For example, in financing agreements, a borrower's default usually gives the lender the right to receive **default interest**—a higher rate of interest than the borrower was paying the lender before the default. So, for example, if a borrower is paying X% interest on a promissory note, the default rate might be X% *plus* 2%.

15.6.2.2.4 Injunctive Relief

The enforceability of provisions entitling a party to injunctive relief remains questionable. Parties cannot require a court to grant injunctive relief. Despite the case law, provisions stating that the parties intended injunctive relief do seem to influence

---

17. This provision is based on a contract in Thomas D. Selz et al., 5 Ent. L. 3d: Leg. Concepts & Bus. Pracs. app. D-13, § 18 (West July 2012) (available at http://web2.westlaw.com/find/default.wl?cite=UU(Ib7c e5de7265a11ddabcef8d187e8c05a)&sr=TC&rs=WLW13.04&pbc=DA010192&vr=2.0&rp=%2ffind%2fdefaul t.wl&sv=Split&fn=_top&findtype=l&mt=Westlaw&db=200165).

courts' decisions.[18] Analyzing and sorting out how these provisions should be written give lawyers agita.

Confidentiality agreements often provide for injunctive relief. They do so as a way of limiting unauthorized disclosures. The following provision is typical. It tries to justify its claim for injunctive relief by explaining why monetary damages are insufficient.

Example 1 — Excerpt from a Confidentiality Agreement

Injunctive Relief. Because of the unique nature of the Confidential Information and the Research, the Executive acknowledges that

(a) the Company will suffer irreparable harm if the Executive breaches any one or more of his obligations stated in Paragraphs 1 through 5 of this Agreement;

(b) monetary damages will be inadequate to compensate the Company for any breach; and

(c) the Company is entitled to injunctive relief to enforce the terms of Paragraphs 1 through 5, in addition to any other remedies available to it at law or in equity.

Sales of real property also often include provisions for specific enforcement of the sale.

Example 2 — Excerpt from a Real Estate Purchase Agreement

Purchaser's Remedies. The Purchaser may enforce specific performance of this Agreement against the Seller, if the Seller intentionally refuses to sell the Property and if the Purchaser is not in breach. In connection with that enforcement, the Seller shall pay the Purchaser's costs and expenses, including reasonable attorneys' fees.

15.6.2.2.5 Liquidated Damages

Liquidated damages can be a versatile remedy when a suit for damages might yield uncertain results. Drafters can fashion these provisions to be transaction specific. But drafting liquidated damages provisions courts danger: Drafters always risk that a court could find the liquidated damages provision to be a penalty and unenforceable. Before drafting such a provision, review how the courts in your state interpret these provisions.

For example, assume a play opens in New York City and has only a short run before the production closes. Then, serendipitously, a new investor appears and wants the play to reopen. The original theater believes it should have first dibs on the play now that it might have a very long run. Unfortunately, the theater owner has already rented

---

18. For an excellent discussion of this issue and case citations, *see* Edward Yorio, *Contract Enforcement: Specific Performance and Injunctions* §§ 19.2-19.3 (Little, Brown & Co. 1989); *see generally* Frederick A. Brodie & Nathan R. Smith, *The False Promises of Injunction Clauses,* 189 Managing Intell. Prop. 92 (May 2009) (available at http://www.pillsburylaw.com/publications/the-false-promise-of-injunction-clauses).

out the theater to another production. What to do? The parties' solution included a transaction-specific liquidated damages remedy.[19]

> **Reopening the Play**. If the Production Company closes the Play and vacates the Theater but desires to reopen the Play in New York City before the 90th day after the Production Company vacates the Theater, at the Theater Owner's option, the Production Company shall either reopen the Play
>
>> (a) at the Theater under this Agreement's terms or[20]
>> (b) at another New York City theater and pay the Theater Owner $10,000 per week or the prorated amount, as appropriate, for the run of the Play at the other New York City theater.
>
> The payments required under subsection (b) constitute liquidated and full damages suffered by the Owner, as determined by the parties, because they cannot determine the future damages at the time of this Agreement.

Here's another example of a transaction-specific liquidated damages provision. Assume an apartment owner wants to renovate. To do so in some cities, she must enter into a contract not only with the contractor, but also with the entity that owns her apartment building (the "Building"). In the excerpt from the construction contract between the owner and contractor that follows, the contractor promises the owner that the contractor will pay the Building a stated sum per day for each day past the contractually imposed construction deadline. (In a separate agreement, the apartment owner promises the Building that it will cause the contractor to pay the Building.) Apartment building managers often demand these types of payments to incentivize contractors to finish on schedule—to minimize disruption in the building and to the apartment dwellers' urban karma.

> **Delayed Completion**. If the Contractor fails to complete Construction on or before April 30, 20X8, the Contractor shall pay $1,000 per day to the Apartment Building until the Construction is completed. After May 30, 20X8, the sum increases to $2,000 per day, until the Contractor completes Construction, including the last day of Construction.[21]

15.6.2.2.6 Indemnities

When Party A promises to pay for the loss for which Party B is financially responsible, Party A **indemnifies** Party B. The indemnity allocates risk between the parties. The contract shifts the risk of loss to the **indemnitor** (the party who will be paying) by the indemnitor's promise to make the indemnitee whole for any loss that the indemnitee sustains. Here is a simple example without any bells or whistles.

---

19. Thomas D. Selz et al., 5 Ent. L. 3d: Leg. Concepts & Bus. Pracs. app. D-13, § 13(d) (West July 2012). *See generally* Eric Fishman & Anne Lefever, *4 Tips for a Better Liquidated Damages Clause,* http://www.law.com/corporatecounsel/PubArticleCC.jsp?id=1202608137407&4_Tips_for_a_Better_Liquidated_Damages_Clause&slreturn=20130709123734 (accessed Aug. 2, 2013).

20. This use of *or* is exclusive and does not require punctuation to precede it.

21. The author can imagine a litigator's arguments that these payments are penalties, not liquidated damages.

> **Indemnity**. The Licensor shall indemnify and defend[22] the Licensee against all losses and liabilities arising from third-party claims that the Software infringes any ownership rights of third parties.

Drafters commonly use sophisticated indemnity provisions in acquisition agreements as an exclusive contractual remedy to supersede the common law remedies. Buyers prefer indemnities, among other reasons, because they expand the scope of losses for which the seller is responsible. For example, in the United States, each party must pay its own litigation expenses. An indemnity can change this common law rule by adding to the matters indemnified: *the Buyer's cost and expenses in enforcing this indemnity, including reasonable attorneys' fees and expenses.* Sellers also seek indemnities because they can impose contractual caps on damages and shorten otherwise lengthy statutes of limitation. A full review of acquisition indemnities is beyond the scope of this book.[23]

Outside the acquisition context, drafters use indemnities in a multitude of transactions—for example, to indemnify an escrow agent against litigation claims and to indemnify licensees against claims of copyright infringement.[24]

Common issues to consider when drafting an indemnity include the following:

- What triggers the indemnity?
- Who is on the hook for the indemnity? Is it just Party X or also its parent company?
- Is notice a condition to the obligation to indemnify or merely a contractual promise to provide notice?
- What kinds of losses are indemnified against—expectation damages, consequential damages, incidental damages?
- For how long is the indemnity available?
- Is the indemnity capped?
- Must the indemnitee sustain a minimum loss before the indemnitor has an obligation to indemnify?

A salient issue that the drafter must also address is whether the indemnitor will defend (and pay to defend) the indemnitee. The common law does not include defense as part of the indemnity, so drafters must explicitly provide for it. If an obligation to defend is included, issues include the following:

- Is there a duty to defend or just to pay costs?
- Who controls the defense (that is, the legal strategy)?
- May the indemnitee participate with its own counsel if it pays for the counsel?
- Does the indemnitee need to approve any settlement?

If your client wants a short contract with a down and dirty indemnity (one sentence), include *defend* along with *indemnify*. Otherwise, address these issues carefully at length because substantial money is at stake.

---

22. See subsequent comments in this section about the use of *defend.*

23. For a full treatment of the subject, *see* Morton A. Pierce & Michael C. Hefter, *Indemnities,* in *Negotiating and Drafting Contract Boilerplate* ch. 10 (Stark et al. eds., ALM Publg. 2003).

24. *Id.* at 248.

15.6.2.2.7 Cumulative vs. Exclusive Remedies

When drafting contracts that provide a remedy beyond the common law remedies, drafters must address whether the contractual remedy is exclusive and supplants the common law remedies or whether the contractual remedy is merely part of the plaintiff's arsenal. Liquidated damages provisions are generally exclusive, but not always.

> **Example 1 — Exclusive Remedy**
>
> **Indemnity as Exclusive Remedy**. The remedies of the parties stated in this Article 10 are exclusive and preclude either party's assertion of any other rights that party may have under the Purchase Agreement, applicable law, or otherwise.
>
> **Example 2 — Cumulative Remedies**
>
> **Cumulative Remedies**. The remedies stated in this Section are cumulative and in addition to all other remedies available under this Agreement, at law, and in equity.
>
> **Example 3 — Cumulative Remedies**
>
> **Cumulative Remedies**. The rights and remedies of the parties under this Article are nonexclusive and are in addition to all other remedies available to the parties at law or in equity.

The exclusive remedy exemplar in Example 1 comes with a caveat. If one of the parties has committed fraud, the equitable remedy of rescission may still be available.[25]

15.6.2.2.8 Payment Provisions

Clients forgive many glitches, but drafting the monetary payment provisions incorrectly is not a glitch—and not generally forgiven. It's critical to *follow the cash*. This means you must understand and track all the monetary consequences, including the reason for each payment and its source. When drafting these provisions, general promises to pay don't suffice. As with the consideration payments in the action sections, a promise to pay money must answer the following questions: *Who is obligated to pay what* to *whom by when* and *how*.

15.6.2.2.9 Setoff Provisions

A setoff provision secures payment to a party by using another party's money that the party has in its possession to pay an amount that the other party owed to it. To restate, using fewer references to unnamed parties and too many antecedents: A setoff payment secures payment by entitling Party A, who rightfully possesses Party B's money for one reason, to use that money to pay itself (Party A) amounts Party B owes it for another reason.

---

25. *Abry Partners V, L.P. v. F & W Acq. LLC*, 891 A.2d 1032 (Del. Ch. 2006).

Banks regularly include a setoff provision in their credit agreements. For example, if a borrower owes money to a bank and has money on deposit with the bank, the bank may take the money on deposit and pay itself all or part of the principal amount of the loan. So, if a borrower owes a bank $10,000 and has deposited $3,000 with the bank, the bank may set off the $3,000 against the $10,000 and reduce the borrower's outstanding principal to $7,000.

Setoffs are also common in leases. Typical provisions state that the landlord may set off against the deposit that the tenant originally paid the landlord money the tenant owes the landlord for damage to the apartment.

The following is a setoff provision from an escrow agreement:[26]

> **Right of Setoff**. Without limiting the Escrow Agent's other rights and remedies against the Seller and the Buyer, the Escrow Agent may satisfy all or part of the Seller and the Buyer's indemnity obligations under Section 4 by setoff against the Escrow Amount. The Escrow Agent shall promptly notify the Seller and the Buyer of any setoff.

15.6.2.2.10 Immediate Termination on Receipt of Termination Notice

This section started with the statement that agreements did not generally terminate on receipt of a termination notice and have no other contractual consequences. But they can terminate in just that way—sometimes. In an acquisition, if a seller fails to satisfy a condition to closing, the buyer has a walk-away right. If the seller has not made any misrepresentations or breached any warranties or covenants, then the buyer has no other rights against the seller. For a detailed discussion of this endgame scenario, see the discussion on endgame provisions in acquisition agreements in Document 6 in Chapter 32.

15.6.2.3 Survival of Common Law Rights and Obligations and Specific Contract Provisions

Whether common law rights and obligations survive will depend on the alternative remedies the parties have negotiated and whether they are cumulative or exclusive. If they're cumulative, rights and obligations survive. If the remedies are exclusive, then no rights and obligations survive.

As to specific contract provisions surviving, you must look at each agreement to determine whether a transaction-specific provision should survive.

15.7 DISPUTE RESOLUTION PROVISIONS

Unfortunately, parties end up litigating many contractual disputes. In anticipation of that litigation, many parties want their contracts to include dispute resolution provisions, provisions that will govern some of the procedural and substantive aspects of the litigation.

Preliminarily, the parties must decide whether they want to adjudicate or arbitrate their disputes, or rely on some other dispute resolution mechanism, such as

---

26. The original bank example discussing setoff provisions can be found in Chapter 20, at footnote 3.

mediation. The parties could also agree to a series of meetings to discuss the issue, elevating the level of the principals participating as the meetings continue.

If the parties agree to adjudicate their disputes, the dispute resolution provisions should include governing law, forum selection, and service of process provisions. Other provisions to consider are a waiver of venue objections, a waiver of the right to a jury trial,[27] and a provision requiring the losing party to pay the prevailing party's attorneys' fees and other expenses. The last is often difficult to obtain.

If the parties agree to arbitrate their disputes, the provisions with respect to the arbitration can be short (a simple statement of the agreement to arbitrate) or detailed. A detailed provision will specify, among other things:

- The disputes to be arbitrated.
- The rules that will govern the arbitration.
- The location of the arbitration.
- The governing law.
- The qualifications of the arbitrators.
- The method of choosing the arbitrators.
- The payments of expenses relating to the arbitration.
- The finality of the arbitration.

15.8 LOCATION OF THE ENDGAME PROVISIONS

Drafters generally place endgame provisions at the end of the contract. The beginning of the contract has the parties' plan for a successful transaction or relationship. The conclusion of the relationship, whether good or bad, is relegated to the end of the contract. It reflects the chronology of a transaction.

Endgame provisions usually appear together in one section or article. This facilitates finding these provisions. Occasionally, drafters integrate an endgame term with substantive business provisions. For example, here is an unedited version of a provision from a distribution and licensing agreement.[28] The Licensor licenses software ("Product") to the Distributor who pays royalties. This provision authorizes the Licensor to audit the Distributor's accounting records to ensure that the Distributor is paying the Licensor the proper amount for sales of the Product. The provision includes the grounds and method of termination if the Distributor's underpayment exceeds a certain amount.

> [**Right to Audit; Understated Payments**.] Licensor or its designated agent may, at Licensor's sole expense (except as provided herein), upon 10 days advance written notice to Distributor during Distributor's business hours examine and/or audit the books and records of Distributor which relate to payments due and Products distributed under this Agreement. Licensor shall not have access to any of Distributor's records beyond those necessary to complete any audit contemplated under this Section 5.5. If any examination or audit should reveal that the License Fees to Licensor under this Agreement for any period was [sic] understated in any Sales Report, then Distributor shall pay to Licensor immediately upon demand the amount understated and any penalty fee due with respect thereto. If any examination or audit discloses an understatement in any Sales Report of five percent (5%) or more, Distributor shall

---

27. Although a waiver of the right to a jury trial is enforceable in most states, some states prohibit a waiver. *See e.g.* Mont. Code Ann. §28-2-708 (2011).

28. Bitrix, Inc., *Distribution and Licensing Agreement,* http://www.bitrixsoft.com/partners/agreement.html (accessed July 31, 2013; provision can be found at Section 5.5, Right to Audit; Understated Statements).

also reimburse Licensor for any and all costs and expenses connected with the examination or audit (including without limitation, reasonable accountants' and attorney's [sic] fees). In the event that any examination or audit discloses . . . an understatement in any Sales Report of ten percent (10%) or more, Distributor shall also pay to Licensor as an underpayment penalty an amount equal to the amount of the underpayment. In the event any of the understatement of ten percent (10%) or more is determined to be intentional, Licensor may at its option terminate this Agreement immediately upon written notice to Distributor. The foregoing remedies shall be in addition to any other remedies Licensor may have hereunder. No provision of this Section 5.5 shall be construed as limiting or restricting any Licensor's rights or remedies provided elsewhere in this Agreement or by law.

Although Section 5.5 is a stand-alone provision, the agreement's termination provision[29] cross-references it when listing the grounds for termination. This aids the reader who has turned to the back of the contract looking for the endgame provisions in their usual location.

Termination. The Parties may terminate this Agreement as provided below:

[Intentionally omitted.]

(a) Licensor may terminate this Agreement as provided in Section 4.2 and 5.5 hereof . . .

One remedy commonly found outside the endgame section or article is the walkaway right that arises from a failure to satisfy a condition to closing (generally, in an acquisition or a financing agreement). The language introducing the conditions article states this remedy, albeit not explicitly.

> **Conditions**. Each of the following conditions must have been satisfied or waived before the Buyer is obligated to close the transactions that this Agreement contemplates. *(If the Buyer is not obligated to close, then the Buyer may walk away.)*

For a more detailed discussion of the role of conditions in endgame provisions in acquisition agreements, see Document 6 in Chapter 32.

15.9   DRAFTING THE ENDGAME PROVISIONS

Conceptually, endgame provisions are a series of *if/then* propositions.

- If this good event happens, then this is the consequence.
- If this bad event happens, then this is the consequence.

While the consequences differ from contract to contract based on the parties' business concerns, they generally fall into one of three categories.

- An obligation to perform (e.g., "The Borrower shall pay default interest.")
- The grant of discretionary authority (e.g., "The Bank may foreclose.")
- A declaration (e.g., "The contract terminates on a party's delegation of its performance without the other party's consent.")

The organization of endgame provisions depends on the contract. If they deal with defaults (something has gone wrong), two schemes are common. The first puts a list

---

29. *Id.* at § 10.2(c).

of the offending events into one section and the consequences into another. Credit agreements and employment agreements often follow this scheme, as the agreements have default provisions relating to only one party.

The second scheme creates an endgame article that has separate sections for each party's defaults. If the consequences of both parties' defaults are the same, a third section can detail the remedies. Otherwise, each party's section should be broken down into subsections, with the first subsection listing the defaults and the second listing the consequences. Remember, these organizational schemes may not be appropriate for all contracts and are merely guidelines.

If the endgame provisions are not related to defaults (a happy endgame), create separate sections or articles as needed to address specific business issues. For example, acquisition agreements sometimes have provisions that apply after the transaction has been successfully consummated, such as the following: covenants requiring that the seller change its name post-closing and covenants not to compete.

A more specific organizational scheme that may apply in many situations creates individual sections to address each of the six major issues that endgame provisions should address.

1. The termination events (or the events triggering a contractual remedy).
2. The contractual consequences (both monetary and nonmonetary) of receipt of the termination notice.
3. The date the contract terminates.
4. Whether common law rights survive.
5. Whether any specific contract provisions survive.
6. Dispute resolution provisions.

Here is an example of an endgame provision from a movie distribution agreement.

---

17. **Termination**

17.1 **Grounds for Termination**.

(a) **Discretionary Authority to Send Notice of Intent to Terminate**. The Distributor may send a notice stating that it has grounds for termination and that it intends to terminate this Agreement (a "**Notice of Intent to Terminate**") in accordance with this Section 17 if any one or more of the following events has occurred and is continuing.

(i) The Movie Owner made any misrepresentation under this Agreement.

(ii) The Movie Owner breached any material covenant under this Agreement that cannot be cured.

(iii) The Movie Owner breached any material covenant under this Agreement that can be cured, and it failed to cure that breach before the 16th calendar day after receiving the Distributor's Notice of Intent to Terminate.

(iv) The Movie Owner becomes insolvent or fails to pay any of its debts when due.

(v) A petition under any bankruptcy or insolvency law is filed by or against the Movie Owner.

(vi) The security interest that the Movie Owner granted to the Distributor in the Collateral ceases to be enforceable or perfected.

continued on next page >

(b)   **Notice of Intent to Terminate**. The Distributor shall include in the Notice of Intent to Terminate

(i)   a statement of all amounts owed;

(ii)   the amount of any setoff to be taken under Section 17.4; and

(iii)   a statement of all obligations due.

17.2   Movie Owner's Obligations Arising from Receipt of Notice of Intent to Terminate. If the Distributor sends a Notice of Intent to Terminate under Section 17.1,

(a)   then no later than five business days after receiving that notice, the Movie Owner shall pay the Distributor by wire transfer of immediately available funds an amount equal to

(i)   the Distributor's out-of-pocket costs incurred in connection with the Picture *plus*

(ii)   the Advance or any portion of the Advance that the Distributor paid to the Movie Owner *minus*

(iii)   the amount of any setoff that the Distributor takes in accordance with Section 17.4, as stated in the Notice of Intent to Terminate; and

(b)   the Movie Owner shall perform all obligations under this Agreement that the Distributor declares due.

17.3   Specific Performance. The Distributor may specifically enforce the Movie Owner's obligations under Section 17.2.

17.4   Setoff. Without limiting any other remedies available to the Distributor under this Agreement or at law, the Distributor may set off against any amount it is obligated to pay under this Agreement to the Movie Owner, sums in the Distributor's possession that are reasonably sufficient to secure the Distributor from and against the Movie Owner's liabilities or the Movie Owner's breach of any of its obligations under this Agreement.

17.5   Cumulative Remedies. In addition to any rights and remedies stated in this Agreement, the Distributor may exercise all of its rights at law or equity, including without limitation, its rights and remedies in and to the Collateral.

17.6   Effective Date of Termination. If the Distributor delivers a Notice of Intent to Terminate under Section 17.1, then termination is effective when the Distributor has both received payment of all money due under Section 17.2(a) and the Movie Owner has performed all its obligations to be performed in accordance with Section 17.2(b).

17.7   Survival of Common Law Rights and Obligations. All rights in law and equity and all obligations arising from any ground for termination stated in Section 17.1 survive this Agreement's termination.

15.10 ENDGAME CHART

The following is an endgame chart, a schematic way to organize information regarding endgame provisions. It doesn't cover every point, but it's often a good way to begin. Some of the exercises that follow will show you how these charts can help you.

Endgame Chart

Ground for Termination	Monetary Consequences of Receipt of Notice of Termination	Other Contractual Consequences of Receipt of Notice of Termination	Date of Contract Termination	Survival of Common Law Causes of Action	Survival of Other Contract Provisions

EXERCISES

Exercise 15-1

Ellsworth Endgame Chart

1. Ellsworth has decided to live in an assisted-living facility that is associated with a charitable institution. Concurrent with entering the facility, Ellsworth donates $25,000 to the charity. She must also pay a monthly fee.
2. The facility has a two-month probationary period during which Ellsworth can decide if she wants to remain in the facility long term. If Ellsworth leaves before the two-month probationary period ends, the charity will return the $25,000 donation. If she leaves afterward, the charity is entitled to keep the donation.
3. The contract must also contemplate Ellsworth's death and what happens to the donation in that event.

Step 1

Fill in the left column of the following chart to reflect all the circumstances (grounds for termination) for which the monetary consequences must be determined.

Step 2

Complete the right column of the following chart by writing whether the donation is kept or returned in each instance.

Follow the Cash — Provide for All Eventualities

Grounds for Termination	Monetary Consequences (Donation kept or returned?)

Exercise 15-2

Healthy Hearts, Inc. has decided to hire Adele Administrator. Healthy Hearts will pay her an annual salary at a rate of $100,000, plus a discretionary bonus. In addition, it will reimburse Administrator for documented business expenses. The parties have agreed on four termination events: failure to perform up to standards, misrepresentations as to previous experience, death, and disability.

Step 1

In the chart that follows, complete the far left column by listing each ground for termination.

Step 2

Because Healthy Hearts is obligated to pay Adele for three reasons, the contract must address the three monetary consequences for each ground of termination. In the first row of the chart that follows, replace the bracketed instructions with the correct information.

Step 3

Complete the endgame chart.

Follow the Cash — Tracking Payment Types and Sources

Grounds for Termination	Monetary Consequences with Respect to [insert type of payment]	Monetary Consequences with Respect to [insert type of payment]	Monetary Consequences with Respect to [insert type of payment]
Ground #1 for Termination			
Ground #2 for Termination			
Ground #3 for Termination			
Ground #4 for Termination			

Exercise 15-3

1. Concurrently with the execution and delivery of an acquisition agreement, the Buyer pays the Seller a $100,000 deposit.

2. The acquisition has a confidentiality provision which by its terms applies regardless whether the transaction closes.

3. For this exercise, the acquisition agreement has the following grounds for termination:

    (a) The Seller may terminate because the Buyer made a misrepresentation.

    (b) The Buyer may terminate because the Seller made a misrepresentation.

    (c) The Buyer may terminate if a nonfault condition to its obligation to close is not satisfied.

4. The parties agree that liquidated damages based on the deposit make sense (if the Buyer makes a misrepresentation).

5. Assume that the transaction does not close and that the indemnification provisions do not apply. Complete the endgame chart that follows.

Full Endgame Chart for a Simple Acquisition

Ground for Termination	Monetary Consequences with Respect to the Deposit (Keep or return?)	Other Contractual Consequence of Receipt of Notice of Intent to Terminate (Do the facts provide for any?)	Date Contract Terminates (Does it vary depending on the facts?)	Survival of Common Law Causes of Action (If the contract provides for liquidated damages, should the common law causes of action survive?)	Survival of Other Contract Provisions (What provision is a candidate for survival?)
Seller may terminate if Buyer's representation was false					
Buyer may terminate if Seller's representation was false					
Buyer may terminate if a condition to the Buyer's obligation to close is not satisfied					

Exercise 15-4

The cure provision in Section 15.6.2.1 has a gap — a situation that it creates through drafting but does not address. What is it?

Exercise 15-5

Draft the endgame provisions for Exercise 5-3. What is missing from these provisions — both from a drafting and business perspective? Review one or two precedents to help you answer the question in the previous sentence. Use the following defined terms and definitions to help with your drafting:

"License" means the license Ralph LP grants in Section 2.1.

"Licensed Products" means caps and t-shirts bearing the Trademark.

"Term" has the meaning assigned to it in Section 2.1.

"Trademark" means a pictorial representation of the cartoon character Ralph.

Exercise 15-6

Draft the endgame provisions of the Aircraft Purchase Agreement. Use the information from the Purchase Offer and the Escrow Agreement, found in Exercise 6-3, and the defined terms that were included in the Aircraft Purchase Agreement excerpt in Exercise 7-7.

Exercise 15-7

Read the following excerpt from an employment agreement and then answer the questions that follow.

Excerpt from an Employment Agreement

10.   Termination. The Executive's employment terminates before the termination date stated in Article 2 as follows:

10.1   Death or Disability. If the Executive dies or becomes permanently disabled, this Agreement terminates effective at the end of the calendar month during which his death occurs or when his disability becomes permanent.

10.2   Cause. If a majority of the disinterested directors of the Company's board of directors vote to remove the Executive from his duties for Cause, this Agreement terminates and the Executive ceases to be an officer of the Company effective on the date specified by the directors. For purposes of this Agreement, "Cause" means the occurrence of any one or more of the following events:

10.2.1   The Executive has been convicted of or pleaded guilty or no contest to

10.2.1.1   any misdemeanor reflecting unfavorably on the Company; or

10.2.1.2   any felony offense.

10.2.2   The Executive has committed fraud or embezzlement, that determination to be made by a majority of the disinterested directors of the Company's board of directors in their reasonable judgment.

10.2.3   A majority of the disinterested directors of the Company's board of directors has determined in their reasonable judgment that

10.2.3.1   the Executive has breached one or more of his fiduciary duties to the Company or has made an intentional misrepresentation to the Company; and

10.2.3.2   the breach or misrepresentation has had or is likely to have a material adverse effect on the Company's business operations or financial condition.

---

continued on next page >

10.2.4 The Executive has failed to obey a specific written direction from the board of directors consistent with this Agreement and the Executive's duties under this Agreement.

10.2.5 After written notice and a 30-day cure period, the Executive has materially neglected or failed to satisfactorily discharge any of his duties or responsibilities, that determination to be made by a majority of the disinterested directors of the Company's board of directors in their reasonable judgment.

Questions

1. Section 10.1 provides for termination on death or permanent disability. While death is relatively certain, the Company and Executive might dispute whether the Executive's disability has become permanent. If you represented the Executive, what substantive changes could you recommend that would provide greater certainty as to when a disability would become permanent?

2. Why are fraud and embezzlement treated differently from misdemeanors and felonies that require conviction?

3. Does subsection 10.2.3 adequately protect the Company if the Executive makes misrepresentations or breaches his fiduciary duties? What if he lied on his resume? Will this lead to a material adverse effect on the Company's financial condition?

4. If you represented the Executive, what change could you ask for in subsection 10.2.4 that would provide your client with greater protection? Use the other subsections as a guide.

5. Assume that the Company pays the Executive an annual salary and a guaranteed bonus of $10,000, and reimburses his expenses. The guaranteed bonus increases each year by 5 percent on a compounded basis. If you represented the Company, what would you suggest that the Company pay the Executive on termination for each of the scenarios in the excerpt? Not precise dollar amounts, but conceptually. What would you recommend if you represented the Executive?

General Provisions

16.1 INTRODUCTION[1]

Drafters often refer to the **general provisions** at the back of the contract as the *boilerplate* provisions. Typical provisions include amendment, governing law, severability, and waiver of jury trial.

These provisions supply a road map, telling the parties how to govern their relationship and administer the contract. The provisions are said to serve housekeeping functions, arguably matters of secondary importance. The placement of these provisions toward the end of the contract, under a caption of *Miscellaneous* or *Administrative Provisions*, furthers the impression that these provisions are but an afterthought. Consequently, lawyers often ignore them, and legal commentators and critics lampoon them.

The term *boilerplate* suggests standardized provisions that can be used in all circumstances. But they cannot. You will regularly find key business issues hidden in these provisions, and they will get you into trouble if you do not redraft them. By learning the business and legal implications of the general provisions, you will know when and how to modify them.

Each section that follows discusses one of the general provisions and begins with an example of the relevant provision.

One general point: If parties are executing multiple agreements as part of a single transaction, make sure that the general provisions are the same in each agreement. For example, when a party borrows money, it may sign not only a credit agreement, but also a security agreement and a pledge agreement. All of these agreements should use exactly the same general provisions. Any divergence creates the potential for litigation.

---

1. Each section in this chapter is based on a chapter in *Negotiating and Drafting Contract Boilerplate* (Stark et al. eds., ALM Publg. 2003) ("*Negotiating and Drafting Contract Boilerplate*"). The text in this chapter either quotes or paraphrases the relevant chapter. At the beginning of each section, the author of the relevant chapter is referenced. I thank each of the authors for his or her contributions to *Negotiating and Drafting Contract Boilerplate* and to this book.

Section 16.1 is based on Tina L. Stark, *Introduction,* in *Negotiating and Drafting Contract Boilerplate* ch. 1.

All material from *Negotiating and Drafting Contract Boilerplate* is used with permission of the publisher—ALM Publishing (www.lawcatalog.com); copyright ALM Props., © 2003. All Rights Reserved.

16.2   ASSIGNMENT AND DELEGATION[2]

> **Assignment and Delegation.** No party may assign any right or delegate any performance under this Agreement. All assignments of rights are prohibited, whether they are voluntary or involuntary, by merger, consolidation, dissolution, operation of law, or any other manner. A purported assignment or purported delegation in violation of this Section X.X is void.

The assignment and delegation provision is one of the general provisions that you will tailor most often. When you do, remember that you must deal with both assignments and delegations, not just assignments. Many provisions in precedents do not even mention delegation.

16.2.1   THE BASICS OF ASSIGNMENTS AND DELEGATIONS

Recall from Chapter 3 that the flip side of every covenant is a right.[3] An assignment is a transfer of those rights to a third party. For example, if Leslie has an obligation to pay Ibrahim $100, Ibrahim has a right to be paid $100, and he may transfer that right—for example, to Mark. Ibrahim is the **assignor**, Mark is the **assignee**, and Leslie is the **nonassigning party**.

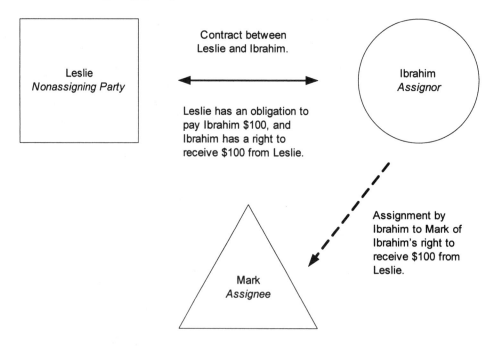

Once Ibrahim assigns his rights, he no longer has a right to Leslie's performance. Instead, Mark has that right, and Leslie has a duty to perform in his favor.[4]

---

2. Section 16.2 is based on Tina L. Stark, *Assignment and Delegation,* in *Negotiating and Drafting Contract Boilerplate* ch. 3.

3. See §3.4.

4. *See Pac. E. Corp. v. Gulf Life Holding Co.*, 902 S.W.2d 946, 958-959 (Tenn. App. 1995) (citing Samuel Williston, *A Treatise on the Law of Contracts* vol. 3, §433 (3d ed., Baker, Voorhis & Co. 1960) and *Restatement (Second) of Contracts* §§280 cmt. e, 323 cmt. a (1979)).

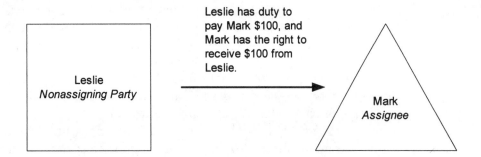

Note that the arrow goes in only one direction. Mark has no duty to perform in favor of Leslie as Ibrahim did not delegate his performance contemporaneously with the assignment—which leads us neatly to delegations.

A party delegates its performance when it appoints someone else to perform in its stead.[5] The party who delegates its performance is the **delegating party**. The person to whom it delegates its performance is the **delegate**, and the other party to the original contract is the **nondelegating party**. Performance refers not only to duties, but also to conditions.[6]

Not all duties are delegable. If a duty is personal in nature or requires the delegating party's unique skills, the would-be delegating party cannot delegate.[7] For example, Billy Joel could not delegate his duty to perform at Madison Square Garden to your professor. Among the nondelegable duties is a party's obligation to execute a promissory note.[8] That duty would become delegable, however, if the delegate were willing and able to tender cash to the nondelegating party at the time of the delegation.[9]

Returning to our earlier hypothetical, assume that Ibrahim has a right to the $100 only if he delivers two boxes of multipurpose paper to Leslie. That is, Ibrahim has not only a right, but also a duty to perform. A delegation would consist of Ibrahim delegating to Mark the former's duty to deliver the paper to Leslie.

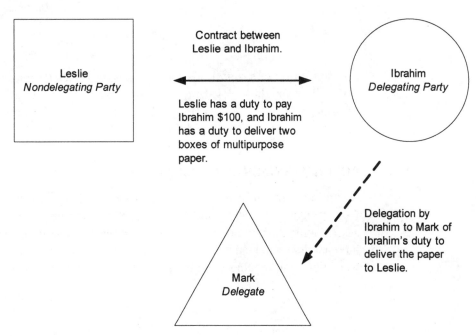

---

5. *See Proriver, Inc. v. Red River Grill, LLC*, 83 F. Supp. 2d 42, 50 n. 14 (D.D.C. 1999).

6. *Restatement (Second) of Contracts* § 319(1) (1981).

7. *In re Schick*, 235 B.R. 318, 323 (Bankr. S.D.N.Y. 1999).

8. *See* Joseph M. Perillo, *Calamari and Perillo on Contracts* 631 (5th ed., West 2009).

9. *Id.*

Delegation alone does not bind a delegate to perform in favor of the nondelegating party. If it did, anyone could become obligated to perform anything even though that person had not agreed to do so. Thus, the delegate must agree with the delegating party that it will perform in favor of the nondelegating party. It must **assume** the delegating party's duties to the nondelegating party.[10] When it does so, the nondelegating party becomes a third-party beneficiary of that assumption. Parties can also create a performance obligation through a novation.[11]

Therefore, in our hypothetical, when Mark assumes Ibrahim's duty to Leslie, Mark becomes obligated to deliver to Leslie the two boxes of multipurpose paper. Because the flip side of every obligation/duty is a right, Leslie has a right to that performance: the delivery of the multipurpose paper. Leslie becomes the third-party beneficiary of Mark's assumption of Ibrahim's duty.

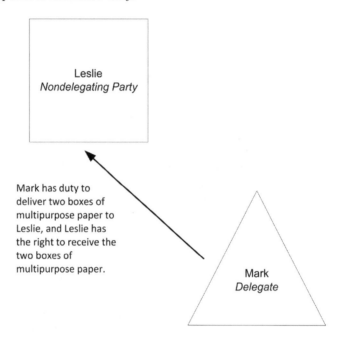

Delegation of a duty does not discharge the delegating party's performance obligation. Rather, the delegating party remains secondarily liable.[12] Were it otherwise, the delegating party could effectively eliminate its performance obligation by delegating it to someone unable to perform.

16.2.2 ANTI-ASSIGNMENT PROVISIONS

An anti-assignment provision is what it sounds like: a provision that prohibits a party from assigning its rights under a contract. Parties insert these provisions to prevent assignments that would materially change the nonassigning party's duties or materially increase its risks.[13] In one line of cases, for example, the anti-assignment provisions were held enforceable because assignment would increase the risk that the nonas-

---

10. *Lumsden v. Roth*, 291 P.2d 88, 89-90 (Cal. App. 1955).

11. *See First Am. Com. Co. v. Wash. Mut. Sav. Bank*, 743 P.2d 1193, 1195 (Utah 1987) (stating that the "essential element of a novation is the discharge of one of the parties to a contract and the acceptance of a new performer by the other party as a substitute for the first original party.").

12. *Lonsdale v. Chesterfield*, 662 P.2d 385, 388 (Wash. 1983).

13. *See Restatement (Second) of Contracts* §317(2)(a) (1981).

signing party would lose certain tax benefits.[14] In addition, parties pair them with anti-delegation provisions to ensure that they need to deal with only one party—the one with whom they originally contracted.

Making an anti-assignment provision enforceable requires a detailed, carefully drawn provision, and it often does not work. The reasons are twofold. First, the provisions of the Uniform Commercial Code (the "U.C.C.") render ineffective any anti-assignment provisions subject to the U.C.C.[15] So, no matter how careful you are, the provision will be ineffective. Second, even if the U.C.C. is inapplicable, courts are hostile to these provisions, and judges are willing to write tortured opinions to find the provisions unenforceable.[16] The hostility stems from their belief that anti-assignment provisions inappropriately restrain commerce.[17]

To prohibit a transfer of rights, draft the anti-assignment provision to prohibit *an assignment of rights under the agreement*. If the provision prohibits only *the assignment of the agreement*, courts generally interpret the provision as an anti-delegation provision. Indeed, both the U.C.C. and the *Restatement (Second) of Contracts* specifically provide canons of interpretation to that effect.[18]

In making their decisions, courts determine whether the parties intended an anti-assignment provision or an anti-delegation provision. As stated by Professor Corbin:

> [If] a building contract provides that the builder shall not assign the contract, it is almost certain that the parties intend that he shall not delegate supervision of the work wholly to another, and leave the job himself. In the absence of very apt words to the contrary, they do not intend that the builder shall not assign his right to instalments [sic] of the price as they fall due. It may be of great importance to have the personal supervision of the builder; but it is of much less importance to whose hands the money is to be paid. If the owner desired to deprive the builder of the power to assign his right to the money, he would have said that the builder's right to the money shall not be assigned, not that the builder shall not assign the "contract."[19]

This reasoning may seem as if the courts are turning themselves inside out to conclude what they want. They are. They dislike anti-assignment provisions and, therefore, as a policy matter, construe them narrowly.[20]

Generally, a simple prohibition against the assignment of rights does not suffice when drafting an anti-assignment provision. You must also reckon with the distinction between the **right** and the **power** to prohibit an assignment.[21] An anti-assignment provision that only prohibits an assignment takes away only the right to assign. In

---

14. *See e.g. Grieve v. Gen. Am. Life Ins. Co.*, 58 F. Supp. 2d 319, 323 (D. Vt. 1999).

15. *See* U.C.C. §2-210(2), U.L.A. U.C.C. §2-210(2) (2004); U.C.C. §§9-406–9-409, U.L.A. U.C.C. §§9-406–9-409 (2002).

16. Calamari & Perillo, *supra* n. 8, at 709 (stating that the cases "have tended to find that the particular provision before the court was not drafted with sufficient clarity to accomplish its purpose of prohibiting assignment. They have often emasculated the provision by holding it to be merely a promise not to assign.").

17. *See Segal v. Greater Valley Terminal Corp.*, 199 A.2d 48, 50 (N.J. Super. App. Div. 1964). The following is an example of how an anti-assignment provision can impede commerce. Assume that Rancher Rob sells Stockyard Sue ten heads of cattle for $500 and that the contract provides that Stockyard Sue can pay Rancher Rob at a later date. Assume further that before the payment date, Rancher Rob needs cash to make an investment. One way that Rancher Rob can fund that investment is to assign his $500 account receivable to Credit Bank. In exchange, Credit Bank would pay Rancher Rob a discounted amount, say $450. The benefit of this assignment is that it gives Rancher Rob access to funds that he would not otherwise have. Thus, the assignment permits a new commercial venture. That venture is not possible, however, if Rancher Rob's contract with Stockyard Sue has an enforceable anti-assignment provision.

18. U.C.C. §2-210(4), U.L.A. U.C.C. §2-210(4) (2004); *Restatement (Second) of Contracts* §322(1) (1981).

19. John E. Murray, Jr., *Corbin on Contracts* vol. 9, §49.9, 214 (rev. ed., Matthew Bender & Co. 2007).

20. *Rumbin v. Utica Mut. Ins. Co.*, 757 A.2d 526, 531 (Conn. 2000).

21. *Bel-Ray Co., Inc. v. Chemrite (Pty) Ltd.*, 181 F.3d 435, 442 (3d Cir. 1999).

that instance, an assignment would be enforceable, although the nonassigning party would have a cause of action for breach against the assignor. That might not be worth much, however. Nonassigning parties generally suffer little damage as their performance usually does not change.

To create an anti-assignment provision that renders an assignment void, you must take away not only the right to assign, but also the power to assign.[22] To do this, a contract must prohibit the assignment of rights under the contract and declare that any purported assignment is void.[23] You do not need to add *null* or *of no further force and effect.* Those terms are synonyms, and *void* suffices.

Finally, in drafting an anti-assignment provision, you must take into account that courts narrowly construe the meaning of the verb *assign*. If you want to prohibit assignments by merger or by operation of law, explicitly prohibit these types of assignment. A general prohibition on assignments does not include them.[24] Indeed, do not rely on general anti-assignment language if the parties agree that a specific assignment is prohibited. Be specific. If the parties want to prohibit all mergers, consider defining *merger* by stating that the term refers to any merger, regardless of which party survives.

Consistent with this advice, explicitly prohibit a **change of control**.[25] A change of control occurs, for example, if a shareholder sells more than 50% of a company's shares to another person. Parties worry about such a change because a new person controlling the other party can dramatically change the parties' relationship.

To prohibit a change of control, provide either that a change of control is deemed an assignment for purposes of the anti-assignment provision or that a change of control is a default. In addition, consider whether the agreement should define change of control.

16.2.3 ANTI-DELEGATION PROVISIONS

Unlike anti-assignment provisions, anti-delegation provisions are generally enforceable[26] and may be drafted in a straightforward manner by stating that neither party may delegate performance.[27] Just as with an anti-assignment provision, include a declaration that any purported delegation in violation of the parties' agreement is void.

If the parties desire an anti-delegation provision but wish to permit a specific delegation, consider whether the right to delegate should be subject to any conditions. A common one requires the delegate to be creditworthy. In addition, drafters often require the delegate to assume, in writing, the delegating party's performance obligations. If you represent a client that is likely to be the delegating party, secure an agreement that the delegating party is deemed released from its performance obligations on the signing of the delegation documents. Otherwise, it remains secondarily liable.

---

22. *See id.*

23. *Pravin Bankers Assocs., Ltd. v. Banco Pop. del Peru*, 109 F.3d 850, 856 (2d Cir. 1997).

24. *Dodier Realty & Inv. Co. v. St. Louis Nat'l Baseball Club, Inc.*, 238 S.W.2d 321, 325 (Mo. 1951).

25. *Segal v. Greater Valley Terminal Corp.*, *supra* n. 17.

26. *See* U.C.C. §2-210(1), U.L.A. U.C.C. §2-210(1) (2004); *Restatement (Second) of Contracts* §318(1) (1981).

27. *Performance* is a better word choice than duty because performance is broader, encompassing not only duties, but also conditions. *Restatement (Second) of Contracts* §319(1) (1981).

16.3 SUCCESSORS AND ASSIGNS[28]

> **Successors and Assigns.** This Agreement binds and benefits the parties and their respective permitted successors and assigns.[29]

The successors and assigns provision is a staple of commercial contracts. Although inserted almost ritualistically, its function and effect are rarely understood. It is sometimes confused with the assignment and delegation provision. But that provision deals with whether the contract permits assignments and delegations, while the successors and assigns provision, properly understood, deals with the consequences of an assignment and delegation.

The case law regarding the successors and assigns provision is muddy, with courts differing as to the provision's purpose and effect.[30] To understand the issues, some additional detail on the law of assignments and delegation is helpful.

As noted in Section 16.2.1, when a party assigns its rights under a contract to a third party, the nonassigning party becomes bound to perform for the benefit of the assignee.[31] But an assignment confers only the benefits of the rights being assigned, not any performance obligations.[32] The assignee is only an assignee—not an assignee and a delegate. Acceptance of the assignment does not create performance obligations.

An assignee may concurrently be a delegate. If a party simultaneously assigns its rights and delegates its performance, the assignee becomes a delegate on assuming the delegating party's duties to the nondelegating party.[33] Unfortunately, assignments are often ambiguous and do not clearly state whether the assignor is simultaneously delegating its performance.[34] In these cases, the courts look to whether the assignee assumed its assignor's performance.[35] If it did, then the court will find a contemporaneous delegation.[36] Unfortunately, no consensus exists as to whether an assumption must be express or whether an implied assumption is also permissible.[37]

The *Restatement (Second) of Contracts* and the U.C.C. prefer the modern approach.[38] Both provide that broad, general words of assignment constitute not only an assignment, but also a delegation.[39] The rationale is that both are generally

---

28. Section 16.3 is based on Tina L. Stark, *Successors and Assigns, in Negotiating and Drafting Contract Boilerplate.*

29. An alternative provision can be found on p. 225.

30. *See infra* nn. 41-45.

31. *See Pac. E. Corp. v. Gulf Life Holding Co.*, *supra* n. 4.

32. *See Petals Factory Outlet of Del., Inc. v. EWH & Assocs.*, 600 A.2d 1170, 1174 (Md. Spec. App. 1992).

33. *Lumsden v. Roth*, *supra* n. 10; *see* John Edward Murray, Jr., *Murray on Contracts* §§136[A][2], 139 (5th ed., Matthew Bender & Co., Inc. 2011); E. Allan Farnsworth, *Farnsworth on Contracts* vol. 3, §11.10, 129 (3d ed., Aspen Publishers 2004).

34. Arthur L. Corbin et al., *Corbin on Contracts* vol. 9, §47.6 (Joseph M. Perillo ed., rev. ed., West Publg. Co. 2007).

35. *See generally Murray*, *supra* n. 33, at §141[E].

36. *Id.*

37. *See Meighan v. Watts Constr. Co.*, 475 So. 2d 829, 833 (Ala. 1985) (stating that the law "in most states" requires an express assumption (citing *Rose v. Vulcan Materials Co.*, 194 S.E.2d 521, 533 (N.C. 1973)); *but see Nofziger Commun., Inc. v. Birks*, 757 F. Supp. 80, 82, 85 (D.D.C. 1991) ("[A]lthough some jurisdictions seem to have accepted the express assumption rule as one of general applicability, [it is not the general rule]. . . . [A] review of the law in other jurisdictions reveals that many jurisdictions have applied the express assumption rule only in a few narrow situations [the sale of land and assumption of liability for past breaches].").

38. *Restatement (Second) of Contracts* §328(1) (1981); U.C.C. §§2-210(4), U.L.A. U.C.C. §2-210(4) (2004).

39. *Id.*

intended, despite the drafting. So, for example, an assignment *of all my rights under the contract* would be both an assignment and a delegation, even though the delegation was unstated and the assumption was implied. Courts have created an exception if evidence demonstrates that the parties intended something different, such as when an assignment is a grant of a security interest. The less modern cases hold that assumptions must be express.[40]

Enter the successors and assigns provision. The better view is that this provision

- eliminates the necessity of an express assumption, binding the assignee to perform as it is also a delegate; and
- restates the common law that the nonassigning party must give the benefit of its performance to the assignee.

Nonetheless, the courts have interpreted the successors and assigns provision in wildly different ways. Although some courts have held that it binds an assignee,[41] others have held that it does not.[42] Other courts have held that the successor and assigns provision demonstrates that the parties intended contract rights to be assignable.[43] Still others have held that it is evidence that a nondelegable duty is delegable.[44] One case even holds that the provision constituted evidence that a preliminary agreement was a binding contract.[45] In the face of these different holdings, you rely on this provision at your own risk. The better approach is to draft a provision that says exactly what the parties intend.

X.X Successors and Assigns.

(a) **The Nonassigning Party's Performance Obligations**. If there is an assignment, the nonassigning party is deemed to have agreed to perform in favor of the assignee.

(b) **The Assignee's Performance Obligations**. If there is an assignment,
(i)   a contemporaneous delegation is deemed to have occurred, and
(ii) the assignee is deemed to have assumed the assignor's performance obligations in favor of the nonassigning party

(except if in either instance there is evidence to the contrary).

---

40. *See Bluebonnet Warehouse Coop. v. Bankers Trust Co.*, 89 F.3d 292, 297 (6th Cir. 1996); *see also Restatement (Second) of Contracts* §328(1) (1981); U.C.C. §2-210(4), U.L.A. U.C.C. §2-210(4) (2004).

41. *See Mehul's Inv. Corp. v. ABC Advisors, Inc.*, 130 F. Supp. 2d 700, 706 (D. Md. 2001) (stating that because the contract included a successors and assigns provision, the parties contemplated that they might assign their rights "and that their assigns and successors would be bound by the contract.").

42. *See Kneberg v. H.L. Green Co., Inc.*, 89 F.2d 100, 103-104 (7th Cir. 1937), and the cases cited therein.

43. *See Baum v. Rock*, 108 P.2d 230, 234 (Col. 1940) ("The courts generally have held that a contract which otherwise might not be assignable, is made so by the insertion therein of a provision binding the assigns of the parties. We follow this rule.").

44. *See Davis v. Basalt Rock Co.*, 237 P.2d 338, 343 (Cal. Dist. App. 1952) (holding that performance could not be delegated despite a recital of "assignability" in the successors and assigns provision as that provision was not "absolutely determinative," and nothing that "the intention of the parties must be gathered from a consideration of the terms and entire tenor of the contract.") (quoting *Montgomery v. De Picot*, 96 P. 305, 307 (Cal. 1908)).

45. *See Plastone Plastic Co. v. Whitman-Webb Realty Co.*, 176 So. 2d 27, 28-29 (Ala. 1965) (Although the successors and assigns provision made no reference to binding the parties, the contract was found to be "binding upon the original parties[.]") (citing *Tex. Co. v. Birmingham S. College*, 194 So. 192 (Ala. 1940)); *but see Normandy Place Assocs. v. Beyer*, 1988 WL 35311 at *1 (Ohio App. 2d Dist. Mar. 16, 1988) (referring to the successors and assigns provision as evidence that a preliminary agreement was a binding contract).

> (c) **Assignability of Rights and Delegability of Performance**. This Section X.X does not address, directly or indirectly, whether
> (i) rights under this Agreement are assignable or
> (ii) performance under this Agreement is delegable.
> Section [insert cross-reference to the anti-assignment provision] addresses these matters.
> (d) **Definitions**. For purposes of this Section X.X,
> (i) **"assignment"** means any assignment, whether voluntary or involuntary, by merger, consolidation, dissolution, operation of law or any other manner;
> (ii) **"assignee"** means any successor or assign of the assignor;
> (iii) **"a change of control"** is deemed an assignment of rights; and
> (iv) **"merger"** refers to any merger in which a party participates, regardless of whether it is the surviving or disappearing party.

By clarifying the parties' obligations under an assignment and expressly stating that a delegation occurs concurrently with assignment, this proposed provision solves the problem presented by the common law and better serves the purpose of the successors and assigns provision.

If you do use the traditional version, include the word *permitted* before *successors and assigns*. That should prevent a party from successfully arguing that the successors and assigns provision allows assignments and delegations.

> This Agreement binds and benefits the parties and their respective *permitted* successors and assigns.

When the words *successors* and *assigns* are used in tandem, *assigns* denotes a party to whom a voluntary transfer of rights has been made.[46] *Successor* does not usually mean *assignee*. Instead, the classic definition of a *successor* is a corporation that by merger, consolidation, or other legal succession has been transferred rights and has assumed the performance obligations of another corporation.[47] Finally, you must tailor whichever version you use if one of the parties is a man or woman.

> **Successors and Assigns**. This Agreement binds and benefits
>
> (a) Roger North and his heirs, executors, administrators, legal representatives, and [permitted] assigns; and
> (b) Telecom Inc. and its [permitted] successors and assigns.

---

46. *See S. Patrician Assocs. v. Int'l Fid. Ins. Co.*, 381 S.E.2d 98, 99 (Ga. App. 1989).

47. *See Enchanted Ests. Community Ass'n, Inc. v. Timberlake Improvement Dist.*, 832 S.W.2d 800, 802 (Tex. App.—Houston [1st Dist.] 1992) ("As applied to corporations, 'successor' does not normally mean an assignee . . . .") (*citing Int'l Ass'n of Machinists, Lodge No. 6 v. Falstaff Brewing Corp.*, 328 S.W.2d 778, 781 (Tex. App.—Houston 1959)).

16.4 GOVERNING LAW[48]

> **Governing Law**
>
> **Governing Law.** The laws of [insert state name] (without giving effect to its conflicts of law principles) govern all matters arising under and relating to this Agreement, including torts.

A governing law provision (also known as a choice of law provision) establishes the law that governs a dispute arising from an agreement. Courts routinely enforce these provisions unless the chosen state has no substantial relationship to the parties or transaction or the application of the law would violate the public policy of a state with a greater interest.[49] In its absence, common law conflicts of law principles govern. In that event, the governing law is that of the state with the most significant relationship to the transaction.[50] In a litigation, the parties may disagree which state that is, particularly when the law in one state favors one party. By choosing the governing law when drafting the contract, the parties may forestall a dispute on this issue. To complement the governing law provision, also include a choice of forum provision that chooses a forum in the state whose law will govern. This enhances the likelihood that a court will enforce the governing law provision.

When choosing which state's law should govern, consider several factors. First, evaluate whether the law of the jurisdiction under consideration is well developed and predictable. Delaware and New York, for example, both have well-developed bodies of corporate law, making an agreement's interpretation more predictable than might be true in other jurisdictions. In addition, evaluate whether the particular body of state law is hostile or friendly to the type of client (and the subject matter) being represented. For example, while California courts have upheld significant punitive damages awards for bad faith denials of insurance coverage, New York courts, as a general matter, rarely make such awards.[51]

When drafting a governing law provision, pay attention to the language defining the scope of the provision. Despite the plain meaning of the words, the following provision is not as broad in scope as it seems to be:

> The laws of Kentucky govern all matters arising under this Agreement.

As drafted, the provision excludes torts and other claims.[52] One way to bring those claims within the provision's embrace is to add the phrase *or relating to*. Courts

---

48. Section 16.4 is based on Brad S. Karp & Shelly L. Friedland, *Governing Law and Forum Selection*, in *Negotiating and Drafting Contract Boilerplate* ch. 6.

49. *See e.g. Elgar v. Elgar*, 679 A.2d 932, 943 (Conn. 1996); *see Restatement (Second) of Conflicts* §187 (1971); *see generally* Symeon C. Symeonides, *Choice of Law in the American Courts in 1996: Tenth Annual Survey*, 45 Am. J. Comp. L. 447, 488 (1997).

50. *See Intercontinental Plan., Ltd. v. Daystrom, Inc.*, 248 N.E.2d 576, 582 (N.Y. 1969); *Restatement (Second) of Conflicts* §188 (1971).

51. *Compare Delos v. Farmers Group, Inc.*, 155 Cal. Rptr. 843, 857 (App. 4th Dist. 1979), *with Rocanova v. Eq. Life Assurance Soc'y of the U.S.*, 634 N.E.2d 940, 944 (N.Y. 1994).

52. *See e.g. Shelley v. Trafalgar House Pub. Ltd. Co.*, 918 F. Supp. 515, 521-522 (D.P.R. 1996) (Where the provision indicated that "this letter shall be subject to and construed in accordance with the laws of the State of New York," the provision did not apply to the tort claim.); *Caton v. Leach Corp.*, 896 F.2d 939, 943 (5th Cir. 1990) (finding that claims of tort, breach of duty of good faith, and fair dealing and claims for restitution were not included in the parties' narrow choice of law clause, which stated that "[t]his Agreement shall

have stated that the phrase extends the scope of the governing law clause to matters beyond the specific contract.[53] This option may be startling because it uses a couplet. Generally, couplets should be banished from contracts as legalese.[54] Here, however, the couplet has meaning.

Alternatively, some drafters expressly state that the governing law will cover matters relating to torts by adding *including torts* immediately after *all matters*.

> **The laws of Kentucky govern all matters arising under this Agreement, including torts.**

Although this addition broadens the coverage to include tort claims, it is narrower than the phrase *arising out of or relating to*, which can even reach different contracts.[55] Not covering torts one way or the other often leads to litigation.[56]

In many commercial transactions, the parties wish New York or Delaware law to govern, even though the transaction has no relationship with the chosen state. This can be done if the amount of the transaction meets statutory thresholds set forth in New York and Delaware law.[57]

If you go this route, pair the New York or Delaware governing law provision with a New York or Delaware choice of forum provision so that the litigation is in a forum that will enforce the governing law provision.[58] Be careful to check the dollar threshold for a particular state because the amount required for the choice of forum provision may exceed that for a governing law provision.[59]

Some choice of law provisions deal with *renvoi*. *Renvoi* is French for *return* or *send back*. It occurs when one state's conflict of law principles require that a second state's principles be used, but that second state's principles require that the first state's principles be used. This referral from one state's principles to another and back to the first creates an endless cycle of return.

be construed under the laws of the State of California."); *Gloucester Holding Corp. v. U.S. Tape and Sticky Prods., LLC*, 832 A.2d 116, 122, 123-125 (Del. Ch. 2003) (holding that torts and statutory claims were outside the embrace of a governing law provision stating the agreement "shall be construed, interpreted and the rights of the parties determined in accordance with the laws of the State of Delaware . . . .").

53. *See Turtur v. Rothschild Registry Int'l, Inc.*, 26 F.3d 304, 309 (2d Cir. 1994) (holding that a governing law provision was broad enough to cover torts when the agreement covered any controversy "arising out of or relating to" that agreement); *Caton v. Leach Corp.*, 896 F.2d 939, 943 (5th Cir. 1990) (comparing the contract's narrow clause that did "not address the entirety of parties' relationship" to broader clause that included "arising from or relating in any way.").

54. *See* F. Reed Dickerson, *The Fundamentals of Legal Drafting* 208 (2d ed., Little, Brown & Co. 1986).

55. *See ePresence, Inc. v. Evolve Software, Inc.*, 190 F. Supp. 2d 159, 162-163 (D. Mass. 2002) (construing California choice of law clause to include a subsequent and independent oral contract where the clause stated that it governed "[the] Agreement and all matters arising out of or relating to [the] Agreement. . . .").

56. *Abry Partners V, L.P. v. F & W Acq. LLC*, 891 A.2d 1032, 1059 (Del. Ch. 2006).

57. Del. Code Ann. tit. 6, § 2708(c) (2013); N.Y. Gen. Oblig. Law §5-1401(1) (2013).

58. *See* Del. Code Ann. tit. 6, §2708(b) (2013); N.Y. Gen. Oblig. Law § 5-1402 (2013); *but see Nutracea v. Langley Park Invs. PLC*, 2007 WL 135699 at *3 (E.D. Cal. Jan. 16, 2007). Although no California court has explicitly overruled *Nutracea*, in 2010 the Federal District Court for Massachusetts held that *Nutracea*'s holding was "no longer supported by the weight of law." *Huffington v. Carlyle Group*, 685 F. Supp. 2d 239, 244 (D. Mass. 2010).

59. For example, New York requires a $250,000 threshold for New York law to be governing law and a $1 million threshold for New York to be the forum. N.Y. Gen. Oblig. Law §§5-1401–5-1402 (2013). California requires a $250,000 threshold for California law to be governing law. Cal. Civ. Code §1646.5 (2013). California also requires a $1 million threshold for California to be the forum. Cal. Civ. Proc. Code §410.40 (2013).

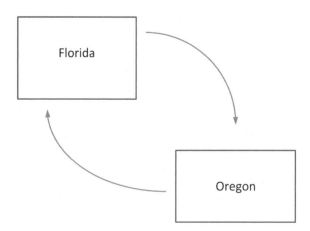

To break this cycle, some lawyers qualify the governing law provisions with the clause, *without regard to its conflict of law principles.* (See the provision introducing this section.)[60] In reality, this clause is unnecessary as the law of the chosen state typically excludes its choice of law rules.[61] However, it has become so commonplace that you will be hard-pressed to convince someone that the provision is superfluous.

16.5 WAIVER OF RIGHT TO A JURY TRIAL[62]

> [Section number XX last section of the agreement]. **Waiver of Right to a Jury Trial**. Each party knowingly, voluntarily, and intentionally waives its right to a trial by jury in any legal proceeding arising out of or relating to this Agreement and the transactions it contemplates. This waiver applies to any legal proceeding, whether sounding in contract, tort, or otherwise. Each party acknowledges that it has received the advice of competent counsel.

The U.S. Constitution and many state constitutions guarantee the right to a jury trial.[63] In most states, a party may waive this right.[64] But before inserting a waiver of jury trial provision into a contract, first consider whether a waiver benefits your client. If your client is a large, commercial corporation, a waiver of jury trial provision might be provident. Jury members often harbor a visceral dislike of large, commercial corporations or see them as having deep pockets.[65]

---

60. *See* p. 226.

61. *See Restatement (Second) of Conflict of Laws* § 187 cmt. h (1971) ("The reference[to the laws of a particular state], in the absence of a contrary indication of intention, is to the 'local law' of the chosen state and not to that state's 'law,' which means the totality of its law including its choice-of-law rules. When they choose the state which is to furnish the law governing the validity of their contract, the parties almost certainly have the 'local law,' rather than the 'law,' of that state in mind (*compare* § 186, cmt. b). To apply the 'law' of the chosen state would introduce the uncertainties of choice of law into the proceedings and would serve to defeat the basic objectives, namely those of certainty and predictability, which the choice-of-law provision was designed to achieve."); *see also* Donald W. Glazer, Scott T. FitzGibbon & Steven O. Weise, *Glazer and FitzGibbon on Legal Opinions: Drafting, Interpreting, and Supporting Closing Opinions in Business Transactions* § 9.12.1 n. 2 (Aspen Publishers 2001).

62. Section 16.5 is based on Lauren Reiter Brody & Frances Kulka Browne, *Waiver of Jury Trial*, in *Negotiating and Drafting Contract Boilerplate* ch. 7.

63. U.S. Const. amend. VI; Cal. Const. art. 1, § 16; Mass. Const. Part the First, art. 12; N.Y. Const. art. 1, §2; Neb. Const. art. 1, §6.

64. *But see* Ga. Code Ann. §9-11-38 (2013); Mont. Code Ann. §28-2-708 (2011).

65. David T. Rusoff, *Contractual Jury Waivers: Their Use in Reducing Lender Liability*, 110 Banking L.J. 4, 5 (1993).

Because the right to a jury trial is a constitutional right, courts disfavor a waiver of this right and require that a waiver be *knowing, intentional, and voluntary.*[66] The key, of course, is to draft the waiver in such a way that a court will reach the "appropriate" conclusion. The following drafting guidelines are derived from the case law:

Guidelines for Drafting a Waiver of the Right to a Jury Trial

1. *Put the waiver of jury trial provision as the last of the general provisions, so that it immediately precedes the signature lines.*[67]

2. *Make the provision prominent by putting it in a bold font and in a font size that is larger than that used in the rest of the contract.*[68]

3. *Use a caption that indicates that the right to a jury trial is being waived.*[69]

4. *List the provision in the table of contents, using a caption that indicates the right to a jury trial is being waived.*[70]

5. *Make the provision bilateral.*[71]

6. *If the other party is a natural person,*

    (a) *require that person to initial the provision;*[72]

    (b) *include a statement that the waiver is knowing, voluntary, and intentional;*[73]

    (c) *require that person to acknowledge that her lawyer explained the provision;*[74] *and*

    (d) *require that person's lawyer to sign a form stating that he has explained the provision and its ramifications to his client.*[75]

---

66. *See Conn. Nat'l Bank v. Smith*, 826 F. Supp. 57, 59 (D.R.I. 1993).

67. *See In re Reggie Packing Co.*, 671 F. Supp. 571, 574 (N.D. Ill. 1987) (enforcing jury waiver where "the waiver clause is located at the end of a paragraph, just two inches above the parties' signatures").

68. *See Luis Acosta, Inc. v. Citibank, N.A.*, 920 F. Supp. 15, 19 (D.P.R. 1996) (ordering jury trial where "the wavier clause is not in boldface and is buried at the end of the contract"). You may also consider putting the provision in all capital letters. Although some commentators believe that a provision using all capital letters is difficult to read, courts have nonetheless suggested that the all capital letters format is an acceptable way to make the waiver of jury trial provision prominent.

69. *Smyly v. Hyundai Motor Am.*, 762 F. Supp. 428, 430 (D. Mass. 1991) (enforcing an agreement that "plainly set out the jury waiver [and] foretold it in capital letters in an introductory table of contents").

70. *Id.*

71. *See e.g. U.S. v. Mt. Village Co.*, 424 F. Supp. 822, 825 (D. Mass. 1976).

72. *Coop. Fin. Ass'n, Inc. v. Garst*, 871 F. Supp. 1168, 1172 n. 2 (N.D. Iowa 1995) (recommending that parties initial clause to demonstrate that it was reviewed).

73. *Bank of Bos. Conn. v. Rusconi*, 1994 WL 506622 at *1 (Conn. Super. Sept. 6, 1994); *cf. In re Pate*, 198 B.R. 841, 843 (Bankr. S.D. Ga. 1996) (upholding contractual waiver of jury trial and preference for arbitration because contract reflected parties' understanding of the nature of the right relinquished).

74. *See* Robert H. MacKinnon & Nathan M. Eisler, *Drafting Lending Documents to Avoid Lender Liability Claims,* in *Lender Liability Litigation 1990: Recent Developments* 27, 49 (PLI Course Handbook Series No. 551, 1990).

75. It has also been suggested that an acknowledgment should describe the counseling provided, including, for example, that the party agreeing to the waiver was told that it was under no compulsion to execute the waiver, that the party exercised independent judgment to act, and that it acted of its free will, without duress, coercion, or compulsion. *See id.* at 43; *cf. Ricker v. U.S.*, 417 F. Supp. 133, 140 (D. Me. 1976) (holding elderly couple's waiver of right to notice and hearing in a mortgage agreement was unenforceable because "[n]o attorney was advising them, and at no time did anyone explain to them that by signing the mortgage they were waiving rights to notice and hearing.").

16.6 NOTICE[76]

> **Notice.**
>
> (a) **Requirement of a Writing; Permitted Methods of Delivery**. Each party giving or making any notice, request, demand, or other communication (each, a "**Notice**") in accordance with this Agreement shall give the Notice in writing and use one of the following methods of delivery, each of which for purposes of this Agreement is a writing:
>   (i)   Personal delivery.
>   (ii) Registered or Certified Mail (in each case, return receipt requested and postage prepaid).
>   (iii) Internationally recognized overnight courier (with all fees prepaid).
>   (iv) Facsimile.
>   (v)   E-mail.
> (b) **Addressees and Addresses**. Any party giving a Notice shall address the Notice to the appropriate person at the receiving party (the "Addressee") at the address listed on the signature page of this Agreement or to another Addressee or another address as designated by a party in a Notice pursuant to this Section.
> (c) **Effectiveness of a Notice**. Except as provided elsewhere in this Agreement, a Notice is effective only if the party giving the Notice has complied with subsections (a) and (b) and if the Addressee has received the Notice.

Notice provisions are ubiquitous. Nearly every contract has one. They do more, however, than list the addresses to which parties should send their notices. They allocate the risk of a notice's nonreceipt.

Notice provisions used to state: "A notice is effective three days after its deposit in a U.S. Postal Service mailbox." This meant that, even if the notice was lost, the sender of the notice had rights against the recipient three days after mailing. The risk of nonreceipt was on the recipient. As this led to inequitable results, many parties now insist that the risk of nonreceipt should be on the sender. To do so, notice must be effective only on its receipt.

A well-drafted notice provision should state the modes by which a party may give notice. Typically, a provision permits notices to be given by fax, by in-person delivery, or by overnight courier. The sender can easily monitor these modes to determine whether the other party has received the notice. Many notice provisions no longer permit delivery by U.S. Postal Service first-class mail because of its unreliability. If the parties insist on delivery through the U.S. Postal Service, a common compromise is delivery by certified or registered mail. The benefit of these two forms of delivery is that a sender can request a return receipt.[77] The delivery of notice by e-mail is becoming more common, but some drafters still have qualms about it. This may change,

---

76. Section 16.6 is based on Steven R. Berger, *Notices*, in *Negotiating and Drafting Contract Boilerplate* ch. 15.

77. "Return receipt service provides a mailer with evidence of delivery (to whom the mail was delivered and date of deliver), along with information about the recipient's actual delivery address." U.S. Postal Serv., *Domestic Mail Manual* §5.2.1, http://pe.usps.com/text/dmm300/503.htm#_top (accessed July 27, 2011).

however, as parties become more comfortable with software technology that provides certainty of delivery and security.

Here are additional points to consider when drafting a notice provision.

- Is delivery of the notice a covenant or condition or both? (The suggested provision is drafted as both).
- If a copy of a notice is to be sent to a person other than a party, is that party's receipt required for the notice to be effective?
- Should the addressee be a specific person (who may well leave the company) or the corporate title of the person in charge of the transaction?
- What accommodation, if any, needs to be made for international deliveries?

16.7 SEVERABILITY[78]

> **Severability**. If any provision of this Agreement is determined to be illegal or unenforceable, the remaining provisions of this Agreement remain in full force, if the essential provisions of this Agreement for each party remain legal and enforceable.

Courts will not enforce obligations arising out of illegal agreements.[79] A contract that contains one illegal provision may, however, also contain legal, enforceable provisions. In these situations, a refusal to enforce the entire contract might prove unduly harsh. Instead, courts often strike the offending provisions, allowing the rest of the agreement to stay in force.[80]

The purpose of a severability provision is to express the parties' intent that a court enforce the valid provisions of a contract, even if it finds a provision to be illegal or unenforceable. Usually, the provision is similar to the one that follows:

> **Severability**. If any provision of this Agreement is illegal or unenforceable, that provision is severed from this Agreement and the other provisions remain in force.

Unfortunately, this typical provision rarely reflects the parties' actual intent. For example, imagine a noncompete agreement that requires an employer to pay an employee $3 million, in return for which the employee agrees not to compete anywhere in the world for ten years. Imagine further that the court holds that the noncompete is overly broad and unenforceable. With the standard severability provision, the noncompete would be severed, but the payment obligation would remain. The likelihood that this would accomplish the parties' intent is low. More likely, they intended that the nonsevered provisions would remain in effect only if the essential provisions of the agreement for each party remained binding and enforceable.

---

78. Section 16.7 is based on C. James Levin & Avery R. Brown, *Severability,* in *Negotiating and Drafting Contract Boilerplate* ch. 17.

79. *See generally* Richard A. Lord, *Williston on Contracts* vol. 6, § 13.25, 831-837 (4th ed., West 2009) (discussing traditional blue-pencil rule).

80. *See Rogers v. Wolfson,* 763 S.W.2d 922, 924 (Tex. App.—Dallas 1989), *cert. denied,* (Tex. Feb. 13, 1989) (holding that clearly severable provision will not render entire contract invalid).

While this rewriting of the more standard formulation may not preclude all intent-related issues, at least it explicitly expresses that the parties cannot do without some provisions. In addition, it gives them the opportunity to argue which provisions are essential in the context of any later dispute.

Keep one other thing in mind when drafting severability provisions: The way you draft the provision should reflect whether the governing law is that of a state that follows the **blue-pencil rule**[81] or that of a state that follows the **rule of reasonableness**.[82]

Under the traditional blue-pencil rule, a court will delete portions of an otherwise unenforceable provision if the deleted portions can be clearly—and grammatically—separated from the remainder of the provision (i.e., if the provision will still be grammatically correct after the offending terms have been deleted). For example, an overbroad covenant forbidding future employment in Connecticut could not be reduced to cover one county in a blue-pencil jurisdiction.[83] By contrast, that result could be reached if the covenant had separately listed each county in Connecticut. Then, a court could salvage the noncompete by deleting specific counties until the list was no longer overbroad. States that have adopted the blue-pencil approach include Connecticut, Indiana, and North Carolina.[84]

The *Restatement (Second) of Contracts* has rejected the blue-pencil approach in favor of the more flexible rule of reasonableness.[85] Under this rule, a court may reform an unenforceable provision to the extent reasonable under the circumstances and then enforce it as so reformed.[86] States that have adopted this approach include Delaware, Florida, New Jersey, New York, Pennsylvania, and Tennessee.[87] Courts have sought to limit the risk of overreaching that this approach might entail by requiring proof that the offending provisions were drafted in good faith and in accordance with standards of fair dealing.[88]

16.8 AMENDMENTS[89]

> **Amendments.** The parties may amend this Agreement only by the parties' written agreement that identifies itself as an amendment to this Agreement.

The no oral amendments provision is classic boilerplate—always present, rarely negotiated. It is also generally unenforceable under the common law. In a Texas case,

---

81. *See generally Lord, supra* n. 79, at § 13.25, 831-837 (discussing traditional blue-pencil rule).

82. *See generally Restatement (Second) of Contracts* § 184 (1979).

83. *See Beit v. Beit*, 63 A.2d 161, 166 (Conn. 1948) (covenant unenforceable where parties intended covenant to apply to a certain county, not a severable portion of it).

84. *See id.* at 165-166; *College Life Ins. Co. of Am. v. Austin*, 466 N.E.2d 738, 744 (Ind. App. 1st Dist. 1984); *Whittaker Gen. Med. Corp. v. David*, 379 S.E.2d 824, 828 (N.C. 1989).

85. *Restatement (Second) of Contracts* § 184 (1979).

86. *Id.*

87. *See Knowles-Zeswitz Music, Inc. v. Cara*, 260 A.2d 171, 175 (Del. Ch. 1969); *Dorminy v. Frank B. Hall & Co.*, 464 So. 2d 154, 157 (Fla. 5th Dist. App. 1985); *Solari Indus., Inc. v. Malady*, 264 A.2d 53, 57 (N.J. 1970); *Karpinski v. Ingrasci*, 268 N.E.2d 751, 754-755 (N.Y. 1971); *Sidco Paper Co. v. Aaron*, 351 A.2d 250, 254-255 (Pa. 1976); *C. Adjustment Bureau v. Ingram*, 678 S.W.2d 28, 37 (Tenn. 1984).

88. *See Lord, supra* n. 79, at § 13.26, 853-854; *Farnsworth, supra* n. 33, at §5.8, 347; *C. Adjustment Bureau v. Ingram, supra* n. 87 (noting that credible evidence that a contract is "deliberately" unreasonable and oppressive will render it invalid).

89. Section 16.8 is based on Brian A. Haskel, *General Provisions,* in *Negotiating and Drafting Contract Boilerplate* ch. 16.

the court stated that a written contract "is of no higher legal degree than an oral one, and either may vary or discharge the other."[90] Similarly, in a New York case, Judge Cardozo said:

> Those who make a contract may unmake it. The clause which forbids a change, may be changed like any other. . . . What is executed by one act is restored by another. . . . Whenever two [persons] contract, no limitation self-imposed can destroy their power to contract again.[91]

To bring greater predictability to contractual relations, some states have enacted laws providing that no oral amendment provisions are enforceable.[92] The courts, however, have undermined these statutory provisions by finding that parties can modify the underlying agreement by an executed (completed) oral amendment, a course of conduct, or estoppel.[93]

A nationwide solution has also been attempted through U.C.C. §2-209(2), which provides that *no oral amendment* provisions are enforceable in contracts.[94] Unfortunately, this solution is limited in scope to contracts subject to U.C.C. Article 2 and is not bulletproof. Specifically, under U.C.C. §2-209(4), a purported amendment that does not satisfy the requirements of the statute of frauds can operate as a waiver of the no oral amendments provision.[95] The rationale is that course of performance during the term of the contract either represents a waiver or is relevant in determining whether a particular act affects the agreement's meaning. In essence, U.C.C. §2-209(4) codifies the estoppel theory under which courts have enforced oral amendments despite contractual prohibitions against them.

With all these obstacles to an enforceable no oral amendments provision, the obvious question is whether it makes sense to try to include one. The answer is *yes*. These provisions evidence the parties' agreement and their intent at the time the contract was signed. Many parties use them as guideposts for their actions during the life of the contract. If a dispute arises as to whether a purported amendment is enforceable, these provisions set the starting point for a court's analysis because they reflect the parties' understanding when they made their agreement.

The no oral amendments provision can be very simple. It needs to state that the parties may amend the provision only by written agreement. You may tailor the provision by specifying who must sign on behalf of each party. You may also include as a condition to the enforceability of the amendment that each party must deliver to the other a board resolution authorizing the amendment. Also consider including language that requires the amendment to identify itself as an amendment to the agreement. This can be helpful in New York, for instance, where the state's highest court held that

---

90. *Mar-Lan Indus., Inc. v. Nelson*, 635 S.W.2d 853, 855 (Tex. App.—El Paso 1982).

91. *Beatty v. Guggenheim Exploration Co.*, 122 N.E. 378, 381 (N.Y. 1919).

92. *See e.g.* Cal. Civ. Code §1698 (2012); N.Y. Gen. Oblig. Law §15-301 (2013).

93. *See Wechsler v. Hunt Health Sys., Ltd.*, 186 F. Supp. 2d 402 (S.D.N.Y. 2002); *S. Fed. Sav. & Loan Ass'n of Ga. v. 21-26 E. 105th St. Assocs.*, 145 B.R. 375, 380 (S.D.N.Y. 1991) ("Under certain conditions . . . a written agreement which provides that it cannot be modified except by a writing, can be modified by a course of conduct or actual performance.") (internal citations omitted).

94. U.C.C. §2-209(2) states:

> A signed agreement which excludes modification or rescission except by a signed writing cannot be otherwise modified or rescinded, but except as between merchants such a requirement on a form supplied by the merchant must be separately signed by the other party.

"Between merchants" is interpreted to mean between sophisticated parties. *Wis. Knife Workers v. Nat'l Metal Crafters*, 781 F.2d 1280, 1284 (7th Cir. 1986).

95. U.C.C. §2-209(4) states: "Although an attempt at modification or rescission does not satisfy the requirements of subsection (2) or (3) it can operate as a waiver."

the minutes of a board of directors' meeting, signed by the corporate secretary, were a sufficient writing to constitute execution of an amendment.[96]

16.9 MERGER[97]

> **Merger.** This Agreement constitutes the final, exclusive agreement between the parties on the matters contained in this Agreement. All earlier and contemporaneous negotiations and agreements between the parties on the matters contained in this Agreement are expressly merged into and superseded by this Agreement.

A merger provision is sometimes called an **integration provision** or a **zipper clause**. Generally speaking, it is the best way (but not a bulletproof way) to ensure that parol evidence cannot be used to supplement the contract. In the absence of a merger provision, courts will examine all of the relevant facts and circumstances to determine whether it is a final and exclusive expression of the parties' agreement.[98] A writing that is a final expression of the parties' agreement is said to be *partially integrated*, while a writing that is both a final and exclusive expression of the parties' agreement is said to be *fully integrated*.

Under the parol evidence rule, if a writing is integrated, whether fully or partially, a term that contradicts the existing writing cannot be admitted into evidence.[99] If the writing is partially integrated, evidence of prior negotiations and agreements are admissible to supplement the writing, but not to contradict it.[100] (Remember: If the agreement is partially integrated, it is not the exclusive statement of the parties' agreement. Therefore, consistent provisions can supplement it.) But if the writing is fully integrated (final and exclusive), generally, not even evidence of an additional, consistent term is admissible.

Despite these rules, parol evidence is always admissible to explain an ambiguous contract term.[101] In addition, courts generally permit a party to introduce parol evidence that the other party fraudulently induced it to enter into the contract. A number of courts have prohibited the introduction of this evidence if the allegedly defrauded party disclaimed reliance in the contract on the representation that it now claims was the basis of the fraud.[102]

When drafting a merger provision, describe the agreement being signed as *final and exclusive* to signal that the parties intend the agreement to be fully integrated. Also state the consequences of the agreement being final and exclusive: that all prior negotiations and agreements are merged into the agreement being signed. If the agreement being signed does not supersede an existing agreement (such as a confidentiality agreement), state the exception.

---

96. *DFI Commun., Inc. v. Greenberg*, 394 N.Y.S.2d 586, 589-590 (N.Y. 1977).

97. Section 16.9 is based on Ronald B. Risdon & William A. Escobar, *Merger,* in *Negotiating and Drafting Contract Boilerplate* ch. 18.

98. *In re William Rakestraw Co.*, 450 F.2d 6 (9th Cir. 1971) (applying California law).

99. Farnsworth, *supra* n. 33, at vol. 2, § 7.3, 226 (quoting *Restatement (Second) of Contracts* §215 (1981)).

100. *Id.*

101. *Id.* (quoting *Restatement (Second) of Contracts* §216(1) (1981)).

102. *See e.g. Consarc Corp. v. Marine Midland Bank, N.A.*, 996 F.2d 568 (2d Cir. 1993) (applying New York law).

If the parties are signing multiple agreements contemporaneously, use a defined term to refer to all the agreements—for example, use *Transaction Documents*. The merger provision should then state that those documents together constitute the final and exclusive agreement of the parties. Be sure that each of the other agreements being executed includes a merger provision that is exactly the same as the one in the primary agreement.

16.10 COUNTERPARTS[103]

> **Counterparts**. The parties may execute this Agreement in one or more counterparts, each of which is an original, and all of which constitute only one agreement between the parties.

A **counterpart** is a duplicate original that parties sign. Drafters use counterparts to expedite transactions when not all the parties attend the agreement's signing and to create multiple originals so that each party can have a fully executed original.

Historically, the rationale for using multiple counterparts was as an antifraud measure for contracts. The use of counterparts originated in real property conveyancing in England.[104] Under English common law, an indenture was used to memorialize an agreement for the purchase or lease of real property.[105] The *indenture*, or *deed indented*, takes its name from the practice of writing as many copies of the deed as there were parties on one large sheet of parchment, and then cutting them apart in an indented or wavy line.[106] Thus, each document was a counterpart to the other. This practice was particularly useful in transactions where one or more parties had continuing covenants, because in these situations each party desired its own copy of the agreement.[107]

The counterparts were signed in one of two ways. In a lease, for example, the landlord signed the portion of the document that contained his promises, and the tenant signed the portion with his promises.[108] Then they would swap their respective signed documents. (Traditionally, the portion of the indenture that the landlord executed was called the *original*, and the remaining sections were termed the *counterparts*.) The second way that indentures could be signed was for all the parties to execute the identically drafted segments of parchment, thereby rendering them all "originals."[109]

---

103. *See Abry Partners V, L.P. v. F & W Acq. LLC*, 891 A.2d 1032, 1059 (Del. Ch. 2006); *Danann Realty Corp. v. Harris*, 5 N.Y.2d 317, 157 N.E.2d, 597 (N.Y. 1959).

104. Section 16.10 is based on Frances Kulka Browne, *Counterparts*, in *Negotiating and Drafting Contract Boilerplate* ch. 19; *see also* § 17.5.2 for details concerning the signing of counterparts.

105. *See* Alvin L. Arnold & Jack Kusnet, *The Arnold Encyclopedia of Real Estate* 402 (Warren, Gorham & Lamont 1978).

106. *Id.*

107. Charles Greenstreet Addison, *A Treatise on the Law of Contracts* 21 (William E. Gordon & John Ritchie eds., 11th ed., Stevens & Sons 1911).

108. *See* Charles Donahue, Jr., Thomas E. Kauper & Peter W. Martin, *Cases and Materials on Property: An Introduction to the Concept and the Institution* 502 (West 1974).

109. The following is a counterparts provision from the Indenture, dated January 25, 1694, between Joseph Reynolds and John Balderston and the Fellows and Scholars of Emanuel College:

Original Old English

In Witness Whereof to one part of these Indentures remaining with . . . Joseph Reynolds[,] the . . . Fellows and Schollars [sic] have put their common seale [sic] [; and] to the other parte [sic] thereof

In either case, in the event of a dispute, the counterparts could be physically pieced together to verify that they came from the same parchment.

The typical counterparts provision in a modern contract provides that the parties may execute the contract in one or more counterparts. This is usually interpreted in two ways: first, to permit each party to sign separate counterparts, which, when collated, together constitute a fully executed original; second to permit multiple originals, each of which is signed by all the parties. In this event, each party leaves the signing with a single document that is a fully executed original. Some drafters prefer to spell out each of the two possibilities.

A well-drafted counterparts provision also states that the counterparts *constitute only one agreement*. This means that each party makes only one set of promises even though the parties may have executed multiple counterparts, creating multiple, fully executed originals. That is, neither party promises to do something as many times as it has executed counterparts.

For details concerning the signing of counterparts, see Section 17.5.2.

---

remaining with the . . . Fellows and Schollars [sic][,] . . . Joseph Reynolds hath put to his hand and seale [sic] the day and year first above written.

Contemporary English redraft

In Witness Whereof, the Fellows and Scholars have executed the part of this Indenture remaining with Joseph Reynolds; and Joseph Reynolds has executed the part of this Indenture remaining with the Fellows and Scholars.

[Contract is from the collection of Tina L. Stark.]

EXERCISES

Exercise 16-1

Rewrite the following provision so that it is well drafted. What drafting change would you make if you wanted to increase the likelihood of the provision's enforceability as a fully integrated agreement?

> **Entire Agreement**. This Agreement, together with the Confidentiality Agreement and the other Instruments delivered in connection herewith, embody the entire agreement and understanding of the parties hereto and supersede any prior agreement or understanding between the parties with respect to the subject matter of this Agreement.

Exercise 16-2

The following provision is intended as an anti-assignment provision. How would you rewrite it to fulfill the parties' intent and to otherwise improve the drafting? If your client was the party most likely to be requesting consent, what additional language might you suggest?

> **Assignment**. This Agreement may not be assigned by either party without the prior written consent of the other.

Exercise 16-3

Rewrite the following provision to improve its drafting. Are *change, waiver, discharge,* and *termination* redundant and legalese? Are *modify, change,* and *amend* redundant and legalese? What cardinal rule of good drafting does the provision violate? How could the heading be improved?

> **Amendments and Waivers**. Neither this Agreement, the Note, nor any terms hereof or thereof may be changed, waived, discharged, or terminated, unless such change, waiver, or discharge is in writing signed by the Company and the Bank.

Exercise 16-4

Rewrite the following provision to improve its drafting.

> **Counterparts**. This Agreement may be executed in one or more counterparts, each of which shall be deemed an original, but all of which together shall constitute one and the same document.

Exercise 16-5

From a business perspective, what are the parties trying to accomplish in the following provision? In the first sentence, to what does the word *respective* refer? The first sentence uses the words *assign or transfer*. The second sentence uses the words *sell, assign, transfer, or grant*. Should *sell* and *grant* be deleted from the second sentence? Does the provision preclude the Company from delegating its obligations under the Agreement? If the Company were to negotiate the prior consent exception, what additional language could it ask for that might make it more likely that the Bank would consent? Rewrite the provision to correct drafting errors, including formatting.

> **Successors and Assigns.** This Agreement shall be binding on and inure to the benefit of the Company, the Bank, all future holders of the Note and their respective successors and assigns, except that the Company may not assign or transfer any of its rights under this Agreement without the prior written consent of the Bank. The Company acknowledges that the Bank may at any time sell, assign, transfer, or grant participations in the Loan to other financial institutions (a "**Transferee**"). The Company agrees that each Transferee may exercise all rights of payment (including rights of setoff) with respect to the portion of such loans held by it as fully as if such Transferee were the direct holder thereof.

Exercise 16-6

When drafting a notice provision, what would you consider when deciding whether to include a provision requiring that counsel receive a copy of the notice for the notice to be effective? (*Hint*: Why might the size and sophistication of the client matter?)

Exercise 16-7

If you were drafting a counterparts provision that allowed each party to sign a different document, what language would you need to add to the provision to create certainty as to the agreement's effective date?

Exercise 16-8

Find a notice provision precedent that addresses e-mail.

Signatures

17.1 INTRODUCTION

With a few exceptions,[1] creation of a contract requires neither a writing nor a signature.[2] Instead, contract formation requires offer, acceptance, consideration, and mutual assent to the agreement's essential terms.[3] But the drafter must make sure that the signature lines are correct if the parties want a written contract to memorialize their contract and intend that signatures evidence their agreement. Attention to detail is essential.

The formal name for the language introducing the signature blocks is the **testimonium clause**. This book refers to it as the **concluding paragraph**. The following is typical:

> In Witness Whereof, the parties have executed and delivered this Agreement on the date hereof.

This chapter will first address the meaning of *executed* and *delivered* and then the benefits of a more contemporary concluding paragraph. It concludes with a discussion of e-signatures, the drafting of signature blocks, and a variety of issues related to signature pages.

17.2 EXECUTION AND DELIVERY

17.2.1 DEFINITIONS

Parties have repeatedly litigated the meanings of *executed* and *delivered,* and whether both of these actions are necessary to create an enforceable contract. The case law is messy.

---

1. Among the exceptions are contracts subject to the statute of frauds. *See e.g.* N.M. Stat. § 55 2-201 (2003).

2. *See e.g. Schaller Tel. Co. v. Golden Sky Sys., Inc.*, 298 F.3d 736, 743 (8th Cir. 2002).

3. *See e.g. Fant v. Champion Aviation, Inc.*, 689 So. 2d 32, 37 (Ala. 1997).

Older, but not overruled, cases distinguish the verb *to execute* from the verb *to sign*.[4] *To sign* means to affix one's name in one's own handwriting, while *to execute* is broader and connotes affixing a signature either in one's own handwriting or through a representative. Other cases use the verbs synonymously.[5] Statutes can also be determinative. The Uniform Commercial Code provides that a signature includes the signing by a person's authorized representative.[6]

In some instances, cases distinguish execution from delivery,[7] while others interpret *execution* broadly to include signing and delivery.[8] When the terms are differentiated, *delivery* means the exchange of signed copies of the agreement.[9]

17.2.2 DELIVERY AND CONTRACT FORMATION

Delivery is not generally required for an agreement to be effective,[10] except for a few documents, such as deeds,[11] contracts under seal,[12] negotiable instruments,[13] and documents of title.[14] That said, the law in several states is that delivery is required.[15] Moreover, if parties intend that delivery should be an element of formation, courts will effectuate that intent.[16] Similarly, if they intend that signing is sufficient, courts will effectuate that intent.[17]

In sophisticated commercial transactions with closings, parties generally intend that the agreements to be signed at the closing be both signed and delivered. As a closing is not certain until the parties successfully complete their negotiations, the signed agreements on the closing table (or exchanged electronically) must remain ineffective until the actual closing. To do this, delivery becomes an additional element of the agreements' formation, and delivery is postponed until the parties agree they are ready to close. Then, they exchange consideration and deliver the agreements. Although many transactions rely on this type of arrangement, it is not always memorialized in writing. It is an unstated understanding.

You can directly address the issue of the parties' intent with respect to delivery by stating in the contract when it becomes effective: on signing, or on signing and deliv-

---

4. *Wamesit Nat'l Bank v. Merriam*, 96 A. 740, 741 (Me. 1916).

5. *Elliott v. Merchants' Bank & Trust Co.*, 132 P. 280, 281 (Cal. App. 1913).

6. U.C.C. §3-401.

7. *See Brown Bros. Lumber Co. v. Preston Mill Co.*, 145 P. 964, 966-967 (Wash. 1915).

8. *See Nodland v. Chirpich*, 240 N.W.2d 513, 517 (Minn. 1976) ("Delivery is ordinarily an essential element of the execution of a written contract."); *Hayes v. Ammon*, 85 N.Y.S. 607, 608 (App. Div. 1904).

9. *See Am. Fam. Mut. Ins. Co. v. Zavala*, 302 F. Supp. 2d 1108, 1117 (D. Ariz. 2003) ("Generally, it is the delivery of an executed document, not the mere signing of the document, that creates a binding contract.").

10. *See Hunts Point Tomato Co., Inc. v. Roman Crest Fruit, Inc.*, 35 B.R. 939, 944-945 (Bankr. S.D.N.Y. 1983).

11. *See Herr v. Bard*, 50 A.2d 280, 281 (Pa. 1947).

12. *See Restatement (Second) of Contracts* §95 (1981). Some states still recognize the vitality of a seal and its consequences, although most states have abolished seals or the distinction between sealed and unsealed agreements. *See* Eric Mills Holmes, *Corbin on Contracts* vol. 3, §10.18 (Perillo ed., rev. ed. 1996).

13. U.C.C. §3-201 (2004).

14. U.C.C. §7-501 (2005).

15. *See Nodland*, *supra* n. 8; *Am. Fam. Mut. Ins.*, *supra* n. 9.

16. *See Schwartz v. Greenberg*, 107 N.E.2d 65, 67 (N.Y. 1952); *Midwest Mfg. Holding, L.L.C. v. Donnelly Corp.*, 1998 WL 59500 at *5 (N.D. Ill. Feb. 6, 1998).

17. *See Bohlen Indus. of N. Am., Inc. v. Flint Oil & Gas, Inc.*, 483 N.Y.S.2d 529, 530 (4th Dept. App. Div. 1984).

ery. Requiring both elements presents the parties with an additional hurdle to contract formation. Whether that will help or hurt your client is generally unfathomable because drafters cannot know at the time of drafting the future factual circumstances that will create the issue. On balance, this author prefers to require delivery as an element of contract formation. People change their minds. Signing an agreement and putting it in a briefcase differs from handing a signed agreement to someone else.

Contract formation is also an issue when parties sign agreements in counterparts. For a discussion of the issues, see Section 17.3.

17.3   THE CONCLUDING PARAGRAPH

As previously noted,[18] the concluding paragraph generally resembles the following:

Wrong

In Witness Whereof, the parties hereto have executed and delivered this Agreement on the date hereof.

This language is replete with legalese and technically unnecessary. It is not, however, without purpose. It evidences that the parties have intentionally signed the agreement, and it reminds them that they have agreed to bind themselves.[19] A more contemporary version follows:

Correct

To evidence the parties' agreement to this Agreement, they have executed and delivered it on the date set forth in the preamble.

This version retains both *executed* and *delivered* to reflect the historical distinction between the terms. You could replace *executed* with the simpler and more contemporary *signed*. This continues to recognize the historical distinction between *executed* and *delivered* but further modernizes the concluding paragraph. Make this change, however, *only* if you change all of the contract's provisions that use *executed* or a form of it. For example, many contracts include a representation and warranty that a party has the power and authority to execute, deliver, and perform the agreement. Legal opinions may also need to be changed. Be careful. Not saying the same thing the same way invites litigation.[20]

The proposed concluding paragraph assumes that the parties wish to retain the historical distinction between *execution* and *delivery*. If they do not, use just *executed* or just *signed*. If you use *signed*, again, be sure to conform the contract's other provisions. Remember, however, that some case law does give *execute* a broad meaning that encompasses delivery.[21] Therefore, you should confirm the interpretation of *execute* under the contract's governing law.

---

18. See §17.1.

19. *See* Lon L. Fuller, *Consideration and Form*, 41 Colum. L. Rev. 799, 800 (1941).

20. See §21.8.

21. *See Hayes v. Ammon, supra* n. 8.

The concluding paragraph also deals with the date of signing and delivery. The proposed language refers to execution and delivery *on* the date set forth in the preamble. If that date is an *as of* date,[22] follow the suggestions in Section 6.2.2.

When the parties sign the agreement in counterparts or on different dates, the contract must reflect the different signing and effective dates. The usual options for effectiveness are *the date that the last party executes and delivers the agreement* or *on delivery of one executed counterpart from each party to the other parties*.[23] Do not rely on a provision that merely states that the provision can be executed in counterparts.[24] Instead, in the action sections, state specifically what constitutes effectiveness.

Version 1

Effective Date. This Agreement is effective when each party has delivered to each other party one executed counterpart of this Agreement.

Version 2

Effective Date. This Agreement is effective on the date that the last party executes and delivers this Agreement to the other party.

In both instances, the concluding paragraph and the signature line must be tailored to fit the facts.

To evidence the parties' agreement to this Agreement, each party has executed and delivered it *on* the *date* indicated under that party's signature.

FURNITURE BY FRANK, INC.

By: _Frank Rabb_
    Frank Rabb, President

Dated: _4-13-20XX_

You can take one of three approaches to the date in the preamble when effectiveness is tied into the date the last party signs. First, the preamble could omit any reference to date and the effective date would be that stated in the provision within the body of the agreement. Second, once you know the date of the last signature (and therefore, the *as of* effective date), you could insert it in a blank left in the preamble for the *as of* date. But this courts trouble. Litigation could ensue if the wrong date is inserted or if the blank is not filled in. Third, the first sentence of the preamble could omit a date and a second sentence be added stating the effective date. In that event, you would omit the effective date provision in the action sections to preclude any possible differences in how the effective date is stated. A difference could create an ambiguity.

---

22. See §6.2.2 for a discussion of as of dates, §8.4 for a discussion of effective dates in contracts for a term of years, and §§16.10 and 17.2.2 for a discussion of effective dates with respect to contracts executed in counterparts.

23. *Bohlen Indus. of N. Am., Inc. v. Flint Oil & Gas Co., Inc.*, *supra* n. 17 (provision stating that contract could be signed in counterparts was "merely for procedural purposes"; delivery was not necessary when subsequent provision states that the agreement was not effective until all had signed).

24. *Id.*

> **This Settlement Agreement** is between Cartoon Characters LLC, a Pennsylvania limited liability company ("**Cartoon**"), and Specialty Manufacturing, Inc., a Texas corporation ("**Specialty**"). It is effective on the date that the last party executes and delivers it to the other party.

The salient point is that the agreement must be internally consistent. The preamble, the action sections' effective date provision, the counterparts provision, and the concluding provision must all work together.

17.4 DRAFTING THE SIGNATURE BLOCKS

17.4.1 THE BASICS

Before drafting the signature blocks, make sure that you have the correct name of the person or entity signing. If the party is an individual, confirm that you have that individual's full legal name rather than a nickname or professional name.[25] Drafting the signature block for an entity can be treacherous. Companies sometimes do not operate under their legal name, but instead use a trade name. Using the trade name could result in making the individual signing personally liable.[26] Because the potential for mistakes is high, check the organizational documents of each party to confirm the details of each name, including any commas and where they go. Then confirm that the name in the preamble is the same as the name in the signature block.

Next, check an entity's organizational documents and bylaws to find out whether more than one signature is necessary. Sometimes two or more signatures are required for a particular kind of contract, such as a loan, or if the contract involves more than a certain amount of money.

Finally, if an entity is signing the agreement, obtain an incumbency certificate—a document that states who is an officer. It should include an original signature of each person with signing authority, so that you can compare the signature of the person signing the documents with the signature on the incumbency certificate. If the entity is a corporation, the corporate secretary should sign the certificate. In addition, an officer other than the corporate secretary needs to certify the portion of the incumbency certificate relating to the corporate secretary.

Signature blocks are typically placed on the right half of a page, one above the other if more than one person is signing. Here are two typical signature lines.

_____
Tanya Williams

Rochester Realty Corp.

By: _____
James Tao, President

---

25. Some women use their given surname for professional purposes, but their married name for all other purposes.

26. *See Lachmann v. Houston Chronicle Publg. Co.*, 375 S.W.2d 783, 784-786 (Tex. Civ. App. 1964).

Some drafters precede each signature block with the role-related defined term for the party, but this is stylistic. If the role-related defined term is included, it typically appears in bold and in all capital letters. This formatting distinguishes it from the name of the entity that immediately follows, which is in bold but capitalizes only the first letter of each word. Although typographers generally frown on using all capital letters, this is a judicious use.

TENANT

Tanya Williams
Tanya Williams

LANDLORD

Rochester Realty Corp.

By: ___*James Tao*___
James Tao, President

17.4.2 DRAFTING THE SIGNATURE BLOCK OF AN INDIVIDUAL

The signature line for an individual is easy to draft. It is a line with the individual's name typed directly under it. The individual then "signs on the dotted line."

John Hancock
John Hancock

17.4.3 DRAFTING THE SIGNATURE BLOCK OF A CORPORATION

The signature block for a corporation must reflect that the person signing is acting in a representative capacity.[27] To do this, first put the name of the corporation on a separate line. Inclusion of the corporate name indicates who is signing the contract.[28] Four lines down from the corporation's name, insert the line on which the officer will sign and precede it with *By*. The use of *by* signals that the entity is acting through its agent.[29] Then, immediately beneath that line, put the officer's name and title. This

---

27. *See Stewart Coach Indus., Inc. v. Moore*, 512 F. Supp. 879, 884 (D. Ohio 1981); *see generally* S. C. Vass, *Personal liability of one who signs or indorses without qualification commercial paper of corporation*, 82 A.L.R.2d 424 (1962).

28. *See 780 L.L.C. v. DiPrima*, 611 N.W.2d 637, 644-645 (Neb. App. 2000).

29. *See Restatement (Third) of Agency* § 6.01 cmt. d(1) (2006) (stating that a contract may indicate the representative capacity of an agent in multiple ways, including "statements of: (1) the principal's name followed by the agent's name preceded by a preposition such as 'by' or per . . . "); *see also id.* cmt. d(2) (stating that "[T]the basic principles discussed in Comment (d)(1) are applicable when a principal is an organization, such as a corporation or limited-liability company. An organizational executive does not become subject to personal liability on a contract as a consequence of executing a document in the executive's organizational capacity . . ."); *but see Bristow v. Adm'r of Isaac Erwin*, 1851 WL 3552 at *1 (La. 1851) (finding that agency was implied by the circumstances, though noting that it would have been "more proper" if "by" or "per" had been used).

information establishes who the agent is and his or her representative capacity.[30] Failure to draft the signature line this way could result in personal liability for the officer.[31]

Example 1 shows what the signature block would look like if the drafter had all the information relating to the officer at the time of drafting. Although that is optimal, it is not always possible. Example 2 shows an alternative that you can use, when you do not have the details on who is signing. If you draft the signature block as in Example 2, fill in the blanks when the parties sign the agreement.

Example 1

Sweat & Toil, Inc.

By: *Elizabeth N Workhorse*
    Elizabeth N. Workhorse, Vice President

Example 2

Sweat & Toil, Inc.

By: _____
    Name:
    Title:

17.4.4 DRAFTING THE SIGNATURE BLOCKS OF A GENERAL PARTNERSHIP, A LIMITED PARTNERSHIP, AND A LIMITED LIABILITY PARTNERSHIP

In the same way that a corporation's signature line must reflect that the corporation acts through its officers, a partnership's signature block must reflect that the partnership acts through its general partners. If the general partner is an individual, use the following format:

Sweat & Toil Partners, a general partnership

By: *Elizabeth N Workhorse*
    Elizabeth N. Workhorse, General Partner

If the general partner is a corporation, then you must add an additional layer to the signature block. The signature block must reflect that the partnership is acting through its general partner, a corporation, which is acting through its officer. Some drafters reflect the relative relationship between the partnership and the corporate partner by indenting the information five spaces with respect to the corporate officer as follows:

---

30. *See Agric. Bond & Credit Corp. v. Courtenay Farmers' Coop. Ass'n*, 251 N.W. 881, 887-888 (N.D. 1933).

31. *See Bissonnette v. Keyes*, 64 N.E.2d 926, 927 (Mass. 1946) (failure to include corporate name resulted in personal liability for agent, even though "agent" followed the agent's name).

Sweat & Toil LP, a limited partnership
By: Sweat Inc., General Partner

By: *Elizabeth N Workhorse*
Elizabeth N. Workhorse, Vice President

Many personal service businesses, such as law firms and accounting firms, are organized as limited liability partnerships (LLPs). A proper signature block for an LLP uses the following format:

Sweat & Toil LLP, a limited liability partnership

By: *Elizabeth N Workhorse*
Elizabeth N. Workhorse, [General] Partner

Although LLPs are a kind of general partnership, a law firm's signature line may follow the signer's name with the title *partner* rather than *general partner*. In part, this is because many law firms are two-tier partnerships that do not want the outside world focusing on how they classify their partners.[32]

If the signature line uses *partner* rather than *general partner*, the other party to the contract relies on the apparent authority of the person holding himself out as a partner. The cure for any concern regarding apparent authority is to ask for a copy of the partnership agreement and then to make sure that the partner signing is duly authorized to act on behalf of the partnership in that transaction. This capacity issue is usually more important in the context of commercial dealings with the LLP (e.g., bank loans, leases, and major commercial contracts) than in professional dealings with the LLP (e.g., opinions, pleadings, confidentiality agreements, and formal advice to clients).

17.4.5   DRAFTING THE SIGNATURE BLOCK OF A LIMITED LIABILITY COMPANY

Limited liability companies (LLCs) may be managed by their members or by managers.[33] In each case, the signature block must reflect who manages the LLC.

Sweat & Toil, LLC

By: *Elizabeth N Workhorse*
Elizabeth N. Workhorse, Member

---

32. In these partnerships, some partners' pecuniary interest in the firm is based wholly on a share of the profits. (These partners are what one ordinarily considers partners in a general partnership.) Other partners' pecuniary interest in the firm is only partially dependent on profits. The rest is usually some form of guaranteed amount. These latter partners are authorized by the firm to hold themselves out as partners and are generally permitted to sign opinions and some agreements.

33. Del. Code Ann. tit. 6, § 18-402 (Lexis, current through 2013).

Sweat & Toil, LLC

By: _____

Elizabeth N. Workhorse, Managing Director

17.4.6 DRAFTING OFFICERS' CERTIFICATES

Officers of entities often sign certificates—statements that a particular fact is true. The following are common certificates:

- A certificate of incumbency (certifying that the signatures are the signatures of the duly elected officers).
- A certificate as to stockholders' and directors' resolutions (certifying that they were duly adopted and are still in effect).
- A certificate with respect to a copy of the certificate of incorporation (certifying the accuracy of the attached copy).

For these certificates, the officer, not the entity, is the signatory. The rationale is that the officer has personal knowledge. The signature block reflects the officer's different role.

_____

Alex Glover, Secretary

In acquisitions and financings, officers are often asked to sign a **bring-down certificate**—a document certifying two things: first, that the representations and warranties made at signing are true at closing; and second, that all covenants to be performed on or before closing have been performed. Officers sometimes balk at signing these certificates in the usual fashion because they fear personal liability. The parties can address this issue in multiple ways, one of which is to have the corporation, rather than the officer, sign the certificate. Should the parties agree to this solution, use a standard corporation signature block. A detailed discussion of the other ways to address this issue is beyond this book's purview.[34]

17.5 MODE OF EXECUTION

Generally, most parties use a pen to sign an agreement, but anything that makes a mark and is identifiable to a party usually suffices.[35] The following sections discuss e-signatures and execution in counterparts.

---

34. For a detailed discussion of officers' certificates, *see* Lou Kling & Eileen Nugent, *Negotiated Acquisitions of Companies, Subsidiaries and Divisions* vol. 2 § 14.02[5] (Law Journal Press 1992).

35. *Haywood Sec., Inc. v. Ehrlich*, 149 P.3d 738, 740 (Ariz. 2007) (quoting from its earlier decision, the court stated that "[t]he signature may be written by hand, or printed, or stamped, or typewritten, or engraved, or photographed, or cut from one instrument and attached to another. . . . [I]t has been held that it is immaterial with what kind of an instrument a signature is made."); *Salt Lake City v. Hanson*, 425 P.2d 773, 774 (Utah 1967) (stating that "[w]hile one's signature is usually made writing his name, the same purpose can be accomplished by placing any writing, indicia or symbol *which the signer chooses to adopt*

17.5.1 E-SIGNATURES

In the Internet age, lawyers are called on to draft contracts that become legally binding electronically.[36] These documents present a modern spin on the classic evidentiary problem of authentication. In today's world, what constitutes a valid *e-signature,* and what safeguards ensure its authenticity?

In the United States, enforceability of e-signatures is principally governed by two pieces of legislation: the federal Electronic Signatures in Global and National Commerce Act (the E-Sign Act),[37] and the Uniform Electronic Transactions Act (UETA),[38] a uniform state law adopted by almost all of the states as of this writing. In accordance with a provision of the E-Sign Act, UETA supersedes the E-Sign Act, but only if a state enacts the uniform law in the form recommended by the National Conference of Commissioners on Uniform State Laws.[39] Therefore, make sure you know which statutory framework governs.

UETA's stated purpose is "to remove barriers to electronic commerce by validating and effectuating electronic records and signatures."[40] It then defines an e-signature as "an electronic sound, symbol, or process attached to or logically associated with a record and executed or adopted by a person with the intent to sign the record."[41] E-signatures include clicking on an *I Accept* button and digital signatures. Digital signatures are created with software that can encrypt and decrypt data.[42] This capability allows a digital signature to be attributable to a specific person and to authenticate a document.[43]

Internationally, different legislative bodies have developed their own laws, such as the European Union's Electronic Commerce Directive.[44] In addition, the United Nations Commission on International Trade has issued model legislation addressing electronic signatures.[45]

A detailed discussion of how to create e-signatures is beyond the scope of this book.[46] If you need to create an electronic signature, be sure to research the law as it is evolving.

---

and use as his signature and by which it may be proved: e.g., by finger or thumb prints, by a cross or other mark . . .").

36. *See generally* Richard A. Lord, *A Primer on Electronic Contracting and Transactions in North Carolina,* 30 Campbell L. Rev. 7 (Fall 2007).

37. The Electronic Signatures in Global and National Commerce Act, 15 U.S.C. §§ 7001-7031.

38. Unif. Elecs. Transactions Act (UETA) §§ 1-21 (2002).

39. 15 U.S.C. § 7002(a).

40. UETA, *supra* n. 38, Prefatory Note, U.L.A. Elec. Trans., Prefatory Note.

41. *Id.* at § 2(8).

42. F. Lawrence Street, Mark P. Grant & Sandra Sheets Gardiner, *Law of the Internet* § 1.05 (Michie 2009).

43. Julian S. Millstein, Jeffrey D. Neuberger & Jeffrey P. Weingart, *Doing Business on the Internet: Forms and Analysis* § 8.05[1] (Law Journal Press 1997).

44. Council Directive 2000/31/EC, O.J. (L 178) 1-16, Directive on electronic commerce (available at http://eur-lex.europa.eu/LexUriServ/LexUriServ.do?uri=CELEX:32000L0031:EN:NOT).

45. UNCITRAL Model Law on Electronic Signatures (2001) (http://www.uncitral.org/pdf/english/texts/electcom/ml-elecsig-e.pdf).

46. *See generally* Street *et al., supra* n. 42; Millstein *et al., supra* n. 43.

17.5.2 COUNTERPARTS[47]

As discussed in Chapter 16, parties cannot always convene to sign an agreement.[48] In these circumstances, lawyers often arrange for each party to sign a separate, duplicate original—a *counterpart*. Once each party has signed its counterpart, the lawyer assembles them to produce a fully executed, original counterpart agreement.

Parties also use counterparts to create multiple originals, so that each party to a transaction has its own fully executed original. To do this, each party signs as many counterparts as the number of parties. So, if there are eight parties, each party signs eight counterparts.

17.5.3 STAND-ALONE SIGNATURE PAGES

Occasionally, drafters create signature pages without text from the agreement. Generally, they do this to resolve a logistical problem. It permits a party who cannot attend a closing to sign while the lawyers continue to draft the agreement. It also creates signatures to be gathered if the transaction is going to have a virtual closing. The party's lawyer then holds the signature pages until the closing and, at that time, appends them to the final version of the agreement.[49]

While convenient, this practice involves risk. First, the parties may dispute whether the signed pages constituted execution and delivery of the contract or whether they were a mere logistical convenience.[50] Second, a drafter risks a malpractice claim. A client could allege that the lawyer had no authority to append the signature pages because it never would have assented to the final version of the agreement had it known and understood its terms. To prevent such a claim, send your client the final text and get its approval of any last minute changes.

17.6 ANTIFRAUD MECHANISMS

As signatures can create an enforceable contract, their misuse can create a contract that at least one party did not intend. You can address this potential fraud in several ways.

Although stand-alone signature pages can be helpful logistically, they also create the possibility of fraud: A nefarious person could attach them to a different document.[51] If all the parties can attend a signing, format the agreement so that the signature lines are on the same page as the final provisions or at least begin on that page. If the signature lines naturally fall on a separate page, stop the text of the agreement about half way down the previous page, space down several lines and insert in bold letters "**INTENTIONALLY LEFT BLANK**" or draw an X through the blank space. Then, on the following page of the agreement, conclude the text of the agreement and add the signature lines.

---

47. See § 16.10 for a more detailed discussion of counterparts.

48. *Id.*

49. *Chariot Group, Inc. v. Am. Acq. Partners*, L.P., 751 F. Supp. 1144, 1151 (S.D.N.Y. 1990) (no contract existed where the one party signed the signature pages for convenience only, the pages remained in the custody of that party's attorney, and the pages were never delivered to the other party).

50. *See Midwest Mfg. Holding, L.L.C. v. Donnelly Corp.*, 1998 WL 59500 at *4 (N.D. Ill. Feb. 6, 1998).

51. *See Winston v. Mediafare Ent. Corp.*, 777 F.2d 78, 79-80, 83 (2d Cir. 1985).

As another antifraud mechanism, the parties should initial each interlineation. Doing so can be used to demonstrate the parties' agreement to the change.[52] In addition, the parties could initial each page of the agreement if a client worries that the other side might replace a page with one that included "nonagreed to" provisions. As initialing every page of a long agreement is onerous, it is not common practice. Therefore, reserve this procedure for the appropriate situations (e.g., separation agreements and settlement agreements with respect to contentious litigation).

Although parties do not typically initial every page in significant commercial transactions in the United States, parties in some foreign jurisdictions almost always do it. Accordingly, be sure to check local custom and practice.

17.7 INITIALING OTHER THAN AS AN ANTIFRAUD MECHANISM

Parties occasionally initial a contract not as an antifraud mechanism but to indicate that they have read and understood a provision. For example, a lawyer sometimes requires a party to initial a jury waiver provision.[53] The lawyer can then use the initials as evidence that the waiver was knowing, voluntary, and intentional—the standard that courts insist be met before enforcing a waiver.[54]

17.8 ACKNOWLEDGMENTS

An acknowledgment is a party's formal declaration before an authorized public official, generally a notary public, that it voluntarily executed an agreement.[55] In some states, it authenticates an agreement,[56] while in others it makes the agreement effective.[57] An acknowledgment is only obligatory when a statute requires one, as in connection with real estate conveyances and mortgages. Because the laws with respect to acknowledgments differ from state to state, check the law in your jurisdiction. If an acknowledgment is required, it follows the signature lines. It may also be on a separate page attached to the agreement.

52. *GBF Eng'r, Inc. v. John*, No. 09-CV-11367, 2010 WL 3342260 at *10 (E.D. Mich. Aug. 25, 2010) (initialing changes manifested assent to them); *Lerman v. Rock City Bar & Grille, Inc.*, No. 09 CV 2444, 2010 WL 2044865 at *4 (N.D. Ohio May 21, 2010) (absence of initials raises question of fact as to whether the parties agreed on the change).

53. *See Coop. Fin. Ass'n v. Garst*, 871 F. Supp. 1168, 1172, n. 2 (N.D. Iowa 1995).

54. *See K.M.C. Co. v. Irving Trust Co.*, 757 F.2d 752, 755-756 (6th Cir. 1985).

55. *Est. of Burleson*, 210 S.E.2d 114, 114 (N.C. App. 1974).

56. *Webster Bank v. Flanagan*, 725 A.2d 975, 980 (Conn. App. 1999).

57. *Lewis v. Herrera*, 85 P. 245, 246 (Ariz. 1906).

EXERCISES

Exercise 17-1

Nathan Nocturne is Managing Director of Nocturne LLC, a manager-managed LLC. Nocturne LLC is the general partner of Nocturne Luminescence LP, which is in turn the general partner of Nitelite LP. Draft the signature line for Nitelite LP.

PART THREE

Drafting Clearly and Unambiguously

Legalese

18.1 INTRODUCTION

Legalese annoys almost anyone who reads contracts—whether client, lawyer, or judge. Obscure words and phrases, hailing from times past, clutter provisions and make them difficult to understand. Not surprisingly, commentators have disparaged legalese for centuries:

> Swift's acid phrase was "a peculiar Cant and Jargon of their own, that no other Mortal can understand." Bentham had a bag of phrases, applied with uncomplimentary impartiality: *law jargon, lawyers' cant, lawyers' language, flash language.* . . . With more or less politeness, [others have complained that lawyers are wordy]. "Words multiplied for the Purpose," "a vicious sea of verbiage," repetitious, verbose, prolix.[1]

Despite this harsh criticism, legalese remained the norm until 1975 when Citibank lawyers rewrote their consumer promissory note.[2] These lawyers did more than revise the bank's contracts. They reconceived how consumer contracts should be written. They began by eliminating legalese and provisions appropriate only for commercial contracts. In addition, they improved the contracts' appearances by using white space and easily readable fonts. They also turned full-page sentences into short, clear sentences and adopted a more informal tone, making the contracts less intimidating. Together, these changes resulted in a new style of contract drafting, dubbed **plain English**.

The benefits of plain English drafting are so apparent and so appealing that some states have mandated by statute that plain English be used in consumer contracts.[3] No such laws have been passed with respect to sophisticated commercial contracts, but, over time, drafters have incorporated plain English concepts into their contracts.[4]

In this chapter and in Chapters 19 and 20, you will learn how to replace legalese with ordinary words; format provisions to make complicated material easier to assimilate; and redraft long, dense sentences into shorter, simpler ones.

---

1. David Mellinkoff, *The Language of the Law* § 2, 3-4, and § 19, 24 (Little, Brown & Co. 1963) (emphasis in the original) (footnotes omitted).

2. *See* Carl Felsenfeld & Alan Siegel, *Writing Contracts in Plain English* 27-30 (West 1981).

3. *See e.g.* N.Y. Gen. Oblig. Law § 5-702 (Westlaw current through L. 2006, ch. 646).

4. Federal regulations do, however, mandate the use of plain English principles in a prospectus. 17 C.F.R. § 230.421 (Westlaw current through Oct. 19, 2006).

18.2 FORMAL AND ARCHAIC WORDS

Legalese creeps into contracts in several ways. One of the most common is the use of formal, archaic words, such as the following:[5]

    above (as an adjective)
    above-mentioned
    aforementioned
    aforesaid
    before-mentioned
    henceforth
    hereby
    herein
    hereof
    hereto
    hereinafter
    hereinbefore
    herewith
    said (as a substitute for "the," "that," or "those")
    same (as a substitute for "it," "he," "him," etc.)
    such (as a substitute for "the," "that," or "those")
    thereof
    therewith
    whatsoever
    whensoever
    whereof
    wheresoever
    whosoever
    within-named
    witnesseth

Some drafters complain that some of these terms are actually helpful and should be used. In fact, in almost all instances, acceptable alternatives are available.

Drafters often use *hereof, hereto,* and similar words to indicate the section, schedule, or exhibit to which a provision is referring. To eliminate these words easily, include an interpretive provision either in the definitions section or with the general provisions:

> **Internal References.** Unless otherwise stated, references to Sections, subsections, Schedules, and Exhibits are to Sections, subsections, Schedules, and Exhibits of this Agreement.

Hereby is also easily replaced. Replace it with the thing to which *hereby* is referring.

---

5. This list is based on a list from F. Reed Dickerson, *The Fundamentals of Legal Drafting* 207 (2d ed., Little, Brown & Co. 1986).

> **Wrong**
>
> **Waiver of Right to a Jury Trial**. Each party waives its right to a jury trial with respect to the transactions contemplated *hereby*.
>
> **Correct**
>
> **Waiver of Right to a Jury Trial**. Each party waives its right to a jury trial with respect to the transactions [contemplated by this Agreement] [that this Agreement contemplates].

The second bracketed phrase is preferable as it changes the phrase from the passive to the active voice.

Thereof can often be replaced with *its*. Alternatively, determine to what *thereof* refers and create a prepositional phrase beginning with *of* and ending with the thing to which *thereof* is referring:

> **Wrong**
>
> **Escrow Fund**. The Escrow Fund shall be held by the Escrow Agent under the Escrow Agreement pursuant to the terms *thereof*.
>
> **Correct**
>
> **Escrow Fund**. The Escrow Agent shall hold the Escrow Funds under the Escrow Agreement pursuant to its terms.
>
> **Better**
>
> **Escrow Fund**. The Escrow Agent shall hold the Escrow Funds pursuant to [the terms of the Escrow Agreement] [the Escrow Agreement's terms].

This redraft also changes the sentence from the passive to the active voice. Look also at this example of how to eliminate *thereof*:

> **Wrong**
>
> Without limiting the generality *thereof* . . .
>
> **Correct**
>
> Without limiting the generality of the preceding sentence . . .[6]

Said and *such* are pointing words. They refer to something previously stated. Replace them with *the*, *a*, *that*, or *those*.

---

6. Drafters use this phrase when they establish a rule in one sentence and then, in a subsequent sentence, want to list specific matters that come within the rule.

Wrong

> **Bonus**. With respect to each year of the Term, the Company shall pay the Executive a bonus equal to 10% of [such] [said] year's Net Profits, except that the Company is not obligated to pay [such] [said] bonus with respect to any year of the Term in which Net Profits are less than $1 million.

Correct

> **Bonus**. With respect to each year of the Term, the Company shall pay the Executive a bonus equal to 10% of *that* year's Net Profits, except that the Company is not obligated to pay *the* bonus with respect to any year of the Term in which Net Profits are less than $1 million.

18.3 COUPLETS AND TRIPLETS

Contracts are often replete with redundancies. A classic example is *null and void.* Drafters frequently fear paring down these couplets and triplets, terrified that any deletion will result in an unknown, disastrous substantive change. This fear is usually unwarranted.

The profusion of couplets and triplets reflects the evolution of the English language.[7] After the Normans invaded England in 1066, French slowly became the language used in English courts and contracts. It predominated from the mid-thirteenth century to the mid-fifteenth century. Not unexpectedly, the English came to resent the use of French and began once again to use English for legal matters. As the use of "law French" began to wane, English lawyers were faced with a recurring problem. When they went to translate a French legal term into an English legal term, they were often unsure whether the English word had the same connotation. The solution was obvious: Use both the French and the English word. For example, *free and clear* is actually a combination of the Old English word *free* and the French word *clair.* Here are a few other examples:[8]

■ acknowledge and confess	Old English and Old French
■ breaking and entering	Old English and French
■ goods and chattel	Old English and Old French
■ right, title, and interest	Old English, Old English, and French

Compounding this penchant for joining French and English synonyms was the English custom of joining synonyms, especially those that were alliterative and rhythmic:[9]

- ■ to have and to hold.
- ■ aid and abet.
- ■ part and parcel.
- ■ rest, residue, and remainder.

---

7. This discussion of the history of the English language is based on the materials in David Mellinkoff, *The Language of the Law* ch. 9 (Little, Brown & Co. 1963).

8. *Id.* at 121-122.

9. *Id.* at 42-46 and 120-122.

The bottom line is that most couplets and triplets reflect our linguistic heritage and not legal distinctions. Therefore, they should be pared down to one word—unless the drafter intends a substantive difference, as in the phrase *represent and warrant*.

The following is a list of word combinations that should not be used:[10]

all and every	known and described as
any and all	made and entered into
alter or change	means and includes
amend, modify, or change	null and of no effect
bind and obligate	null and void
by and between	over and above
by and with	perform and discharge
convey, transfer, and set over	relieve and discharge
covenant and agree	remise, release, and forever quit-
due and owing	claim (except in states where
each and all	required by statute)
each and every	sole and exclusive
final and conclusive	suffer or permit
for and in behalf of	then and in that event
full force and effect	true and correct
furnish and supply	type and kind
kind and character	understood and agreed

18.4 PRETENTIOUS AND VERBOSE EXPRESSIONS

Look closely at the lists that follow. The words in the *Don't Use* column are either pretentious or verbose. Replace them, as appropriate, with the words in the *Use* column.[11]

Don't Use	Use
above	[refer to the specific provision]
attains the age of	becomes . . . years old
at the time	when
below	[refer to the specific provision]
by means of	by
by reason of	by, because of
cease	stop
commence	begin
consequence	result
contiguous to	next to
dated as of even date hereof	dated the date of this Agreement
does not operate to	does not
during such time as	during
during the course of	during
effectuate	carry out
endeavor (verb)	try
enter into a contract with	contract with

continued on next page >

---

10. This list is from Dickerson, *supra* n. 5, at 208.

11. These lists are derived from lists in *id.* at 209-213.

Don't Use	Use
for the duration of	during
for the purpose of holding	to hold
for the reason that	because
forthwith	immediately
in case	if
in cases in which	when, where (use "whenever" or "wherever" only when needed to emphasize the exhaustive or recurring applicability of the rule)
in lieu of	instead of, in place of
inquire	ask
institute	begin, start
in the event that	if
is able to	can
is authorized	may
is binding upon	binds
is unable to	cannot
loan (as a verb)	lend
mutually agree	agree
necessitate	require
notwithstanding anything to the contrary in this Agreement	despite any other provision in this Agreement
notwithstanding the foregoing	despite the previous [sentence]
party of the first part	[the party's name]
prior to	before
provision of law	law
purchase (as a verb)	buy
State of Kansas	Kansas
suffer (in the sense of *permit*)	permit
sufficient number of	enough
until such time as	until
utilize, employ (in the sense of "use")	use

CHAPTER EIGHTEEN

EXERCISES

Exercise 18-1

The following provision is from a shareholders' agreement:

Definition of Cause. For purposes hereof, "Cause" with respect to the termination of any Shareholder's employment has the meaning set forth in said Shareholder's employment agreement with the Company.

Exercise 18-2

Term. The term of this Agreement commences as of the date set forth in Section 8.6 hereof.

Exercise 18-3

Delivery of Financial Statements. No later than 90 days after the end of each fiscal year, the Borrower shall provide the Bank a copy of the Borrower's year-end financial statements. Such financial statements shall be certified by the Borrower's chief financial officer to fairly present the financial condition of the Borrower.

Exercise 18-4

Release. Except as herein to the contrary provided, each party releases, remises, and forever discharges the other from any and all actions, suits, debts, claims, and obligations whatsoever, both in law and equity, that either of them ever had, now has, or may hereafter have, against the other by reason of any matter, cause, or thing to the date of the execution of this Agreement.[12]

---

12. This provision is based on a general release in Gary N. Skoloff, Richard H. Singer, Jr., & Ronald L. Brown, *Drafting Prenuptial Agreements* VII-61 (Aspen 2003).

Exercise 18-5

Waiver. In the event of the failure of the Borrower aforesaid to comply with the terms of the aforementioned Note, the undersigned Guarantor waives notice of acceptance of this Guaranty, diligence, presentment, notice of dishonor, demand for payment, any and all notices of whatever kind or nature, and the exhaustion of legal remedies available to the holder of said Note.

Exercise 18-6

Lease. The Lessor leases to the Lessee, and the Lessee leases from the Lessor, all the machinery, equipment, and other property described in

(a) the schedule executed by the parties concurrently herewith; and

(b) any schedule hereafter executed by the parties hereto.

All said machinery, equipment, and other property described in all said schedules are hereinafter collectively called the "equipment," and all said schedules are hereinafter collectively called the "schedules."

Exercise 18-7

Compliance with Communications Act. The Merger's consummation does not violate the Communications Act or the rules and regulations promulgated thereunder.

Clarity through Format

19.1 INTRODUCTION

Imagine if this book had no page numbers, no paragraphs separating ideas, and no chapters—instead, from start to finish, it was all one long, continuous, dense block of words. Daunting—it would be a nightmare to read. But the publisher has spent considerable money and effort to enhance the book's clarity through format. Many lawyers, however, expend little effort enhancing their contracts' clarity through format.

In the remainder of this chapter, you will learn formatting techniques that will improve the clarity of the contracts you draft.

19.2 SECTIONS AND SUBSECTIONS

One of the easiest ways of formatting a contract is to use sections and subsections. By using a greater number but shorter sections, a contract becomes easier to read.

Look at the following provision from a joint venture agreement. It states the procedure for appointing officers and indemnifies the officers.

Wrong

9.3 Officers of the Joint Venture. The Managing Venturer shall appoint the chief executive officer, chief financial officer, and other officers of the Joint Venture. The officers are to perform those duties and have those responsibilities that the Managing Venturer assigns to them. The Non-Managing Venturer must approve the appointment and replacement of the chief executive officer and shall not unreasonably withhold or delay its approval. The Managing Venturer may appoint one or more officers of either Venturer to be an officer of the Joint Venture, but only if that officer intends to devote substantially full time to the Joint Venture. If that officer fails to devote substantially full time to the Joint Venture, the Managing Venturer shall terminate that officer's employment. The Managing Venturer may determine, in its sole discretion, the benefits to be offered to any officer appointed in accordance with this subsection. The Joint Venture shall indemnify and defend each officer of the

continued on next page >

Joint Venture against all claims, losses, damages and liabilities, including reasonable attorneys' fees, relating to any act or failure to act by that officer, but only if the officer's act or failure to act was in good faith and, in both cases, in a manner that officer reasonably believed to be in, or not opposed to, the Joint Venture's best interests; or if the officer relied on the opinion or advice of competent legal counsel. Any indemnity under this Section is to be paid from the Joint Venture's assets, and no Venturer has any individual liability on account of the indemnity under this Section 9.3.

No doubt, this provision gave you MEGO—*my eyes glaze over*. Truth be told, did you even finish reading the provision? Provisions drafted like this make it difficult, if not impossible, to carefully analyze and comment on a contract. What follows is the same provision, but formatted. No other changes have been made. It is now much easier to read because it has been broken down into multiple sections, each section separated from the next by white space, and each with a heading to signal its substance. It is still long and not as interesting as a Tom Clancy novel, but it is better than before.

Correct

9.3   The Joint Venture's Officers.

9.3.1   **Appointment of Officers**. The Managing Venturer shall appoint the chief executive officer, chief financial officer, and other officers of the Joint Venture. The officers are to perform those duties and have those responsibilities that the Managing Venturer assigns to them.

9.3.2   **Approval of Chief Executive Officer's Appointment**. The Non-Managing Venturer must approve the appointment and replacement of the chief executive officer and shall not unreasonably withhold or delay its approval.

9.3.3   **Appointment of a Venturer's Officer**. The Managing Venturer may appoint one or more officers of either Venturer to be an officer of the Joint Venture, but only if that officer intends to devote substantially full time to the Joint Venture. If that officer fails to devote substantially full time to the Joint Venture, the Managing Venturer shall terminate that officer's employment. The Managing Venturer may determine, in its sole discretion, the benefits to be offered to any officer appointed in accordance with this subsection.

9.3.4   **Indemnity of Officers**. The Joint Venture shall indemnify and defend each officer of the Joint Venture against all claims, losses, damages and liabilities, including reasonable attorneys' fees, relating to any act or failure to act by that officer, but only if

9.3.4.1   the officer's act or failure to act was in good faith and, in both cases, in a manner that officer reasonably believed to be in, or not opposed to, the Joint Venture's best interests; or

9.3.4.2   the officer relied on the opinion or advice of competent legal counsel.

9.3.5   **Source of Funds**. Any indemnity under this Section 9.3 is to be paid from the Joint Venture's assets, and no Venturer has any individual liability on account of the indemnity under this Section.

19.3   TABULATION

19.3.1   EXPLANATION OF TABULATION AND WHEN TO USE IT

Look again at Section 9.3.4 in the "correct" provision.[1] In that section, a long sentence is broken down into two subsections, each of which is grammatically independent of the other. They are conceptually related, which is why they are subsections of the same section. Subsections can also be used to join two or more related sentences. This reduces the length of the contract and aids the reader by showing how the sentences are related. In both cases, each subsection is indented and separated from the other by white space. This formatting is known as **tabulation**. It takes its name from the use of the keyboard *Tab* key that is used to indent the tabulated material.

The following example shows how tabulation can be used to join two related sentences. The sentences are from a noncompetition agreement.

> **Version 1—Untabulated Sentences**
>
> **Noncompetition**. For a one-year period after the Term, the Executive shall not employ any person who was an employee during the Term. In addition, during that period, the Executive shall not interfere with the relationship between the Company and any of its employees.
>
> **Version 2—Tabulated Sentence**
>
> **Noncompetition**. For a one-year period after the Term, the Executive
>
> (a) shall not employ any person who was an employee during the Term; and
>
> (b) shall not interfere with the relationship between the Company and any of its employees.

The next example shows a long, untabulated sentence from a construction contract[2] and the same sentence, but tabulated.

---

1. See § 19.2.

2. This provision is based on a provision from Stanley P. Sklar & Gregory R. Andre, *Design and Construction Contracts,* in *Commercial Contracts: Strategies for Drafting and Negotiating* vol. 2, ch. 29, 29-85 (Morton Moskin ed., Aspen Publishers 2006).

Version 1 — Untabulated Sentence

Contractor's Right to Terminate. The Contractor may terminate this Agreement for cause if work is stopped for 30 days or more through no fault of the Contractor or because of a court order, if the Architect unjustifiably refuses to approve a payment request, or if the Owner refuses to pay a payment request that the Architect approved.

Version 2 — Tabulated Sentence

Contractor's Right to Terminate. The Contractor may terminate this Agreement for cause if

(a) work stops for 30 days or more through no fault of the Contractor or because of a court order;

(b) the Architect unjustifiably refuses to approve a payment request; or

(c) the Owner refuses to pay a payment request that the Architect approved.

Deciding when to use tabulation requires a judgment call. If you are deciding whether to join two or more sentences through tabulation, the subject matter of the sentences should be related. For example, if both sentences relate to the rights of a bank on its borrower's default, tabulation is probably appropriate. If the subject matter is not related, create separate sections and insert them in the appropriate place in the contract. If you are deciding whether to break down one sentence into a tabulated format, any sentence with a compound or a series is a candidate. For these purposes, a **compound** refers to two items in a sentence joined by *and* or *or*. A **series** refers to three or more items in a sentence joined by *and* or *or.*

The length and complexity of the sentence are also considerations. Any sentence that is already a candidate becomes a stronger candidate if it is three lines or longer—the so-called **three-line rule**. The ultimate deciding factor is whether tabulation makes it easier for a reader to assimilate the information.

Beware of tabulation overkill. Tabulating a sentence just because it has a compound or series is inappropriate. The following sentence should not have been tabulated; it is short and easy to understand in its untabulated state.

Version 1 — Untabulated Sentence

Corporate Power and Authority. The Licensor has full corporate power and authority to execute, deliver, and perform this Agreement.

Version 2 — Tabulated Sentence

Corporate Power and Authority. The Licensor has full corporate power and authority to

(a) execute,

(b) deliver, and

(c) perform

this Agreement.

19.3.2 HOW TO TABULATE

The guidelines for tabulating are relatively simple.

General Tabulation Guideline 1

Use parallel drafting to construct the tabulated sentence.[3] To do this, draft the language that introduces the tabulated subsections and the language of each subsection so that the introductory language creates a coherent, grammatically correct sentence when joined with each subsection. In addition, if the sentence continues after the tabulated subsections, then that concluding language must also create coherent sentences when joined with the introductory language and each subsection.

Consider the tabulated sentence that follows, which uses parallel drafting. You can test this by joining together the introductory language with each of the subsections and create two separate sentences. The sentence is from an agreement between a company and a software developer.[4]

> **Version 1 — Tabulated Sentence**
>
> **Developer's Representations and Warranties**. The Developer represents and warrants that the Software
>
> (a) is unique and original;
>
> (b) is clear of any claims or encumbrances; and
>
> (c) does not infringe on the rights of any third parties.
>
> **Version 2 — Untabulated Sentences**
>
> ■ The Developer represents and warrants that the Software is unique and original.
> ■ The Developer represents and warrants that the Software is clear of any claims or encumbrances.
> ■ The Developer represents and warrants that the Software does not infringe on the rights of any third parties.

The following sentence also uses parallel drafting. Test it the same way. Join the introductory language, a subsection, and the concluding language.

> **Version 1 — Tabulated Sentence**
>
> **Employee Sanctions**. Each time an Employee
>
> (a) is absent from work for an unexcused reason,
>
> (b) takes a coffee break longer than 15 minutes, or
>
> (c) smokes a cigarette in a designated no smoking area,
>
> that Employee loses one vacation day.

---

3. See § 23.12 for a discussion of parallel drafting as craftsmanship.

4. The provision is from Gregory J. Battersby & Charles W. Grimes eds., *License Agreements: Forms and Checklists* 4-27 (Aspen Publishers 2003).

Version 2 — Untabulated Sentences

- Each time an Employee is absent from work for an unexcused reason, that Employee loses one vacation day.
- Each time an Employee takes a coffee break longer than 15 minutes, that Employee loses one vacation day.
- Each time an Employee smokes a cigarette in a designated no smoking area, that Employee loses one vacation day.

The following tabulated sentence does not use parallel drafting. Why?

Version 1 — Wrong

Landlord's Rights on Termination. If this Lease terminates because of a default by the Tenant, the Landlord may

(a) immediately enter the Premises by any legal proceeding; and

(b) has the right to evict any person on the Premises.

The problem is with subsection (b). When joined with the introductory language, it creates an incoherent sentence. The problem is clear when the tabulation is removed, as follows:

Version 1 — Wrong

Landlord's Rights on Termination. If this Lease terminates because of a default of the Tenant, the Landlord *may has the right to* evict any person on the Premises.

To fix the tabulated sentence so that it uses parallel drafting and makes sense, drop the words *has the right to* from subsection (b).

Version 2 — Correct

Landlord's Rights on Termination. If this Lease terminates because of a default of the Tenant, the Landlord may

(a) immediately enter the Premises by any legal proceeding; and

(b) evict any person on the Premises.

General Tabulation Guideline 2

The grammar of the sentence determines its punctuation. The application of this guideline breaks down tabulated sentences into two formats:

1. The **sentence format** in which each tabulated subsection creates a full sentence when joined with the introductory language.
2. The **list format** in which the introductory language is a complete sentence and each tabulated subsection is part of an enumerated list. A strong clue that

a list format is appropriate is if the introductory language includes some form of the word *follow.*

Each tabulated sentence that was used as an example in the discussion of Guideline 1 used the sentence format. The following example of tabulation uses the list format.

Events of Default. Each of the following events is an Event of Default:

(a) The Borrower has failed to pay interest when due.

(b) The Borrower has failed to pay principal when due.

(c) Any representation or warranty of the Borrower stated in Article 3 was false when made.

(d) The Borrower has breached any covenant in Article 4.

Sometimes, with a little editing, you can draft a provision using either the list format or the sentence format. Look at the following provision, which is drafted using the sentence format.

Version 1 — Sentence Format

Employee Sanctions. Each time an Employee

(a) is absent from work for an unexcused reason,

(b) takes a coffee break longer than 15 minutes, or

(c) smokes a cigarette in a designated no smoking area,

that Employee loses one vacation day.

Here is the sentence revised to use the list format.

Version 2 — List Format

Employee Sanctions. An Employee loses one vacation day each time the Employee does any one of the following:

(a) The Employee is absent from work for an unexcused reason.

(b) The Employee takes a coffee break longer than 15 minutes.

(c) The Employee smokes a cigarette in a designated no smoking area.

In this instance, the list format is preferable because it is easier to read. The sentence format has introductory language, subsections, and concluding language — three separate components that must be joined before the reader can take in all the information. But the list format has only two components, the introductory language and the enumerated items in the subsections. The less work that a reader has to do, the easier it is for the reader to assimilate the information.

Now, for the specific guidelines applicable for each of the formats. (This chapter's appendix provides an abbreviated version of these guidelines for ease of use when drafting. Examples follow the guidelines.)

Guidelines for Sentence Format Tabulation

1. *Include in the introductory language all the words common to each tabulated subsection, with four exceptions.* First, do not separate an article (e.g., *the, a,* or *an*) from the noun it precedes. Doing so makes the reading of the tabulated subsections awkward. The second exception is stylistic and not followed by all drafters: If the tabulated subsections are a series of negative covenants introduced with *shall not,* put *shall not* with each subsection, rather than in the introductory language. This change acts as a reading aid, reminding the reader that the provision prohibits the acts in each of the subsections. The third exception is also stylistic, and its use depends on the specific provision. Sometimes a provision is easier to read if the *to* of an infinitive is kept together with the present form of its verb (e.g., to see, to walk, to draft). But this is not always the case. The final exception requires a drafter to analyze how the tabulation affects a provision's substance: If putting all the common words in the introductory language affects a subsection's substantive meaning, then repeat the words in each subsection.

2. *Punctuate the introductory language as you would if the sentence were untabulated.* If you would not put punctuation after the last word in the introductory language if the sentence were untabulated, then do not use any punctuation when the sentence is tabulated. But if the introductory language would end with a comma if the sentence were untabulated, then that comma should remain when the sentence is tabulated.

3. *Begin each tabulated subsection with a lowercase letter.*

4. *If no concluding language is common to each subsection, do the following:*

    (a) *End each tabulated subsection (other than the last) with a semicolon.* This way, each tabulated subsection results in a complete sentence when combined with the introductory language. A semicolon signals the conclusion of each such sentence.

    (b) *Insert* and *or* or *as appropriate after the semicolon of the next-to-last subsection.*

    (c) *End the last tabulated subsection with a period.*

5. *If concluding language is common to each subsection, do the following:*

    (a) *End each tabulated subsection with whatever punctuation would be used (if any) if the sentence were untabulated.* To determine the punctuation, join the introductory language with each subsection to see if any punctuation is appropriate.

    (b) *Insert* and *or* or *as appropriate after the punctuation of the next-to-last subsection.*

    (c) *Begin the concluding language at the left margin so that it has the same margin as the introductory language.*

    (d) *End the concluding language with a period.*

As noted earlier, a tabulated sentence with both introductory and concluding language is more difficult for a reader to take in than a tabulated sentence that has only introductory material. If your initial draft includes concluding language, try to redraft the provision to eliminate it.

Example 1 is a classic example of a provision tabulated using the sentence format: All the common words are in the introductory language; that language does not conclude with any punctuation; and each subsection, other than the last, ends with a semicolon.

> **Example 1**
>
> **Architect's Obligations**. The Architect shall
>
> (a) consult with the Owner at least once a week; and
>
> (b) deliver to the Owner an accounting of expenses incurred each month in connection with the Project, no later than five business days after the end of each month.

Example 2 is a variation on Example 1. It differs in that the introductory language ends with a comma because that language is a prepositional phrase that would end with a comma if the sentence were untabulated. In addition, although *the* is common to both subsections, it is omitted from the introductory language as articles should be kept with their nouns.

> **Example 2**
>
> ***Force Majeure* Event**. If a *Force Majeure* Event occurs,
>
> (a) the Contractor shall advise the Owner of its existence as soon as possible after its occurrence; and
>
> (b) the Contractor's obligation to perform is suspended until the *Force Majeure* Event ends.

In Example 3, unlike Examples 1 and 2, the provision has both introductory and concluding language. Although no punctuation ends the first subsection (because there would be none if the sentence were untabulated), a comma ends the second subsection because the sentence would have a comma if it were untabulated.

> **Example 3[5]**
>
> **Type of Film**. The Photographer shall photograph in
>
> (a) black and white or
>
> (b) color,
>
> as requested by the Client.

Example 4 revises Example 3 and demonstrates how a tabulated provision with concluding language can be drafted to eliminate that language.

> **Example 4**
>
> **Type of Film**. The Photographer shall comply with the Client's request to photograph in
>
> (a) black and white or
>
> (b) color.

---

5. This provision is sufficiently simple that it would not be tabulated in an agreement. It is used here to demonstrate how to tabulate this type of provision.

If a sentence is to be tabulated using the list format, the following guidelines apply:

Guidelines for List Format Tabulation

1. *Draft the introductory language so that it includes the phrase* as follows *or* the following *or otherwise incorporates that concept and end it with a colon.*

2. *Draft the introductory language, if appropriate, so that it signals whether the items in each subsection are cumulative or alternative.*

3. *Begin each subsection with a capital letter and end it with a period.*

4. *Do not insert* and *or* or *after the next-to-last subsection.*

The following examples show how introductory language can signal whether the items in each subsection are cumulative or alternative.

Example 1

Termination. The Company may terminate the Executive for any one or more of the following reasons:

Example 2

Notice. When the Company sends a notice, it shall use one of the following methods, but it may choose which one:

Example 3

Duties. During the Term, the Executive shall perform all of the following duties:

19.3.3 MULTILEVEL TABULATION

Some sentences are sufficiently complex that they require more than one level of tabulation. If so, follow the numbering system for the sublevels as set out in Section 19.4. The following termination provision is in both untabulated and tabulated formats.[6] The tabulated version has two levels of subsections.

Version 1—Untabulated Sentence

9.1 Termination. Either party may terminate this Agreement if the other party breaches any covenant in this Agreement, but only if that breach remains uncured for 30 days after written notice of it to the breaching party, and as a result of that breach, the nonbreaching party cannot substantially realize the benefits that it would have realized from this Agreement absent that breach, or if the other party files a petition for bankruptcy in any court pursuant to any statute of the United States or any state.

---

6. A real termination provision would include other termination events.

Version 2 — Tabulated Sentence

9.1 Termination. Either party may terminate this Agreement if the other party

    (a) breaches any covenant in this Agreement, but only if

        (i) that breach remains uncured for 30 days after written notice of it to the breaching party and

        (ii) as a result of that breach, the nonbreaching party cannot substantially realize the benefits that it would have realized from this Agreement absent that breach;

    or

    (b) files a petition for bankruptcy in any court pursuant to any statute of the United States or any state.

When drafting a multilevel tabulated sentence, indent each subordinate level five more spaces than the previous level so that the reader can see the subordinate relationship between one level and the next. In establishing the relative relationship between the levels, make each section or subsection parallel with its subordinate subsection to prevent a garbled or ambiguous provision.

Subsection (i) does not end with a semicolon because the end of the clause is at the end of subsection (ii). Finally, note the placement of the bolded *or*. Although some drafters would place this *or* after the semicolon in subsection (ii), others put it on its own line at the same indentation of the subsections that it joins. It provides another useful, visual clue as to how the levels relate to each other. Of course, the *or* would not be bolded in an actual contract.

19.3.4 DOUBLE TABULATION

Double tabulation occurs in a sentence that has two or more independent sets of subsections at the same level. In the following representation and warranty from a loan agreement, the double tabulation occurs because subsections (i) and (ii) are not subsections of either subsection (a) or (b). Subsections (i) and (ii) are not labeled (c) and (d) because that would mislead the reader. It would suggest that the introductory language that applies to subsections (a) and (b) also applies to subsections (i) and (ii).

Leases. **Schedule 3.11** lists each lease to which the Borrower is a party. With respect to each lease listed in **Schedule 3.11**,

    (a) no default has occurred and is continuing, and

    (b) no event has occurred and is continuing which, with notice or lapse of time or both, would constitute a default on the part of the Borrower,

except for those defaults and events of default, if any, that

    (i) are not material in character, amount, or extent; and

    (ii) do not, severally or in the aggregate, materially detract from the value of or materially interfere with the present use of the property subject to the lease.

As this example demonstrates, double tabulation is unwieldy. You can, however, usually avoid it by breaking down the sentence into two or more sentences, as has been done in the following redraft.

3.11 Leases.

(a) **Borrower's Leases**. Schedule 3.11(A) lists each lease to which the Borrower is a party.

(b) **Defaults**. Schedule 3.11(B) lists each lease to which the Borrower is a party and where either

   (i) a default has occurred and is continuing; or

   (ii) an event has occurred and is continuing which, with notice or lapse of time or both, would constitute a default by the Borrower.

(c) **Materiality of Defaults**. The defaults and events listed in Schedule 3.11(B)

   (i) are not material in character, amount, or extent; and

   (ii) do not, severally or in the aggregate, materially detract from the value or materially interfere with the present use of the property subject to the lease.

19.4 NUMBERING SYSTEMS

In the same way that a brief or a memorandum can be organized into main ideas and subsidiary ideas, so too can a contract. To reflect the different organizational levels in a contract, use one of the common numbering systems. Most firms have templates for numbering systems, as do most word-processing programs. The key is to use an outline format, white space, and indentations to clarify the relative relationship between the provisions. Discussion and examples of three common numbering systems follow:

Numbering System 1

Article 1 — How to Format a Contract

One of the most common numbering systems divides an agreement into articles, each article comprising a set of related provisions. The House Purchase Agreement, Document 1 in Chapter 32, uses this numbering system. So, for example, Article 3 states the Seller's representations and warranties, and Article 4 states the Buyer's representations and warranties.

Each article number and its title are bolded and centered. Although many drafters number the articles using roman numerals, arabic numerals are easier for a reader. Do not put a period at the end of the title of the article.

1.1 Sections. Each article is broken down into sections and then subsections. Each section number is in bold and is not followed by a period. Each section has a bold heading followed by a period in regular font. The word *Section* should not precede a section's number, although many lawyers do include it. They feel that the slightly longer heading helps the reader find a specific section. Drafters using a more contemporary style omit *Section*. The provision is in the regular font and immediately follows the period after the heading unless the section has only subsections.

(a) **Subsections**. The formatting of subsections resembles the formatting of sections, although the subsection referent (e.g. *(a)*) is not in bold. If a subsection includes one or more sentences, it should have its own heading as should every other subsection at that level. But if the subsections are part of a tabulation,

    (i) do not use a heading; and

    (ii) follow the punctuation guidelines for tabulation stated in Section 19.3.2.

(b) **Indentation of Subsections**. All subsections at the same level should be indented relative to the indentation of the section or subsection that precedes it. This visually shows the reader the logical relationship between the contract's parts. Each level is indented five more spaces than the previous sublevel. (This takes advantage of the default tab indents.)

(c) **More on Subsections**. In the same way that an outline must have a subsection 2 if it has a subsection 1, a contract must have at least two subsections at each level.

1.2 More on Numbering System 1. If additional levels of subsections are required beyond the first level, those subsections should adhere to the following numbering system:

(a)

    (i)[7]

    (ii)

        (A)

        (B)

            (1)

            (2)

(b)

Numbering System 2

1. **How to Format a Contract**. This level is the equivalent of an article in Numbering System 1. Typically, the only text is a heading, but drafters sometimes begin the provision immediately after the heading.

    1.1 **Using Numbering System 2**. The guidelines with respect to headings and fonts are the same for both formats. Only the numbering and margins differs. It adheres to the following system:

    1.2

        1.2.1

        1.2.2

            1.2.2.1

            1.2.2.2

    1.3 **Why Some Drafters Prefer this Numbering System**. Some drafters prefer the precision of this numbering system. Specifically, it helps a reader who flips through a contract looking

---

7. Drafters sometimes refer to this level as *one in the hole* or *romanettes* followed by the appropriate number (e.g., *romanette three*).

for a particular provision. Rather than a page having merely a series of subsection referents (e.g., *(a)*, *(b)*, and *(c)*), each referent tells the reader a provision's location relative to the contract's other provisions.

1.4 **Variation**. Some drafters modify this numbering system, using lettered and numbered subsections after the third level, concerned that subsequent referents become long and harder to follow. Usually, the benefits of this numbering system are not forfeited because the contract will include at least one numbered referent on each page.

1.4.1

(a)

(i)

Numbering System 3

1. **Short Contracts**. Some contracts are relatively short and do not require articles. For these contracts, the provisions can be set up as a series of numbered sections, each section with a bolded heading. If no subsections are required, the text of the provision immediately follows the heading. If subsections are required, they should adhere to the following numbering system:

(a) **Nomenclature**. Some drafters refer to provisions using this numbering system as **paragraphs** and **subparagraphs**, which is perfectly acceptable alternative nomenclature.

(i)

(ii)

(A)

(B)

(1)

(2)

(b)

2. **Second Section**. Contract provisions in this book use all three numbering systems.

19.5 HEADINGS

Integral to any numbering scheme are the headings that identify for the reader the substance of the provision. Readers often flip through contracts looking for a specific provision. Headings that accurately relate a provision's substance facilitate a reader's review.

When choosing a heading, take care that it accurately describes the provision's contents. Do not rely on the general provision that headings do not affect the contract's construction or interpretation. Relying on that provision results in sloppy drafting.

Headings are sometimes too short. Consider the following provision from an agreement between a publisher and an author:

> **Too Short**
>
> **Copies**. No later than ten days before the Book's publication, the Publisher shall provide the Author with five free copies of the Book.

Although the heading *Copies* is descriptive, it could be more so. By changing the name to *Free Copies*, just one more word, the heading becomes more informative.

> **Better**
>
> **Free Copies**. No later than ten days before the Book's publication, the Publisher shall provide the Author with five free copies of the Book.

Headings, of course, can also be too long, trying to encapsulate too much of a provision. Generally, if the heading must list more than two topics to be accurate, divide the provision into two or more sections. If the heading has multiple topics, separate them with a semi-colon.

> **Free Print Copies; E-book Access**. No later than ten days before the Book's publication, the Publisher shall provide the Author with five free print copies of the Book and access to the Book's E-book version.

19.6 TABLE OF CONTENTS

A table of contents is particularly handy in long contracts. It permits a reader to find a specific provision quickly. Generally, a sophisticated word-processing program can automatically create a table of contents if you use automatic numbering.

19.7 TYPOGRAPHY

Contracts are long and arduous to read. Anything that facilities their reading is a boon. Font is one of the factors in the mix, but which font should you select? Typographers classify fonts into two types: **serif** and **sans serif**. A serif font has extra small lines at the ends of the horizontal and vertical strokes of a letter.

The dog wagged its tail.

Sans serif fonts are simpler; they do not have the extra small lines. (*Sans* is French for *without*.)

The dog wagged its tail.

The accepted wisdom has long been that serif fonts, such as Times New Roman, are easier to read. But multiple studies have questioned whether that is correct.[8]

---

8. *See* Alex Poole, *Which Are More Legible: Serif or Sans Serif Typefaces?*, http://alexpoole.info/blog/which-are-more-legible-serif-or-sans-serif-typefaces (last updated March 2012; accessed July 4, 2013) (explaining the rationale for each of serif and sans serif fonts and reviewing the literature comparing the two fonts); Ruth Anne Robbins, *Painting with print: Incorporating concepts of typographic and layout design into the text of legal writing documents*, 2 J. Ass'n Leg. Writing Dirs. 108, 119-120 (Fall 2010).

Indeed, some studies suggest that the easiest font to read is the one with which the reader is most familiar.[9]

The advent of computers has added an additional layer of complexity to the mix. The issue is no longer simply which font facilitates reading a *printed* document. Lawyers must take into account that they now draft and review contracts both in hard copy and on their computers. Therefore, lawyers must also consider which fonts facilitate reading documents on LCD screens, such as laptops, tablets, and flat-panel monitors.

Beginning with the Windows XP version of its operating system, Microsoft has offered a new font-rendering software technology, ClearType®, which makes text on LCD screens sharper and easier to read.[10] To take advantage of this technology, Microsoft has created six new fonts.[11] Several of these fonts are also intended to be easily read in print. Microsoft offers two of these fonts as default fonts in the Windows Vista®, Windows 7®, and Windows 8® operating systems: Cambria (a serif font)[12] and Calibri (a sans serif font).[13]

Here are examples of both.

Cambria

This Confidentiality Agreement, dated March 1, 20X9, is between Wonder Drugs, Inc., a Delaware corporation ("**Wonder Drugs**"), and Still Viable Venture Capital Fund LP, a Delaware limited partnership ("**VC Fund**").

[Other provisions intentionally omitted.]

19.2 Definition of Confidential Information. "Confidential Information" means all information that Wonder Drugs discloses to VC Fund that is in

(a)   tangible form and clearly labeled as confidential when disclosed; or

(b)   non-tangible form and that is both

(i)   identified as confidential when disclosed and

(ii)   summarized and designated as confidential in a written memorandum delivered to VC Fund no later than 10 business days after the information was first disclosed.

19.3 Confidentiality Period. VC Fund shall hold in confidence and shall not disclose any Confidential Information for a period of five years, beginning on the date this Agreement is executed and delivered and ending on the day immediately preceding the fifth anniversary of its execution and delivery.

---

9. Poole, *supra* n. 8.

10. Microsoft Corp., *What is ClearType*, http://www.microsoft.com/typography/WhatIsClearType.mspx (updated Jan. 16, 2002).

11. Microsoft commissioned these fonts from designers and engineers. *See* Microsoft, ClearType Font Collection, http://www.microsoft.com/typography/ClearTypeFonts.mspx (accessed July 4, 2013); Ascender Corporation, *ClearType® FontCollection®* 2, http://www.ascendercorp.com/pdf/MSClearTypeFontCollection.pdf (accessed July 4, 2013).

12. Microsoft, *Cambria Poster*, http://www.microsoft.com/typography/ctfonts/CambriaPoster.xps (accessed July 4, 2013).

13. Microsoft, *Calibri Poster*, http://www.microsoft.com/typography/ctfonts/CalibriPoster.xps (accessed July 4, 2013).

Calibri

This Confidentiality Agreement, dated March 1, 20X9, is between Wonder Drugs, Inc., a Delaware corporation ("**Wonder Drugs**"), and Still Viable Venture Capital Fund LP, a Delaware limited partnership ("**VC Fund**").

[Other provisions intentionally omitted.]

19.2   Definition of Confidential Information. "Confidential Information" means all information that Wonder Drugs discloses to VC Fund that is in

    19.2.1   tangible form and clearly labeled as confidential when disclosed; or

    19.2.2   non-tangible form and that is both

        (a)   identified as confidential when disclosed and

        (b)   summarized and designated as confidential in a written memorandum delivered to VC Fund no later than 10 business days after the information was first disclosed.

19.3   Confidentiality Period. VC Fund shall hold in confidence and shall not disclose any Confidential Information for a period of five years, beginning on the date this Agreement is executed and delivered and ending on the day immediately preceding the fifth anniversary of its execution and delivery.

Despite Microsoft's intent to create fonts that are readable both on-screen and in print, one commentator has criticized these default system fonts and suggested that lawyers use alternative "professional" fonts.[14] These alternatives indeed work well for lawyers from a single firm writing briefs and motions that others will eventually read in print. But for transactional lawyers who are writing contracts, professional fonts can be problematic.

Transactional lawyers exchange drafts of contracts electronically and edit them on-screen. If the lawyers involved use different professional fonts, the exchange of well-formatted documents becomes more challenging. Formatting may be lost in the transmission and repeated conversion from one font to another. Lawyers could remedy this problem by drafting in a default system font and then converting to a professional font for the printing of execution copies. Although this can be done, it is an extra step in the drafting process. If a lawyer does not choose this remedy, she must choose between the default system fonts, Calibri and Cambria.

As between the two default system fonts, one commentator prefers Calibri on the general principle of it being a "better" font.[15] But the choice between the two fonts is not scientific.[16] Each of these fonts has a different personality.[17] Cambria, as a serif font, is more formal; while Calibri, as a sans serif font, is more progressive and

---

14. Matthew Butterick, *Typography for Lawyers: Essential Tools for Polished & Persuasive Documents* 82, 116-131 (Jones McClure Publg. 2010). Mr. Butterick is a practicing lawyer who does double-duty as a commentator on typography in legal documents. See *infra* n. 15 for Mr. Butterick's view of which fonts should be used in contracts as opposed to other legal documents.

15. Telephone Interview with Matthew Butterick, author of *Typography for Lawyers: Essential Tools for Polished & Persuasive Documents* (Jones McClure Publg. 2010).

16. Email from William Davis (Monotype Imaging Inc., formerly Ascender Corp.) to Tina L. Stark (Aug. 4, 2010) (Monotype designs and sells fonts, including Microsoft fonts). *See also* Robbins, *supra* n. 8, citing Linda L. Lohr, *Creating Graphics for Learning and Performance: Lessons in Visual Literacy* 71 (2d ed., Pearson 2003).

17. E-mail from Davis, *supra* n. 16.

friendly.[18] Lawyers accustomed to a serif font, such as Times New Roman, may prefer Cambria's formality. Indeed, Cambria was intended to be the ClearType® alternative to Times New Roman.[19] Other lawyers may prefer the more modern quality of Calibri. Lawyers might also take into account that sans serif fonts are generally more readable on-screen.[20] The author uses Calibri for documents to be read on-screen and Century Schoolbook for documents of significant length to be read as printed documents.

---

18. *Id.*

19. Barbara S. Chaparro, A. Dawn Shaikh, & Alex Chaparro, *Examining the Legibility of Two New ClearType Fonts,* 8 Usability News (newsltr. of Software Usability Research Laboratory at Wichita St. U.), 2 (Feb. 2006), http://psychology.wichita.edu/surl/usabilitynews/81/pdf/Usability%20News%2081%20-%20 Chaparro.pdf.

20. Robbins, *supra* n. 8.

EXERCISES

All of the following exercises are available on the *Drafting Contracts* Website.

Exercise 19-1

Mark up the following provision to indicate how you would tabulate it. Do not change anything else.

> **6.1 Audit by Licensor**. With respect to each Royalty Period, the Licensor may cause an independent accounting firm to audit or review all the Licensee's books and records and to issue a report pertaining to the Royalties earned in that Royalty Period. The Licensor shall give the Licensee reasonable prior written notice of the audit or review. The Licensee shall make its books and records available to the Licensor during normal business hours. If the Licensor wants to object to the Licensee's determination of Royalties for a Royalty Period, it must deliver to the Licensee a statement describing its objections not later than 60 days after the Licensor receives the applicable report obtained. Each party shall use reasonable efforts to resolve the Licensor's objections. If the parties do not resolve all objections on or before the 30th day after the Licensee received the statement of the Licensor's objections, the parties shall promptly submit those objections for resolution to an independent accounting firm acceptable to both parties. If the parties cannot agree on an independent accounting firm, the parties shall select a "big-four" accounting firm by lot. Each party may eliminate one firm by objecting to it in writing. The determination of the independent accounting firm selected in accordance with this provision is conclusive and binding on the parties. The following provisions apply with respect to each audit or review pursuant to this Section 6.1: If an audit or review as finally determined pursuant to this Section 6.1 determines that the Licensee has underpaid Royalties for a Reporting Period, the Licensee shall promptly pay to the Licensor the amount equal to the Royalties owing *minus* the Royalties paid *plus* interest of 10% per year on that amount, accruing from and including

the date on which that amount was due to, but excluding, the date on which that amount is paid.

If an audit or review as finally determined pursuant to this Section 6.1 determines that the Licensee

has overpaid Royalties for a Reporting Period, the Licensor shall promptly pay to the Licensee the

amount equal to the Royalties paid *minus* the Royalties owing. With respect to each audit and review

conducted in accordance with this Section 6.1, the Licensor shall pay the fees of the independent

accounting firm that conducted that audit or review and the fees of any other independent account-

ing firm selected in accordance with this Section 6.1. Despite the immediately preceding sentence,

if the audit or review, as finally determined, determines that the Royalties for the applicable Report-

ing Period are understated by 2% or more, then the Licensee shall pay the fees of the independent

accounting firm that audited or reviewed the Licensee's books and records and the fees of any other

independent accounting firm selected in accordance with this Section 6.1.

Exercise 19-2

Tabulate each of the following provisions, and correct any drafting errors.

Termination of Agreement. On the termination or expiration of this Franchise Agreement, the

Franchisee shall immediately cease to operate the Franchised Business. The Franchisee further cov-

enants that it will no longer represent to the public that it is a franchisee of the Franchisor.[21]

Limitations on Dividends, etc. No dividend or other distribution or payment shall be declared,

paid, or made by the Seller in respect of shares of its capital stock. No purchase, redemption, or

other acquisition shall be made, directly or indirectly, by the Seller of any outstanding shares of its

capital stock.

Use of Premises. The Tenant shall use and occupy the Premises for the purposes of a sand-

wich café, and the Tenant's use of the space will be for the sale of quality food for consumption on or

---

21. This provision is based on a provision from Andrew J. Sherman, *Franchise Agreements,* in *Commercial Contracts: Strategies for Drafting and Negotiating* vol. 2, ch. 21, 21-58 (Morton Moskin ed., Aspen Publishers 2006).

off the Premises or for take-out or for delivery, for the operation of catering services and for the sale of

nonalcoholic beverages for consumption on or off the Premises or for take-out or delivery.

Exercise 19-3

Mark up the following provision to correct any drafting errors.

> **Covenants of the Borrower**. From and after the Effective Date and through the end of the
>
> Lending Term, the Borrower hereby agrees to
>
> (a) provide the Lender with fiscal year-end financial statements no later than 60 days after the
>
> end of each fiscal year; and
>
> (b) the insurance currently in place will continue throughout the term of the Agreement.

Exercise 19-4

Tabulate the following provision from a settlement agreement, and correct any drafting errors. In addition, determine what substantive changes you would recommend to a client making these representations and warranties.[22]

> Each of the Parties warrants and represents for itself that each has been represented by legal counsel of their own choice in the negotiation and joint preparation of this Agreement, has received advice from legal counsel in connection with this Agreement and is fully aware of this Agreement's provisions and legal effect, that all agreements and understandings between the Parties are embodied and expressed in this Agreement, and that each of the Parties enters into this Agreement freely, without coercion, and based on each of the Parties' own judgment and not in reliance on any representations or promises made by any of the other Parties, apart from those expressly set forth in this Agreement.

Exercise 19-5

On page 266, review Version 2 of the provision *Contractor's Right to Terminate.* How could ambiguity be avoided by using the list format? (Big Hint: See Guideline 2 on page 272.)

---

22. This provision is excerpted from CD Form 7, *Settlement Agreement with Detailed Provisions Dealing with Potential Claims-by-Non-Settling Entities,* in *Settlements Agreements in Commercial Disputes: Negotiating, Drafting & Enforcement,* vol. 1 (Richard A. Rosen ed., Aspen 2003).

APPENDIX

Tabulation Guidelines

Sentence Format

1. Use the sentence format for tabulation when the introductory language and an enumerated item form a complete, grammatical sentence.

2. The punctuation at the end of the introductory language is what it would be—or not be—if the introductory language and the enumerated item were actually joined to create a sentence. So, if the introductory language would not be followed by any punctuation when joined with one of the enumerated items, there would be no punctuation in the tabulated format.

3. The first word of each enumerated item is lowercase—because it is the continuation of a sentence.

4. Each enumerated item ends with a semi-colon, *except* for the last item, which ends with a period. *And* or *or* follows the semi-colon of the next-to-last enumerated item.

Examples

Architect's Obligations. The Architect shall

(a)   consult with the Owner at least once a week; and

(b)   deliver to the Owner an accounting of expenses incurred each month in connection with

the Project, no later than five business days after the end of each month.

Force Majeure Event. If a *Force Majeure* Event occurs,

(a)   the Contractor shall advise the Owner of its existence as soon as possible after its occur-

rence; and

(b)   the Contractor's obligation to perform is suspended until the *Force Majeure* Event ends.

List Format

1. Use the list format when the introductory language includes some form of *follow*.

2. Draft the introductory language, if appropriate, so that it signals whether the items in each subsection are cumulative or alternative.

3. End the introductory language with a colon.

4. Each enumerated item begins with a capital letter and ends with a period — even if the enumerated item is a single word.

5. Neither *and* nor *or* follows the period in the next-to-last enumerated item.

Example

Events of Default. Each of the following events is an Event of Default:

(a) The Borrower has failed to pay interest when due.

(b) The Borrower has failed to pay principal when due.

(c) The Borrower has made a misrepresentation or breached a warranty in Article 3.

(d) The Borrower has breached any covenant in Article 4.

Clarity through Sentence Structure

20.1 INTRODUCTION

Chapter 19 examined how an agreement's formatting can affect its clarity. In this chapter, we examine how an individual sentence's organization can affect its clarity.

20.2 SHORT SENTENCES

In Chapter 19, you learned one aspect of the **three-line rule**: Any sentence longer than three lines is a good candidate for tabulation if it includes a compound or a series. A variation on the three-line rule is that any sentence longer than three lines is also a candidate for being recast as two or more sentences. As with tabulation, the shorter sentences facilitate a reader's assimilation of a sentence's substance.

The following sentence comes from a lease. Compare it to the corrected version. Note how much easier the latter is to read. Subsections would help even more.

Wrong

Termination on Fire or Casualty. If a fire or other casualty destroys the Building, the Landlord may terminate the Lease by notifying the Tenant in writing, and then, all Base Rent and Additional Rent due under this Lease ceases as of the date of the casualty, and the Tenant shall remove its trade fixtures and personal property from the Premises no later than 35 calendar days after it receives the Landlord's termination notice, whereupon both parties are released from all further obligations under this Lease, except for any obligations previously incurred.

Correct

Termination on Fire or Casualty. If a fire or other casualty destroys the Building, the Landlord may terminate the Lease by notifying the Tenant in writing. In that event, all Base Rent and Additional Rent due under this Lease ceases as of the date of the casualty. The Tenant shall remove its trade fixtures and personal property from the Premises no later than 35 calendar days after it receives the Landlord's termination notice. On completion of that removal, both parties are released from all further obligations under this Lease, except for any obligations previously incurred.

20.3   SENTENCE CORE

20.3.1   KEEP THE CORE TOGETHER

Every sentence has core words: the subject, verb, and object. These words convey a sentence's critical information. In the sentence, *Bob ate a sandwich*, *Bob* is the subject, *ate* is the verb, and *sandwich* is the object. A writer could expand the sentence by telling the reader the kind of sandwich and when Bob ate it, but the core words have conveyed the sentence's essence.

To facilitate a reader's understanding of a sentence, keep the core words next to each other. If they are separated, a reader must work harder to synthesize a sentence's information. This is especially so when the subject is separated from the verb. Instead of reading all the core information at once, a reader must put the core information on hold while wading through the noncore information. By the time the reader reaches the remainder of the core words, she may have lost the thread of the sentence.

In the provision that follows, underscore the core words of the sentence. Notice how the *if* clause inserted in the middle of the core words interrupts the sentence's flow.

Wrong

Revised Architectural Plans. The Architect shall, if the Owner agrees to pay the Architect's additional fee in accordance with Section 2.2, revise the Final Plans for the house.

This sentence can easily be revised by beginning the sentence with the *if* clause.

Correct

Revised Architectural Plans. If the Owner agrees to pay the Architect's additional fee in accordance with Section 2.2, the Architect shall revise the Final Plans for the house.

20.3.2   REDUCE THE NUMBER OF WORDS PRECEDING THE CORE WORDS

A sentence's core words should be as close to the beginning of a sentence as possible. If they are not, the reader becomes overburdened with the ancillary information that precedes them. By reducing the number of words preceding the core words, a reader can more readily absorb all the information in the sentence.

Drafters sometimes have problems adhering to this rule because they begin a sentence with a long introductory clause that precedes the sentence's core words. For example:

> **Wrong**
>
> **Bankruptcy**. If a party makes a general assignment of all or substantially all of its assets for the benefit of creditors, or applies for, consents to, or acquiesces in, the appointment of a receiver, trustee, custodian, or liquidator for its business or all or substantially all of its assets, the other party may immediately terminate this Agreement by sending written notice.

In the preceding provision, the sequence of clauses makes logical sense because it establishes an *if/then* relationship. If *x* condition exists, then *y* consequence follows. The sequence reflects the temporal order in which the events must occur. But because the core information comes so late in the sentence, the reader has difficulty assimilating the sentence's information. The remedy is to flip the clauses' sequence.

> **Better**
>
> **Bankruptcy**. A party may immediately terminate this Agreement on written notice if the other party makes a general assignment of all or substantially all of its assets for the benefit of creditors, or applies for, consents to, or acquiesces in, the appointment of a receiver, trustee, custodian, or liquidator for its business or all or substantially all of its assets.

This provision becomes even clearer when the rearranged sentence structure is tabulated.

> **Preferred**
>
> **Bankruptcy**. A party may immediately terminate this Agreement on written notice if the other party
>
> (a) makes a general assignment of all or substantially all of its assets for the benefit of creditors; or
>
> (b) applies for, consents to, or acquiesces in, the appointment of a receiver, trustee, custodian, or liquidator for its business or all or substantially all of its assets.

20.4 SHORT BEFORE LONG

20.4.1 PUT SHORT PHRASES BEFORE LONG PHRASES

Often a drafter may choose the order in which two or more phrases appear in a sentence. Generally, you should put the short phrase first. Again, this helps the reader assimilate information by reducing what must be remembered before the second phrase appears. Read the two versions of the following sentence and notice where the italicized language appears in each.

Version 1

Maintenance of the Building. The Landlord shall maintain the Building's Common Areas, including lobbies, stairs, elevators, corridors, and restrooms, the windows in the Building, the mechanical, plumbing, and electrical equipment serving the Building, and the structure of the Building *in reasonably good order and condition*.[1]

Version 2

Maintenance of the Building. The Landlord shall maintain *in reasonably good order and condition* the Building's Common Areas, including lobbies, stairs, elevators, corridors, and restrooms, the windows in the Building, the mechanical, plumbing, and electrical equipment serving the Building, and the structure of the Building.

While either version is grammatically correct, the latter version is preferable. In its new location in Version 2, the italicized language is easy to assimilate and does not impede the assimilation of the other information in the sentence.

The sentence can be further improved by tabulating it.

Version 3

Maintenance of the Building. The Landlord shall maintain *in reasonably good order and condition*

    (a) the Building's Common Areas, including lobbies, stairs, elevators, corridors, and restrooms;

    (b) the windows in the Building;

    (c) the mechanical, plumbing, and electrical equipment serving the Building; and

    (d) the structure of the Building.

20.4.2 PUT THE SHORT EQUIVALENT AS THE SUBJECT IN A DECLARATION

Some declarations are drafted as if the verb is a mathematical equal sign, making the language before and after it equivalents. Definitions are an example:

"Alphabet" means the letters *a through z*.

Thus, *alphabet* equals the letters *a* through *z*. If this type of sentence occurs outside of the definitions section, putting the shorter equivalent before the verb generally facilitates a reader's comprehension.

---

1. This provision is based on a provision from Mark A. Senn, *Commercial Real Estate Leases: Preparation, Negotiation, and Forms* 17-4 (3d ed., Aspen Publishers 2004).

Version 1

Exclusive Remedy. After the Closing, a party's sole remedy with respect to any claim (including any torts claim) relating to this Agreement and the Transaction Documents is the indemnity stated in Article 10.

Version 2

Exclusive Remedy. After the Closing, the indemnity stated in Article 10 is a party's sole remedy with respect to any claim (including any torts claim) relating to this Agreement and the Transaction Documents.

EXERCISES

Mark up the provision in each exercise to create clarity through sentence structure. If appropriate, make other drafting changes that improve the provision. In Exercise 20-3, consider how to revise the language to reflect modern technology. All of the following exercises are available on the *Drafting Contracts* website.

Exercise 20-1

"**Agreement**" means this Manufacturing Agreement, as it may from time to time be amended.

Exercise 20-2

Updating of Disclosure Schedules. The Seller shall, in the event of any omission or misstatement in the Disclosure Schedules, or any change in the underlying facts with respect to any matter disclosed in the Disclosure Schedules, amend and update the Disclosure Schedules so that they are at all times true and correct.

Exercise 20-3

Reproduction of Documents. This Agreement and all documents relating thereto, including, without limitation, (a) consents, waivers, and modifications that may hereafter be executed, (b) documents received by the Lender on the Closing Date (except the Notes themselves), and (c) financial statements, certificates, and other information previously or hereafter furnished to the Lender, may be reproduced by the Lender by any photographic, photostatic, microfilm or other process and the Lender may destroy any original document so reproduced.

Exercise 20-4

Share Ownership. On the transfer of the certificate or certificates evidencing the Shares owned by each Seller to the Buyer, each Seller will have transferred good and valid title to the Shares to the Buyer, free and clear of all Liens.

Exercise 20-5

Increase to Contract Price. If the Contractor is required to pay or bear the burden of any new federal, state, or local tax, or of any rate increase of an existing tax (except a tax on net profits) taking effect after May 30, 20XX, the Contract Price increases by the amount of the new tax or the increased tax resulting from the rate increase.[2]

Exercise 20-6

Setoff.[3] In addition to any rights and remedies of the Bank provided by law, the Bank shall have the right, without prior notice to the Company, any such notice being expressly waived by the Company to the extent permitted by applicable law, on the filing of a petition under any of the provisions of the federal Bankruptcy Act or amendments thereto, by or against; the making of an assignment for the benefit of creditors by; the application for the appointment, or the appointment, of any receiver of, or of any of the property of; the issuance of any execution against any of the property of; the issuance of a subpoena or order, in supplementary proceedings, against or with respect to any of the property of or the issuance of a warrant of attachment against any of the property of; the Company, to set off and apply against any indebtedness, whether matured or unmatured, of the Company to the Bank, any amount owing from the Bank to the Company, at or at any time after, the happening of any of the above-mentioned events, and the aforesaid right of setoff may be exercised by the Bank against the Company or against any trustee in bankruptcy, debtor in possession, assignee for the benefit of creditors, receiver or execution, judgment or attachment creditor of the Company, or against anyone else claiming through or against the Company or such trustee in bankruptcy, debtor in possession, assignee for the benefit of creditors, receiver, or execution, judgment or attachment creditor, not-

---

2. This provision is based on a provision in Glower W. Jones, *Alternative Clauses to Standard Construction Contracts* 455 (2d ed., Aspen 1998).

3. This provision is from a bank loan agreement. It describes when a bank has a **set-off right**. It provides that if a borrower owes money to the bank and has money on deposit with the bank, the bank may use the money on deposit to reduce the principal amount of the loan. For example, if a borrower owes a bank $10,000 and has $3,000 on deposit with the bank, the bank may *set off* the $3,000 against the $10,000 and reduce the borrower's outstanding principal to $7,000.

withstanding the fact that such right of set off shall not have been exercised by the Bank prior to the

making, filing or issuance, or service on the Bank of, or of notice of, any such petition; assignment for

the benefit of creditors; appointment or application for the appointment of a receiver; or issuance or

execution of a subpoena, order or warrant.

Ambiguity

21.1 INTRODUCTION

Ambiguity can be expensive. If parties dispute the meaning of a provision, they must either renegotiate it or litigate. In either event, clients pay attorneys' fees and bear the cost of time not spent on more productive matters. In this context, the old adage that an ounce of prevention is worth a pound of cure was never more true. You should derive little solace from canons of interpretation that may resolve an ambiguity. Those canons are most useful when parties are disputing a provision's meaning, but your job is to draft to preclude that dispute. In the remainder of this chapter, you will learn about common causes of ambiguity and how to prevent them.[1]

21.2 AMBIGUITY AND VAGUENESS

21.2.1 DEFINITION OF AMBIGUITY

An ambiguity arises when a provision can be interpreted in two or more mutually exclusive ways. Imagine a contract between a Canadian manufacturer of ski equipment and a U.S. retailer that provides for payment of $10,000 on the retailer's receipt of the merchandise. But what kind of dollars—U.S. or Canadian? This type of ambiguity, which arises because a word has multiple dictionary meanings, is known as *semantic ambiguity*.[2]

The two other types of ambiguity are **syntactic** and **contextual** ambiguity. Syntactic ambiguity occurs when it is unclear what a word or phrase refers to or modifies. In the following example, it is unclear whether each Seller is obligated to sell its Shares to the Buyer, or whether the Sellers are obligated to sell their jointly owned Shares to the Buyer.

---

1. For an excellent treatment of the law of contract interpretation, *see* Steven J. Burton, *Elements of Contract Interpretation* (Oxford U. Press 2009).

2. Not all words that have multiple dictionary meanings create ambiguities. Some words necessarily reveal their meaning in context. "Examples of these multipurpose words abound: 'If the bear escapes, the owner shall bear the cost.'" F. Reed Dickerson, *Materials on Legal Drafting* 55 (West Publg. Co. 1981). These words are known as *homonyms*.

> **Sale of Shares**. The Sellers shall sell their Shares to the Buyer.

Contextual ambiguity occurs when two provisions are inconsistent. The two provisions can be in the same or different agreements. The following example is more obvious than most ambiguities, but demonstrates the point:

> **Provision 1**
>
> **Tenant's Obligations**. The Tenant shall maintain the entire Building.
>
> **Provision 2**
>
> **Landlord's Obligations**. The Landlord shall maintain the lobby of the Building.

In the long run, it does not matter whether you can name the three types of ambiguity. What matters is developing a sensitivity to ambiguities, so that you do not draft them, and so that you can recognize them.

21.2.2 VAGUENESS DISTINGUISHED FROM AMBIGUITY

Vagueness is not the same as ambiguity. A word or a phrase is vague if its meaning varies depending on the context or if its parameters are not plainly delineated. For example, *reasonable* is vague. What is reasonable in one context may be wholly unreasonable in another. *Blue* is also vague. It could be anything from a pale, robin's egg blue to midnight blue. One blue shades into the next.[3]

In his contract drafting treatise, Reed Dickerson distinguishes ambiguity from vagueness:

> Language can be ambiguous without being vague. If in a mortgage, for example, it is not clear whether the word "he" in a particular provision refers to the mortgagor or the mortgagee, the reference is ambiguous without being in the slightest degree vague or imprecise. Conversely, language can be vague without being ambiguous. An example is the written word "red."[4]

Vagueness is neither inherently good nor bad. It depends on what concept best expresses the parties' agreement and on what best protects your client or advances his interests. Assume that you represent a senior executive in the negotiation of his employment agreement with a large, privately held company. The company's first draft of the employment agreement states that it will lend the executive "$500,000 at 3.5% per year for the purchase of a house in Manhattan." *House* is problematic. It is too specific. Manhattan has very few houses. It has cooperatives, condominiums, townhouses, and lofts. While *house* might be perfectly appropriate in most parts of the country, in Manhattan, a more vague, more inclusive term such as *residence* or *home* is more appropriate.[5]

---

3. *See* F. Reed Dickerson, *The Fundamentals of Legal Drafting* 39 n. 3 (2d ed., Little, Brown & Co. 1986).

4. *Id.* at 40.

5. *See* Albert Choi & George Triantis, *Strategic Vagueness in Contract Design: The Case of Corporate Acquisitions*, 119 Yale L.J. 848 (2010) (discussing why a vague material adverse change provision in an acquisition agreement may be superior to a more precise provision).

21.3 AMBIGUITIES ARISING FROM *AND* AND *OR*

Provisions that include *and, or,* or *and* and *or* are cannon fodder for the creation of ambiguity. Sections 21.3.1 through 21.3.3 that follow explain the mayhem that these simple, short words can create.[6]

21.3.1 THE MEANING OF *AND* AND *OR*

Grade school grammar rules often state as axioms that *and* is **conjunctive** and inclusive,[7] meaning that it joins two or more things; and that *or* is **disjunctive**, meaning that it establishes alternatives between two or more things.[8] Look at the following two sentences:

Conjunctive *and*

Fred likes cake *and* cookies.

Disjunctive *or*

Samantha may have a dog *or* a cat as a pet.

The first sentence uses *and* in its traditional role, conjunctively, to signal that Fred likes both cake and cookies. The second sentence uses *or* in its traditional role, disjunctively, to signal that Samantha may have only one pet, either a dog or a cat. This is the exclusive use of *or*. But contract drafting is rarely so simple. Both *and* and *or* can be used in ways that your sixth-grade English teacher never mentioned.

In addition to being used disjunctively, *or* can signal that matters that seem to be exclusive alternatives may also exist concurrently, creating a third alternative or changing the standard from alternatives to a single cumulative standard.[9] Look at the following provision:

Wrong

Default. If the Landlord makes a misrepresentation or breaches a covenant, then the Tenant may pursue all remedies to which it is entitled under the law.

If *or* is only disjunctive, this provision permits the Tenant to sue for damages if the Landlord either makes a misrepresentation or breaches a covenant. But what happens if the Landlord does both? Has the Tenant lost all its remedies? That makes no business sense. Instead, the parties probably intended that if the Landlord both misrepresented and breached, the Tenant would have two causes of actions and that it could pursue all its remedies. This interpretation results in three alternatives, instead of

---

6. *See* Maurice B. Kirk, *Legal Drafting: The Ambiguity of "And" and "Or",* 2 Tex. Tech. L. Rev. 235 (1970-1971).

7. *The New Oxford American Dictionary* 57 (Erin McKean ed., 3d ed., Oxford U. Press 2010); *see also Ace Cash Express, Inc., v. Silverman,* 2004 WL 101684 at *3 (Tex. App.—Austin Jan. 23, 2004).

8. *The New Oxford American Dictionary, supra* n. 7, at 1232; *see also Perkins & Will v. Sec. Ins. Co. of Hartford,* 579 N.E.2d 1122, 1126 (Ill. App. 4th Dist. 1991).

9. *Vinograd v. Travelers' Protective Ass'n of Am.,* 258 N.W. 787, 788-789 (Wis. 1935).

two, that will give rise to remedies: (1) a misrepresentation, (2) a breach of covenant, and (3) a misrepresentation and a breach of covenant. The following revised provisions reflect the parties' actual intent:

Correct — Version 1

Default. If the Landlord makes a misrepresentation, breaches a covenant, or makes a misrepresentation and breaches a covenant, then the Tenant may pursue all remedies to which it is entitled under the law.

Correct — Version 2

Default. The Tenant may pursue all remedies to which it is entitled under the law if the Landlord does one or both of the following:

(a) Makes a misrepresentation.

(b) Breaches a covenant.

Which of the "Correct" provisions do you prefer? Why?

This use of *or* is known as the **inclusive** use.[10] Some contracts include an interpretive provision that any use of *or* is inclusive rather than exclusive. As contract provisions do use *or* in its exclusive sense, such an interpretive provision could wreak havoc within an agreement. Adding the phrase, *unless the context otherwise requires*, renders the interpretive provision a nullity. One side can always contend that the context otherwise requires. Instead, scrutinize each use of *or* and draft the provision so it says what you intend. One easy way to indicate the exclusive sense of *or* is to use *either* in conjunction with *or.*

Purchase Price Payment. The Buyer shall pay the Seller *either* $8.6 million in immediately available funds on the Closing Date *or* $10 million in immediately available funds on the third anniversary of the Closing Date.

Although *and* is often used conjunctively, it can have the same connotation as the inclusive *or*.[11] In the following example, both provisions permit the Contractor to paint the house using employees, subcontractors, or both employees and subcontractors.

Version 1

Painters. The Contractor may use its employees or subcontractors to paint the House.

Version 2

Painters. The Contractor may use its employees and subcontractors to paint the House.

---

10. *Shaw v. Nat'l Union Fire Ins. Co. of Pitt.*, 605 F.3d 1250, 1254 n. 8 (11th Cir. 2010).

11. *See id.* at 1254 (citing Maurice B. Kirk, *Legal Drafting: The Ambiguity of "And" and "Or"*, 2 Tex. Tech. L. Rev. 238 (1970-1971) (citing F. Reed Dickerson, *The Fundamentals of Legal Drafting* 77 (Little, Brown & Co. 1965))).

Finally, courts will interpret *and* to mean *or* and *vice versa* if it is necessary to implement the parties' intent.[12] Given the inherent ambiguity of *and* and *or*, look carefully at each use of these words to determine whether a provision requires tailoring to clarify the parties' intent.

21.3.2 *AND* AND *OR* IN THE SAME SENTENCE

When *and* and *or* appear in the same sentence to join items in a series, their joint presence almost always creates an ambiguity. To demonstrate how the ambiguity arises, we will work with the following provision:

Wrong

Registration for Litigation Clinic. A student may register for the Litigation Clinic only if that student has taken Evidence or Advanced Civil Procedure and is a third-year student.

This sentence has three standards.

1. The taking of Evidence.
2. The taking of Advanced Civil Procedure.
3. Being a third-year law student.

The ambiguity stems from the different ways in which the standards can be combined. Looking at the alternatives as mathematical symbols can be helpful.

- A = the taking of Evidence.
- B = the taking of Advanced Civil Procedure.
- C = being a third-year student.

Using the letter equivalents, the provision, as drafted, can be restated as follows:

- A or B and C.

Now, using parentheses to establish the relationship between the letter equivalents, here are the two possibilities:

Version 1

(A or B) and C = the student must have taken either Evidence or Advanced Civil Procedure and, in addition, must be a third-year student

Version 2

A or (B and C) = the student must have taken Evidence, or, as an alternative, must have taken Advanced Civil Procedure and must be a third-year student

---

Tabulation easily cures an ambiguity arising from *and* and *or* appearing in the same sentence by showing the relative relationship between the sentence's parts.

---

12. *Noell v. Am. Design Inc., Profit Sharing Plan*, 764 F.2d 827, 833-834 (11th Cir. 1985) (citing *Dumont v. U.S.*, 98 U.S. 142, 143 (1878)).

Correct — Version 1

Registration for Litigation Clinic. A student may register for the Litigation Clinic only if that student

    (a) has taken either Evidence or Advanced Civil Procedure

    and

    (b) is a third-year student.[13]

Here, subsections (a) and (b) establish a cumulative standard.

Correct — Version 2

Registration for Litigation Clinic. A student may register for the Litigation Clinic only if that student

    (a) has taken Evidence

    or

    (b) has taken Advanced Civil Procedure and is a third-year student.

Here, subsections (a) and (b) establish alternative standards.

21.3.3 *AND/OR*

When used in a contract, *and/or* is usually intended to mean *either Choice 1 or Choice 2 or, if not either one of those choices, then both Choice 1 and Choice 2 concurrently*. Judges and commentators have little love for *and/or*. Actually, many forcefully deride it, often penning vitriolic language to describe it.[14] The phrase rouses such anger because its imprecision repeatedly causes litigation. Look at the following language from an employment contract.[15]

[The Company shall hire the Executive to act] as president and/or general manager.

The sentence has at least three possible meanings, all mutually exclusive, based on context.

1. The Company shall hire the Executive to act only in the capacity of president.
2. The Company shall hire the Executive to act only in the capacity of general manager.
3. The Company shall hire the Executive to act as both the president and the general manager.

---

13. An alternative redraft is the following:

    Only third-year students who have taken either Evidence or Civil Procedure may register for the Litigation Clinic.

Some readers may find this version more difficult to understand because of the long *who* clause that separates *students* from *may*.

14. *See* Maurice B. Kirk, *Legal Drafting: The Ambiguity of "And" and "Or", supra* n. 6, at 235.

15. This language paraphrases the contract language at issue in *Hicks v. Haight*, 11 N.Y.S.2d 912 (N.Y. Sup. Ct. 1939).

The case from which this language derives actually posits a fourth meaning: that the executive was actually the company's chief executive officer because he was hired to act as both the president and general manager.[16]

Although *and/or* may seem an innocuous, shorthand solution to a drafting quandary, its long-term risks outweigh the short-term benefits. Don't use it.

21.4 AMBIGUITIES ARISING FROM SENTENCE STRUCTURE

21.4.1 MODIFIERS OF ITEMS IN A COMPOUND OR SERIES

Whenever a modifier follows a compound or a series, an ambiguity may be created. The issue is whether the qualifier modifies each item in the compound or series or only the closest item. (The use of *and* or *or* does not directly cause the ambiguity here, but their use to create the compound or the series is a prerequisite. Again, their presence should signal potential ambiguity.) The grammatical rule is known as *the rule of the last antecedent*. When the rule applies, the qualifier qualifies the noun or phrase that immediately precedes it.[17]

In the following representation and warranty, the qualifier, *to the Borrower's knowledge*, follows *pending or threatened*.

> **Wrong**
>
> **Litigation**. No litigation against the Borrower is pending or threatened to the Borrower's knowledge.

This provision's meaning differs significantly depending on whether the knowledge qualifier modifies both *pending* and *threatened* or only *threatened*. Usually, a bank insists that a borrower make a flat representation and warranty with respect to pending litigation. It will argue that the borrower should know what litigation is pending and if it does not know, then it should perform the necessary due diligence so that it can give an unqualified representation and warranty. In contrast, a bank will usually accept a knowledge qualifier with respect to threatened litigation. It recognizes that a borrower might not know that a third party has been injured and is threatening to sue. To make the representation and warranty reflect the agreed-on risk allocation, *to the Borrower's knowledge* needs to be moved so that it follows the *or* and immediately precedes *threatened*.

> **Correct**
>
> **Litigation**. No litigation against the Borrower is pending or, to the Borrower's knowledge, threatened.

---

16. *Id.* at 914.

17. *See In re Enron Creditors Recovery Corp.*, 380 B.R. 307, 319-323 (Bankr. S.D.N.Y. 2008) (The rule of the last antecedent "provides that, where no contrary intention appears, a limiting clause or phrase should ordinarily be read as modifying only the noun or phrase that it immediately follows.") (citing Norman J. Singer & J.D. Shambie Singer, *Sutherland Statutes and Statutory Construction* vol. 2A, § 47:33 (7th ed., Thomson/West 2007)).

21.4.2 MULTIPLE ADJECTIVES

An ambiguity can arise if two or more adjectives or adjectival phrases modify the same noun. (Once again, *and* is implicated in causing the ambiguity.) Do the adjectives describe two required characteristics of a particular thing, or do they describe two kinds of things? To test which it is, ask whether the sentence could be redrafted as two separate sentences. If yes, the adjectives signal two kinds of things.

For example, the phrase *charitable and educational institutions* is ambiguous.[18]

> **Original**
>
> **Identity of Donee**. The Trust may donate funds only to charitable and educational institutions.

The issue is how the two adjectives, *charitable* and *educational*, relate to each other and to the noun *institutions*. The phrase may contemplate institutions that are concurrently charitable and educational; that is, it contemplates one thing that has two characteristics. Thus, the adjectives are cumulative, the typical interpretation of a string of adjectives modifying a noun.[19]

> **Revision 1**
>
> **Identity of Donee**. The Trust may donate funds only to an institution that is both charitable and educational.

Alternatively, the phrase could contemplate two kinds of institutions: charitable institutions and educational institutions. This could be demonstrated by drafting the provision as two separate sentences.

> **Revision 2 — Version 1**
>
> **Identity of Donee**. The Trust may donate funds to charitable institutions, and the Trust may donate funds to educational institutions.[20]
>
> **Revision 2 — Version 2**
>
> **Identity of Donee**. The Trust may donate funds only to an institution that is either charitable or educational.

A third possibility exists. The Trust could have authority to donate funds to three kinds of institutions: (1) charitable institutions, (2) educational institutions, and (3) institutions that are both charitable and educational.

---

18. *See* F. Reed Dickerson, *The Fundamentals of Legal Drafting, supra* n. 3, at 110.

19. *Id.*

20. The actual provision would need to indicate that these are the only kinds of institutions to which the Trust could donate funds, as in Version 2.

Revision 3

Identity of the Donee. The only institutions to which the Trust may donate funds are the following:

(a) Institutions that are charitable only or educational only.
(b) Institutions that are both charitable and educational.

When using multiple adjectives, repeat the nouns as necessary to create clarity. Tabulation may also help.

21.4.3   SENTENCE ENDING WITH A *BECAUSE* CLAUSE

Sentences that end with a *because* clause are often ambiguous. As explained by Reed Dickerson:

> A terminal "because" clause is often ambiguous in that it is not clear whether the clause applies to the entire statement or merely to the phrase immediately preceding. For example, in the sentence, "The union may not rescind the contract because of hardship," it may not be clear whether the draftsman intends to say, "The union may not rescind the contract, because to do so would cause hardship," or "The union may not rescind the contract, using hardship as the justification."[21]

When faced with such an ambiguity, redraft the sentence to clarify the intent.

21.4.4   SUCCESSIVE PREPOSITIONAL PHRASES

Ambiguity can occur when one prepositional phrase immediately succeeds another. In such a case, the provision generally does not indicate whether the second prepositional phrase modifies only the immediately preceding prepositional phrase or the preceding prepositional phrase and that which came before it. For example, the following sentence is ambiguous in the absence of any other context. Specifically, does the second prepositional phrase, *in New York*, modify *cooperative apartment* or *owner of a cooperative apartment*? Once you know the answer, you can easily rewrite the provision.

Wrong

Entitlement to Tax Rebates. Every owner of a cooperative apartment in New York is entitled to a tax rebate.

Correct — Version 1

Entitlement to Tax Rebates. Every owner of a cooperative apartment *that* is in New York is entitled to a tax rebate.

Correct — Version 2

Entitlement to Tax Rebates. Every owner of a cooperative apartment *who* is in New York is entitled to a tax rebate.

---

21. F. Reed Dickerson, *The Fundamentals of Legal Drafting*, *supra* n. 3, at 103.

Although the redraft cured the ambiguity caused by the successive prepositional phrases, a second ambiguity remains: the use of *New York*. That could refer to New York State, New York City (which includes its five boroughs), or Manhattan (one of the five boroughs).

21.5 SAY THE SAME THING THE SAME WAY

21.5.1 ESTABLISHING STANDARDS

Practically every word or phrase in a contract establishes a standard, and by changing a few words, a drafter can change that standard. Must a party take an action in *no later than three days*, *reasonably promptly*, or *as soon as practicable*? Each of these time frames represents a different standard. By changing the standard, you change the time frame in which a party must perform its obligation. Therefore, by choosing between the standards, the parties allocate risk by making it more or less likely that the party with the obligation will breach the standard.

Because a change of a word can change the meaning of a contract provision, a cardinal principle of good drafting is to **say the same thing the same way**. If you do not, a court may hold that the difference in wording is substantive, even if sloppy drafting caused it.[22]

Here is a lawyer's nightmare:

You are drafting the purchase agreement in connection with your client's purchase of a chain of gyms. During a negotiation, you agreed to add a knowledge qualifier to four of the Seller's representations and warranties. When redrafting the contract, you use the phrase *to the knowledge of each of the Seller's officers* in the first three representations and warranties, but in the fourth you use *to the knowledge of each of the Seller's executive officers*. (The fourth is a more lenient standard from the Seller's perspective because the Seller is liable for the knowledge of a smaller group of people.) In the real world, this could occur inadvertently (but inexcusably) because you copied and pasted the fourth representation and warranty from another contract and failed to notice the different knowledge qualifier.

Now, the disaster. Post-closing, your client discovers that the fourth representation and warranty is materially false, and that one of the Seller's officers knew it at the time of the contract's signing. Outraged, your client tells you to draft the complaint and to claim $100,000 in damages. You are now in a most unfortunate predicament. The fourth representation and warranty, as drafted, stated that none of the Seller's *executive* officers knew that the representation and warranty was false. That representation and warranty is, in fact, true. It was a lower-level officer who knew of the falsity. Therefore, your client has no cause of action against the Seller. If you had used the same qualifier in all four representations and warranties (*to the knowledge of each of the Seller's officers*), the representation and warranty would have been false, and your client would have had a viable cause of action.

---

22. *See Int'l Fid. Ins. Co. v. Co. of Rockland*, 98 F. Supp. 2d 400, 412 (S.D.N.Y. 2000) (stating that "sophisticated lawyers . . . must be presumed to know how to use parallel construction and identical wording to impart identical meaning when they intend to do so, and how to use different words and construction to establish distinctions in meaning."); *Pac. First Bank v. New Morgan Park Corp.*, 876 P.2d 761, 767-768 (Or. 1994) (determining that a lease intentionally did not require a landlord to be reasonable when rejecting a tenant's transfer of the lease but required any rejection of a sublease to be reasonable).

21.5.2 CRAFTSMANSHIP

Although saying the same thing the same way is generally a matter of substance, it is not always. Sometimes, it is a matter of craftsmanship. For example, no substantive consequences result if you use both the following phrases in a contract: *includes, without limitation* and *including, but not limited to.*[23] However, by using only one of these phrases throughout a contract, you show the attention to detail that is the hallmark of a careful lawyer.

In the following sections, we will look at some of the more sophisticated ways that drafters apply the say the same thing the same way principle.

21.5.3 ISSUES IN ACQUISITION AND CREDIT AGREEMENTS: REPRESENTATIONS AND WARRANTIES VS. COVENANTS

In acquisition agreements, representations and warranties, on the one hand, and covenants, on the other, often deal with the same subject matter. For example, in the representation and warranty that follows with respect to property, plant, and equipment, a seller states the current condition of those assets. Then, in the covenants, the seller promises how it will maintain those assets from signing to closing. If the standards in the representations and warranties and the covenants differ, a seller could be obligated to upgrade the condition of the assets. A parallel issue arises in a credit agreement in which a borrower often makes representations and warranties on a topic that is also a subject of a borrower covenant.

Look at the following provisions from the perspective of the seller and determine what modifications you would ask the buyer for and why.

From the representations and warranties

> **4.12 Condition of Property**. Except as set forth in **Schedule 4.12**, the Seller's property, plant, and equipment are in customary operating condition, subject only to ordinary wear and tear.

From the covenants

> **5.10 Maintenance of Properties, etc**. The Seller shall maintain all of its properties in good order, reasonable wear and tear excepted.

As a close read of these provisions reveals, the standard for upkeep differs. The representation and warranty is vague. The reader does not know whether the condition is poor or good—only that it's customary. (In what other way do these provisions violate the *say the same thing the same way principle*?) In these circumstances, an aggressive buyer might reasonably argue that the covenant obligates the seller to upgrade the condition of the properties to good order, reasonable wear and tear excepted.

---

23. It is clunky drafting to use either of these phrases. See § 23.5.5 for an alternative.

21.5.4   SIMILAR PROVISIONS IN MORE THAN ONE AGREEMENT

Just as different standards in representations and warranties and covenants can create a problem, different standards in different agreements can create a problem. The classic scenario occurs when a buyer purchases all the outstanding shares of a target company and borrows money to fund its acquisition. In the acquisition agreement, the seller makes representations and warranties to the buyer. In the financing agreement, the buyer turns into the borrower who makes representations and warranties to the lender about the target. (The bank wants these representations because its risk is as to the target.) Although the representations and warranties in the two agreements will be similar, they will not be the same. For example, compare the following representations and warranties from an acquisition agreement and a financing agreement:

> **The Seller's Representation and Warranty to the Buyer**
>
> **Condition of Property.** The Seller's equipment and machinery are in the condition that industry standards require.
>
> **The Borrower's Representation and Warranty to the Lender**
>
> **Property, Plant, and Equipment.** All of the Target's property, plant, and equipment are in good order, reasonable wear excepted.

If the buyer/borrower believes that the two standards materially differ and that the financing agreement standard is tougher, the buyer/borrower must decide whether it otherwise knows enough facts to make a truthful statement to the lender. If it does not, the buyer/borrower has four options. First, it can ask the seller to change its representation and warranty so that it mirrors the one that the buyer/borrower must give in the financing agreement. Second, it can ask the lender to change its representation and warranty so that it mirrors the one the buyer/borrower receives in the purchase agreement. Third, it can ask the lender for some other change in the representation and warranty, such as a qualification. Fourth, it can leave the representation and warranty unchanged, but only after performing additional due diligence so that it can truthfully make the representation and warranty.

The same issue can arise when memorializing a transaction requires multiple contracts. For example, imagine the repercussions if two agreements in an integrated transaction unintentionally had different governing law provisions. To prevent these mistakes, always take the time to conform all the general provisions in each of a transaction's agreements.

21.5.5   CONTRACT PROVISIONS AND DOCUMENTS BASED ON STATUTORY PROVISIONS

Contract provisions and documents are sometimes based on statutory provisions. For example, a certificate of incorporation reflects the requirements of the statute authorizing the formation of corporations. Although most drafters use a treatise form as the basis of a certificate of incorporation, that form, when it was first created, was based on the statute.

When creating a provision or a document based on a statute, parrot the words of the statute: Say exactly what it says. Although a difference between the two may not cause a difference in substance, it could.[24] And if it does, it may prevent your firm from opining that the document meets the statute's requirements. Think of it as sanctioned plagiarism (yes, an oxymoron). To draft the document, you must copy it, meaning: Copy and paste the statute into your document. Then, change only what is necessary to tailor the document to your transaction.

The following example shows a provision from a certificate of incorporation based on the statutory provision.

Delaware General Corporation Law § 102 (a)(3) *(contents of certificate of incorporation)*

The certificate of incorporation shall set forth . . . [t]he nature of the business to be conducted or promoted. It shall be sufficient to state, either alone or with other businesses or purposes, that *the purpose of the corporation is to engage in any lawful act or activity for which corporations may be organized under the General Corporation Law of Delaware* . . . (emphasis added).

Statement of Purpose in Certificate of Incorporation

The purpose of the Corporation is to engage in any lawful act or activity for which corporations may be organized under the General Corporation Law of Delaware (emphasis added).

21.6 DATES, TIME, AND AGE

Drafters regularly cause ambiguities by the ways in which they express dates, age, and time. A modicum of care can banish these ambiguities from an agreement.

21.6.1 DATES

21.6.1.1 The Problems

Misuse of prepositions causes many of the ambiguities with respect to dates. Common problem prepositions are *by, within, between, from,* and *until.* Here are some examples. (Section 21.6.1.2 sets out correct revisions of each of the following provisions.)

Provision 1 — by [a stated date]

Samples. The Manufacturer shall submit a sample *by* November 15, 20XX.

This use of *by* raises the issue of whether November 14 or November 15 is the last day on which the Manufacturer may submit the sample.[25]

---

24. *See* Vincent L. Teahan, *Why Don't Our Clients Like Their Wills?,* 69 N.Y. St. B.J. 26, 30 (1997) (stating that "the lawyer has to hold a mirror to the language of the GST statute and its regulations" in order for a particular tax exemption to apply to a will).

25. *Phoenix Newsps., Inc. v. Molera,* 27 P.3d 814, 819 (Ariz. App. Div. 1 2001) ("The word 'by' when used before a date certain may mean 'before a certain date,' but it just as readily may mean 'on or before a certain date.'").

> **Provision 2—within [x days of]**
>
> **Notice to the EPA.** The Buyer shall notify the Environmental Protection Agency of the sale *within* 30 days of the Closing.

Here, it is unclear whether the 30 days precedes or follows the Closing, or both. (Most likely, it is a pre-closing covenant.) In addition, it is unclear whether the 30 days includes the day of the Closing.[26]

> **Provision 3—between [date 1] and [date 2]**
>
> **Tender of Bids.** A potential buyer may tender bids for the Target *between* November 1, 20XX and November 15, 20XX.

The ambiguity is whether the dates are bookends surrounding the dates on which a party may tender bids, or whether the dates are also dates on which a party may tender bids.[27]

> **Provision 4—from [date 1] until [date 2]**
>
> **Tender of Bids.** A potential buyer may tender bids for the Target *from* November 1, 20XX *until* November 15, 20XX.

This provision creates the same ambiguity as does *between*: Are the stated dates also dates on which a party may tender bids, or are they bookends?[28]

21.6.1.2 THE CURES

To prevent ambiguities in provisions with dates, state the beginning and ending dates and, if appropriate, specify the time on each date. As an alternative, use one of the following:

---

26. *See Reifke v. State*, 31 A.D.2d 67, 70 (N.Y. App. Div. 4th Dept. 1968) ("[T]he word 'within' fixes the limit beyond which action cannot be taken, but does not fix the first point of time at which action shall be taken. It prescribes the end, not the beginning; it means 'not longer in time than' or 'not later than.'"); *Glenn v. Garrett*, 84 S.W.2d 515, 516 (Tex. Civ. App.—Amarillo 1935) ("The word 'within,' used relative to time, has been 'defined variously as meaning: any time before; at or before; at the end of; before the expiration of; not beyond; not exceeding; not later than.'"); *Kramek v. Stewart*, 648 S.W.2d 399, 401 (Tex. App.—San Antonio 1983) ("The term 'within' has numerous definitions including 'not later than,' 'anytime before,' and 'before the expiration of.'").

27. *Atkins v. Boylston Fire & Marine Ins. Co.*, 46 Mass. 439, 440 (Mass. 1843) ("[Between] . . . has various meanings . . . . The most common use of the word is to denote an intermediate space of time or place.").

28. *See Hecht v. Powell*, 240 Ill. App. 124, 130 (Ill. App. 1st Dist. 1926) ("Strictly etymologically, [until] is a word of exclusion, but as commonly used, it is just as likely to be used in an inclusive as an exclusive sense."); *Fetters v. Des Moines*, 149 N.W.2d 815, 818 (Iowa 1967) ("The words 'from' and 'to' when used with respect to measurement of time have no fixed or specific meaning. Standing alone they are ambiguous and equivocal."), *overruled in part on other grounds by, Mease v. Fox*, 200 N.W.2d 791 (Iowa 1972); *Conway v. Smith Mercantile Co.*, 44 P. 940, 940 (Wyo. 1896) ("The word 'until' may either, in a contract or a law, have an inclusive or exclusive meaning, according to the subject to which it is applied, the nature of the transaction which it specifies, and the connection in which it is used, and this rule extends to the correlatives of the word.").

- Before.
- On or before.
- After.
- On or after.
- No later than.

Provision 1, corrected — by [a stated date]

Samples. The Manufacturer shall submit a sample

- *no later than* November 15, 20XX.
- *on or before* November 15, 20XX.
- *before* November 16, 20XX.

Although each of the three alternatives cures the ambiguity, clients often prefer the first and second alternatives as they state the last permissible date for submission, the date a client will circle in red on its calendar. The third alternative, however, requires a client to determine (albeit rather easily) the deadline.

Provision 2, corrected — within [x days of]

Notice to the EPA. The Buyer shall notify the Environmental Protection Agency of the sale

- no later than 30 days before the Closing.
- no later than 30 days after the Closing.

Determining which alternative to include in the contract requires a review of the statute and knowing the business deal. In either alternative, the 30-day period excludes the day of the Closing.

Provision 3, corrected — between [date 1] and [date 2]

Tender of Bids. A potential buyer may tender bids for the Target beginning on November 1, 20XX at 9:00 a.m. and ending on November 15, 20XX at 5:00 p.m.

The inclusion of the time on each of the two days avoids any issues as to how early or late in the day a potential buyer may tender a bid.

Provision 4, corrected — from [date 1] until [date 2]

Tender of Bids. A potential buyer may tender bids for the Target beginning on November 1, 20XX at 9:00 a.m. and ending on November 15, 20XX at 5:00 p.m.

As *from/until* creates the same ambiguities as does *between*, the same cure works.

21.6.2 TIME

Time ambiguities fall into two broad categories: the measurement of a time period and the statement of the time of day.

21.6.2.1 Measurement of Time Periods

Parties often need to refer to time periods—for example, the length of a loan or the number of days' notice to be given. The best alternative is to use exact dates, but that is not always possible. Notice provisions operate in the future and no one knows when the provisions will come into play. In addition, precedents regularly try to limit the number of blanks to be filled in by expressing time periods in words. To avoid any ambiguity when doing so, follow these rules:

When measuring years

- Use the concept of an anniversary date.
- Refer to calendar years only to refer to the period from and including January 1 through December 31 of the same year.[29]
- Check the consequences of leap years.
- Confirm that a future date is a Business Day by using a perpetual calendar or provide that the event must occur on the next Business Day.

For example:

Version 1

Due Date. The Note is due on May 6, 20XX.

Version 2

Due Date. The Note is due on the day immediately preceding the fifth anniversary of its issuance, except if that day is not a Business Day, then it is due on the next Business Day.

When measuring months, determine which of the following possibilities the parties intend and draft accordingly:

- Calendar months, meaning from the first day of a named month through its last day.
- 30-day periods, beginning on any day.[30]

---

29. *See Draper v. Wellmark, Inc.*, 478 F. Supp. 2d 1101, 1108 (N.D. Iowa 2007) ("The term 'calendar year' has been construed in several cases, though not without exception to indicate the period from January 1 to December 31, inclusive.") (citing E.L. Strobin, *What 12-Month Period Constitutes "Year" or "Calendar Year" as Used in Public Enactment, Contract, or Other Written Instrument*, 5 A.L.R.3d 584, § 4[d] (1966)). Failure to do so can create ambiguity. *See also Gottesman & Co., Inc. v. Int'l Tel. & Telegraph Corp.*, 477 N.Y.S.2d 139, 140 (N.Y. App. Div. 1st Dept. 1984) (The meaning of "full years of operation" was interpreted by one party to mean the full calendar year from January 1 to December 31 and by the other party to mean successive twelve-month periods.).

30. *Mercer v. Aetna Life Ins. Co.*, 593 P.2d 23, 24-25 (Kan. App. 1979) ("While the term 'calendar month' means a month as designated in the calendar, without regard to the number of days it may contain, 'thirty days' and 'one month' are not synonymous terms and do not necessarily nor ordinarily mean the same periods of time.").

■ The period beginning on a specific date and ending on the day in the next month which numerically corresponds to the day in the starting month *minus* one (March 18, 20XX through April 17, 20XX).[31]

Ambiguity can easily arise when using months as the standard of measurement. In ordinary parlance the meaning of a calendar month is clear: from the first day of the month through the last day — May 1 through May 31. In contracts the expected meaning is not necessarily the meaning that a court will attribute to the phrase. Moreover, certain types of contracts have conventions that determine the meanings of *month*, such that a month is the period from a day in the calendar month to the corresponding numerical day of the next month (not the corresponding numerical day, *minus* one).[32] When weighing what language to use, look at whether changing the reference from a number of months to a number of days clarifies an ambiguity or makes the provision easier to draft. Here are some examples:

Version 1

Term. The term of this Lease is *six calendar months*. If the parties sign this Lease on the first day of a calendar month, then the term begins on that date, and the month in which the Lease is signed is the first calendar month. If the parties do not sign this Lease on the first day of a calendar month, then the term begins on the first day of the next calendar month, which is then the first calendar month of the term. In either event, the term ends at 5:00 p.m. on the last day of the sixth calendar month of the term.

Version 2

Term. The term of this Lease is *six months*. The first day of the term is the date that the parties sign this Lease. If that date is

(a) the first day of a calendar month, the term ends at 5:00 p.m. on the last day of the sixth calendar month of the term; and

(b) not the first day of a calendar month, the term ends at 5:00 p.m. in the sixth month following the month in which the parties signed this Lease, on the day of the month numerically corresponding to the day on which the parties signed this Lease, *minus* one.

Version 3

Term. The term of this Lease is 180 days, beginning on the date that the parties sign this Lease and ending at 5:00 p.m. on the 180th day.

Version 4

Term. The term of this Lease begins on March 14, 20XX and ends on September 13, 20XX.

---

31. *Ruan Transport Corp. of Neb. v. R.B. 'Dick' Wilson, Inc. of Neb.*, 79 N.W.2d 575, 577 (Neb. 1956) ("The term calendar month, whether employed in statutes or contracts, and not appearing to have been used in a different sense, denotes a period terminating with the day of the succeeding month numerically corresponding to the day of its beginning, less one. If there be no corresponding day of the succeeding month, it terminates with the last day thereof.").

32. For the definition of "interest period" *see* Prac. L. Co., *Loan Agreement: Borrowing Mechanics*, http://us.practicallaw.com; search "loan agreement: borrowing mechanics" (accessed June 18, 2013).

When measuring weeks, determine which one of the following possibilities the parties intend:

- The seven-day period beginning on Sunday and ending on Saturday.[33]
- The seven-day period beginning on a specific day and ending one day before the same day in the following week (Wednesday through Tuesday).
- The five-day period beginning on Monday and ending on Friday.

Also, think through the effect of holidays, and look at whether changing the reference from a number of weeks to a number of days clarifies an ambiguity or makes the provision easier to draft. Compare the following provisions:

Version 1

Beginning of Production. The Manufacturer shall begin production of the Item no later than two weeks after the Retailer approves the Item. The two-week period begins on the day after the Manufacturer's receipt of the Retailer's approval and ends at 5:00 p.m. on the last day of the two-week period.

Version 2

Beginning of Production. The Manufacturer shall begin production of the Item no later than 9:00 a.m. on the 14th day after the Manufacturer's receipt of the Retailer's approval. The 14-day period includes weekends and holidays.

When measuring days, determine the following:

- Which is the first day and which is the last.
- Whether days should be limited to business days.
- Whether a time of day should be specified.

In making these determinations, parties often rely on statutes,[34] interpretive provisions, and definitions. For example, when a mathematical formula includes the number of days in a time period, an interpretive provision can prevent disputes by resolving which are the first and last days of the period.[35] The following provision is from a credit agreement.

Determining the Number of Days of Interest Accrual. When calculating the amount of interest owed, the number of days as to which interest accrues includes the first day of a period but excludes the last day of that period.

---

33. *Syversen v. Saffer*, 140 N.Y.S.2d 774, 778 (Sup. Ct. 1955) (noting that calendar week "is a definite period of time, commencing on Sunday and ending on Saturday") (citing *In re Wright's Will*, 171 N.Y.S. 123, 124 (App. Div. 4th Dept. 1918)), *aff'd*, 150 N.Y.S.2d 551 (App. Div. 2d Dept. 1956).

34. *See e.g.* Cal. Civ. Code §10 (1872) (stating that time is "computed by excluding the first day and including the last"); Ind. Code §34-7-5-1 (1998) (stating that time "shall be computed by excluding the first day and including the last."); N.Y. Gen. Constr. Law § 20 (1988) (stating that "[t]he day from which any specified period of time is reckoned shall be excluded in making the reckoning").

35. A day is ordinarily considered a calendar day, but in construing an agreement the court must factor in the intention of the parties. *U.S. v. Sargent-Tyee Co.*, 376 F. Supp. 1375, 1376 (E.D. Wash. 1974) (stating that the term "days" as used in the contract at issue referred to "days of the ordinary 5-day work week during which the Bell 205 helicopter was available to the defendant").

Similarly, to avoid disputes as to whether weekends and holidays are part of a time period, parties often define *business day* to distinguish it from other days. These definitions usually use local bank holidays as their starting point because a bank holiday in Hawaii might not be a bank holiday in Nebraska.

Definition

"**Business Day**" means a day other than a Saturday, Sunday, or other day on which commercial banks in [insert location] are authorized or required by law to close.

Provision

Version 1

Response to Notice of Arbitration. If a party gives the other party a Notice of Arbitration, the other party shall respond no later than *five days* after the date of its receipt of the Notice of Arbitration.

Version 2

Response to Notice of Arbitration. If a party gives the other party a Notice of Arbitration, the other party shall respond no later than *five Business Days* after the date of its receipt of the Notice of Arbitration.

If a time period keys off the date of a notice's receipt, parties often include the following two interpretive provisions in the general provisions' notice section:

Date of Receipt. If a party receives a notice on a day that is not a Business Day or after 5:00 p.m. on a Business Day, it is deemed received at 9:00 a.m. on the next Business Day.

Rejection or Nondelivery. If a party rejects a notice, or the notice cannot otherwise be delivered in accordance with this Agreement, then the notice is deemed received on its rejection or the inability to deliver it.

21.6.2.2 Time of Day

When stating the time of day as of when something should be determined, state whether it is *a.m.* or *p.m.* Do not use 12:00 a.m. or 12:00 p.m. as they can be ambiguous.[36] To deal with which day midnight belongs to, write either 11:59 p.m. or 12:01 a.m. If the two-minute differential matters (which it generally does not), write 11:59:59 p.m. or 12:00:01 a.m.

21.6.3 AGE

When referring to a person's age,

- state the age as of which a right begins; or
- refer to the *celebration* of a particular birthday.

---

36. *See State v. Hart*, 530 A.2d 332, 333-334 (N.J. Super. App. Div. 1987) (noting the inconsistency of New Jersey opinions deciding the meaning of 12:00 p.m.); *see also Warshaw v. Atlanta*, 299 S.E.2d 552, 554 (Ga. 1983) (finding that zoning ordinance's use of "12:00 p.m." referred to midnight).

> **Example 1**
>
> **Authority of Officers**. Only a corporate officer who is 21 or older may bind a party.
>
> **Example 2**
>
> **Drinking Age**. Only a person who has celebrated that person's 21st birthday may drink alcoholic beverages.

21.7 USING *IF/THEN* FORMULATIONS TO DRAFT CONDITIONS

When drafting a condition using an *if/then* formulation, an ambiguity can be created if the *if* clause includes a time or date.

> **Wrong**
>
> **Additional Air-conditioning**. If the Landlord provides Additional Air-conditioning before 5:00 p.m. on any day, then the Tenant shall pay Additional Rent as computed in accordance with **Exhibit C**.

As *before 5:00 p.m. on any day* immediately precedes *then*, the Landlord could argue that the Tenant owes the Additional Rent on the day the Landlord provides the Additional Air-conditioning. The following redraft eliminates the ambiguity by deleting *then* and stating how to determine the time of payment, although it is only a general statement.

> **Correct**
>
> **Additional Air-conditioning**. If the Landlord provides Additional Air-conditioning on any day, the Tenant shall pay Additional Rent in accordance with the provisions of this Agreement, including **Exhibit C**.

21.8 PLURALS

Using the plural form of nouns or possessives invites ambiguity. Whenever possible, contracts should be drafted using singular nouns and singular possessives.[37] This applies to nouns that are the subject of the sentence and those used elsewhere.

Look at the three circles below and notice how they intersect with each other. Imagine that Circle A represents the knowledge of Seller A, that Circle B represents the knowledge of Seller B, and that Circle C represents the knowledge of Seller C.

---

37. *See BP Amoco Chem. Co. v. Flint Hills Resources LLC*, 600 F. Supp. 2d 976, 982 (N.D. Ill. 2009) (finding that the use of the plural noun, "production units," was "ambiguous as to whether the parties intended the representation to refer to the simultaneous or individual production capacity of the three units").

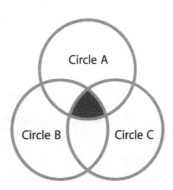

Now assume that the Buyer has drafted the following representation and warranty for the Sellers.

Wrong

> **Defaults**. To the Sellers' knowledge, the Target is not in material default under any contract.

To determine whether the representation and warranty is true, we would need to know what constitutes the Sellers' knowledge. A reasonable argument could be made that the Sellers' knowledge is not the aggregate knowledge of the Sellers, as represented by the aggregate area of the three circles. Instead, it is only the knowledge that all three Sellers share, as represented by the shaded area where the three circles intersect. To prevent this latter interpretation, the knowledge qualifier must be rewritten to clarify that the Buyer is asking about the knowledge of each Seller.

Correct

> **Defaults**. To each Seller's knowledge, the Target is not in material default under any contract.

Here is another example of ambiguity caused by plurals. In the original version, it is unclear whether each shareholder must exchange only that shareholder's shares or whether the shareholders must also exchange the shares they own jointly. The revised provision contemplates that some shares might be jointly owned but by fewer than all the shareholders.

Wrong

> **Exchange of Shares**. On December 31, 20XX, the Shareholders shall exchange their preferred shares for common shares.

Correct

> **Exchange of Shares**. On December 31, 20XX, each Shareholder shall exchange for common shares all of the preferred shares that Shareholder owns, whether individually or jointly with one or more other Shareholders.

In the next example, the ambiguity is whether the schedule must list agreements to which not all of the Sellers are a party. The revision refers to *each* agreement but could have referred to *all* agreements or *every* agreement without creating any ambiguity, but that is not always the case. *Each* is preferable because it distinguishes separately all of the contracts, limiting the possibility of ambiguity. Draft in the singular.

Wrong

Agreements. **Schedule 3.6** lists and describes all agreements to which the Sellers are a party.

Correct

Agreements. With respect to each Seller, **Schedule 3.6** lists and describes each agreement to which that Seller is a party.

Ambiguity can also arise when parties are listed individually but joined by *and*. For example:

Wrong

Notice of Borrowing Amount. Borrower A and Borrower B shall notify the Bank of the Borrowing Amount at least three days before the Borrowing Date.

The ambiguity is whether each Borrower is obligated to notify the Bank or whether the Borrowers must act jointly.

Correct — Version 1

Notice of Borrowing Amount. Borrower A and Borrower B shall each notify the Bank of the Borrowing Amount at least three Business Days before the Borrowing Date.

Correct — Version 2

Notice of Borrowing Amount. Borrower A and Borrower B shall jointly notify the Bank of the Borrowing Amount at least three Business Days before the Borrowing Date.

21.9 PROVISOS

Drafters use provisos for three purposes.

1. To state a condition.
2. To state an exception to a rule.
3. To add additional material.

All these uses might suggest that provisos are an indispensable drafting tool. They are not. Instead, the multiplicity of purposes creates serious problems for a drafter because of their potential for ambiguity — as in the following provision:

Wrong

Disclosure of Assets. Mr. Nowicki shall disclose all of his assets to Mrs. Nowicki, *provided* that Mrs. Nowicki discloses all of her assets to Mr. Nowicki.

The proviso in this example has two possible meanings. First, Mrs. Nowicki's previous disclosure of her assets could be a condition to Mr. Nowicki's obligation to disclose his assets. (A condition to an obligation and the obligation.) Second, the proviso could merely be signaling an additional covenant—a covenant that Mrs. Nowicki is also obligated to disclose her assets.[38] With two alternative meanings that are mutually exclusive, the provisio creates a classic ambiguity.

Correct—Version 1

If Mrs. Nowicki discloses all of her assets to Mr. Nowicki, Mr. Nowicki shall disclose all of his assets to Mrs. Nowicki. *(Condition to an obligation and the obligation.)*

Correct—Version 2

Mr. Nowicki shall disclose all of his assets to Mrs. Nowicki, and Mrs. Nowicki shall disclose all of her assets to Mr. Nowicki. *(Reciprocal covenants.)*

Finally, provisos can create an interpretive nightmare because they often travel in packs—like wolves. Where one resides, another lurks. This results from the usual back and forth of negotiation. First, the drafter crafts a provision, believing that it memorializes the parties' agreement. The other party readily agrees—with one proviso. The drafter then acknowledges that the proviso seems right, except for one issue that can be cured—with another proviso. And on it goes until the provision has three or even four provisos. The accumulation of provisos exacerbates the difficulty of analyzing the provision. The reader gets lost trying to puzzle out what each proviso means (condition, exception, or additional material) and how each proviso relates to the others and to the main provision.

In drafting contemporary commercial agreements, purge documents of provisos. They may have been a staple of commercial drafting for centuries, but they are a staple destined for the wastebasket.

When faced with a provision that typically might be handled with a proviso, first determine the proviso's purpose. Then, redraft the proviso, but use the alternative, appropriate language.

Rule 1

To state a condition, use *must, if*, or *it is a condition that*. (If you use *must*, add an interpretive provision.)[39]

Rule 2

To state an exception to a rule, use *except that, but*, or *however*.

---

38. *Hohenberg Bros. Co. v. George E. Gibbons & Co.*, 537 S.W.2d 1, 3 (Tex. 1976) (stating that "in the absence of such a limiting clause, whether a certain contractual provision is a condition, rather than a promise, must be gathered from the contract as a whole and from the intent of the parties").

39. See §11.3.

Rule 3

To add additional material, use a new sentence or subsection or a connective such as *furthermore* or *and*.

If a provision has more than one proviso, determine how each one relates to the other and to the main purpose of the provision. Then use formatting to establish how they relate to each other. Depending on the provision, tabulation, multiple sentences, multiple sections, or multiple subsections may be appropriate.

The following are examples of improperly drafted provisos and appropriate redrafts:

Proviso as a condition

Wrong

> **Change Order**. The Owner may change the bathroom tile, *provided that* the new tile does not cost more than the original tile.

Correct

> **Change Order**. The Owner may change the bathroom tile, if the new tile does not cost more than the original tile.

Proviso as an exception to a rule

Wrong

> **Consents**. The Contractor shall obtain all Consents; *provided, however,* the Owner shall obtain the Community Board's Consent.

Correct

> **Consents**. The Contractor shall obtain all Consents, *except* that the Owner shall obtain the Community Board's Consent.

When drafters used typewriters, they underscored *provided, provided that,* and *provided, however,* to highlight the exception. The contemporary equivalent is to italicize *except*.

Proviso as additional material

Wrong

> **Consents**. The Contractor shall obtain the Consent of the Housing Department *provided, however,* it shall also obtain the Community Board's Consent.

Correct

> **Consents**. The Contractor shall obtain the Consent of both the Housing Department and the Community Board.

CHAPTER TWENTY-ONE

EXERCISES

Exercise 21-1

Read the following provision. Two words are vague, and one phrase is ambiguous.
What are they? Mark up the provision to clarify the ambiguity.

Assignment. Neither party may assign any right under this Agreement to any Person without

the prior written consent of the other party. Manufacturer consents, without any further consent

being required, to the assignment by Purchaser to any affiliate of Purchaser that is as creditworthy as

Purchaser.

Exercise 21-2

Mark up the following provisions to clarify the ambiguities and to correct any drafting errors.

Compliance with Applicable Law. The Borrower has complied with all Laws and is currently

in compliance with all Laws, except for any noncompliance which would not have a material adverse

effect on the Borrower.

Conditions to Closing. The Buyer's obligation to perform is subject to the fulfillment of each of

the following conditions: The representations and warranties of the Seller must be true on and as of

the Closing Date with the same force and effect as if made on the Closing Date. The Seller must have

complied with the covenants to be complied with by the Closing Date. The Seller must have delivered

to the Buyer a certificate to the foregoing effect.

Exercise 21-3

The following provision comes from a website development agreement. Determine
how *and* and *or* are used in it and whether their use creates any ambiguities. Mark
up the provision to clarify any ambiguities.

Third-party Content. The Developer shall use commercially reasonable efforts to secure for the

Client the broadest possible rights to any third-party content that the Developer incorporates into the

Website. The Developer may either purchase the third-party content or license it. Any use of third-party content is subject to the Client's final approval. The Client shall pay all costs or fees for third-

party content, either by directly paying the third party or by reimbursing the Developer, after receiving

appropriate documentation.

Exercise 21-4

Mark up the following provisions to correct the drafting errors. The provisions create a substantive business issue. What is it?

Provision 1

Article 5 — The Landlord's Covenants

Throughout the term of the Lease, the Landlord agrees as follows:

[Provisions Intentionally Omitted]

5.4 Alterations. The Landlord shall not unreasonably withhold permission from the Tenant in

determining whether the Tenant may proceed with making alterations to the Premises.

Provision 2

Article 6 — The Tenant's Covenants

Throughout the Lease Term, the Tenant agrees as follows:

[Provisions Intentionally Omitted]

6.6 Alterations. The Tenant shall not make any changes or alterations to the Premises without

the Landlord's prior written consent.

Exercise 21-5[40]

Big Ten University (Big Ten) entered into a collective bargaining agreement with the Local Union (the Local Union) on January 1, 20XX.

1. As drafted, do the following provisions require Big Ten to contribute to the Welfare Fund and the Employees' Pension Fund on behalf of each probationary employee? What do you think was the parties' intent?

2. Redraft the provisions to clarify that the agreement does not require a contribution with respect to any probationary employee.

The provisions are available on the *Drafting Contracts* website.

---

40. This exercise is based on *In re Teamsters Indus. Employees Welfare Fund*, 989 F.2d 132 (3d Cir. 1993).

2.2 New Employees. New employees may be disciplined or discharged with or without cause for a trial period of sixty days. New employees must become members of the Local Union by the sixty-first day of their employment, at which time they shall be deemed to be regular employees covered by this Agreement and entitled to all health and retirement benefits of this Agreement. Trial period employees will sometimes be referred to as probationary employees.

[Provisions Intentionally Omitted]

10.1 Contributions to Benefit Funds. Big Ten will contribute to the Employees' Welfare Fund and the Employees' Pension Fund on behalf of each employee.

Exercise 21-6

Mark up the following sentence from an employment agreement to correct the ambiguity and any other drafting errors. Assume that the Closing Date is not January 1, 20XX and that the parties intend a term based on the number of days in a calendar year.

Term. This Agreement and the employment hereunder shall commence on the Closing Date (as such term shall be defined in the Purchase Agreement) and shall continue in effect for a period of five calendar years from such Closing Date.

Exercise 21-7

Mark up the following provisions to clarify the ambiguities and correct any other drafting errors.

Due Date. The Note is due one year from its date of issuance. Interest is to be computed on the basis of a 360-day year.

Interest Accrual. Interest accrues on the Note from the date of the Note's issuance until the Prepayment Date.

Acceptance of Bids. Seller shall accept all bids (for the purchase of Blackacre) delivered to its offices between April 3, 20XX, and April 16, 20XX.

Trust. Never trust anyone over 30.

Expiration of Option. This option expires at 12:00 midnight Tuesday, July 9, 20XX.

Exercise 21-8

Memorandum

To: Andrew McKenzie

From: Sasha Petrov

Our client, Coffee & Cream Corp. (Coffee), owns a chain of high-end, company-operated retail stores that sell and serve coffee. They are merging with Tea for Two, Inc. (Tea), a similar chain of stores, but one that sells and serves tea. The parties signed the Merger Agreement on April 18, 20XX. Tea agreed to merge into Coffee, making Coffee the surviving corporation.

Both Tea and Coffee are Delaware corporations. Between now and the Closing, which will be on June 1, 20XX, each of the parties will submit the Merger Agreement to its stockholders in accordance with the requirements of Section 251 of the Delaware General Corporation Law. Instead of filing and recording the Merger Agreement as required by Section 251(c), Coffee has decided to file a certificate of merger as permitted by Section 251(c). Please draft the Certificate of Merger. Attached as Exhibit A are the relevant statutory provisions. In your draft you may assume that each of the constituent corporations will comply with all of the statutory provisions relating to mergers and that there will be no amendments or changes to the certificate of incorporation of Coffee. Coffee's principal place of business is located at 445 Tenth Avenue, New York, New York 10022.

The President of Coffee is Carla Cappuccino, and the President of Tea is Larry Lipton.

Exhibit A

Delaware General Corporation Law § 251(c)

The agreement required by subsection (b) of this section shall be submitted to the stockholders of each constituent corporation at an annual or special meeting for the purpose of acting on the agreement. Due notice of the time, place, and purpose of the meeting shall be mailed to each holder of stock, whether voting or nonvoting, of the corporation at the stockholder's address as it appears on the records of the corporation, at least 20 days prior to the date of the meeting. The notice shall contain a copy of the agreement or a brief summary thereof, as the directors shall deem advisable. At the meeting, the agreement shall be considered and a vote taken for its adoption or rejection. If a majority of the outstanding stock of the corporation entitled to vote thereon shall be voted for the adoption of the agreement, that fact shall be certified on the agreement by the secretary or assistant secretary of the corporation. If the agreement shall be so adopted and certified by each constituent corporation, it shall then be filed and shall become effective, in accordance with § 103 of this title. In lieu of filing the agreement of merger or consolidation required by this section, the surviving or resulting corporation may file a certificate of merger or consolidation, executed in accordance with § 103 of this title, which states:

(1) The name and state of incorporation of each of the constituent corporations;

(2) That an agreement of merger or consolidation has been approved, adopted, certified, executed, and acknowledged by each of the constituent corporations in accordance with this section;

(3) The name of the surviving or resulting corporation;

(4) In the case of a merger, such amendments or changes in the certificate of incorporation of the surviving corporation as are desired to be effected by the merger, or, if no such amendments or changes are desired, a statement that the certificate of incorporation of the surviving corporation shall be its certificate of incorporation;

(5) In the case of a consolidation, that the certificate of incorporation of the resulting corporation shall be as set forth in an attachment to the certificate;

(6) That the executed agreement of consolidation or merger is on file at an office of the surviving corporation, stating the address thereof; and

(7) That a copy of the agreement of consolidation or merger will be furnished by the surviving corporation, on request and without cost, to any stockholder of any constituent corporation.

Delaware General Corporation Law § 103

(a) Whenever any instrument is to be filed with the Secretary of State or in accordance with this section or chapter, such instrument shall be executed as follows:

(1) The certificate of incorporation, and any other instrument to be filed before the election of the initial board of directors if the initial directors were not named in the certificate of incorporation, shall be signed by the incorporator or incorporators (or, in the case of any such other instrument, such incorporator's or incorporators' successors and assigns). If any incorporator is not available by reason of death, incapacity, unknown address, or refusal or neglect to act, then any such other instrument may be signed, with the same effect as if such incorporator had signed it, by any person for whom or on whose behalf such incorporator, in executing the certificate of incorporation, was acting directly or indirectly as employee or agent, provided that such other instrument shall state that such incorporator is not available and the reason therefor, that such incorporator in executing the certificate of incorporation was acting directly or indirectly as employee or agent for or on behalf of such person, and that such person's signature on such instrument is otherwise authorized and not wrongful.

(2) All other instruments shall be signed:

a. By any authorized officer of the corporation; or

b. If it shall appear from the instrument that there are no such officers, then by a majority of the directors or by such directors as may be designated by the board; or

c. If it shall appear from the instrument that there are no such officers or directors, then by the holders of record, or such of them as may be designated by the holders of record, of a majority of all outstanding shares of stock; or

d. By the holders of record of all outstanding shares of stock.

Exercise 21-9

Mark up the following provision to eliminate the provisos and to correct any other drafting errors.

> **Nonsolicitation.** During the Noncompetition Period, Wagner shall not employ or seek to employ any employee of Sugarcane Corp.; provided, however, Wagner may employ or seek to employ Mark Bender, provided that Wagner first notifies Sugarcane Corp. in writing at least 10 days prior to contacting him with respect to any such employment; provided further, that this provision does not apply to the employment of any hourly employee.

Exercise 21-10

Mark up the following provision to clarify the ambiguity.

> **Allocation of Losses.** Losses shall be borne by the General Partner and the Limited Partners in equal shares.

Exercise 21-11

Find the ambiguity in the following sentence and then rewrite it twice to show each of the possibilities.

> The Buyer shall pay for the House to be inspected by an engineer within 10 days of signing the contract.

_____

_____

_____

_____

Numbers and Financial Provisions

22.1 INTRODUCTION

Clients may forgive many things, but getting the monetary provisions wrong is not one of them. To draft them properly often requires an understanding not only of the business deal, but also financial accounting practices and even tax law in some cases. Therefore, drafting these provisions is generally a collaborative effort, involving the client's accountants and tax advisors. You should bring these specialists into the process as early as possible, so that any business issues related to the monetary provisions can be resolved as early on as possible.

This chapter teaches you how to draft numbers and mathematical formulas used in agreements. In addition, the final section discusses how to draft provisions involving financial statement concepts and practices.[1]

22.2 HOW TO DRAFT PROVISIONS USING NUMBERS

Historically, drafters have written numbers both in words and arabic numerals.

> **Wrong**
>
> **Samples**. The Licensee shall deliver to the Licensor a sample of any Product that it wants to manufacture at least thirty (30) days before manufacturing is to begin.

This unnecessary duplication makes a contract more difficult to read.

Write the numbers one through ten in words and the numbers higher than ten in arabic numerals, unless the first word of a sentence begins with a number and other numbers are in the sentence. Then, write out all of the numbers in words.

This format is consistent with good writing generally, and readers will recognize this format.

---

1. See §22.4.

> **Correct**
>
> **Samples**. The Licensee shall deliver to the Licensor a sample of any Product that it wants to manufacture at least 30 days before manufacturing is to begin.

Although many drafters have stopped drafting numbers in both words and arabic numerals, they continue to draft dollar amounts both ways. Instead, generally, only arabic numerals should be used.

> **Wrong**
>
> **Payment of Rent**. The Tenant shall pay the Landlord Ten Thousand Dollars ($10,000.00) for each calendar month of the Term, no later than the third Business Day of that calendar month of the Term.
>
> **Correct**
>
> **Payment of Rent**. The Tenant shall pay the Landlord $10,000 for each calendar month of the Term, no later than the third Business Day of that calendar month of the Term.

This reiteration of dollar amounts is ingrained in our everyday habits. Think of the checks that you write. You write the amount both in numerals and in words.

The rationale for the duplication is that the words act as a safety net in case, inadvertently, an extra numeral is added, numerals are transposed, or some other error occurs. Indeed, a statutory canon of construction addresses this possibility and provides that the words are to be given effect if the words and the numbers differ.[2] But what happens if the number is correct and the words are wrong (*60* vs. *six*)? The better approach is to *draft dollar amounts using only numerals* and to proof what you have written—carefully. Some drafters who generally follow this rule make an exception for promissory notes and mortgages and use both numerals and words for these documents. But the proofing admonition still holds.

You can reduce the likelihood of miswriting dollar amounts in two ways. First, omit the pennies—the last two digits ($XX.00) of any dollar amount that has no cents. Write $345,286, rather than $345,286.00. Second, for dollar amounts greater than $1 million, express the millions or billions of dollars in words if the last three numbers of the dollar amount are all zeros. Write $103.255 million, rather than $103,255,000.

Whether a number should be rounded and how that should be done depends on context and convention. Dollar amounts in publicly disclosed information are adjusted upward or downward to the nearest whole number. Payment amounts are sometimes rounded to the nearest whole number. If not, they are generally rounded to two decimal points. Here is a rounding provision from a credit agreement.

---

2. U.C.C. § 3-114, U.L.A. § 3-114 (2004) states: "If an instrument contains contradictory terms, typewritten terms prevail over printed terms, handwritten terms prevail over both, and words prevail over numbers." *See Yates v. Com. Bank & Trust Co.*, 432 So. 2d 725, 726 (Fla. 3d DCA 1983) ($10,075 vs. Ten hundred seventy-five dollars [$1,075]).

> **Rounding**. Any financial ratio that the Borrower is required to maintain in accordance with this Agreement is to be calculated by
>
> (a) *dividing* the first appropriate component by the second appropriate component;
>
> (b) carrying the result to one place more than the number of places by which the ratio is expressed in this Agreement; and
>
> (c) rounding the result up or down (with a rounding up if there is no nearest number).

Subsection (c) addresses the possibility that the numeral in the last decimal place is "5," which is, of course, equidistant between two numbers. To prevent a dispute in this situation, the contract provides a default rule: round up.

22.3 HOW TO DRAFT MATHEMATICAL FORMULAS

Mathematical calculations are commonplace in contracts. Parties often calculate royalties, cost-of-living adjustments, bonuses, purchase price adjustments, profit and loss allocations, earnouts, mandatory prepayments, clawbacks, interest-rate changes, currency-exchange rates, financial covenants, and more. Drafting these provisions requires an understanding of the business purpose of the formula as well as the ability to express mathematical concepts and calculations clearly.

22.3.1 BASIC MATHEMATICAL OPERATIONS

A formula begins with the four basic mathematical operations: addition, subtraction, multiplication, and division. Signal these operations by using mathematical terms to avoid any ambiguity that might arise from the use of colloquial expressions. For example, the mathematical operation of *six over two* can be interpreted two ways. If a court interprets it to signal subtraction, the result is four. But, *six over two* could also signal a ratio, the numerator of which is six and the denominator of which is two. If that is how a court interprets the language, the result would be three, not four.

Addition

the *sum* of (a) _____ *plus* (b) _____

Subtraction

the *difference* of (a) _____ *minus* (b) _____

Multiplication

the *product* of (a) _____ *times* (b) _____

Division

the *quotient* of (a) _____ *divided* by (b) _____

In addition to the four basic mathematical operations, you may need to express a fraction or a percentage. For example, an executive fired without cause might be entitled to a percentage of her previously agreed-on bonus. Although the contract could refer to a prorated percentage of the bonus, the following language is more precise, thereby reducing the likelihood of a dispute as to the calculation.

Version 1

Ratio: Expressed as a fraction

the fraction, the numerator of which is _____ and the denominator of which is _____

Version 2

Ratio: Expressed as a percentage

the fraction, expressed as a percentage, the numerator of which is ____ and the denominator of which is _____

When writing a formula, bold or italicize the mathematical terms. The emphasis makes it easier for a reader to follow the mathematical operations. Do not precede a mathematical term with a comma. Here's a simple example.

Wrong

Purchase Price. The Buyer shall pay the Seller the Purchase Price which is the amount equal to

(a) $100,000, plus

(b) the Adjusted Net Worth.

Correct

Purchase Price. The Buyer shall pay the Seller the Purchase Price which is the sum of

(a) $100,000 *plus*

(b) the Adjusted Net Worth.

22.3.2   THE ORDER OF MATHEMATICAL OPERATIONS

If calculating a result requires more than one mathematical operation, indicate the order in which the operations are to occur by using parentheses. A change in the order might result in a change in the answer. For example:

Formula: $6 + 3 \div 3$

Alternative 1: $(6 + 3) \div 3$
$= 9 \div 3 = 3$

Alternative 2: $6 + (3 \div 3)$
$= 6 + 1 = 7$

Were no parentheses used and the contract to have no other instructions, the answer would be determined by using the default mathematical order of operations:

multiplication, division, addition, and subtraction.[3] In this example, Alternative 2 would be the correct answer because division precedes addition in the order of operations.

As discussed in the next section, tabulation excels as a way to indicate the order in which mathematical operations are to be performed as it shows the relative relationship between the operations.[4]

22.3.3 DRAFTING THE FORMULA

You can draft a formula three ways.

- Using **an algebraic equation** in which each component of the formula is defined and mathematic notation is used to indicate the operations.
- Using **narration and tabulation** to indicate each component of the formula and the order of the operations.
- Using a **narrative cookbook approach** to chronologically order or describe the intended mathematical operations.[5]

To illustrate how these different approaches work, we will use a simple hypothetical based on a provision for annual rent increases under a lease.[6] Many long-term leases include such provisions to protect landlords from increased operating costs resulting from inflation. As part of analyzing how to draft the formula that calculates the rent increase, we will look at some of the business considerations that might arise during the drafting process.

Before drafting any formula, understand how it works. To test your understanding, make up numbers and plug them into the tentative formula. Always test whether the result of the formula could be a negative number.

For example, assume that the base rent at the time a lease begins is $100 per month. In addition, the lease provides that rent increases each year by the same percentage that the cost of living increases from the lease's commencement date. So, if as of the first anniversary of the lease's commencement date, the cost of living has increased by 5%, then the base rent increases by 5%, or $5 ($.05 \times 100$), for a total of $105. Similarly, if as of the second anniversary of the lease's commencement date, the cost of living has increased by a cumulative 8% from the commencement date (not from the first anniversary of the commencement date), then the base rent of $100 increases for the third year of the lease by 8%, or $8 ($.08 \times 100$), for a total of $108. Because these increases could be substantial over the course of a long-term lease, a tenant might want to negotiate a cap—that is, a limit by which the base rate could be increased in any year or a total over the lease term.

But what happens if the cost of living decreases between the first and second anniversaries, so that the cumulative increase from the commencement date is 3% at the end of the second year? The parties must decide between two possibilities. The rent could remain at $105 (no decreases allowed), or it could decrease to $103 to reflect the decreased cost of living. Assume that decreases are permitted. The parties must next address whether the rent could decrease below the base rent on the com-

---

3. This order is also the default setting in electronic spreadsheets.

4. See discussion in §22.3.3.

5. *See* F. Reed Dickerson, *The Fundamentals of Legal Drafting* 202 (2d ed., Little, Brown & Co. 1986).

6. For a detailed discussion of cost-of-living adjustments in real estate leases, *see* Mark A. Senn, *Commercial Real Estate Leases: Preparation, Negotiation, and Forms* §6.04 (5th ed., Aspen Publishers 2012). *See generally* Carla J. Garrett, Hayden J. Trubitt & Contributing Authors, *Lawyer's Guide to Formulas in Deal Documents and SEC Filings* (Swartz ed., Law Journal Press 2008).

mencement date. Although a tenant would love that, a landlord might insist that the base rent established a floor below which the rent could not fall. If the tenant agrees to this, the rent to be paid beginning on the second anniversary of the commencement date could be less than $105 per month (the monthly rent paid between the first and second anniversaries), but not less than $100.

With that background, let us turn to the drafting of the provision. Based on the discussion in the previous paragraphs, you now know that the formula must

(a) calculate the annual percentage increase in the cost of living from the commencement date to a specific anniversary date; and
(b) use that percentage to calculate the annual increase in the base rent.

Here is a quick math review: To determine a percentage change between two numbers, first determine how big a change there is from the first to the second number. To do this, start with the second number and subtract from it the first number. Then, to get the percentage change, divide the first calculation's result by the first number. So, for example, if you have six oranges (the first number) and buy two more for a total of eight (the second number), the percentage increase is calculated as follows:

Step 1: 8 (the second number) *minus* 6 (the first number), which is equal to 2.

Step 2: 2 *divided by* 6, which is 1/3, which may also be stated as 33.33% or .33.[7]

To determine the cost-of-living adjustment, parties typically rely on the Consumer Price Index (CPI), an index that "represents changes in prices of all goods and services purchased for consumption by urban households."[8] That index provides data by geographic regions, permitting parties to choose the most applicable index. Each index establishes a base year with a value of 100. All increases in an index are keyed off the base year. Therefore, to determine a change in the CPI, calculate the difference in the value as of any two dates. Assume a base year of 20X5 with an index value of 100. So, if the CPI in 20X6 is 140, the CPI has changed by 40 (140 − 100), resulting in a 40% increase (40/100) since the base year in the index.

With this background, you can begin to draft.

To draft a formula, break down the financial business deal into its components, determine the mathematical operation for each component, and then state the formula using one of three methods: algebraic equation, narration and tabulation, or the cookbook approach. You will see how each of these methods works as you read through the following examples.

No matter which method you include in a contract, always draft the formula using an algebraic equation first. It will test your understanding of the formula. If you cannot draft it this way, you will probably also have a difficult time drafting using either of the narrative methods, as each one expresses the equation in words. If you cannot draft the formula, it's possible that the parties have not clearly articulated their intent. The following provisions show how the rent increase formula can be drafted using each of the three methods:[9]

---

7. Algebraically, this is represented as (8 − 6) ÷ 6. This represents a one-third (33.33%) increase and not a 25% increase since the original number of oranges was six.

8. *See* U.S. Dept. of Lab., Bureau of Lab. Statistics, *Consumer Price Indexes,* http://www.bls.gov/cpi/cpiovrvw.htm#item1 (last accessed July 4, 2103; last modified date October 16, 2001). Because this index represents a broad "market basket" of consumer items, the parties may agree on a different index more closely related to the subject matter of their contract.

9. The provisions do not address the subtleties of what happens if the CPI decreases.

X.X Amount of Annual Rent.

(a) **Definitions**. For the purposes of this Section, each of the following terms has its assigned meaning:

    (i) "**Annual Rent**" means the annual rent as stated in Section X.X(b)(i) or as calculated in accordance with Section X.X(b)(ii), as the case may be.

    (ii) "**CPI 1**" means the value of the Consumer Price Index on January 1, 20X6.[10]

    (iii) "**CPI 2**" means the value of the Consumer Price Index on January 1 of the Term Year with respect to which the Annual Rent is being calculated.

    (iv) "**Rent Increase**" is the amount calculated in accordance with Section X.X(c).

    (v) "**Term Year**" means each calendar year during this Agreement's Term.

(b) **Annual Rent**.

    (i) **Annual Rent for Term Year Beginning January 1, 20X6**. The Annual Rent for the Term Year beginning on January 1, 20X6 is $45,000.

    (ii) **Annual Rent for Term Years Beginning After December 31, 20X6**. The Annual Rent for each Term Year beginning after December 31, 20X6 is $45,000 *plus* the Rent Increase.

    (iii) **Negative Number as Result of Calculation of Rent Increase**. If the calculation of the Rent Increase for any Term Year results in a negative number, the Annual Rent for that Term Year is $45,000.

(c) **Calculation of the Rent Increase**. The formula for calculating the amount of the Rent Increase is as follows:

$$\text{Rent Increase} = \left(\frac{\text{CPI 2} - \text{CPI 1}}{\text{CPI 1}} \right) \times 45{,}000$$

By tinkering with this formula, you can calculate the total new annual rent, rather than the amount of the increase. To do this, put the entire formula for the Rent Increase inside a set of parentheses (which means that the formula inside the parentheses is a separate calculation) and precede the parentheses with the following: $45,000 +$. The full formula would look like this:

$$\text{Annual Rent} = 45{,}000 + \left(\frac{\text{CPI 2} - \text{CPI 1}}{\text{CPI 1}} \times 45{,}000 \right)$$

---

10. An actual provision would specify the CPI to be used and detail what the parties should do if the government stopped publishing the chosen CPI. It would also deal with the reality that the parties would not know of the change in the CPI for some period of time after the end of each calendar year.

Narration and Tabulation

(a) **Definitions**. [The definitions are the same as those in the Algebraic Equation example, except the definitions for CPI 1 and CPI 2 are omitted.]

(b) **Annual Rent**. [The same provisions as those in the Algebraic Equation example.]

(c) **Calculation of the Rent Increase**. With respect to any Term Year for which a Rent Increase must be calculated, the amount of the Rent Increase is equal to the product of $45,000 *times* the amount equal to

    (i)   the value of the Consumer Price Index on January 1 of the term year with respect to which the Annual Rent is being calculated minus the value of the Consumer Price Index on January 1, 20X6

        divided by

    (ii)   the value of the Consumer Price Index on January 1, 20X6.

X.X Amount of Annual Rent.

(a) **Definitions**. [The following definitions are in addition to those in the Narration and Tabulation example.]

    (i)   "**CPI Difference**" has the meaning assigned in Section X.X(c)(i).

    (ii)   "**Percentage Change**" has the meaning assigned in Section X.X(c)(ii).

(b) **Annual Rent**. [The same provisions as those in the Algebraic Equation example.]

(c) **Calculation of the Rent Increase**. With respect to any Term Year for which a Rent Increase must be calculated, the amount of the Rent Increase is calculated as follows:

    (i)   *Subtract* the value of the Consumer Price Index on January 1, 20X6 from the value of the Consumer Price Index on January 1 of the term year with respect to which the Annual Rent is being calculated (the difference, the "CPI Difference").[11]

    (ii)   *Divide* the CPI Difference by the value of the Consumer Price Index on January 1, 20X6 (the quotient, the "Percentage Change").

    (iii) *Multiply* the Percentage Change times $45,000.

After drafting the formula, review it with the client and have the client approve it. Do more than merely send the contract provision. Also send multiple examples of how the formula works, including examples demonstrating what could happen in unusual circumstances (e.g., a decrease in the cost-of-living index or the impact of high, sustained inflation over five years). Save the client's approval either in electronic form or hard copy (or both) and file it in the appropriate place. If you speak with the client, write a memo to the file memorializing your discussion or send the client an e-mail confirming the conversation. These contemporaneous documents may help you if the client ever claims it did not approve the formula.

---

11. Note that the defined terms in subsection (c) are used only once. Although, generally, you should not create a defined term unless you will use it more than once, here, the use of the defined terms clarifies the substance by making the calculations easier to understand.

Once the client approves the formula, with the client's permission, send it and the examples of the formula's application to the other side. If the other side agrees with what you have drafted and the examples, consider including those examples as an exhibit to the contract. If they are included, the parties and the court will be able to refer to those examples—as a type of "legislative history"—when later determining the parties' intent.[12]

22.4 HOW TO DRAFT PROVISIONS INVOLVING FINANCIAL STATEMENT CONCEPTS

If you have not taken an accounting course, the following discussion may be difficult to understand. Nonetheless, by reading it, you should come away with at least one point: Drafting provisions using financial statement concepts can be tricky.

Many contract provisions that require calculations use accounting concepts and practices. For example, a publisher will pay an author based on a book's "**net sales**," an accounting concept; and a bank will have the right to declare a default if a company's "**net worth**" (another accounting concept) falls below an agreed-on dollar amount. You cannot draft those provisions without understanding those concepts. However, a minicourse in accounting concepts is beyond the scope of this book. Nonetheless, this section will address the role that standard corporate accounting plays in drafting provisions using financial concepts.

GAAP is the acronym for *generally accepted accounting principles*. The principles and practices codified in GAAP guide the preparation of a company's financial statements and how it maintains its books and records. All public companies, as SEC registrants, are required to report their results using GAAP, and many private companies do so, because their lenders or shareholders require it. This agreed-on set of principles and methods benefits users of financial statements by making companies comparable to one another and more transparent to a variety of users. GAAP is a "common language" for communicating financial results.

GAAP does not establish just one method of accounting to which all companies must adhere. GAAP is like a six-lane highway. Multiple, optional methods for some items coexist. Some methods allowed under GAAP are very conservative (the far right lane), while others are very aggressive (the far left lane). Companies may choose which lane to drive in. They may even "change lanes" from time to time. These choices determine a company's financial reporting "personality"—some are consistently aggressive; others are consistently conservative.[13]

Many unsophisticated drafters react with a knee-jerk response to drafting provisions involving accounting issues: They require all calculations to be made in accordance with GAAP. Unfortunately, that approach may mire the client in some unfortunate trap or deprive the client of a contractual advantage that a more thoughtful analysis could have created.

Among the points to consider are the following:

- GAAP is an evolving set of principles and practices. What is accepted and practiced today may not be tomorrow—or over the term of the contract.
- GAAP allows different accounting treatments for the same event.
- A non-GAAP principle or calculation may better protect your client.

---

12. See Howard Darmstadter, *Precision's Counterfeit: The Failures of Complex Documents, and Some Suggested Remedies*, 66 Bus. Law. 61, 73-82 (Nov. 2010).

13. Companies with conservative reporting practices tend to report lower rates of income, assets, and equity than their more aggressive peers do but are considered to have "high-quality" earnings.

22.4.1   GAAP AS AN EVOLVING STANDARD

GAAP is an evolving set of practices, one that tries to stay relevant in a changing commercial environment. Thus, new disclosures of financial information and new methods of accounting for transactions and events are constantly being mandated.[14] As many, if not most, calculations required by an agreement are not made on the date of signing, contractual provisions dealing with GAAP-based calculations must contemplate the consequences of changes in GAAP. The types of provisions in which this issue arises include purchase price adjustments, contingent earnouts, financial covenants in loan agreements, and buy-sell agreements in partnership and stockholder agreements.

Parties can address that GAAP evolves over time in several ways. First, parties can ignore the changes. In this case, the parties would provide for *calculations to be made in accordance with GAAP as in effect as of the date of this Agreement*. Many parties, especially borrowers, prefer this formulation.[15] It provides certainty. The borrower knows what GAAP is and how it is applied in the contract as of the contract date and that it can comply with the financial covenants. While this may provide the borrower with a business advantage, it does have a disadvantage: The borrower's record keeping becomes more onerous. Specifically, its records for reporting to the SEC and others must comply with whatever GAAP is in effect from time to time. In addition, it must also keep whatever records are necessary to compute the financial covenants in accordance with GAAP as it existed on the date the parties signed the contract.

As an alternative, the parties can provide that the calculations be made *in accordance with GAAP [as in effect from time to time] [as in effect on the calculation date]*—that is, whatever the evolving GAAP is on the calculation date.[16] While this method avoids the record keeping issue, it creates a different problem for borrowers: They must be able to comply with financial covenants based on a future GAAP that they neither know nor control.

Although these uncertainties may generate angst for borrowers, the borrower's "friendly" banker may not be similarly perturbed. While the lender cannot be certain how GAAP may change, the change in GAAP may require a more conservative presentation of the borrower's financial position—a result that appeals, of course, to a banker's conservative nature. This issue's resolution depends on many factors, but many borrowers accede to lenders' provisions because of the latter's superior bargaining power.

Other alternatives for resolving the issue of which GAAP to use include the following:

■ With respect to a proposed change in a generally accepted accounting principle, the parties may agree during their original negotiations how the change, once implemented, will affect the agreement's calculations. This depends, to some degree, on anticipating what changes may occur in GAAP.

■ The parties may agree to negotiate in good faith the contractual consequences of any change in GAAP that materially affects any calculation in the agreement. Be careful with this provision. It is only an agreement to negotiate. The parties may not reach an agreement. To deal with this possibility, some agreements pro-

---

14. For example: GAAP has evolved to recognize the **fair value** of some assets, such as securities and intellectual property. Fair value is what an asset is worth (as defined) in the marketplace (as defined). This recognition of fair value departs from GAAP's long-standing focus on **historical cost**—what a company paid for an asset. Another relatively recent addition to GAAP is the expensing of the **cost of stock options**.

15. *See* Sandra S. Stern, *Structuring and Drafting Commercial Loan Agreements* ¶ 7.01[3] (A.S. Pratt & Sons 2010).

16. *Id.*

vide that if the negotiations fail, the change in GAAP will not be implemented automatically.

22.4.2 GAAP'S AUTHORIZATION OF ALTERNATIVE METHODS

GAAP's flexibility in permitting users to choose among alternative acceptable methods can help or harm your client. Which it is generally depends on whom you represent.

Imagine that a borrower's loan agreement requires it to earn a minimum level of net income, as determined in accordance with GAAP. Unfortunately, our hypothetical borrower has had a dismal year, and it seems likely that it will breach the minimum net income covenant.

The borrower's chief financial officer (CFO) has, however, carefully reviewed the loan agreement and has hit on an idea to boost the bottom line for purposes of covenant compliance: By changing the method it uses to account for sales, the borrower can now "recognize" (or book) sufficient revenues[17] to allow the borrower to meet the income test. Although the borrower's chief executive officer (CEO) professes concern that this method differs from the one that the borrower has been using, the CFO reassures the CEO that the change presents no problem. ("It's just a small, perfectly acceptable 'lane change,'" he explains.) He reminds the CEO that GAAP does not mandate a particular method to recognize revenue but instead permits users to choose among allowable alternatives. Moreover, the loan agreement gave the company this flexibility by not prohibiting changes in GAAP methods to create compliance with the financial covenants.

Most lenders are, of course, sufficiently sophisticated to avoid this type of manipulation. Thus, their standard form agreements invariably require that the GAAP methods to be used to determine covenant compliance must be consistent with the borrower's past practice[18] or that the practices used in calculating compliance are the same ones used in reporting the borrower's results to others (like the SEC). Lenders do not always insist, however, that the requirement be applied to all methods in all instances. Sometimes, a lender will permit a borrower to deviate from past practice and use an alternative GAAP method for a particular calculation.

For example, some companies value their inventory on a LIFO[19] basis. Assuming that inflation is causing the price of inventory to increase, LIFO reduces a company's net income and income taxes by maximizing its reported cost of sales. It also simultaneously minimizes the reported value of the company's inventory.[20] This minimization is in many instances irrelevant. It can, however, be a distinct disadvantage. For example, a lower reported value of inventory may limit the amount a company can borrow under its loan agreement. In this situation, the borrower will probably want

---

17. Accountants use the term **revenue recognition** to describe the rules for determining when (or if) a sale has taken place. If a company has not met the rules' requirements, it cannot "recognize" (include) the additional revenue on its income statement. For example, a company may be using a "completed contract" method for recognizing revenue on a long-term contract. Under this approach, the company only books the "sale" when the contract is completed. By "changing lanes" to a percentage of completion method, the company could recognize some income in the current period. "Lane changes" make auditors and lenders nervous, especially when they result in higher income.

18. *See* Stern, *supra* n. 15.

19. **LIFO** is the acronym for *last in, first out*. It assumes that the most recent inventory items that the company manufactured or bought for resale are the first ones sold. Typically, when a company reports inventory on the LIFO basis, it reports higher costs for its sales of goods and, therefore, lower profits compared to alternative methods.

20. This may not be the case with respect to a product new to the market. In this case, rather than the cost of the product increasing over time to reflect inflation, the price may fall because of increased manufacturing efficiencies and the debugging of the product.

to report a higher inventory number to increase the amount it can borrow. Often, a borrower can achieve this goal by negotiating for the right to revalue its inventory for measuring compliance using the FIFO method[21] — but only to calculate the amount it can borrow.

22.4.3   NON-GAAP ALTERNATIVES

In the same way that parties may need to replace one accepted accounting method with another to reflect the true economic substance of a transaction, sometimes parties need to use a non-GAAP method in valuing an asset or in making a calculation. Imagine that the buyer of a business has agreed to pay the seller "the book value of its assets," as stated on its balance sheet, plus $100,000. Included among these assets is a building that the seller has owned for 20 years. As GAAP requires buildings to be depreciated, the building's low book value may not reflect its true value. In this instance, the seller could reasonably insist that the building be valued at its fair market value for purposes of the transaction, even though that does not accord with GAAP.

22.4.4   PROVISIONS USING BALANCE SHEET ACCOUNTS

Typical provisions that rely on calculations based on balance sheet accounts include the following:

- Purchase price adjustment provisions keyed into changes in **net worth**[22] or **working capital**.[23]
- Financial covenants requiring borrowers to maintain minimum net worth, working capital, or current ratio.
- Borrowing base formulas.

When negotiating the accounting-related provisions in any of these contexts, the lawyer and her client must track through the balance sheet and think through on a line item basis whether any one or more of the accounts requires special treatment. For example, the purchase price in some acquisition agreements is based on the seller's reported or book net worth, which in turn is based on the seller's total reported assets and its total reported liabilities. Thus, the value attributed to each asset and each liability directly impacts the purchase price.

When you represent a seller in such a case, think through which assets on the balance sheet do not reflect that asset's true fair market value. Because GAAP is generally conservative, it tends toward understating assets. For that reason, parties may prefer to value assets using something other than GAAP. As noted before, buildings can be revalued to their fair market value. Other assets that may not be reflected at their actual values are an assembled workforce, a patent portfolio, favorable leases, a

---

21. **FIFO** is the acronym for *first in, first out*. It assumes that the first inventory items that the company manufactured or bought for resale are the first ones sold.

22. **Net worth** is often used synonymously with **equity** in describing the value of the owners' interest in a business. Both terms describe the amount equal to the sum of a business's assets minus the sum of its liabilities.

23. **Working capital** describes the assets a firm uses in its operations. It is shorthand for the result of the following calculation: the sum of a company's current assets (cash, accounts receivable, and inventory) minus the sum of its current liabilities (accounts payable, notes payable, and current portion of long-term debt). It is a measure of short-term liquidity because the only assets included in the calculation are those that can typically be converted into cash quickly. Working capital is what's left over if it is assumed that all current assets are used to pay all current liabilities.

catalog of creative works, trade secrets, and goodwill. Most of these intangible assets, when created internally, are typically carried at a value of zero in accordance with GAAP.

While sellers want to maximize price, buyers fear being saddled with unforeseen liabilities and claims. Therefore, they seek to ensure that the net worth calculation accurately reflects all the company's liabilities—not only those on the balance sheet, but also those that GAAP does not require a company to report. Significant areas of concern include the following:

- Pending litigation.
- Environmental cleanup liabilities.
- Guaranties.
- Purchase obligations.
- Unfunded pension obligations.

If you represent a buyer, consider dealing with these contingent liabilities by establishing a reserve, even though GAAP would not require one.[24] Of course, the parties must work through the specifics of such an approach collaboratively with their lawyers and accountants.

22.4.5 PROVISIONS USING REVENUE AND EARNINGS CONCEPTS

Revenues and earnings formulas appear in a wide variety of agreements, including:

- Purchase price provisions in acquisition agreements.
- Compensation provisions in employment agreements.
- Royalty provisions in license and franchise agreements.
- Buyout provisions in partnership and stockholder agreements.
- Profit and loss sharing provisions in joint ventures or partnerships.

In these situations, the amount being paid or received can be significantly affected by the accounting choices made in the documents. To make certain that the documents reflect the intended economics, the formulas need to be crafted carefully.

A salient concern for parties is who controls the accounting. If your client controls it, then, generally, a bottom-line, profits-based formula is best; if it does not control the accounting, the superior alternative is a top-line, revenues-based formula.

The theory behind this dichotomy is that the party lacking control (say, the seller) risks the bottom line being artificially reduced—either by the inclusion of expenses that might be allowable under GAAP, but not reflective of the transaction's true economics, or by the acceleration of some expenses. Alternatively, if the earnout formula is tied to gross revenues (the "top line"), rather than net profits, the party who controls the accounting has much less leeway in manipulating the payment due. Obviously, if you represent the party with control, the ability to "refine" the bottom line has a certain attraction.[25]

If you represent the party without control and are unsuccessful in negotiating a revenue-based formula, all is not lost. Prophylactic countermeasures can be negotiated. Specifically, negotiate covenants limiting the types of expenses and the amount of each expense included in net income. The goal is to reduce the other side's flex-

---

24. Other possibilities include an indemnity, a holdback, insurance, or a purchase limited to the target's assets.

25. See §25.2.4 for a description of the facts in *Buchwald v. Paramount Pictures Corp.*, 1990 WL 357611 (Cal. Super. Jan. 8, 1990).

ibility as much as possible, putting your client in a position as close to a revenue-based formula as possible.

For example, a seller who is negotiating a contingent payout in connection with an acquisition might argue that the impairment[26] of any goodwill created in connection with the acquisition should be an excluded expense. Analytically, this item arises wholly because of the acquisition and, therefore, arguably, distorts the real earnings picture. From the seller's perspective, any other expenses new to the business (e.g., additional overhead) would also be fair game for exclusion. Finally, consider including language that requires the accounting to be consistent with prior years, thus precluding artificial expense or revenue recognition in selected periods.

Obviously, if you represent the buyer, resist any attempt to shackle your client's flexibility. Your client now owns the business, and it should have the ability to run it, including the accounting.

---

26. Accountants use the term **impairment** to describe the decline in value of intangibles like goodwill and customer lists. The amount of the decline can be a highly subjective determination. New management of a purchased business regularly writes off (takes as an expense) assets like goodwill to reduce post-acquisition income immediately after transaction. This act makes income higher in the long term because the write-offs were already taken in the first year after the transaction. Management prefers the higher income in the future because that is probably when their shares vest or their employment contracts are renewed.

CHAPTER TWENTY-TWO

EXERCISES

Exercise 22-1

Shareholders A, B, C, and D wish to enter into a shareholders' agreement, but they would like to see one provision before you draft the entire agreement. They want the agreement to provide that if any shareholder wants to sell shares to a third party, that shareholder must first offer the shares to the other shareholders. (This is known as a **right of first refusal**.) The shareholders were not terribly good at explaining how to determine the number of shares each nonselling shareholder could buy. Instead, they gave the following example:

> Assume that the corporation has 50 shares issued and outstanding, and that A wants to sell the ten shares she owns. B, who owns 20 shares, could purchase 50% of those ten shares because B owns 50% of the shares not being sold. Draft the formula for determining the number of shares that each nonselling shareholder may purchase when a shareholder is selling all the shares it owns. Use the method that you think will make it the easiest for the reader to understand the provision's purpose and how it functions.

Exercise 22-2

Arthur Wright, a quarterback for the San Jose Dragons, has hired Davis Reynolds to represent him in contract negotiations with the Dragons and in connection with product endorsements. (This kind of contract is known as a *representation agreement.*) The parties have agreed that Wright will pay Reynolds the amount that is the greater of Reynolds's standard hourly rate for the type of services Reynolds provides under their agreement multiplied by the hours spent on providing the services and 15% of the gross amount of all monies received by Wright or on his behalf from contracts that Reynolds negotiated. The parties have already negotiated the definition of Services, so don't worry about that. They're the standard services for representation agreements.

Reynolds has asked you to draft the payment provision and to let him know of any questions with respect to the provision.

Exercise 22-3

Redraft the following provision so that it is one sentence and uses appropriate mathematical language. It is available on the book's website.

Purchaser's Payments. The Purchaser covenants that it shall pay the Seller the difference

between the Purchase Price and the amount of any loan obtained by the Purchaser from a Lending

Institution. The Purchaser also covenants that the Purchaser will pay all costs in connection with the

closing as required by the Lending Institution.

A Potpourri of Other Drafting Considerations

23.1 GENDER-NEUTRAL DRAFTING

When drafting a contract that has parties who are individuals (rather than entities), make all pronouns referring to individuals gender specific. So, in an employment agreement between a corporation and its executive Sadie Kendler, make sure that *she* and *her* appear wherever appropriate, and not *he* or *him*. If you are working with a precedent on a computer, you can easily do this. Use your word-processing program's Find and Replace function to help you find all the instances that need to be changed. Alternatively, keep two versions of the precedent on your computer, one for men and the other for women.

The drafting becomes a little more complicated if both men and women are parties, or if men, women, and entities are parties. It is awkward to use *he, she,* and *it* and *him, her,* and *it*. Instead, replace the pronouns with the defined term used to refer to these parties.

Awkward

Shareholder Eligibility. To be eligible to vote for the members of the Board of Directors, a Shareholder shall submit *his, her, or its proxy* no later than 5:00 p.m., May 18, 20XX.

Better

Shareholder Eligibility. To be eligible to vote for the members of the Board of Directors, a Shareholder shall submit *that Shareholder's proxy* no later than 5:00 p.m., May 18, 20XX.

As an alternative, delete unnecessary pronouns.

> **Awkward**
>
> **Transfer of Shares**. A Shareholder proposing to transfer *his*, *her*, or *its* Shares . . .
>
> **Better**
>
> **Transfer of Shares**. A Shareholder proposing *to transfer Shares* . . .

Do not use a plural form of a defined term. While this works perfectly well in narrative writing, it can create ambiguity in a contract, as in the following provision:

> **Wrong**
>
> **Deadline**. The Students shall submit their exercises no later than 5:00 p.m., Friday, June 10, 20XX.

At least four interpretations of this provision are possible.

> **Correct — Version 1**
>
> **Deadline**. Each Student shall submit *that Student's exercise* no later than 5:00 p.m., Friday, June 10, 20XX.
>
> **Correct — Version 2**
>
> **Deadline**. Each Student shall submit *that Student's exercises* no later than 5:00 p.m., Friday, June 10, 20XX.
>
> **Correct — Version 3**
>
> **Deadline**. Each team of Students shall submit *its exercise* no later than 5:00 p.m., Friday, June 10, 20XX.
>
> **Correct — Version 4**
>
> **Deadline**. Each team of Students shall submit *its exercises* no later than 5:00 p.m., Friday, June 10, 20XX.

If individuals are not parties to an agreement, gender-neutral drafting issues still arise if any of the contract's provisions refer to individuals. For example, references to *firemen*, *policemen*, and *workmen* are no longer appropriate. Contract provisions should use gender-neutral terms, such as *firefighters*, *police officers*, and *workers*.

23.2   THE CASCADE EFFECT

The **cascade effect** occurs when the drafting of a business term in one provision requires a change in, or the addition of, a second business term. A simple example: Assume that you are drafting an employment agreement that requires your client to pay its executive an annual salary of $100,000. The contract also includes an endgame provision that obligates the company to pay the executive his salary through his last day of employment if the company terminates him for cause. Now assume that after the first round of negotiations, the client agrees to pay the executive a $10,000 annual bonus. Here is where the cascade effect kicks in. You will need to make two changes. First, you will need to change the compensation provision in the payment section in the action sections to provide for the bonus. Second, you will need a new endgame provision that spells out how much of the bonus, if any, the client will pay if it fires the executive for cause. One change causes another. The cascade effect plays a significant role in the review of a contract. What cascade effects did the drafter put in and how do you address them? Also, what new provisions should you add as part of the cascade effect?

23.3 EXCEPTIONS

When drafting or reviewing an agreement, a lawyer must carefully analyze each provision to determine whether it should apply in all circumstances. When it does not—and it often does not—the contract must provide for an exception.

23.3.1 HOW TO SIGNAL AN EXCEPTION

Exceptions are signaled in several ways: *except, except as otherwise provided, other than, unless, provided,* and *provided, however.* All of these signals, other than *provided* and *provided, however* are acceptable. *Provided* and *provided, however* have multiple meanings that create the possibility of ambiguity.[1]

23.3.2 PLACEMENT OF THE EXCEPTION

As a general rule, when drafting a provision that includes an exception, put the rule first, then the exception. If the order is reversed, the provision often becomes more difficult to understand because the reader does not have the context to understand the exception. In addition, with a long exception, the reader has too much information to remember before getting to the provision's main point.

Wrong

Enforceability. Except to the extent that enforcement is limited by

(a) applicable bankruptcy, insolvency, reorganization, moratorium, or other similar laws affecting creditors' rights generally, or

(b) general equitable principles, regardless of whether the issue of enforceability is considered in a proceeding in equity or at law,

this Agreement is the Publisher's legal, valid, and binding obligation, enforceable against the Publisher in accordance with its terms.

Correct

Enforceability. This Agreement is the Publisher's legal, valid, and binding obligation, enforceable against the Publisher in accordance with its terms, except to the extent that enforcement is limited by

---

1. See §21.8.

> (a) applicable bankruptcy, insolvency, reorganization, moratorium, or other similar laws affecting creditors' rights generally; or
>
> (b) general equitable principles, regardless of whether the issue of enforceability is considered in a proceeding in equity or at law.

Although you should generally put the exception at the end of a provision, it may work better at the beginning of a provision if

- it is short and quickly alerts the reader to the exception or
- it provides helpful context.

In the following examples, the first version is acceptable, while the second is preferred.

Acceptable

Investments. Except for a $400,000 investment in a subsidiary, the Borrower shall not make any investments.

Better

Investments. The Borrower shall not make any investments, except for a $400,000 investment in a subsidiary.

The following is classic drafting in an acquisition agreement where a short exception precedes a representation and warranty:

Litigation. Except as stated in **Schedule 3.15**, the Seller is not a party to any pending or, to its knowledge, threatened litigation.

If a provision and its exception result in a long sentence, consider breaking it down into subsections. Put the general rule in the first subsection and the exception in the next. The captions for the subsections should signal their content: *General Rule* and *Exception*.

Correct

Duty of Nondisclosure.[2]

(a) **General Rule**. The Executive shall not disclose any item of Confidential Information in any form to any Person.

(b) **Exception**. Despite subsection (a), the Executive may disclose Confidential Information to any one or more of the following Persons:

    (i) A member, manager, or agent of the LLC.

    (ii) A person to whom the LLC has authorized the Executive to make disclosure.

---

2. This provision is based on a provision in John M. Cunningham, *Drafting Limited Liability Company Operating Agreements Form* 17, § 7.1 (Aspen Publishers 2006).

If a rule and its exception are in separate sentences or subsections, their relationship should be explicitly stated in one of the two sentences or subsections.

> Except as set forth in the next [sentence] [subsection], [state the general rule].
>
> *or*
>
> Despite the previous [sentence] [subsection], [state the exception].

Drafting Hint: Do not use *foregoing* instead of a specific reference. It is invariably ambiguous.

Although you can generally draft the exception either way, use the second format if the contract states the general rule in a section or subsection captioned *General Rule*. *General rules* do not include exceptions. Of course, if the provision were rewritten without subsections and captions, the sentence with the general rule could contain the reference to the exception, as in the following provision.

> **Correct**
>
> **Duty of Nondisclosure**. The Executive shall not disclose any item of Confidential Information in any form to any Person, except in accordance with the remainder of this Section X. The Executive may disclose Confidential Information to any one or more of the following Persons:
>
> (a) A member, manager, or agent of the LLC.
>
> (b) A person to whom the LLC has authorized the Executive to make disclosure.

Putting an exception at the end of a provision or a sentence may create an ambiguity if the exception follows a compound or a series. It may be unclear whether the exception modifies only the word or phrase immediately adjacent to it, or whether it modifies each of the items in the compound or the series.[3] To cure any potential ambiguity, draft the exception so it specifically applies to each item in the compound or series. Alternatively, tabulate the compound or the series and then, after the last item, put the exception on a new line at the left margin. In the provision that follows, the ambiguity is whether the exception, including its reasonableness requirement, applies only to subletting.

> **Wrong**
>
> **Assignments and Sublets**. The Tenant shall not assign its rights under this Lease or sublet the Apartment, except with the Landlord's prior written consent.

---

3. See § 21.3 for a discussion of how modifiers following a compound or series can create ambiguity.

Correct

> **Assignments and Sublets**. The Tenant shall not assign its rights under this Lease or sublet the Apartment, except in either instance with the Landlord's prior written consent.

Correct

> **Assignments and Sublets**. The Tenant shall not
>
> (a) assign its rights under this Lease or
>
> (b) sublet the Apartment,
>
> except with the Landlord's prior written consent.

Drafters sometimes put exceptions both at the beginning of a sentence and at the end. Generally, this reflects the drafter's thinking process. She knows of one exception as she begins drafting the provision, but then has a brilliant insight and puts another exception at the end. Instead, put all of the exceptions together at the end of the sentence and, if necessary to enhance clarity, tabulate them.

Wrong

> **Assignments and Sublets**. Except as permitted by Section 4.7, the Tenant shall not assign its rights under this Lease or sublet the Apartment, except with the prior written consent of the Landlord.

Correct

> **Assignments and Sublets**. The Tenant shall not assign its rights under this Lease or sublet the Apartment, except that it may do either in each of the following circumstances:
>
> (a) As permitted by Section 4.7.
>
> (b) With the Landlord's prior written consent.

23.3.3   *EXCEPT AS OTHERWISE PROVIDED*

The phrase *except as otherwise provided* signals an exception. The exception, however, appears not in the provision being read, but elsewhere in the contract. The two provisions are related but, for a structural reason, are not together.

Some drafters specify where the other provision is, but others do not. Those who do not generally cannot articulate a persuasive reason for not including a section reference. The proffered rationale often focuses on the danger of an incorrect cross-reference or on the flexibility to argue later that the contract includes more than one exception—even if the parties contemplated only one at the time of drafting. Include the cross-reference. To prevent an incorrect cross-reference, keep it in brackets or in a large, bold font until you finalize the agreement. Then, check the cross-reference, insert it, and delete any brackets or return it to its regular font, as the case may be. Alternatively, code the cross-reference using your word-processing program, so that the section references update automatically. Although the automatic updates should work, the drafter should do a final check to confirm that the program worked properly.

If you discover multiple cross-references to the same section, it may mean that you need to reorganize the contract and put related provisions together.

23.4 *NOTWITHSTANDING ANYTHING TO THE CONTRARY*

The phrase *notwithstanding anything to the contrary in this Agreement* signals a reader that one provision trumps all of the others. No matter what those other provisions say, this provision supersedes them. This phrase may also be used in a more limited way: *notwithstanding anything to the contrary in Section X.*

Be careful when you use this phrase, especially if the contract uses it more than once. If the two instances contradict each other, an ambiguity will result. Ambiguity can even result if it is used only once.[4] If you use this phrase-trumping provision, be sure you mean it.

A contemporary alternative to *notwithstanding anything to the contrary in this Agreement* is *despite any other provision of this Agreement.*

23.5 *INCLUDING*

The word *including* ignites passion in drafters. Some adamantly assert that it should always be accompanied by a qualifying phrase — either *without limitation* or *but not limited to.* Others fervently insist that those phrases are superfluous, that *including* necessarily encompasses those concepts. If all were right in the world, the latter common, ordinary meaning of *including* would prevail. But then conflicting case law arises from three lines of cases.[5]

23.5.1 *INCLUDING* IS RESTRICTIVE

In the first line of cases, courts hold that *including* is restrictive, that the enumerated items after *including* compose all the items that relate to the noun preceding *including*.[6] Consider the following definition from a statute. In construing it, the court held that "shall include" was restrictive and that air transportation companies were not included within the embrace of the defined term "transportation company."

> [T]he term "transportation company" shall include any company . . . owning, leasing or operating for hire a railroad, street railway, canal, steamboat line, and also any freight

---

4. *See United Rentals, Inc. v. RAM Holdings, Inc.*, 937 A.2d 810 (Del. Ch. 2007) (Poor drafting and the use of notwithstanding anything to the contrary resulted in ambiguity as to which provision trumped which other provision.).

5. Indeed, the cases themselves acknowledge the ambiguity of the term. *See e.g. Auer v. Cmmw.*, 621 S.E.2d 140, 144-145 (Va. App. 2005) ("Generally speaking, the word 'include' implies that the provided list of parts or components is not exhaustive and, thus, not exclusive. . . . However, the word 'include' is also commonly used in a restrictive, limiting sense. . . . Used in this limiting sense, the term typically introduces an exhaustive list of all of the components or members that make up the whole. . . . Thus, when a statute uses the word 'include' in this restrictive, limiting sense to define a term, it sets forth the entire definition, and no other elements or items are includable. . . . Because the word 'include' is susceptible to more than one meaning and because it is not immediately clear from the word's context which meaning is meant to apply . . . we conclude that the statute's provision . . . is ambiguous.") (interpreting a statute).

6. *See In re Est. of Meyer*, 668 N.E.2d 263 (Ind. App. 1996) (interpreting a will).

car company, car corporation, or company . . . in any way engaged in such business as a common carrier over a route acquired . . . under the right of eminent domain.[7]

23.5.2   *INCLUDING* IS A TERM OF ENLARGEMENT

In the second line of cases, the courts hold that *include* is a term of enlargement, meaning that the enumerated items following *include* expand the meaning of the noun or phrase that precedes *include*.[8] For example, the meaning of "use of the automobile" would typically be limited to acts involving movement of the automobile. But an insurance policy expanded the meaning of that phrase when it defined "use" to include "loading and unloading."[9]

23.5.3   *INCLUDING* SIGNALS THAT ILLUSTRATIONS FOLLOW

In the third line of cases, the courts hold that *include* signals that the enumerated items that follow are illustrations of the general principle exemplified in the noun that precedes *include*.[10] For example, in a contract between a utility company and a consumer, the contract provided that the sewerage lines would "include those located within the boundaries of the Consumer's property." The court held that the consumer was responsible for the construction and maintenance of sewerage lines outside its property boundaries, noting that "shall include . . . connotes simply an illustrative application of the general principle."[11]

23.5.4   WHAT SHOULD THE DRAFTER PUT IN THE CONTRACT?

With the case law mixed, the drafter must assess the risk of the judge ruling one way or another. Will the judge decide that *include* has a restrictive, an expansive, or an illustrative meaning? If a drafter believes that the risk of a "wrong" decision is small, the drafter can omit a qualifying phrase. But many drafters are risk averse. Litigation roulette is not for them. They would prefer not to learn how a court would rule in a particular instance. These drafters (including this author) choose the more conservative route and include a qualifying phrase—either *including without limitation* or *including but not limited to*.

In making this decision, a drafter could reasonably take into account the efficacy of the qualifying phrases. That is, do they work? The answer is that mostly they do. When interpreting these qualifiers, courts generally acknowledge their significance in turning the enumerated items that follow the qualifier into a nonexclusive list.[12]

---

7. *See In re C. Airlines, Inc.*, 185 P.2d 919, 923-925 (Okla. 1947) (interpreting a statute).

8. *See State ex rel. Nixon v. Estes*, 108 S.W.3d 795, 800 (Mo. App. W. Dist. 2003) ("While the plain meaning of the word 'include' may vary according to its context in a statute, it is ordinarily used as a term of enlargement, rather than a term of limitation.") (interpreting a statute).

9. *See Pac. Automobile Ins. Co. v. Com. Cas. Ins. Co. of N.Y.*, 161 P.2d 423, 427-428 (Utah 1945) (interpreting a contract).

10. *See Fed. Land Bank of St. Paul v. Bismarck Lumber Co.*, 314 U.S. 95, 99-100 (1941) (interpreting a statute); *DIRECTV, Inc. v. Crespin*, 2007 WL 779232 at *3 (10th Cir. 2007) (interpreting a statute); *Pottsburgh Utils., Inc. v. Daugharty*, 309 So. 2d 199, 201-202 (Fla. 1st Dist. App. 1975) (interpreting a contract).

11. *Pottsburgh Utils., Inc. v. Daugharty*, *supra* n. 10, at 201 (interpreting a contract).

12. *See People v. Clark-Van Brunt*, 205 Cal. Rptr. 144, 149 (Super. App. Dept. 1984) (stating that, "The clear import of the phrase 'but is not limited to' signifies that the Legislature intended the definition of 'drug paraphernalia' to be expansive and flexible. Thus the expressly enumerated items are simply exemplary of those items which may constitute 'drug paraphernalia' rather than delineating the parameters of the subject.") (interpreting a statute); *McCabe v. Comm'r, Ind. Dept. of Ins.*, 949 N.E.2d 816, 819-821 (Ind. 2011) ("'[M]ay include but are not limited to' . . . is a standard expression designating the permissive inclusion of

Indeed, one court, which held that *including* had a restrictive meaning, indicated that the result would have differed had the parties included "but not in limitation of the foregoing."[13] Another court indicated that the qualifying phrase buttressed its decision that *includes* had an illustrative or expansive connotation.[14] Not surprisingly, some cases also find that a qualifying phrase is unnecessary to turn *including* into an expansive term.[15]

23.5.5 AVOIDING CLUNKY AND REDUNDANT DRAFTING

When a drafter prefers to include a qualifying phrase, the drafter must use that same phrase each time she uses *including* in the contract. Not doing so invites litigation because then the drafter would have violated a cardinal rule of good drafting: saying

---

an open-ended class of items not to be limited by designation of specific items that follow." The court noted that in the context of this case, certain decisions might "restrain the outer limits" of the qualifying phrase.) (interpreting a statute); *In re Forfeiture of $5,264*, 439 N.W.2d 246, 255 (Mich. 1989) ("Contrary to the interpretation of the Court of Appeals in Ewing Road, we do not view the proviso, 'including, but not limited to,' to be one of limitation. Rather, we believe the phrase connotes an illustrative listing, one purposefully capable of enlargement.") (interpreting a statute); *In re Est. of Littlejohn*, 698 N.W.2d 923, 926 (N.D. 2005) ("The words 'includes, but are not limited to' ordinarily includes a partial and non-exclusive list.") (interpreting a power of attorney); *but see Shelby Co. State Bank v. Van Diest Supply Co.*, 303 F.3d 832, 837-838 (7th Cir. 2002) (This case held that "including but not limited to" modified the phrase that preceded it ("all inventory") by restricting it to what followed the "including but not limited to." The contested language was the collateral description in a U.C.C. financing statement drafted by a supplier of goods, Van Diest. A third party creditor, a bank, argued that the collateral was limited to inventory that Van Diest sold to its purchaser as suggested by the language following "including but not limited to." Van Diest argued that it had a security interest in all inventory, not just what it sold. The court found both interpretations reasonable and that the security description was ambiguous. In reaching its decision that the only collateral was the inventory sold to the purchaser, the court first called the listing of items "bizarre" when the broad phrase "all inventory" preceded "including but not limited to." Then, in the same paragraph, it noted that there were "use[s] for descriptive clauses of inclusion, so as to make clear the kind of entities that ought to be included." It concluded its decision as follows: "The most compelling reason to construe the language of this agreement against Van Diest [the supplier] is the fact that it was Van Diest that drafted the security agreement, and that the language of that agreement plays an important part for third-party creditors [that is, the bank].") (citation omitted). The case's facts make it somewhat anomalous and, therefore, weak authority for the proposition that the additional qualifying language is not reliable.

13. *In re Est. of Meyer*, *supra* n. 6, at 265 ("If he had intended to use the word 'including' as a term of enlargement rather than a term of limitation, [the deceased] could have modified 'including' with the phrase 'but not in limitation of the foregoing.'") (interpreting a will).

14. *Jackson v. Concord Co.*, 253 A.2d 793, 800 (N.J. 1969) ("We have earlier held, in analogous interpretation situations under this act, that terms like 'include' are words of enlargement and not of limitation and that examples specified thereafter are merely illustrative . . . This is especially so where the word 'including' is followed by the phrase 'but not limited to'") (citations omitted; interpreting a statute); *see also St. Paul Mercury Ins. Co. v. Lexington Ins. Co.*, 78 F.3d 202, 206-207 (5th Cir. 1996) (stating that "'including' . . . "is generally given an expansive reading, even without the additional if not redundant language of 'without limitation.'") (interpreting a contract); *Leach v. State*, 170 S.W.3d 669, 672-673 (Tex. App.—Fort Worth 2005) (acknowledging the expansive scope of "but not limited to" in another statute, but stating that that use did not limit the expansive scope of "including" in the statute being interpreted, the court having earlier noted that the Code Construction Act explicitly gave "including" an expansive meaning) (interpreting a statute); *cf. Horse Cave State Bank v. Nolin Prod. Credit Ass'n*, 672 S.W.2d 66, 66-67 (Ky. App. 1984) (In this case, the court had to determine whether the description in a U.C.C. financing statement sufficiently described the collateral. The court relied on an earlier case in stating that "farm machinery," without more, did not give third parties the ability to readily identify the collateral from its description. The court held that the listing of specific machinery after an including but not limited to clause described the collateral sufficiently. Here is the provision at issue: "all farm machindry [sic], including but not limited to tractor, plow and disc . . . plus all property similar to that listed . . . .") (interpreting a U.C.C. financing statement).

15. *St. Paul Mercury Ins. Co. v. Lexington Ins. Co.*, *supra* n. 14, at 206-207; People v. Perry, 864 N.E.2d 196, 208-209 (Ill. 2007) (The court first notes, "[t]he legislature has on many occasions used the phrases 'including but not limited to' or 'includes but is not limited to' to indicate that the list that follows is intended to be illustrative rather than exhaustive. An electronic search of the Illinois Compiled Statutes reveals 1,749 statutes using the phrase 'including but not limited to' and 249 containing the phrase 'includes but is not limited to.'" It then adds that, even in the absence of the qualifying phrases, "includes" should be given its plain and ordinary meaning—that the enumerated items that follow are illustrative, not exclusive).

the same thing the same way.[16] But this drafting often seems redundant and clunky. An interpretive provision placed in either the definitions article or with the miscellaneous provisions solves the problem.

> The words "including," "includes," and "include" are deemed to be followed by the words "without limitation."

23.5.6 *WITHOUT LIMITING THE GENERALITY . . .*

If the sentence's grammatical structure precludes inserting *including* immediately after the statement of the general concept, a drafter should end the sentence and begin the next new sentence with the phrase *without limiting the generality of the preceding [section, sentence].* For example:

> **Duties**. The Company shall employ the Performer as a broadcast anchor for sports programming on the Station. In this capacity, the Performer shall render those services that the Company requires, subject to its direction, control, rules, and regulations. *Without limiting the generality of the preceding sentence*, the Performer's services include
>
> (a) preparing for, rehearsing, delivering, and performing on the Station's programs, whether live or recorded;
>
> (b) operating all kinds of technical equipment; and
>
> (c) writing, producing, and directing programs on which the Performer is to appear.

If *including* had been inserted after *regulations*, then *including* would appear to refer to *regulations*, which is its immediate antecedent.

The phrase *without limiting the generality of the preceding [section, sentence]* is a contemporary alternative *to without limiting the generality of the foregoing.* Do not use the traditional formulation. In addition to being legalese, it can cause ambiguity because *foregoing* does not specify to what it refers; it could be referring to one or more sentences or sections.

23.6 *EJUSDEM GENERIS*

Ejusdem generis, a Latin phrase, means *of the same kind or class*. Courts apply this canon of construction where a list of specific items concludes with general language intended to expand that list. In determining how that list should be expanded, courts limit the breadth of the general language by finding it embraces only other items of the same kind or class as those already listed. The preceding specific words limit the scope of the general language.

A classic application of *ejusdem generis* arises in the context of a *force majeure* definition. For example:

---

16. See §21.9.

> **"*Force Majeure* Event"** means storm, flood, washout, tsunami, lightning, drought, earthquake, volcanic eruption, landslide, cyclone, typhoon, tornado, or any other event beyond a party's control.

Although the concluding language *any other event beyond a party's control* is broad, a court would likely look to the characteristics of the specific events preceding that language to determine what other events would be within its scope. As the listed events are all natural catastrophes, a court, relying on *ejusdem generis*, could reasonably find that a hurricane fits within the general language, but that a war does not. This may or may not be what the parties intended.

Parties can attempt to overcome the application of *ejusdem generis* by stating that it does not apply.

23.7 *EXPRESSIO UNIUS EST EXCLUSIO ALTERIUS*

Expressio unius est exclusio alterius, another Latin phrase, means the expression of one thing excludes the other.[17] When used as a canon of construction, it limits a provision to what it states expressly.

Suppose, for example, that a contract obligates the tenant to pay for specific repairs.

> The Tenant shall at his own cost repair the walls, ceilings, light fixtures, plumbing work, pipes, and fixtures.[18]

Were the landlord to argue that the tenant was also obligated to repair the roof, the tenant could rebut that argument by contending that the provision's failure to mention the roof meant that it was excluded: The expression of one thing excludes the other.

23.8 *CONTRA PROFERENTEM*

A classic rule of construction is *contra proferentem*: A contract should be construed against the party who drafted it.[19] The rationale is that the drafter is better able to prevent an ambiguity. Although this rule of construction makes sense when parties have unequal bargaining power, it loses force when a contract is between sophisti-

---

17. *See generally* Clifton Williams, *Expressio Unius Est Exclusio Alterius*, 15 Marq. L. Rev. 191 (1931).

18. This example is based on the contract provision in *Zbarazer Realty Co. v. Brandstein*, 113 N.Y.S. 1078, 1079 (App. Div. 1909).

19. *See Diversified Energy, Inc. v. Tenn. Valley Auth.*, 223 F.3d 328, 339 (6th Cir. 2000); *S. Energy Homes, Inc. v. Washington*, 774 So. 2d 505, 513 (Ala. 2000); David Horton, *Flipping the Script: Contra Proferentem and Standard Form Contracts*, 80 U. Co. L. Rev. 431 (2008) (arguing for a strict application of contra proferentem in standard form contracts); *see also Restatement (Second) Contracts* §206 (1981) ("In choosing among the reasonable meanings of a promise or agreement or a term thereof, that meaning is generally preferred which operates against the party who supplies the words or from whom a writing otherwise proceeds.").

cated commercial parties that are each represented by counsel.[20] To rebut the presumption, the drafting parties can include a provision specifically stating that *contra proferentem* does not apply. Each contract has its own peculiarities, but the following provision is a good start:

> **Construction of Contract**. Each party acknowledges that it
>
> (a) is a sophisticated commercial party and that it participated in negotiating this Agreement, and
>
> (b) has been represented by counsel of its choice who either participated in the drafting of this Agreement or had ample opportunity to review and comment on it.
>
> Accordingly, neither party is presumptively entitled to have the contract construed against the other party in accordance with the canon of construction known as *contra proferentem*. It does not apply to this Agreement.

23.9 *DEEM*

Use *deem* or *deemed* to turn something contrary to reality into a contractual reality. *Deem* creates the fiction that something is true, even though it is not.

> **Example 1**
>
> **Wrong**
>
> **Notice**. A notice *is deemed effectively given* only if the notice is in writing and the intended recipient receives it.
>
> **Correct**
>
> **Notice**. A party gives an effective notice only if the notice is in writing and the intended recipient receives it.
>
> **Example 2**
>
> **Correct**
>
> **Notice**. Any notice or instruction received after 5:00 p.m. on a Business Day or on a day that is not a Business Day is deemed received at 9:00 a.m. on the next Business Day.

---

20. *See Dawn Equip. Co. v. Micro-Trak Sys., Inc.*, 186 F.3d 981, 989 n. 3 (7th Cir. 1999); *see also Restatement (Second) Contracts* §206, Reporter's Note to cmt. a (1981) (doctrine "has less force when the other party . . . is particularly knowledgeable"); Meredith R. Miller, *Contract Law, Party Sophistication and the New Formalism*, 75 Mo. L. Rev. 493, 504 (2010).

23.10 NOMINALIZATIONS

Nominalizing a word converts it from a verb into a phrase that includes the noun form of the verb. For example, the previous sentence could be rewritten by converting *nominalize* into *nominalization* and *convert* into *conversion*.

> The *nominalization* of a word is the *conversion* of a verb into a phrase that includes the noun form of the verb.

When you have a choice between using a verb or a noun phrase, choose the verb. It makes the sentence shorter and punchier by making it more direct. Here are two other examples:

Example 1 — Wrong

On the expiration of the term of this Agreement . . . .

Example 1 — Correct

When this Agreement expires . . . .

Example 2 — Wrong

A party shall give the other party a notification . . . .

Example 2 — Correct

A party shall notify the other party . . . .

Common nominalizations and their verb forms include the following:

Noun	Verb
administration	administer
alteration	alter
application	apply
compensation	compensate
consideration	consider
contribution	contribute
notification	notify
payment	pay
submission	submit
violation	violate

23.11 PARALLEL DRAFTING

In Chapter 19, you learned about parallel drafting in connection with tabulating a single sentence.[21] Parallel drafting also applies to multiple sentences dealing with similar subject matter. To be parallel, the grammatical structure of each of those sentences must be the same. Fixing parallel structure sometimes also requires that you redraft the provisions so that they say the same thing the same way. Generally, an absence of

---

21. See § 19.3.2.

parallel drafting in this context does not affect substance. Instead, the issue is one of craftsmanship.

Here are two provisions from an employment agreement that are not parallel, as well as a revision that fixes the problem. The caption dealing with death in the corrected version has been revised so that the two captions also parallel each other. As with any two provisions, either could be redrafted to make it parallel to the other. Here, the *if* clauses are relatively short, so they can be at the beginning of each sentence.

Wrong

Disability During Employment. The compensation payable to the Executive is reduced by 50% if the Executive is disabled for more than six months.

Death Benefits. If the Executive dies during the Term, the Employer shall pay the Executive's estate the Executive's salary through the date of his death.

Correct

Disability During Employment. If the Executive is disabled for more than six months, the compensation payable to the Executive is reduced by 50%.

Death During Employment. If the Executive dies during the Term, the Employer shall pay the Executive's estate the Executive's salary through the date of his death.

23.12 *RESPECTIVELY*

Use *respectively* to establish that two or more items create concurrent relationships when joined with two or more other items in the same sentence: If A, B, and C occur, then D, E, and F are true, respectively. A relates to D; B relates to E; and C relates to F, all at the same time.

Example 1 — Version 1

Maximum Borrowings. Subsidiary A, Subsidiary B, and Subsidiary C may borrow a maximum of $2 million, $4.5 million, and $8 million, respectively.

As an alternative, the information could be displayed in a chart with introductory language. This might be easier for the reader to understand the correlations.

> **Example 1 — Version 2**
>
> **Maximum Borrowings**. Each Subsidiary may borrow at a maximum the dollar amount adjacent to its name.

	Maximum Borrowing
Subsidiary A	$2 million
Subsidiary B	$4.5 million
Subsidiary C	$8 million

Here is another example.

> **Example 2**
>
> **Election of Directors**. The Group A Shareholders and the Group B Shareholders shall cast their votes for Group A Directors and Group B Directors, respectively.

23.13 *AS THE CASE MAY BE*

Use *as the case may be* to establish that two or more items create alternative relationships when joined with two or more other items in the same sentence. If A occurs, then B occurs, *or* if C occurs, then D occurs. The relationships are alternative, not concurrent.

> **Allocation of Income and Losses**. All *net income* or *net loss* allocated to a Partner in accordance with the terms of this Article 6 is to be *credited* or *charged*, as the case may be, to that Partner's capital account.
>
> (Here the correlations are between *net income* and *credited* and then, separately between *net loss* and *charged*.)

Some drafters use *as the case may be* to clarify that an *or* in a sentence is being used in its exclusive sense. Typically, the additional language is superfluous because there are not two or more sets being correlated.

> **Wrong**
>
> **Death and Retirement Benefits**. The Partnership shall pay the amount calculated in accordance with **Exhibit A** in 60 equal monthly installments, beginning on the first day of the month following the month in which the Partner died or retired, as the case may be.

> **Correct**
>
> **Death and Retirement Benefits**. The Partnership shall pay the amount calculated in accordance with **Exhibit A** in 60 equal monthly installments, beginning on the first day of the month following the month in which the Partner died or retired.

23.14 *THERE IS* AND *THERE ARE*

You can often eliminate *there is* and *there are* from a sentence, making it tighter. Look for the sentence's core meaning, and use those words to create a new subject and verb.

Wrong

Litigation. There is no litigation pending or threatened against the Licensor with respect to the Trademark.

Correct

Litigation. No litigation is pending or threatened against the Licensor with respect to the Trademark.

23.15 THE POSSESSIVE

Many lawyers shy away from using a noun's possessive form. But its use shortens a sentence, making it easier to read while doing no harm to its substance.

Wrong

Confidentiality. During and after the term *of this Agreement*, each party shall protect the secrecy of the Confidential Information *of the other party*. All Confidential Information remains the exclusive property *of the disclosing party. (33 words)*

Correct

Confidentiality. During and after this *Agreement's* term, each party shall protect *the other party's* Confidential Information. All Confidential Information remains *the disclosing party's* exclusive property. *(24 words)*

CHAPTER TWENTY-THREE

EXERCISES

Exercise 23-1

The following provision comes from an employment agreement between Vera Ward and Scuba Vacations, Inc. Mark it up so that it applies only to Ward. What changes would you make so that it could be used in any employment agreement? If you were Vera Ward, which version would you prefer, and why?

> The Company shall provide Ward with the Company's full range of health and insurance benefits and shall provide him with an office suite similar to the one he had at his previous employer.

Exercise 23-2

Mark up the following provisions to correct the drafting errors.

> **Assignments.** Except for delegations to affiliates, the Contractor shall not assign its performance under this Agreement to any Person, other than Hughes Contracting Corp.

> **Severability.** If any provision of this Agreement is deemed by the final decree of a court to be unenforceable, the enforceability of the remaining provisions is unimpaired.

> **Consents.** Other than the approval of the Seller's shareholders, the Seller is not required to obtain any consent or approval or give any notice in connection with the execution and delivery of this Agreement or the consummation of the transactions contemplated hereby, except for notification to and consents and approvals from the persons listed in **Exhibit D.**

Deconstructing Complex Provisions

24.1 THE SIX-STEP PROCESS

In the preceding chapters, you learned multiple skills that will help you write clear and unambiguous provisions. Although each can be used separately, you can also use them together to deconstruct long, difficult provisions in a precedent or draft from the other side. Many times these provisions are so dense that you cannot be sure of their substantive effect. To understand them, you need to take them apart, reorganize them, and clean up the language. Only then can you find the ambiguities and incorrect statements of the business deal.

Deconstructing these provisions can be intimidating. Often, so much seems wrong. But by deconstructing a provision in steps, the process becomes manageable. This chapter describes a six-step process for deconstructing — and reconstructing — complex provisions. You already know five of the six steps, so learning the process should be relatively easy. As the chapter explains each of the steps, it will deconstruct a provision so you can see the process being applied.

Here are the six steps:

1. Explicate.
2. Create clarity through format.
3. Create clarity through sentence structure.
4. Clarify ambiguities.
5. Root out legalese.
6. Check substance.

We will now look at each of them in turn.

24.1.1 EXPLICATE

Explicating a provision breaks it down into its component parts. It permits you to look at each sentence, clause, and modifier to see how each relates to the other.

Before explicating a provision, copy, paste, and save it into a new document. Then, using the *Enter* key, begin breaking the provision down by separating each sentence from the others. Number each of the sentences. To break down a sentence, press Enter before any introductory prepositional clause so that it appears on its own line. Also find each compound and series and move each item to a line alone and indent it. As your skill in explicating improves, you may decide not to tabulate every item in a compound or series, but do it in the beginning. Show the relationship of the items in the compound or series to the preceding language by indenting each item, just as you would if you were formatting. If a word or phrase qualifies the compound or series, put it on a separate line. Finally, put each proviso and exception on a separate line.

The following are an unexplicated provision and the same provision after explication.

Unexplicated Provision

Maintenance and Location. The Lessee shall, at its own expense, maintain the Equipment in good operating condition and repair and protect the Equipment from deterioration other than normal wear and tear. The Lessee shall not make any modification, alteration, or addition to the Equipment without the prior written consent of the Lessor, which shall not be unreasonably withheld, provided that no consent is required for engineering changes recommended by and made by the manufacturer; and shall keep the Equipment at the location shown in the Schedule, and shall not remove the Equipment without the prior written consent of the Lessor. The Lessee shall during the term of this Lease, at its own cost, enter into and maintain in force a contract with the manufacturer or other acceptable maintenance company, covering the maintenance of the Equipment.

Explicated Provision

Maintenance and Location.

1. The Lessee shall, at its own expense,
    - maintain the Equipment in
        - good operating condition and
        - repair and
    - protect the Equipment from deterioration other than normal wear and tear.

2. The Lessee
    - shall not make any
        - modification,
        - alteration, or
        - addition
    - to the Equipment without the prior written consent of the Lessor, which shall not be unreasonably withheld,
    - provided that no consent is required for engineering changes recommended by and made by the manufacturer;
    - shall keep the Equipment at the location shown in the Schedule, and
    - shall not remove the Equipment
    - without the prior written consent of the Lessor.

3. The Lessee shall during the term of this Lease, at its own cost,
　　　　enter into and
　　　　maintain in force
　　　a contract with
　　　　the manufacturer or
　　　　other acceptable maintenance company,
　　　covering the maintenance of the Equipment.

24.1.2　CREATE CLARITY THROUGH FORMAT

Once you explicate a provision, it becomes relatively easy to format. First, look at each sentence and decide whether the subject matter of another sentence is sufficiently related that the sentences should be combined to create a section or joined into one tabulated sentence. In addition, look at each sentence to decide whether it deals with only one subject. If it does not, then two sentences or sections may be appropriate. Then, look at each indented item from a compound or series and decide whether it should be a subsection or joined with the rest of the sentence. If any indented items are preceded or followed by a qualifier, keep the qualifier on a separate line. Later you will decide whether its placement creates an ambiguity. Write yourself a note, so that you remember to check this point later. (For now, we will strictly adhere to the order of the six-step process. But as you become more proficient, you may decide to perform multiple steps simultaneously.)

Applying this analysis to our example, we see that sentences one and three both deal with maintenance of the equipment. So, the redraft will put them together into one section. The second sentence, however, covers two unrelated topics: changes to the Equipment and location of the Equipment. Thus, two sections should be created from this sentence.

Now we will look at the indented items for each sentence and decide whether they should become subsections. The first sentence has two levels of indentation. *Good operating condition* and *repair* should be rejoined with the preceding language. They both qualify *Equipment*, which precedes them in the sentence, and they are short with no potential for ambiguity. Deciding whether to keep the remaining tabbed items as subsections is more difficult. Because the qualifier *other than normal wear and tear* follows the tabbed items, it creates an ambiguity: Does the language qualify each of the tabbed items or only the second? This issue of ambiguity can also be postponed.

In the second sentence, *modification, alteration,* and *addition* need not be tabulated as they are short. As to the other two indented items, we earlier decided that they should be in their own section. They are, however, long enough that they should be tabulated in that new section. The last line, *without the prior written consent of the Lessor,* makes substantive sense only as an exception to the prohibition that precedes it. Therefore, the prohibition and the exception can be joined.

In the third sentence, neither set of indented items needs to be drafted as subsections, although that may be revisited when the sentence is moved to become a part of the first section.

Here's the reformatted provision.

7.1 Maintenance. The Lessee shall, at its own expense,

(a) maintain the Equipment in good operating condition and repair and

(b) protect the Equipment from deterioration,

other than normal wear and tear. The Lessee shall during the term of this Lease, at its own cost, enter into and maintain in force a contract with the manufacturer or other acceptable maintenance company, covering the maintenance of the Equipment.

7.2 Alterations and Additions. The Lessee shall not make any modification, alteration, or addition to the Equipment without the prior written consent of the Lessor, which shall not be unreasonably withheld, provided that no consent is required for engineering changes recommended by and made by the manufacturer.

7.3 Equipment's Location. The Lessee

(a) shall keep the Equipment at the location shown in the Schedule and

(b) shall not remove the Equipment without the prior written consent of the Lessor.

24.1.3 CREATE CLARITY THROUGH SENTENCE STRUCTURE

To create clarity through sentence structure, apply the rules that you learned in Chapter 20 as well as other rules that you have learned that deal with sentence structure. For example, redraft nominalizations, place exceptions after the general rule, use the active voice, and use possessives.

Let's look at each of the sections of the example provision. In the first sentence of Section 7.1, *at its own expense* appears in the middle of the verb, violating the rule that a sentence's core words should be kept together. That can be corrected by moving it to the beginning of that sentence. The second sentence has the same issue. In addition, *during the term of this Lease,* is superfluous. That phrase can be deleted. The remainder of the sentence is wordy and should be made more concise. (See the redraft.)

Section 7.2 violates the three-line rule. This fix is easy. The "proviso" can be turned into its own sentence and rewritten to omit *provided.* In the new first sentence, three changes must be made. First, the nominalizations *modification, alteration,* and *addition* must be changed to their verb forms. Second, *without the prior written consent of the Lessor* must be redrafted so that it uses the possessive. Third, *which shall not be unreasonably withheld* must be changed from the passive to the active voice. In addition, *recommended by and made by the manufacturer* must also be changed from the passive to the active voice.

In Section 7.3, *without the prior written consent of the Lessor* must be changed so that it uses the possessive form of *Lessor.*

Here's the redraft.

7.1   Maintenance. At its own expense, the Lessee shall

(a)   maintain the Equipment in good operating condition and repair and

(b)   protect the Equipment from deterioration,

other than normal wear and tear. At its own cost, the Lessee shall enter into and maintain in force an equipment maintenance contract with the manufacturer or other acceptable maintenance company.

7.2   Alterations and Additions. The Lessee shall not modify, alter, or add to the Equipment without the Lessor's prior written consent, which the Lessor shall not unreasonably withhold. Despite the previous sentence, no consent is required for engineering changes that the manufacturer recommends and makes.

7.3   Equipment's Location. The Lessee

(a)   shall keep the Equipment at the location shown in the Schedule; and

(b)   shall not remove the Equipment without the Lessor's prior written consent.

24.1.4 CLARIFY AMBIGUITIES

Section 7.1 presents three issues of ambiguity.

- First, should the phrase *other than normal wear and tear* qualify only subsection (b), or both subsections (a) and (b)? It probably qualifies both, although that would have been hard to tell from the original version of the provision. As a drafting matter, the phrase (really an exception) could be left where it is. The alternative would be to include it with each of the subsections.

- Second, the second sentence seems inconsistent with the first. The first sentence requires the Lessee to maintain the Equipment, while the second sentence requires the Lessee to enter into a maintenance agreement so that someone else can maintain the equipment. One way to reconcile the two would be to state that the second covenant is in furtherance of the first.

- Third, the two sentences do not say the same thing the same way. The first sentence uses the phrase *at its own expense,* while the second sentence uses the phrase *at its own cost.*

A second issue of not saying the same thing the same way arises when we compare Section 7.2 to Section 7.3. Section 7.2 provides that the Lessor *shall not unreasonably withhold its consent,* while Section 7.3 does not have that limitation on the Lessor's granting of its consent. Before deciding on this redraft, you would need to consult with your client to find out whether a difference was intended.

Here's this redraft:

7.1 Maintenance. At its own expense, the Lessee shall

(a) maintain the Equipment in good operating condition and repair and

(b) protect the Equipment from deterioration,

except for normal wear and tear. At its own expense and in furtherance of its obligations in the preceding sentence, the Lessee shall enter into and maintain in force an equipment maintenance contract with the manufacturer or other acceptable maintenance company.

7.2 Alterations and Additions. The Lessee shall not modify, alter, or add to the Equipment without the Lessor's prior written consent, which the Lessor shall not unreasonably withhold. Despite the previous sentence, no consent is required for engineering changes that the manufacturer recommends and makes.

7.3 Equipment's Location. The Lessee

(a) shall keep the Equipment at the location shown in the Schedule and

(b) shall not remove the Equipment without the Lessor's prior written consent
[, which the Lessor shall not unreasonably withhold].

24.1.5 ROOT OUT LEGALESE

When performing this step, ruthlessly delete legalese. In addition, clean up any language problems that you have not already fixed.

This sample provision did not have much legalese. The only triplet in the provision is found in Section 7.2: *modify, alter, or add. Modify* and *alter* are synonyms, but *add* arguably is not. If the original equipment is left unchanged, but a new piece of equipment is added to it, that addition, in this business, might not be an alteration.

The provision's defined terms, *Lessor* and *Lessee,* are problematic. As discussed in Chapter 7 on definitions, many readers find it difficult to read contracts with defined terms ending in *or* and *ee.* Alternative defined terms might be *Owner* and *Renter.* If the owner regularly leases equipment, it might nonetheless prefer to retain the traditional defined terms. In either event, the article *the* does not always precede *Lessor* and *Lessee.* The rewrite must use — or not use —*the* consistently.

Both Section 7.1 and 7.2 provide for *prior written consent.* If the general provision on notices requires notices to be in writing, then *written* should be deleted as superfluous.

The following rewrite is minimal:

7.1 Maintenance. At its own expense, the Renter shall

(a) maintain the Equipment in good operating condition and repair and

(b) protect the Equipment from deterioration,

except for normal wear and tear. At its own expense and in furtherance of its obligations in the preceding sentence, the Renter shall enter into and maintain in force an equipment maintenance contract with the manufacturer or other acceptable maintenance company.

7.2 Alterations and Additions. The Renter shall not alter or add to the Equipment without the Owner's prior consent, which the Owner shall not unreasonably withhold. Despite the previous sentence, no consent is required for engineering changes that the manufacturer recommends and makes.

7.3 Equipment's Location. The Renter

(a) shall keep the Equipment at the location shown in the Schedule and

(b) shall not remove the Equipment without the Owner's prior consent
[, which the Owner shall not unreasonably withhold].

24.1.6 CHECK SUBSTANCE

Checking substance is the final step of the six-step process. At this stage, you must step back and look at the redrafted provision and confirm that it accurately states the business deal. You may have discovered earlier in the process that the provision was incorrect. Correcting it when you discover an error makes sense. That way, the other changes can work with the new substance. Also, use this step as an opportunity to see if anything else in the provision must be changed. Some changes do not fall neatly into one of the steps, but they must still be made.

For our purposes, we will assume that the provision comports with the business deal. One point that might be raised with the client is a standards issue.[1] Section 7.1 ends with the statement that the maintenance company must be *acceptable.* Presumably, that means *acceptable to the Owner.* If representing the Renter, you might suggest changing that standard to *reasonably acceptable.*

---

1. See §25.5.

EXERCISES

Exercise 24-1

Apply the six-step process to the following provisions. Both are available on the *Drafting Contracts* website.

> **Assignment.** No assignment or delegation of the rights, duties, or obligations of this Agreement shall be made by either party except as provided herein without the express written approval of a duly authorized representative of the other party; provided, however, that the Company may assign any or all of its rights and obligations hereunder to a wholly owned subsidiary of the Company; and provided further that the Company may delegate certain of its duties hereunder to ABC Healthcare Systems, Inc.

> **Use of Mark on Invoices, etc.** The use of the Mark by Licensee on invoices, order forms, stationery, and related material and in advertising in telephone or other directory listings is permitted only upon Licensor's prior written approval of the format in which the Mark is to be so used, the juxtaposition of the Mark with other words and phrases, and the content of the copy prior to the initial such use of the Mark and prior to any material change therein, which approval shall not be unreasonably withheld and shall be granted or denied within ten (10) business days of the submission of such format; provided, however, that such use of the Mark is only in conjunction with the sale of Licensed Items pursuant to this Agreement and further provided that should Licensor require a change in such format due to a revision, change, or modification by Licensor of the Mark, Licensor shall provide Licensee with reasonable notice of any such change or modification of the Mark in order to afford Licensee a reasonable period of time to revise and substitute invoices, order forms, stationery or other material reflecting the new Mark and shall permit Licensee to use, until the earlier of six months or depletion, such existing invoices, order forms, stationery, or other material without objection.

PART FOUR

Drafting from the Client's Perspective

Adding Value to the Deal

25.1 INTRODUCTION

Drafting contracts is more than translating the business deal into contract concepts and writing clear, unambiguous contract provisions. Sophisticated drafting requires a lawyer to understand the transaction from a client's business perspective and to add value to the deal. Looking at a contract from the client's perspective means understanding what the client wants to achieve and the risks it wants to avoid. Adding value to the deal is a euphemism for finding and resolving business issues. These skills are problem-solving skills and are integral components of a deal lawyer's professional expertise. They require an understanding not only of contracts, but of business, the client's business, and the transaction at hand. At a law firm or general counsel's office, having these skills is generally the province of the senior lawyers, and not necessarily all of them.

In a totally unscientific survey, partners were asked how they identified business issues. The following are some of the responses:

- "Identifying business issues requires a sixth sense."
- "A business issue is any issue you find that the client should resolve."
- "I know one when I see one."

The nub of these answers is that the partners learned by experience how to discern business issues.

Although you will find no substitute for experience, this chapter proposes a framework that will help you learn how more experienced practitioners think. The framework consists of five prongs, each of which is a business issue that appears in almost every transaction — albeit in different guises. The prongs of the framework are as follows:

- Money.
- Risk.
- Control.
- Standards.
- Endgame.

The subsequent sections of this chapter discuss these prongs and show how they manifest themselves in transactions. Afterward, you will work through a series of exercises in which you will apply the five-prong framework to fact patterns.

25.2 MONEY

25.2.1 AMOUNT TO BE PAID OR RECEIVED

The first money issue to consider is always whether a client is entitled to receive more money or to pay less. Although clients generally negotiate and agree on the amount, lawyers can often add value because of their deal-specific expertise. For example, perhaps your client, a major bank, wants to purchase a corporate jet. The client's expertise is finance, not the purchase and sale of airplanes, which is your specialty. If the client consults you before it negotiates the purchase price of the plane, you may be able to add value by explaining that the plane's proposed purchase price exceeds current market value because of the glut of planes on the market.

As part of this analysis, consider whether any of the payment should be contingent. For example, buyers and sellers may value a seller's business differently. This is especially true for a new business. The seller is sure that it is the next Google, and the buyer certainly hopes so but questions the seller's valuation because the business has no track record of profitability. To bridge the difference in valuation, a buyer can pay the seller a small amount at closing and additional payments in the future. The parties will determine that amount based on a formula tied to the business's performance after the acquisition. This arrangement is known as an **earnout**.[1]

25.2.2 TIMING OF PAYMENTS

When analyzing a transaction, think through any issues with respect to the timing of monetary payments. These are known as **time value of money**[2] issues. It is almost always better for a client to pay later, but to receive money sooner. The longer a client has the money, the longer that money can be invested and earning money. (Of course, tax considerations or other matters might require postponing the receipt of money.)

If your client must pay the other party, ask whether it can spread out the payments over time, or whether the other party will give your client a discount for immediate payment. If the other side must pay your client, negotiate for receipt of the payment as soon as possible. If the other side objects, find out from your client whether it could benefit from an immediate but smaller payment. For example, if the client receives the funds immediately, it may be able to invest in a new deal.

25.2.3 CREDIT RISK

Credit risk is always a business issue when the other party is obligated to pay your client in the future. Although the other party may be flush with cash when the parties make their deal, it may be less strong when payment is due. Therefore, whenever your client has agreed to receive a delayed payment, consider whether the risk of a payment default is significant. If it is, then negotiate a mechanism to secure the payment.[3]

---

1. For a more detailed discussion of earnouts, *see* Lou R. Kling & Eileen T. Nugent, *Negotiated Acquisitions of Companies, Subsidiaries and Divisions* vol. 2, §17.01 (Law Journal Press 1992).

2. For an excellent discussion of time value of money, *see* Terry Lloyd, *Present Value Concepts and Applications, in Accounting for Lawyers 1996: Using Financial Data in Legal Practice* 257 (PLI Course Handbook Series No. B-965, 1996).

3. For a detailed discussion of ways to minimize credit risk, see the materials on risk in §25.3.3.

25.2.4 ISSUES RELATING TO PAYMENT FORMULAS

Parties often use a formula to determine a contract's consideration. For example, formulas are used to calculate the following:

- Purchase price adjustment provisions in acquisition agreements.
- Compensation provisions in employment agreements.
- Royalty provisions in license and franchise agreements.
- Buy-out provisions in partnership and stockholder agreements.

When reviewing a formula, begin by analyzing whether the theoretical basis for the payment amount is analytically correct. Stated differently, is the formula neutral, or does it favor your client or the other party?

Buchwald v. Paramount Pictures Corp. brought the problem of a flawed formula into sharp relief.[4] That case made "Hollywood accounting" infamous. The trouble began when Alain Bernheim, the producer of *Coming to America*,[5] agreed that Paramount would pay him a percentage of the movie's net profits, in addition to a modest upfront fee. Apparently, Bernheim expected the movie to be a success and anticipated that he could earn much more money by receiving a percentage of net profits rather than a one-time upfront fee.

The movie was a huge hit. Bernheim, no doubt, was elated. Unfortunately, that elation was short-lived: The studio reported that it lost money on the movie and that Bernheim was entitled to no additional money. The problem stemmed from the way the studio accounted for the movie's expenses. It included as expenses not only the direct expenses of the movie, but also some of the studio's overhead expenses. Thus, Bernheim would have been far better off receiving a percentage of the movie's gross revenues — before any expenses were deducted. Alternatively, Bernheim and the studio could have agreed on which expenses were allocable to the movie.

Assuming that your client and the other party have agreed on a formula for calculating the payment amount, confirm that the formula is properly stated. Is each variable unambiguous? Is the formula as a whole unambiguous?

Some of the most common drafting errors occur when crafting a formula.[6] To make certain that a formula works as intended, run multiple hypotheticals to see what answers are obtained when numbers are plugged into the formula. Be sure to include in the hypotheticals numbers far outside the range that the client expects. Calculations sometimes result in negative amounts, and the parties need to address what happens in that circumstance.

After running the numbers, send the hypotheticals to your client to make sure that he understands how the formula will work, both when the transaction succeeds and when it fails. (Clients do not like surprises.) Once your client approves the formula and the hypotheticals, send them to the other side for its review and approval. With luck, this process will root out any differences at a time when they can be resolved — without litigation. As the final step in this process, with the approval of all the principals, annex the hypotheticals as an exhibit to the contract. They will become a legislative history of sorts, setting forth the parties' understanding of the formula at the time of contracting.

---

4. *See Buchwald v. Paramount Pictures Corp.*, 1990 WL 357611 (Cal. Super. Jan. 8, 1990); *see also* Pierce O'Donnell & Dennis McDougal, *Fatal Subtraction: The Inside Story of Buchwald v. Paramount,* appendix B (Doubleday 1992).

5. Eddie Murphy starred.

6. See Chapter 22 for a fuller discussion of formulas.

25.2.5 TRANSACTION EXPENSES

Parties do not always address the allocation of transaction expenses—especially at the preliminary stages of negotiation. As they can run to a tidy sum, you and your client should think through whether each party should pay its own expenses or whether the expenses should be shifted from one party to the other.

25.2.6 ACCOUNTING AND TAX ISSUES

The accounting and tax issues in a contract can be quite sophisticated. These issues may determine the structure of the transaction and sometimes even whether the transaction can be done. If you do not have the background to address these issues, you *must* obtain the assistance of a qualified practitioner.[7]

25.2.7 WHO, WHAT, WHEN, WHERE, WHY, HOW, AND HOW MUCH?

As you may recall from Chapter 8 on the action sections, whenever you draft a provision dealing with the payment of money, you should always answer the questions, *who, what, when, where, why, how,* and *how much*?[8]

25.2.8 ENDGAME

Every contract ends—either happily or unhappily. A borrower can repay the loan or default; a joint venture can conclude successfully or fail; and an acquisition can close or fail to be consummated. No matter which way a contract ends, the parties will have issues to address. Often, they include money. Therefore, when drafting endgame provisions, think through what should be the monetary consequences of the contract's end. *Follow the cash.* For example, when a real estate lease term ends, consider what should happen with the tenant's deposit: The landlord should be required to return it, but should be able to offset against it any costs incurred because of the tenant damaging the apartment.[9]

Monetary endgame issues also include whether the prevailing party in a litigation should be contractually entitled to recover its attorneys' fees and other litigation expenses.[10]

25.3 RISK

25.3.1 TYPES OF RISK

As we have seen, representations and warranties, covenants, and conditions are all risk allocation mechanisms. In addition, risk can manifest itself in multiple other ways in a transaction. First, a contract can raise the specter of tort liability—fraudulent inducement, product liability, and tortious interference with contract. Second, the provisions can create contract law risk. For example, a noncompetition provision could be unenforceable. Third, a contract can create statutory liability, such as liability under the securities laws. Fourth, a risk, such as credit risk, can be inherent in the transaction.

---

7. See Chapter 22 for a discussion of accounting-related drafting issues.

8. See §8.3.

9. For a detailed discussion of endgame issues, see Chapter 15.

10. Under the common law, each litigant is responsible for its own attorneys' fees. The parties can, however, agree that the losing party (whether plaintiff or defendant) must pay the prevailing party's attorneys' fees.

25.3.2 EVALUATING THE RISK

Lawyers are terrific at ferreting out risks in a transaction. Law school primes them to issue spot. If that is all they do, however, they will quickly earn justifiable reputations as deal killers.

Determining the risks only begins a lawyer's risk analysis. Next, she must assess the probability that the risk will occur. In addition, she should try to quantify the risk and do a risk/reward analysis. With this information, the client can evaluate the risk more completely. It may decide, for example, not to elevate the matter to a business issue because it believes that the risk will probably not occur and that the financial consequences would be relatively small. Alternatively, the client could decide that the benefit does not justify the risk, even with a low probability of occurrence.

Whether a risk develops into a business issue often depends on a client's risk aversion profile. How comfortable is the client with taking risk? Is the client an entrepreneur ready to roll the dice, or is it a small, local bank willing to assume only minimal risks?

25.3.3 METHODS TO MITIGATE RISK

A lawyer's reputation as a dealmaker often depends on his ability to resolve risk issues creatively. Although a transaction may require an innovative solution, you can often rely on the techniques discussed in this section.

If credit risk is the concern, one party can take a security interest in the other party's assets. If you use this technique, determine which assets are the most valuable and which will be the easiest to liquidate. Be sure that the security interest applies to these assets. As an alternative (or additional) technique for reducing credit risk, a third party's credit can be added to the credit of the party with the payment obligation. Typically, the third party will agree to serve either as a **co-obligor** or as a **guarantor**. Of course, this party must be creditworthy.

Escrows are another technique that parties use to lessen credit risk. To create an escrow, the parties deposit cash or other property with a neutral third party, who agrees to release it only in accordance with the terms of the escrow agreement. The Exhibit to the book discusses escrow agreements, including their use and some of the salient business issues.[11]

Other methods of reducing risk include **indemnity agreements, letters of credit, insurance**, and **deal-specific methods**. In an indemnity agreement, one party promises to pay the other party for its losses, even if the indemnified party did not cause the loss. For example, when a lateral partner joins a firm, the firm generally indemnifies the lateral partner against any existing malpractice claims.

In a letter of credit transaction, a bank substitutes its credit for that of a party's. For example, imagine a manufacturer in Italy wants to sell goods to a small company in New York but will not do so unless it can be assured of payment. To provide this assurance, the buyer arranges for a letter of credit under which a bank will pay the manufacturer on the fulfillment of certain conditions.

Typically, the conditions require that the manufacturer deliver documents to the bank indicating that the proper goods are being shipped. The bank does not, however, undertake to inspect the goods. It *only* examines documents.[12] If the buyer wants an inspection of the goods, the buyer must arrange for a third party to inspect the goods and issue a certificate that the inspected goods were the proper items in the appropriate condition.

---

11. Chapter 6 includes an escrow agreement. See p. 91.

12. Because a bank will only look at documents, a letter of credit is sometimes referred to as a **documentary letter of credit**.

After all the parties have agreed to the conditions, the bank issues its letter of credit in favor of the manufacturer. The letter of credit is the bank's promise to pay the manufacturer on its presentation to the bank of the appropriate documents. Thus, the bank substitutes its credit for the buyer's. The buyer reimburses the bank after it pays the manufacturer.

Parties also use insurance to reduce risk. Companies generally purchase multiple kinds of insurance.

- General liability insurance.
- Directors' and officers' insurance.
- Health insurance.
- Environmental insurance.
- Business interruption insurance.

Knowing that a party has insurance is insufficient. You must know, among other things, the deductible (the amount the insured must pay before the insurer is liable), the maximum the insurer is obligated to pay, how much of that amount has already been paid, and whether the insurer is creditworthy.

As noted, parties sometimes need to rely on deal-specific methods to reduce risk. For example, the parties could reduce a buyer's risk by changing a stock acquisition to an asset acquisition. The risk is reduced because of the different structure. In an asset acquisition, a buyer chooses which assets it will buy and chooses which liabilities it will assume. If the buyer does not specifically assume a liability, it remains with the seller. So, if the seller had significant litigation liabilities, the buyer could choose not to assume those liabilities. In contrast, in a stock acquisition, no assets are assigned or liabilities assumed. Instead, the shareholders of the target sell their shares to the buyer who becomes the new shareholder. Nothing happens to the business. Thus, any liability of the target continues to be its liability. Only its shareholders have changed.

25.4 CONTROL

In analyzing control as a business issue, the initial inquiry must be whether having control is good or bad from a client's perspective. For example, limited partners are entitled to limited liability because they exercise no control over the limited partnership. In this context, lack of control is good. However, limited partners do not generally want to abdicate to the general partner all control over their investment. They want the ability to protect their investment. Thus, the limited partners will seek as much control as the general partner will tolerate and as much control as the limited partners can accrete without becoming general partners under the relevant state law. Thus, control is actually a two-edged sword for limited partners.

Control is always an issue when your client is subject to a risk. Indeed, whenever your client worries about risk, ask yourself how the agreement can diminish or control it.

Control and risk business issues often coexist when negotiating and drafting covenants. With respect to each promise, determine whether your client can control the outcome. If not, it is gambling when it agrees to the covenant because it could end up in breach through no fault of its own. To protect your client, negotiate a covenant that reduces the risk by changing the degree of obligation. For example, a party may not want to promise that it will obtain an environmental permit because it cannot control the agency's decision. That party may be willing, however, to promise that it will prepare and submit the necessary papers by a certain date and that it will enter into good faith negotiations with the agency.

When thinking about control issues, think through which party is in control, whether that is the correct party, or whether control should be shared, and if so, how. Imagine two companies have entered into a joint venture to build a skyscraper. Should one party decide (that is, control) who the subcontractors will be? If the decisions are to be joint, how will the parties break a deadlock?

Once controls are in place, they need not remain at the same level throughout a relationship. For example, after first making a loan, a bank may justifiably insist that the agreement prohibit the borrower from making any capital expenditures. The bank has made the loan for working capital purposes and does not want the loan proceeds sidelined into fixed assets not immediately involved in producing profits. However, the bank may be willing to moderate this restriction once the borrower has repaid an agreed-on percentage of the principal.

Parties can also increase controls. Preferred shareholders often negotiate for this. Generally, they have no voting rights. But if the parties agree, they could earn the right to have one or more board members if the company fails to pay dividends for three consecutive quarters.

25.5 STANDARDS

Almost every word or phrase in a contract establishes a standard. For example, every representation and warranty establishes a standard of liability. If the standard is not met, the recipient of the representation and warranty may sue the maker. This is a macro standard. That macro standard can, however, be changed at the micro level. By changing a word or a phrase in a representation, the standard changes. Are property, plant, and equipment in *good repair, customary repair,* or *in compliance with statutory standards*? Covenants and conditions are also standards, as is every adjective (*good* repair) and adverb (*promptly* deliver). Definitions are also standards (how a financial ratio is defined determines the standard to be incorporated into a loan covenant). Thus, each time a definition changes, so do a party's rights and duties.

Once you determine what the standards are, determine whether the standard favors your client, and if not, how it can be modified.

Some drafters insist that vague standards are inherently wrong.[13] That is incorrect. While vagueness may invite a dispute over a standard, sometimes it is the only way to bridge disparate positions or to provide a party with flexibility. Vagueness is the drafter's equivalent of the reasonable person standard. Parties use it to establish a facts and circumstances test. For example, if a *force majeure* event occurs, how quickly must the nonperforming party tell the other party of the occurrence? Immediately? Within 24 hours? What if the nonperforming party is cut off from all communication because of the *force majeure* event? Under those circumstances, the 24-hour cutoff is unreasonable. More equitable would be *as soon as feasible.*

Although vague standards may sometimes further a transaction, they can also disadvantage a client. It depends on the business deal. As noted earlier, sometimes a seller of a business will agree to an earnout. To memorialize this arrangement, the purchase agreement will state the formula for determining the income on which the earnout is based. The value of the seller's earnout could be destroyed, however, if that formula merely states that *revenues minus expenses equals income.* In that case, the vagueness of the standard *expenses* would permit the buyer to decrease the income by deducting inappropriate expenses. Therefore, do not start drafting with

---

13. See Chapter 21 for a more detailed discussion of vagueness.

a preconceived notion that vagueness is good or bad. Instead, each time a provision establishes a vague standard, analyze whether it helps your client or whether a more specific, concrete standard would improve the client's position.

When you contemplate negotiating a change in a standard, think through the business risk of asking for that change. If your client has limited negotiating leverage, a request for a change will focus the other party's attention on that standard and could result in an even more stringent standard.

You and your client must also consider who should decide whether a standard has been met. Sometimes, a party decides. For example, a landlord and tenant could agree that the tenant may assign the lease to a third party, but only *if the landlord grants consent in its sole discretion.*

If the parties disagree as to whether a standard has been met, they have several options. They can adjudicate the matter in court, or they can arbitrate or mediate their disagreement. Alternatively, they can appoint an individual with subject matter expertise to resolve any disputes outside a proceeding. In sophisticated construction agreements, owners and contractors sometimes appoint a third-party engineer to settle any differences in a timely manner—sometimes in just a few days.

Contracts, sometimes, but not always, address the consequences of breaching a standard.[14]

25.6 ENDGAME

As noted earlier in this chapter and as discussed in Chapter 15, every contractual relationship terminates in either a friendly or an unfriendly manner. Either way, the parties must think through the consequences. These critical provisions deserve your studied attention.

Before turning to the exercises in this chapter, review Chapter 15 and its discussion of the business issues that endgame provisions raise.

---

14. See Chapter 15 for an in-depth discussion of this matter.

EXERCISES

Exercise 25-1

On the next page is a short letter agreement between a broker and an owner of an apartment. The agreement raises multiple business issues. In order to analyze what those issues are, you will use the chart on the following pages.

The chart is composed of an X axis and a Y axis. Along the X axis, each in a separate column, are the five prongs of the framework. Going down the Y axis, each sentence of the letter agreement is separately set forth. To complete the chart, determine with respect to each sentence which of the five business issues is present and indicate the issue in the appropriate box. Thus, with respect to the first sentence, first consider if it raises any money issues. If so, note them in the appropriate box. Then consider whether the sentence raises any risk issues, and if so, note them in the appropriate box. Follow the same procedure with respect to each of the other prongs and then with respect to each of the other sentences. Not every sentence involves all of the prongs. In addition, an issue may straddle two or more prongs. If this occurs, just indicate that in your notes.

Two additional exercises follow Exercise 25-1. Complete them the same way.

Mr. Robert Best
Best Brokerage, Inc.
200 Real Estate Way
Burgeoning City, Wyoming

Dear Mr. Best:

This letter sets forth the agreement between Best Brokerage, Inc. ("Best"), and the undersigned.

By signing this letter, I grant Best the exclusive right to act as broker for the sale of my apartment for a three-month period (the "Brokerage Period") beginning the day you countersign this letter agreement. I will pay Best a commission of 5% of the sales price of the apartment if during the Brokerage Period the apartment is sold to someone other than someone I have already identified as a prospective purchaser.

On the signing of this letter agreement, I will give you a set of keys to my apartment. You promise to give me sufficient notice before bringing any prospective purchaser to the apartment. If any prospective purchaser damages my apartment or its furnishings in any way, Best agrees to indemnify me in full for the cost of replacement or repair.

If this letter correctly sets forth our agreement, please countersign this letter.

Sincerely yours,

Oren Oglethorpe
_____
Oren Oglethorpe, Owner

AGREED:
BEST BROKERAGE, INC.
By: _____
Robert Best, President

Exercise 25-1 Chart

	Money	Risk	Control	Standards	Endgame
By signing this letter, I grant Best the exclusive right to act as broker for the sale of my apartment for a three-month period (the "Brokerage Period") beginning the day you countersign this letter agreement.					
I will pay Best a commission of 5% of the sales price of the apartment if during the Brokerage Period the apartment is sold to someone other than someone I have already identified as a prospective purchaser.					
On the signing of this letter agreement, I will give you a set of keys to my apartment.					
You promise to give me sufficient notice before bringing any prospective purchaser to the apartment.					
If any prospective purchaser damages my apartment or its furnishings in any way, Best agrees to indemnify me in full for the cost of replacement or repair.					

Exercise 25-2

To: Alice Associate

From: Peter Partner

Our client is Ralph Products LP (Ralph LP). Ralph LP owns all rights in the cartoon character Ralph — a short, frumpy, bespectacled, eight-year-old for whom life never goes quite right. For reasons that no one can fathom, anything with a likeness of Ralph on it sells like hotcakes. Ralph LP has been making millions by licensing the character to different companies who manufacture and then market products bearing Ralph's likeness.

Earlier today, Ralph Randolph, the president of Ralph LP, called to tell me that he and Merchandisers Extraordinaire, Inc. (Merchandisers), had agreed to the salient terms of a license agreement with respect to Ralph merchandise. Randolph asked me whether I could foresee any business or legal issues with respect to the manner in which the parties had structured the royalty payments. I understand that aspect of the deal as follows: With respect to each year of the contract term, Merchandisers must pay royalties equal to 15% of all gross sales under $7 million; 10% with respect to sales that equal or exceed $7 million; but in no event less than an aggregate of $600,000 per year. In addition, Ralph LP will have the right to terminate the contract if Merchandisers' net worth is less than $10 million as of the end of its fiscal year.

As you know, I am on my way to Paris and do not have time to analyze this issue now. Please think it through and be prepared to explain any problems when I call you from the plane. I know that there are lots of other issues with respect to this license agreement, but right now just stick to the money, standards, and endgame issues.

Exercise 25-2 Chart

	Money	Risk	Control	Standards	Endgame
With respect to each year of the contract term, Merchandisers must pay royalties equal to 15% of all gross sales under $7 million; 10% with respect to sales that equal or exceed $7 million; but in no event less than an aggregate of $600,000 per year.					
In addition, Ralph LP will have the right to terminate the contract if Merchandisers' net worth is less than $10 million as of the end of its fiscal year.					

Exercise 25-3

To: Leo Pard

From: Ty Gere

Subject: Clark Partnership Agreement

Two siblings, Margo and Bob Clark, have asked us to consider their plan to form a general partnership for their new business: Diets-Are-Us. DAU intends to manufacture and market a line of freshly cooked, high-end diet meals. It will sell the meals directly to specialty food stores. The Clarks are confident that the business will do well. Their secret ingredient is a genetically engineered food supplement that makes you feel full — even though the amount consumed is relatively small. The inventor of the ingredient is their cousin Roberta who has given them the go-ahead to use the ingredient in the business.

The Clarks intend to capitalize the business with $100,000. Margo will contribute $75,000, and Bob will contribute $25,000. Bob has significant experience in the diet food industry, having just completed a three-year stint as executive vice president of the company that is the industry leader — albeit in frozen foods. Accordingly, the plan is that he will run the business on a day-to-day basis. Margo will be in charge of advertising and back-office operations. Bob hopes that the new business will keep Margo's mind off her recent illness. He confided that the long-term prognosis is not good.

The business deal with respect to profits is that the first $75,000 goes to Margo, while the next $25,000 in cash that is distributed is Bob's. Thereafter, the money is split 50-50.

Please provide me with a list of the business issues that I should raise with the Clarks at my meeting with them later today. It would be helpful if your list comported with the framework we recently discussed.

Exercise 25-3 Chart

	Money	Risk	Control	Standards	Endgame
Two siblings, Margo and Bob Clark, have asked us to consider their plan to form a general partnership for their new business: Diets-Are-Us. DAU intends to manufacture and market a line of freshly cooked high-end diet meals. It will sell the meals directly to specialty food stores. The Clarks are confident that the business will do well.					
Their secret ingredient is a genetically engineered food supplement that makes you feel full—even though the amount consumed is relatively small. The inventor of the ingredient is their cousin Roberta who has given them the go-ahead to use the ingredient in the business.					
The Clarks intend to capitalize the business with $100,000. Margo will contribute $75,000, and Bob will contribute $25,000.					

continued on next page >

Money	Risk	Control	Standards	Endgame
Bob has significant experience in the diet food industry, having just completed a three-year stint as executive vice president of the company that is the industry leader—albeit in frozen foods. Accordingly, the plan is that he will run the business on a day-to-day basis.				
Margo will be in charge of advertising and back-office operations. Bob hopes that the new business will keep Margo's mind off her recent illness. He confided that the long-term prognosis is not good.				
The business deal with respect to profits is that the first $75,000 goes to Margo, while the next $25,000 in cash that is distributed is Bob's. Thereafter, the money is split 50-50.				

Exercise 25-4

To: Budding Associate

From: Proud Partner

Our client is a member of the acquisition committee of a London venture capital fund. What follows is a preliminary report from one of the fund's analysts. Please review the report to determine the business issues that might arise if the fund decides to acquire the target. I will need your report as quickly as possible.

* * * *

1. Wonder Drugs Limited is a privately held British company specializing in biotechnology. Its primary product is Getbetter, a drug that the founder created to help his son who is afflicted with a rare disease. Because the number of patients with the disease is relatively small, Getbetter has never been particularly profitable despite its effectiveness. Wonder Drugs manufactures only 100,000 doses of the medicine a year. To make matters worse, Wonder Drugs' patent on Getbetter ends December 31, 20X9. With the loss of the patent, other companies may begin to manufacture a generic version of Getbetter. If they do, Getbetter's marginal profitability could turn into a loss. As of December 31, 20X8, 40% of the assets of Wonder Drugs consisted of inventory in Getbetter.

2. Despite the issues mentioned in paragraph 1, we believe that Wonder Drugs is a strong acquisition candidate. It has a possible best-seller in a drug that it has been working on for ten years. Feelbetter is an antidepressant for children, which in clinical trials, has proven quite effective in relieving the symptoms of depression. Management of Wonder Drugs projects that it could sell over 30 million doses each year. Antidepressants for children are, however, controversial. Research in England and the United States has demonstrated that some antidepressants increase the likelihood that some children will commit suicide.

3. Although the French regulatory authorities have approved Feelbetter, other countries have not. Wonder Drugs believes that Feelbetter will be profitable only if it can be sold in the Commonwealth and the United States. Accordingly, these approvals are key. Wonder Drugs expects these approvals by the end of June of this year. Final approval of the patent is also expected around the same time.

4. The ownership structure of Wonder Drugs is relatively simple. Dr. Niles Smith, the founder of the company, owns 60% of the company's shares. (He has an excellent reputation within the biomedical community.) Various members of his family own the remainder of the shares. Dr. Smith is now 65 and wants to sell his business as part of his estate plan. He has requested that the transaction be structured as a stock sale to minimize the taxes he and the other shareholders must pay. Dr. Smith believes that he can persuade all the other members of his family to sell their respective shares. His only concern is whether his oldest daughter will sell. They have not spoken in five years, and he is concerned that she might refuse to sell just to be difficult.

5. Dr. Smith has told us that once the sale is complete, he does not want to have any post-closing liabilities to the buyer. He told us that he needed the full amount of the purchase price to fund a trust for his son and to pay for some other activities he is contemplating as part of his retirement. Dr. Smith is refusing to give any representations and warranties on

the efficacy or the safety of Getbetter and Feelbetter. He said that those were the buyer's risks. He has, however, offered to permit us to review all of the research on Getbetter and Feelbetter. (That is, we can do all the due diligence we want.) In addition, he and his assistant would meet as often as needed with representatives of the buyer (for example, their scientists).

6. Dr. Smith is the chief executive at Wonder Drugs and its primary researcher. He is brilliant and has done a fine job managing the company. He has told us, however, that he does not want to work for Wonder Drugs after its sale. He has never worked for anyone and doesn't want to start that now. But in 20X7, as part of a succession plan, Dr. Smith hired Sara Jones as his research assistant. She has top-notch scientific credentials and has been instrumental in bringing Feelbetter through its regulatory trials. To induce Sara to join Wonder Drugs, the company granted her options to purchase 1,000 shares of Wonder Drugs at a price of £100 per share, the options to vest on receipt of the English and American regulatory approvals.

7. Our purchase price discussions with Wonder Drugs have been difficult. Dr. Smith has been insisting on a very high per-share price relative to what the company earns on Getbetter and what it may earn once its patent lapses. He insists the company will generate huge income once Feelbetter receives its regulatory approvals, and he wants the price to reflect the projected income. While it is our hope that the new drug will make the company hugely profitable, the new medicine has no track record. The high level of projected income is completely speculative. In addition, we feel that the price has to factor in the possibility of litigation should the antidepressant cause suicides — despite the results of the drug's current trials. We will continue to negotiate the purchase price with Dr. Smith.

8. The company's financial records are adequate for a privately held company. We have no reason to believe that there is any fraud. But the company has been using a small accounting firm. Bringing in a big name accounting firm may be expensive, but it's an essential element for our exit strategy.

9. Wonder Drugs has been selling Getbetter through pharmaceutical distributors. Those distributors then sell the medicine to hospitals and pharmacies. One of these distributors has not paid Wonder Drugs in six months and owes the company £200,000, over 10% of last year's revenues.

10. The production facility machinery was state of the art when Wonder Drugs purchased it ten years ago. This machinery can last 20 years if it is well-maintained. Dr. Smith told us that Wonder Drugs has been negotiating to purchase new machinery for the production of Feelbetter.

Exercise 25-4 Chart

	Money	Risk	Control	Standards	Endgame	Other
Paragraph 1 Seller's Issues						
Paragraph 1 Buyer's Issues						
Paragraph 2 Seller's Issues						
Paragraph 2 Buyer's Issues						

continued on next page >

	Money	Risk	Control	Standards	Endgame	Other
Paragraph 3 Seller's Issues						
Paragraph 3 Buyer's Issues						
Paragraph 4 Seller's Issues						
Paragraph 4 Buyer's Issues						

	Money		Risk		Control		Standards		Endgame		Other
Paragraph 5 Seller's Issues											
Paragraph 5 Buyer's Issues											
Paragraph 6 Seller's Issues											
Paragraph 6 Buyer's Issues											

continued on next page >

	Money	Risk	Control	Standards	Endgame	Other
Paragraph 7 Seller's Issues						
Paragraph 7 Buyer's Issues						
Paragraph 8 Seller's Issues						
Paragraph 8 Buyer's Issues						

	Money	Risk	Control	Standards	Endgame	Other
Paragraph 9 Seller's Issues						
Paragraph 9 Buyer's Issues						
Paragraph 10 Seller's Issues						
Paragraph 10 Buyer's Issues						

PART FIVE

Putting a Contract Together

Organizing a Contract and Its Provisions

26.1 INTRODUCTION

A well-written contract has an organizational framework that makes it easy to read. It has **structural integrity**.[1] A reader knows where to look for a provision and understands how the contract's provisions relate to each other. By ordering them in a "meaningful sequence,"[2] a drafter reduces a reader's work.

There is no single way to organize a contract. Drafters can conceptualize the same contract differently. If an approach facilitates a contract's reading, then it is a legitimate alternative. Nonetheless, over time, through custom and practice, the organization of some types of contracts has become standardized. An acquisition agreement is a paradigmatic example. If you were to look at a dozen precedents from a dozen different firms, their organization would be almost exactly the same. In instances like this, hewing to the accepted organization facilitates the contract's reading. Changing it requires the reader to hunt for a provision that is not in its usual place, a frustrating and time-wasting exercise. In addition, the client may refuse to pay for the time spent reorganizing the contract.

In practice, you will draft very few contracts from scratch. Instead, you will use a precedent—either one from your firm or one that you find in a secondary resource. Someone else will have already spent the time to impose order and organize the contract's provisions. You may want to fine-tune that organization, but most of your organizational responsibilities will be limited to inserting new provisions in the appropriate place and organizing individual provisions. These are not insignificant tasks, and a reader will appreciate your careful rendering of this work.

The remaining sections of this chapter discuss the typical organization of a contract, how to organize the business provisions of a contract, and how to organize individual provisions.

---

1. The author of this book first heard the phrase *structural integrity* from Ernest Rubenstein, then a partner at Paul, Weiss, Rifkin, Wharton & Garrison LLP.

2. Alan Siegel, *Language Follows Logic: Practical Lessons in Legal Drafting,* remarks made at Conference of Experts in Clear Legal Drafting, National Center for Administrative Justice, Washington, D.C., June 2, 1978, in F. Reed Dickerson, *Materials on Legal Drafting* 150 (West 1981).

26.2 A CONTRACT'S ORGANIZATIONAL STRUCTURE

Contracts are organized at both a macro and a micro level. The macro level is the organization of the contract as a whole: What are the beginning, middle, and ending provisions? Micro-level organization refers to the organization of the individual provisions—no matter where in the contract they occur.

26.2.1 ORGANIZATION AT THE MACRO LEVEL

At the macro level, the organization of contracts rarely differs, except for the organization of business provisions. As you have seen, virtually all contracts begin with the introductory provisions: the preamble, recitals, and words of agreement—in that order. (Exceptions exist, of course. Drafters sometimes omit recitals because they are superfluous for the particular contract.) Although practice varies, most drafters place the definitions after the introductory provisions.

The next provisions are almost always the action sections, and their order is, again, fairly standard: Typically, the subject matter performance provision appears first, followed by the provision setting forth the payment, whether monetary or otherwise. Then come the provisions relating to the agreement's term, date, time, and place of closing, and the closing deliveries (in each instance, if appropriate for the transaction).

The remaining business provisions follow the action sections. These provisions set out the parties' representations and warranties, covenants, conditions, rights, and discretionary authority. Significant policies are also stated. The organization of these business provisions varies from contract to contract, but generally the last business provisions are the endgame provisions. These provisions usually adhere to a common organizational scheme: first, the defaults; then, the remedies; and finally termination. This order mimics the events in the business world: defaults occur, and then a party seeks remedies.[3]

After the endgame provisions are the general provisions, the final provisions of a contract. Most drafters insert these provisions without giving any thought to the order in which they should appear (but, one hopes, with some thought as to their substance). Nonetheless, you can organize these provisions by grouping them by subject matter: communication provisions, provisions determining the elements of the contract, provisions relating to third parties, financial and risk allocation provisions, interpretive provisions, and dispute resolution provisions. (The outline at the end of this section details the specific provisions.) In some agreements, a general provision may be of particular importance—for example, the indemnity provision or the *force majeure* provision. In that case, break the provision out and give it its own article or section, as appropriate.

Case law suggests that a contract's last provision should be the waiver of a right to jury trial.[4] Although courts will enforce a jury waiver, they do so reluctantly and insist that a waiver be knowing, voluntary, and intentional.[5] In deciding whether this standard has been met, courts look at whether the provision was conspicuous, thereby making it more likely that the waiving party read it. Putting the jury waiver provision last is one way of making it conspicuous.

Of course, the contract ends with the parties' signatures.

---

3. For further detail on the organization and drafting of endgame provisions, see Chapter 15.

4. *See Reggie Packing Co. v. Lazere Fin. Corp.* (*In re Reggie Packing Co.*), 671 F. Supp. 571, 572 (N.D. Ill. 1987).

5. See § 16.5 for a detailed discussion of the provision waiving jury trial.

Outline of Typical Contract Structure

- Preamble.
- Recitals.
- Words of agreement.
- Definitions.
- Action sections.

    ◆ Subject matter performance provision.
    ◆ Monetary provisions.
    ◆ Term (if applicable).
    ◆ Closing details: when and where (if applicable).
    ◆ Closing deliveries (if applicable).

- Other business provisions.
- Endgame provisions.

    ◆ Defaults.
    ◆ Remedies.
    ◆ Termination.

- General provisions.

    ◆ Communication (notices, publicity, and confidentiality).
    ◆ Third parties (assignment, delegation, successors and assigns, and third-party beneficiaries).
    ◆ Financial and risk allocation (indemnities and *force majeure*).
    ◆ Determination of contract elements (amendment, waiver, merger, counterparts, and severability).
    ◆ Interpretive provisions (number, gender, and captions).
    ◆ Dispute resolution (arbitration, mediation, governing law, choice of forum, service of process, cumulative remedies, and waiver of jury trial).

- Signature lines.
- Schedules.
- Exhibits.

26.3 ORGANIZATION OF THE BUSINESS PROVISIONS AND INDIVIDUAL PROVISIONS

The five primary organizing principles for arranging a contract's business provisions are the following:

- Subject matter.
- Relative importance.
- Contract concepts.
- Chronology.
- Party.

Many contracts use more than one of these principles, with one acting as the primary organizing principle and one or more of the others as subsidiary principles.[6]

---

6. In *The Fundamentals of Legal Drafting,* the seminal treatise on drafting, F. Reed Dickerson discusses how to use division, classification, and sequence as tools to create a contract's organization—or "architecture," to use his terminology. F. Reed Dickerson, *The Fundamentals of Legal Drafting* 81-91 (2d ed., Little, Brown & Co. 1986). But Dickerson, himself, had reservations about the utility of these tools: "All the composition books tell you to make an outline, but none that I have seen gives an adequate account of how it should be conceptualized. I tried to remedy the situation in chapter 5 of *The Fundamentals of Legal*

26.3.1   SUBJECT MATTER AND RELATIVE IMPORTANCE

Organizing a contract's business provisions by subject matter is the most common way to put together a contract at the macro level. The process resembles the process used when organizing an outline for a brief or a memorandum. For those documents, a writer first determines the main points and the subsidiary points, and then orders them to create a cohesive and persuasive document. Before settling on the final organizational scheme, the writer may try several different ones.

The parallel process in contract drafting begins with a drafter grouping together business terms on the same or similar topics and creating subject matter groups. These groups become provisions that must be further organized, often with the more important provisions appearing earlier in the contract. As noticed earlier, the endgame provisions are generally placed, however, toward the end of the contract. This reflects the transaction's chronology, and is a nod to the parties' psychological reaction to endgame provisions: Bad news should be deferred.

In determining the relative importance of provisions, consider, among other things, whether the parties will refer to a provision frequently (more important) or infrequently (less important). In addition, generally, the statement of a rule should precede its exception[7] to facilitate understanding of the exception. Knowing what the rule is puts the exception in context.

As a test of whether an agreement's organization works, determine the number of cross-references used in the agreement. Sometimes a cross-reference cannot be avoided. Two provisions must be read in conjunction with each other; one may supersede the other in limited circumstances, or the second provision qualifies the first. But if multiple cross-references relate to the same topic, consider reorganizing the contract or creating a new section to deal with that topic. Assembling the related provisions in one place may make it easier for the reader.

To make these organizing principles concrete, imagine that your client is a chain of big-box stores (think Target) that is contracting with a photo-finishing lab for its few customers who do not use digital cameras. Your client informs you that the parties have agreed to the following business terms (in no particular order):

1. The lab will develop and print the photographs that each store's customers have dropped off for developing.
2. For nondigital photographs, the lab must use developer manufactured by Chelsea Photo Chemicals, which is located in New York City.
3. The lab must pick up film from each store every day, but after 5:00 p.m.
4. The lab must provide a first-quality product.
5. The lab must return the finished photographs no later than noon the day after it picks up the film.
6. For nondigital photographs, the lab must use fixer manufactured by Berkshire Photo Materials, which is located in Egremont, Massachusetts.
7. All photographs are to be printed on Axon photographic paper with a matte finish, unless a customer specifies otherwise.
8. If a customer drops off more than ten rolls of film at a store on any day, the lab may return the photographs developed from that film later than noon the day after it picks up the film, but no later than 5:00 p.m.

Drafting, but I'm afraid that I left the reader awash in a sea of abstraction." F. Reed Dickerson, *Materials on Legal Drafting* 103 (West 1981) (quoting F. Reed Dickerson, *Legal Drafting: Writing as Thinking, or, Talk-back from Your Draft and How to Exploit It,* 29 J. Leg. Educ. 373, 374 (1978)).

7. See § 23.3 for a more detailed discussion of how to draft exceptions.

To organize these eight business points, first group together related matters: Four points relate to the quality of the product and the materials to be used (#2, #4, #6, and #7); three relate to pickups and deliveries (#3, #5, and #8); and one (#1) is part of the subject matter performance provision. Next, determine in which order these groups should appear. The first decision—an easy one—is to put the subject matter performance provision in with the other action sections. After this, you must decide which of the remaining provisions should be first: the provisions dealing with pickups and deliveries or the ones dealing with the product's quality.

In the hypothetical described above, timing may be the more important business term because of its primacy in the store's marketing efforts. A drafter could decide, however, that quality is more important because without it, timing does not matter. Both analyses are reasonable, and either order would be acceptable based on the facts available.

After deciding the order of these two provisions, you must organize the individual provisions. This is organization at the micro level. With respect to the provisions on pickups and deliveries, how could you order them to help a reader understand them? Chronological order is an obvious possibility. In addition, the general rule as to the delivery of the photographs by noon should precede the exception that permits delivery after noon but no later than 5:00 p.m. of that same day. In the draft of this provision that follows, note how the formatting enhances its clarity.

"**Delivery Day**" means, with respect to each roll of film, the day after the day that the Lab picks up that roll of film from a Store.

Schedule of Pickups and Deliveries.

(a) **Pickups**. The Lab shall

  (i) pick up from each Store every day all rolls of film that its customers have deposited with that Store; and

  (ii) make that pickup after 5:00 p.m.

(b) **Deliveries**.

  (i) **General Rule**. With respect to each roll of film picked up from each Store, the Lab shall return to that Store the photographs developed from that roll no later than noon of that roll's Delivery Day.

  (ii) **Exception**. Despite subsection (i), if a customer of a Store deposits more than ten rolls of film on any one day, the Lab

    (A) may return the photographs developed from those rolls to that Store later than noon of their Delivery Day, but

    (B) shall return them no later than 5:00 p.m. of their Delivery Day.

Next you must analyze and organize the provisions dealing with the quality of the photographs and the purchase of the materials. You must first decide whether the lab's obligation to deliver first-quality photographs should be drafted as one section or two—one for the general obligation as to quality and the other as to the lab's obligation to use specific products. As the obligation to deliver a quality product is short, it can be combined easily with its related business points. Again, formatting is used to enhance the provision's clarity.

Quality of the Finished Photographs. The Lab shall print first-quality photographs. Without limiting the generality of the preceding sentence, the Lab shall

(a) use, for all nondigital photographs,

    (i) developer manufactured by Chelsea Photo Chemicals, located in New York, New York; and

    (ii) fixer manufactured by Berkshire Photo Materials, located in Egremont, Massachusetts;

and

(b) print all photographs on Axon photographic paper with a matte finish, unless a customer specifies a different finish.

This provision has two levels of micro-organization, both of which rely on chronology. The substance of subsection (a) appears before subsection (b) as the lab must use the chemicals to develop the photographs before it prints them. Subsections (a)(i) and (ii) list the developer first and the fixer second as developer is the first chemical used in the developing process.

26.3.2 CONTRACT CONCEPTS

Contract concepts rarely provide the overarching organizational scheme of a contract's business provisions. Acquisition and financing agreements are the exceptions. Nonetheless, a drafter will sometimes use a contract concept to organize part of a contract that is otherwise organized by subject matter. For example, drafters often appropriately put all of a party's representations and warranties in one section, as was done in Section 10 of the Website Development Agreement (Version 1) (Chapter 32, Document 2).

26.3.3 CHRONOLOGY

Drafters can use chronology to organize provisions, especially in situations where one party's actions depend on the occurrence—or nonoccurrence—of the other party's actions. For example, suppose that a licensor must approve a sample of a trademarked product before its licensee may manufacture it. A well-drafted provision will need to provide a timetable for the approval process: When must the licensee submit a sample of the product? How soon afterwards must the licensor respond, and by when does the licensee need to address the licensor's response? Putting these provisions in chronological order provides the reader with an easy roadmap to follow.

26.3.4 PARTY

Modern contracts are not usually organized so that all of the provisions relating to one party precede all of the provisions relating to the second party. Instead, organization by party is often a secondary level of organization. For example, in an indemnity agreement, each party usually indemnifies the other party against certain risks. Although a drafter could craft the indemnity so that each party indemnifies the other in one section, often the drafter creates separate sections for each party's indemnification obligation. Generally, the remaining provisions of an indemnity agreement are organized by subject matter.

26.4 ORGANIZATION OF ACQUISITION AGREEMENTS

Acquisition agreements are intriguing creatures from an organizational perspective because their organization is multi-layered and uses all of the organizing principles. The overarching organizational principle is contract concept. After the action sections, the agreement's provisions appear in the following order: representations and warranties, then covenants, and finally conditions. The contract concept provisions appear in this order to reflect the chronology of the transaction. The parties represent and warrant to each other on the signing date; covenant with respect to the gap period between signing and closing; and establish conditions to the closing on the closing date.

Each set of contract concept provisions is sub-organized first by party. The seller's provisions precede the buyer's provisions. Finally, each party's provisions are organized by subject matter. As a matter of common practice, these provisions are not organized by relative importance. If they were, the seller's representations and warranties with respect to the financial statements would appear first because they are of the utmost importance to the buyer—who determines the purchase price based on them. Instead, the representations and warranties first establish that the party exists as a legal entity, that it has the authority to enter into the transaction, and that the contract is legal, binding, and enforceable.

Following the articles establishing the conditions to closing, the agreement concludes with the endgame provisions (termination, indemnities, change of name, and noncompete) and the general provisions.

EXERCISES

Exercise 26-1

Determine the organizational scheme of the Escrow Agreement in Chapter 6.

Exercise 26-2

The provisions in the following list regularly appear in employment agreements. They are not in the order in which they would appear in a contract. Reorder the list so that the provisions are in an appropriate order.

1. No oral amendments. _____

2. Anti-assignment provision. _____

3. Bonus. _____

4. Change of control of the Employer (What happens to the Executive on a change of control of the Employer: forced retirement, bonus to keep on working, nothing?). _____

5. Death and disability (financial and contractual ramifications of death or disability). _____

6. Duties (a description of the Executive's responsibilities). _____

7. Effects of the termination of the Executive's employment. _____

8. The Executive represents that entering into this employment agreement does not violate any other agreement to which the Executive is a party. _____

9. The Employer agrees to employ the Executive, and the Executive agrees to work for the Employer. _____

10. Merger (all prior writings and negotiations are merged into this contract; sometimes referred to as the *integration provision*). _____

11. Expense account. _____

12. Extent of service (e.g., full-time or part-time). _____

13. Governing law. _____

14. Waiver of jury trial. _____

15. Insurance and other employee benefits. _____

16. Notices. _____

17. Salary. _____

18. Severability. _____

19. Successors and assigns. _____

20. Term of contract: three years. _____

21. Termination for cause. _____

22. Working facilities (windowed, corner office, or claustrophobic cubicle?). _____

The Drafting Process

27.1 INTRODUCTION

Despite the sarcastic comments of some of your colleagues, drafting a contract requires much more than pulling out a dog-eared precedent and changing the names and the dates. The drafting process is sophisticated. It requires you to integrate your knowledge of business, the business deal, the client's business, the law, and your writing skills. This task is not easy, and it is time-consuming. But it is intellectually rewarding.

This chapter describes the ideal drafting process—what you would do with unlimited time and financial resources. You will rarely have the luxury of being able to follow the process step by step. Instead, you will take shortcuts and find your own way of doing things. But by understanding the full process, you can create a process that works for you and your client.

27.2 AGREEING TO THE BUSINESS TERMS

Most contracts enter the world in the same way. They begin with the parties agreeing to do a deal. It may be as prosaic as the purchase and sale of a house, or as exceptional as a multibillion-dollar joint venture. In a transaction, the parties generally negotiate the key business terms, including price.[1] Once they have done so, each party contacts its lawyers. One of the lawyers will probably draw up a list of the main business points for all parties to review, so that they can confirm the deal's basic terms.

At this juncture, the parties decide whether to enter into a **letter of intent**, also known as a **term sheet** or a **memorandum of understanding**. In it, the parties state the business terms to which they have agreed.

When properly used, letters of intent save the parties time and money. By forcing the parties to think about the transaction's details early on, with luck, the parties will discover any deal breakers or other roadblocks to completing the transaction.

---

1. Other scenarios are, of course, possible. Sometimes an unsophisticated client will meet with a lawyer at a deal's inception. The lawyer will then help the client structure and negotiate the transaction's material terms.

The list of business terms in a letter of intent can be quite short or very detailed, covering almost everything that would appear in a signed agreement. Which approach is chosen depends on how the parties intend to use the document.

Some parties use the letter of intent as a mini-agreement, intending to be bound, but also intending to memorialize the deal in a traditional, full-fledged agreement. Other parties use a letter of intent as a nonbinding, general statement of interest in a transaction on the listed terms. In this context, the letter of intent is the basis of future negotiations, rather than the culminating expression of the negotiations. Nonetheless, the parties may choose to include binding terms with respect to confidentiality, payment of expenses, and the obligation to negotiate in good faith.

If the lawyers do not properly draft the letter of intent, it can become the source of litigation. One party will claim that it bound the parties to the transaction; the other will claim it was merely a preliminary statement of interest. To prevent this, the lawyers must clarify the letter of intent's purpose. If the parties intend it to be nonbinding, it should state clearly that the parties have significant, substantive business issues to negotiate and that the transaction is not binding until memorialized in a definitive, written agreement.

27.3   DETERMINING WHO DRAFTS THE CONTRACT

Before drafting begins, the parties and their lawyers must decide who will draft the contract. Often, however, no one discusses this. Instead, custom and negotiating leverage are determinant. For example, the lender's lawyers always draft the credit agreement and any ancillary agreements; the employer's lawyers always draft the employment agreement; and the publisher's lawyers always draft the book contract. They are risking their money, so they set the ground rules—subject to negotiation.

If custom does not dictate who drafts the contract, and if the other side gives you the opportunity to draft the contract, take it—not because the billings will be greater, but because your client will gain a strategic advantage if you control the drafting process. Specifically, as you begin to incorporate the agreed-on business points into the contract, you will face a myriad of issues that the parties did not discuss. For example, should a representation and warranty be flat or qualified, and if qualified, how? Because you are drafting the contract, you and your client can decide each of these issues to your client's advantage, without violating any ethical proscriptions. You are not changing the deal. You are addressing matters not previously negotiated.

Depending on her caliber, the lawyer on the other side may not question any of the provisions you craft, giving your client a win at no cost. If she does spot an issue, she must ask for a change and negotiate. Although any redraft may tilt the provision toward the other side, the ultimate provision may still be more favorable to your client than if the other side had produced the first draft.

Drafting the contract also means that you can control the deal's tempo. If your client is eager to close the transaction, you can turn around drafts quickly. But if it wants to slow the tempo, you can take your time in drafting and distributing the first draft or revisions.

27.4   LEARNING ABOUT A TRANSACTION

Generally, you will learn about a transaction when a client or supervising lawyer calls you or sends you an e-mail. Although your responsibilities are similar in each situation, they are not the same. This section will first discuss your responsibilities if you are dealing directly with the client and then if you are dealing with a supervising lawyer.

27.4.1 LEARNING ABOUT A TRANSACTION FROM A CLIENT

When a client calls and announces a new transaction, listen carefully to the details. He will probably start by giving you headlines.

> We are hiring a new Executive Vice President, Antoine Johnson. He will be starting June 15th, and we are going to pay him $150,000 per year.

Although these are certainly salient facts, they are not all the facts that you will need to write the contract. If you have been practicing for several years and you specialize in employment law, you may be able to rattle off ten questions without any further research. But if that is not the case, ask the questions that you can think of and then suggest a meeting to discuss the transaction in more detail. Before ending the call, ask the client to bring to the meeting any relevant documents, including any deal memos, letter of intent, correspondence, previous contracts, and notes.

A follow-up meeting is generally better than a follow-up phone call. At a meeting, the conversations tend to be more wide-ranging, and you are more likely to gain a thorough understanding of the deal and the client's goals. The reality, however, is that parties conduct a great deal of business by phone and e-mail.

To prepare for the client meeting, create a checklist of the questions that you want to ask. The checklist should cover all the business terms to be incorporated into the agreement. If you are working at a firm, it may have a checklist for each type of transaction that the firm regularly handles. You can add to this checklist (or create your own) by reviewing agreements from prior transactions. If you are creating your own checklist, always look at more than one agreement, so that you review as wide a variety of provisions as possible. Also, look at forms in treatises, continuing legal education materials, and industry association materials. In addition, you can find agreements online, but take care that they come from reputable sources, so that you can have confidence in their quality.

As part of your preparation for the meeting, draw a diagram of the transaction. If you are drafting a simple lease, the diagram will probably not be of much help. But, with a more sophisticated transaction with multiple parties and mini-transactions, the visual may help you see how these mini-transactions fit together. For example, imagine that your client, a bank, intends to lend $100 million to a corporation. Because the borrower has had some financial trouble in the past, it has agreed to grant a security interest in its assets to the bank. In addition, each of its two subsidiaries will guarantee the borrower's debt and back up its guaranty by granting a security interest in its assets. This may sound complex, but it is actually a relatively simple transaction. Take a look at the diagram on the following page.

At the client meeting, begin by getting an overview of the transaction and the client's attitude toward it. If the client is eager to discuss the details of the transaction, then postpone this preliminary discussion or integrate it into the discussion of deal points.

Assuming that you begin with a general discussion about the transaction, some of the questions that you might ask follow:

- What is the impetus behind the transaction?
- What are the client's business goals and expectations?
- What would constitute a big win?

- What does the client want to avoid?
- What are the hot-button issues and the deal breakers?
- Is the transaction necessary to the company's survival?
- Is timing a factor? Is time of the essence?
- Do the parties have a previous business relationship? If so, are they parties to any other agreements that will affect the new transaction?
- Is the price a bargain, or is it steep?
- Is it a good deal but one that the client will forego if the other side is unreasonable or intransigent?
- Which party has the negotiating leverage?
- How much risk is the client willing to take?

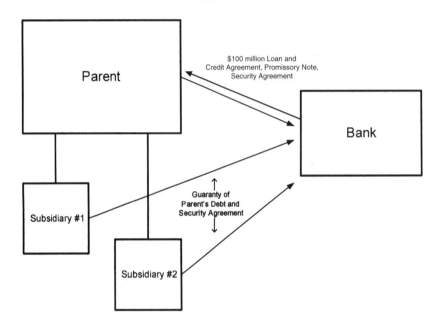

Knowing the answers to these questions will help you to be more than a scrivener. Your advice will be more strategic, and you will be better able to craft a contract that serves the client's needs.

As part of this discussion, go over negotiating strategy with the client. It may seem premature as you have not yet drafted the contract, but this is exactly the right time for the first of these discussions. A contract's first draft opens the bidding for the next round of the negotiations, so how you write its provisions affects how the other side responds. Does the client want to start out with extreme positions on the theory that you cannot get what you do not ask for? Or does the client want to start with more moderate positions to expedite final agreement? If the latter, the unstated message to the other side is that the moderate provisions are close to final, leaving little room for negotiation. In practice, the negotiation strategy will most likely differ depending on the deal and the provision.

As part of the discussion of negotiating strategy, look at the contract from the other side's perspective. What does the other side need to make a deal? Much of this will already have been discovered in the earlier negotiations between the principals. But as you discuss the business issues with your client, discuss whether your client will be more likely to get what it needs if the contract's first draft reflects the other side's needs. At the same time, discuss how the other side may react to specific provisions. If you think that it will have a strong, negative reaction, it may be more strategic for the client to raise the issue directly with the other side's principal.

Next, ask the client how sophisticated the agreement should be. Should you "pull out all the stops" and address every business point that you can think of? If not, should you draft a "down and dirty" contract—that is, a contract that covers only the salient business points? If the latter, the answer may reflect concerns both as to timing and cost. If cost matters, discuss with your client the consequences of not dealing with certain issues. The associated risks may convince her that you should draft a more detailed contract. You could also decide that some points should be dealt with summarily and others, such as the endgame provisions, should be drafted in detail. Of course, these decisions may change during the negotiation.

With these preliminary matters concluded, begin asking specific questions about the transaction. Be sure to keep accurate notes. You will discuss too many issues to rely on your memory.

Use your checklist as a guide for what needs to be discussed. Although the client will need to answer your specific questions, encourage expansive answers. The more you know, the better you can tailor the contract to the client's needs. If the client raises matters that are not on your checklist, explore them or add them to a list for follow up. Also add to that list any questions that the client cannot answer.

As you go through the specific issues on your checklist, the client may instruct you not to address a specific business or legal matter. If so, explore the client's rationale. It may be a negotiating strategy. The client may lack negotiating leverage and fear that raising the issue means losing it. By omitting the issue from the contract, the client postpones the problem until a time when he may be in a stronger position.

The client may also see the risk as sufficiently remote or small that he does not want to spend time and money on it. If so, provide the client with the information needed to knowledgeably decide what to do, and then respect that business decision.

Alternatively, the client may tell you that he has established a terrific working relationship with the other side and can rely on its good faith to work out any issues. If so, gently remind the client that his contact person on the other side could change jobs, leaving him with just the contract and its provisions.

As you discuss this matter with the client, keep in mind that his focus on the relationship reflects a legitimate approach to negotiating and drafting contracts. Indeed, it prevails in Japan. Because the Japanese focus on the relationship, they usually put less emphasis on memorializing the deal and will agree to a much less detailed, shorter contract. Nonetheless, American contracts are negotiated in a different culture, where failing to address an issue can be dangerous. Ultimately, again, your client must decide.

Finally, a client may want to avoid contentious or unpleasant issues. This can be particularly true with endgame provisions. When putting together a deal, clients often want to focus on its success, not its potential failure. They will resist attempts to address the consequences of the deal foundering. Here, your objectivity can be quite valuable to a client. You can lay out the advantages and disadvantages of including the endgame provisions, as well as the relative merits of specific provisions. Again, the client must decide, but that decision will be a considered one if you do your job right.

As part of this interview, you may also want to ask whether you or the client will take the "laboring oar" in the negotiations. Although lawyers often negotiate contracts, some business executives are excellent negotiators and want to take the lead on key business terms.

Before the meeting concludes, discuss timing. When does the client want to see a draft, and how quickly does he want to distribute it to the other side? In addition, review what you are to do and any matters on which the client should follow up.

The initial meeting will give you plenty of information with which to work. As you start using it and other information that you gather, you will think of more questions. This is as it should be.

27.4.2 LEARNING ABOUT A TRANSACTION FROM A SUPERVISING LAWYER

Learning about a new transaction from a supervising lawyer resembles, but is not the same as, learning about it from a client. As a junior lawyer, you should consider more senior lawyers in your office to be your first clients. Therefore, your interactions with them will in many ways mirror the interaction that you will have with a client. But receiving an assignment is often a more passive interaction than meeting with a client. When you learn about a transaction from a supervising lawyer, she will probably have already discussed the transaction with the client. When you meet with your supervising lawyer, your job is to ensure that she thoroughly and accurately transfers all that information to you.

Listen carefully to confirm that you understand the nature of the transaction. Are you to draft a sublease or a lease assignment? If you are to draft an employment agreement, should you also draft a noncompetition agreement? You should leave the meeting with all the information and documents that you would have had if you had been to a client meeting, including deal memos, letters of intent, correspondence, previous contracts, and notes. If you need other information, ask for it. Also ask questions if you do not understand something. Do not be embarrassed. As a junior lawyer, you can ask *almost* any question without others thinking it a dumb question. Senior lawyers expect you to ask questions at the initial meeting and to return later with more questions.

Before you leave, find out the deadline. The supervisor may give you any one or more of three deadlines.

1. The date by which you must submit your draft to the supervising lawyer.
2. The date by which the supervising lawyer must submit a draft to the client.
3. The date by which your office must deliver the agreement to the other party.

27.5   PREPARING TO DRAFT A CONTRACT

27.5.1 RESEARCHING THE LAW AND OBTAINING THE ADVICE OF SPECIALISTS

Before beginning to draft, determine what legal issues the transaction raises. For example, will the endgame provisions include a liquidated damages provision? If so, you may need to research the law to help you and your client choose a dollar amount that adequately compensates the injured party, but does not convert the provision into an unenforceable penalty provision. Similarly, you must also consider whether any statutes affect the agreement. Must you deal with securities regulations, environmental laws, or U.C.C. provisions?

You cannot — and should not — research all of an agreement's legal issues before you begin drafting. First, you may not know about an issue until you are working on a specific provision. Second, the client may want to distribute a draft to the other side as quickly as possible. Third, others in your office may have subject matter expertise. Speaking with those lawyers will often save you time and the client money.

In any transaction, you *must* obtain the advice of an accountant or a tax lawyer, or both, unless you understand the subtleties of all the issues raised. Almost always, these issues require a specialist's expertise because of their implications. In more sophisticated transactions, these issues might require the transaction's structure to be changed or the deal to be abandoned. Because of these consequences, talk with the accountants and tax lawyers as early as possible in the transaction.

27.5.2 RESEARCHING THE PARTIES AND THE INDUSTRY

As this book repeatedly explains, before drafting a contract, you must fully understand the business deal. Often, to do this, you must research the client, the other side, and their industry. What you learn will enable you to add value to the deal because of your ability to find and resolve issues that you might otherwise have missed.

For example, assume that your client, a bank, has agreed to lend $5 million to a jewelry manufacturer. As part of the transaction, the borrower has agreed to grant the bank a security interest in its inventory. Taking the security interest may be more complicated than you would expect. In the jewelry industry, manufacturers often consign individual pieces of jewelry to their customers, retail stores. Sometimes, these consignments are properly documented with U.C.C. filings. Frequently, however, a manufacturer and its customer operate on a more informal basis. The manufacturer gives the retailer the jewelry "on memo," a short document that recites that the manufacturer has transferred the jewelry to the retailer. The parties file no U.C.C. forms. Without knowing how the borrower's industry functions, you could not draft the proper papers to document the bank's security interest.

With the advent of the Internet, researching a client, the other side, and the parties' industry has become much easier. By going online, you can find annual reports, recent articles, and research analysts' reports. As you sift through this information, try to determine the issues with which the industry—and the parties—are grappling. Then, assess the information and how you can use it to your client's advantage.

If the other side is a public company, also check the SEC's EDGAR database for agreements that it has entered into.[2] If you find one for a transaction similar to the one you are working on, you may be able to use it against the other side during the negotiations. For example, if the other side insists on a materiality qualifier for a specific representation and warranty, but previously gave it flat,[3] you can argue more forcefully that no qualifier is required.

27.6 DRAFTING WITH AND WITHOUT A PRECEDENT

27.6.1 CHOOSING A PRECEDENT

In a drafting context, **precedent** refers to a contract from an earlier transaction, but lawyers also use it to refer to forms. In both cases, lawyers use the precedent as the basis of a new agreement. Think of a precedent as a template that you tailor for each transaction.

Almost all drafting done today begins with a precedent for two reasons. First, it is efficient. Precedents save time and money. Rather than reinventing the wheel for each new deal, a lawyer gets a head start. Second, if the precedent is a good one, using it will reduce errors and improve a contract's quality.

Precedents abound. Generally, you will not have a problem finding them. The more difficult task will be choosing the right one. If you are working directly with a client, ask whether it has a preferred form that it would like you to use. Carefully review it, however, to confirm that it is appropriate for the new transaction. Clients generally are not lawyers and may not understand why a particular form is inappropriate.

---

2. http://www.sec.gov/edgar.shtml.

3. See §3.2.4 for an explanation of a *flat representation*.

If you are working for a supervising lawyer, ask that person to recommend a precedent. Lawyers tend to use the same precedent again and again because they are familiar with it and comfortable with its quality. If you use a different one, the supervising lawyer will compare your draft to her precedent, which may only result in your changing the draft so that it more closely resembles that precedent.

If no one gives you a precedent to use, you will need to look for one. If you work in a firm or a general counsel's office, ask your colleagues whether they have a contract from an earlier deal that would work for your transaction. In addition, find out whether your firm or company has a form bank. Many firms and general counsel offices create forms for each type of transaction they handle. Some even annotate the form's provisions with explanations and instructions on how to tailor them. These forms and contracts should be your first choice because of their quality. In addition, you may have ready access to the precedent's drafter, who can explain the purpose behind provisions that you do not understand.

If you do not obtain a precedent from someone in your office or from the client, you can obtain forms from industry associations, treatises, continuing legal education materials, and online. Be wary of all these precedents; quality varies.

In addition to finding forms online from various vendors, you can search the SEC's EDGAR database. It includes contracts that public companies have entered into and then filed to comply with their disclosure obligations.

When choosing between precedents, follow these guidelines:

Guidelines for Choosing Precedents

1. *Choose a precedent that is for the same type of transaction.* Do not choose a share purchase agreement if your transaction is a merger.

2. *Choose a precedent where the party in your client's position had the greater negotiating leverage.* For example, assume that you represent the landlord in the lease of a 35-story building at a time when demand for space is high and first-class space is generally unavailable. In this case, you would want to avoid leases that were negotiated when the real estate market was in the doldrums and tenants had the negotiating leverage. A lease from a time when the market was thriving would probably include more landlord-friendly provisions.

3. *Do not use an executed agreement as a precedent.* It includes all the concessions that the party in your client's position made, so it is not a good place from which to start. Instead, look for a draft of the agreement, preferably one several iterations earlier than the executed agreement. If you can find it, the first draft sent to the other side makes a good precedent. It will include your colleagues' and the client's comments and will reflect your side's opening positions.

In addition to choosing a precedent to use as the base document for your draft, retain other good precedents that you find. You can use them as additional resources as you draft. Analyzing multiple versions of the same provision will help you assess the precedent's provision and give you ideas on the different ways to draft its substance.

27.6.2 USING A PRECEDENT

A case precedent guides the court as it decides how to rule. But because a case is rarely on "all fours" with another, judges must find the similarities and the differences and tailor their opinions accordingly. You should approach a precedent's provisions the same way. They should *guide* you as you draft the agreement for your transaction. A precedent's words are not engraved in stone. If you are using a form, it represents what others have considered a good starting place. Those who created it intended drafters to modify it to memorialize each new transaction. Similarly, if you are using a contract from an earlier deal, the provisions are not specific to your deal, so you must change them.

Using a contract from an earlier deal can be a nightmare when you first begin working as a lawyer. At this stage in your career, you may have trouble discerning whether a provision is deal specific or is simply something you do not understand. You cannot "punt" and leave it in the contract, assuming that it must be correct. This would result in a "mindless markup." Neither can you just delete it, assuming that it is wrong or inapplicable. You must determine its purpose and then decide whether to keep it, modify it, or delete it. If you have access to several drafts of the agreement that you are using as a precedent, comparing them may help you determine a provision's role. Having a treatise at hand while drafting may also be helpful.

You will confront one other problem with precedents: Many are poorly drafted from a stylistic perspective, even those whose substance is top-notch. In a perfect world, you would redraft each of these provisions, using what you have learned in your law school drafting course and your practice experience. Unfortunately, you generally will not have that option. Redrafting a provision is time-consuming, and you probably will not have that time in a fast-paced transaction. In addition, your firm will want to bill that time to the client, who may resist paying the firm for work it considers unnecessary.

When at a firm and confronted with a poorly drafted provision, determine whether the existing language creates an ambiguity. If it does, redraft it, but mention your change in the cover memo to the supervising lawyer.[4] Her perspective may differ from yours. If the provision is unambiguous, but otherwise is poorly drafted, use the provision as is and then deal with its problems after the transaction finishes. Then, consult with the firm's "keeper of the forms," who will probably appreciate your input. Do not change the firm's master form without permission.

You may be able to change your approach to redrafting poorly drafted provisions as you become a more experienced lawyer. As you gain the confidence of your supervising lawyers, they may give you greater latitude to rework a form's provisions.

If you have your own firm, you will probably be unable to clean up a precedent all at once, even if you want to, because of the other demands on your time. Instead, redraft one or two provisions each time you use the precedent. By spreading out the work over time, you will be able to manage the task more readily.

27.6.3 DRAFTING WITHOUT A PRECEDENT

Occasionally, you may need to draft a contract for which you can find no precedent. If this occurs, take a step back and think about the substantive provisions that the contract will need. Do other contracts have similar provisions, even if they are not exactly on point? Can you draft the contract by patching together relevant provisions from different agreements?

For example, suppose a shareholder requests a new share certificate to replace the one that he has lost. Your client, the corporation that issued the share certificate, is willing to replace it but does not want to be liable if someone subsequently presents the original. The corporation asks that you draft something to protect it. You agree to do so but then cannot find a precedent.

---

4. See §27.8.4.1.

Although you lack an exact precedent, you can borrow and modify the substantive provisions of other contracts. From a business perspective, your client has two goals. First, it wants the shareholder's assurance that he still owns the shares and that the reason the share certificate is "missing" is that he lost it, not because he transferred it to a third party. Second, your client wants to be able to sue the shareholder for damages if someone else presents the original certificate.

To accomplish these business goals, you can borrow substantive provisions from two agreements. To address your client's first concern, you could modify a representation and warranty on share ownership from a share purchase agreement.

> **Shareholder's Representations and Warranties**. The Shareholder represents and warrants to the Corporation that the Shareholder
>
> (a) owns the shares represented by Certificate No. 3345;
>
> (b) has not transferred to any third party the shares represented by Certificate No. 3345; and
>
> (c) has lost Certificate No. 3345.

To deal with your client's second concern, you could draft an indemnity provision, tailoring the subject matter performance provision of almost any indemnity agreement.

> **Indemnification**. The Shareholder shall indemnify and defend the Corporation against any liabilities and losses arising from the Shareholder's loss of Certificate No. 3345.

With these key business provisions in place, you can draft the remainder of the contract.

27.7 THE LOGISTICS OF DRAFTING A CONTRACT

If you are drafting a contract using a precedent, first copy the precedent and put the original aside. Always keep the precedent unchanged, so that it can be used again. Do this whether you are working with an electronic precedent or a hard copy.

If you are going to hand-mark changes on a hard copy of the precedent, photocopy the original onto 8½ by 14-inch paper and reduce the size of the photocopy to 90%. This will give you more room for your mark-up and will make it easier for you or your assistant to read the changes to be made.

Every draft of the contract that you distribute, whether internally where you work, to the client, or to third parties, should be numbered and dated, in the right or left header.

> **Draft #1**
> **June 13, 20XX**

This information not only distinguishes one draft from the next, but also may be some evidence that the draft was not intended as a final and binding agreement.[5]

Be sure to distinguish internal drafts from those sent to third parties. If you distribute two drafts at your firm before sending the agreement outside the firm, those distributions could be *Internal Draft #1* and *Internal Draft #2*. The first distribution outside the firm would be *Draft #1*.

Next, set up electronic file systems to keep track of the internal and external drafts. With respect to the electronic copies of the agreement, create a folder for each draft and keep in it the draft that was distributed and any electronic comments that you receive. By keeping a copy of each draft, you can always easily reinsert into Draft #4, for example, the provision that you deleted from Internal Draft #2. In addition, you will have electronic precedents available for future transactions.

You may also want hard-copy files. If so, use one accordion-type expandable folder for each draft. In it, put a hard copy of the draft, along with all the comments that you received from your colleagues, whether electronically or on a hard copy of the agreement. In addition to keeping you organized, this system signals to your supervising lawyer that you are organized and in control of what you are doing. Partners and other supervising lawyers worry. They worry about every aspect of a transaction, including whether you know what you are doing. If you can reduce their worry quotient, that will reduce the pressure on you.

27.8 DRAFTING A CONTRACT

27.8.1 OTHER DRAFTERS

Although you may draft most of the contract, others in your office may be responsible for drafting portions of it. For example, when drafting a bank loan agreement, you might need inserts drafted by members of the environmental, labor, tax, and real estate departments. Those lawyers will appreciate your giving them as much lead time as possible.

27.8.2 TRANSLATING THE BUSINESS DEAL INTO CONTRACT CONCEPTS

Before beginning to draft, list all the provisions that you have to draft. Use the deal memo or letter of intent as a starting point. Then check your notes from discussions with the client or supervising lawyer, and go through the precedents and secondary materials. (You may have already done the latter if you created your own checklist or added to one that you obtained from your firm or elsewhere.) In addition, consider whether the cascade effect[6] will require you to draft any new provisions or change any existing provisions. Also, use the five-prong framework (discussed in Chapter 25) to analyze whether the contract must address any other deal-specific business issues. Finally, review the different ways that the parties' relationship could evolve, and confirm that you and the client have settled on a way to deal with each of them—ask "What if?" All of this is time-consuming but critical to the drafting process.

Once you have listed all the business terms, translate them into contract concepts. Then, reorganize the list so that the business terms appear in the order in which they

---

5. *See In re Windsor Plumbing Supply Co., Inc.*, 170 B.R. 503, 522-523 (Bankr. E.D.N.Y. 1994); *Girardi v. Shaffer*, 2003 WL 23138445 at *7 (Bankr. E.D. Va. Jan. 17, 2003).

6. See §23.2.

will appear in the contract. Use your precedent and the principles that you learned in Chapter 26 to help you order the list. As a help for organization, consider having a separate piece of paper for each aspect of what you are organizing. If you're drafting an acquisition agreement, then gather all the needed representations on one page, covenants on a second page, and conditions on a third. (Of course, you could alternatively do this in an electronic document.) As you are doing this, keep asking yourself if there is a cascade effect—a covenant that you need because you added a representation and warranty. If you're organizing the contract by subject matter, each subject should have its own page. When you have finished all this (of course, you can do this electronically), you are ready to draft. After you have practiced for a while, you should be able to truncate this process. But, in the beginning, it will help you to go through all the steps.

27.8.3   DRAFTING THE FIRST DRAFT

27.8.3.1   How to Begin

Where do you begin? How do you actually decide what to write? Drafters differ in their approach, and your approach may change depending on the agreement. You may not want to start with the introductory provisions. You may have an idea for a tough provision and want to try drafting it right away. But absent a good reason to start somewhere else, start with the introductory provisions. Drafting these provisions first will establish the defined terms for the parties and will begin to put words on the page. Writer's block can be as much of a problem when writing contracts as when writing memos and briefs.

27.8.3.2   The Definitions

Although the definitions article generally follows the words of agreement, drafting *all* the definitions is *not* the next thing to do. Many drafters prefer to skip the definitions article entirely and deal with a definition only when they need the defined term to draft a provision. This practice works well because it forces the drafter to see the definition in the context in which it will be used. It also works well for lawyers who place definitions in context.

Some drafters do draft some of the definitions before they turn to the contract's substantive provisions. Those who do so generally work on definitions that they know they need to revise. (The ability to do this develops as you work on multiple deals and become familiar with the regularly used definitions.) These drafters then deal with the remaining definitions as needed.

Whether you skip the definitions or draft some of them early on, stay sensitive to the need to draft new ones. Draft them while you are working on the relevant provisions.

As you work with the definitions, remember that they are being incorporated into substantive contract provisions and that they will have substantive consequences. They are standards that, when changed, affect the business deal and the parties' rights and obligations. Accordingly, make sure that each definition works each time its defined term is used.

27.8.3.3   The Business Provisions

After the definitions, turn to your list of business points. If you have organized that list so that it coordinates with the sequence of the contract's provisions, you have a roadmap for working through the contract. But you will probably not stay on a straight path to the signature lines. Drafting is not linear.[7] Contracts evolve, and the process is often messy.

As you work through the contract, you will constantly refine your ideas and what you have drafted. You will see issues that were not apparent when you started drafting. You may decide on a new provision or do wholesale redrafts of provisions you thought you had finished. You may also decide not to revise all of the provisions your first time through the contract. You may prefer to make the easy changes in one round of revisions and then, in the next, return to the more sophisticated provisions. Or, you may draft all the points in the letter of intent in the first mark up and turn to all the other provisions in the next. Most drafters go through three or four rounds of revisions before they have a first draft to distribute.

Some provision hopping should be part of your planned approach to drafting. Indeed, it is good practice to work on related provisions at the same time. For example, if you are drafting an acquisition agreement, you should draft the seller's representation and warranty about its equipment and the related covenant about maintaining that equipment at the same time. This will decrease the possibility that the provisions will have different standards and violate the *say the same thing the same way* rule.[8] Similarly, provision hopping makes sense if you add a new provision that causes a cascade effect. If you choose not to draft related provisions at the same time, make a margin note in the precedent at the intended location of the second provision to remind yourself of what you still have to do.

As you work through the contract, you will have questions. Do not stop drafting and wait to get an answer. Instead, do one or more of the following:

- Create a list of questions to ask your client or supervising lawyer. (Do not call or e-mail every time you have a question.)
- Put the provision about which you have a question in brackets. (This option works well if you will not be able to ask a question before submitting your draft.)
- Craft two or more versions of the provision, putting each in brackets. (This shows the reader the options.)
- Describe the issue in the cover memo to your supervising lawyer or the client. (By explaining the issue, you may help the reader decide how to handle it.)

Also, set up a system to deal with cross-references. As you draft, you may find that one provision needs to refer to another. Because provisions will change their location as you work through the drafting process, you need to track the cross-references so that you can update them properly when you finalize the contract. To deal with this, insert the correct cross-reference at the time of the initial drafting in a large bold font inside a set of brackets. Then, later, you can search for a bracket or the bold reference, and insert the revised cross-reference. Alternatively, some word-processing programs can keep track if you properly code the cross-reference.

Choosing the right words to express the deal is challenging—and fun. As you have seen throughout this book, the smallest change in a word or a phrase affects the parties' rights and obligations. Use your knowledge of the business and legal consequences of the contract concepts to guide you in tailoring the provisions. For example, draft a representation and warranty broadly and with no qualifiers if your client will receive the representations and warranties. Keep the following guidelines in mind while you are drafting:

---

7. Scott J. Burnham, *Drafting and Analyzing Contracts* 318 (3d ed., LexisNexis 2003).

8. See §21.5.

Contract Drafting Guidelines

1. *Do not recut the deal.* Although you are more than a scrivener, you are not a principal. Do not draft a provision so that it favors your client more than the agreed-on deal intended. Doing so could be an ethical violation.

2. *Determine whether one party will have more control.* If you represent the less-powerful party, you may be able to protect it better with detailed provisions that spell out its rights.

3. *Determine whether vagueness or specificity will benefit your client.* The answer is usually provision specific.

4. *If the contract establishes a relationship that will exist for a term of years, build in flexibility so that each change in circumstances does not create a contractual crisis.*

5. *Use the canons of construction to give you insight into how a court might interpret a provision.* Then, rewrite the provision if the parties' intent differs from that possible interpretation.

6. *Do not rely on the canons of interpretation to put a gloss on what you are drafting.* Instead, clarify any unclear or ambiguous provisions. The canons of interpretation are a last resort — something to give you and your client comfort if a provision cannot be clarified because of the client's weak negotiating position. (Once you raise the problem with the provision, if the other party has superior negotiating leverage, that party may try to strengthen the provision so that it favors it even more.)

7. *Draft the contract to deal with all the possibilities of an* if/then *scenario.* As you have seen, covenants, discretionary authority, and declarations can be subject to conditions. When you draft a provision that sets out an *if/then* business term, think through what happens if the opposite fact pattern occurs. Does the contract already provide for this possibility? If not, discuss with your client how to handle this new situation. For example, the endgame provisions of most employment agreements deal with the possibility of a termination for cause.

> **Termination for Cause.** If the Company terminates the Executive for Cause, the Company shall pay the Executive . . .

This *if/then* scenario should make you think of another: termination without cause.

8. *Draft a real-world, pragmatic contract that reflects how the parties will interact.* Good writing alone does not make a good contract. If a contract's provisions are impractical and will not work on a day-to-day basis, redraft them.

As noted earlier, it may take three or four rounds of revisions to produce your "first draft." As you refine it to reflect the business deal as accurately as possible, also look at the contract from a good writing perspective and do the following:

- Create clarity through format.
- Create clarity through sentence structure.
- Eliminate legalese.
- Eliminate ambiguity.

27.8.3.4   Finalizing the Contract

To finalize the contract, run your word-processing program's Spell Check. But beware: Spell Check does not pick up a misspelled word that creates another word (e.g., *there*

v. *their*). Also, check that all cross-references are correct. Then, print out a hard copy and proofread it carefully. No matter how facile you are with a computer, you will find substantive errors and glitches when reviewing a hard copy that you will not find when looking at the contract on a computer screen. Read the contract slowly and look at what you wrote and see if it coincides with what you thought you wrote.

27.8.4 REDRAFTING THE CONTRACT

No contract is ever finished after the first draft. Most lawyers are inveterate revisers and cannot read a document without a pencil in hand to mark comments. Anyone who reads your draft, whether a supervising lawyer or a client, will have comments. Receiving comments does not mean that you did a poor job. It is part of the drafting process. Even senior lawyers will have other lawyers review their drafts. In a large firm, you may need to take comments from several lawyers — generally lawyers in other departments who did not give you their input as you were working on your first draft. By working through all these comments, the contract will improve, and you will learn a great deal about drafting.

You will receive comments in several ways. Some readers will talk through their comments with you. This can be helpful because it gives you an opportunity to ask questions. You can take notes on these conversations in two basic ways: by hand or on your computer. Some drafters like to use Microsoft Word's Comment function, taking notes in a "balloon" adjacent to the applicable draft language. Other drafters prefer to take handwritten notes. If you prefer the latter, create extra room for note-taking by photocopying the draft onto 8½ by 14-inch paper and reducing the copy to 90%. When you take notes, consider using a different color pen or pencil for each person. By color-coding readers' comments, you will find it easier to report who made which comments. Your client or supervising lawyer may need this information to reconcile conflicting comments.

Some readers mark their comments on a copy of the draft and then give you the draft. Always follow up if you cannot decipher a notation. Others will use a word-processing program's Comment function[9] or input changes on an electronic copy of the contract and give you a redlined version. (A redlined[10] document shows changes by underlining new language and striking through deleted language.)

As you receive or read through comments, think through whether they are correct. They may not be. You may have already dealt with a point elsewhere, or the comment may be inconsistent with your understanding of the business deal or another comment you have received. If you disagree with a comment, discuss it with the person who made the comment.

Look carefully at each provision before you modify it. You may need to change additional language in that provision so that the requested change works properly. You may also need to change another provision or draft a new one because of the cascade effect. If you cut and paste in a new provision from another agreement, check that the relevant standards in the revised contract are consistent. Sometimes you will inadvertently introduce a new standard.

When you finish making the requested changes, read the entire contract. Inevitably, you will find glitches and substantive issues that you and others did not see. You

---

9. The Comment function in Microsoft Word permits a reader to insert a balloon in a document's margin and to write a comment in the balloon. Each balloon is connected to the relevant part of the document by a dotted line.

10. A synonym for *redlined* is *blacklined*.

may be the only one readily able to spot these problems because of your familiarity with the contract.

With that, you have completed your first draft for external distribution.

27.8.4.1 The Cover Memo

When you distribute the first draft of the contract (indeed, any draft), send it with a cover memo that

- tells the reader where to find the provisions that deal with hot-button issues;
- explains the risks and benefits of provisions not previously discussed; and
- describes open issues and proposes ways of resolving them.

If you take notes on these points as you draft, writing this memo will be much easier.

Spend time on the memo. Keeping the client (or supervising lawyer) informed is part of your job. Indeed, you have an ethical obligation to keep the client informed.[11] A short, well-written memo that highlights the salient issues will help you do that.

Choose the recipients of your memo carefully. If it contains privileged information, sending it to the wrong person could destroy the attorney/client privilege.

Document 7 in Chapter 32 discusses in more depth the drafting of memoranda to the client. Section 28.7.2 discusses memoranda to the other side after reviewing its draft.

---

11. Model R. of Prof. Conduct 1.4(a)(3) (2006). See §30.3.

EXERCISES

Exercise 27-1

Your client has called and wants to come in for a meeting. She has decided to create a website for her business and must sign a contract with a marketing company. Create a checklist of questions to ask her. Use the Website Development Agreement (Version 1)—Document 2 in Chapter 32—as a starting place. In addition, find at least two other website development agreements and use their provisions to create additional checklist questions.

Exercise 27-2

Diagram the following transaction: A corporation (Parent) is the sole shareholder of Sub A and owns 51% of the outstanding shares of Sub B. The target (Target) is a wholly owned subsidiary of Target-Parent. Target is to merge into Sub A, with Sub A the surviving corporation. Sub A will pay Target-Parent with funds it borrows from Big Bank. Sub A has agreed to secure its debt by granting a security interest in all its assets to Big Bank. Parent will guarantee Sub A's debt and will back up the guaranty by pledging the shares it owns in Sub A and Sub B.

Exercise 27-3

Research letters of intent and then draft the language that you would use to clarify that a letter of intent did not bind the parties to consummate the transaction.

How to Review and Comment on a Contract

28.1 INTRODUCTION

Every contract has two drafters: the lawyer who writes the initial draft and the lawyer who reviews that draft. In some ways, reviewing a contract is more difficult than writing it. Not only must a reviewing lawyer prepare for that review in the same way a drafter prepares to draft, the reviewing lawyer must also try to determine what the drafter was thinking when the provision was written. A provision that seems reasonable on its face may be problematic. The drafting lawyer knows what was intended. The reviewing lawyer must divine that intent by reverse engineering. He must look at the finished product and figure out the thinking process that created it.

In this chapter, you will learn how to analyze a contract, identify key issues, and give comments. Just as drafting requires more than changing the names and dates in a precedent, analyzing a contract requires more than reading it. Here are the five steps:

1. Prepare.
2. Get your bearings.
3. Read and analyze the key business provisions.
4. Read and analyze the entire contract.
5. Mark up the contract and give comments.

28.2 PREPARE

Before you read the other side's draft, you must prepare in exactly the same way you would have if you had been the drafter. You must

- obtain all available information about the business deal;
- create a checklist of questions for the client;
- thoroughly interview the client;
- research the law, the other party, and the parties' industry;
- find appropriate precedents;
- create a list of business issues and deal terms (both those that the parties have agreed to and any new ones to be incorporated);

■ translate them into contract concepts; and

■ organize the business terms in the sequence in which you expect that they will appear in the contract.

Without this preparation, you cannot effectively review a contract. You will not have the knowledge of the business deal or the tools to determine whether the draft appropriately memorializes that deal.

28.3   CONTRACT ANALYSIS: HOW TO READ AND UNDERSTAND A CONTRACT PROVISION

Every lawyer who confronts an unread contract has (or should have) a knot in her stomach. The task on which she is about to embark tests the mettle of even the best lawyers. She is going to *read* the contract. But what does that mean? It is much more than reading words on the page. The lawyer must understand the implications of the words from a business, legal, and practical perspective.

To read a contract, you must break it down provision by provision and analyze each provision separately. You must ask and answer at least six questions virtually simultaneously.

■ What is the business purpose of the provision?
■ Does the provision properly incorporate the agreed-on business deal?
■ Can the provision better protect the client and reduce the risk?
■ Can the provision further advance the client's goals?
■ Are there legal issues?
■ Are there drafting issues?"

These questions are the short-form framework for contract analysis. The long-form framework has eight questions with a total of 14 subparts.[1] So contract reading . . . is contract analysis, but contract analysis is not the same as contract interpretation.

Contract interpretation assumes an ambiguity or a lack of clarity. Contract analysis precedes this determination. It asks the questions that provide the insight into the provision's meaning and effect. Contract analysis may well lead you to conclude that a provision is ambiguous, but it goes way beyond and . . . asks, "What business, legal, and drafting issues are shrouded here?"

The ability to perform contract analysis is a deal-critical skill. To analyze a contract means to disassemble it to understand the other side's objectives and the contract's business, legal, and drafting nuances and the issues raised. Stated differently, a deal lawyer eats what she kills;[2] that is, she protects her client by determining what must be negotiated after reading the other side's draft contract. Each point found counts as a kill, a point to be negotiated and possibly won. If the lawyer instead concludes, "It all seems good to me," she and her client will not celebrate with a lavish lunch. Instead, the lawyer will starve, having squandered negotiating points that she never found or raised. Because there was no kill, the lawyer has surrendered points not ever subject to negotiation.[3]

---

1. The appendix to this chapter sets out the long-form framework.

2. The phrase, *a lawyer eats what she kills,* is a play on the large-firm method of compensating its partners. When this method is used, a firm pays a lawyer only for the business she has originated; that is, what she killed and brought home to the firm.

3. Tina L. Stark, *At the Heart of the Matter: Reading Contracts Dealing with Risks in Transactions,* 14 Tenn. J. of Bus. L. 309, 310-311 (special ed. 2013).

You have spent the semester learning how to analyze a contract. You just may not have been aware of it. The lessons were integrated into learning to draft. First, you learned the contract concepts and their respective business and legal purposes. Then, you practiced reading a contract and recognizing what contract concept was used to memorialize the business term. You also learned the *close reading skill*: What did individual words mean and what was the client's business perspective on these words? (Adding value to the deal.) Finally, you engaged in *guided reading*, where you reviewed unfamiliar contracts, but you worked your way through them with the help of annotations that explained new concepts and others that asked "thinking" questions. With this expertise, you are ready to analyze a contract's provisions.

28.4 GET YOUR BEARINGS

The first time you look at a contract, you should "eyeball" it. "Eyeballing" a contract is less than skimming it. It means looking through the pages to obtain an overview. How is the contract organized? By subject matter? By contract concept? Is its organization similar to the precedents? How does it differ? Where are the action sections? Do the captions look familiar, or does the contract contain provisions that you had not expected?

With this information, you will gain a sense of the contract in the same way that you would gain the sense of a history textbook by looking at its table of contents and flipping through the pages. You will not have the details, but you will know where the details are and whether the contract at least appears to be within the expected norm.

28.5 READ THE KEY BUSINESS PROVISIONS

Once you have your bearings, review the key business provisions to see if the contract has correctly stated the most significant business terms. Clients frequently call shortly after you receive a contract—often before you could have reasonably been expected to have reviewed it fully. By looking at the key business provisions first, you will be able to address the client's immediate concerns. When reading, focus on the substance of the business deal, not on how you might change specific wording. You will deal with that when you do the markup.

Generally, you should read the payment provisions in the action sections first. Clients often consider these to be a contract's most important provisions. Has the other side gotten the money right? If not, the contract has either been poorly drafted, or the parties have had a serious misunderstanding.

Next, look at the endgame provisions. Look at them from two perspectives: When does the other side have rights against your client, and when does your client have rights against the other side? Also, confirm that the contract ties up all the loose ends—for example, look to see if the contract provides for the return of deposits and post-termination payments. Finally, remember that endgame and money provisions often go hand in hand. Under what circumstances will your client lose the benefits of the contract, and how much will that cost?

Then, turn to the provisions dealing with the most significant other business terms. These may not be intuitively obvious. Sometimes, these points reflect concerns specific to your client. For example, assume that you represent an executive in connection with the negotiation and drafting of her employment agreement. The executive may have a special interest in a charity because of her family's circumstances (an illness, for example). As a partial inducement, the employer may have agreed to donate $50,000 a year to that charity. This issue probably does not appear on any treatise checklist or in any precedent, but it may matter greatly to your client.

28.6   READ THE ENTIRE CONTRACT

After reading the key business provisions, read the entire contract. Start from the beginning. Imagine that you are drafting the contract and marking up a precedent. As you look at each provision, think about what changes you would make. These provisions are not engraved in stone. Many are merely the other side's opening bid with respect to issues that the parties did not discuss. You cannot recut the business deal, but you can negotiate how it is memorialized.

If the contract includes a definitions article, you may take two different approaches to its review. If you have not previously drafted or reviewed this type of contract, consider initially skipping the article entirely, but then returning to it each time you confront a defined term. If you have previously drafted or reviewed this type of contract, look for key definitions and skim them to see if they seem relatively standard. If not, pay special attention to the provisions that include the related defined terms. The drafter may have made substantive changes to relatively standard provisions by changing the definitions. In either event, physically separate the definitions article from the rest of the contract. This will enable you to place it and the contract side by side, so that you can look at a definition and a provision at the same time.

As you continue through the contract, do not be tied in your review to the order of the contract provisions. Instead, mimic the drafting process. Provision-hop as necessary so that you review related provisions at the same time. Once you deal with a point, go back to where you left off, so that you cover every provision. Some drafters check off each provision after they have read it.

As you go through the contract, you will analyze provisions as prosaic as the introductory provisions and as substantive as the action sections. To help you focus on the business issues, use the five-prong framework from Chapter 25 the same way you would have had you been the drafter. Review the contract slowly or you will miss issues.

You may have stylistic comments: legalese, lack of formatting, and so on. Generally, you should defer to the drafter on these matters. If she still drafts as if she were in eighteenth-century England, so be it. Do not spend negotiating capital on whether the contract should say *aforesaid* or *previously*. Although stylistic comments are generally inappropriate, some drafters appreciate them. It is bad form, however, to raise these points at a negotiating session, especially if clients are present. Instead, mark up the relevant provisions and give them to the drafter privately. You may appropriately note in these comments any misspellings, missing, or incorrect words, or other "glitches."

Look not only at what is in the contract, but for what is missing. Reviewing lawyers tend to focus on the words on the page, not on what is absent. Use your checklist to determine whether all the business terms were included. Also, step back and think about your client's goals. Does the contract achieve those goals, or are other provisions needed?

As you go through the contract, make notes in the margin, circle problem language, or otherwise indicate any concern that you have with the language. Do not make the comments too cryptic, or you will have trouble recalling your point, especially if the contract is long. Also, do not do a detailed markup or draft inserts as you go through the contract this time. Subsequent provisions may affect your view of a provision. In addition, you will need the client's input.

That said, here are some questions that you should ask each time you review a contract. Some are pure drafting issues, others part of your contract analysis.

1. Are the parties' names and other information in the preamble correct? Are the correct parties being bound? (See Chapter 6.)
2. Are the recitals accurate? What would be the effect on your client if they became stipulated facts in a lawsuit? Did the drafter put any substantive provisions in the recitals? (See Chapter 6.)
3. Does each definition work each time a provision uses its defined term?[4] Are any substantive provisions in the definitions? (See Chapter 7.)
4. Are the provisions in the action sections correct? (See Chapter 8.)

   (a) Carefully analyze the monetary provisions. Do they work? Does the contract appropriately restrict your client's obligation to pay? Should the other party be paying your client more? Is the other party creditworthy? Should the conditions to the other party's obligation to pay be more easily satisfied? In all instances, do the payment provisions answer the following questions: *who, what, when, where, why, how,* and *how much*? (See Chapter 8.)

   (b) Does the contract include an effective date? If it does, is the trigger for the effective date properly stated? (See Chapters 6 and 8.)

   (c) If the contract is for a stated term, what could prematurely terminate it?[5] Should the contract term automatically renew? (See Chapter 8.)

5. Are the representations and warranties that your client is being asked to make accurate? Do they allocate too much risk to your client? How can they be qualified to reduce the risk? Does the contract ask your client to make representations and warranties that are unrelated to the transaction? (See Chapters 3 and 9.)
6. Has the other side made representations and warranties? Are they too weak? If so, how can they be strengthened? What additional representations and warranties should they make? (See Chapters 3 and 9.)
7. Can your client perform its covenants? Are they too difficult? Does your client have control over the outcome of each of its covenants? What would decrease the degree of obligation? Should any of the covenants instead be conditions to the other party's obligation to perform? Should any of the covenants include an exception? (See Chapters 3 and 10.)
8. Has the other side made the necessary covenants? If not, what additional or different covenants are needed? How should the degree of obligation be changed? Should any of the covenants include an exception? (See Chapters 3 and 10.)
9. Are any conditions to the other side's obligation to perform inappropriate? Should any condition to the other side's obligation to perform be recast as a covenant? (See Chapters 4 and 11.)

---

4. To check, use your word-processing program's Find function.

5. Most contracts deal with this issue in the endgame provisions. Sometimes, however, drafters deal with it in the action sections.

10. Should the conditions to the client's obligation to perform be more stringent? Should any of the client's covenants be recast as a condition? (See Chapters 4 and 11.)

11. Have you carefully examined the endgame provisions? Do they provide for early termination? What constitutes *default* or *cause*? What are the remedies? Does the contract provide for a friendly termination? Are all the loose ends tied up? Should one or more provisions survive the contract's termination? If an endgame provision involves money, does it answer the *who, what, when, where, why, how,* and *how much* questions? Should disputes be litigated, arbitrated, or mediated? (See Chapter 15.)

12. Does the contract include all the appropriate general provisions? If any are omitted, what are the consequences? Has each provision been tailored to reflect the parties' agreement? (See Chapter 16.)

13. Are the signature blocks properly set up? Are the names correct? Are they the same names as those in the preamble? If a party is an entity, does its signature line indicate the signatory's title? (See Chapter 17.)

14. Is there legalese that should be deleted? (See Chapter 18.)

15. Does the contract use formatting to enhance clarity? (See Chapter 19.)

16. Does each sentence's structure enhance its clarity? (See Chapter 20.)

17. Is any provision ambiguous? Are two or more provisions ambiguous when read together? (See Chapter 21.)

18. Do the contract provisions say the same thing the same way? If the standards differ, should they? (See Chapter 21.)

19. With respect to each mathematical formula, have you created hypotheticals to check whether the formula is properly stated? Have you received accounting and tax advice? (See Chapter 22.)

20. Have you used the five-prong framework to analyze the contract's provisions? (See Chapter 25.)

21. Does the contract's organization facilitate its reading? (See Chapter 26.)

22. Has each business point been incorporated? Does the contract deal with all the scenarios that you and the client discussed? If not, do you need to include any of the missing scenarios, or has the client reached a business judgment not to deal with them? Is your client adequately protected? (See Chapter 27.)

23. Do the contract's provisions reflect an understanding of the parties and their industry? (See Chapter 27.)

24. Does the contract raise any legal issues? Are all the provisions enforceable? Have the parties received all the required governmental approvals? (See Chapter 27.)

25. Is the contract pragmatic, one that the parties can actually perform?

26. Has the contract built-in flexibility to address changed circumstances?

28.7 PREPARE COMMENTS

Once you have been through the contract and conferred with your client, you must prepare your comments for the other side. You have three choices, in declining order of preference.

- A detailed markup of the contract, along with an accompanying memorandum. The markup will show the changes you want, while the memorandum will explain proposed changes and raise issues.

- A memorandum discussing the major points, plus a markup of small issues, glitches (typographical errors), and stylistic points (if appropriate).
- Oral comments, conveyed by telephone or at a meeting.

Before concluding which approach to take, talk with your client about the time, cost, and the strategic benefits of one approach rather than another.

28.7.1 MARKUPS

If you mark up the contract, you regain some of the leverage that you lost when the other side took on the role of drafter. Now, you and your client can shape the contract in ways both obvious and subtle. In addition, by making the comments in writing, you permit the drafter to concede the point without doing so in front of you, your client, and the drafter's client. It is easier on the ego, and the need to look tough in front of the client is not directly put into play. It also gives the other side time to think through your side's comments. A point that it might have rejected in person may be easier to win this way. You will not settle all the points with your markup. Key business issues will remain, but you may winnow down the issues, making it easier to complete the negotiations.

If your client is worried about the markup's cost, explain its strategic advantage. Point out that the markup allows you to shape the negotiation and the deal through drafting.

Markups may be done by hand or by making changes using an electronic copy of the agreement. Ask the drafter which she prefers. Some drafters dislike electronic markups because they lose control over the document. Others prefer it because it reduces the work of inputting agreed-on changes. Some firms prefer not to ask and produce new electronic versions.

Before marking up a contract electronically, check the firm's or company's procedures. Most firms and companies have special software to prevent the other side from reviewing the metadata created during the drafting process.

Most lawyers today use electronic markups. But you should also know how to do it by hand. The logistics are relatively easy. An example follows these instructions. To indicate that you wish to delete one or more words, put a straight line through those words. To indicate that you wish to insert words, put a **caret** where you want the words. (A caret is a proofreading mark that looks like an upside down "v".) Then, draw a line from the top of the caret into the margin. Write the words you want inserted, circle them to create a balloon, and connect the balloon to the line connected to the caret.

If an insert consists of more than a few words, type it on a separate page. Use a caret, a line, and a balloon to indicate where the insert goes. Rather than putting the proposed language in the balloon, put an **insert number** there. An insert number consists of the page number on which the change is to be made and a capital letter to distinguish multiple inserts on the same page. Use the capital letters in alphabetical order. For example: *Insert 22A* and *Insert 22B*. Although each insert should appear on a separate page, you do not need to create a separate document for each insert. Instead, use a page break to move each insert onto its own page.

If you wish to move language to another page, circle it, draw a line from it to the margin, and attach it to a balloon. Inside the balloon, give the circled language an insert number, just as if you were adding language. Then, indicate the page to which the language should be moved: *Insert 22C to page 34*. On the page where the language is to be inserted, put a caret at the insertion point and attach it to a balloon in

[handwritten box: Insert 5A]
[handwritten: t]

2.10   Corporate Organization. The Licensee shall ~~within thirty (30) days of~~ *[handwritten: either]* *[handwritten: ¶ 2.10.1]*

~~the date hereof,~~ establish a separate division of its company dedicated

exclusively to the sale of Licensed Products throughout the Territory ~~,~~ *[handwritten: ; or]* *[handwritten box: Insert 5B]*

2.11   Production Team.

    2.11.1   Definition. For the purposes of this Section 2.11, "Production

        Team" means a head of sales, a production manager, ~~and~~ *[handwritten: a]*

        production assistant ~~,~~ *[handwritten: ,)]* *[handwritten: and a stylist .]*

    2.11.2   Exclusivity. At its sole expense, the Licensee shall

        (a)   employ a Production Team; and

        (b) *[handwritten: cause]* each member of the Production Team ~~shall~~ *[handwritten: to]* work

            exclusively with the Licensor's representatives on the

            Licensee's business arising under this Agreement.

    2.11.3   Prior Approval. ~~These individuals will be hired~~ *[handwritten box: Insert 5C]* with the

        Licensor's prior approval.

    ~~**2.11.4**~~   *[circled]* **Sales Force.** Licensee shall maintain a separate sales force for

        the sale of the Licensed Products.

[handwritten: Insert 5D to page 8]

[handwritten: 2.11.4] *[handwritten box: Insert 7A, from page 7]*

the margin. Inside the balloon, put language along the following lines: *Put Insert 22C here.*

When you add language or move it, the numbering of sections and subsections may change. Mark those changes too, or write a general comment.

28.7.2 A MEMORANDUM

You can use a memorandum two ways: as a stand-alone document or as a supplement to a markup. If you use it as a stand-alone document, use it to explain the changes that you want and why. List the comments in ascending section number order and include the section's title. The memo's introduction can direct the reader to the numbered paragraphs that have the most important changes.

1. **Section 2.4** — [title of section]
2. **Section 3.6** — [title of section]
3. **Section 8.7** — [title of section]

Use the memorandum as a negotiating tool, explaining the business and legal reasons for each change. Laying out the issues for the other side gives it the opportunity to think through the issues privately, without time pressure and without ceding the point in your presence or the clients'. A memorandum resembles a markup in this regard.

Tone is important, as in any negotiation. Diplomatic is generally best, but use a more aggressive tone if appropriate in the context of the transaction.

Although a memorandum allows you to argue your position, it does not, unfortunately, generally allow you to propose specific language changes. By not drafting the language, you cede a strategic advantage to the other side. But you may be able to regain some of the advantage—in two ways. First, include proposed inserts as attachments to the memo. Second, as you draft the memorandum, phrase the discussion so it uses words or phrases that you think should be incorporated into the agreement. The drafter might just use them as an easy way to make agreed-on changes.

Some drafters accompany a stand-alone memorandum with a markup of glitches and minor points. This will advance the later negotiation by permitting the parties to focus on the primary business issues.

If you use the memorandum with a markup, do not elaborate on every change. Instead, use it as a negotiating tool, just as you would with a stand-alone memorandum.

28.7.3 ORAL COMMENTS

Oral comments are generally the least favorable option from a strategic perspective because you do not propose specific language. But, you can compensate to some degree. In preparing for the negotiation, draft inserts for key business provisions. This way, you know not only the substance of what you are asking for, but also the details. During the negotiation, make specific comments, using words and phrases from your inserts. As the other side takes notes, it may pick up your language and then, later, incorporate it into the contract. Having the draft inserts also enables you to offer them to the other side if it assents to a proposed change.

EXERCISE

Exercise 28-1

This exercise requires you to redraft, and perhaps negotiate, an employment agreement between Carrie Richards, a neophyte television reporter, and her soon-to-be new employer, a television station. All the documents for this exercise are on the book's website, and your professor will distribute them to you.

APPENDIX

Framework for Contract Analysis—Long Form

1. What is the provision's business purpose?

    (a) What does your client want from this provision?

    (b) How does the other side perceive this provision? What will be its most significant issue with it?

2. From a neutral perspective, as drafted, does the provision accomplish its purpose?

    (a) Does it properly state the business deal? Stated differently, are the business terms incorporated correctly?

    (b) Does the provision follow the guidelines for drafting this type of provision? (For example: If it is a monetary payment, does the provision include both a statement of the amount and the obligation to pay for each type of consideration? If it is a covenant, has it answered the *who, what, when, where, why, how,* and *how much* questions?)

3. As drafted, does the provision accomplish the client's business goal? Does this provision hurt the client? Can the client's interests be further advanced or protected?

4. Does the provision implicate any legal issues?

5. Are there any industry- or practice-specific points to be considered?

6. Does the provision implicate any other provision (cascade effect)?

7. Does analysis reveal any other business issues? Use the five-prong framework.

    (a) Money—Does the contract follow the cash?

    (b) Risk—Has risk been allocated appropriately?

    (c) Control—Who is the decision maker? Can the right to decide be expanded or limited? How can the client control a risk?

    (d) Standards—Can the standards be made more client-friendly? What kind of standard is best: one that is vague or one that is specific?

    (e) Endgame—Does the agreement include the appropriate defaults, remedies, exit provisions, and provisions for a happy ending?

8. Are there drafting issues?

    (a) Is there ambiguity?

    (b) Does the statement of each business term use the right contract concept and the right signal for that contract concept?

(c)   Is there legalese to be deleted?

(d)   Can clarity be created through formatting?

(e)   Can clarity be created through a change in sentence structure?

Amendments, Consents, and Waivers

29.1 INTRODUCTION

Business deals change: An existing provision no longer works, a new business issue arises, a party fails to perform, or a one-time event requires special handling. As the relationship between the parties evolves, so too must the agreement that memorializes their transaction. To deal with these changes, drafters rely on amendments, consents, and waivers.

29.2 AMENDMENTS — GENERAL INFORMATION

An amendment changes a contract. It can be on any topic covered — or not covered — by the contract. Under the common law, new consideration is generally necessary for an amendment to be enforceable.[1] Nonetheless, courts have frequently surmounted this requirement by refusing to look at the adequacy of consideration.[2] In addition, they have shown a willingness to enforce amendments if the contract is purely executory (unperformed by both parties).[3] Statutes can also play a role in determining an amendment's enforceability. The Uniform Commercial Code[4] and other statutes in some jurisdictions[5] include provisions that override the common law. They provide that an amendment is enforceable without consideration — although a writing may be required. Bottom line: the law is a bit of a hodgepodge and knowing the law of the relevant jurisdiction is a must.

As was discussed in Chapter 16, amendments can be either oral or written, and oral amendments are often enforceable — despite a no oral amendments provision.[6] Because of this, discussions about possible amendments, or what could be construed as discussions about possible amendments, can be delicate. In the appropriate

---

1. *Alaska Packers Ass'n v. Domenico*, 117 F. 99 (9th Cir. 1902).

2. Brian A. Haskel, *Amendment and Waiver,* in *Negotiating and Drafting Contract Boilerplate* 507-509 (Stark et al. eds., ALM Publg. 2003).

3. *Id.; see also Restatement (Second) of Contracts* §89 (1981).

4. U.C.C. §2-209(1) (an agreement modifying a contract need not have consideration to be binding).

5. *See e.g.* Mich. Comp. L. Ann. §566.1.

6. See Chapter 16.

situation, consider sending a letter to the other side acknowledging negotiations with respect to an amendment but stating, for the record, that the parties did not reach an agreement.

An amendment may be drafted as an agreement or a letter. A letter is more informal and quicker, but it is just as binding. This book will refer to amendments stated in a full, formal agreement as *inside-the-contract amendments* and amendments made in letter agreements as *outside-the-contract amendments*. The following sections discuss each of these amendment types in turn.

29.3   INSIDE-THE-CONTRACT AMENDMENTS

This section details how to draft inside-the-contract amendments—those in a formal agreement format. In this format, the actual amendments compose the subject matter performance provision, and the other contract parts play their usual, respective roles. Appendix 1 to this chapter sets forth complete agreement with inside-the-contract amendments.

29.3.1   THE INTRODUCTORY PROVISIONS AND THE DEFINITIONS

When drafting the preamble of an amendment, name the agreement *Amendment* or *Amending Agreement*. If the parties have previously amended the existing agreement, the amendment's title should reflect the number of amendments: for example, *Fourth Amendment*. The preamble should also state which agreement is being amended by including that agreement's name, its parties, and the original signing date or *as of* date. By properly titling the amendment and including the information about the existing contract, a drafter quickly conveys to the reader the contract's purpose. Some drafters exclude the information about the existing agreement from the preamble and put it in the recitals. But that style of preamble delays giving the reader critical information. The better style is to include all of the information on the existing agreement in the preamble. The following preamble is typical:

> **This Third Amendment**, dated January 17, 20X8, amends the Employment Agreement, dated February 23, 20X6, as amended, between Buckeye Pharmaceuticals Inc., an Ohio corporation (the "**Company**"), and Mohammed Ahmed (the "**Executive**").

Although recitals may be omitted from some agreements, they are often helpful in an amendment. Use them to explain why the parties are amending their agreement. This puts the amendment in context for the reader.

> **Background**
>
> 1. The Company has employed the Executive as Executive Vice President of Research for approximately two years and now desires to promote him to President.
> 2. The parties desire to amend the Employment Agreement, dated February 23, 20X6, as amended to the date of this Amendment (the "**Existing Agreement**"), to reflect the Executive's new duties, compensation, and other matters.

If the parties are not exchanging consideration for the amendment, do not state that they have. Keep the words of agreement simple:

Accordingly, the parties agree as follows:

The amending agreement may need to distinguish between the agreement as it exists before it is amended and the agreement that exists after it is amended. *Existing Agreement* is a good defined term to use for the agreement before the amendment. The definition of Existing Agreement should incorporate all previous amendments, whether the term is defined in context, as in the recitals above, or in a separate definition.

> **"Existing Agreement"** means the Employment Agreement between the Company and the Executive, dated February 23, 20X6, as amended to the date of this Amendment.

As previously suggested, *Amendment or Amending Agreement* works for the agreement that sets out the amendments, and *Resulting Agreement* can be used to refer to the Existing Agreement, as amended by the Amendment.

Other definitions may also be necessary. If so, the customary drafting guidelines apply.[7] If the amendment uses terms defined in the existing agreement, do not redefine them. Instead, incorporate them into the amending agreement, using the following provision:

> **Definitions**. Capitalized terms used in this Amendment without definition have the meanings assigned to them in the Existing Agreement.

29.3.2 DECIDING WHAT TO AMEND

When discussing a proposed amendment with a client, focus on the business goal, rather than on specific provisions. Once you understand the goal, carefully review the *entire* contract for provisions that will need to be changed. Often a change in one section leads to a change in another—*the cascade effect*.[8] You may need to change a cross-reference, rewrite a provision, delete a provision, or add a provision.

29.3.3 THE ACTION SECTIONS

The subject matter performance provision of an amending agreement is composed of the provisions that implement the changes to the existing agreement—that is, the inside-the-contract amendments. These provisions explicitly state what language is to be deleted from the existing agreement and what language is to be inserted. If a reader wanted to, she could cut and paste the changes into the existing agreement and end up with an amended agreement that could be read from beginning to end.

The following examples from an employment agreement demonstrate different ways to draft inside-the-contract amendments. Commentary explaining the differences follows the examples. (Although the form of these amendments is correct, they

---

7. See §7.5.
8. See §23.2.

include substantive drafting errors. You will analyze these errors as part of an exercise. For now, focus on the style of the amendments.)

1. Section 2.2 (a) of the Existing Agreement is amended by deleting "Executive Vice President for Research" and inserting in its place "President."

2. Section 2.2 (b) of the Existing Agreement is amended by deleting the period at the end of the sentence and inserting in its place the following:

   > , except if the Company consents, and the Company shall not unreasonably withhold its consent.

3. Section 2.3 of the Existing Agreement is amended by deleting the period at the end of the sentence and inserting in its place the following:

   > , except that the Executive may perform volunteer work for the March of Dimes without violating this provision.

4. Section 2.4 of the Existing Agreement is amended by deleting that Section and inserting in its place the following:

   > **2.4 Term**. The term of employment under this Agreement is from March 1, 20X5 through December 31, 20X9 (the "**Employment Term**").

   > *(The employment term of the existing agreement was from March 1, 20X5 through December 31, 20X6.)*

5. Section 2.5 is amended to read as follows:

   > **2.5 Salary**.
   >
   > (a) **March 1, 20X5 through December 31, 20X6**. The Company shall pay the Executive at a rate of $140,000 a year during the Employment Term. The annual salary is to be prorated for the period from March 1, 20X5 through December 31, 20X6. The Company shall pay the annual salary in approximately equal monthly payments on the last business day of each month. *(This is the original provision, now recast as a subsection with a caption.)*
   >
   > (b) **January 1, 20X7 through December 31, 20X9**. For the period beginning on January 1, 20X7 through December 31, 20X9, the Company shall pay the Executive at a rate of $180,000 a year. *(This is the new provision.)*

6. The Existing Agreement is amended by deleting Section 3 and inserting in its place "Section 3 has been intentionally omitted."

7. The Existing Agreement is amended by inserting the following provision as Section 6 after the end of the Existing Agreement's Section 5:

   > **6. The Company's Location**. The Company shall not locate its headquarters outside of the greater metropolitan Cleveland, Ohio, region without the Executive's consent, which consent the Executive shall not unreasonably withhold.

8. The Existing Agreement is amended to change the section numbers of Sections 6, 7, 8, 9, and 10 to Sections 7, 8, 9, 10, and 11, respectively.

Note the different ways in which an amendment can be effected. Paragraphs 1, 2 and 3 are short. None of them includes the full amended provision, just the changes. This lack of context can obscure the amendment's effect, as in Paragraph 2.

Paragraphs 4 and 5 take a different approach. They include the entire provision, as amended. This method makes it easier for the reader but results in a longer amending agreement.

The amendment in Paragraph 6 deletes a section and inserts as a placeholder the statement that Section 3 was intentionally omitted. This language reduces a drafter's work by eliminating the need to renumber successive provisions and to revise cross-references that become incorrect because of the renumbering.

Paragraph 7 amends the existing agreement by adding a new section. It has the ancillary effect of throwing off the numbering of the subsequent sections. The amendment in Paragraph 8 corrects that problem by renumbering the subsequent sections.

Some drafters put a new provision as the last provision of the existing agreement.[9] This keeps the numbering intact and avoids the need to change cross-references. Similarly, if a new subsection is added to a tabulated enumeration, drafters put it last. Then, the other changes to that provision will be limited to changes to the punctuation of the tabulated items. For example:

> Section 4 of the Existing Agreement is amended by
>
> (a) deleting "and" at the end of subsection (c);
>
> (b) deleting the period at the end of subsection (d) and inserting in its place "; and"; and
>
> (c) adding the following as a new subsection (e): "[insert new language]."

29.3.4 OTHER PROVISIONS

Amending agreements occasionally include representations and warranties. For example, each party might represent and warrant to the other that

- its board of directors has authorized the amendments;
- it has duly executed and delivered the amending agreement;
- the amending agreement is enforceable against it in accordance with its terms; and
- the representations and warranties made at the signing of the existing agreement are also true as of the signing of the amending agreement.[10]

In addition to representations and warranties, amending agreements may also include conditions. These are usually directed towards postponing an amendment's effectiveness until the conditions have been satisfied. (Note that the amending agreement itself is effective, but not the actual amendments to the existing agreement.) For example:

---

9. This should not be done, however, if you are restating the agreement or amending and restating it. See §29.3.

10. This may not always be true. Carefully review and accurately state the then-current facts in the amending agreement.

> **Amendments' Effectiveness.** The amendments in this Amendment are effective on the satisfaction of the following condition: The Borrower's counsel must have delivered to the Bank an opinion that the Borrower's board of directors has duly authorized this Second Amendment and the amendments set forth in it. If this condition is not satisfied before June 1, 20XX, this Second Amendment terminates, and the Existing Agreement continues unchanged and in full force.

Drafters differ as to which of the general provisions should be included in an amending agreement. Some drafters incorporate all of them by reference; others restate the governing law provision, but no others.

One principled approach is to include only the following provisions: governing law, choice of forum, counterparts, severability, and merger. The governing law and choice of forum provisions are included to ensure that the amending agreement and the existing agreement are governed by the same law and can be adjudicated in the same court. The rationale for including the last three provisions is that they deal directly with the amending agreement's creation. The language of all of these provisions should duplicate the language in the existing agreement but with a tweak for the merger provision. (Say the same thing the same way.) It should refer not to the existing agreement but the amending agreement.

> **Merger.** This Second Amendment constitutes the final and exclusive agreement between the parties on the matters contained in this Second Amendment. All earlier and contemporaneous negotiations and agreements between the parties on the matters contained in this Second Amendment are expressly merged into and superseded by this Second Amendment.

Once the amending agreement is executed, the resulting agreement must reflect that the final and exclusive agreement consists of what was the existing agreement plus the amending agreement. You can approach the drafting in one of two ways. If the existing agreement's definition of *Agreement* includes *as amended,* the original merger provision necessarily takes into account the amendment.

> **"Agreement"** means this Website Development Agreement, as amended from time to time.

If the existing agreement's definition of *Agreement* does not include *as amended,* then that definition or the merger provision must be amended. That way, each time the defined term *Agreement* is used in a general provision, or any other provision, it refers to the resulting agreement.

Following this approach, the other general provisions do not need to be restated in the amending agreement. Once the parties execute and deliver the amending agreement, each of the general provisions applies to the resulting agreement—that is, the existing agreement after the amendments.

If you decide to incorporate by reference into the amending agreement all of the general provisions from the existing agreement, you may need to address a technical drafting issue. Specifically, when those provisions are incorporated, they will probably bring with them references to *this Agreement.* But those references will be wrong because they will be referring to the existing agreement. Instead, they should refer to the amending agreement because the general provisions are being incorporated so that they become part of the amending agreement. Therefore, to make the incorporation by reference work, add a sentence to the following effect in the provision that incorporates the general provisions from the existing agreement:

> Each reference to "this Agreement" in the provisions incorporated by reference from the Existing Agreement into this Amendment is deemed a reference to "this Amendment."

Amending agreements generally conclude with a provision along the following lines:

> **Continued Effectiveness of the Existing Agreement**. Except as amended by the amendments in this Amendment, the Existing Agreement continues unchanged and in full force.

This declaration precludes any inference that the amendments have caused a change to any provision in the existing agreement, other than those changed in the amending agreement.

29.4 RESTATED AGREEMENTS

Occasionally, parties enter into so many amendments that the then-existing agreement becomes difficult to read. Imagine trying to analyze a section of a contract that has its subsections in four different amending agreements! To deal with this event, parties can create a **restated** agreement or an **amended and restated** agreement.

To create a restated agreement, the drafter inserts all of the previous amendments into a master document, which then is the exclusive expression of the parties' agreement. An amended and restated agreement not only restates an agreement, but also amends one or more provisions at the same time.

When restating an agreement, move any provisions that were added to the end of the existing agreement—to keep numbering intact—to their appropriate place within the contract. Now that the agreement will exist on a stand-alone basis (without amendments), the contract's structural integrity should be restored. This will facilitate the reading and analysis of the contract because when a reader looks for a provision in its logical place, it will be there.

Before deciding to restate an agreement, consider whether the benefits of the restated agreement outweigh the following disadvantages:

- The time and cost of preparing the restatement.
- The possibility of introducing errors into the existing agreement.
- The risk that the other side will see the restatement as an opportunity to renegotiate points that it conceded during the original negotiations.

When drafting a restated or an amended and restated agreement, think through the effect of changing the date in the preamble from the date the parties signed the existing agreement to the date that the parties sign the restatement. One problem that this change causes relates to the representations and warranties. As you have learned, representations and warranties speak as of a moment in time, generally the date that the parties sign the contract.[11] When a restatement is signed, the date in the preamble is the date of that signing. But the existing agreement's representations and warranties should not speak as of the day of the restatement's signing. Instead, they should continue to speak as of the day of the existing agreement's signing. To preclude disputes on this matter, the introductory language to these representations and warranties should state explicitly that they continue to speak as of the original signing date.

> **Version 1**
>
> The Borrower represents and warrants to the Bank that the following statements were true as of [insert date of original signing of the contract]:

If the parties also want to add new representations and warranties or to have the existing representations and warranties also speak as of the date of the restatement's signing, additional language can be inserted.

> **Version 2**
>
> The Borrower represents and warrants to the Bank that the following statements were true as of the [insert date of original signing of the contract] and are true on the date of this Restated Agreement:

Be careful about the passage of time. The facts underlying some of the representations and warranties may have changed. For example, a statement of the level of the inventory on the date of the restatement is unlikely to be the same as the level of inventory on the date of the signing of the original agreement. If the parties agree to representations and warranties both as of the original signing date and the restatement date and the facts differ, create separate subsections for each date as of which the representations and warranties speak. Move representations and warranties to their own section and introduce them with language along the following lines:

> **Version 3**
>
> The Borrower represents and warrants to the Bank that the statements in subsection (a) were true as of the [insert date of original finding of the contract] and that the statements in subsection (b) are true on date of this Restated Agreement.
>
> (a) **Inventory Representations and Warranties as of Signing**. [Provision intentionally omitted.]
>
> (b) **Inventory Representations and Warranties as of the date of this Restated Agreement**. [Provision intentionally omitted.]

---

11. See §3.2.1.

29.5 OUTSIDE-THE-CONTRACT AMENDMENTS

An outside-the-contract amendment differs and yet is similar to an inside-the-contract amendment. The two formats differ with respect to the material that surrounds the amending provisions. An outside-the-contract amendment

- begins with the typical features of any letter—the addressee's name and address and a salutation;
- states that, when signed, the letter constitutes an amendment to the existing agreement;
- incorporates by reference the defined terms from the existing agreement;
- amends the existing agreement;
- requests that the addressee indicate its agreement to the amendments by signing the letter and the enclosed duplicate original (if hard copy is used, rather than PDFs); and
- requests that the addressee return one of the two originals to the sender.

In an outside-the-contract amendment, the amending provisions can be the same as those of an inside-the-contract amendment or they can differ. If they differ, it's generally because the parties and the drafter are taking a short cut and trying to save transaction costs, or they are being strategic and trying to make the changes seem innocuous, when they are not. In these instances, rather than amending specific words, the amendments state the effect of the amendment. This leaves the reader, the litigators, and the judge to figure out which words were actually changed. These amendments lack precision and invite litigation. You should avoid using them—unless you have a strategic reason to do otherwise.

See Appendix 2 to this chapter for an example of a letter agreement that uses outside-the-contract amendments that only state the amendments' consequences.

29.6 CONSENTS

29.6.1 DEFINITIONS

A **consent** permits something that the contract otherwise prohibits. For example, many contracts prohibit a party from delegating its performance under the contract without the other party's consent.

> **Delegation.** The Contractor shall not delegate any of the Work without the Owner's prior written consent.

If the Contractor wants to delegate the painting of the house without violating its covenant, the Contractor must obtain the Owner's consent.

29.6.2 DRAFTING THE REQUEST FOR CONSENT AND THE CONSENT

Guidelines for Drafting Consents

When drafting the request for a consent, keep the following guidelines in mind:

1. *The first paragraph of the consent should refer to the agreement requiring the consent and create the parties' defined terms.*

> We refer to the Credit Agreement, dated November 12, 20X6, between Big Bank N.A. ("**Big Bank**") and Worldwide Shipping Inc., a Florida corporation ("**Worldwide**").

2. *The second paragraph should state what your client wants and why.* Postponing these details to later in the letter will annoy the other side. Use the subsequent paragraphs to provide details.

3. *When drafting the cover letter and the consent, track the language in the agreement that prohibits the act for which your client is seeking consent.* Say the same thing the same way.

4. *Draft the scope of the requested consent so that it meets your client's needs.* While your client might like the latitude of a broadly drafted consent, requesting that may not be the best strategy. If the other side perceives the consent as overreaching, it may reject the request.

5. *Make it as easy as possible for the other side to consent.*

  (a) Draft the consent and include it with the request.
  (b) Include the appropriate materials for return by overnight courier. Alternatively, if an original, hard copy is not required, request that the signed copy be returned by e-mail as a PDF or in another appropriate format.

29.7 WAIVERS

29.7.1 DEFINITION

From a practitioner's perspective, waivers typically arise in response to three events.

- The failure of a condition.
- The occurrence of a misrepresentation, breach of warranty, or breach of covenant.
- The likely breach of a covenant.

If any of these offending events occurs, the party entitled to a remedy or walk-away right may choose to waive the event's occurrence. A **waiver** is a party's agreement that it will perform as if the event had not occurred and that it will not exercise its remedies or walk-away right.[12] A waiver does not amend a contract. All of the agreement's provisions, including the problematic provision, remain unchanged and enforceable. If the offending event occurs again, the party entitled to the remedy or walk-away right may once again choose whether to waive.

For example, imagine that a buyer of a house has bargained for the receipt of the house's architectural plans as a condition to closing. If the seller cannot deliver the plans, the buyer may decide not to close and to exercise his walk-away right, or he may waive the failure of the condition and purchase the house. If the seller also promised to deliver the plans, its nondelivery would be a breach of covenant. The buyer would then need to decide whether he also wanted to waive the breach and forego any remedies available to him.

As noted, a party may waive the application of a provision in anticipation of a breach. A bank might do this if its borrower announces that it will be unable to comply with one of its financial covenants. The pre-breach waiver would be advantageous to

---

12. See § 4.2.2 for an example of a waiver of a condition to an obligation.

both parties. The bank would avoid having a borrower in default, and the borrower would avoid the ancillary consequences of a breach, such as a cross-default or disclosure obligations if it is a publicly held corporation.

29.7.2 DRAFTING THE WAIVER

Waivers can be drafted in the form of a letter or as a stand-alone agreement. In either case, the subject matter performance provision is the waiver. It is a self-executing provision,[13] effective on the waiver's execution.

> **Waiver.** [By signing this Waiver] [By countersigning this letter], the Landlord waives the Tenant's failure to comply with Section 6.8 of the Lease.

To establish that the waiver is a one-time event, most waivers include language to the following effect:

> **Limited Waiver.** This Waiver is effective only on this occasion and only for the purpose given and is not to be construed as a waiver on any other occasion, for any other purpose, or against any other Person.

If the contract between the parties has a general provision dealing with waivers with language to this effect, parrot that language in the waiver. Remember: Say the same thing the same way.

29.8 CHOOSING BETWEEN A CONSENT AND A WAIVER

Consents and waivers are kissing cousins. Which one is appropriate depends on the contract's language. If a covenant absolutely prohibits something without exception, the piece of paper to be obtained is a waiver. It renders the prohibition unenforceable on this one occasion. If a covenant provides for an exception to the prohibition with the other party's consent, then, in accordance with the contract, the piece of paper to be obtained is a consent.

---

13. See §8.2.

EXERCISES

Exercise 29-1

Review the inside-the-contract amendments in Section 29.3.3. What business and drafting issues do the amendments in Paragraphs 4 and 5 raise? Read both provisions before trying to answer the question.

Exercise 29-2

Review Appendix 2 to this chapter. What business issues might there be because of the way the amendments are drafted? Use the information in Appendix 1 to help you with your analysis.

Exercise 29-3

Using the information in the letter that follows, mark up the Consent to Assignment that follows it. Alternatively, redraft the Consent using the Consent that is available on the book's website.

January 26, 20X9

Mr. James Smith
425 West Haven Corp.
425 West Haven Avenue
El Paso, Texas 79905

Re: Request for Consent to Assignment and Release

Dear Mr. Smith:

We refer to the Lease (the "Lease"), dated July 1, 20X6, between 425 West Haven Corp. ("West Haven") and Maria's Muffins Inc. ("Muffins"). In accordance with Section 7.8 of the Lease, we request that West Haven consent to Muffins's assignment of its rights under the Lease to Sammy's Sweets Inc. ("Sweets").

Muffins is going out of business and desires to assign its rights under the Lease to Sweets. Sweets has agreed to assume all of Muffins's obligations under the Lease that arise and are due and payable on and after March 1, 20X9, the date that Muffins will assign its rights under the Lease to Sweets (the "Assignment Date").

Sweets manufactures and distributes chocolate truffles to candy stores in Texas. Enclosed for your information are (a) a description of Sweets's business and (b) Sweets's audited financial statements for the period ended December 31, 20X8.

Section 7.8 of the Lease prohibits the assignment of the Lease without West Haven's consent. Thus, in accordance with the Lease, Muffins requests that West Haven

(a)   consent to Muffin's assignment to Sweets, on March 1, 20X9, of all Muffins's rights under the Lease; and

(b)   release Muffins from all of its obligations under the Lease that arise and are due and payable on and after March 1, 20X9.

Muffins also requests that you acknowledge that no other consent or consideration is required for the assignment to be effective. Your consent and release will apply only to the transaction described in this letter and is subject to Sweets's assumption of all of Muffins's obligations under the Lease that arise and are due and payable on and after March 1, 20X9. We will mail you a copy of the assumption promptly after Sweets signs it.

To consent to the assignment and to grant the release, please

•   sign the two duplicate original consent forms accompanying this letter; and

•   return the duplicate original by [national courier in the enclosed, prepaid envelope] [PDF by e-mail to lawyer@gmail.com], as soon as possible, but in no event later than February 20, 20X9.

If you desire any further information concerning the transaction, please do not hesitate to call me at (915) 555-5555. We appreciate your assistance in this matter.

Very truly yours,

Maria's Muffins Inc.

By: _____

Maria Rodriguez, President

Consent to Assignment

Subject to the proviso set forth in the last sentence hereof, West Haven Rental Corp. (the

"**Lessor**") hereby consents to the assignment by Maria's Muffins Inc. ("**Muffins**") of all its right,

title, and interest under the Lease, dated July 1, 20X6, (the "**Lease**") to Sammy's Sweets Inc.

("**Assignee**"), and Lessor hereby releases Muffins from all its obligations and liabilities under the

Lease arising and due and payable on and after the date that Muffins assigns its rights under the

Lease to the Assignee (the "**Assignment Date**"). Notwithstanding the foregoing, the consent and

the release granted herein shall only be effective if, on the Assignment Date, Assignee shall have assumed all of Muffins's obligations and liabilities under the Lease arising and due and payable on

and after the Assignment Date.

425 West Haven Corp.

By: _____

James Smith, President

Dated: _____

Exercise 29-4

Amend the Aircraft Purchase Agreement in accordance with the instructions in
Exercise 31-4.

APPENDICES

Appendix 1: An Inside-the-Contract Amendment

Second Amendment[14]

Second Amendment, dated January 17, 20X7, to the Employment Agreement, dated February 23, 20X5, as amended, between Buckeye Pharmaceuticals Inc., an Ohio corporation (the "**Company**"), and Mohammed Ahmed (the "**Executive**").

Background

The Company has employed the Executive as Executive Vice President of Research for approximately two years and now desires to promote him to President. The parties desire to amend the Employment Agreement, dated February 23, 20X5, as amended (the "**Existing Agreement**"), to reflect the Executive's new duties, compensation, and other matters.

Accordingly, the parties agree as follows:

1. **Definitions.**

    (a) Terms defined in the preamble and recitals of this Amendment have their assigned meanings, and capitalized terms used in this Amendment without definition have the meanings assigned to them in the Existing Agreement.

    (b) "**Amendment**" means this Second Amendment.

2. **Amendments.**

    (a) Section 2.2 (a) of the Existing Agreement is amended by deleting "Executive Vice President for Research" and inserting in its place "President."

    (b) Section 2.2 (b) of the Existing Agreement is amended by deleting the period at the end of the sentence and inserting in its place the following:

    > , except if the Company consents, and the Company shall not unreasonably withhold its consent.

    (c) Section 2.3 of the Existing Agreement is amended by deleting the period at the end of the sentence and inserting in its place the following:

    > , except that the Executive may perform volunteer work for the March of Dimes without violating this provision.

    (d) Section 2.4 of the Existing Agreement is amended by deleting that section and inserting in its place the following:

    > **2.4 Term**. The term of employment under this Agreement is from March 1, 20X5 through December 31, 20X9 (the "**Employment Term**").

    (The employment term of the existing agreement was from March 1, 20X5 through December 31, 20X6.)

---

14. This fact pattern was inspired by one created by the author's colleague, Alan Shaw.

(e) Section 2.5 is amended to read as follows:

2.5 Salary.

(a) **March 1, 20X5 through December 31, 20X6**. The Company shall pay the Executive at a rate of $140,000 a year during the Employment Term. The annual salary is to be prorated for the period from March 1, 20X5 through December 31, 20X6. The Company shall pay the annual salary in approximately equal monthly payments on the last business day of each month. *(This is the original provision, now recast as a subsection with a caption.)*

(b) **January 1, 20X7 through December 31, 20X9**. For the period beginning on January 1, 20X7 through December 31, 20X9, the Company shall pay the Executive at a rate of $180,000 a year. *(This is the new provision.)*

(f) The Existing Agreement is amended by deleting Section 3 and inserting in its place "Section 3 has been intentionally omitted."

(g) The Existing Agreement is amended by inserting the following provision as Section 6 after the end of the Existing Agreement's Section 5:

> **6. The Company's Location**. The Company shall not locate its headquarters outside of the greater metropolitan Cleveland, Ohio, region without the Executive's consent, which consent the Executive shall not unreasonably withhold.

(h) The Existing Agreement is amended to change the section numbers of Sections 6, 7, 8, 9, and 10 to Sections 7, 8, 9, 10, and 11, respectively.

3. **Continuation of Existing Agreement**. Except for the amendments made in this Amendment, the Existing Agreement remains unchanged and in full effect.

4. **General Provisions**.

(a) **Choice of Law**. [Intentionally omitted.]

(b) **Choice of Forum**. [Intentionally omitted.]

(c) **Counterparts**. [Intentionally omitted.]

(d) **Merger**. [Intentionally omitted.]

(e) **Severability**. [Intentionally omitted.]

To evidence their agreement to this Amendment's terms, the parties have executed and delivered this Amendment on the date set forth in the preamble.

Buckeye Pharmaceuticals Inc.

By: _____

Betsy Rice, Chief Executive Officer

_____

Mohammed Ahmed

Appendix 2: An Outside-the-Contract Amendment in Letter Format

January 17, 20X7

Mr. Mohammed Ahmed
322 Westland Road
Shaker Heights, Ohio 12345

Dear Mr. Ahmed:

Please refer to the agreement dated February 23, 20X5 between Buckeye Pharmaceuticals Inc. (the "Company") and you relating to your employment by the Company (that agreement, as amended, the "Existing Agreement"). When signed by you, this letter constitutes an amendment of the Existing Agreement.

Capitalized terms used in this letter without definition have the meanings assigned to them in the Existing Agreement.

1. You are promoted to President.
2. You may do volunteer work for the March of Dimes without breaching our agreement.
3. All references to December 31, 20X6 are changed to December 31, 20X9.
4. Your annual salary for the period January 1, 20X7 through December 31, 20X9 is $180,000.
5. As you will be President, you no longer have to report to the President.
6. The Company promises not to relocate its headquarters outside of Cleveland, Ohio, without your consent. You have agreed not to withhold your consent unreasonably.
7. Once you have signed this letter, the amendments are effective as of January 1, 20X7.
8. Except as stated in this letter, the Existing Agreement remains unmodified and in full force.

To indicate your agreement to these amendments, please sign this letter and the enclosed duplicate original in the space provided at the end of the letter. In addition, please return [one original to the Company by [a recognized national courier] in the enclosed, pre-paid envelope] [a PDF of the signed original by e-mail to glawyer@gmail.com].

Very truly yours,

Buckeye Pharmaceuticals Inc.

By: _____
Betsy Rice, Chief Executive Officer

Agreed to on _____

_____
Mohammed Ahmed

PART SIX

Drafting Ethically

Ethical Issues in Drafting

30.1 INTRODUCTION

The ABA Model Rules of Professional Conduct (the "Model Rules")[1] primarily address ethical issues that arise in litigation. This focus creates problems for deal lawyers who turn to them when faced with ethical dilemmas. They find, with limited exceptions,[2] no rule on point or one that applies only tangentially or by analogy.

The litigation bias of the Model Rules has its roots in the failures of its predecessors, the Model Code of Professional Responsibility[3] and the 1908 Canons of Ethics:[4]

> The [Model] Code's failure to state standards and objectives for the advisor is probably due to many factors. Perhaps the most easily understandable is historical. Traditionally the lawyer's function was almost solely that of a courtroom advocate, and as a result, the original Canons of Professional Responsibility [1908] dealt almost exclusively with the dilemmas of that role. . . .
>
> Several reasons help explain why this historical bias has not been remedied. While the result of the advocate's effort is often of extreme public import, and occasionally political in nature, the advisor's effort is generally private and seemingly important only to the immediate parties. Frequently the advisor's most important decisions are designed to remain confidential. Because the Model Rules serve partly as a public relations device, it is only natural that the Rules should focus on the more public, and more publicized, role of an attorney.
>
> Another reason for the limited viewpoint . . . is that the advocate's role has been better defined by a well-delineated legal process. In contrast, the advisor performs many diverse functions for the client and generally is unconstrained by formal procedures. As a result, it is more difficult to state comprehensively the ethical considerations for an advisor.[5]

---

1. All citations to the Model Rules are to the 2013 American Bar Association Model Rules of Professional Conduct. The full commentary to each Model Rule is available on the textbook's website.

2. *See e.g.* Model R. Prof. Conduct 2.1 ("In representing a client, a lawyer shall exercise independent professional judgment and render candid advice. In rendering advice, a lawyer may refer not only to law but to other considerations such as moral, economic, social and political factors, that may be relevant to the client's situation.").

3. Model Code of Prof. Resp. (ABA 1981).

4. Canons of Prof. Ethics (ABA 1908).

5. Louis M. Brown & Harold A. Brown, *What Counsels the Counselor? The Code of Professional Responsibility's Ethical Considerations—A Preventive Law Analysis,* 10 Val. U. L. Rev. 453, 454-456 (1976) (footnotes omitted).

Exacerbating this paucity of rules is a paucity of case law and ethical opinions. This scarcity undoubtedly reflects the private nature of transactional work. Litigation is audible, visible, and public—it takes place in a forum where the proceedings are recorded. Transactions are generally negotiated in the privacy of a conference room, and contracts drafted in the privacy of an office. Because no record is made, disciplining a lawyer becomes much more difficult.

The remainder of this chapter highlights key ethical issues that contract drafters face. The exercises at the end of the chapter take you past the generalities to specific, real-world applications of the ethics rules.

30.2 THE DRAFTER'S ROLE

Model Rule 1.2(a) allocates the responsibilities and authority of lawyers and their clients. It states:

> [A] lawyer shall abide by a client's decisions concerning the objectives of representation and, as required by Rule 1.4, shall consult with the client as to the means by which they are to be pursued. A lawyer may take such action on behalf of the client as is impliedly authorized to carry out the representation.[6]

Stated more colloquially, the client's role is to establish the representation's objective, while the lawyer's role is to determine the means to accomplish the objective and to take the actions necessary to accomplish it.

Comment 2 to Model Rule 1.2 adds a gloss on the objective/means dichotomy in the context of a lawyer and client disagreeing about the means the lawyer should use. Although the Comment does not state how lawyers and clients should resolve their disagreements, it notes the following:

> Clients normally defer to the special knowledge and skill of their lawyer with respect to the means to be used to accomplish their objectives, particularly with respect to technical, legal and tactical matters. Conversely, lawyers usually defer to the client regarding such questions as the expense to be incurred and concern for third persons who might be adversely affected.[7]

This gloss carefully hedges its assertion by including the adverbs *normally* and *usually*. In the transactional context, the gloss's applicability depends to some degree on the client's sophistication. The more sophisticated the client is, the more likely that the client will want to participate in technical, legal, and tactical matters. Sophisticated clients often have as much experience as their lawyers in negotiations and will have specific ideas on what to broach, how, and when. In addition, as more lawyers have moved out of the legal profession into business positions, more clients have legal expertise. In these situations, deferring to the client as to the means is appropriate. If you vehemently disagree with the client's decisions, consider resigning.[8]

Although no Model Rule deals directly with contract drafting, the objective/means dichotomy does provide some guidance as to the drafter's role. That role is to facilitate, through drafting (the means), an agreement between the parties (the client's objective). But this role does not render the drafter a mere scrivener. By working with a client to flesh out the business deal, a drafter adds value to the deal and advances

---

6. Model R. Prof. Conduct 1.2(a).

7. *Id.* at cmt. 2.

8. *Id.* ("If [efforts to reach agreement] are unavailing and the lawyer has a fundamental disagreement with the client, the lawyer may withdraw from the representation.")

the client's objective. A drafter may not, however, recut the parties' business deal by adding or changing provisions to which the parties have agreed. Doing so steps over the line.

30.3 THE DRAFTER'S RESPONSIBILITY

Model Rule 1.1 states that "[a] lawyer shall provide competent representation to a client."[9] This rule raises at least two issues for drafters. First, what body of knowledge must a drafter have to be competent, and second, may a lawyer draft a contract if the lawyer has no prior experience with that type of contract? Comment 2 to Model Rule 1.1 should give you *some* comfort as you begin your career:

> A lawyer need not necessarily have special training or prior experience to handle legal problems of a type with which the lawyer is unfamiliar. A newly admitted lawyer can be as competent as a practitioner with long experience . . . . A lawyer can provide adequate representation in a wholly novel field *through necessary study*.[10] (Emphasis added.)

The italicized words are the key. You may represent a client despite little practical experience, but only if you gain the requisite knowledge through study. For a contract drafter, requisite knowledge means, at a bare minimum, a thorough grounding in contract law. (E.g., You should know the consequences of drafting a covenant rather than a condition.) In addition, according to some commentators, it includes an understanding of arbitration's role in dispute resolution.[11] It also entails subject matter expertise—either in a field of law or an industry. Finally, you must understand business, including financial statement concepts.[12] You cannot draft an agreement reflecting a business deal if you do not understand business and the client's business. Remember: A failure to have (or gain) the requisite expertise could subject you not only to disciplinary action but also to malpractice liability.

A drafter's responsibilities also include regularly informing the client about the status of the agreement and the transaction—how business and legal issues have been resolved and which issues remain open.[13] What this entails varies, depending on what Comment 5 to Model Rule 1.4 calls the **guiding principle**: The degree of communication depends on the client's expectations.[14] Some clients are hands-on and want to know everything about everything. Other clients are concerned only with the big picture. They want information on deal points, but not on other, subsidiary business issues. What and how much you communicate is client specific.

---

9. Model R. Prof. Conduct 1.1.

10. *Id.* at cmt. 2 (emphasis added).

11. Donald Lee Rome, *It's a New Day for ADR: From Boilerplate to Professional Responsibility,* 8 Bus. L. Today 11, 12, 15 (1999); *see also* David Hricik, *Infinite Combinations: Whether the Duty of Competency Requires Lawyers to Include Choice of Law Clauses in Contracts They Draft for Their Clients,* 12 Williamette J. Int'l L. & Dis. Res. 241, 258 (2004) (suggesting that in some circumstances, the duty of competency requires the inclusion of a choice of law provision).

12. Lawrence A. Cunningham, *Sharing Accounting's Burden: Business Lawyers in Enron's Dark Shadows,* 57 Bus. Law. 1421, 1449-1459 (2002).

13. Model R. Prof. Conduct 1.4(a)(3) ("A lawyer shall . . . keep the client reasonably informed about the status of the matter[.]"); *id.* at 1.4(b) ("A lawyer shall explain a matter to the extent reasonably necessary to permit the client to make informed decisions regarding the representation.").

14. Model R. Prof. Conduct 1.4 cmt. 5 ("The guiding principle is that the lawyer should fulfill reasonable client expectations for information consistent with the duty to act in the client's best interests, and the client's overall requirements as to the character of representation.").

458   Chapter 30   Ethical Issues in Drafting

30.4 INTERACTIONS WITH THIRD PARTIES

Transactional lawyers deal with third parties on a regular basis, particularly in negotiations. These dealings are often strewn with ethical landmines through which you must navigate carefully, and they do not disappear because you are negotiating on paper through dueling drafts and markups.

The key ethical proscriptions in connection with contract drafting are the following Model Rules:

■ Model Rule 1.2(d) — "A lawyer shall not counsel a client to engage, or assist a client, in conduct that the lawyer knows is criminal or fraudulent . . . ."[15]

■ Model Rule 4.1(b) — "In the course of representing a client a lawyer shall not knowingly . . . fail to disclose a material fact to a third person when disclosure is necessary to avoid assisting a criminal or fraudulent act by a client, unless disclosure is prohibited by Rule 1.6."[16]

■ Model Rule 8.4(c) — "It is professional misconduct for a lawyer to . . . engage in conduct involving dishonesty, fraud, deceit or misrepresentation . . . ."[17]

Model Rules 1.2(d) and 4.1(b) require an understanding of **intersectionality**.[18] Intersectionality determines whether a lawyer's actions are ethical by looking at where in the spectrum of behavior the client's actions fall. Imagine that the following diagonal represents the range of a client's actions, moving from legal and not fraudulent at Point A to criminal and fraudulent at Point D.

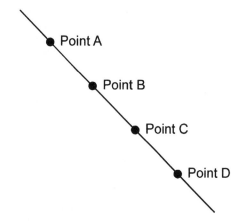

As the client's activities move down the diagonal, the lawyer's actions move in tandem from ethical to unethical. So, at Point A, when the client's actions are legal, his lawyer's actions are ethical. But at Point D, when the client's actions are criminal or fraudulent, the lawyer violates the ethical duty not to assist a client in criminal or fraudulent activities.

To apply the concept of intersectionality to drafting, imagine that the diagonal represents varying degrees of truthfulness in the client's representations and warranties. If the representations and warranties are true, then the lawyer's drafting of the contract does not violate any ethical proscriptions. But, if they are intentionally false,

---

15. Model R. Prof. Conduct 1.2(d).

16. Model R. Prof. Conduct 4.1(b).

17. Model R. Prof. Conduct 8.4(c).

18. Former Dean Mary C. Daly of St. John's University School of Law introduced me to the concept of *intersectionality.*

they constitute fraudulent misrepresentations, and drafting the contract assists the client in perpetrating a fraud.

Violation of Model Rule 8.4(c) does not require as a prerequisite that the client commit a crime or fraud. Instead, the focus is on the lawyer's actions. Has the lawyer done something, independently of the client's actions, that involves dishonesty, fraud, deceit, or misrepresentation? For example, one ABA Opinion concludes that a lawyer's failure to alert the drafter of a scrivener's error that the latter made would constitute fraud by the lawyer.[19] Although the opinion also adverts to Model Rules 1.2(d) and 4.1(b), the violation of Model Rule 8.4(c) is included as a separate violation.

---

19. ABA Informal Op. 86-1518.

CHAPTER THIRTY

EXERCISES

Exercise 30-1

Skating on Thin Ice

Part A

Assume that you are Sandy Plage, an up-and-coming corporate partner at Good Ethics & Law. Over time, you have developed an excellent business relationship with Bob Hansell. Bob has sent you substantial business from whatever company was his then-current employer.[20] Currently, he is general counsel at Speedskates, Inc. (Speedskates). Speedskates is the U.S. operating subsidiary of Speedskates International, Inc. (International), a privately held multinational corporation with its headquarters in Singapore.

The sole shareholders of International are two siblings (Robert and Sara Marlat), who are also the directors and officers of Speedskates. At the moment, your law firm is representing International in connection with tax and corporate issues relating to International's operations both in the United States and worldwide. In addition, you are the primary outside counsel in connection with a loan agreement Speedskates is negotiating.

Bob just called sounding somewhat distressed. He first reviewed the deal facts with you.

1. Speedskates is in the midst of negotiating for a $50 million line of credit from Big Bank NA ("Big Bank"). International will guarantee the debt. (Speedskates already has $200 million in long-term debt from a multi-bank group.) The new line would provide Speedskates with some badly needed additional working capital. (See the diagram on page 462.)
2. As a condition to the consummation of the Credit Agreement, Big Bank has requested Bob, as in-house counsel, to deliver a legal opinion on certain corporate matters. (This is common practice. The theory is that in-house counsel can deliver these opinions more cheaply than outside counsel because in-house counsel has superior knowledge.) Bob wants you to review the Credit Agreement and his overall opinion and to advise him whether the individual opinions he is being asked to give are appropriate. His initial inclination is that he should be able to give the opinions as they are all true. Those opinions are as follows:
    (a) Speedskates is duly incorporated and in good standing; the Credit Agreement is duly authorized, executed, and delivered.
    (b) The consummation of this transaction does not violate any existing agreements to which Speedskates is a party.

Issue

Is it appropriate for you to discuss these matters with Bob?

---

20. Translation: Bob is important to you. You are paid not only for your brains, but because you bring in business. Bob = business.

Part B

In your preliminary review of the Credit Agreement, you discover two representations and warranties that raise concern:

■ The draft of the Credit Agreement states that Speedskates has complied with all the covenants in the other loan agreement. That agreement requires Speedskates and its affiliates to meet certain net worth tests. Because of operating losses incurred during the past two years, Speedskates has failed to meet the net worth tests and has breached the loan agreement. Therefore, leaving the representation and warranty as is in the Credit Agreement would result in an untrue statement.

■ In Section 5.7 of the Credit Agreement, Speedskates represents that International and each of its subsidiaries (including Speedskates) has filed the tax returns required to be filed and has paid all required taxes, other than those that could not have a material adverse effect.

    (i)   Based on the work that your firm has done, you know that Speedskates France, one of International's subsidiaries, may owe some taxes to the United States. No one yet knows whether the amount at stake is material as the detailed review and analysis that would be required to make such an assessment has not been done. An assessment of materiality would need to contemplate not only the consequences of any payment on International's net worth but also on its liquidity. Neither the firm nor Speedskates' auditors has the time to finish the assessment before the loan closes.

    (ii)   Bob Hansell knows, of course, all about the tax issues, as he has been acting as International's point person.

After reviewing these representations and warranties with several of your colleagues, you call Bob back.

Issues

1. What do you advise Bob about the legal consequences of Speedskates making the representation and warranty with respect to the no violation of other agreements? Why does this matter? If Speedskates makes the representation and warranty and you continue with your representation, will you violate your ethical duties?

2. What do you advise Bob about the legal consequences of Speedskates making the representation and warranty with respect to the tax payments and the financial statements? Why does this matter? If Speedskates makes the representation and warranty and you continue with your representation, will you violate your ethical duties?

3. May Bob deliver his opinion without violating any ethical rules?

4. Assume that

    (a)   you and Bob have raised grave concerns about the tax returns with the president of International; and

    (b)   International's president tells Bob that the amount at stake with regard to the tax returns is not material, and that the materiality exception in the representation and warranty permits Speedskates to make the representation and warranty without further disclosure.

Can you and Bob rely on what the president has said?

5. Assume that

    (a) Bob tells International's president that he will not deliver his opinion without changes to the representations and warranties; and

    (b) the president responds by telling Bob that if he fails to deliver the opinion, he will be in breach of his employment agreement with International.

    Bob then calls you and asks what his rights are if he quits, or in the alternative, if International fires him. You respond. . . .

6. Bob goes home to mull over his options. The next morning he calls to report that the deal has closed, the bank having decided to waive the condition requiring Bob's opinion. May you tell the bank? What are your ethical obligations in terms of reporting this matter to the local disciplinary authority?

Diagram of the Speedskates Transaction

Exercise 30-2

You're Too Kind

To: Exhausted, but Still Going, Associate

From: Compassionate, but Demanding, Corporate Partner

As you know, I am representing HiTech Inc. in the sale of substantially all of its assets. Unfortunately, in connection with that deal, I now have an ethical dilemma: The Buyer's lawyers have crafted a provision that is too generous to our client. Specifically, they have drafted the representation and warranty with respect to defaults under existing contracts as follows:

"No material defaults exist under any material agreements."

According to my recollection of the negotiation (and also the recollection of our client), the representation and warranty was supposed to provide that no defaults exist under any material agreement. (No double dip on materiality.)

Our client insists that we say nothing. I am thinking that maybe we should say something. What are our ethical obligations? Do you have any suggestions as to how we should deal with our client on this matter?

I have no idea whether it will be helpful to you, but attached is ABA Informal Opinion 86-1518. Do not do any other research on this matter; our client does not want to pay.

ABA Informal Opinion 86-1518
Notice to Opposing Counsel of Inadvertent Omission of Contract Provision
February 9, 1986

Where the lawyer for [A] has received for signature from the lawyer for [B] the final transcription of a contract from which an important provision previously agreed upon has been inadvertently omitted by the lawyer for [B], the lawyer for [A], unintentionally advantaged, should contact the lawyer for [B] to correct the error and need not consult [A] about the error.

A and B, with the assistance of their lawyers, have negotiated a commercial contract. After deliberation with counsel, A ultimately acquiesced in the final provision insisted upon by B, previously in dispute between the parties and without which B would have refused to come to overall agreement. However, A's lawyer discovered that the final draft of the contract typed in the office of B's lawyer did not contain the provision which had been in dispute. The Committee has been asked to give its opinion as to the ethical duty of A's lawyer in that circumstance.

The Committee considers this situation to involve merely a scrivener's error, not an intentional change in position by the other party. A meeting of the minds has already occurred. The Committee concludes that the error is appropriate for correction between the lawyers without client consultation.[1]

---

1. Assuming for purposes of discussion that the error is "information relating to [the] representation," under Rule 1.6 disclosure would be "impliedly authorized in order to carry out the representation." The Comment to Rule 1.6 points out that a lawyer has implied authority to make "a disclosure that facilitates a satisfactory conclusion"—in this case completing the commercial contract already agreed on and left to the lawyers to memorialize. We do not here reach the issue of the lawyer's duty if the client wishes to exploit the error.

A's lawyer does not have a duty to advise A of the error pursuant to any obligation of communication under Rule 1.4 of the ABA Model Rules of Professional Conduct (1983). "The guiding principle is that the lawyer should fulfill reasonable client expectations for information consistent with the duty to act in the client's best interests and the client's overall requirements as to the character of representation." Comment to Rule 1.4. In this circumstance there is no "informed decision," in the language of Rule 1.4 that A needs to make; the decision on the contract has already been made by the client. Furthermore, the Comment to Rule 1.2 points out that the lawyer may decide the "technical" means to be employed to carry out the objective of the representation, without consultation with the client.

The client does not have a right to take unfair advantage of the error. The client's right pursuant to Rule 1.2 to expect committed and dedicated representation is not unlimited. Indeed, for A's lawyer to suggest that A has an opportunity to capitalize on the clerical error, unrecognized by B and B's lawyer, might raise a serious question of the violation of the duty of A's lawyer under Rule 1.2(d) not to counsel the client to engage in, or assist the client in, conduct the lawyer knows is fraudulent. In addition, Rule 4.1(b) admonishes the lawyer not knowingly to fail to disclose a material fact to a third person when disclosure is necessary to avoid assisting a fraudulent act by a client, and Rule 8.4(c) prohibits the lawyer from engaging in conduct involving dishonesty, fraud, deceit, or misrepresentation.

The result would be the same under the predecessor ABA Model Code of Professional Responsibility (1969, revised 1980). While EC 7-8 teaches that a lawyer should use best efforts to ensure that the client's decisions are made after the client has been informed of relevant considerations, and EC 9-2 charges the lawyer with fully and promptly informing the client of material developments, the scrivener's error is neither a relevant consideration nor a material development and therefore does not establish an opportunity for a client's decision.[2] The duty of zealous representation in DR 7-101 is limited to lawful objectives. *See* DR 7-102. Rule 1.2 evolved from DR 7-102(A)(7), which prohibits a lawyer from counseling or assisting the client in conduct known to be fraudulent. See also DR 1-102(A)(4), the precursor of Rule 8.4(c), prohibiting the lawyer from engaging in conduct involving dishonesty, fraud, deceit, or misrepresentation.

---

2. The delivery of the erroneous document is not a "material development" of which the client should be informed under EC 9-2 of the Model Code of Professional Responsibility, but the omission of the provision from the document is a "material fact" which under Rule 4.1(b) of the Model Rules of Professional Conduct must be disclosed to B's lawyer.

Exercise 30-3

Lower than Loew

You are Lydia Grant, a junior associate at Good Ethics & Law LLP. Your client is Acquisitions Inc. (Acquisitions), a privately held investment firm. One of Acquisitions's subsidiaries, Newco, is purchasing substantially all of the assets of a candy manufacturer. To finance the purchase, Newco is borrowing the necessary funds from Megabank USA. You have been representing the subsidiary in connection with the loan negotiations. You've been working with Henry Loew, vice president of Acquisitions.

The terms of the borrowing are fairly standard and include mandatory prepayments as determined by a formula.[21] Unfortunately, the formula does not work

---

21. Mandatory prepayment provisions generally provide that a borrower must repay the bank a percentage of any cash that it receives from an additional bank borrowing, the issuance of equity or debt securities, or the sale of substantially all of its assets. The bank insists on the prepayment because a lower outstanding loan balance reduces the credit risk.

properly according to your understanding of the provision from earlier discussions with the bankers and their lawyers. It seems as if the formula's results significantly understate the amount Newco must prepay. As the parties did not draft a term sheet, you have no statement of terms with which to compare the provision. Moreover, as Acquisitions and Megabank have not done a deal before, you can't even look at an earlier deal for guidance.

Loew is adamant that you say nothing. To obtain an additional perspective, you speak with the Ralph Adams, the firm's partner responsible for legal ethics. He gives you the attached case, thinking that it might provide you with some much needed guidance.

Issues

1. Must you disclose the problem with the prepayment provision?

2. Assume that you conclude that you must disclose the problem with the prepayment provision. On hearing your conclusion, Loew marches into Ralph Adams's office and declares you to be "a lily-livered coward." Ralph is less abusive, but not much. He tells you and Loew that although it is a close question, he thinks the deal can go forward without disclosing the problem with the prepayment formula. What are your ethical obligations? May you follow your superior's instructions without violating your ethical obligations?

Stare v. Tate
21 Cal. App. 3d 432, 98 Cal. Rptr. 264 (2d Dist. 1971)

KAUS, [Presiding Justice].

Plaintiff appeals from an adverse judgment in an action to reform a property settlement agreement with her former husband, the defendant, and to enforce the agreement as reformed.

Facts

The agreement in question was signed by both parties [who were divorcing] on February 21, 1968. It was the culmination of protracted negotiations which had been going on for several years. Both sides were represented by counsel at all times.[1]

In the negotiations both sides apparently agreed that the community property was to be evenly divided. They did not agree, however, on the value of certain items and on the community property status of certain stocks that stood in the husband's name alone.

These disagreements centered principally on items which, it was understood, were to be retained by the husband. . . .

To sum up: if Joan was correct with respect to the value of the Holt property, her community property interest in it was about $25,000 higher than Tim conceded; if she were to succeed on her contentions with respect to the stock, Tim would have had to pay her roughly $40,000 more than he was willing.

In January, 1968, Joan's attorney prepared a document entitled "SECOND PROPOSAL FOR A BASIS OF SETTLEMENT—TATE v. TATE" which, among other things, arrived at a

---

1. The attorneys who represent the husband on this appeal did not act for him in the negotiations.

suggested figure of $70,081.85 for the value of Joan's share in the Holt property. This value was arrived at by a computation set forth in the proposal. It is copied in the footnote.[4]

It is obvious that Joan's attorney arrived at the figure of $70,081.85 for the community equity in the property only by making two substantial errors. First, the net value after deducting the encumbrances from the asserted gross value of $550,000 is $241,637.01, not $141,637.01; second, one-half of $141,637.01 is substantially more than $70,081.85. The correct figure for the equity should have been $120,818.50 or, roughly $50,000 more.

The mistake did not escape Tim's accountant who discovered it while helping Tim's attorney in preparing a counteroffer. He brought it to the attention of the attorney who, in his own words, reacted as follows:

> I told him that I had been arguing with (the wife's attorney) to use the value that was on the—on the real property tax statement, but I knew that that was low and (he) would never go for it, that the appraisal had been $425,000.00 when the building had been purchased by said owners, and I thought that until we got it, that we would use something like a $450,000.00 value, and he said, "Fine." It is my recollection that I said to him, "You know, you might as well use the figure that Walker [the wife's attorney] has there because his mistake is a hundred thousand dollars and we value it at a hundred thousand dollars less, so it is basically the same thing, so give it a $70,000.00 equity," and that is what he did and that is how it came about.

A counteroffer was then submitted to Joan and her lawyer. It lists all of the community assets, with the property in question being valued at $70,082.00, rounding up the erroneous figure in Joan's offer to the nearest dollar. There can be no reasonable doubt that the counteroffer was prepared in a way designed to minimize the danger that Joan or her attorney would discover the mistake. While all other encumbered properties are listed at an agreed gross value, with encumbrances shown as a deduction therefrom, the only figure that appears next to the Holt property is the equity!

.   .   .

The rule that the party who misleads another is estopped from claiming that the contract is anything but what the other is led to believe, appears to be quite generally accepted. Citing many cases from other jurisdictions and noting no contrary authority Corbin says: "Reformation may be a proper remedy even though the mistake is not mutual. If one of the parties mistakenly believes that the writing is a correct integration of that to which he had expressed his assent and the other party knows that it is not, reformation may be decreed. The conduct of the other party in permitting the first to execute the erroneous writing and later attempting to enforce it may be regarded as fraudulent; but it is enough to justify reformation that he knows the terms proposed by the first party and the meaning thereof and leads that party reasonably to believe that he too assents to those terms. This makes a contract; and the writing may be reformed to accord with it. The fact that the first party was negligent in failing to observe that the writing does not express what he has assented to does not deprive him of this remedy. The ground for estoppel is against the other and non-mistaken party, not against the mistaken party even though he is negligent." (3 Corbin on Contracts, §614, pp. 730-732.) The rule is also in accord with the Restatement of Contracts.

.   .   .

Stephens, J., and Aiso, J., concurred.

---

4. "888 East Holt Avenue, Pomona
   (Note: value as per previous offer)

Total value	$550,000.00
Less encumbrance	- 308,362.99
Net value	$141,637.01
One-half community	$70,081.85"

Exercise 30-4

WCBA's Technical Problems

You are Pat E. Kake, a partner at Good Ethics & Law, a New York City law firm with 450 lawyers in the United States and abroad. You have a broad-ranging corporate practice, having successfully resisted several attempts by the firm to pigeonhole you into a niche practice.

Part A

One of your clients is WCBA, one of New York City's premiere television stations. Your contact at WCBA is Lila Bartley, senior vice president and general counsel.

Lila just called and related the following: WCBA's longtime sportscaster, Ray Statler, passed away recently. His death has created a significant business problem for WCBA, as its ratings for the evening broadcasts have fallen precipitously since he died. Lila tells you that all is not lost, however. WCBA has learned through the grapevine that Bob Jacobs, WXYZ's longtime sportscaster, is disaffected with his present employer and wants to jump ship as soon as possible. As a result of the intervention of an intermediary, Bob gave his employment agreement to another employee of WCBA, and that agreement has been passed on to Lila.

Lila tells you that she has reviewed the contract and that one provision gives her pause. It states the following:

> **Noncompete**. During the Term and for a period of 90 days afterwards, Employee shall not
>
> (a)　accept employment from,
> (b)　negotiate for employment with, or
> (c)　solicit any proposal from
>
> any Person in connection with a position as a radio or television sportscaster.[22]

She then states the obvious: If Bob were to sign a contract with WCBA, he will have violated his contract with WXYZ, and WCBA may be subject to a suit for tortious interference with contract. Lila then continues that WCBA is willing to accept the business risk of the lawsuit. Lila is worried, however, about the risk to her. Is she somehow acting unethically by participating in the negotiation and drafting of Bob's employment contract with WCBA?

Issues

1.　What do you advise Lila? Should she alert Bob to the issue?

2.　How (if at all) does this differ from aiding a client who intends to violate a law?

Part B

Lila calls you and informs you that WCBA has made the business decision to employ Bob. She asks that you negotiate the contract. You are, of course, delighted to do so. (Your hours this month have been a little low.) Lila tells you that Dave Winslow will be negotiating on behalf of Bob.

After marking up an employment agreement from the firm's precedents files, you send a copy to Lila who blesses it. You then send a PDF copy of the agreement by e-mail to each of Bob Jacobs and Dave Winslow.

---

22. For the purposes of this exercise, assume that this contract provision is enforceable.

About three days later, Dave calls to give you comments on the draft. Most of his comments are reasonable; others give you pause.

Issues

1. Dave asks for a bonus if ratings improve 5% or more within the first 30 days of the employment term. Lila approves the bonus. When you go to draft the bonus provision, you note that the parties did not address whether a pro rata bonus should be payable on death or disability. Are you ethically obligated to provide for the pro rata bonus in the revised contract? What nonethical reason could you give to encourage Lila to raise the issue with Dave?

2. Dave states that the proposed noncompete provision is probably unenforceable both in terms of time and geographic scope. You agree to a reasonable, shorter time period, but insist on a larger geographic scope, arguing that it is the industry standard. It is, but it is also highly unlikely that a court would enforce it.

   (a) Will you be violating your ethical duties if the contract includes an unenforceable geographic scope provision?
   (b) Would your answer change if you were drafting a standard form contract that all of WCBA's employees would sign and you knew that the courts had held the provision unenforceable?

Exercise 30-5

Pine Greene

In addition to WCBA, one of your long-time clients is By'em Inc. (By'em). By'em buys undervalued companies and sells off the subsidiaries and divisions at prices that are, in the aggregate, greater than the value of the company as a whole. You have strong relationships with both the in-house counsel, Stanley Leech, and the executive vice president, Reena Pixley.

Reena called about two weeks ago to tell you about a new deal. By'em plans to purchase Conglomerate Inc. (Conglomerate). She asked that you mark up and distribute By'em's standard form purchase agreement. The deal is on a fast track. Negotiations and due diligence proceed apace, and the closing is scheduled for the end of the month. The transaction is basically friendly; you even established a good working relationship with Roger Pine, president of Conglomerate.

As part of the negotiations, By'em and Conglomerate agree to a term. When drafting the insert, you craft the insert in such a way that Conglomerate arguably takes on more of the risk than had been agreed to. You blackline the entire provision so that Conglomerate's counsel will know that it has been changed. In your cover letter, as has been your practice, you point out the significant changes in the revised draft—except this one provision.

Issues

1. Did you violate your ethical duties by drafting the provision the way you did, or by failing to note the change in your cover letter?

2. Does your answer change if the client instructs you to make the change? Consider *In re Rothwell*, 296 S.E.2d 870 (S.C. 1982).

In re ROTHWELL

296 S.E.2d 870 (S.C. 1982)

PER CURIAM:

The Hearing Panel and the Board of Commissioners on Grievances and Discipline recommend respondent Donald Erwin Rothwell be publicly reprimanded for professional misconduct. We agree.

Respondent was retained by Richard Mowery to represent him in negotiations with Mowery's former employer, W.W. Williams Company, who had transferred Mowery from Columbus, Ohio to Columbia. To facilitate the transfer, Williams Company loaned Mowery $47,000 to purchase a house in Columbia.

Mowery was discharged from Williams Company after he moved to Columbia, but before he had repaid the $47,000. Williams Company offered to buy Mowery's Ohio house and apply the equity to the debt, leaving a deficiency of $7,201.04.

Williams Company prepared and mailed to respondent a deed along with a letter requesting that respondent have his client, Mowery, execute and return the deed to Williams Company for filing. The letter also stated, "[w]e will expect your call if there are any questions."

Respondent surreptitiously altered the deed by inserting a paragraph satisfying the entire debt from Mowery to Williams Company, and mailed the deed to Williams Company with a letter which stated only:

> We are returning herewith your package to you duly executed. Once you have filed the deed of record, please forward on a clocked copy of same for our files. Thank you.

No notice was given Williams Company that the deed had been altered.

Williams Company filed the deed and sued Mowery for the deficiency. Respondent raised the altered deed as a defense.

Respondent contends the deed prepared by Williams Company was merely an offer, and his alteration of the deed constituted a counteroffer. Clearly, Williams Company expected respondent to either (1) have his client execute the deed or (2) telephone Williams Company. Respondent's letter to Williams Company gave no notice of the alteration, but rather, led Williams Company to believe he had complied with their request.

We agree with the Panel that respondent engaged in conduct involving dishonesty, fraud, deceit, and misrepresentation which is prejudicial to the administration of justice and adversely reflects on his fitness to practice law, all in violation of DR1-102(A)(1), (4), (5) and (6); DR7-102(A)(3); and sections 5(b) and (d) of the Rule on Disciplinary Procedure of the Supreme Court of the State of South Carolina. Accordingly, respondent Donald Erwin Rothwell stands publicly reprimanded for his acts of professional misconduct.

PART SEVEN

Additional Exercises

Additional Exercises

Exercise 31-1[1]

Revised Car Purchase Agreement

Revise your draft of the Car Purchase Agreement (Exercise 5-1) based on the material that you have covered so far this semester. In addition, include appropriate provisions to reflect the following changes to the transaction's terms:

1. The Buyer has decided that it may want to do a bit of due diligence and not rely solely on the Seller's representations and warranties. The Seller has agreed that the Buyer has the right not to close if a mechanic of the Buyer's choice determines that the car is not in the condition represented. The Buyer has agreed to pay for the inspection.

    You may create whatever facts you want to draft these business terms. Think about how the inspection would actually take place. What would be the sequence of events? For example, how does the car get to the mechanic? How will the parties know what the mechanic concluded? Draft these provisions from the Buyer's perspective, but in a manner that would be reasonably acceptable to the other side.

    In deciding how to draft the provisions about the inspection, also think about the contract's organization. Would it be more helpful to the reader to separate the provisions by contract concept or to put all the related provisions together or do some combination?

2. The Seller is insisting on a 10% down payment to be paid concurrently with the execution and delivery of the parties' agreement. She also wants an additional 10% down payment after completion of the mechanic's inspection.

3. The car's Vehicle Identification Number is 23456.

4. The Buyer has been looking for a job as an associate at a law firm and has received an offer from Hie Power & Stress LLP. He wants to be able to call off the closing if he does not receive the promised $5,000 sign-on bonus. To induce the Seller to accept this proposal, the Buyer agreed that if the Buyer did not close because he did not receive his sign-on bonus, the Seller could keep the first down payment. The Seller would also like some assurance in the contract that the Buyer has received an offer from Hie Power.

---

1. This exercise is based on an exercise that Alan Shaw created.

5. The Seller has agreed to deliver the car, the keys, and any manuals to the Buyer's home on the Closing Date.

6. The Seller has told the Buyer that the car is still under the manufacturer's warranty and that she has its documentation. The Buyer was delighted to learn this but wants to know what the warranty provides. He is not a trusting fellow and is unwilling to rely on the Seller's assessment of the quality of the manufacturer's warranty. If the warranty is not reasonably acceptable, he does not want to purchase the car. Without stating the details of the warranty, provide the Buyer with the comfort he has asked for.

7. If either party makes a misrepresentation or breaches a warranty or covenant, the contract should terminate.

8. When working through the endgame provisions, *follow the cash* and provide for all appropriate contingencies as to the down payments—both if the transaction closes and if it does not close. You must separately analyze how the contract will deal with each down payment in each situation. If the facts do not state which party is entitled to one or both of the down payments under a particular circumstance, think through what makes sense from the Buyer's business perspective and draft accordingly. Write a memo no longer than one page explaining which down payments went to which party and why.

9. The closing will take place at 1:00 p.m. at the office of the Buyer's lawyers: Workhard & Succeed LLP. Its address is 278 Appletree Lane, Glencoe, Illinois.

Assume that the contract has not yet been executed. Each of these provisions, therefore, is part of the original contract and does not amend an existing agreement. In addition, as in Exercise 5-1, assume that no statutes apply to this transaction.

Exercise 31-2

Aircraft Purchase Agreement

Follow the instructions in the memorandum that follows:

Memorandum

To: D. Fender

From: H. Flighty

Date: October 10, 20X2

Re: Purchase of the Icarus I-800

As you know, I have not finalized my deal with Rob Robertson. I think that deal will fall through. If it does, I suspect my entire net worth will be at risk as I have yet to find financing to consummate the I-800 purchase from Samson's company.

Last evening, Sam called and asked why my lawyers hadn't sent out a draft agreement. I told him that I would see what was holding you up. Obviously, what was holding you up was that I hadn't asked you to draft the rest of the agreement. Now, however, we must go forward.

Please do not reinvent the wheel on this transaction. I have attached to this memo as **Exhibit A** a document that combines

(a) the draft I gave you that had the preamble, recitals, words of agreement, and definitions (the First Draft); and

(b) representations and warranties, covenants, and conditions from an Asset Purchase Agreement that a friend of mine used in another transaction. I have also attached a photo of the I-800 and some marketing literature. I thought you might be interested to see what I'm buying.

To complete the draft for my review, please do the following:

(i)   Redraft Exhibit A to take into account our previous discussion of the First Draft. If we didn't discuss something but it needs revision, do it.

(ii) Insert the action sections that you previously worked on, making any necessary revisions.

(iii) Redraft the remaining provisions of Exhibit A to reflect our deal. They will probably need a fair amount of revision. Do not use any supplementary sources other than those distributed to you in that drafting course you took at law school.

In order to save money, do not draft provisions other than the ones I've specifically asked for or those that are required because of the cascade effect.

In your redraft, please take into account the following:

1. In our discussions, Sam advised me that Wings is not in default under the Pilot Agreement, but that it is in default under the Maintenance Agreement. The default has given rise to a $250,000 lien against the I-800 in favor of Greasemonkeys, Inc. I told Sam that I considered this lien material. Sam specifically stated that no other liens had been filed against the Aircraft — material or otherwise. He then promised me that between now and the Closing, the Greasemonkeys' lien would be removed. Obviously, this point needs to be covered wherever appropriate in the Aircraft Purchase Agreement. If that lien is not removed by Closing, I

would like the right not to close as well as the right to sue for damages. I think the Purchase Offer also had a provision about liens.

2. Delete in whole or in part any representation and warranty, covenant, or condition that is inapposite, or change it to fit the facts as I have described them to you. One thing I am certain of is that I cannot represent and warrant that I have financing now. I doubt that Sam will go for it, but try drafting a financing out.

   As I'm sure you know, a financing out provides a buyer with a walk-away right if it is unable to obtain financing. Sellers generally dislike financing outs, fearing that they transform an obligation to purchase into an option to purchase. Specifically, they worry that a buyer may decide it dislikes a deal and then try to get out of it by claiming it could not obtain any financing or could not obtain financing on commercially reasonable terms. If that happens, a seller could end up losing other sale opportunities, while tied up for months in a contract with the buyer. If you can think of a way to demonstrate that my interest is real, something that might make the financing out more tolerable to Sam, please add it to the draft. Whatever it is, it must be something that is not too hard to do.

3. Do not delete from your agreement Sections 7.4 and 7.5 and Sections 8.4 and 8.5. (You may redraft, but you may not delete.)

4. As far as I know, Wings' only asset is the I-800. Please make sure that the contract reflects this. I want it explicitly covered because if Wings does own any spare parts or anything else related to the Aircraft, I want them to be part of this deal. I'm certainly paying enough.

5. My recollection is that I inappropriately included at least one substantive provision in the definitions article of the Aircraft Purchase Agreement. Please move it to the appropriate section in the body of the agreement. Also include whatever representations and warranties, covenants, and conditions that the Purchase Offer requires. If it is unclear whether a term is a covenant or a condition, I'd like to be able to sue as well as to get out of this deal.

6. The parties have agreed that they may agree to terminate the agreement at any time.

7. Samson told me that the I-800's maximum range with eight passengers and four crewmembers is 8,000 nautical miles at Mach 90. That's a fabulous distance and speed. Please make sure that the contract includes this information.

8. Samson told me something else that he wants changed. The representations and warranties have lots of language dealing with material adverse changes to Wings' business. He says that language would be appropriate for the sale of a business, but I'm buying only a single asset—the jet. Please come up with a material adverse change standard that is more transaction specific.

9. Sam has agreed to have the Aircraft's tail painted by the Closing with Fly-by-Night's logo. But, the paint shop may have trouble fitting in the I-800 between now and the Closing. If the Aircraft is not painted on time, we've agreed that I don't have to close. Because that is a fairly extreme outcome for something relatively minor, he has good incentive to get it done. Just this one provision should do it.

10. The draft attached as Exhibit A is rife with drafting errors. There's legalese, provisions are way too long, and there's a total lack of craftsmanship. Please clean it up.

11. Please spell out how the escrowed amount is to be distributed if we don't close. Figure out all the reasons we might not close and make sure that the escrow is distributed appropriately. Remember: *Follow the cash.* Also, my recollection is that the Purchase Offer requires me to pay $3 million if the deal doesn't close because of something I did wrong. Please figure out how this interacts with the financing out.

12. I've been doing some more thinking on Section 5.5. Only some of those restrictions make sense for our deal. Choose those that you think apply and make them transaction specific.

13. The Seller and the Buyer each have conditions to their closing obligations related to litigation. Please decide whether each condition should cover litigation against
    (a) the Seller and the Buyer, each as individual defendants or jointly, or
    (b) against just one party, and if so, which party.
    Please explain your decision in your memo to me.

14. Do not draft any Exhibits.

15. For clarity, the $3 million payment referred to in Paragraph 9 of the Purchase Offer is intended by the parties to be liquidated damages. Assume that the provision is enforceable. Do not research this issue.

16. If a representation and warranty includes a schedule and you have the relevant information, please draft the schedule and attach it to the agreement. Assume that the only facts that exist are those that you know. (Stated differently, if you don't have facts, then don't draft a schedule.) Eliminate references to any unnecessary schedules. Of course, you could always omit the schedule and put the information in the agreement—if appropriate. Which you do is a judgment call. (In making that judgment call, consider the amount of information and whether including it in the agreement or a schedule facilitates reading the contract.)

17. Define *Escrow Amount* as $300,000. This definition differs from the Escrow Agreement's definition of *Escrow Amount*. This revised definition will permit you to separately treat the $300,000 and the accrued interest on the Escrow Amount. Remember: The Escrow Agreement and the Aircraft Purchase Agreement are separate agreements and need not have identical defined terms and definitions. They must, however, work together.

18. As you know from our due diligence, Wings is the current registered owner of the Aircraft. I want to make sure that Wings gives us any documentation that we need from it so that we can register the Aircraft. Please determine what that is and make sure that the agreement provides that we receive it at the Closing. Do we need the consent of the FAA? Let me know what you find out.

19. Do not add a representation and warranty about existing litigation.

20. I'm wondering whether the definitions of Maintenance Agreement and Pilot Agreement should treat amendments the same way and whether there's a cascade effect (hint) from the way the definitions do treat amendments.

21. I've also been worrying about the Engines. My mechanic didn't think that they were properly maintained. I don't think that the Seller can say more than that they are in adequate condition. The rest of the Aircraft, however, is in good condition, except for ordinary wear and tear. Please provide that between now and the Closing the Aircraft will be maintained and repaired in accordance with its FAA Approved Maintenance and Inspection Program. That should bring the Engines to an appropriate maintenance level before the Closing. Also, please make sure that the Seller is obligated to keep the Aircraft's logbook and other flight maintenance records accurate, complete, and current.

22. Here's some additional information with respect to my financing plans. So far, I am negotiating with three banks and have submitted full applications to two: First National Bank of Lex and Lex Banking, N.A. I mentioned this to Sam, and it gave him comfort to know this. He wants it in the agreement—of course.

23. Samson confirmed to me that Wings doesn't do business outside of its state of incorporation. Neither does Fly-by-Night. Please figure out how and where this should be reflected in the agreement.

24. There are no defaults under the Purchase Offer or the Escrow Agreement.

25. Please include the necessary provisions so that the Aircraft Purchase Agreement, once signed, supersedes the Purchase Offer. My recollection is that Chapter 16 from your law

school drafting textbook might have something that could help you here. Do not draft any other "boilerplate" provisions. Sam and I have agreed to deal with those issues in a later draft.

26. Include the appropriate signature lines.

27. When you send me the finished agreement, please include a cover memo of no more than two pages. Follow the guidelines on drafting memos to clients in Chapter 32, Document 7 of your law school drafting textbook.

Finally, please draft an agreement that favors me, but that is not so one-sided or overly aggressive that it impedes negotiations. We want to get the deal done, so no gratuitously demanding provisions just to appear tough.

H.F.

Note to students: The following draft of the Aircraft Purchase Agreement is on the *Drafting Contracts* website.

EXHIBIT A

Aircraft Purchase Agreement

AGREEMENT, dated October 30, 20XX, by and among Supersonic Wings Corp., a Delaware corporation, (the "Seller") and Fly-by-Night Aviation, Inc., a New York corporation having its principal place of business at 987 East 48th Street, New York, New York 10036 ("Buyer").

WHEREAS, the Seller desires to sell to Buyer, and Buyer desires to purchase from the Seller, the Aircraft; and

WHEREAS, the Buyer hereby agrees to pay the Seller $23,000,000 in immediately available funds.

NOW, THEREFORE, in consideration of the mutual promises herein set forth and subject to the terms and conditions hereof, the parties agree as follows:

Article 1 — Definitions

1.1 Defined Terms. As used in this Agreement, terms defined in the preamble and recitals of this Agreement have the meanings set forth therein, and the following terms have the meanings set forth below:

"**Agreement**" means this Agreement of Sale and all Schedules and Exhibits hereto, as the same may be amended from time to time.

"**Aircraft**" means the Airframe, equipped with the two Rolls-Royce engines, Model No. BR710, bearing Serial Nos. 72725 and 72726, together with all appliances, avionics, furnishings, and other components, equipment, and property incorporated in or otherwise related to the Airframe or engines.

"**Airframe**" means the Icarus Aerospace Corporation I-800 aircraft, bearing United States Registration No. N765BW and Manufacturer's Serial No. 8181.

"**Assigned Contracts**" means the Maintenance Agreement (as hereafter defined) and the Pilot Agreement (as hereafter defined).

"**Assumed Liabilities**" means, collectively, all liabilities and obligations of the Seller that arise under either (a) the Maintenance Agreement on or after the Closing Date or (b) the Pilot Agreement on or after the date of the Closing.

"**Aviation Fuel**" means the gas or liquid that is used to create power to propel the aircraft. At the time of the Seller's delivery of the Aircraft to Buyer, the fuel gauge of the Aircraft shall register as full.

"**Closing**" means the closing of the sale of the Aircraft contemplated by this Agreement in New York, New York on the Closing Date.

"**Closing Date**" has the meaning specified in Section 2.04(a).

"**Consent**" shall mean any consent of, approval of, authorization of, notice to, or designation, registration, declaration or filing with, any Person.

"**Contract**" shall mean any contract, lease, agreement, license, arrangement, commitment or understanding to which the Buyer or any Seller is a party or by which it or any of its properties or assets may be bound or affected.

"**Engines**" means the two Rolls-Royce engines, Model No. BR710, bearing Serial Nos. 72725 and 72726.

"**Laws**" means all federal, state, local or foreign laws, rules and regulations.

"**Lien**" means any lien, charge, encumbrance, security interest, mortgage, or pledge.

"**Maintenance Agreement**" means that certain Maintenance Agreement, dated as of April 3, 20X0 between Greasemonkeys, Inc., and Seller, as the same may be amended from time to time.

"**Order**": any judgment, award, order, writ, injunction or decree issued by any federal, state, local or foreign authority, court, tribunal, agency, or other governmental authority, or by any arbitrator, to which any Seller or its assets are subject, or to which the Buyer or its assets are subject, as the case may be.

"**Person**" shall mean any individual, partnership, joint venture, corporation, trust, unincorporated organization, government (and any department or agency thereof) or other entity.

"**Pilot Agreement**" means that certain Pilot Agreement between Seller and Ace Pilots, Inc., dated as of May 12, 20X1, as of the date of this Agreement.

Article 2 — Purchase and Sale

[To be inserted.]

Article 3 — Representations and Warranties of the Seller

The Seller represents and warrants to the Buyer as follows:

3.1 Organization; Good Standing. The Seller is a corporation duly organized, validly existing and in good standing under the laws of the state of its incorporation as set forth in Schedule 2, with all requisite corporate power and authority to own, operate and lease its properties, and to carry on its business as now being conducted. The Seller is duly qualified to do business and is in good standing in each jurisdiction where the conduct of its business or the ownership of its property requires such qualification. The jurisdictions in which the Seller is qualified to do business are set forth in Schedule 2 hereto.

3.2 Authority. The Seller has full corporate power, authority and legal right to execute and deliver, and to perform its obligations under this Agreement and to consummate the transactions contemplated hereunder, and has taken all necessary action to authorize the purchase hereunder on the terms and conditions of this Agreement and to authorize the execution, delivery, and performance of this Agreement.

3.3 Enforceability. This Agreement has been duly executed and delivered by the Seller and constitutes a legal, valid, and binding obligation of the Seller enforceable against Seller in accordance with its terms, except as such enforceability may be limited by applicable bankruptcy, insolvency, or other similar laws from time to time in effect, which affect the enforcement of creditors' rights in general and by general principles of equity regardless of whether such enforceability is considered in a proceeding in equity or at law.

3.4 Noncontravention. Neither the execution and the delivery of this Agreement by Seller nor the consummation of the transactions contemplated hereby will (i) conflict with or result in any violation of the certificate of incorporation or the bylaws of the Seller, (ii) result in the violation of any Law or Order applicable to the Seller or any of its assets, or (iii) will conflict with, result in the breach of (with or without notice or lapse of time or both), or constitute a default under (with or without notice or lapse of time or both), any Contract to which the Seller is a party or to which the Seller or its assets is subject.

3.5 Governmental and Other Consents, etc. No consent, approval or authorization of or designation, declaration, or filing with any governmental authority or other persons or entities on the part of the Seller is required in connection with the execution or delivery of this Agreement or the consummation of the transactions contemplated hereby.

3.6 Title to Assets. A description of all real property owned by the Seller is set forth in Schedule 5. Except as set forth in said Schedule 5 or in any title insurance policy obtained by the Buyer prior to the execution of this Agreement by the Buyer, the Seller has good title to all its properties and assets, real, personal and intangible, subject to no mortgage, pledge, lien, security interest, lease, charge, encumbrance or conditional sale or other title retention agreement, except for such imperfections of title, liens, easements or encumbrances, if any, as are not material.

3.7 Agreements. A list and brief description of all agreements to which the Seller is a party is set forth in Schedule 6. All such agreements are valid and effective in accordance with their respective terms. Except as set forth in Schedule 6, there are no existing defaults or events which with notice or lapse of time or both would constitute defaults thereunder, the consequences of which in the aggregate would have a material adverse effect on the business and operations of the Seller.

3.8 Condition of Property. Except as set forth in **Schedule 3.9**, the plants, structures, and equipment of the Seller are in good operating condition and repair, subject only to ordinary wear and tear.

3.9 Law Compliance. The Seller has complied with and is not in default under any Laws the violation of which could have a material adverse effect on the business, properties, assets, or operations, or on the condition, financial or otherwise, of the Seller. Seller agrees to comply in all material respects with any Law the violation of which could have a material adverse effect on the Seller.

Article 4 — Representations and Warranties of the Buyer

The Buyer represents and warrants to the Seller as follows:

4.1 The Buyer is a corporation duly incorporated, validly existing and in good standing under the laws of its jurisdiction of incorporation and has all requisite corporate power and authority and legal right to own, operate, and lease its properties and assets and to carry on its business as now being conducted.

4.2 Authority. The Buyer has full corporate power, authority, and legal right to execute and deliver, and to perform its obligations under this Agreement and to consummate the transactions contemplated hereunder, and has taken all necessary action to authorize the purchase hereunder on the terms and conditions of this Agreement and to authorize the execution, delivery, and perfor-mance of this Agreement. This Agreement has been duly executed by the Buyer, and constitutes a legal, valid and binding obligation of the Buyer enforceable against Buyer in accordance with its terms except as such enforceability may be limited by applicable bankruptcy, insolvency, or other similar laws from time to time in effect, which affect the enforcement of creditors' rights in general and by general principles of equity regardless of whether such enforceability is considered in a proceeding in equity or at law.

4.3 Compliance with Instruments, Consents, Adverse Agreements. Neither the execution and the delivery of this Agreement by Buyer nor the consummation of the transactions contemplated hereby will conflict with or result in any violation of or constitute a default under any term of the certifi-cate of incorporation or the bylaws of the Buyer, or conflict with or result in any violation of or consti-tute a default under any Law or Contract by which the Buyer is, or its properties or assets, are bound.

4.4 Financing. Buyer has all monies or appropriate binding commitments from responsible financial institutions to provide Buyer with funds sufficient to satisfy the obligations of Buyer to Seller under this Agreement.

Article 5 — Covenants of the Seller

The Seller agrees that from the date the parties execute and deliver this Agreement until the Closing, the Seller shall do the following:

5.1 Cooperation. To use its commercially reasonabale efforts to cause the sale contemplated by this Agreement to be consummated, and, without limiting the generality of the foregoing, to obtain the Consents, permits and licenses that may be necessary or reasonably required in order for the Seller to effect the transactions contemplated hereby.

5.2 Transactions Out of Ordinary Course of Business. Except with the prior written consent of the Buyer, the Seller shall not enter into any transaction out of the ordinary course of business.

5.3 Maintenance of Properties, etc. To maintain all of its properties in customary repair, order and condition (taking into consideration the age and condition thereof), reasonable wear and tear excepted.

5.4 Access to Properties, etc. The Seller shall give to the Buyer and to its counsel, accountants, and other representatives access during normal business hours (on reasonable prior notice) to copies of all of its Contracts and Permits, books and records, and shall furnish to the Buyer all such documents and information with respect to the affairs of the Seller as the Buyer may from time to time reasonably request.

5.5 Ordinary Course. The Seller shall not (i) enter into any contract to merge or consolidate with any other corporation, (ii) change the character of its business, or sell, transfer or otherwise dispose of any material assets other than in the ordinary course of business or (iii) declare or pay any dividend or other distribution in respect of shares of capital stock. In addition, the Seller agrees not to make any purchase, redemption or other acquisition, directly or indirectly, of any outstanding shares of its capital stock or purchase any assets or securities of any Person, except with the prior written consent of the Buyer.

Article 6 — Covenants of the Buyer

The Buyer agrees that from the date the parties execute and deliver this Agreement until the Closing, the Buyer shall do the following:

6.1 Cooperation. The Buyer shall use its commercially reasonable efforts to cause the sale contemplated by this Agreement to be consummated, and, without limiting the generality of the foregoing, to obtain the Consents and Permits which may be necessary or reasonably required in order for the Buyer to effect the transactions contemplated hereby.

Article 7 — Conditions to the Seller's Obligations

The Seller is obligated to consummate the transactions that this Agreement contemplates only if each of the following conditions has been satisfied or waived on or before the Closing Date.

7.1 Buyer's Representations and Warranties. The representations and warranties of the Buyer set forth herein shall be true in all material respects on and as of the Closing Date, except as affected by transactions contemplated or permitted by this Agreement.

7.2 Buyer's Covenants. The Buyer shall have performed all its obligations and agreements and complied with all its covenants contained in this Agreement to be performed and complied with by the Buyer prior to the Closing Date.

7.3 Buyer's Closing Certificate. The Seller must have received a certificate of the Buyer, certifying to the truth of the statements in Sections 7.1 and 7.2.

7.4 No Litigation. No action, suit or proceeding before any court or any governmental or regulatory authority shall have been commenced and still be pending, no investigation by any governmental or regulatory authority shall have been commenced and still be pending, and no action, suit or proceeding by any governmental or regulatory authority shall have been threatened against the Seller or the Buyer (i) seeking to restrain, prevent or change the transactions contemplated hereby or questioning the validity or legality of any of such transactions, or (ii) which if resolved adversely to such party would materially and adversely affect the financial condition, business, property, assets or prospects of any such Person.

7.5 Documentation. All matters and proceedings taken in connection with the Acquisition as herein contemplated, including forms of instruments and matters of title, shall be reasonably satisfactory to the Seller and to its counsel.

Article 8 — Conditions to the Buyer's Obligations

The Buyer is obligated to consummate the transactions that this Agreement contemplates only if each of the following conditions has been satisfied or waived on or before the Closing Date.

8.1 Seller's Representations and Warranties. The representations and warranties of the Seller contained herein shall be true and correct in all material respects on and as of the Closing Date, except as affected by transactions contemplated or permitted by this Agreement.

8.2 Seller's Covenants. The Seller shall have performed all of its obligations and agreements and complied with all of its covenants contained in this Agreement to be performed and complied with by it prior to the Closing Date.

8.3 Seller's Closing Certificate. The Buyer must have received a certificate of the Seller, certifying to the truth of the statements in Sections 8.1 and 8.2.

8.4 No Litigation. No action, suit or proceeding before any court or any governmental or regulatory authority shall have been commenced and still be pending, no investigation by any governmental or regulatory authority shall have been commenced and still be pending, and no action, suit or proceeding by any governmental or regulatory authority shall have been threatened against the Seller or the Buyer (i) seeking to restrain, prevent or change the transactions contemplated hereby or questioning the validity or legality of any of such transactions or (ii) which if resolved adversely to such party, would materially and adversely affect the financial condition, business, Property, assets or prospects of any such Person.

8.5 Documentation. All matters and proceedings taken in connection with the Acquisition as herein contemplated, including forms of instruments and matters of title, shall be reasonably satisfactory to the Buyer and to its counsel.

Note to Students: Add endgame provisions and signature lines.

Icarus Aerospace Corporation
Icarus I-800 Specifications
You're safe with us. You'll never burn.

Range —7,200 nautical miles when traveling at Mach 85 with four passengers and eight crew.

High speed — 5,500 nautical miles at Mach 90 with four passengers and eight crew.

Engines — Two GE Passport engines.

DIMENSIONS

Exterior
Length: 95.6 feet
Wingspan: 100.7 feet
Height overall: 27 feet

Interior
Cabin length: 55 feet
Cabin maximum width: 7.98 feet
Cabin height: 6.25 feet

Exercise 31-3

Revised Aircraft Purchase Agreement

Follow the instructions in the memorandum that follows:

To: D. Fender
From: H. Flighty
Re: Purchase of the I-800

Thanks for that last draft. It was very helpful in moving things along. Please do another one incorporating the comments that I gave you recently. In addition, Sam and I negotiated the following points that should also be incorporated:

1. I had my mechanic thoroughly inspect the I-800. He reported that one of the engines (Serial No. 72725) is not working properly. Sam promised to get it fixed after we sign. He also promised that my mechanic could reinspect it and that I would only have to purchase the Aircraft if the mechanic determines that the engine is in good working order, ordinary wear and tear excepted. Keep out of the contract the details of when and how the reinspection will occur. Also, don't worry about the serial number. I know that's correct even though Sam got the model number wrong in the last draft.

2. Sam mentioned that he had spoken to Wright Aviation LLC, aircraft brokers, but had never hired the company to sell the I-800 on his behalf. I told Sam that I wanted that in the contract. He agreed. It would also be good to know that he didn't speak with anyone else.

3. Sam also told me that he had heard that I had tried to assign my rights under the Purchase Offer to Rob Robertson, his longtime business adversary. He was not happy. He has insisted on an anti-assignment and an anti-delegation provision in the Aircraft Purchase Agreement. He wants the contract to be clear that if I try to assign my rights, the assignment is unenforceable. He also wants to amend the Purchase Offer to include the same provision. Is that necessary? Please draft accordingly.

4. Please research whether Wings is required to obtain its stockholders' approval to sell the I-800. According to Sam, its board of directors has already authorized the transaction. What about my company? Is any authorization required to purchase? (As you know, the board of directors has already authorized the transaction.) If stockholder approval is required in either instance, please assume that it won't be obtained until after the agreement is signed. If approval of the Seller's stockholders is required, the Seller must be obligated to use its commercially reasonable efforts to get it. That way, the Seller can't get out of the deal by sloughing off its responsibilities and then claiming it couldn't get the approval. Essentially, that would give the Seller an option. By the way, do we need a separate section obligating the Seller to use its commercially reasonable efforts to obtain the stockholder consent (if required), or does another contract provision already address this point? Finally, if any approval is required, please decide for whom receipt of the approval should be a condition to closing. Please explain in your memo to me how you decide to address each of these issues in the agreement.

5. As you know, the wrong kind of fuel can damage a jet's engines. Sam told me that since he has owned the I-800, he has always used the appropriate fuel. I asked him about the period before his company owned the jet. He said that the manufacturer's sales agent had

assured him that the proper fuel had been used for all test flights. I told him that this point needed to be addressed in the contract.

6. Create a definition "Litigation Event" for Sections 7.4 and 8.4.

7. Please add the following additional provisions: merger, severability, and amendments.

Please send me both clean and redlined drafts so that I can easily see the changes you have made. In addition, write me a memo explaining anything significant I should know about. Keep the memo to one page, single spaced.

H.F.

Exercise 31-4

Amendment to the Aircraft Purchase Agreement

Follow the instructions in the memorandum that follows:

To: D. Fender
From: H. Flighty
Re: Purchase of the I-800

Thanks for that last draft. It was very helpful in moving things along. The parties executed the APA on October 30th. But, of course, we thought of some more points that we want incorporated into the agreement. Please draft an amendment to the APA incorporating the following points that Sam and I just negotiated:

1. Sam mentioned that he had spoken to Wright Aviation LLC, aircraft brokers, but had never hired the company to sell the I-800 on his behalf. I told Sam that I wanted that in the contract. He agreed. It would also be good to know that he didn't speak with anyone else. He mentioned something about mutuality.

2. Sam also told me that he had heard that I had tried to assign my rights under the Purchase Offer to Rob Robertson, his longtime business adversary. He was not happy. He has insisted on an anti-assignment and an anti-delegation provision in the Aircraft Purchase Agreement. He wants the contract to be clear that if I try to assign my rights, the assignment is unenforceable. Do we need to amend the Purchase Offer?

3. I had my mechanic thoroughly inspect the I-800. He reported that one of the engines (Serial No. 72725) is not working properly. Sam promised to get it fixed before closing. He also promised that my mechanic could re-inspect it and that I would only have to purchase the Aircraft if the mechanic determines that the engine is in good working order, ordinary wear and tear excepted. Keep out of the contract the details of when and how the re-inspection will occur. Also, don't worry about the serial number. I know that's correct even though Sam got the model number wrong in the last draft.

4. Please research whether Wings is required to obtain its stockholders' approval to sell the I-800. According to Sam, its board of directors has already authorized the transaction. What about my company? Is any authorization required to purchase? (As you know, the board of directors has already authorized the transaction.) If stockholder approval is required in either instance, please assume that it won't be obtained until after the agreement is signed. If approval of the Seller's stockholders is required, the Seller must be obligated to use its commercially reasonable efforts to get it. That way, the Seller can't get out of the deal by sloughing off its responsibilities and then claiming it couldn't get the approval. Essentially, that would give the Seller an option. By the way, do we need a separate section obligating the Seller to use its commercially reasonable efforts to obtain the stockholder consent (if required), or does another contract provision already address this point? Please think carefully about this point and address it in your memo to me. Finally, if any approval is required, please decide for whom receipt of the approval should be a condition to closing. Please explain in your memo to me how you decide to address each of these issues in the agreement.

H.F.

Exercise 31-5

Shoeless Joe Jackson Exercise[2]

Below is an excerpt from the 1919 standard form American League Player's Contract between Shoeless Joe Jackson and Charles Comiskey, owner of the Chicago White Sox. For those of you who are not baseball historians, Shoeless Joe Jackson is a legendary baseball figure. He is remembered for his performance on the field and for his association with the Black Sox Scandal, when members of the 1919 Chicago White Sox participated in a conspiracy to "fix" the World Series. As a result of Jackson's association with the scandal, Kenesaw Mountain Landis, Major League Baseball's first commissioner, banned Jackson from playing after the 1920 season.

Please redraft this excerpt from the contract, including its organization and format. Remember that subject matter is the most common way of organizing a contract. Look again at the Website Development Agreement (Chapter 32, Document 2) and note how it uses both subject matter and contract concepts for organization.

You may add a stand-alone definitions article. In addition, you may amplify the provision to address business points that the provision raises but does not answer. Stated differently, you may add additional material and facts so long as they deal with the specific issues raised by the information that you have. Mr. Comiskey is your client, so provisions should be drafted with his interests in mind. The provisions should not be so one-sided that Shoeless Joe would reject them out of hand.

Do **not** draft a complete contract—just the provisions necessary to address the points raised in the provision that you have been given. In addition, please draft a one-page cover memorandum to Mr. Comiskey explaining the basis for any drafting or business decisions you make. This is a memorandum to the client, not to your professor.

Paragraph 3 of the 1919 American League Player's Contract

(1) The player agrees to render for the club owner, at such times and places during the term of this contract as the club shall designate, his best services as a ball player; and he agrees to keep himself in the best possible physical condition from the date hereof until the termination of the contract; and a violation of either of the foregoing provisions of this paragraph shall be such a breach of contract as (2) shall entitle the club owner either to terminate this contract forthwith, by written notice, or to suspend the player, by written notice, without pay until the club owner is satisfied that the player is ready, able and willing to resume his services in the manner in this paragraph provided. The player further agrees (3) that, during the term of this contract, he will not, except with the consent of the American League, engage, either during the American League season or at any other time, in any game or exhibition of baseball, football, basketball, or other athletic sport, except as herein provided.

---

2. I thank Richard Neumann for suggesting this contract excerpt as an exercise.

Exercise 31-6

National Security Exercise

MEMORANDUM

To: Barbara Chin

From: Daniel Petrowski

Date: July 15, 20X7

Re: Dissolution of National Security Inc.

Attached is a draft notice from National Security Inc. to all of its creditors. Please review it to make sure that it is properly drafted. If you find any problems, please redraft the notice and write me a memo about any drafting or substantive issues that you think I should know about. We're going to have to give an opinion that this notice complies with the statute, so the notice has to be right. I've attached the pertinent provisions of the Delaware statute.

NATIONAL SECURITY INC.

236 Road to Ignominy

Los Angeles, CA 00000

July 15, 20X7

To Whom It May Concern:

National Security Inc., a Delaware corporation (NSI), hereby advises you that it has been dissolved in accordance with the procedures set forth in the General Corporation Law of the State of Delaware (GCL). You are further advised that all individuals having a claim against NSI must present their claims against NSI in accordance with this letter, as follows:

1. All claims must be in writing and must contain all the information necessary to inform NSI of the identity of the claimant and the substance of the claim.
2. The mailing address to which a claim must be sent is:

   National Security Inc.
   236 Road to Ignominy
   Washington, D.C. 00000
   Attention: Benedict Arnold, Vice President

3. The date by which a claim must be received is August 31, 20X7.
4. A claim will be barred if not received by August 31, 20X7.
5. NSI or a successor entity may make distributions to other claimants and NSI's stockholders or persons interested as having been such without further notice to you, as claimant.
6. The aggregate amount of all cash dividends made by NSI to its stockholders for the three years prior to the date NSI dissolved is $3,650,000.

Please address any questions that you have concerning making a claim to Benedict Arnold, Vice President. Mr. Arnold's telephone number is (202) 555-5555.

Sincerely yours,

National Security Inc.

By: _____

Marcus Junius Brutus

Title: President

Delaware General Corporation Law § 280—Notice to claimants; filing of claims.

(a)(1) After a corporation has been dissolved in accordance with the procedures set forth in this chapter, the corporation or any successor entity may give notice of the dissolution, requiring all persons having a claim against the corporation other than a claim against the corporation in a pending action, suit or proceeding to which the corporation is a party to present their claims against the corporation in accordance with such notice. Such notice shall state:

    a. That all such claims must be presented in writing and must contain sufficient information reasonably to inform the corporation or successor entity of the identity of the claimant and the substance of the claim;

    b. The mailing address to which such a claim must be sent;

    c. The date by which such a claim must be received by the corporation or successor entity, which date shall be no earlier than 60 days from the date thereof; and

    d. That such claim will be barred if not received by the date referred to in subparagraph c. of this subsection; and

    e. That the corporation or a successor entity may make distributions to other claimants and the corporation's stockholders or persons interested as having been such without further notice to the claimant; and

    f. The aggregate amount, on an annual basis, of all distributions made by the corporation to its stockholders for each of the 3 years prior to the date the corporation dissolved.

Exercise 31-7

Closing Certificate Exercise

From: Lester Lawyer
To: Nicholas Neophyte
Date: November 24, 20X8
Re: Closing Certificates

On September 1, 20X8, Marvelous Magic Corp., a Delaware corporation ("Marvelous Magic"), entered into a Purchase Agreement with Tricky Tricks, Inc., an Alaska corporation ("Tricky Tricks"). In accordance with the Purchase Agreement, Marvelous Magic will be purchasing substantially all of the assets of Tricky Tricks at a closing to be held at our offices on December 31, 20X8.

Please draft the closing certificates referred to in Section 7 of the Purchase Agreement as soon as possible. I have attached to this memo a closing certificate from a past deal as well as a copy of the relevant provisions of the Agreement. Thomas Titan is the president of Tricky Tricks.

CERTIFICATE

Reference is made to that certain Asset Purchase Agreement (the "**Agreement**") dated as of March 15, 20X3, between Startup Inc., New York corporation (the "**Seller**"), and Colossal Conglomerate Corp., a Massachusetts corporation (the "**Buyer**"). Capitalized terms used in this Certificate without further definition have the meaning ascribed thereto in the Agreement.

The Seller hereby certifies in accordance with Section 12(c) of the Agreement as follows:

1. The representations and warranties of the Seller contained in the Agreement are true on and as of the date hereof with the same force and effect as though made on and as of the date hereof, except as affected by transactions contemplated or permitted by the Agreement.

2. The Seller has performed all of its obligations and agreements and complied with all of its covenants contained in the Agreement to be performed and complied with by it prior to the date hereof.

IN WITNESS WHEREOF, the undersigned has executed this Certificate as of the 30th day of June, 20X3.

COLOSSAL CONGLOMERATE CORP.

_____

By:
Title:

Excerpts from the Purchase Agreement between Marvelous Magic and Tricky Tricks

Article 7 — Conditions to Purchaser's Obligations

The obligation of the Purchaser to complete the purchase of the Purchased Assets under this Agreement is subject to the satisfaction or waiver of, on or before the Closing Date, each of the following conditions precedent:

7.1 Representations and Warranties. All of the representations and warranties of the Seller made in or pursuant to this Agreement must be true and correct on the Closing Date with the same effect as if made on the Closing Date (except to the extent such representations and warranties may have been affected by the occurrence of events or transactions expressly contemplated and permitted by this Agreement) and the Purchaser must have received a certificate from the President of the Seller, confirming, to the best of his knowledge, information and belief (after due inquiry), the truth and correctness of the representations and warranties of the Seller.

7.2 Performance of Obligations. The Seller must have performed or complied with, in all respects, all its obligations, covenants and agreements under this Agreement, and the Purchaser must have received a certificate from the Seller certifying to the foregoing.

Exercise 31-8

Endgame Exercise

This provision is an exemplar from Chapter 15—straight from the original contract. Rewrite the provision to fix the substantive and drafting errors.

> **Termination**. If either Party believes that the other Party is in material breach of this Agreement . . . , then the non-breaching Party may deliver notice of such breach to the other Party. In such notice, the non-breaching Party will identify the actions or conduct that it wishes such Party to take for an acceptable and prompt cure of such breach (or will otherwise state its good faith belief that such breach is incurable); provided, however, that such identified actions or conduct will not be binding on the other Party with respect to the actions that it may need to take to cure such breach. If the breach is curable, the allegedly breaching Party will have ninety (90) days to either cure such breach (except to the extent such breach involves the failure to make a payment when due, which breach must be cured within thirty (30) days following such notice) or, if a cure cannot be reasonably effected within such ninety (90) day period, to deliver to the non-breaching Party a plan for curing such breach which is reasonably sufficient to effect a cure within a reasonable period. If the breaching Party fails to (a) cure such breach within the ninety (90) day or thirty (30) day period, as applicable, or (b) use Commercially Reasonable Efforts to carry out the plan and cure the breach, the non-breaching Party may terminate this Agreement by providing written notice to the breaching Party.

Exercise 31-9[3]

Ellsworth Agreement

You worked on a version of this exercise in Exercise 15-1. Now that you've learned about ambiguity and structuring a provision, it is time to work with the full provision—clarify its ambiguities and organize it to make sense conceptually.

On December 15, 20XX, Bertha Ellsworth (Ellsworth) was admitted to the Home for the Aged (the Home) and signed an agreement stating the terms of her stay at the Home. The agreement provided that for the first two months of her stay she would be a probationary member and that afterwards she would become a life member. On the same day, Ellsworth paid $100,000 to the Home by a check that stated: "In Payment of Life Membership for Bertha Ellsworth in the Home, as specified in the Agreement dated December 15, 20XX."

Ellsworth died on December 29, 20XX, before her probationary period ended. The administrator of the estate wants to recover the $100,000 gift as Ellsworth never became a life member. The Home claims it is entitled to keep the money. The agreement is ambiguous. Assume that you represented Ellsworth when the contract was negotiated. How would you have drafted the following provisions to protect her?

The lines of the provisions are numbered to facilitate class discussion. The provisions are available on the book's website.

1	**1.1** Ellsworth having this day given the Home,
2	without reservation, the sum of $100,000 to be used and
3	disposed of in the furtherance of its benevolence and
4	charitable work as it may deem best, the Home admits
5	Ellsworth into the Home as a member thereof during the
6	period of her natural life.
7	**1.5** It is clearly understood that Ellsworth has been
8	received in accordance with the new regulations on a
9	probation period of two months in which time she has the
10	opportunity of finding out whether she desires to remain in
11	the Home. If it should be found advisable to discontinue her
12	stay in the Home, then her gift, with the exception of $2,000
13	per month shall be refunded.
14	**12.1** Probationary membership means a short trial
15	period while the member becomes adjusted to life at the
16	Home. The probationary membership shall not continue for
17	a longer period than two consecutive months. If for any
18	reason the trial member does not desire to remain in the
19	Home, she shall have the privilege of leaving. Only
20	members who do not have the money to pay for their life
21	Membership shall be granted the privilege of paying by the
22	month.

---

3. This exercise is based on *First Nat'l Bank of Lawrence v. Methodist Home for the Aged*, 309 P.2d 389 (Kan. 1957).

Exercise 31-10

Trademark Licensing Agreement

Draft the trademark licensing agreement described in the deal memo in
Exercise 5-3.

PART EIGHT

Exemplars and Guided Reading Exercises

Exemplars and Guided Reading Exercises

Document 1

House Purchase Agreement[1,2]

This House Purchase Agreement, dated [date to be inserted], 20X5, is between Sally Seller (the "**Seller**"[3]) and Bob Buyer (the "**Buyer**").[4]

Background

This Agreement[5] provides for the sale to the Buyer of the Seller's house at 7221 Perada Drive, Walnut Creek, California 94595 (the "**House**") and the land on which it is situated.[6]

The Seller and the Buyer agree as follows:[7]

Article 1 — Definitions

1.1 Definitions. The terms defined in the preamble and recital have their assigned meanings, and each of the following terms has the meaning assigned to it:[8]

"**Agreement**" means this House Purchase Agreement, its Schedules, and Exhibits, each as amended from time to time.[9]

"**Closing**" means the consummation of the transaction that this Agreement contemplates.

"**Closing Date**" has the meaning assigned to it in Section 2.3.[10]

"**Premises**" means the House, the land described in **Exhibit A**, and the household items that **Schedule 1.1** lists.

Article 2 — Purchase and Sale[11]

2.1 Purchase and Sale. At the Closing, the Seller shall sell the Premises to the Buyer, and the Buyer shall purchase the Premises from the Seller.[12]

---

1. This House Purchase Agreement is a simplified exemplar of a contract that parties would actually use. Notably, the agreement provides for no down payment.

2. Centered title above preamble uses the same title as that in the preamble, but font is larger.

3. *The* precedes the defined term *Seller,* so *the* is used in the body of the agreement each time the defined term *Seller* is used.

4. Preamble. Contemporary sentence format.

5. Although *Agreement* has not yet been defined, the defined term is used. This use violates the drafting guidelines for definitions and defined terms, but is common practice.

6. Brief recital stating property to be purchased. As defined, *House* does not include the land on which the House is situated.

7. Short statement of the words of agreement. Longer one unnecessary as the consideration is evident.

8. Introduction incorporates the terms previously defined in the preamble and recitals.

9. Definition makes explicit that the Schedules and Exhibits are part of the Agreement. The language referring to amendments simplifies any future amendments by not requiring the definition of *Agreement* to be amended.

10. Definition by cross-reference.

11. The provisions in this article are what the textbook refers to as the action sections.

12. Subject matter performance provisions (covenants).

13. This agreement does not mimic a real transaction in that it has no provision for a down payment.

14. The phrase *the date the transaction closes* prevents an ambiguity. Because *Closing Date* is defined in context, an issue could arise as to how much of what precedes the parenthetical is part of the definition of the defined term created in the parenthetical. Without the additional language, a party might argue that the meaning of *Closing Date* is limited to only the original date or only an alternative date. While that might not be a winning argument, it is enough to cause trouble.

15. In an acquisition agreement, the asset purchased must be conveyed and money must be paid to consummate the transaction.

This section is only for acts that are to take place at Closing or afterward. Therefore, the reference to *Payment of Purchase Price* refers only to payments to be made at Closing. Any down payments would be dealt with in a separate section after the statement of the purchase price.

16. The warranty deed is the document that conveys ownership of the Premises.

17. This *further assurances* provision operates at Closing. It requires the Seller to fix any glitches that might arise at Closing in connection with conveying the Premises.

18. The payment provision must cover *who* is paying *how much* to *whom* and *the manner of payment*.

19. This further assurances provision applies only after the Closing.

20. The representations and warranties should include all the information on which a party (here, the Buyer) is relying.

2.2   Purchase Price. The purchase price for the Premises is $200,000.[13]

2.3   The Closing. The Closing is to occur on [date to be inserted], 20X5, or another date as to which the Seller and the Buyer agree (the date the transaction closes, the "**Closing Date**").[14] It is to take place at the offices of Abbott & Peabody LLP, 100 Geary Street, San Francisco, California, beginning at 9:00 a.m. local time.

2.4   Instruments of Transfer; Payment of Purchase Price; Further Assurances.[15]

(a)   **Seller's Deliveries.** At the Closing, the Seller shall execute and deliver to the Buyer

   (i)   a general warranty deed[16] for the Premises, substantially in the form of **Exhibit B**; and

   (ii)   any other instrument or instruments of transfer that may be necessary or appropriate to vest in the Buyer good title to the Premises.[17]

(b)   **Buyer's Deliveries.** At the Closing, the Buyer shall deliver to the Seller by wire transfer $200,000 in funds immediately available in San Francisco, California.[18]

(c)   **Further Assurances.** Following the Closing, at the request of the Buyer, the Seller shall deliver any further instruments of transfer and take all reasonable action that may be necessary or appropriate to vest in the Buyer good title to the Premises.[19]

Article 3 — Seller's Representations and Warranties

The Seller represents and warrants to the Buyer as follows:[20]

3.1   The House. The House was built in 1953, along with the other houses in the neighborhood.

3.2   The Roof. The roof of the House is four years old.

3.3   Appliances. All of the appliances in the House are in excellent condition, except for the dishwasher, which is not working.

3.4 Cable. The House is wired for cable television, and the cable is functioning properly.

3.5 Swimming Pool.

(a) **The Pool**. A swimming pool is in the backyard of the House. Its dimensions are 30 feet by 10 feet.

(b) **Water Heater**. A water heater that uses propane gas heats the pool. The water heater is on the Premises and is in good working condition, ordinary wear and tear excepted.

(c) **Propane Gas Tank**. The propane gas tank is on the Premises, and it is exactly one-half full with propane gas.

3.6 Living Room Paint Color. The living room's walls are painted eggshell white and were painted one year ago.

3.7 Premises. The land on which the House is situated is a one-acre lot that is accurately described in Exhibit A.[21]

Article 4 — Buyer's Representations and Warranties

The Buyer represents and warrants to the Seller as follows:

4.1 Financing. The Buyer has sufficient funds to purchase the Premises without obtaining a loan.[22]

Article 5 — Seller's Covenants

From the date of this Agreement to the Closing Date, the Seller shall perform as follows:[23]

5.1 Dishwasher. The Seller shall cause the dishwasher to be repaired.[24]

5.2 Paint. The Seller shall not paint the walls of any room in the House.

5.3 Propane Gas Tank. The Seller shall cause the propane gas tank to be at least one-third full on the Closing Date.

21. The exhibit is a metes and bounds description of the Premises from the deed.

22. Buyers often refuse to give this representation and warranty because they do not have the funds. They need a mortgage.

23. This introductory language is appropriate because all the covenants are pre-closing covenants. If the parties agree to other covenants, omit the introductory language and state the time frame within each covenant.

24. This covenant contemplates that the Seller may not herself fix the dishwasher, but establishes that she is contractually responsible if it is not fixed.

25. From a business perspective, the Seller cannot promise to settle the dispute. She has no control over the other owner. What kind of covenant could the Seller give the Buyer to assure him that the Seller will do what is necessary to settle the dispute?

26. This provision is tabulated. To enhance clarity through format, two subsections were created, one for each of the covenants. They are joined in one section because of the related subject matter.

5.4 Settlement of Border Dispute. The Seller shall pay all costs related to settlement of the border dispute with the owner of the house at 7221 Perada Drive, Walnut Creek, California 94595.[25]

5.5 Carpet Cleaning.[26] The Seller shall

(a) cause all carpeting in the House to be professionally cleaned before the Closing Date; and

(b) pay the cost for the cleaning, but no more than $500, no later than the Closing Date.

Article 6 — Conditions to the Seller's Obligations

The Seller is obligated to consummate the transactions that this Agreement contemplates only if each of the following conditions has been satisfied or waived on or before the Closing Date.

27. Lawyers refer to this provision colloquially as a *bring-down* because it updates the representations and warranties down to the date of the Closing.

28. This is a broad condition and applies not only to pre-closing covenants but those necessary to consummate the transaction at the Closing. Therefore, if the Buyer does not pay the purchase price at Closing, the Buyer will have failed to satisfy this condition to the Seller's obligation to close. See covenant in Section 2.4(b).

29. Without the certificate, the Seller has no written evidence of the Buyer acknowledging that he satisfied the two previous closing conditions. The Seller may sue if the certified statements are not true.

30. The bracketed language contemplates that some of the facts true at signing may not be true at Closing. This is usually only an issue for a seller. For example, the amount of propane in the gas tank may have changed.

6.1 Representations and Warranties. The Buyer's representations and warranties must have been true on the date that they were made and must be true as of the Closing Date with the same force and effect as though made on and as of the Closing Date.[27]

6.2 Covenants. The Buyer must have performed each of the covenants to be performed by him on or before the Closing Date.[28]

6.3 Buyer's Closing Certificate.[29] The Seller must have received a certificate of the Buyer, certifying to the truth of the statements in Sections 6.1 and 6.2.

Article 7 — Conditions to the Buyer's Obligations

The Buyer is obligated to consummate the transactions that this Agreement contemplates only if each of the following conditions has been satisfied or waived on or before the Closing Date.

7.1 Representations and Warranties. The Seller's representations and warranties must have been true on the date that they were made and must be true as of the Closing Date with the same force and effect as though made on and as of the Closing Date, [except to the extent that this Agreement contemplates changes.][30]

7.2 Covenants. The Seller must have performed each of the covenants to be performed by her on or before the Closing Date.

7.3 Seller's Closing Certificate. The Buyer must have received a certificate of the Seller, certifying to the truth of the statements in Sections 7.1 and 7.2.

7.4 Property Line Dispute Resolution.[31] The Seller and the owner of the house at 7221 Perada Drive, Walnut Creek, California 94595 must have settled their dispute as to the property line establishing the boundaries of the land between the two houses.

Article 8 — Termination[32]

8.1 Seller's Right to Terminate.

(a) **Grounds for Termination and Notice of Termination**. The Seller may send a notice[33] to the Buyer regarding this Agreement's termination if any one or more of the following events has occurred on or before the Closing Date:

   (i) **Misrepresentations and Breaches of Warranties**. The condition stated in Section 6.1 has not been satisfied or waived.

   (ii) **Covenants**. The condition stated in Section 6.2 has not been satisfied or waived.

   (iii) **Closing Certificate**. The condition stated in Section 6.3 has not been satisfied or waived.

(b) **Effective Date of Termination**. If the Seller sends a notice regarding this Agreement's termination as permitted by Section 8.1(a), this Agreement terminates on the day the Buyer receives the notice.

(c) **Consequences of Termination**. On termination of this Agreement under this Section 8.1, neither party has any further rights or obligations under this Agreement, except for the Seller's rights and the Buyer's obligations arising from any Buyer misrepresentation, breach of warranty, or breach of covenant.

31. The Buyer will insist on this condition because the covenant only addresses the payment of settlement costs. Only through this condition does the Buyer have the right to walk away if the dispute is not resolved. How could the drafting of this condition be improved from the Buyer's perspective? Re-read Annotation 25. Does there need to be an express condition that the Seller has paid all the associated costs?

32. Termination provisions are some of the most difficult to negotiate and draft. If this is your first time reading these provisions, just try to get a sense of them. We'll spend time on them during the semester.

33. The provision does not require written notice because Section 9.7 states that all notices must be in writing. That provision covers all notices sent under the agreement.

8.2 Buyer's Right to Terminate.

(a) **Grounds for Termination**. The Buyer may send a notice to the Seller regarding this Agreement's termination if any one or more of the following events has occurred on or before the Closing Date:

(i) **Misrepresentations and Breaches of Warranties**. The condition stated in Section 7.1 has not been satisfied or waived.

(ii) **Covenants**. The condition stated in Section 7.2 has not been satisfied or waived.

(iii) **Seller's Closing Certificate**. The condition stated in Section 7.3 has not been satisfied or waived.

(iv) **Property Line Dispute**. The condition stated in Section 7.4 has not been satisfied or waived.

(b) **Termination under Sections 8.2(a)(i), 8.2(a)(ii), or 8.2(a)(iii)**.

(i) **Effective Date of Termination**. If the Buyer sends a notice regarding this Agreement's termination under any one or more of Sections 8.2(a)(i), 8.2(a)(ii), and 8.2(a)(iii), this Agreement terminates on the date the Seller receives the notice.

(ii) **Consequences of Termination**. On termination of this Agreement under any one or more of Sections 8.2(a)(i), 8.2(a)(ii), and 8.2(a)(iii), neither party has any further rights or obligations, except for the Buyer's rights and the Seller's obligations arising from any Seller misrepresentation, breach of warranty, or breach of covenant.

(c) **Termination under Section 8.2(a)(iv)**.

(i) **Effective Date of Termination**. This Agreement terminates on the day the Buyer receives the notice regarding termination.[34]

34. If a down payment had to be repaid, the contract would include the specifics of *who* pays *what, when,* and *how*. In addition, the termination of the agreement would be postponed until the required payment had been received.

(ii) **Consequences of Termination**. On termination of this Agreement under Section 8.2(a)(iv), neither party has any further rights or obligations.

Article 9 — General Provisions

9.1 Assignment and Delegation. Neither party may assign its rights or delegate its obligations under this Agreement without the consent of the other party, which party shall not unreasonably withhold its consent.[35]

9.2 Assigns. This Agreement binds and benefits the parties and their respective permitted assigns.[36]

9.3 Merger. This Agreement states the final and exclusive agreement between the parties regarding the transaction that this Agreement contemplates. It supersedes all previous negotiations and agreements.[37]

9.4 Counterparts. The parties may execute this Agreement in counterparts, each of which is an original, but all of which constitute only one agreement between the parties.[38]

9.5 Severability. If any provision of this Agreement is illegal or unenforceable, that provision is severed from the Agreement, and the other provisions remain in effect only if the essential business and legal provisions are legal and enforceable.[39]

9.6 Governing Law. The laws of California, without regard to its conflict of laws principles, govern all matters arising under or relating to this Agreement, including torts.

9.7 Notices.[40] The parties must send all notices in writing. No notice is deemed received until the addressee has received it.

9.8 Waiver of Right to a Jury Trial.[41] Each party waives its right to a trial by jury in all matters relating to and arising under this Agreement, including torts. Each party has initialed this provision to indicate that the party has read the

35. This language is typical, but it does not void an assignment.

36. This language no longer serves its original purpose — to clarify whether a delegation occurred contemporaneously with an assignment and whether the delegate assumed the obligations. Chapter 16 suggests alternative language, which has yet to be widely accepted. This provision typically also refers to *successors*, but that is a corporate concept.

37. To prevent the inclusion of parol evidence, an agreement must be both *final* and *exclusive.*

38. This provision permits signatories to sign separate copies of the agreement, collate them, and create a complete original. It also authorizes multiple originals. (Never have multiple originals of a promissory note.)

39. Often, these provisions state simply that the other provisions remain in effect. But that does not typically reflect the real business deal: The contract should continue only if the economic and legal terms stay intact.

40. Notices are risk allocation provisions. Specifically, they allocate the risk of nonreceipt of the notice.

41. Because this waiver is of a constitutional right, courts insist the waiver be knowing, intentional, and voluntary. The drafter's challenge is to demonstrate through contract language that the waiver was given under those circumstances. One factor that courts have used in deciding whether a waiver met the constitutional standard is whether the provision was prominent. Making the waiver the last provision and using a larger font are two ways of doing so.

provision and makes the waiver knowingly, intentionally, and voluntarily.

To evidence the parties' agreement to this Agreement, they have executed and delivered it on the date stated in the preamble.[42]

42. Contemporary concluding paragraph language.

Seller

_____

Sally Seller

Buyer

_____

Bob Buyer

Document 2

Website Development Agreement (Version 1)

This **Website Development Agreement** is dated January 8, 20XX and is between Go-Karts Corp., a California corporation (the "**Client**"), and Website Designs, Inc., a Michigan corporation (the "**Developer**").

This Agreement provides for the Developer's development of a website for the Client.

The parties agree as follows:

1. **Definitions and Defined Term.**

    1.1 **Defined Terms**. Terms defined in the preamble have their assigned meanings and each of the following terms has the meaning assigned to it.

    "**Agreement**" means this Website Development Agreement, including **Exhibit A**, as each may be amended from time to time.

    "**Business Day**" means any day other than a day that a bank in San Jose, California is required or permitted to be closed.

    "**Change Order**" means an agreement that changes or supplements the Services.

    "**Content**" means all text, images, sound, graphics, and other materials describing the Client's business and industry.

    "**Developer Programming**" has the meaning assigned to it in Section 8.1.

    "**Down Payment**" has the meaning assigned to it in Section 4.2.1.

    "**Effective Date**" means the date the second party to execute and deliver this Agreement delivers the executed Agreement to the other party, the date of delivery to be the date of the other party's receipt of the executed Agreement.

    "**Services**" means the services listed in the Scope of Services section in **Exhibit A**.

    "**Team**" means the employees the Developer assigns to perform the Services.

    "**Website**" means a collection of interconnected web pages on the Internet, pertaining to the Client.

    "**Works**" means the Website and all other deliverables, including all derivative deliverables, resulting from the performance of the Services.

    1.2 **Interpretive Provisions**.

        1.2.1 **References to Sections, etc**. References to Sections, subsections, and Exhibit A are references to Sections, subsections, and Exhibit A of this Agreement.

        1.2.2 **References to a Person**. References to a person include that person's permitted successors and assigns and, in the case of any governmental person, the person succeeding to the governmental functions of that person.

        1.2.3 *Including* **and** *Its* **Variations**. The words *including*, *includes*, and *include* are deemed to be followed by the words *without limitation*.

2. **Development of Website**.

    2.1 **Hiring of the Developer.** By executing and delivering this Agreement, the Client hires the Developer to design and develop the Website for the Client.

    2.2 **Design and Development of the Website**. Subject to the provisions of this Agreement, the Developer shall design and develop the Website by performing the Services.

3. **Effective Date**.

    3.1 **Effective Date**. This Agreement is effective on the Effective Date.

    3.2 **Termination of Agreement**. This Agreement terminates on the third Business Day after the Effective Date at 5:00 p.m., San Jose, CA time, if the Developer has not received the

Down Payment required by Section 4.2 by that time. In that event, neither party has any rights or obligations against the other.

4. **Fees**.

    4.1   **Estimate and Cap**. The Developer estimates that its fee for performing the Services will be between $12,000 and $15,000. Despite the preceding sentence, the maximum that the Client is obligated to pay the Developer for the Services, as described in Exhibit A, is $17,000. If the parties agree to a Change Order, the new cap is the amount the parties agree to at that time. If the parties do not agree to a new cap, but only an estimated range, then the new cap is the higher number of any estimated range *plus* 10% of that number.

    4.2   **Down Payment**.

        4.2.1   **Amount of the Down Payment**. The down payment is $6,000 (the "**Down Payment**").

        4.2.2   **Obligation to Pay the Down Payment**. The Client shall wire transfer the Down Payment in immediately available funds (San Jose, CA) to the Developer's bank account no later than three Business Days after the Effective Date. The Client shall use the following wire instructions:

            Big City Bank, 738 Fulton Ave., San Jose, California

            Website Designs, Inc. #485930284

            ABA 0390000000

            Swift Code BCBUS33

    4.3   **Additional Payments**.

        4.3.1   **Billing Rates**. The billing rates for Team members range from $75 to $225 an hour. The Developer may increase these rates only after having given the Client at least 30 days prior notice.

        4.3.2   **Amount to Be Paid**. The Client shall pay the Developer for each quarter hour that a Team member works, except if the cap has been reached. In that event, the Client's obligation to pay any amount in excess of the cap is discharged. In determining the amount that the Client is obligated to pay, the Developer shall give the Client a credit equal to the amount of the Down Payment.

        4.3.3   **Form of Invoice**. With respect to each month that the Developer provides Services, the Developer shall send an invoice to the Client indicating

            (a)   the number of hours each Team member worked;

            (b)   the billing rate for each Team member;

            (c)   the aggregate invoiced fee for each Team member;

            (d)   the aggregate invoiced fee for the Team; and

            (e)   the amount by which the invoice has been reduced to reflect any outstanding credit arising from the Down Payment.

        If the cap has been reached, the Developer shall continue to send invoices to the Client, but the Developer shall indicate on the invoice that the Client is not obligated to pay the invoiced amount.

        4.3.4   **Form and Timing of Payment**. The Client shall pay each month's invoice by company check or by wire transfer. In either case, the Client shall cause payment to be received no later than ten Business Days after the Client's receipt of that month's invoice.

5. **Provision of Services**.

    5.1   **Quality of Services**. The Developer shall perform the Services using sound professional practices and in a competent and professional manner by knowledgeable and qualified employees.

    5.2   **Content**. The Client shall not deliver any Content to the Developer that

        5.2.1   it does not own or have a right to use; or

5.2.2   is defamatory, libelous, or otherwise actionable.

5.3   **The Developer's Employees**. No later than five Business Days after the Effective Date, the Developer shall assign the following employees to be the Team members providing the Services to the Client: Omar Adams, Kyla Rubin, and Marla Wojinsky. The Developer may replace one or more of these employees with other employees, but only after it receives the Client's prior consent. The Client shall not unreasonably withhold its consent.

5.4   **Schedule**. The Developer shall use commercially reasonable efforts to provide the Services as efficiently as possible with the goal of completing the Services no later than April 30, 20XX.

5.5   **Liens**. The Developer shall perform the Services so that each Work is free of liens or other encumbrances at the time that it is delivered.

5.6   **Change Orders**. If from time to time the Client wants to change or supplement any Service, the parties must execute and deliver a Change Order. A Change Order is effective when the first party to execute and deliver the Change Order receives the fully executed Change Order from the other party. This Agreement's provisions govern if this Agreement and a Change Order conflict.

5.7   **Compliance with Laws**. In performing the Services, the Developer shall comply with all federal, state, local, or foreign laws, rules, and regulations, as each is in effect from time to time.

6.   **Client Representative**. No later than five Business Days after the Effective Date, the Client shall assign a representative to work with the Team and notify the Developer who that representative is. The Client shall give the representative the authority to sign Change Orders and to make all other decisions concerning the Website and the Services. At any time, the Client may remove the then-current representative and assign another representative to work with the Team.

7.   **Content**.

   7.1   **Initial Content**. No later than ten Business Days after the Effective Date, the Client shall deliver to the Developer the following:

     7.1.1   The Website's URL.

     7.1.2   The Content that it wants incorporated into the Website.

   7.2   **Additional Content**. If the Client wants to change the Content after the Developer has incorporated it into the Website, the Developer is entitled to an additional fee, which the Client shall pay, all of which must be documented by a Change Order that both parties sign.

8.   **Ownership**.

   8.1   **Definition**. "**Developer Programming**" means any programming or software that the Developer creates, or has created, outside of this Agreement but uses in the Works.

   8.2   **Work for Hire**.

     8.2.1   **Rights to the Works**. The Works are works made for hire and all rights to them vest in the Client. The Developer has no right to them or any interest in them and shall not use them to benefit anyone other than the Client.

     8.2.2   **Assignment of Rights in the Works**. By signing this Agreement, the Developer assigns to the Client

       (a)   all rights in each Work that do not vest in the Client by operation of law; and

       (b)   all copyright interests in each Work for the entire period of that Work's copyright protection.

   8.3   **Developer Programs**. The Developer retains all rights to all Developer Programming, but grants to the Client a perpetual, nonexclusive license to use all Developer Programming in connection with the Works.

9.   **Warranties**. The Developer warrants that the Works will

   9.1   be usable by the Client for the purposes for which they were intended;

9.2   operate in conformity with the specifications listed in Exhibit A; and

9.3   be free of viruses, Trojan horses, and other software that could damage the Website or the computer of any user of the Website.

10. **Representations and Warranties**.

    10.1   Developer. The Developer represents and warrants to the Client as follows:

        10.1.1   **Organization**. The Developer is a corporation duly organized, validly existing, and in good standing under the laws of its jurisdiction of incorporation.

        10.1.2   **Corporate Power and Authority**. The Developer has all requisite corporate power and authority

            (a)   to own, operate, and lease its properties, and to carry on its business as now being conducted; and

            (b)   to execute, deliver, and perform this Agreement.

        10.1.3   **Authorization**. The Developer has taken all necessary corporate action to authorize the execution, delivery, and performance of this Agreement.

        10.1.4   **Enforceability**. The Developer has duly executed and delivered this Agreement, and it constitutes the Developer's legal, valid, and binding obligation. This Agreement is enforceable against the Developer in accordance with its terms, except to the extent that enforcement is limited by either one or both of the following:

            (a)   Applicable bankruptcy, insolvency, reorganization, moratorium, or other similar laws affecting creditors' rights generally.

            (b)   General equitable principles, regardless of whether the issue of enforceability is considered in a proceeding in equity or at law.

        10.1.5   **Team Members**. The Team members listed in Section 5.3 are knowledgeable and qualified to perform the Services.

    10.2   Client. The Client represents and warrants to the Developer as follows:

        10.2.1   **Organization**. The Client is a corporation duly organized, validly existing, and in good standing under the laws of its jurisdiction of incorporation.

        10.2.2   **Corporate Power and Authority**. The Client has all requisite corporate power and authority

            (a)   to own, operate, and lease its properties, and to carry on its business as now being conducted; and

            (b)   to execute, deliver, and perform this Agreement.

        10.2.3   **Authorization**. The Client has taken all necessary corporate action to authorize the execution, delivery, and performance of this Agreement.

        10.2.4   **Enforceability**. The Client has duly executed and delivered this Agreement, and it constitutes the Client's legal, valid, and binding obligation. This Agreement is enforceable against the Client, except to the extent that enforcement is limited by either one or both of the following:

            (a)   Applicable bankruptcy, insolvency, reorganization, moratorium, or other similar laws affecting creditors' rights generally.

            (b)   General equitable principles, regardless of whether the issue of enforceability is considered in a proceeding in equity or at law.

11. **Development Credit**. The Client shall acknowledge the Developer as the Website developer on the Website page entitled "About the Site." The Client may remove the acknowledgment if it materially changes the Website after this Agreement terminates.

12. **Termination**.

    12.1   Termination. Except as provided in Section 3.2 and Section 12.2, this Agreement terminates when the Developer has completely performed the Services and the Client has paid all fees in accordance with Section 4.

12.2 Termination for Cause. A nonbreaching party may earlier terminate this Agreement by notifying the alleged breaching party of the former's intent to terminate if the allegedly breaching party did one or more of the following:

12.2.1 Materially misrepresented a fact.

12.2.2 Materially breached either a warranty or covenant.

This Agreement terminates on the tenth Business Day after a party receives a notice of intent to terminate. On termination, the terminating party has all rights and remedies that law and equity provide. Despite the previous sentences in this Section 12.2, if the Client does not pay the Down Payment in accordance with Section 4.2.2, then Section 3.2 governs termination, not this Section 12.2.

13. General Provisions.

13.1 Governing Law. The internal laws of California govern all matters arising under or relating to this Agreement, including torts.

13.2 Assignment and Delegation. The Developer shall not assign its rights or delegate its performance under this Agreement without the Client's prior consent. The Client may assign its rights and delegate its performance. For the purposes of this Section, an assignment includes a change of control.

13.3 Successors and Assigns. This Agreement binds and benefits the parties and their respective permitted successors and assigns.

13.4 Notices. The parties shall send all notices in writing and give all consents in writing. A notice or consent is effective when the intended recipient receives it.

13.5 Merger. This Agreement is the final and exclusive statement of the parties' agreement on the matters contained in this Agreement. It supersedes all previous negotiations and agreements.

13.6 Amendments. The parties may amend this Agreement only by an agreement in writing that both parties execute.

13.7 Counterparts. The parties may execute this Agreement in counterparts, each of which constitutes an original, and all which, collectively, constitute only one agreement. The delivery of an executed counterpart signature page by facsimile or PDF is as effective as delivering this Agreement in the presence of the other party to this Agreement. This Agreement is effective as stated in Section 3.

To evidence the parties' agreement to this Agreement, each party has executed this Agreement on the date stated beneath that party's name.

Website Designs, Inc.

By: _____
Walter Kelley, President

Dated: _____

Go-Karts Corp.

By: _____
Esther Grant, President

Dated: _____

Exhibit A

Scope of Services

- Creative consulting.
- Creation of site map.
- Three mock-ups of home page.
- Two revisions of chosen home page.
- Three mock-ups of secondary page.
- Two revisions of chosen secondary page.
- Programming for 30 static pages.
- Launch and testing of Website.

Specifications

- Website to work with multiple browsers.
- Website to work with multiple operating systems, including those created by Microsoft or Apple.
- Client to be able to make changes to the Website using a commercially available software application.

Document 3

Assignment and Assumption Agreement[1]

Assignment and Assumption Agreement (this "**Assignment**"), dated September 10, 20XX, between Virginia Vendors, Inc., a Delaware corporation (the "**Assignor**"), and Complete Nutrition LLC, a Colorado limited liability company (the "**Assignee**").[2]

Background[3]

1. The Assignor is a party to the agreements [more particularly][4] listed in Exhibit A to this Assignment (the "**Exhibit A Agreements**"[5]).

2. The Assignor and the Assignee have entered into the Asset Purchase Agreement, dated July 15, 20XX (the "**Asset Purchase Agreement**"[6]), which provides for, among other things,

   (a) the Assignor to assign its rights [and delegate its performance][7] under the Exhibit A Agreements to the Assignee; and

   (b) the Assignee to assume the Assignor's performance under the Exhibit A Agreements [that arise and are payable after the date of this Assignment].[8]

The parties agree as follows:

1. **Assignment**. By executing and delivering this Assignment, the Assignor assigns to the Assignee, its successors and assigns, all of the Assignor's rights under the Exhibit A Agreements.[9]

2. **Delegation**. By executing and delivering this Assignment, the Assignor delegates to the Assignee, its successors and assigns, all of the Assignor's performance obligations under the Exhibit A Agreements.[10]

3. **Acceptance and Assumption**. By executing and delivering this Assignment, the Assignee

   (a) accepts the assignment[11] from the Assignor of its rights under each of the Exhibit A Agreements;

---

1. This agreement could easily be properly named "Assignment, Delegation, and Assumption Agreement" as a delegation is included. In many assignments, the assignor only "assigns" the agreement. But both the *Restatement (Second) of Contracts* and the U.C.C. interpret a party's assignment of a contract to include a delegation, unless there is evidence to the contrary. That evidence would exist, for example, in a borrower's assignment of a contract to a bank as security for a loan.

2. Could use "Seller" and "Buyer" for ease of reading.

3. What is the purpose of these recitals?

4. Is this language necessary, helpful, or legalese?

5. Although the defined term could be *Agreements*, using *Exhibit A Agreements* is arguably easier for the reader because *Agreement* generally refers to the agreement being signed. One could reasonably disagree with this.

6. Does this agreement really need to be defined?

7. This language is not always included. See Comment 1.

8. What is the purpose of the bracketed language?

9. Is this a promise of performance or a self-executing provision, that is, the performance?

10. As noted in Annotation 1, many practitioners would not include a specific delegation. Including it avoids any need to interpret *assign* to include *delegate*.

11. Technically, an assignee must accept the rights assigned to it.

12. What provision does this echo? Why is the language repeated?

13. Why doesn't the language in subsection (b) make subsection (c) unnecessary?

(b)   assumes all of the Assignor's performance obligations under the Exhibit A Agreements that arise and are payable after the date of this Assignment;[12] and

(c)   agrees to be bound by all of the provisions in the Exhibit A Agreements.[13]

To evidence the parties' agreement to the provisions of this Assignment, they have executed and delivered it on the date stated in the preamble.

Virginia Vendors, Inc.

By: _____
          Name and title

Complete Nutrition LLC

By: _____
          Name and title

Document 4

The Action Sections of an Asset Purchase Agreement

Article 1 — Definitions

1.1 **Definitions**. Terms defined in the preamble and recitals of this Agreement have their assigned meaning, and each of the following terms has the meaning assigned to it.

(a) "**Assumed Liabilities**" means the following liabilities and obligations of the Seller:

[The agreement lists the liabilities that the Buyer will be assuming.][1]

(b) "**Closing**" means the closing of the transactions that this Agreement contemplates in Memphis, Tennessee on the Closing Date.[2]

(c) "**Closing Date**" has the meaning assigned to it in Section 2.3.

(d) "**Note**" has the meaning assigned to it in Section 2.2(a)(ii).

(e) "**Purchased Assets**" means [the contract lists the assets the Buyer is purchasing].[3]

Article 2 — Purchase and Sale

2.1 **Sale of Properties and Assets**. At the Closing, the Seller shall sell, transfer, assign, convey, and deliver the Purchased Assets to the Buyer, and the Buyer shall purchase, accept, and acquire the Purchased Assets from the Seller.[4]

2.2 **Purchase Price**.[5] The purchase price is

(a) $25 million, consisting of[6]

---

1. Does every asset sale include assumed liabilities?

2. Why is this definition substantively wrong? Look at Section 2.3.

3. Why might a drafter delete this defined term? What should replace it?

4. What's wrong with this section from a drafting perspective?

5. Section 2.2 is definitional. The Buyer's obligation to pay the purchase price at Closing is in Section 2.4.

If part of the purchase price were due concurrently with the signing of the agreement or after signing but before closing, the drafter would add a section to deal with those payments. They would not belong in Section 2.4 because that section deals exclusively with closing conveyances and closing payments. Neither would they belong in the covenant article, despite their being covenants. Covenants are not restricted to the covenant article. (The covenants in the covenant article generally apply during the gap period or post closing.) All payments of purchase price belong in the action sections.

6. Each part of the consideration aggregating $25 million has its own subsection.

7. What is the purpose of the Exhibit? What is the benefit of defining *Note* here rather than in the definitions article?

8. The *p* from *plus* lines up under the dollar sign to indicate it is joining subsections (a) and (b).

9. What is wrong with the bracketed language from a drafting perspective?

10. Why is the defined term *Closing Date* placed where it is?

11. Section 2.4 is only for actions that occur at closing and for the further assurances provision that applies at the time of the closing.

Section 2.4 does NOT cover any payments of the purchase price before closing. It is only for payments that a buyer makes at closing.

12. In an asset sale, some piece of paper must convey each asset from the seller to the buyer. A bill of sale is used for tangible and intangible assets; a deed is used for real property; and an assignment is used to convey contractual rights. Document 3 is an exemplar of an assignment and assumption agreement. Document 5 is an exemplar of a bill of sale.

A seller must execute and deliver each conveyancing document because the seller is the entity that is doing the conveying. Why must a buyer execute the assignment and assumption agreement?

13. The bracketed language establishes a standard. What risk does this standard pose to the Seller?

Often in an acquisition, the seller must not only legally convey the asset to the buyer using a conveyancing document, but also physically deliver the asset. That may not be possible when what is being sold is a business. But if the asset is a single tangible asset that readily moves, the seller should also be obligated to deliver the asset to the buyer. The promise to deliver the asset belongs in the *Seller's Deliveries*. Carefully review the language that introduces what is to be delivered and confirm that the introductory language parses properly with each enumerated item. If not, perhaps the contract needs an additional delivery section.

(i) $10 million in immediately available funds; and

(ii)   a $15 million promissory note payable to the order of the Seller, substantially in the form of **Exhibit A** (the "**Note**"[7]);

plus[8]

(b)   an assumption by the Buyer of the [Assumed Liabilities of the Seller].[9]

2.3   The Closing. The Closing is to occur on December 22, 20X2, or another date as to which the Seller and the Buyer agree, but no later than December 31, 20X2 (the date the sale is consummated, the "**Closing Date**"[10]). It is to take place at the offices of Workhard & Playlittle LLP, 1180 Avenue of the Americas, New York, New York, beginning at 9:00 a.m. local time.

2.4   Closing Deliveries; Further Assurances.[11] [Instruments of Transfer; Payment of Purchase Price and Assumption of Liabilities; Further Assurances]

(a)   **Seller's Deliveries.** At the Closing, the Seller shall execute and deliver to the Buyer the following:[12]

(i)   A bill of sale for the Purchased Assets, [in a form [reasonably] satisfactory to the Buyer].[13]

(ii)   An assignment of each lease under which the Seller is tenant, in a form satisfactory to the Buyer.

(iii)   Such other instrument or instruments of transfer as may be necessary or appropriate to vest in the Buyer good title to the Purchased Assets.[14]

(b)   **Buyer's Deliveries.**[15] At the Closing, the Buyer shall deliver [or cause to be delivered] to the Seller the following:

(i) $15 million in funds immediately available in New York, New York.

(ii)   The Note, executed by the Buyer.

(iii)   An instrument, executed by the Buyer, in a form reasonably satisfactory to the Seller, whereby the Buyer assumes the Assumed Liabilities.[16]

14. This is a further assurances provision — a promise to deliver other documents at the time of the Closing, if necessary to convey the assets. This differs from the further assurances provision in subsection (c). That applies to the post-closing period.

15. Section 2.4(b) is the Buyer's promise to pay the purchase price at closing. (Section 2.2 merely stated the amount of the purchase. It was not joined with an obligation to pay it.) Because the purchase price in this transaction has three components, the payment provision must have three corresponding provisions to spell out how each component is to be paid or delivered.

In some transactions, the parties may have put into escrow a portion of the purchase price. That is irrelevant to the drafting of the buyer's covenant to pay the full purchase price (minus any down payments). The seller wants this buyer's promise because it protects the seller against the risk that the escrow agent breaches and fails to pay the escrowed amount at closing. If that should occur, the contract provisions ensure that the seller will nonetheless be paid in full: The buyer promised to pay the full purchase price and must, therefore, make up any deficit. Assuming the buyer pays the escrowed amount to the seller, the buyer would have a cause of action against the escrow agent.

The contract must reflect that the buyer itself will not actually be paying the full amount. The language introducing subsection (b) reflects that the buyer is promising a result (full payment), but not promising that it will be the actor that causes the result. The salient language is *cause to be delivered*. In the vernacular, *cause to be delivered* means that a party promises that something will get done, but makes no promises as to how it will get done.

16. The Buyer's assumption is listed under *Buyer's Deliveries*. Generally, one agreement — an Assignment and Assumption Agreement — contains both the seller's assignment and the buyer's assumption. Nonetheless, the promises to assign and assume must be separately stated.

17. This further assurances provision kicks in post-closing. Compare the two further assurances provisions. What differs, and is it problematic?

18. Note the parallel structure of subsections (i) and (ii). Each one begins with an infinitive followed by a reference to the Buyer. This is a matter of good drafting and craftsmanship.

19. As with all provisions, before using this subsection, think through whether it applies to the agreement being drafted.

(c) **Further Assurances.**[17] Following the Closing, at the request of the Buyer, the Seller shall execute and deliver any further instruments of transfer and take all reasonable action as may be necessary or appropriate

(i) to vest in the Buyer good title to the Purchased Assets; and[18]

(ii) to transfer to the Buyer all licenses and permits necessary for the operation of the Purchased Assets.[19]

Document 5[1]

Bill of Sale[2]

State of New Jersey, Bergen County

1. **Purchase Agreement.**[3] This Bill of Sale ("**Bill of Sale**") refers to the Boat Purchase Agreement, dated October 1, 20XX (the "**Purchase Agreement**"), between Richard Hunter (the "**Seller**") and Dana Jackson (the "**Buyer**"). The Seller's current address is 1231 Forest Ave., Paramus, NJ 07652. The Buyer's current address is 721 Hickory Ave., Tenafly, NJ 07670. Capitalized terms used without definition in this Bill of Sale have the meanings assigned to them in the Purchase Agreement.

2. **Sale and Transfer of the Boat.**[4] The purchase price for this sale is stated in the Purchase Agreement, and the Buyer is paying it contemporaneously with the execution and delivery of this Bill of Sale. By executing and delivering this Bill of Sale, the Seller sells to the Buyer all of the Seller's rights to the Boat and the Related Assets and transfers to the Buyer title to the Boat and the Related Assets.

3. **Further Assurances.**[5] Following the Closing, the Seller shall execute and deliver to the Buyer any further instruments of transfer and take all reasonable action as may be appropriate

    (a) to vest in the Buyer good title to the Boat and the Related Assets; and

    (b) to transfer to the Buyer all licenses and permits necessary to operate the Boat.

4. **Power of Attorney.**[6]

    (a) **Appointment.** Without limiting Paragraph 3 of this Bill of Sale, the Seller appoints Joseph Solomon, 80 Park Plaza, Newark, NJ 07101 as the Seller's attorney in fact (Joseph Solomon and his successors and assigns, the "**Seller's Attorney**") for the following purposes:

        (i) To exercise any right or perform any obligation that the Seller now has or may acquire relating to the Bill of

---

1. This Bill of Sale has been drafted as an exemplar. Consult local laws, including those of New Jersey, before drafting a bill of sale for a transaction.

2. What is the business purpose of this document?

3. What are Paragraph 1's functions?

4. Paragraph 2
(a) What is the legal purpose of the first sentence?
(b) What is the purpose of the second sentence?
(c) What language achieved the purpose?

5. Paragraph 3
(a) What is the business purpose of this provision?
(b) In this transaction, in what document would you expect to see similar language?
(c) What drafting considerations should you have when writing this provision?

6. Paragraph 4
(a) What is the business purpose of this provision?
(b) What is wrong with the language constituting the definition for the defined term *Seller's Attorney*?

Sale and the transaction that the Purchase Agreement contemplates.

(ii) To demand, receive, recover, and collect

    (A) any money related to the transaction that the Purchase Agreement contemplates; or

    (B) the Boat and the Related Assets.

(iii) To give receipts and releases for the Boat and the Related Assets.

(iv) To institute and prosecute, in the name of the Seller, any legal and equitable remedies and any other means that the Seller's Attorney may deem proper to collect or reduce to possession the Boat and any Related Asset.

(v) To do all things legally permissible, required, or that the Buyer reasonably requests to ensure that the Buyer acquires the Seller's rights to the Boat and the Related Assets.

(vi) To use the Seller's name in any manner the Seller's Attorney may reasonably deem necessary to complete the transactions contemplated by either or both of this Bill of Sale and the Purchase Agreement.

(b) **Scope of Power of Attorney**. This Paragraph 4 is to be construed as a power of attorney only for the transactions that are contemplated by either or both of this Bill of Sale and the Purchase Agreement. The enumeration of specific items, acts, rights, or powers does not limit or restrict, and is not to be construed or interpreted as limiting or restricting, the general powers granted to the Seller's Attorney.

5. **Term of the Power of Attorney.**[7] The Seller's Attorney may begin exercising the rights, powers, and authority granted in Paragraph 4 when this Bill of Sale is executed and delivered. The power of attorney ends on the 30th day after the Closing.

7. Paragraph 5
(a) What is the business purpose of this provision?
(b) If the closing of the boat sale is October 15, 20XX, on what date does the power of attorney end?

6. Governing Law. The internal laws of New Jersey govern all matters arising under or relating to this Bill of Sale, including torts.

The Seller has executed and delivered this Bill of Sale on October 15, 20XX.[8]

Seller[9]

_____

Richard Hunter

8. What would be the consequence of rewriting the concluding paragraph as follows? "The Seller has executed this Bill of Sale on October 15, 20XX."

9. Why doesn't the Buyer sign this document?

Document 6

Endgame Provisions in Acquisition Agreements

The conditions article and the termination article in an acquisition agreement are inextricably intertwined. The conditions article lists each condition that must be satisfied or waived before a party has an obligation to perform the agreement's subject matter performance provision. These conditions can be divided into three categories.

1. Conditions requiring that representations and warranties be true.
2. Conditions requiring that covenants be performed.
3. Conditions unrelated to either representations and warranties or to covenants.

The failure to satisfy or waive one or more of these conditions creates the grounds for terminating an acquisition agreement. But the conditions article only creates conditions. It does not contractually turn the failure to satisfy or waive a condition into a ground for termination, nor does the conditions article state the consequences of termination. Instead, the termination article does both these things.

The termination article typically consists of the following sections.

1. Grounds for termination.
2. Contractual monetary consequences of receipt of notice of termination.
3. Other contractual consequences of receipt of notice of termination.
4. Effective date of termination.
5. Consequences of termination—survival of common law rights and remedies and survival of specific contract provisions.
6. Dispute resolution provisions.

The *Grounds for Termination* section gives a party the discretionary authority to notify the other party that it has grounds for termination if one or more of the conditions to its obligation to close has not been satisfied or waived. Parties colloquially refer to this notice as a **termination notice** or **notice of termination**. But the notice alone may or may not terminate the agreement. Instead, it notifies the other party that the first party is exercising its right to terminate. Termination may or may not occur immediately. The effective date of termination depends on the ground for termination.

An acquisition agreement has the same number of grounds for termination as it has conditions to closing, and the agreement enumerates each ground for termination in its own subsection. Therefore, a one-to-one correlation exists between the conditions to a party's obligation to perform and the reasons a party may terminate a contract.[1] A ground for termination subsection does not restate the language of a condition, but instead cross-references the subsection stating the condition. So, for example, assume Section 6.2 states that performance of all covenants to be performed on or before closing is a closing condition. Therefore, in the section stating the grounds for termination, the ground for termination is the failure to satisfy or waive the condition stated in Section 6.2. It's indirect, but the way it's done. If the condition were restated, the drafter would have to be extraordinarily careful to say the same thing the same way. A divergence between the condition and the ground for termination would invite litigation. The cross-reference obviates the problem.

---

1. The one-to-one correlation disappears if the contract states that the parties may terminate the agreement at any time.

7.1 Termination by the Seller.

(a) **Grounds for Termination**. The Seller may notify the Buyer that it has grounds for this Agreement's termination if any one or more of the following events has occurred on or before the Closing Date:

    (i) **Misrepresentations and Breaches of Warranty**. The condition stated in Section 5.1 has not been satisfied or waived. *(Section 5.1 states the condition that the representations and warranties must have been true on the signing date and must also be true on the closing date.)*

    (ii) **Breach of Covenants**. The condition stated in Section 5.2 has not been satisfied or waived. *(Section 5.2 states the condition that all covenants must have been performed on or before the closing date.)*

Depending on the business deal, receipt of the notice of termination may trigger contractual obligations, monetary obligations, or rights. The section dealing with these terms should precede the *Effective Date of Termination* section to reflect the chronological sequence of events.

If receipt of the notice of termination triggers a contractual obligation, include a section with a title that describes the required performance; for example, *Required Purchase of Unsold Licensed Products*.

If a party must pay money, include a section, *Payment Obligations*. The payment could be a return of funds or it could be liquidated damages. In either event, it should explicitly address all the *who, what,* and *when* questions attendant to the payment of money. If the payment constitutes liquidated damages, the provision should state that the payment is the exclusive remedy. You must, of course, check applicable law so that the provision has the best chance of being enforceable.

If the notice of termination triggers the right to retain money, include a section *Right to Retain [insert descriptive name]*. If the right to retain money constitutes liquidated damages, the provision should state that the retention of the money is the exclusive remedy, again, if that is the business deal.

The section *Effective Date of Termination* states the date when an agreement terminates. The date depends on whether the termination process includes an obligation to be performed or money to be paid. If no payment or performance is required, then termination is effective on a party's receipt of the notice of termination. If a payment or performance is required, the effective date of termination is the date the payment is received or the obligation performed. This postponement ensures that all of the agreement's provisions apply during the period between the receipt of the notice of termination and the receipt of the payment or performance. These provisions would include the dispute resolution provisions, such as governing law, choice of forum, and waiver of the right to a jury trial.

Finally, the agreement must address the consequences of its termination. The aptly named section, *Consequences of Termination,* takes the laboring oar. Generally, the salient issue in this section is whether the terminating party has the common law right to sue for damages. It would have that right if the other party had made a misrepresentation, breached a warranty, or breached a covenant. To memorialize these rights, the section states that on termination, neither party has any rights or obligations, *except for Party A's rights and Party B's obligations arising from any misrepresentation, breach of warranty, or breach of covenant.* When these rights and obligations are preserved, they are said to **survive** the agreement's termination. (In a real-world, sophisticated acquisition, these rights and obligations would probably not survive because a negotiated, contractual indemnity would be the exclusive remedy.) No rights or obligations survive if the breaching party paid liquidated damages because if they did, the terminating party could receive double damages.

Specific contract provisions sometimes also survive termination. For example, the parties might want the confidentiality provision to survive the contract's termination. If a provision is to survive, the contract must explicitly state that it does.

If the ground for termination is not a misrepresentation, breach of warranty, or breach of covenant, no rights or obligations survive because damages only arise from misrepresentations and breaches. For example, the agreement might include a condition that seller's counsel must have delivered its opinion to the buyer. As discussed, the agreement would include a correlative ground for termination if the opinion were not delivered. If a party were to terminate the contract because the opinion was not delivered, the only remedy would be the common law walk-away right. The agreement would state that on termination under Section X, neither party has any rights or obligations.

Dispute resolution provisions are key to any contract's endgame provisions, but a detailed discussion is beyond the scope of this book.

Beginning on page 532 is an exemplar of a conditions article in an acquisition agreement.

Beginning on page 534 is an exemplar of termination provisions in an acquisition agreement. Finally, beginning on page 537 is a drafting exercise.

Conditions in an Acquisition Agreement[1]

Article 6 — Conditions to the Seller's Obligation to Perform

The Seller is obligated to consummate the transactions that this Agreement contemplates only if each of the following conditions has been satisfied or waived on or before the Closing Date:[2]

6.1 **The Buyer's Representations and Warranties**. The Buyer's representations and warranties stated [in this Agreement][in Article 4][3] must have been true on the date this Agreement was executed and delivered, and they must be true on and as of the Closing Date as if they were made on that date[, except as affected by transactions that this Agreement contemplates.][4]

6.2 **The Buyer's Covenants**. The Buyer must have performed all of its covenants to be performed on or before the Closing Date.[5]

6.3 **The Buyer's Closing Certificate**. The Buyer must have delivered a certificate to the Seller, signed by its Executive Vice President, certifying as to the truth of the statements in Sections 6.1 and 6.2.[6]

Article 7 — Conditions to the Buyer's Obligation to Perform

The Buyer is obligated to consummate the transactions that this Agreement contemplates only if each of the following conditions has been satisfied or waived on or before the Closing Date:

7.1 **The Seller's Representations and Warranties**. The Seller's representations and warranties stated [in this Agreement] [in Article 3] must have been true on the date this Agreement was executed and delivered, and they must be true on and as of the Closing Date as if they were made on that date[, except as affected by transactions that this Agreement contemplates.][7]

1. Only the conditions to closing are in this article. The failure to satisfy a condition and its consequences are stated in the termination article.

2. This introductory sentence follows the article heading, but is unnumbered.

3. Which cross-reference is better? Condition requires that the representations and warranties be accurate as of two dates. Why should the buyer care if the reps were inaccurate on signing, so long as they are accurate on closing?

4. The bracketed language is only appropriate if the contract contemplated a change in the facts underlying the representations and warranties. Look at each representation and warranty and see if the parties expect that the underlying facts will change. Typically, these facts do not change with respect to the buyer.

5. Why would this condition not refer to the article that contains the buyer's covenants between signing and closing? Why does this condition refer to covenants to be performed *on the Closing Date*?

6. Why is the certificate necessary?

7. Here is the same language that was the subject of Annotation 4. This language is needed more frequently with respect to the seller's representations and warranties. During the gap period, facts relating to a seller's business may well change.

7.2 **The Seller's Covenants**. The Seller must have performed all of its covenants to be performed on or before the Closing Date.

7.3 **The Seller's Closing Certificate**. The Seller must have delivered a certificate to the Buyer, signed by its President, certifying as to the truth of the statements in Sections 7.1 and 7.2.

7.4 **Consents**. All of the Consents listed in Schedule X.X must have been obtained.[8]

8. Why would Section 7.4 be necessary as a business and legal matter to protect a buyer? Assume the seller promised that, during the gap period, it would use commercially reasonable efforts to obtain all consents.

Termination Provisions in an Acquisition Agreement[1]

Article 8 — Termination

8.1   Written Agreement. The parties may terminate this Agreement at any time by written agreement.[2]

8.2   Termination by the Seller.

(a)   **Grounds for Termination**. The Seller may notify the Buyer that it has grounds for this Agreement's termination if any one or more of the following events has occurred on or before the Closing Date:

  (i)   **Misrepresentations and Breaches of Warranty**.[3] The condition stated in Section 6.1 has not been satisfied or waived.

  (ii)   **Breach of Covenants**. The condition stated in Section 6.2 has not been satisfied or waived.

  (iii)   **The Buyer's Closing Certificate**. The condition stated in Section 6.3 has not been satisfied or waived.

(b)   [**Payment Obligations**.[4] If the Buyer receives a notice of termination under Section 8.2(a), it shall pay the Seller $X no later than three days after its receipt of the notice of termination. To effect this payment, X shall

  (i)   wire transfer $X of funds immediately available in Chicago, Illinois no later than three days after its receipt of the notice of termination; and

  (ii)   do any other act necessary to the transfer the funds.][5]

or

(b)   [**Right to Retain** [*Insert defined term that identifies the money — for example, the Y Payment.*] If the Buyer receives a notice of termination under Section 8.2, it is entitled to retain the [Y Payment].][6]

(c)   **Effective Date of Termination**. If the Seller sends a notice of termination of this Agreement under Section 8.2(a), the termination is effective when [the Buyer receives the Seller's notice of

---

1. These provisions tie into the preceding conditions articles.

2. This provision does not need to be more detailed because the parties will enter into an agreement concerning the termination. Technically, the provision is not even required because the parties may always amend or terminate their agreement. Parties tend to include it because it reflects their understanding.

3. The grounds for termination are created by cross-reference to the sections stating the conditions. Each condition has its own ground for termination. The headings make it easier for the reader to understand the ground for termination.

4. Subsection (b) addresses whether money is paid or retained or if a contractual performance is required. If a party has a payment obligation, how could it be legally characterized, and what are the business and drafting consequences? The alternative to this provision is that a party might be entitled to retain funds. That right should be stated explicitly to avoid any dispute as to the right to those funds.

5. Draft provisions that specify the other acts necessary to transfer the funds. Don't use general language.

6. Why is *entitled* used and not the discretionary language *may*?

termination] [the Seller receives the payment required by Section 8.2(b)].[7]

7. Why do the termination dates differ?

(d) **Consequences of Termination**. On termination of this Agreement under Section 8.2, neither party has any further rights or obligations under this Agreement[, *except for the Seller's rights and the Buyer's obligations arising from any one or more of the Buyer's misrepresentations, breach of warranty, or breach of covenant*].[8]

8. What determines whether the bracketed language is included?

Write in the appropriate contract language for each of the following provisions, using the conditions on pages 536-537 to determine grounds for termination.

8.3 Termination by the Buyer.

(a) **Grounds for Termination**. The Buyer may send the Seller a notice stating that it has grounds to terminate this Agreement if any one or more of the following events has occurred on or before the Closing Date:

(i) **Misrepresentations and Breaches of Warranty**.

    _____

    _____

    _____

(ii) **Breach of Covenants**.

    _____

    _____

    _____

(iii) **The Seller's Closing Certificate**.

    _____

    _____

    _____

(iv) **Failure to Obtain Consents**.

    _____

    _____

    _____

(b) **Contract Obligation/Payment Obligations/Right to Retain**.

[Assume for this exercise that neither party has a payment or performance obligation.]

(c) **Effective Date of Termination**. If the Buyer terminates this Agreement under Section 8.3(a), the termination is effective when

_____

_____

_____

(d) **Consequences of Termination**.

(i) **Termination under Section 8.3(a)(i), (ii), and (iii)**. On termination of this Agreement under any one or more of Sections 8.3(a)(i), (ii), and (iii),

_____

_____

_____

_____

_____

(ii) **Termination under Section 8.3(a)(iv)**. On termination of this Agreement under Section 8.3(a)(iv),

_____

_____

_____

_____

_____

8.4 Survival of Confidentiality Provisions. Despite any termination of this Agreement under Section 8.2 or 8.3, the parties' obligations under Article 9 — Confidentiality survive to the extent stated in that Article.

Document 7

Drafting Client Memoranda

Client memoranda are used for multiple purposes, including the following:

- To describe important business or legal issues that arose when drafting or negotiating and to obtain client input so that the issues can be resolved.
- To describe how drafting or negotiation resolved important business or legal issues.
- To report, in general, on negotiations that lawyers conducted.
- To pose specific questions (transaction structure; negotiation strategy).
- To answer specific questions that the client posed. (Is government consent required?)
- To inform the client of important information that the lawyer learned from the other side. (The other side is having trouble meeting payroll.)
- To describe a problem and to propose a solution.
- To report on the status of the deal.

These memoranda are some of the most important communications you will write to clients. Ethically, you have an obligation to keep a client up to date on the status of negotiations. Equally important is the client relations issue. The client will receive many memos, e-mails, and letters from you and will judge the quality of your work by what you write. Can you write informally without legalese, so that a nonlawyer can understand the salient points? Do you waste her time with minor issues or with long, nonessential, prefatory material? Can you state the law succinctly and, even more important, why it matters to the client as a business matter? She will make these judgments independently of your negotiation success and contract drafting ability.

The following guidelines will be helpful to you as you learn how to write memoranda. Of course, formal memoranda are often less common today because so many people correspond through e-mail. These guidelines apply also to e-mails to clients. After reviewing the guidelines, you can read two exemplar memos that relate to a house purchase agreement.

Guidelines for Drafting a Client Memorandum

1. *A formal memo has "To," "From," "Date," and "Re" or "Subject" lines.*

> To: Sara Nottingham
> From: Jake Rice
> Date: November 17, 20X5
> Re: Revised Trademark Licensing Agreement

2. *The introduction should be short so that the reader gets to the substance as quickly as possible.* The introduction should state the subject matter of the memo and where the conclusion or action items are (if any). Use language along the following lines:

> In reviewing the revised draft of the Trademark Licensing Agreement, please note the following. The memo concludes with three action items for you.

If the memorandum discusses just a few points, it may be helpful to precede the body of the memo with a list of bullet points. This crystallizes the purpose of the memo, facilitating its reading.

> This memorandum addresses the two key issues that remain outstanding:
>
> - Whether the Contractor will pay liquidated damages if it fails to keep on schedule.
> - Whether the parties will be obligated to mediate a dispute before resorting to litigation.

3. *Number each paragraph of the memorandum.*

> **Example 1**
>
> 1. First point
>
> 2. Second point

In addition, organize the memorandum in numerical order by section number and section heading to alert the reader to the topic of each paragraph.

> **Example 2**
>
> 1. **Section 3.2 — License Term**
>
> 2. **Section 4.1 — Royalties**

Finally, if you know a topic that particularly interests the client, address its location in the prefatory material, so that the client can immediately find it.

> **Example 3**
>
> In reviewing the revised draft of the Trademark Licensing Agreement, please note that the issues are addressed in the order in which they appear in the agreement. The memorandum addresses the exclusivity issue in Paragraph 6.

4. *Avoid legalese and draft simply.* The client may not be a lawyer, so technical legal terminology only impedes understanding. Often, technical language can be avoided by focusing on what the provision is intended to accomplish from a business perspective. Draft in a conversational tone, but with the recognition that a memo communicates information to the client and requires a degree of formality. It is not an e-mail to a friend.

5. *Draft succinctly.* The goal is a one-page memo—a case on a page. Business people have little time and less patience. The transaction or circumstances may require a longer memo, but that takes nothing away from the advice to draft succinctly. Should you somehow reasonably end up with a multi-page memo, consider including an *Executive Summary* at the memo's beginning.

6. *Don't bury the headline.* For each new point included in the memo, tell the reader in the first sentence of the paragraph why it is important. For the client, that's usually the business consequence.

7. *The memo should avoid the first person.* When describing the contract, do not state what you did as the drafter. Instead, describe what the contract provides.

Wrong

I drafted Section 6.2 so that the Manufacturer is obligated to use first-quality raw materials.

Correct

Section 6.2 obligates the Manufacturer to use first-quality raw materials.

8. *If the draft changes the substance of a provision, explain how the redraft changes the provision, describe the business or legal consequences, and summarize the original provision.* This three-part discussion can be quite short if the language is focused. If appropriate, consider suggesting alternative language for the client to consider.

Example

Revised Section 4.2 requires the Manufacturer to inform you [the Retailer] promptly if it knows that a production delay is reasonably likely. This early notice should help in making timely merchandising decisions. The original draft had no notice requirement.

The *promptly* standard is vague. Would you prefer to make it more specific by replacing *promptly if* with *no later than three business days after*?

9. *Don't provide the client with a detailed discussion of the law unless the client needs the information to understand a business issue or to make a business decision.* Explain first what the contract needs to provide from the business/legal perspective and then tie it into the statute.

Wrong

The statute requires that the Corporation give 30 days' notice before it can do X. The initial draft provided for only 25 days' notice. The new date of March 13, 20XX complies with the statute.

Correct

Revised Section 15.2 extends the deadline for receipt of notice from potential claimants to March 13, 20XX—an extra ten days. The new date now complies with the statutory requirement. The time period in the earlier draft was too short.

10. *Don't quote the agreement or a statute.* Instead, summarize the relevant language using nonlegal terminology and explain why, from a business perspective, the client should care.

11. *Do more than spot and list issues and problems.* Propose ways to resolve these matters and move the deal forward.

12. *Use formatting to enhance clarity.* For example, if five business issues remain, set them out indented with bullets. Then address each of the issues in turn.

13. *Remember that you are not the decision maker with respect to business issues.* Issues of fairness are ultimately business issues and for the client's approval. That said, as you become more senior, some clients may turn to you for business and strategic advice. Wait until you are asked.

Wrong

I think that Section 6.7 as revised is fair to both parties. Mr. Sanchez will be deemed disabled if he cannot work because of illness or injury for 60 consecutive business days. This reflects an equitable number of days missed from work to warrant termination. It will cover most ailments that have a long recovery, but still allow the Company to replace Mr. Sanchez reasonably quickly if necessary.

Correct

Section 6.7, as revised, provides that Mr. Sanchez is deemed disabled if he is absent for 60 consecutive business days because of illness or injury. At that time, you could replace him. Please let me know if this time frame works from your perspective.

---

14. *Do not refer to a provision without providing details of why it is important.*

15. *Do not recite every change made to the contract.* Include only what is important as a business or legal matter. The client is not your professor. Even your professor probably doesn't want that detail.

16. *Single space the memo and insert a blank line between paragraphs.*

17. *Do not discuss formatting or other drafting matters.*

18. *Spend time editing the memo and proofreading it.* Neatness counts. Glaring spelling errors suggest inattention to detail, calling into question all that you have done.

19. *End the memo by addressing action points.* What are the next steps? Does the client need to do something? Is there a critical deadline that the client must meet?

Matters requiring attention:

- Please provide the unaudited quarterly financials for the last fiscal year.
- Consult with the other side to determine whether they will agree to mediation before beginning litigation.

Client Memorandum — Exemplar 1

To: Bob Buyer
From: Attentive Lawyer
Date: August 15, 20X5
Re: House Purchase Agreement

Attached is the first draft of the House Purchase Agreement. Please review the noted sections. Paragraph 4 of this memo discusses the mold inspection and its consequences.

1   **Section 2.1 — Assets Purchased**. As you requested, window treatments are included in the schedule of household items also being purchased. As we did not previously discuss this with the other side, I will mention it in my cover memo to them.

2.   **Section 2.2 — Purchase Price**. This section provides for the following two adjustments to the purchase price:

(a)   The purchase price will increase or decrease based on the amount of oil in the tank on the closing date.

(b)   The purchase price will decrease to reflect an allocation between the parties with respect to county taxes that you previously paid.

If the seller agrees to your request with respect to the carpet cleaning, the purchase price provision will also need to include an adjustment for the related costs. The carpets are discussed in the next paragraph.

3.   **Section 5.2 — Carpets**. In this section, the contract provides that the seller is obligated to have the carpets professionally cleaned no later than the closing date. If they are cleaned, the purchase price will be reduced by the cost of the service, but no more than $500.

4.   **Sections 5.3, 7.2, and 9.1 — Mold Inspection**. These sections permit you to have the house inspected for mold and give you the right not to close if the inspector finds the house is not mold-free. If you do not purchase the house because of mold, you are entitled to the return of your $5,000 down payment.

The other side has asked that we get them the first draft of the House Purchase Agreement no later than Friday. Accordingly, I would appreciate any questions or comments about this draft no later than Thursday, 5:00 p.m. If this timing is problematic, I will arrange for a later delivery to the other side. Just let me know.

A. L.

Client Memorandum — Exemplar 2

To: Bob Buyer
From: Attentive Lawyer
Date: August 23, 20X5
Re: Revised House Purchase Agreement

Enclosed is a draft of the House Purchase Agreement, marked to show changes from the first draft and reflecting yesterday's negotiation. The two key issues are proposed purchase price increases (discussed in Paragraph 1) and the Seller's refusal to delay the closing date. Paragraph 2 discusses her counterproposal.

1.   **Article 2 — Purchase Price**.

   (a)   **Window Treatments** (First draft, Section 2.1). The Seller wants you to pay an additional $500 for the window treatments. You may, of course, make a lower counteroffer or choose not to purchase the window treatments.

   (b)   **Carpet Cleaning** (First draft, Section 5). The Seller has agreed to have professionals clean the carpets, but will pay no more than $300, not the $500 you requested. Are you willing to pay the difference as part of the purchase price? Do you want to stipulate the carpet cleaner to be used?

2.   **Section 2.4 — Closing Date**. The Seller has refused to extend the closing date to November 30th to give you time to obtain financing. She wants to close no later than September 15th, but has offered short-term seller financing of $150,000 at 5%. (That means you must pay $50,000 of the purchase price at closing.) The borrowing, plus accrued interest, would be due no later than the date of your closing with a lender. If you do not pay the Seller before November 30th,

   (a)   the full amount of the financing, plus accrued interest, is due on November 30th;

   (b)   ownership of the house reverts to the Seller on November 30th; and

   (c)   the Seller is obligated to repay you $40,000 by wire transfer on November 30th, meaning she is entitled to keep $10,000 of the $50,000 paid at closing as liquidated damages.

3.   **Termite Inspection — new**. Local law requires that the house be professionally inspected for termites. The Seller has requested that we include the standard provision requiring a buyer to pay for the inspection. The usual cost is about $750.

Please let me know if you have any questions or comments and how you would like to address the purchase price and closing date issues.

A. L.

Document 8

Website Development Agreement (Version 2)

This **Website Development Agreement** is dated January 8, 20XX and is between Go-Karts Corp., a California corporation (the "**Client**"), and Website Designs, Inc., a Michigan corporation (the "**Developer**").

This Agreement provides for the Developer's development of a website[1] for the Client.

The parties agree as follows:

1.   Definitions and Defined Term.

1.1   Defined Terms. Terms defined in the preamble have their assigned meanings and each of the following terms has the meaning assigned to it.

"**Agreement**" means this Website Development Agreement, including **Exhibit A**, as each may be amended from time to time.

"**Business Day**" means any day other than a day that a bank in San Jose, California is required or permitted to be closed.

"**Change Order**" means an agreement that changes or supplements the Services.[2]

"**Content**" means all text, images, sound, graphics, and other materials describing the Client's business and industry.

"**Developer Programming**" has the meaning assigned to it in Section 8.1.

"**Down Payment**" has the meaning assigned to it in Section 4.2.1.

"**Effective Date**" means the date the second party to execute and deliver this Agreement delivers the executed Agreement to the other party, the date of delivery to be the date of the other party's receipt of the executed Agreement.[3]

"**Services**" means the services listed in the Scope of Services section in **Exhibit A**.

"**Team**" means the employees the Developer assigns to perform the Services.

1. Should website be defined in the recital?

2. Would the following definition be better? *"Change Order" means an agreement executed and delivered by the parties that changes or supplements the Services.*

3. Why does it matter that the Effective Date requires delivery of the executed agreement to the first party who signed?

"**Website**" means a collection of interconnected web pages on the Internet, pertaining to the Client.

"**Works**" means the Website and all other deliverables, including all derivative deliverables, resulting from the performance of the Services.

4. What interpretive provisions might you consider adding to the three already in the agreement?

1.2   **Interpretive Provisions.**[4]

    1.2.1   **References to Sections, etc**. References to Sections, subsections, and Exhibit A are references to Sections, subsections, and Exhibit A of this Agreement.

    1.2.2   **References to a Person**. References to a person include that person's permitted successors and assigns and, in the case of any governmental person, the person succeeding to the governmental functions of that person.

    1.2.3   ***Including* and Its Variations**. The words *including*, *includes*, and *include* are deemed to be followed by the words *without limitation*.

2.   **Development of Website.**

2.1   **Hiring of the Developer.** By executing and delivering this Agreement, the Client hires the Developer to design and develop the Website for the Client.

2.2   **Design and Development of the Website**. Subject to the provisions of this Agreement, the Developer shall design and develop the Website by performing the Services.

5. Would it work to make the Effective Date contingent on receiving the Down Payment?

3.   **Effective Date.**

3.1   **Effective Date**. This Agreement is effective on the Effective Date.[5]

6. Why does the agreement terminate at 5:00 p.m. on the stated date? Do not just restate what is in the provision. What is the intent from the Developer's business perspective? Does Section 3.2 need a cross-reference to Section 12.2?

3.2   **Termination of Agreement**. This Agreement terminates on the third Business Day after the Effective Date at 5:00 p.m., San Jose, CA time, if the Developer has not received the Down Payment required by Section 4.2 by that time. In that event, neither party has any rights or obligations against the other.[6]

4.   **Fees**.

7. Is this use of *will* in the first sentence correct?

4.1   **Estimate and Cap**. The Developer estimates that its fee for performing the Services will be between $12,000 and $15,000.[7]

Despite the preceding sentence, the maximum that the Client is obligated[8] to pay the Developer for the Services, as described in Exhibit A, is $17,000. If the parties agree to a Change Order, the new cap is the amount the parties agree to at that time.[9] If the parties do not agree to a new cap, but only an estimated range, then the new cap is the higher number of any estimated range *plus* 10% of that number.[10]

4.2 Down Payment.

4.2.1 **Amount of the Down Payment**. The down payment is $6,000 (the "**Down Payment**").

4.2.2 **Obligation to Pay the Down Payment**. The Client shall wire transfer the Down Payment in immediately available funds (San Jose, CA) to the Developer's bank account no later than three Business Days after the Effective Date. The Client shall use the following wire instructions:

> Big City Bank, 738 Fulton Ave., San Jose, California
> Website Designs, Inc. #485930284
> ABA 0390000000
> Swift Code BCBUS33

4.3 Additional Payments.

4.3.1 **Billing Rates**. The billing rates for Team members range from $75 to $225 an hour. The Developer may increase these rates only after having given the Client at least 30 days prior notice.[11]

4.3.2 **Amount to Be Paid**. The Client shall pay the Developer for each quarter hour that a Team member works, except if the cap has been reached. In that event, the Client's obligation to pay any amount in excess of the cap is discharged. In determining the amount that the Client is obligated to pay, the Developer shall give the Client a credit equal to the amount of the Down Payment.

4.3.3 **Form of Invoice**. With respect to each month that the Developer provides Services, the Developer shall send an invoice[12] to the Client indicating

(a) the number of hours each Team member worked;

8. Should *is obligated* be replaced with *shall*?

9. Note the parallel language in the third and fourth sentences and that the contract avoids any gap by stating what happens in the two alternative situations. What happens if the parties do not agree to an estimated range?

10. Even simple financial calculations should use mathematical language.

11. Should this sentence provide for *written notice*?

12. What is wrong with the following sentence? *The invoice shall state the following:*

(b)   the billing rate for each Team member;

(c)   the aggregate invoiced fee for each Team member;

(d)   the aggregate invoiced fee for the Team; and

(e)   the amount by which the invoice has been reduced to reflect any outstanding credit arising from the Down Payment.

If the cap has been reached, the Developer shall continue to send invoices to the Client, but the Developer shall indicate on the invoice that the Client is not obligated to pay the invoiced amount.[13]

13. Why is *is not obligated to pay* correct and *shall not pay* incorrect?

4.3.4   **Form and Timing of Payment.** The Client shall pay each month's invoice by company check or by wire transfer. In either case, the Client shall cause payment to be received no later than ten Business Days after the Client's receipt of that month's invoice.

5.   **Provision of Services.**

5.1   **Quality of Services.** The Developer shall perform the Services using sound professional practices and in a competent and professional manner by knowledgeable and qualified employees.

14. Is *or* inclusive or exclusive? What drafting might make the intent more explicit?

5.2   **Content.** The Client shall not deliver any Content to the Developer that

5.2.1   it does not own or have a right to use; or[14]

5.2.2   is defamatory, libelous, or otherwise actionable.

15. Assume the penultimate sentence in Section 5.3 were drafted as follows: *The Developer may replace any employee with another employee, but only after it receives the Client's prior consent.* How could the Client argue that the contract permitted the Developer to change only one member of the Team?

5.3   **The Developer's Employees.** No later than five Business Days after the Effective Date, the Developer shall assign the following employees to be the Team members providing the Services to the Client: Omar Adams, Kyla Rubin, and Marla Wojinsky. The Developer may replace one or more of these employees with other employees, but only after it receives the Client's prior consent.[15] The Client shall not unreasonably withhold its consent.

16. What was the Developer's business intent in drafting this covenant? How is the Client protected? How could the parties elaborate on this covenant to guide the parties as to the parameters of *commercially reasonable efforts?*

5.4   **Schedule.** The Developer shall use commercially reasonable efforts to provide the Services as efficiently as possible with the goal of completing the Services no later than April 30, 20XX.[16]

5.5 **Liens**. The Developer shall perform the Services so that each Work is free of liens or other encumbrances at the time that it is delivered.

5.6 **Change Orders**. If from time to time the Client wants to change or supplement any Service, the parties must execute and deliver a Change Order. A Change Order is effective when the first party to execute and deliver the Change Order receives the fully executed Change Order from the other party. This Agreement's provisions govern if this Agreement and a Change Order conflict.

5.7 **Compliance with Laws**. In performing the Services, the Developer shall comply with all federal, state, local, or foreign laws, rules, and regulations, as each is in effect from time to time.[17]

6. **Client Representative**.[18] No later than five Business Days after the Effective Date, the Client shall assign a representative to work with the Team and notify the Developer who that representative is. The Client shall give the representative the authority to sign Change Orders and to make all other decisions concerning the Website and the Services.[19] At any time, the Client may remove the then-current representative and assign another representative to work with the Team.

7. **Content**.

7.1 **Initial Content**. No later than ten Business Days after the Effective Date, the Client shall deliver to the Developer the following:

7.1.1 The Website's URL.

7.1.2 The Content that it wants incorporated into the Website.

7.2 **Additional Content**. If the Client wants to change the Content after the Developer has incorporated it into the Website, the Developer is entitled to an additional fee,[20] which the Client shall pay, all of which must be documented by a Change Order that both parties sign.

8. **Ownership**.

8.1 **Definition**. "**Developer Programming**" means any programming or software that the Developer creates, or has created, outside of this Agreement but uses in the Works.[21]

17. What is wrong with this covenant from the Developer's perspective?

18. What are the business purposes of Sections 5.3 and 6? Despite their similarity, Section 6 does not require the consent for a change in representative, although Section 5.3 requires the Client's consent for a change in the Team members. Why would the parties agree to different procedures?

19. The second sentence in Section 6 includes a nominalization. How could that be corrected?

20. Have the parties erred in drafting this provision as an entitlement of the Developer rather than a covenant of the Client? How would you redraft this provision so that it conforms to Section 5.6?

21. Why is *Developer Programming* defined in context?

8.2   **Work for Hire**.

8.2.1   **Rights to the Works**. The Works are works made for hire and all rights to them vest in the Client.[22] The Developer has no right to them or any interest in them and shall not use them to benefit anyone other than the Client.

8.2.2   **Assignment of Rights in the Works**. By signing this Agreement, the Developer assigns to the Client

(a)   all rights in each Work that do not vest in the Client by operation of law; and

(b)   all copyright interests in each Work for the entire period of that Work's copyright protection.

8.3   **Developer Programs**.[23] The Developer retains all rights to all Developer Programming, but grants to the Client a perpetual, nonexclusive license to use all Developer Programming in connection with the Works.

9.   **Warranties**.[24] The Developer warrants that the Works will

9.1   be usable by the Client for the purposes for which they were intended;

9.2   operate in conformity with the specifications listed in Exhibit A; and

9.3   be free of viruses, Trojan horses, and other software that could damage the Website or the computer of any user of the Website.

10.   **Representations and Warranties**.

10.1   **Developer**. The Developer represents and warrants to the Client as follows:

10.1.1   **Organization**. The Developer is a corporation duly organized, validly existing, and in good standing under the laws of its jurisdiction of incorporation.

10.1.2   **Corporate Power and Authority**. The Developer has all requisite corporate power and authority

(a)   to own, operate, and lease its properties, and to carry on its business as now being conducted; and

---

22. In analyzing this contract, this sentence should cause a full stop. Why?

23. What contract concepts are used in this sentence? As of what is the grant effective? What alternative date might the Developer want and why? Is the issue more technical than real? If a client wanted minimal changes, what would you suggest with respect to this provision?

24. How do these warranties differ from the warranties in the next section?

(b)   to execute, deliver, and perform this Agreement.

10.1.3   **Authorization**.[25] The Developer has taken all necessary corporate action to authorize the execution, delivery, and performance of this Agreement.

25. What is the substantive difference between subsections 10.1.2 and 10.1.3?

10.1.4   **Enforceability**. The Developer has duly executed and delivered this Agreement, and it constitutes the Developer's legal, valid, and binding obligation. This Agreement is enforceable against the Developer in accordance with its terms, except to the extent that enforcement is limited by either one or both of the following:

(a)   Applicable bankruptcy, insolvency, reorganization, moratorium, or other similar laws affecting creditors' rights generally.

(b)   General equitable principles, regardless of whether the issue of enforceability is considered in a proceeding in equity or at law.

10.1.5   **Team Members**. The Team members listed in Section 5.3 are knowledgeable and qualified to perform the Services.

10.2   **Client**. The Client represents and warrants to the Developer as follows:[26]

26. Note that the two sets of representations and warranties parallel each other in the order that the representations and warranties are stated.

10.2.1   **Organization**. The Client is a corporation duly organized, validly existing, and in good standing under the laws of its jurisdiction of incorporation.

10.2.2   **Corporate Power and Authority**. The Client has all requisite corporate power and authority

(a)   to own, operate, and lease its properties, and to carry on its business as now being conducted; and

(b)   to execute, deliver, and perform this Agreement.

10.2.3   **Authorization**. The Client has taken all necessary corporate action to authorize the execution, delivery, and performance of this Agreement.

10.2.4   **Enforceability**. The Client has duly executed and delivered this Agreement, and it constitutes the Client's legal, valid, and binding obligation. This Agreement is enforceable against the Client, except to the extent that enforcement is limited by either one or both of the following:

(a) Applicable bankruptcy, insolvency, reorganization, moratorium, or other similar laws affecting creditors' rights generally.

(b) General equitable principles, regardless of whether the issue of enforceability is considered in a proceeding in equity or at law.

11. Development Credit. The Client shall acknowledge the Developer as the Website developer on the Website page entitled "About the Site." The Client may remove the acknowledgment if it materially changes the Website after this Agreement terminates.

27. Explain the interaction between Section 12 and Section 3.2.

12. Termination.[27]

    12.1 Termination. Except as provided in Section 3.2 and Section 12.2, this Agreement terminates when the Developer has completely performed the Services and the Client has paid all fees in accordance with Section 4.

    12.2 Termination for Cause. A nonbreaching party may earlier terminate this Agreement by notifying the alleged breaching party of the former's intent to terminate if the allegedly breaching party did one or more of the following:

        12.2.1 Materially misrepresented a fact.

        12.2.2 Materially breached either a warranty or covenant.

28. Why is the second sentence required?

    This Agreement terminates on the tenth Business Day after a party receives a notice of intent to terminate. On termination, the terminating party has all rights and remedies that law and equity provide. Despite the previous sentences in this Section 12.2, if the Client does not pay the Down Payment in accordance with Section 4.2.2, then Section 3.2 governs termination, not this Section 12.2.[28]

13. General Provisions.

    13.1 Governing Law. The internal laws of California govern all matters arising under or relating to this Agreement, including torts.

13.2 Assignment and Delegation. The Developer shall not assign its rights or delegate its performance under this Agreement without the Client's prior consent. The Client may assign its rights and delegate its performance. For the purposes of this Section, an assignment includes a change of control.[29]

13.3 Successors and Assigns. This Agreement binds and benefits the parties and their respective permitted successors and assigns.

13.4 Notices. The parties shall send all notices in writing and give all consents in writing. A notice or consent is effective when the intended recipient receives it.

13.5 Merger. This Agreement is the final and exclusive statement of the parties' agreement on the matters contained in this Agreement. It supersedes all previous negotiations and agreements.

13.6 Amendments. The parties may amend this Agreement only by an agreement in writing that both parties execute.

13.7 Counterparts. The parties may execute this Agreement in counterparts, each of which constitutes an original, and all which, collectively, constitute only one agreement. The delivery of an executed counterpart signature page by facsimile or PDF is as effective as delivering this Agreement in the presence of the other party to this Agreement. This Agreement is effective as stated in Section 3.

To evidence the parties' agreement to this Agreement, each party has executed this Agreement on the date stated beneath that party's name.

Website Designs, Inc.

By: _____
       Walter Kelley, President

Dated: _____

Go-Karts Corp.

By: _____
       Esther Grant, President

Dated: _____

29. How would you change this provision to make any purported assignments by the Developer unenforceable?

Exhibit A

Scope of Services

- Creative consulting.
- Creation of site map.
- Three mock-ups of home page.
- Two revisions of chosen home page.
- Three mock-ups of secondary page.
- Two revisions of chosen secondary page.
- Programming for 30 static pages.
- Launch and testing of Website.

Specifications

- Website to work with multiple browsers.
- Website to work with multiple operating systems, including those created by Microsoft or Apple.
- Client to be able to make changes to the Website using a commercially available software application.

Exhibit

Escrow Agreements

Parties use escrow agreements to safeguard property. They deposit the property with a neutral third party, the escrow agent, to ensure that neither party has access to the property, except under agreed-on circumstances. The escrow agent holds the escrowed property until it distributes it in compliance with the escrow agreement's terms. Escrowed property may be cash, securities, or other property.

The reasons for using an escrow are transaction-specific. In connection with the purchase of a house, the buyer usually places his deposit in escrow with an escrow agent. Typically, the escrow agent will release the deposit to the seller if the transaction closes or to the buyer if it does not. In a business acquisition, the parties may deposit a portion of the purchase price in escrow to secure the seller's post-closing indemnification obligations.

The parties to an escrow agreement are the escrow agent and the parties to the primary transaction. The escrow agreement does not state the terms of the primary transaction (e.g., the purchase and sale of the house), although its recitals will describe the transaction. The escrow agreement does do the following:

- It details the circumstances under which the escrow agent will take the property and how it will invest it.
- It establishes the terms in accordance with which the escrow agent will distribute the escrowed property.
- It requires the parties to the primary transaction to pay the escrow agent's fees and to indemnify it for any losses arising out of its service as escrow agent.

The key provisions in the escrow agreement set out the circumstances under which the escrow agent will distribute the escrowed property. Typically, escrow agents require either joint written instructions if the parties agree as to the property's disposition, or, if they do not, a court order that cannot be appealed. Some escrow agents insist on being able to resign if the parties cannot resolve a dispute. In addition, they may require the right to begin a lawsuit seeking a declaratory judgment as to which party is entitled to the escrowed property. If they require such a provision, the escrow agreement usually also provides that the escrow agent may deposit the escrowed property with the court and resign without further liability.

Drafters get into trouble with escrow agreements in two ways. First, they fail to think through all of the scenarios under which the property might need to be distributed. Second, they do not sufficiently explain to the client the circumstances under which the escrowed property will remain undistributed.

Exercise 6-5 includes a Purchase Offer for the sale of an aircraft and an Escrow Agreement in accordance with the escrow agent will hold the buyer's $300,000 deposit. Section 2 of the Escrow Agreement provides for the escrow agent's distribution of the deposit. Note the use of the Exhibit as a means of establishing the content of the notice that the parties must deliver. How does this protect the escrow agent?

Index